Read Chapters: 1

7
8
9
10
11
12
13
15

CONTEMPORARY PHYSICAL DISTRIBUTION

THE PPC MARKETING SERIES

Louis E. Boone, Consulting Editor

Louis E. Boone, The University of Tulsa
CLASSICS IN CONSUMER BEHAVIOR

Louis E. Boone, The University of Tulsa
James C. Johnson, St. Cloud State University
MARKETING CHANNELS, Second Edition

James C. Johnson, St. Cloud State University
READINGS IN CONTEMPORARY PHYSICAL DISTRIBUTION,
  Second Edition

James C. Johnson, St. Cloud State University
Donald F. Wood, San Francisco State University
CONTEMPORARY PHYSICAL DISTRIBUTION

Stephen K. Keiser, University of Delaware
Max E. Lupul, California State University, Northridge
MARKETING INTERACTION: A DECISION GAME

Howard A. Thompson, Eastern Kentucky University
THE GREAT WRITINGS IN MARKETING

CONTEMPORARY

PHYSICAL

DISTRIBUTION

James C. Johnson
St. Cloud State University

Donald F. Wood
San Francisco State University

Division of
THE PETROLEUM PUBLISHING CO.
Tulsa, Oklahoma

TO *Cammy* AND *Doreen*

Manufactured in the United States of America.

Library of Congress Catalog Card Number 76–57500

ISBN 0–87814–025–5

1 2 3 4 5 — 82 81 80 79 78

Preface

PHYSICAL DISTRIBUTION is a fascinating, dynamic subject filled with both problems and opportunities for practicing and future managers. *Contemporary Physical Distribution* has been designed to convey these challenges to the reader.

Too often, college students regard their textbook as a necessary evil. *Contemporary Physical Distribution* is designed to be the most readable textbook available. Its approach focuses on the relevance of physical distribution both as an academic subject and as a potential career.

The traditional functional areas of physical distribution are examined, along with a number of subjects which are frequently given only cursory treatment. These include chapters on international physical distribution, systems controls, and the future trends.

The objectives of *Contemporary Physical Distribution* are threefold:

1. The text examines the latest concepts, techniques, and problems in physical distribution management using current illustrations.

2. The text is written in a fast-moving, uncomplicated writing style. Overly descriptive materials are eliminated and historical discussions are minimized.

3. The text has a managerial orientation. It is designed to help prepare future physical distribution managers by introducing students to the essential elements of physical distribution. In addition, specific decision areas are isolated and the general techniques for solving these problems are presented. Two cases are found at the end of each chapter. They illustrate key aspects of the chapter and serve as an excellent vehicle for stimulating class discussion. The cases also help to integrate the various functional areas of physical distribution.

A number of individuals read portions of our text in its earlier stages and we would like to thank them for their helpful suggestions—as well as hold them blameless for remaining errors and omissions. These persons are: Glen Adams of Standard Oil Company; Folger Athearn, Jr. of Athearn & Co.; Donald W. Baldra of Schering Corp.; James F. Briody of Crown Zellerbach Corp.; W. R. Callister of Del Monte Corporation; Neil D. Chaitin of Challenge Equipment Corporation; W. M. Cheatham of Specialty Brands, Inc.; George Derugin of the Center for World Business at San Francisco State University; W. R. Donham of Standard Brands Foods; Jay P. Hamerslag of Hamerslag Equipment Co.; Lowell Hedrick of Phillips Petroleum Co.; Weldon G. Helmus of Levi Strauss International; Lynn Hill of Heublein, Inc.; Donald E. Horton of the American Warehousemen's Association; Creed Jenkins of Consolidated Distribution Services; J. M. Johnson of Johnson & Johnson; R. L. Kemmerer of California Canners and Growers; Art LaPlant of Schlage Lock Co.; Joseph R. Larsen of C. I. B. A. Pharmaceutical Co.; Don Marsh of United Air Lines Maintenance Operations; Chinnubbie McIntosh of Warren Petroleum Co.; Edward J. Meyers of Pacific Gas & Electric Co.; Donald D. Mickel of the Sacramento Army Depot; Paul R. Neff of Boeing Computer Services, Inc.; Donald Pefaur of Trammell Crow Distribution Corp.; Ray Perin of Perin Co.; Richard L. Rickenbacher of Safeway Stores; Charles S. Shuken of Metropolitan Warehouse Co.; Melvin Silvester; F. J. Spellman; Joseph J. Stefanec of Agrico Chemical Co.; Wendell M. Stewart of A. T. Kearney, Inc.; T. M. Tipton of USCO Services, Inc.; Teddy N. Toklas of the Oakland Naval Supply Center; Terry C. Whiteside of Montana State Department of Agriculture; and Ronald S. Yaros of Cutter Laboratories, Inc.

Special thanks are due to Professors Louis E. Boone of the University of Tulsa, Gary N. Dicer of the University of Tennessee, Stanley J. Hille of the University of Alabama, Jack M. Starling of North Texas State University, and Roy D. Voorhees of Iowa State University, who read the entire manuscript and made many thought provoking suggestions. Also, thanks to Rory K. Miller of the California Maritime Academy for "pre-testing" some of our cases in his class. Finally, Mrs. Margaret Carpenter provided outstanding assistance in the preparation of the manuscript for publication.

St. Cloud, Minnesota   JAMES C. JOHNSON
San Francisco, California   DONALD F. WOOD
January, 1977

Contents

Prologue

DURING WORLD WAR II, General George S. Patton, Jr. had little time or patience for the function of physical distribution (logistics). General of the Army Omar N. Bradley, who served under Patton at one point, has noted:

> On the several occasions I appealed to Patton for more supply support, he would respond as though I had come to chide him on a minor detail and he would brush my complaint aside. Although Patton bossed his Army tactically with an iron hand, he remained almost completely indifferent to its logistical needs. In war, as Patton knew it then, there was little time for logistics in the busy day of a field commander.*

Nevertheless, Patton felt the sting of inadequate physical distribution support when his attacking Third Army was stopped dead in its tracks for lack of fuel. Patton called this situation the "iron grip of logistics." Bradley referred to it as the "tyranny of supplies."

Physical distribution is as important to private business as it is to military operations. The following chapters will examine how business firms can successfully implement physical distribution in order to achieve corporate objectives and to avoid the problems associated with the "tyranny of supplies."

* *A Soldier's Story* (New York: Popular Library, 1951), p. 152.

Part One.

Overview of Physical Distribution

Part I sets the stage for the entire text by introducing the many dimensions of the complex and dynamic subject of physical distribution. The first three chapters of *Contemporary Physical Distribution* are designed to serve as the structural foundation upon which the remainder of the text is built.

Chapter 1 discusses the physical distribution concept and examines the reasons for its recent growth in importance in business firms.

Chapter 2 analyzes the interfaces that the physical distribution department encounters *internally* with an organization's other functional areas—marketing, production, finance, accounting. This chapter clearly reveals the importance of each functional area recognizing the mutual interdependency of each aspect of the firm relative to the others.

Chapter 3 examines the *external* relationships between physical distribution and the firm's ability to successfully meet customer service standards. The importance of the order processing cycle is emphasized in this chapter.

This Boeing 747C can either carry passengers or cargo. *Credit*: World Airways.

CHAPTER ONE

The Physical Distribution System: Its Concept and Growth

Prior to recent years, American management's philosophy has typically been: "If you're smart enough to make it, aggressive enough to sell it—then any dummy can get it there." And now we're paying for it.

—BERNARD J. LaLONDE

Physical distribution is thus today's frontier in business. It is the one area where managerial results of great magnitude can be achieved. And it is still largely unexplored territory.

—PETER F. DRUCKER

WHAT IS PHYSICAL DISTRIBUTION?

Few terms in the vocabulary of most business people are less understood than physical distribution (PD). Physical distribution is somewhat like beauty—each beholder has his or her own preconceived notion of what it is. The cause of this problem lies in the pervasiveness of the subject. PD issues are constantly making headlines of both regular and business-oriented publications. Examples from the early and mid-1970's include port, rail, and shipping bottlenecks resulting from large sales of wheat to Russia and China; the northeastern railroad "problem" resulting from the Penn-Central bankruptcy; and adjustments made throughout the transportation industry due to the higher prices of fuel.

Of all PD activities, transportation receives the most public attention. This is because of its high visibility. Nevertheless, many business people have a rather murky concept of what PD involves; when pressed for a definition, they explain that PD is just an unnecessarily sophisticated term for transportation. *Is this true?*

No, it is not! The prestigious National Council of Physical Distribution Management defines physical distribution as *the integration of two or more activities for the purpose of planning, implementing, and controlling the efficient flow of raw materials, inprocess inventory, and finished goods from point of origin to point of consumption. These activities may include, but are not limited to, customer service, demand*

3

*forecasting, distribution communications, inventory control, material handling, order processing, parts and service support, plant and warehouse site selection, procurement, packaging, return goods handling, salvage and scrap disposal, traffic and transportation, and warehousing and storage.** Transportation is but an integral part of PD.

WHY DID PD INCREASE IN IMPORTANCE?

To answer the question, we must look briefly at the history of American business. Starting with the Industrial Revolution in the early 1800's, the emphasis was on production. A firm stressed its ability to decrease the cost of production of each unit. In the early 1900's, production started to catch up with demand, and business firms began to recognize the importance of sales. But physical distribution, as we now know it, was still ignored. A few marketing scholars had recognized its importance, but the business community failed to accept its importance until much later.[1]

During World War II, military forces made effective use of logistical models and forms of systems analysis to ensure that materials were at the right place when needed. These techniques appeared to be forgotten after the war because of the surge in economic activity. Marketing managers turned their attention to the job of filling the post-war demand for goods. It was not until the recessions of the 1950's that managers started to examine their physical distribution network. The 1958 recession and profit squeeze created an environment in which business people began searching for more effective cost control systems. Almost simultaneously, many firms realized that physical distribution was a major cost item that had never been carefully studied and coordinated.[2] A number of other trends were becoming apparent and they made it necessary to focus attention on product distribution. Six trends can be identified.

First, transportation costs were rising rapidly. Traditional methods of distribution were becoming more costly and management became aware of the need for action to offset this rising expense item.

* The National Council of Physical Distribution Management, general information pamphlet, 1977. Because of the relative infancy of PD many terms are currently being used to define approximately the same subject area: *business logistics, physical distribution, materials management, distribution engineering,* and *logistics management.* The authors of this book have no philosophic preference for any of the above terms, but they do prefer the term *physical distribution,* because it is the most readily recognized term in most business vocabularies.

[1] Bernard J. LaLonde and Leslie M. Dawson, "Early Development of Physical Distribution Thought," in Donald J. Bowersox, *et al.,* editors, *Readings in Physical Distribution Management* (New York: The MacMillan Co., 1959), pp. 9–18.

[2] Donald J. Bowersox, "Physical Distribution Development, Current Status and Potential," *Journal of Marketing* (January 1969).

Second, production efficiency had reached a point where it was becoming very difficult to generate significant additional cost savings. The "fat" had been taken out of production, while physical distribution was still a relatively untouched area.

The third factor was a fundamental change in inventory philosophy. At one time retailers held approximately half of the finished product inventory and wholesalers and manufacturers held the other half. During the 1950's more sophisticated inventory control techniques, especially in the grocery business, reduced total amounts of inventory and changed the ratio to only 10 percent held by the retailers and 90 percent by distributors and manufacturers.[3]

The fourth consideration was the proliferating product lines. This was a direct result of the marketing concept of giving each customer the exact product he or she desires. For example, until the mid-1950's products such as typewriters, light bulbs, appliances, tissue paper, etc. were largely functional in nature. Differences in the products represented real structural dissimilarities. This no longer held. A typewriter dealer could no longer stock the standard black office electric typewriter with pica type. The dealer must be able to match the typewriter color to the decor of the office with the type face chosen to support the image that the buyer wants to project. One writer observed.

> Want to . . . get your glasses fixed? American Optical Company stocks some 60,000 line items. Get a tire for your car? Firestone carries some 48,000 line items. Or maybe after your shopping ordeal you feel you need some beautification—Revlon offers 33,000 items to satisfy your specific needs.[4]

Each product variation, from a physical distribution point-of-view, is an additional product which requires its own inventory system and transportation planning.

The fifth consideration involved computer technology. This was because of the tremendous detail and amount of data that had to be dealt with in order to manage the physical distribution approach. The following are examples of the information that had to be available: (a) location of each customer; (b) size of each order; (c) location of production facilities, warehouses, and distribution centers; (d) transportation costs from each warehouse or plant to each customer; (e) available carriers and the service levels they offer; (f) location of the suppliers; and (g) inventory levels currently available in each warehouse and distribution center. The sheer magnitude of these data rendered manual analysis virtually impossible. Luckily, just as the physical distribution concept was being developed, along came the mathematical beast-of-burden—the computer—which allowed the concept to be put into practice. With-

---

[3] Donald J. Bowersox, "Physical Distribution in Semi-Maturity," *Air Transportation* (January, 1966).

[4] Warren Blanding in "The Fernstrom Moving System" *Feedback* (March-April, 1974), p. 1.

out the development and use of the computer at this time, the physical distribution concept would have remained an interesting theory with few "real-world" applications.

The sixth factor was that as computers gained a foothold into business analysis, it became possible for firms to systematically study the quality of the service they received from their suppliers. Based on this analysis, many firms were able to pinpoint suppliers who consistently offered substandard levels of physical distribution. Offending suppliers could be singled out. Many firms were rudely awakened and made to realize the need to upgrade their distribution systems.

These six factors are still at work. Many firms have adopted a PD outlook and the original PD concepts are being broadened. These will be discussed in later chapters.

THE "TOTAL-SYSTEM" CONCEPT OF PHYSICAL DISTRIBUTION

Physical distribution is a classic example of the systems approach* to business problems. From a company's point-of-view, the systems approach indicates that the company's objectives can be realized by recognizing the mutual interdependence of the basic functional areas of the firm (marketing, production, and finance). The same reasoning can be applied to the area of physical distribution. The physical distribution manager must balance each functional area of physical distribution, and no area can be overstressed to the point that it becomes detrimental to the overall functioning of the PD operation.

THE OBJECTIVE OF PHYSICAL DISTRIBUTION

The objective of a physical distribution system can be stated as follows: With a specified level of service provided to customers, to minimize the costs involved in physically moving and storing the product from its production point to the point where it is purchased.[5] To achieve this objective, the physical distribution manager uses three inter-related

---

* One definition of systems approach is: "The systems approach to a problem involves not only a recognition of the individual importance of the various elements of which it is composed, but an acknowledgment of their interrelationship. Whereas the field specialist concentrates restrictively on his own particular bailiwick, the more versatile systems man, in his capacity as generalist, seeks the optimum blend of many of these individual operations in order to fulfill a broader objective." Colin Barrett, "The Machine and Its Parts," an editorial, *Transportation and Distribution Management* (April, 1971), p. 3.

[5] Customer service is discussed in Chapter 3. An alternative goal would be to maximize return on investment.

concepts of the systems approach: (a) total-cost approach, (b) avoidance of sub-optimization, and (c) cost-trade offs.

THE TOTAL-COST APPROACH

The total-cost approach to distribution is built on the premise that *all* relevant functions in physically moving and storing products should be considered as a whole and *not individually*.‡ The following functions should be included in the total-cost approach to physical distribution.

1. Transportation
2. Warehousing
3. Inventory location and plant location selection
4. Inventory control
5. Materials handling
6. Information flow, including order processing
7. Packaging

The key to the total-cost concept is that all cost items are considered simultaneously when attempting to meet specified customer service levels. When testing alternative approaches, costs of some functions will increase, some will decrease, and some will stay the same. The objective is to find the alternative with the lowest *total* cost.

AVOIDANCE OF SUB-OPTIMIZATION

Sub-optimization occurs where each member of an organization attempts to do the best job possible, but where the total results are less than optimal. The logistics consultant, John F. Magee, observed,

> There is in business today, however, a growing tendency to recognize that the *efficiency* of an individual function examined in isolation may be quite different from the *effectiveness* of the function as part of the total logistic process. Compromises must be found among all the functions to obtain a total system operation that achieves a better cost/effectiveness balance. For example, low cost per ton shipped may be a very expensive target for the system as a whole if the traffic function achieves this target by sacrificing speed and particularly reliability of service or if the mode of transportation chosen makes special packaging necessary.[6]

Why does sub-optimization exist in physical distribution? The answer lies in the fact that each separate logistics activity is being judged

‡ Some firms integrate the movement of inbound raw materials with the outbound movement of finished goods. Where this is done, purchasing and production scheduling must be included within the "total-cost" framework.

[6] John F. Magee, *Industrial Logistics* (New York: McGraw-Hill Book Co., 1968), p. 31. See also; Paul T. McElhiney and Charles L. Hilton, *Introduction to Logistics and Traffic Management* (Dubuque, Iowa: Wm. C. Brown Co. Publishers, 1968), p. 340.

by its abilities to achieve given management objectives, which are often at cross purposes with each other. For example, a warehouse manager in a firm which owns both warehouses and trucks may decide not to pay warehouse workers overtime to load a company truck. This keeps warehouse expenses down but may be very costly to the firm because the truck's schedule is interrupted. Or in other cases, departments not in the logistics area of responsibility may cause another department to operate at less than full efficiency. Thus, the production department may desire to minimize the cost of production per unit of output. To achieve its goal, it schedules long production runs with as few changeovers as possible. The result of this action is excess inventory awaiting sale and the added costs of holding this inventory.

COST TRADE-OFFS

The final concept of physical distribution is the understanding of cost trade-offs. This acknowledges that changing patterns or functions of distribution will result in some costs increasing, while other costs will decrease. The net effect, however, should be an *overall cost decrease* for providing a given level of customer service.

The concept of cost trade-offs can be well illustrated by the following two examples.

1. The Gillette Company, the world's largest producer of safety razors, was faced with an ever expanding assortment of products because it had expanded into a broad range of toiletry products. To give good customer service the company started using air freight, an expensive form of distribution. Upon studying their distribution system, they discovered that their problem was in the slowness with which orders were processed. By simplifying paperwork they were able to reduce the time required to process orders. Gillette was able to return to lower-cost surface transportation and still be able to meet delivery schedules. The cost trade-off was between order processing costs which *increased* and transportation costs which *decreased*; and the net result was that total distribution costs *decreased*.

2. The Montgomery Ward Company found that significant inventory reductions could be achieved by consolidating all their slower-moving products into one central warehouse. This facility is located only seven miles from Chicago's O'Hare Airport. When a slow-moving product or part is needed, the Chicago warehouse is notified and the requirement is often sent via air freight to the requesting party. While this procedure greatly increases the transportation charges involved in sending a product or part to a customer, the inventory holding cost reduction more than offsets the increased per-unit transportation charges.

THE PHYSICAL DISTRIBUTION CONCEPT

We have now discussed the three basic considerations of physical distribution: (1) the total-cost approach, (2) the avoidance of sub-optimization, and (3) the use of cost trade-offs. These three sub-parts, when combined in the decision-making process, form what is commonly called the *physical distribution concept*. The uniqueness of the physical distribution concept is not in the individual functions, since each function (traffic, warehousing, etc.) was performed prior to the concept's inception. Instead, the uniqueness came from the integration of all of these functions into a *unified whole* that seeks the objective of minimizing distribution costs, for a given level of customer service.

THREE PHYSICAL DISTRIBUTION SYSTEMS IN ACTION

This section provides capsule descriptions of PD systems of three well-known firms. Although details differ, they all focus on customer service.

JOSEPH SCHLITZ BREWING COMPANY

In 1973 the Joseph Schlitz Brewing Company shipped more than 20 million barrels of beer, and had a freight bill of more than $75 million. Because of the growing costs involved in PD activities and the continual need to provide a high level of customer service, the company had organized a corporate-level physical distribution department in 1969. This department, headed by a vice-president, is responsible for the traffic and transportation function, production scheduling, packaging, and distribution warehouse locations.

Approximately 60 percent of Schlitz's beer production is shipped by rail and the remainder by truck. The majority of the motor carrier transportation takes place within a 400 mile radius of production plants. Current transport problems include inconsistency of railroad service, particularly in the country's eastern section where rail car availability complicates the situation. Other railroad trouble spots include unreasonable variation in the inside rail car temperature, which results in the product spoiling; pilferage; and product damage.

Schlitz's wholesale customers demand consistent and dependable deliveries from their supplier. To meet this demand, Schlitz has installed a computer assisted car control system called SCOT—Schlitz Customer-Oriented Transportation. SCOT is a computer link-up between production plants, railroads and the Schlitz office in Milwaukee. The system constantly monitors each rail car shipment and prints out exception reports if a car appears to be falling behind a predetermined schedule. It then becomes possible to correct rail problems before they result in an unexpected late delivery. The SCOT program provides Schlitz with periodic carrier performance reports. These reports specify for each railroad the percentage of on-time deliveries that it has achieved, as compared with other—frequently competing—carriers.[7]

LIBBY, MCNEIL & LIBBY

Libby is one of the world's largest producers of canned goods, frozen foods and ready-to-eat frozen dinners. In the U. S. alone, more than 50 million cases are transported through a distribution system that contains more than 100 plants and warehouses. This involves shipping annually approximately 25,000 rail cars and 40,000 truck loads of processed food. In addition, over 25 million cases of products are shipped in international operations.

Libby has been a pioneer in PD innovations. The firm helped develop the concept of *regional distribution centers*. These are warehouses strategically located to facilitate the distribution of products in large quantities. Libby was also active in developing the concept of *unitized shipments*, which involves binding or strapping products together on pallets to achieve greater efficiency in materials handling.

One area of customer service that Libby has stressed is rapid order-processing. Nearly all orders are shipped within 72 hours after receipt and 95 percent of the time the order is shipped within 24 hours. The heart of this order-processing system is a computerized ordering system. Customers (brokers) enter their orders to Libby on a teletype communication network routed directly to Libby's computer center. The order is processed and the best shipping point is notified of the order, via a teletype system.[8]

INTERNATIONAL BUSINESS MACHINES

IBM has the responsibility for rapidly repairing their computer hardware when it malfunctions. To accomplish this, the firm has a distribution parts system which consists of 23 distribution centers. The problem faced by IBM is determining which and how many parts to carry at each of its centers. This is important, since there are 400,000 parts which can "shut down" the computer. IBM determined that of these 400,000 parts, a replacement stock of only 75,000 different items will fill approximately 97.5 percent of all requirements. The remaining 325,000 parts are required only 2.5 percent of the time.

In addition, IBM has prearranged the modes of transportation to be used in any given situation. Shipments to customers or distribution

---

[7] Bob Pettay, "Distribution with Gusto," *Handling and Shipping* (September, 1973), p. 44.
[8] "Profiles of PDM: Libby's," *Handling and Shipping* (October, 1972), p. 74.

centers are labeled as *regular, rush,* or *emergency-machine down.* For example, *regular* shipments to St. Louis from Mechanicsburg, Pennsylvania of 50 pounds or less go by a parcel carrier. If the shipment is greater than 50 pounds, a predetermined motor common carrier is used. *Rush* shipments up to five pounds are transported by air parcel post. Packages between six and fifty pounds go by air forwarder and those greater than 50 pounds are shipped by air freight. The *emergency-machine down* shipments are sent the fastest way possible. For short distances, messengers, private autos, or taxis are used. For longer hauls, the company has chartered airplanes.[9]

RESPONSIBILITIES OF PHYSICAL DISTRIBUTION

The PD manager has a highly complex and challenging position. The major reason is that he or she must be both a *technical expert* and a *generalist.* In the first capacity, the PD manager must have an understanding of freight tariffs, warehouse layouts, inventory analysis, transportation law, etc.

In their capacity as generalists, the PD managers must understand the relationship between all PD functions. In addition they must relate PD to other operations of the firm.

> The emphasis is on the importance of the *modern* distribution man thinking in terms of the whole business system with which he is concerned. He must not only think of a flow of materials within his company, his thoughts must go beyond the shipping dock to the customer's doorstep . . . sometimes backward to the sources of supply. His thinking must cut across traditional organization lines. It must reach out to include competitors, potential markets . . . in short, the physical distribution manager must think big.[10]

At any level, the PD manager must be concerned with profits. Burr Hupp, a well-known PD consultant said:

> . . . remember the equation: Profits equal sales minus cost. The Physical Distribution Manager's job is to give good service at low cost. He can therefore generate profits in two ways. He can influence sales, and he can influence costs. He can generate profits, first of all, by giving good service—service that increases sales because it gets customers to buy and then keeps them coming back to buy again and again. And he can generate profits by cutting costs through more efficient methods.[11]

[9] Phil Schreiner, "A PDM Pyramid," *Handling and Shipping* (August, 1972), pp. 50–53.

[10] Harry J. Bruce, "Distribution History in the Making," *Pacific Traffic* (November, 1973), p. 50.

[11] Burr Hupp, "The Physical Distribution Manager: Tomorrow," an address to N.C.P.D.M.'s 1975 meeting (Chicago: N.C.P.D.M., 1976), p. 27.

PHYSICAL DISTRIBUTION CAREERS

The career opportunities in PD are excellent.[12] Many firms, both large and small actively seek two-year and four-year college graduates, and MBA's who desire to work in the PD area. Michael J. Walsh, vice-president of transportation and distribution for St. Regis Paper Company, noted that his hiring practices have changed "drastically" in recent years. Instead of depending almost exclusively on carrier personnel to become future employees, the firm now prefers college educated people who are generalists in business and who do not necessarily possess a specialty.[13]

Entry-level positions in PD are generally of two types. The first is often as a line supervisor in one of the functional activities such as traffic, warehousing, purchasing, materials management, or inventory control. The second, often staff in nature, is assisting in the coordination and management of several different functions. Large firms have training programs for PD personnel, exposing them to a variety of closely-supervised job assignments.

Many corporations have senior executive positions for their top PD personnel. Figures 1-1, 1-2, and 1-3 present sketches of successful PD practitioners who are firm vice-presidents, including Mr. Walsh. All three were recognized as PD "leaders" by *Traffic Management* magazine. Interestingly, all three have traffic backgrounds, although this pattern is less likely to occur in the future.

A further advantage for PD career professionals is that this aspect of business offers many opportunities for advancement. Charles Rader, General Manager, Corporate Physical Distribution for Cities Service Company, believes that PD is an excellent training-ground for senior management because PD personnel have a high degree of visibility in the firm. This is because PD is an "integrating" function and PD people are constantly in touch with the other functional areas of the firm such as marketing, production, finance, accounting, research and development. Rader stated that because of this high level of contact outside the PD department a large percentage of his employees have the opportunity to be promoted to positions outside of PD.

PD training is also valuable for individuals who hope to work for carriers because it gives them a better understanding of shippers' needs.

Professor Bernard LaLonde of Ohio State University continually surveys career patterns in physical distribution and his findings are reported at annual meetings of the National Council of Physical Distribution

---

12 For an excellent discussion of PD career opportunities and challenges, see: *Traffic Management* (November, 1975), pp. 40–46 and *Traffic Management* (February, 1976), pp. 30–35.

13 "The Physical Distribution Profession: Opportunities Unlimited," *Traffic Management* (Special Reprint, 1972), p. 6.

Fig. 1-1 Physical Distribution Careers.

DONALD G. GRIFFIN began working in the distribution field during his employment with Dow Chemical Company, where he also held production, construction and marketing jobs during the period from 1947 to 1970. He joined his present firm, PPG Industries, Inc., in November, 1970 and now holds the position of vice president, traffic and transportation.

Mr. Griffin is active in the National Freight Traffic Association, Transportation Association of America, Manufacturing Chemists Association and the National Industrial Traffic League.

Mr. Griffin graduated from Texas A&M with a B.S. degree in chemical engineering.

An organization chart of Mr. Griffin's department is illustrated below.

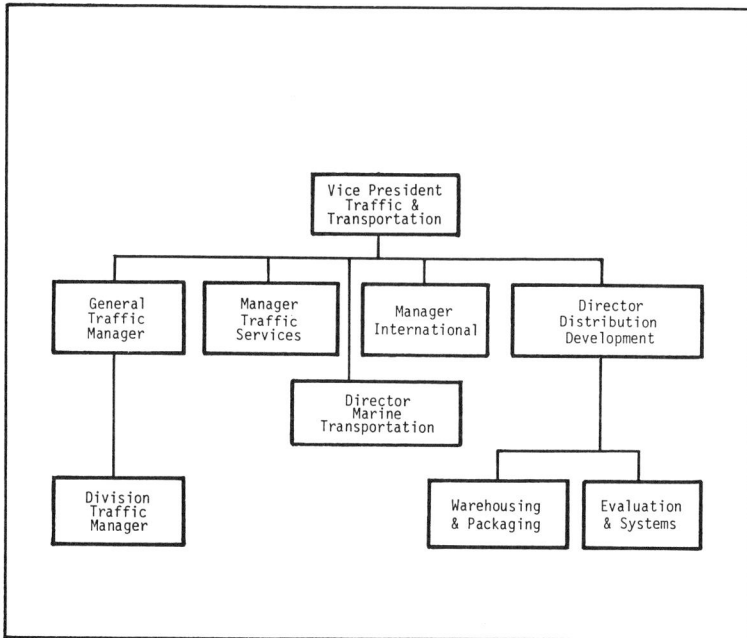

SOURCE: Jack W. Farrell, "The Physical Distribution Profession: A Decade of Growth," *Traffic Management* (Special Reprint, 1972), p. 6.

Fig. 1-2 Physical Distribution Careers.

MICHAEL J. WALSH, JR. joined St. Regis Paper Company in 1947 and has since held management positions in its transportation and distribution department. Prior to his appointment in April, 1971 as vice president of transportation and distribution, he served as assistant vice president and director of transportation and distribution for several years.

Admitted to practice before the Interstate Commerce Commission, Mr. Walsh is a graduate of the Academy of Advanced Traffic.

Mr. Walsh is first vice president of the Traffic Club of New York, a founder-member of the American Society of Traffic and Transportation and has served as chairman of the Transportation and Distribution Committee of the American Paper Institute.

An organization chart of Mr. Walsh's department is illustrated below.

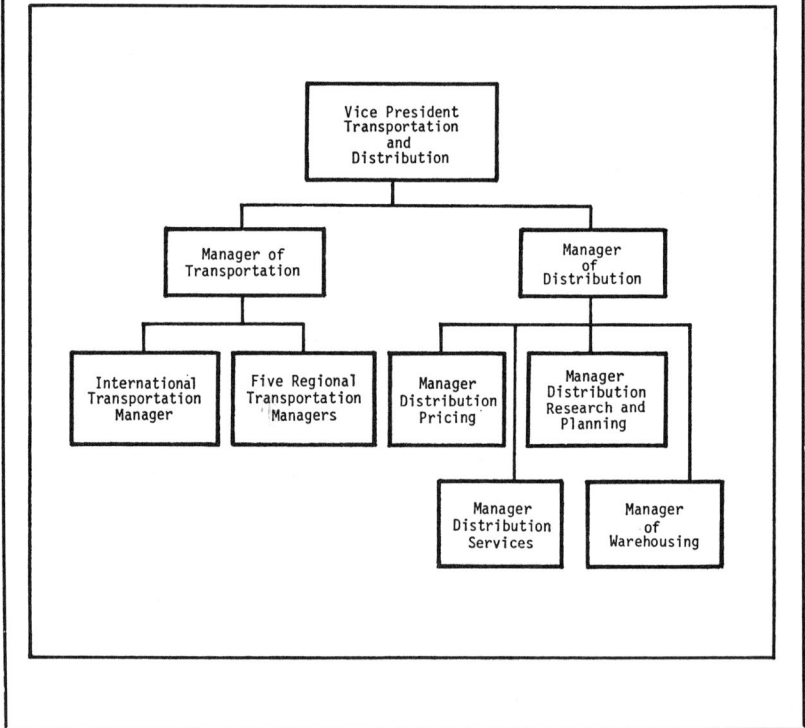

SOURCE: Jack W. Farrell, "The Physical Distribution Profession: A Decade of Growth," *Traffic Management* (Special Reprint, 1972), p. 12.

Fig. 1-3 Physical Distribution Careers.

WILLIAM F. WENDLER joined Westinghouse Electric Corporation in 1951, serving in diversified technical and supervisory traffic positions until 1964, when he became general traffic manager of Alberto-Culver Company. In 1965, he joined the Noxell Corporation in his present position of vice president-distribution services.

National secretary of the National Council of Physical Distribution Management, Mr. Wendler is active also in other professional groups.

Mr. Wendler received a B.S. in marine transportation from the U.S. Merchant Marine Academy in 1947 and has subsequently done post-graduate work in business administration at Temple University.

An organization chart of Mr. Wendler's department is illustrated below.

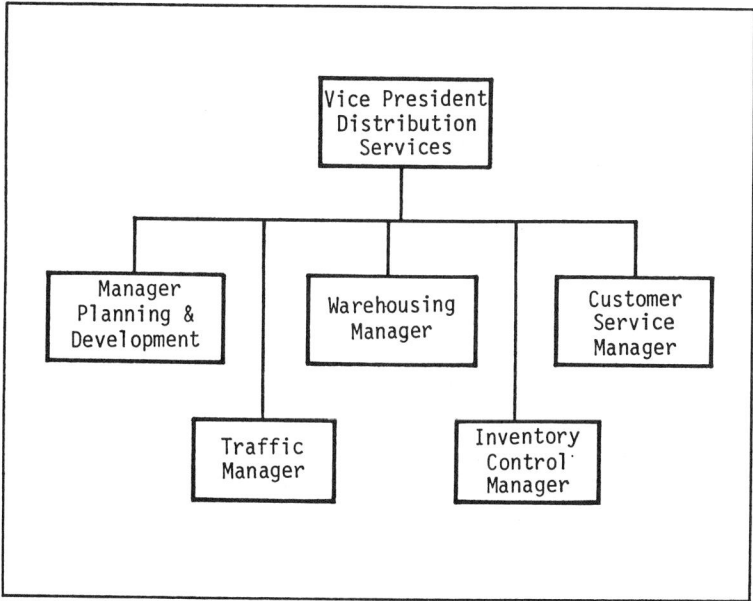

SOURCE: Jack W. Farrell, "The Physical Distribution Profession: A Decade of Growth," *Traffic Management* (Special Reprint, 1972), p. 13.

Management. He collects information from the highest ranking distribution executive in major firms. What follows is a brief summary of his 1975 survey results of 132 executives. Nearly all of his respondents had college degrees; about one third had a master's degree. Seventy percent of those whose title was vice-president had their undergraduate education field listed as business administration. Respondents were asked to indicate which PD functions occupied more than ten percent of their time. The answers were: packaging, four percent; warehousing, 55 percent; traffic management, 42 percent; order processing, 25 percent; warehouse location, 12 percent; product planning, seven percent; and sales forecasting, three percent. Nearly half of the respondents also indicated that more than ten percent of their time was devoted to "general management." LaLonde concluded that the "distribution manager in 1975 is most concerned with his ability to identify and control costs and distribution investment in a period of rapid change in the economy."[14]

PD PROFESSIONALISM

Because of the growing importance of PD activities, this area is moving rapidly toward a true professional status.[15] There are a number of professional organizations in PD and transportation which are dedicated to advancing the professional knowledge of their members. The rationale for these professional associations is that the state-of-the-art is changing so rapidly that professionals must be constantly educating and reeducating themselves.

NATIONAL COUNCIL OF PHYSICAL DISTRIBUTION MANAGEMENT (NCPDM)

This organization is dedicated "to develop the theory and understanding of the physical distribution process, to promote the art and science of managing physical distribution systems and to foster professional dialogue in the field operating exclusively without profit and in cooperation with other organizations and institutions." Further information can be obtained by writing to: NCPDM, 222 West Adams Street, Chicago, Illinois 60606.

AMERICAN SOCIETY OF TRAFFIC AND TRANSPORTATION (AST&T)

AST&T was founded to help its members achieve, "high standards of education and technical training, requisite to the proper performance

14 Bernard J. LaLonde, "The Distribution Manager Today," a paper presented at the 1975 Annual Meeting of the NCPDM (Chicago: NCPDM, 1976), pp. 1–12.
15 See Richard A. Lancioni, "Physical Distribution Management: Is It A Profession?," a paper presented at 1975 Annual Meeting of the NCPDM (Chicago: NCPDM, 1976), pp. 105–108.

of the various functions of traffic, transportation and physical distribution management." To become a certified member of AST&T, one must pass four comprehensive tests over various aspects of traffic, transportation, and PD and write an original research paper. For further information, write: AST&T, 547 West Jackson Boulevard, Chicago, Illinois 60606.

DELTA NU ALPHA (DNA)

DNA is a transportation fraternity dedicated to the education of its members. DNA chapters are very active at the local level and stress the learning process by small educationally-oriented discussion groups. For further information, write: DNA, 15017 Detroit Avenue, Cleveland, Ohio 44107.

TRANSPORTATION RESEARCH FORUM (TRF)

TRF is a "joint endeavor of interested persons in academic life, government service, business logistics, and the various modes of transportation. The Forum's purpose is to provide a common meeting ground or forum for the discussion of ideas and research techniques applicable to economic, management, and public policy problems involving transportation." Additional information can be obtained from: TRF, P.O. Box 330, Ocean City, N.J. 08226

ASSOCIATION OF ICC PRACTITIONERS (AICCP)

This group is dedicated, "to promote the proper administration of the Interstate Commerce Act and related Acts, to uphold the honor of practice before the Interstate Commerce Commission; to cooperate in fostering increased educational opportunities and maintaining high standards of professional conduct, and to encourage cordial communication among the practitioners." To belong to this organization, one must be an ICC practitioner. This is accomplished by passing a comprehensive test administered by the ICC on transportation law. For further information write: Association of ICC Practitioners, 1112 ICC Building, Washington, D. C. 20423.

NATIONAL INDUSTRIAL TRAFFIC LEAGUE (NITL)

The NITL is a shippers' organization which promotes by conference, publicity and other means an understanding of the current transportation needs of the country. NITL's educational program is aimed at the general public, the carriers, and state and national governmental units. For further information write: The National Industrial Traffic League, 711 14th St. N.W., Washington, D. C. 20005.

TRANSPORTATION ASSOCIATION OF AMERICA (TAA)

TAA is a carrier-shipper group which has three primary objectives. The first is to resist government ownership or operation of any form of transportation; and the second is to develop a favorable climate assuring the best possible transportation service at reasonable cost. The final objective is "promoting and nurturing public understanding of the importance of sound transportation, and public awareness of transport problems." For further information, write: The Transportation Association of America, 1101 17th St., N.W., Washington, D. C. 20036.

AMERICAN PRODUCTION AND INVENTORY CONTROL SOCIETY (APICS)

This group attempts to develop professional, scientific approaches to methods of inventory control. Information is available from the group's headquarters at Suite 504, Watergate Building, 2600 Virginia Avenue, N.W., Washington, D. C. 20037.

SUMMARY

This chapter presented an overview of the physical distribution systems. Many businesspeople believe that traffic and transportation management are synonymous with PD management. In actuality, traffic and transportation is but one part (although the most important one) of the PD system. Additional functional areas of PD include warehousing, material handling, packaging, inventory control, plant and warehouse site location, order processing, and customer service.

The increasing importance of PD is the result of several factors, These factors include: the significant increases in transportation rates since World War II; the fact that production had been over-analyzed while PD was ignored; the trend towards reduced inventories at all levels within the marketing channel; and the proliferation of products in the marketplace.

The goal of an effective PD system can be stated as follows: to minimize, for a specified level of customer service, the costs involved in physically moving and storing the product from its production point to the point where it is ultimately purchased.

QUESTIONS FOR DISCUSSION AND REVIEW

1. "Traffic management and physical distribution management are really the same thing! The latter term just sounds more sophisticated,

but it's really nothing more than the purchasing of transportation services." Is this a valid statement? Why?

2. Discuss the functional areas that combine to form the PD department.

3. That PD is an important business function has become more and more recognized during the past decade. Discuss the reason(s) for this.

4. Why is the *phenomenon* of product proliferation so difficult from a PD manager's point-of-view?

5. Explain Professor LaLonde's comment that appears on page 3.

6. Discuss the basic objective of a PD system.

7. Give an example of sub-optimization. Give an example of a PD cost trade-off.

8. Compare and contrast the three distribution organization charts that appear in Figures 1-1, 1-2 and 1-3. Why do you think they differ?

9. Discuss briefly the career potentials in PD management.

10. It has been said that the PD manager should ideally be both a *generalist* and a *technician*. Discuss why this relationship should be true. Does it help to explain why PD managers are in relatively short supply?

CASE 1-1   THELMA'S STAMPS

Thelma Jorgenson had been confined to a wheelchair since she was stricken by polio as a teenager. She lived alone in a one-story house next door to her married brother in Mason City, Iowa. Her needs were fairly modest and she supported herself by selling stamps by mail to stamp collectors. An envelope containing a card which displayed the stamps would be mailed out on request. The stamps were sent "on approval"; the customer would return the unwanted stamps along with cash or check for the stamps wanted and purchased.

Thelma had many old time customers who would buy only one or two stamps a month but enclose newsy notes. Most of her customers were in isolated sections of the United States, far from large cities where specialized collectors' stamps were available in shops. Most of the requests that Thelma received from regular customers were quite detailed. One customer might be interested in stamps used in Portugal in the 1930's; another might be specializing in stamps showing descendants of Queen Victoria; and so on. Only because she did not value her time highly was Thelma able to honor such requests. It might take her an hour to assemble 15 to 20 stamps to mail to the customer who might buy only two for a total of $1.50, out of which Thelma had to pay her wholesale price of 60 cents for the stamps and 10 cents for outgoing postage.

Despite her customers' relative isolation, she apparently benefitted from "word of mouth" advertising and was as busy as she wanted to be.

Each day she received between 20 and 25 letters, usually enclosing payment for stamps previously sent on approval plus requests saying what type of stamps they would like to see next. The average cycle for this type of order was one month. Every month she handled about 400 orders.

Thelma's one problem was inventory. There are hundreds of thousands of stamps that have been issued and some collectors want used stamps, some want unused stamps, some want "blocks of four" and some want first day covers.* She kept her stamps in over 100 large binders containing pages with special slots for holding stamps.

One catalog is used by most stamp collectors and dealers to identify each stamp and to give an estimated value. For stamps with a retail value of twenty cents or less, Thelma just kept inventory by count; for those with a greater value, she kept track of the stamp by its catalog number. The same held for stamps she sent out on approval; her records might show that she had sent out 15 stamps worth 20 cents apiece or less plus specific catalog numbers for the more valuable stamps. For stamps worth several dollars or more, she even noted the stamp's condition and location of cancellation marks, so that the customer could not substitute a more heavily cancelled stamp for a less heavily cancelled copy of the same issue. (Valuable used stamps are worth more if lightly cancelled or if the cancellation does not obliterate the picture on the stamp.) When dealing with regular customers, Thelma did not take as many precautions.

The second inventory problem Thelma encountered was the capital investment required. Her inventory, based on cost to her, was valued at $10,000. At any one time, half of this would be in the room she used as her office and the other half would be "out on approval."

Thelma always used commemorative stamps on outgoing letters, since she knew her customers would clip and save the stamp. In August 1975, when her brother and his family were away on vacation, Thelma ran out of new ten cent first class mail stamps. She wanted to mail out the orders and, since she could not reach the post office herself, she had to choose between using older ten cent U.S. commemoratives (which were more valuable to collectors) or 13 cent airmail stamps with which she was temporarily overstocked. She used the airmail stamps on 25 outgoing packets of stamps being sent out on approval.

A week later she was surprised when three of the customers who had received the airmail letters responded with a note accompanying the payment and the returned stamps. The notes apologized for having formerly kept the approval stamps so long. The customers had assumed

---

* Stamps attached to special-design envelopes which are cancelled on the first day the stamp is released.

that because Thelma was using air mail she was trying to speed up the approval process. The next day ten of the customers who had received the air mail letters responded, again with similar notes. By the end of two weeks, nearly all of those who had received the letters with air mail stamps had responded. Thelma calculated that the length of time the stamps had been out on approval had been cut in half.

Question One: Based on the information given so far, should Thelma switch to using 13 cent airmail rather than 10 cent first class mail stamps on outgoing letters containing stamps for approval? Why?

Question Two: How do you think the postal rate changes in early 1976 would have affected Thelma's operation?

CASE 1-2 SUPERIOR PAPER PRODUCTS COMPANY

Superior Paper Products Company is located in a medium size southern city. The firm is 55 years old and has been controlled by the Sylvester family. Julius Sylvester (1888–1963) founded the firm and ran it until his death. His son George (1921–1968) ran it until his untimely death (struck by lightening on a golf course). Frank Sylvester (1941–) became president in 1968 and with the help of Morris Blackman, who has been with the firm since 1937 and is currently executive vice president, has managed to do a satisfactory job despite his youth and the fact that many of his grandfather's antiquated practices are still in force.

In 1974 the firm's sales were nearly $350 million. Products were marketed in all states east of the Rocky Mountains and about three percent of the sales were exported to European markets. In 1974 profit margins were much lower than for the industry as a whole and this was attributed to Superior's accumulation of embarrassingly large inventories.

In the 1974 slump several large customers who had carried both Superior's products and those of one or more of Superior's competitors, dropped the Superior line claiming they wanted to reduce the number of different product lines they had to maintain in their own stocks. The reason given for dropping the Superior line was "poor customer service." This was especially true in the Northeast where the railroad situation was chaotic and some of Superior's competitors had enlarged their fleets of private trucks.

At the insistence of some of the family members who still owned large blocks of stock, Frank Sylvester (and Blackman) had retained Merlin Associates, a well-known physical distribution consulting firm. They paid Merlin Associates $100,000 to conduct a study of Superior's distribution system and recommend how it could be made more competitive.

Irwin Buchanan, 62 years old, had been traffic manager of Superior

Paper Products since 1940. He had been with the firm since 1931 when, barely out of high school and working in a service station, he impressed Julius Sylvester with the enthusiasm he showed for washing the windows on the elder Sylvester's Packard. Even at washing windows on autos, Buchanan was a perfectionist. After finishing, he would ask permission to stick his head inside the car and then peer through each freshly-washed window to make certain no streaks remained. Even though this was the depths of the depression and Superior Paper Products was not hiring, the elder Sylvester decided to make room for young Buchanan who was assigned to Superior's three-man traffic department which oversaw rates and dealings with rail carriers.

The elder Sylvester never regretted his choice. Buchanan was an outstanding traffic manager. He was one of the leading participants in the I.C.C.'s class rate investigations of the 1940's which ultimately resulted in a restructuring of the nation's entire rate structure so it was more equitable to the South. In 1953 the railroads in the Southern Territory named him "shipper of the year." In 1967 the state's chamber of commerce awarded him the title "Mr. Transportation."

Buchanan was an I.C.C. practitioner and had participated in over 200 I.C.C. proceedings and an equal number of hearings held by state transportation regulatory bodies in states where Superior Paper Products had intrastate shipments. He had appeared numerous times before state legislative committees and congressional committees. He had represented both his industry and southern shippers before the various congressional committees which were considering legislation which finally became the Transportation Act of 1958. At present Buchanan was on a shipper-carrier committee that was studying possibilities of computerizing tariffs. He was also considered to be an "expert" in the field of loss and damage claims.

Because Superior Paper Products spent over $20 million annually for transportation, Buchanan had considerable leverage with carriers. He constantly strove to obtain the lowest rates possible. He had a "sixth sense" for knowing routes over which railroads had large "backhauls" of empty cars. Buchanan would then advise Superior's timber buyers to buy timber at points near the beginning of the rail's empty haul and then Buchanan would offer the rails a large tonnage if they would lower the rate.

He also saw to it that Superior Paper Products' finished product warehouses were located in relatively isolated spots where, again, he could take advantage of a railroad "backhaul" situation and obtain low rates to the warehouse site because there was no other traffic moving to that community. Warehousing costs in these communities were also low; labor was nonunionized and very productive. Because of the large capacity of these warehouses it was possible to store large lots of Superior's finished products, and these large lots were the cushion between production and sales. Buchanan had developed a warehousing system with such large capacity that fluctuations in sales did not affect levels of production. The elder Sylvester had liked this system. It allowed him to run his plants at a constant pace for 50 weeks per year—no layoffs and no overtime. (The plant closed for two weeks in mid-August for vacations.)

When the Merlin Associates' report was completed, one copy was sent to Frank Sylvester and both he and Blackman read it. It confirmed their suspicions that Superior Paper Products' distribution setup was too "transportation-savings" oriented. Sylvester and Blackman spent a long time discussing the report, whether to show it to Buchanan, and how to implement its recommendations. "I sure hate to move against Buchanan," said Frank Sylvester, sadly. "Both Gramps and Dad thought the world of him, and when I was growing up he used to take me to Mobile and to Tampa to see car unloading equipment installations. I know you two are about the same age, but you realize that times have changed and some of Gramp's ideas no longer hold. Buchanan doesn't realize this. The Merlin report says we've got the lowest transportation rates and the biggest inventories in the industry. What am I going to do?"

"Irwin and I are old buddies," said Blackman, softly. "When I tell you what I recommend, I feel like I'm knifing my own brother."

"I appreciate that," said Sylvester, "but I think we're also agreed that something has to be done. Now, what do you recommend?"

Blackman responded: "First of all, I agree with the Merlin Associates report. Second, we need a new physical distribution division and Buchanan's traffic office will become part of the new division. Third, Buchanan will *not* head the new division."

"We're agreed," said Frank Sylvester. "Who's going to tell Buchanan?"

Question One: What do you think the contents of the Merlin Associates' report probably stated?

Question Two: How should Blackman and Frank Sylvester go about informing Buchanan of their decision? What should they say?

CHAPTER REFERENCES

BARRETT, COLIN; "The Machine and Its Parts," *Transportation and Distribution Management* (April, 1971).

BATES, D. L. and John E. Dillard, Jr.; "Physical Distribution: Current Application of Theory," *Transportation Journal* (Winter, 1975), pp. 28–30.

BLANDING, WARREN; *Feedback* ("The Fernstrom Moving System," March-April, 1974).

BOWERSOX, DONALD J.; "Physical Distribution Development, Current Status and Potential," *Journal of Marketing* (January, 1969).

———; "Physical Distribution in Semi-Maturity," *Air Transportation* (January, 1966).

BRUCE, HARRY J.; "Distribution History in the Making," *Pacific Traffic* (November, 1973).

CAVINATO, JOSEPH L.; "Some Pointers on Conducting an AST&T Study Group," *Transportation Journal* (Summer, 1974), pp. 46–49.

CHERINGTON, PAUL W. and Lewis M. Schneider; "Transportation and Logistics Education in Graduate Schools of Business Administration—A Summary Report," *Transportation Journal* (Winter, 1967), pp. 19–26.

DANIEL, NORMAN E. and J. Richard Jones; "The PDM Literature: Practitioner Views," *Transportation Journal* (Fall 1975), pp. 40–46.

DAVIS, GRANT M. and Joseph Rosenberg; "Physical Distribution Management—A Collage of 1973 Observations," *Transportation Journal* (Summer, 1974), pp. 50–56.

DUNN, ROBERT J., Claude H. Ryan, and Keith H. Clark; "Polishing the Silver—The Challenge Answered," *Transportation Journal* (Spring, 1974), pp. 24–29.

ERB, NORMAN H., "A Note on the Meaning of Physical Distribution Management (PDM)," *Transportation Journal* (Summer 1975), pp. 56–57.

FARRELL, JACK W.; "The Physical Distribution Profession: A Decade of Growth," *Traffic Management* (Special Reprint, 1972).

FARRIS, MARTIN T., Douglas C. Cochran, Grant M. Davis, and David R. Gourley; "Transportation Education—An Inter-Disciplinary Approach," *Transportation Journal* (Fall 1969), pp. 33–44.

GILL, LYNN E., "Through the PD Looking Glass," *Distribution Worldwide* (August, 1971), pp. 31–33.

HUPP, BURR; "The Physical Distribution Manager: Tomorrow," an address to N.C.P.D.M.'s 1975 meeting (Chicago: N.C.P.D.M., 1976).

LALONDE, BERNARD J. and Leslie M. Dawson; "Early Development of Physical Distribution Thought," in Donald J. Bowersox, et al., editors, *Readings in Physical Distribution Management* (New York: The MacMillan Co., 1959).

———; "The Distribution Manager Today," an address to N.C.P.D.M.'s 1975 meeting (Chicago: N.C.P.D.M., 1975).

LANCIONI, RICHARD A.; "Physical Distribution Management: Is It a Profession?," an address to N.C.P.D.M.'s 1975 meeting (Chicago: N.C.P.D.M., 1975).

LeKASHMAN, RAYMOND and John F. Stolle; "The Total Cost Approach to Distribution," *Business Horizons* (Winter, 1965), pp. 33–46.

LYNAGH, PETER M., "Physical Distribution: Seventies Style," *Business Perspectives* (Summer, 1973), pp. 28–31.

——— and Richard R. Poist; "Women and Minority Group Involvement: Frontier for Social Activism in PDM," *Transportation Journal* (Summer, 1975), pp. 31–39.

MAGEE, JOHN F.; *Industrial Logistics* (New York: McGraw-Hill Book Co., 1968).

MCELHINEY, PAUL T. and Charles L. Hilton; *Introduction to Logistics and Traffic Management* (Dubuque, Iowa: Wm. C. Brown Co. Publishers, 1968).

PETTAY, BOB; "Distribution with Gusto," *Handling and Shipping* (September, 1973).

PLOWMAN, E. G.; "Physical Distribution Management—How We Got From There," *ICC Practitioners' Journal* (May-June, 1970), pp. 567–575.

"Profiles of PDM: Libby's," *Handling and Shipping* (October, 1972).

ROSE, WARREN; "Is There a Need for Transportation Education at the College Level?," *Transportation Journal* (Spring, 1967), pp. 26–33.

SCHREINER, PAUL; "A PDM Pyramid," *Handling and Shipping* (August, 1972).

"The Physical Distribution Profession: Opportunities Unlimited," *Traffic Management* (Special Reprint).

Traffic Management (November, 1975 and February, 1976).

SCHARY, PHILIP B.; "The Dimensions of Physical Distribution," *Transportation Journal* (Fall, 1970), pp. 5–16.

WAGNER, WILLIAM B.; "A Survey of the Elementary Transportation Course at Selected Universities," *Transportation Journal* (Spring, 1971), pp. 40–46.

WILLIAMS, ERNEST W., JR., Sheldon R. Lewis, Charles S. Davis, Duane F. Semon, James F. Morse, George Dahm, and Earle Compton; "Applications of the Distribution Concept," *Transportation Journal* (Spring, 1968), pp. 35–54.

A General Motors built locomotive being loaded at New Orleans for shipment to Algeria. *Credit:* Lykes Brothers Steamship Co., Inc.

CHAPTER TWO

Physical Distribution
Interfaces Within the Firm

One thing seems sure: the choice of distribution system each company makes will have a significant impact on product design, plant investment, and organization. Industrial logistics and trends in logistics technology will receive increasing attention from business, along with markets, capital resources, and product development, in the formulation of corporate plans for the decade ahead.

—JOHN MAGEE
Harvard Business Review
July-August, 1960

Physical distribution management, once an arcane little sector, has been generally accepted as a full-fledged management science, both in the U.S. and abroad. Corporate executives from other departments all the way to the front office are feeling the influence of traffic and distribution.

Traffic Management
January, 1975

A CONSTANT AND PERVASIVE INTERACTION

Physical distribution managers are constantly interacting with the other functional areas of the firm, such as marketing, production, finance, and purchasing. Recall Charles Rader's comment that one of the major advantages to individuals working in PD is the high level of exposure they receive as they interact with the others in the firm. The purpose of this chapter is to examine the interfaces between the PD department and the firm's other major functional areas.

MARKETING INTERACTIONS

While the physical distribution staff interacts with all the functional areas, the most important interface is with marketing. Figure 2-1 illustrates the integral relationship between physical distribution and the other parts of the firm's marketing "mix." Although Figure 2-1 looks

Fig. 2-1 Physical Distribution As A Step In The Marketing Process.

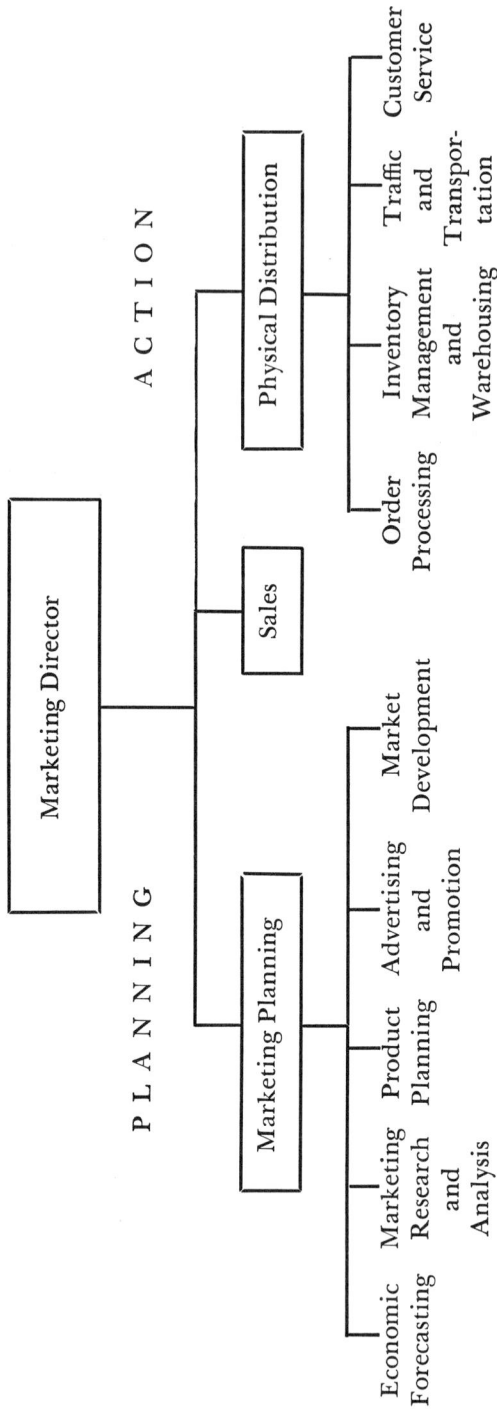

PLANNING   A C T I O N

Marketing Director

Marketing Planning — Sales — Physical Distribution

Marketing Planning:
- Economic Forecasting
- Marketing Research and Analysis
- Product Planning
- Advertising and Promotion
- Market Development

Physical Distribution:
- Order Processing
- Inventory Management and Warehousing
- Traffic and Transportation
- Customer Service

like an organization chart, and it could be, it is also a form of "flow" chart where the earlier actions are always shown on the left side. PD is the last step in the process.

The most important reason that those responsible for marketing have embraced physical distribution in recent years is that effective physical distribution is now recognized as a positive sales-generating asset. The following pages will examine how physical distribution interfaces with each of the four basic parts of the marketing mix: place, price, product, and promotion (sometimes known as the "4 P's").

PLACE DECISIONS

From a marketing viewpoint, place decisions involve two types of networks. The first network involves *physical distribution*, which addresses the issues of how most effectively to transport and store the product from where it is produced to where it is finally sold. (This is, of course, the subject of this entire book.)

Consider briefly the second type of network, known as the *marketing channel*; which is the arrangement of intermediaries (wholesalers, retailers, brokers, manufacturer's representatives, etc.) the firm uses to accomplish its marketing objectives.[1] An effective physical distribution system can provide positive support by allowing the firm to attract—and utilize—the channel members believed to be the most productive. Frequently, the intermediary channel members are in a position to "pick and choose" which manufacturer's products they wish to merchandise. If a manufacturer is not able to consistently provide the right product, at the right time, in the right quantities, and in an undamaged condition, the channel members will either terminate their relationship with the supplier or—at least—not actively promote the supplier's product.

Marketing channel management for the manufacturer is extremely complex, because typically the members (such as wholesalers and retailers) are independent firms which often have conflicting goals and aspirations. Warren J. Wittreich noted that manufacturers tend to be *growth* oriented, whereas many retailers, especially family-owned individual stores, tend to be more satisfied with maintaining the *status-quo*.[2]

Conflict is often present between channel members and the supplier's physical distribution department. Retailers and wholesalers want to "push" the inventory holding function back onto the manufacturer, in order to reduce their own inventory holding costs. The supplier's PD department, on the other hand, would prefer that wholesalers and re-

[1] For further information on marketing channels see: Louis E. Boone and James C. Johnson, (eds.) *Marketing Channels* (2nd ed.; Tulsa, Oklahoma: PPC Books, 1977).

[2] Warren J. Wittriech, "Misunderstanding the Retailer," *Harvard Business Review* (May-June, 1962).

Fig. 2-2 The Exchange and Transaction Function.

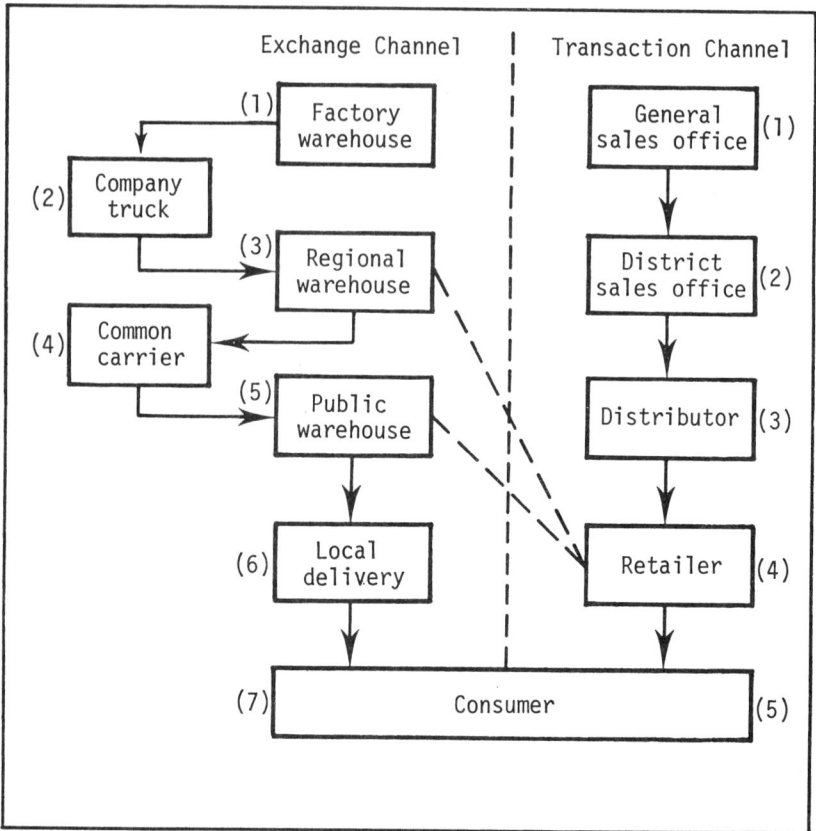

SOURCE: Donald J. Bowersox, *Logistical Management* (New York: Macmillan Publishing Co., Inc., 1974), p. 49.

tailers maintain large inventories. Chapter seven, which discusses inventories, covers this matter in more detail.

A methodology for analyzing the *place decisions* of the marketing mix has been suggested by Professor Bowersox. He feels that there are two basic flows between the manufacturer and the ultimate consumer. The first involves the intermediaries engaged in physically getting the product from the manufacturer to the ultimate consumer, and Bowersox calls this the *exchange function*. This includes the manufacturer's physical distribution department, as well as warehouses and carriers. The second flow is called the *transaction function*, and is devoted exclusively to selling the product to the various channel members. Figure 2-2 illustrates these two functions. The goods physically move through the exchange channel. Title to, or ownership of, the goods moves through the transaction channel. Geographic or "place" decisions regarding movement of goods through the exchange channel are covered elsewhere in this book. Place decisions involving the transactions channel are not covered in this book. They would follow the firm's overall marketing strategy of selecting the best channel member to serve each and every market.

It is both impossible and unwise to assume that either the exchange or the transaction function is the more important. This is because both functions are *mutually dependent* on each other. If either fails, the firm will not be able to sell its products.

PRICING ACTIVITIES

The effectiveness and efficiency of the physical distribution department has significant impact on the firm's selling price of its products.

> It is axiomatic that the price of a product must cover all costs in the long run. It seems equally axiomatic that in the long run any wastes in physical distribution efficiency must be passed on to the consumer in the form of either a higher price or poor product quality. The inability of a firm to control costs in the physical distribution sector can impair profit in the short run and survival in the long run.[3]

Transportation cost factors are also influential in determining the method used to quote the firm's selling price.[4] There are basically two alternatives that a firm can use regarding its handling of the transportation costs. One method is to price F.O.B. origin* and the other is a delivered-pricing system. F.O.B. origin pricing indicates that the seller quotes a price to the buyer which does *not* include any transportation costs to the purchaser. In this type of pricing, the buyer is responsible for the selection of the transport mode, because he or she assumes the expense of the transportation incurred. This system of pricing is easy to administer from the seller's viewpoint and it always yields the same net return for each sale.

A drawback of F.O.B. origin pricing is that it complicates marketing strategies which call for a uniform retail price for the product on a regional or national basis. Retailers are reluctant to follow the manufacturer's suggested retail price because their "landed" price‡ varies depending on the distance between the retailer and the manufacturer.

* This stands for "free on board."

‡ "Landed" price is product price plus transportation costs.

[3] Edward W. Smykay, *Physical Distribution Management*, 3d edition (New York: Macmillan, 1973), pp. 36–37.

[4] This section is based on a discussion in: Donald V. Harper, *Price Policy and Procedure* (New York: Harcourt, Brace & World, Inc., 1965), pp. 203–220.

Since retailers typically have a predetermined margin based on total landed costs, the result is that each retailer would have a different retail price.

Another problem is more subtle, and it is probably the most important. Donald V. Harper observed that ". . . it may mislead the manufacturer into thinking that outbound transportation costs are no concern to him although, in fact, they are still quite important to him to the extent that the buyer of a product is concerned with the total landed cost of the product, rather than just the price of the product alone."[5]

If the vendor quotes a price to the purchaser which includes both the price of the product and the transportation cost of the product to the purchaser's receiving dock, this is known as *delivered pricing*. This type of pricing is often designated "F.O.B. buyer's dock." The seller has the prerogative to select both the mode and the carrier to deliver the product.

An *average* amount of transportation costs is added to each product to determine the uniform delivered price. Some customers are paying either too much or too little freight costs compared to the actual transportation charges paid to the carriers. Buyers located relatively close to seller are forced to pay more than their share of freight charges, and it is said that these buyers pay *phantom freight*.

The opposite situation occurs when the buyer actually pays less freight than the seller incurs in shipping the product. This situation is known as *freight absorption*, because the seller is absorbing part of the transportation costs involved in the shipment. Freight absorption, and phantom freight are illustrated in Figure 2-3 for shipments originating in Omaha.

There are a number of advantages to delivered pricing. The first is that it allows a manufacturer to expand the geographic area to which his or her product is sold, because distant customers in a region do not pay the full costs of transportation. Second, this system of pricing simplifies the usage of suggested retail pricing by the manufacturer. It is more feasible because each retailer in the region pays the same landed cost. Third, delivered pricing is favored by the manufacturer's sales force because they can easily quote the total cost of the product to the buyer. Finally, product distribution is managed by the seller who can control the exchange network, making it function in a manner which is most beneficial to the firm's overall objectives.

There are also some *negative* aspects to delivered pricing systems. The first is that the firm does *not* receive the same net for each purchase. This is because an average transportation cost rather than actual cost was added to the purchase price of each product. Second, over time, the

---

[5] Harper, *op. cit.*, p. 206. Note also that if a firm chooses to sell all products on an F.O.B. origin basis, it is abdicating most physical distribution management functions.

Fig. 2-3 Phantom Freight and Freight Absorption.

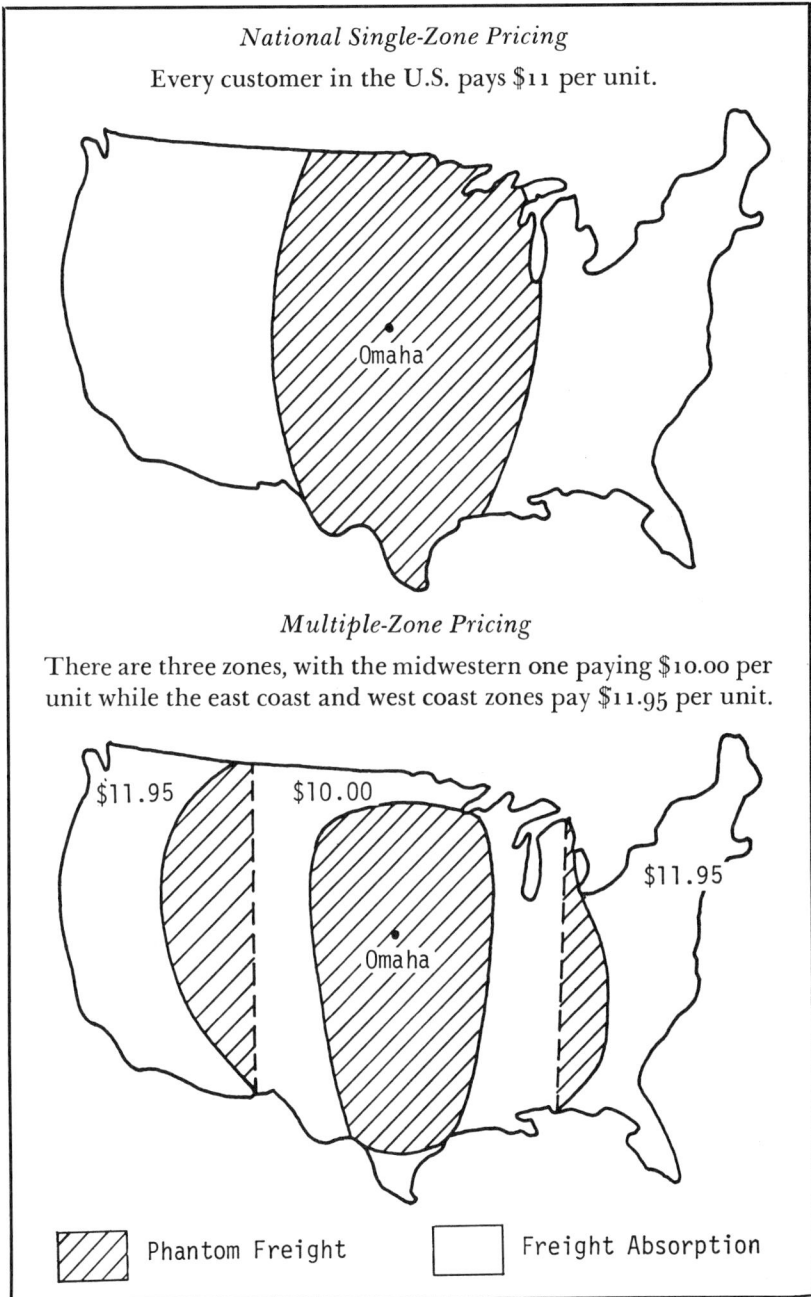

National Single-Zone Pricing
Every customer in the U.S. pays $11 per unit.

Multiple-Zone Pricing

There are three zones, with the midwestern one paying $10.00 per unit while the east coast and west coast zones pay $11.95 per unit.

$11.95 $10.00

$11.95

Omaha

▨ Phantom Freight   ☐ Freight Absorption

locational "mix" of customers can change. This can be especially troublesome if sales continue to increase in the more distant markets in which the firm is already absorbing a portion of the freight charges. A problem also occurs when astute customers realize that since they are located relatively close to the vendor, they are being forced to pay phantom freight. Some sellers, to avoid alienating these customers, allow customers the option to order F.O.B. origin if they so desire. F.O.B. plant prices may also be used by buyers who have their own truck fleets. The Federal Trade Commission (FTC) has questioned the use of delivered pricing systems and whether they are unjustly discriminatory. For example, the FTC ordered some plywood manufacturers to sell F.O.B. origin to any customer who believes he is paying an excessive amount of phantom freight.[6]

Physical distribution managers play an important role in product pricing. They are expected to know the costs of providing various levels of customer service (see Chapter 3) and therefore must be consulted to determine the trade-offs between costs and customer service. Since many distribution costs enjoy per unit savings when larger volumes are handled, the physical distribution manager can also help formulate the firm's "quantity discount" pricing policies.

PRODUCT DECISIONS

The most important interface between the firm's production and physical distribution departments is to insure that the product itself arrives where and when it is needed (and in an undamaged state). If this objective is not met, a *stock-out* may occur. A stock-out occurs when a customer requests and is ready to buy a specific product but is told that the item desired is not in stock. There are three possible outcomes when a stock-out takes place. The first is that the retail customer is extremely brand loyal—and therefore, refuses to purchase a substitute. This customer will wait until the stock-out has been corrected. A second and more likely event is that the customer purchases a substitute product. However, when that substitute product needs replacing, the customer goes back to the original brand. The third potential outcome is when the customer purchases a competitor's substitute product, and later decides he or she *prefers* the competitor's product.

Both the production and physical distribution departments must agree on protective packaging and other materials handling procedures which will result in a minimum of product damage. The subject of freight loss and damage control is discussed in chapters five and six, and

6 "FTC Accepts Orders on Plywood Shipment Practices of Two Firms," *The Wall Street Journal* (April 24, 1974), p. 36. See also: James C. Johnson and Louis E. Boone, "How Competitive Is Delivered Pricing?," *Journal of Purchasing and Material Management* (Summer, 1976), pp. 26–30.

Fig. 2-4 A Product Protection Program.

A PRODUCT PROTECTION PROGRAM

AS PART OF a continuing program designed to insure that its customers receive the best quality possible when they purchase its electric and gas appliances, the Caloric Corporation, a subsidiary of Raytheon Company, undertook a complete finished goods packaging evaluation program in 1971.

Top management initiated and gave its full support to the program, assigning to Paul A. Cloutier, packaging engineer, the task of organizing and coordinating it. His first step was to call a meeting of the company's major packaging material suppliers to discuss the aims and requirements of this program. All suppliers agreed to submit to a competitive design procedure whenever a new or revised package was needed. The following criteria were established:

1. Vendors would be furnished with finished goods samples whenever required.

2. They would be advised of ancillary packaging requirements as well as the testing parameters which had to be met.

3. Vendors could submit as many concepts as they desired.

4. All concepts and samples had to be submitted within 15 days from receipt of prototypes.

5. In addition to testing requirements, the proposed concept had to be able to withstand testing equivalent to double (X2) that required by the National Safe Transit Committee.

6. The proposed concept had to be priced competitively.

7. Vendor submitting the winning concept would be guaranteed a full year as sole supplier of the required material.

Next step was to talk to the Quality Assurance and Consumer Relations departments, which are in close contact with Caloric's sales force and its service people, as well as in direct contact with end product users. A letter from the company's president is included with every item shipped. It invites direct customer comment of the product, including its packaging. A review of such records and the "Product Quality Reports," which are a communication medium between the field and the factory, was instituted to determine the most pressing protective packaging problem area. This turned out to involve the "built-in" product line.

Two specific problems were discovered concerning built-in units. First, oven door kits, which are shipped separately from the ranges, were experiencing a high rate of enamel chippage. At the time, Caloric was using an expensive combination of molded Styrofoam end caps and accordian-pleated inserts within a corrugated carton. Subjecting these kits to the standard NSTC pre-shipment test indicated the packaged product could not pass the prescribed drop test. Inspection of the dropped kits revealed exactly the damage pattern being evidenced in the field.

Sample kits were taken to the company's vendors, and specific parameters were established. Two vendors submitted samples, and testing began immediately. End result was an all-new corrugated package able to withstand repeated drops from 36 inches. Two side benefits were realized: The overall size of the exterior container, a 200-pound test, C-flute, full overlap carton, was reduced by one-fourth, and a substantial material and labor savings also resulted.

Sales people in the high-volume areas were then contacted and advised of the changes. A group of test shipments were set up under control conditions, and arrangements were made for personal follow-up.

"The test shipment results were outstanding," reports Mr. Cloutier, "and not one of the kits in the new package was damaged, while 25% of those in the old one were. Since we started using the new package, we have shipped in excess of 12,000 kits and have had only 43 cases of reported damage."

SOURCE: Lowell E. Perrine, "A Product Protection Program," *Traffic Management* (April, 1973), pp. 44–45.

protective packaging is covered in chapter ten. At this time, note Figure 2-4 which shows a packaging-distribution-marketing interface.

Magee noted that from an inventory control point-of-view, new products being designed should contain as many standardized components as possible. The effect is to reduce the total number of different product parts that must be in inventory at any one time. Regardless of what products are actually assembled, a smaller number of different basic components is used. If, on the other hand, each product requires many unique inputs, then the necessary inventory would have to carry many more different items to support the diversified product line.[7] The same problem would be repeated when it became necessary to stock repair parts.

PROMOTIONAL ACTIVITIES

An important support function provided by physical distribution is to insure that when "specials" are highly advertised, the products will be physically available in the stores to meet the surge in customer demand. It is often said by marketing experts that there are few things more damaging to a firm's goodwill than to be stocked-out of an item that is being heavily promoted in a large sales campaign. There are many situations which require close cordination between the promotion department and the physical distribution personnel. Peter R. Attwood, a British consultant, related the following situation which would be amusing if it weren't so serious.

> An example to illustrate the need for unified planning concerns an American manufacturer who ran a massive sales promotion campaign a few years ago. Customers were given a large discount for orders requiring twenty-five cases of goods at one time. It had been planned that this discount would be covered by the savings from processing large orders. Unfortunately, the campaign flopped, because distribution costs increased out of proportion. These increases were due to handling in uneconomic batches, because a pallet load of goods comprised twenty-four cases.[8]

The Scott Paper Company continually monitors the size of shipments being sent to customers. Whenever it appears that relatively small increases in the order would substantially reduce freight charges per unit, the sales department is notified.[9]

---

[7] John F. Magee, *Industrial Logistics* (New York: McGraw-Hill Book Co., 1968), p. 45.

[8] Peter R. Attwood, *Planning a Distribution System* (London: Gower Press, Ltd., 1971), p. 55.

[9] Janet Bosworth, "What Does a Traffic Manager Do?," *Distribution Worldwide* (March, 1971).

Professors Sampson and Farris have noted that sales personnel always prefer to sell large orders, but will sell in any quantities if the large orders cannot be obtained. If the traffic department establishes too many esoteric rules about minimum order quantities accepted, consolidated shipments, etc; frequently the result is that the sales people will ignore these rules unless they have true respect for the traffic department.[10]

Physical distribution systems need not be thought of as a "neutral" promotional tool. An outstanding distribution system is a selling point in itself. This is true for items such as wallpaper, where retailers cannot carry large stocks but must rely on fast deliveries from some centralized distribution point. Another example is a product to which repair parts are essential.

INBOUND TRAFFIC AND PRODUCTION INTERFACES

In chapter one the inference was created that traffic functions become subordinate to physical distribution functions. This is true, but in many instances only applies to outbound shipments. For many firms, the traffic management problem associated with inbound materials is as important—if not more important—than the traffic management of outbound products. Sometimes managing movement of materials between various plants of the same firm is a major undertaking. Figure 2-5 shows the travels of raw materials which eventually become a DuPont toothbrush. Reading down the table, one would classify the movements to the DuPont Texas plant as inbound raw materials. Responsibility for coordinating these moves would be shared by the firm's purchasing and production staffs. The moves from the Texas operations to West Virginia and then to Massachusetts are of company-owned material in semi-processed form. These moves would involve the traffic and production departments. Finally, the movements from the DuPont Massachusetts plant are of finished products, and could be classified as being physical distribution.

Traditionally, the firm's traffic department handled inbound, interplant, and outbound shipments. With the historical emphasis on production efficiency, inbound and interplant shipments were both considered to be of higher priority than were outbound shipments destined for customers. In many firms, one of the bureaucratic struggles that occurred when the physical distribution concept gained acceptance was between marketing and traffic. The traffic department had to be con-

---

[10] Roy J. Sampson and Martin T. Farris, *Domestic Transportation: Practice Theory and Policy*, 3rd ed. (Boston: Houghton Mifflin Co., 1975), p. 294.

Fig. 2-5 From Desert to Doorstep: The Travels of a Toothbrush.

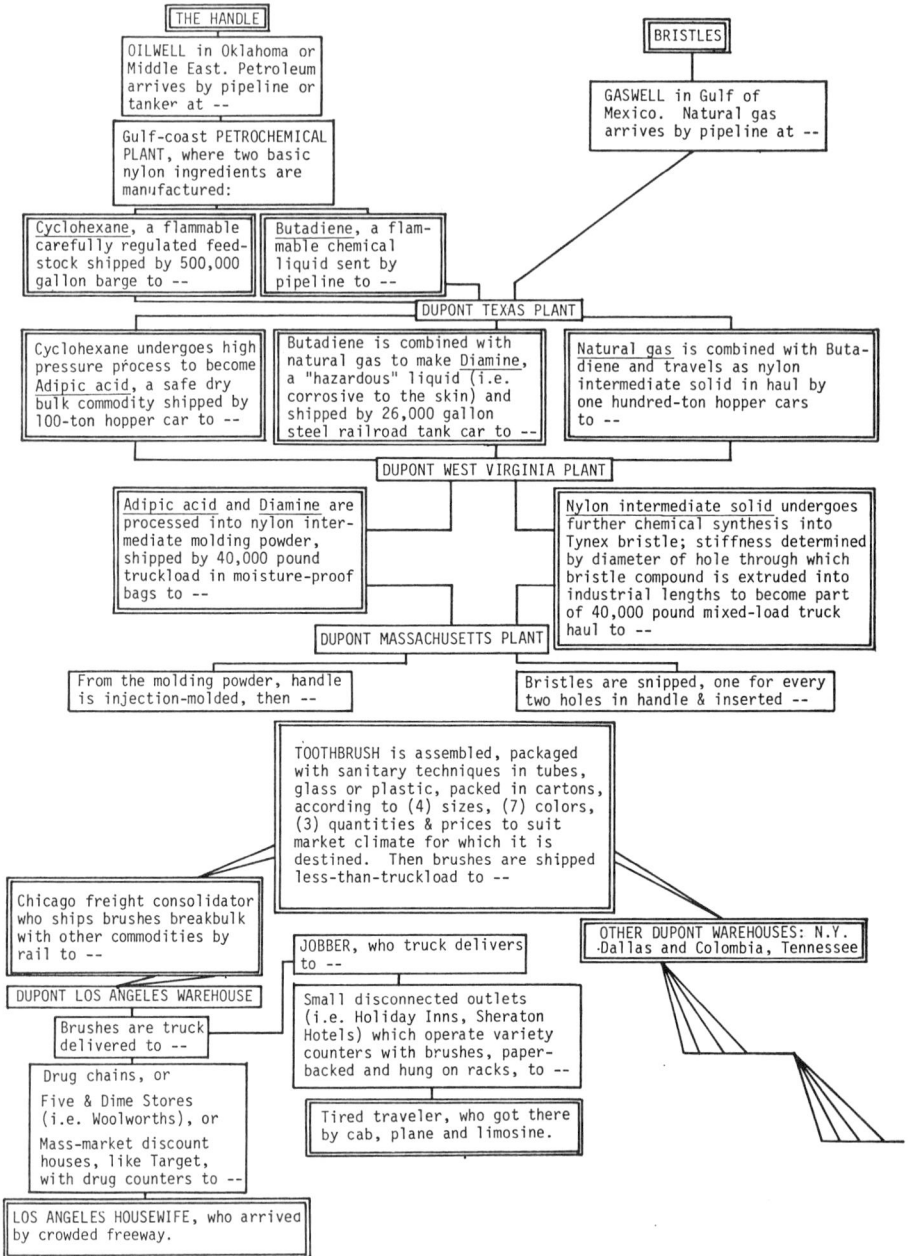

THE HANDLE

OILWELL in Oklahoma or Middle East. Petroleum arrives by pipeline or tanker at --

Gulf-coast PETROCHEMICAL PLANT, where two basic nylon ingredients are manufactured:

BRISTLES

GASWELL in Gulf of Mexico. Natural gas arrives by pipeline at --

Cyclohexane, a flammable carefully regulated feedstock shipped by 500,000 gallon barge to --

Butadiene, a flammable chemical liquid sent by pipeline to --

DUPONT TEXAS PLANT

Cyclohexane undergoes high pressure process to become Adipic acid, a safe dry bulk commodity shipped by 100-ton hopper car to --

Butadiene is combined with natural gas to make Diamine, a "hazardous" liquid (i.e. corrosive to the skin) and shipped by 26,000 gallon steel railroad tank car to --

Natural gas is combined with Butadiene and travels as nylon intermediate solid in haul by one hundred-ton hopper cars to --

DUPONT WEST VIRGINIA PLANT

Adipic acid and Diamine are processed into nylon intermediate molding powder, shipped by 40,000 pound truckload in moisture-proof bags to --

Nylon intermediate solid undergoes further chemical synthesis into Tynex bristle; stiffness determined by diameter of hole through which bristle compound is extruded into industrial lengths to become part of 40,000 pound mixed-load truck haul to --

DUPONT MASSACHUSETTS PLANT

From the molding powder, handle is injection-molded, then --

Bristles are snipped, one for every two holes in handle & inserted --

TOOTHBRUSH is assembled, packaged with sanitary techniques in tubes, glass or plastic, packed in cartons, according to (4) sizes, (7) colors, (3) quantities & prices to suit market climate for which it is destined. Then brushes are shipped less-than-truckload to --

Chicago freight consolidator who ships brushes breakbulk with other commodities by rail to --

JOBBER, who truck delivers to --

OTHER DUPONT WAREHOUSES: N.Y. ·Dallas and Colombia, Tennessee

DUPONT LOS ANGELES WAREHOUSE

Brushes are truck delivered to --

Small disconnected outlets (i.e. Holiday Inns, Sheraton Hotels) which operate variety counters with brushes, paper-backed and hung on racks, to --

Drug chains, or

Five & Dime Stores (i.e. Woolworths), or

Mass-market discount houses, like Target, with drug counters to --

Tired traveler, who got there by cab, plane and limosine.

LOS ANGELES HOUSEWIFE, who arrived by crowded freeway.

SOURCE: Daniel K. Chapman, "Untangling Industry's Toughest Knot: Physical Distribution Systems in the Seventies," a paper distributed by Robertson Distribution Systems, Inc., Houston 1973.

vinced that outbound shipments were fully as important as were inbound and interplant movements.*

The physical distribution department constantly interfaces with the traffic function. An example is the use of private truck fleets (discussed in chapter six) which are frequently advantageous only if a firm can balance movements in two directions. In such an instance, coordination would be needed between a firm's purchasing department, its physical distribution department, and the traffic department which is responsible for obtaining high utilization of the firm's fleet of trucks.

A classic area of conflict between production and physical distribution regards the length of production runs. Production managers prefer long runs in order to minimize the "down" time between runs when the equipment is being retooled. Physical distribution personnel, while appreciating large runs from a transportation savings point-of-view, must consider the ramifications of the increased inventory holding costs which also result. The longer the product run, the greater the average length of time between the manufacturing of the product and its ultimate sale. As will be discussed in chapter seven, inventory holding costs can be very substantial, often running twenty-five percent per year of the value of the products.

Another issue that arises between production and PD staffs concerns plant location. As will be examined in chapter eight, a major input in any plant location decision is the cost of transportation. The structure of the transportation industry, which is examined in chapters four, five and six reveals a highly intricate system which can have substantial impact on plant location decisions.

An area of necessary coordination between production and physical distribution is customer service, which is the subject of the next chapter. Magee tells of a firm, producing electronic assemblies, which decided to pay its production employes on a team incentive basis. Most of the firm's products were assembled from common components and, when orders were received, they were sent immediately to the assembly department. There was a large backlog of orders waiting to be assigned to the assembly groups. Even though the incentive standards were basically equitable, the assembling teams had definite preferences regarding which products earned the largest incentive. Each assembly team, within reason, was able to follow its own preferences regarding which products it assembled. Overall, the factory was able to produce statistics to substantiate that a high proportion of the orders were completed either on

* A large scale management survey in the mid-1970's asked, "In which area of physical distribution management would the positive results of profit and/or service improvement most 'easily' be realized?" The most frequently cited function was "outbound transport." However, when respondents were grouped by title, those whose title was chairman or president ranked "inbound transport" the highest. See Roger Meissner and Paul Nelson, "Where Do We Start?" *Handling and Shipping* (February, 1976), pp. 41–44.

time or ahead of schedule. Nevertheless, Magee's research indicated that a hard core of orders were not being processed within a reasonable amount of time, and that this situation was a continuing source of customer irritation. The plant manager was completely unaware his supervision and scheduling techniques were creating a customer service problem.[11]

To achieve the required smooth flow of inputs into the production or manufacturing process, it is necessary for the purchasing department to coordinate its activities with both the production and physical distribution departments. Physical distribution can assist the purchasing department in arranging for the most advantageous transportation of the inputs into the production facility. This assistance is of prime importance if the firm buys its inputs F.O.B. origin. It is often possible that even if the vendors sell on a delivered price basis, it may be advantageous for the company to purchase F.O.B. origin. This assumes that the firm has been paying a degree of phantom freight in the past. Or, the firm may be operating a truck fleet which currently returns empty.*

FINANCIAL AND ACCOUNTING INTERFACES

The physical distribution department constantly interfaces with both the financial and accounting departments. A key reason for this interdependency is that physical distribution managers can not make any better decisions than the quality of the cost data with which they are working.[12] The finance staff, which is always predicting future cash flows, may be dependent upon the PD staff for information concerning the status of finished products which are somewhere between the end of the firm's production line and the purchaser's receiving dock.

The finance staff often is charged with the responsibility of allocating the firm's limited funds to the projects which are desired by the various operating departments. Finance personnel use several methods such as the return on invested capital method to determine which projects should be funded.

Assume, for example, that the physical distribution department wants to purchase pallet storage racks which allow loaded pallets to be stored higher since they are not resting on the pallets below them. While the racks and their installation will cost $10,000, it will allow the firm to

* Many physical distribution practices discussed throughout this book are applicable to inbound movements as well.

[11] *Industrial Logistics, op. cit.* p. 42.

[12] George G. Smith, "Knowing Your P.D. Costs," *Distribution Age* (January, 1966), p. 21.

avoid using additional public warehouse space which would cost $2,000 per year. Therefore, the pallet racks yield an annual return on invested capital of twenty percent. If this project has a relatively high enough return on invested capital, compared with all other investment opportunities being considered, the finance department will authorize this expenditure.[13]

Physical distribution personnel are constantly interacting with the accounting department. Dr. Michael Schiff, chairman of the Department of Accounting at New York University, was commissioned by the National Council of Physical Distribution Management to study and write a report regarding suggestions as to how accounting can assist physical distribution. The final report entitled *Accounting and Control in Physical Distribution Management* stated that at present most data required for efficient control of physical distribution were already available. The problem was that the required information was scattered in many sundry accounts and difficult to assemble. Schiff argued that the best procedure would involve a controller (senior accountant) who would work directly for the manager of the physical distribution department. This person would then assemble the accounting data for presentation and analysis by the senior physical distribution executives. Schiff noted that eight of fourteen firms which he studied already possessed physical distribution controllers.[14]

Accounting systems that are attuned to the needs of physical distribution can be extremely beneficial. Stern reports that in many cases, effective physical distribution (supported by proper accounting reports) can switch a sales territory from operating in the "red" to one in the "black." In one situation a firm consolidated orders into a sales territory and it was able to produce a twenty-five percent freight savings.[15] In addition, accounts can help to determine the cost of lost sales resulting from a stock-out of the firm's product.[16] Also, they can provide valuable inputs in establishing a zone-type delivered pricing system.[17]

Accounting is a powerful tool for controlling a firm's operations. This is discussed in more detail in chapter fourteen, which deals with physical distribution system controls.

[13] For a good discussion of the preparation of a return on investment report, see Creed H. Jenkins, *Modern Warehouse Management* (New York: McGraw-Hill, 1968).

[14] Michael Schiff, *Accounting and Control in Physical Distribution Management* (Chicago: National Council of Physical Distribution Management, 1971).

[15] George L. Stern, "Traffic: Clear Signals for Higher Profits," *Harvard Business Review* (May-June, 1972), p. 79.

[16] Paul A. Wassmansdorf, "Identifying and Controlling the Costs of Physical Distribution," in *Management of the Physical Distribution Function*, Management Report No. 49 (New York: American Management Association, 1960), pp. 34-36.

[17] H. C. Miller, "Accounting for Physical Distribution," *Transportation and Distribution Management* (December, 1961), pp. 10-11.

PHYSICAL DISTRIBUTION FIRMS

At the risk of over-simplification, this book is written to make it appear that PD functions are performed within a firm, usually by a section or department within the marketing function. In many cases this is so.

However, there are some exceptions and they will be mentioned briefly here. First, there are firms which contract to perform physical distribution services for others. One such firm is Martin-Brower which handles all of distribution functions for food chains such as McDonalds, Baskin-Robbins, etc. Martin-Brower operates 165 tractors and 300 trailers and also controls the inventory levels for their customers. The firm also handles purchasing, pricing, sales analysis and planning functions for their clients.[18]

Public warehouse personnel perform many distribution functions and in some states they also perform deliveries. Recall the discussion of channel members, i.e. firms that act as intermediaries between a manufacturer and the ultimate consumer. Some intermediaries perform more PD functions for the manufacturer than do others. And, of course, for doing this, they expect to be additionally compensated.

Chapter eleven, which deals with international distribution, will discuss additional types of firms which specialize in handling all or portions of a firm's overseas distribution operations.

SUMMARY

This chapter examined the fundamental interfaces between physical distribution and the other functional areas of the firm. By far the most important relationship exists between marketing and physical distribution. There are four basic aspects of the marketing mix: place, price, product and promotion. *Place* decisions involve channels of distribution and physical distribution. Place decisions can be thought of as either part of the *exchange* function or as part of the *transaction* function.

Pricing activities are affected by physical distribution costs. The firm's products can be sold either F.O.B. origin or a delivered pricing system can be used. Because an average amount of freight is added to each product sold in the zone, *phantom freight* and *freight absorption* are encountered.

Product decision interfaces involve insuring that the product arrives at its destination at the right time, in the correct quantities, and in an undamaged condition. If this objective is achieved, the *stock-out* can be avoided.

Promotional activities center around assuring that when highly ad-

---

[18] "Putting the FAST in Fast Food," *Distribution Worldwide* (June, 1975), p. 30.

vertised "specials" are held, the products involved will be physically available in the stores to meet customer demand.

Physical distribution also interfaces with purchasing and production activities. Physical distribution can assist the purchasing department in arranging for the most advantageous transportion of the inputs into the production facility. Production and physical distribution staffs are primarily responsible for new plant and warehouse location analysis.

The finance department is often responsible for deciding which capital expenditures should be authorized by the firm each fiscal year. Therefore, whenever physical distribution personnel request capital improvements, they must work closely with the financial people.

In the past the accounting department and physical distribution group have not supported each other properly. This situation is starting to correct itself, as witnessed by Professor Schiff's research. Effective accounting systems can help allocate sales incentive programs, develop delivered pricing systems, and help "control" PD activities.

QUESTIONS FOR DISCUSSION AND REVIEW

1. Physical distribution necessarily interfaces with all the other functional areas of the firm. Which interaction do you believe is: (a) the *most* important? (b) the *least* important?

2. Discuss briefly each of the four basic aspects of the marketing mix and how *each* interfaces with the physical distribution department.

3. It has been suggested by many marketing executives that physical distribution activities are really a sub-part of the overall marketing function. Take a position regarding this issue and argue your case.

4. How can physical distribution activities provide a positive sales generating situations? Discuss.

5. What is a channel of distribution? What is the relationship between them and physical distribution?

6. Warren J. Wittreich wrote a classic article regarding the different long-term objectives of manufacturers versus small independent retailers. Discuss this basic conflict of objectives.

7. Compare and contrast the *exchange* function versus the *transaction* function.

8. Regarding the exchange and the transaction functions, which do you believe is ultimately the more important to the long-run success of the firm? Defend your answer.

9. What does F.O.B. origin imply? What are the *pluses* and *minuses* of using this type of a pricing system? Discuss.

10. Are there any viable alternatives to F.O.B. origin pricing? If so, discuss them briefly.

11. What is the basic theory or rationale of zone pricing? Why is it

done and what information is necessary to implement such a pricing system?

12. Discuss briefly the concepts of phantom freight and freight absorption.

13. It is often said that zone pricing systems have the potential to produce customer ill-will. Discuss why there may be validity to this statement.

14. The importance of coordinating physical distribution with product decisions is well known. Discuss briefly why this situation is true.

15. What is a *stock-out*? Why are they important?

16. Discuss briefly the possible outcomes which can be precipitated by a stock-out.

17. Does physical distribution have any interfaces with the firm's promotional activities? How, if at all?

18. What can physical distribution do to help the purchasing department?

19. Discuss briefly the interfaces between the firm's manufacturing (production) department and physical distribution.

20. What activity is typically assigned to the finance group which directly affects physical distribution activities?

21. Discuss a number of situations in which physical distribution and accounting can assist each other in performing more efficiently.

CASE 2-1 SUDSY SOAP, INC.

Frank Johnson was traffic manager for Sudsy Soap, Inc. He had held the job for the past five years and had just about every distribution function well under control. His task was made easier because shipping patterns and volumes were unchanging routines. The firm's management boasted that it had a steady share in "a stable market" although a few stockholders grumbled that Sudsy Soap had a declining share in a growing market.

The Sudsy Soap plant was in Akron, Ohio. It routinely produced 100,000 48-ounce cartons of soap each week. Each carton measured about ½ cubic foot and each working day, three or four carloads were loaded and shipped to various food chain warehouses and to a few large grocery brokers. Johnson had worked with the marketing staff to establish prices so nearly all soap was purchased in carload lots. Shipments less than a full carload did not occur very often.

Buyers relied on dependable deliveries and the average length of time it took for a carton of soap to leave the Sudsy production line and reach a retailer's shelf was 19 days. The best time was six days (mainly to chains distributing in Ohio) and the longest time was 43 days (to retailers in Hawaii).

Sudsy Soap's president was worried about the stockholders' criticism regarding Sudsy's lack of growth so he hired a new sales manager E. Gerard Beever (nicknamed "Eager" since his college days at a Big Ten university). Beever had a one-year contract and knew he must produce. He needed a "gimmick."

At his university fraternity re-union he ran into one of his fraternity roommates who was now sales manager for an imported line of kitchen dishes which were manufactured in Hong Kong. Their quality was good, but competition was intense. It was difficult to get even a "toe-hold" in the kitchen dish market. He and Beever shared a common plight; they were responsible for increasing market shares for products with very little differentiation from competitors' products. They each wished they could help the other, but could not. The re-union ended and each went home.

The next week Beever was surprised to receive a telegram from his old roommate. It read:

WE PROPOSE A TIE-IN PROMOTION BETWEEN SUDSY SOAP AND OUR DISHES. WE WILL SUPPLY AT NO COST TO YOU ONE HUNDRED THOUSAND EACH TWELVE INCH DINNER PLATES, SEVEN INCH PIE PLATES, NINE INCH BREAD AND BUTTER PLATES, COFFEE CUPS, AND SAUCERS. EACH WEEK YOU MUST HAVE A DIFFERENT PIECE IN EACH PACKAGE STARTING DINNER PLATE IN WEEK ONE, PIE PLATES IN WEEK TWO, AND SO ON THROUGH END OF WEEK FIVE. RECOMMEND THIS BE DONE WEEKS OF OCTOBER THREE, OCTOBER TEN, OCTOBER SEVENTEEN, OCTOBER TWENTY-FOUR AND OCTOBER THIRTY-ONE OF THIS YEAR. TIMING IMPORTANT BECAUSE NATIONAL ADVERTISING LINKED TO NEW TELEVISION SHOW WE ARE SPONSORING. WE WILL GIVE BUYERS OF FIVE PACKAGES OF SUDSY SOAP, PURCHASED FIVE WEEKS IN A ROW, ONE FREE PLACE SETTING OF OUR DISHES. ENOUGH OF YOUR CUSTOMERS WILL WANT TO COMPLETE TABLE SETTING SO THEY WILL BUY THREE, FIVE OR SEVEN MORE PLACE SETTINGS FROM OUR RETAILERS. TIMING IS CRUCIAL. ADVISE IMMEDIATELY.

Beever was pleased to receive the offer but realized a lot of questions had to be asked and answered before he could recommend that the offer be accepted. He sent a copy of the telegram to Johnson attached to an interoffice memo. The memo said:

Note attached telegram offering "tie-in" with dishes. Dishes are of good quality. What additional information do we need from dish distributor and what additional information do you need before we know whether to recommend acceptance? Please advise A.S.A.P.* Thanks.

* As Soon As Possible.

Question One: Draft Johnson's response to Beever's memo.

CASE 2-2   HAPPY CAMPING GUIDEBOOK

The *Happy Camping Guidebook* was published in Larkspur, California. It came out once a year, in early spring, and listed campsites in Washington, Oregon, and California. In 1974, 200,000 copies were printed and sold. The retail price was five dollars a copy, postage paid. Ms. Tammy Wood was business manager and one of her responsibilities was distribution of the printed copies. Since *Happy Camping Guidebook* contained no advertising, copies were mailed at the special 4th class book rates which were 18 cents for the first pound plus 8 cents for each additional pound to any point in the 50 states. Copies of the most recent *Happy Camping Guidebook* weighed just under two pounds apiece.

Copies were distributed in two ways. About 150,000 copies were mailed to individual purchasers who submitted a five dollar payment with their order. The others were distributed through bookstores and newsdealers. These copies were packaged five to a package because all commercial orders were sold and distributed only in multiples of five. These orders were also mailed in packages of five. (Most orders were for only five at a time but of course if 30 were ordered, then six packages of five would be mailed simultaneously to fill that order.)

Last year, the *Happy Camping Guidebook* enterprise lost money mainly because of increased paper costs. The publisher was debating whether to introduce advertising into the next edition. Over the years a number of camping equipment manufacturers and numerous campsites had indicated they would willingly buy advertisements in *Happy Camping Guidebook*. Anticipated ad revenues were quite high. However, there were three disadvantages that had to be considered.

1. The editorial staff was against carrying advertisements because they felt the "prestige" of the publication would be reduced. In addition, some readers might think that the magazine's text favored advertisers.

2. There would be considerable administrative and production problems associated with accepting and publishing ads. The size of the book would be increased which would mean more paper, printing, etc. would be needed. The book's estimated weight would increase to 2¾ lbs.

3. If it carried advertising, the book would move under parcel post rates which were much more than the book rate. Parcel post rates also increased as distance increased while the book rates were uniform, independent of distance. Assuming the new book with ads weighed 2¾ lbs., the applicable rates would be:

Local zone		$.65
Zone	1	.78
"	2	.78
"	3	.83
"	4	.92
"	5	1.04
"	6	1.18
"	7	1.32
"	8	1.45

All of the rates were higher than the 26 cents (18¢ + 8¢) presently paid on the two pound Guidebook (without ads.) Similar figures for containing five guidebooks in one package (weighing 14 lbs) would be:

Local zone		1.09
Zone	1	1.44
"	2	1.44
"	3	1.65
"	4	1.91
"	5	2.36
"	6	2.88
"	7	3.46
"	8	4.09

The current cost for ten pounds at the book rate was 90 cents.

A record of all last year's sales was kept for promotional purposes. They were stored on computer tape. Working with the local post office, Tammy developed a computer program which sorted zip codes by "zone" distance from Larkspur's post office. Figures for 1974 were:

		Single Book orders	*Five-book* orders
Local zone		2,200	500
Zone	1	2,800	1000
"	2	12,000	1500
"	3	33,000	2000
"	4	30,000	1500
"	5	20,000	1000
"	6	25,000	1000
"	7	20,000	1000
"	8	10,000	500

Question One: Assuming the Happy Camping Guidebook accepts advertising, and sales remain the same, what will the new distribution cost be?

Question Two: At present, the Guidebooks sell for five dollars a copy, postage paid, for orders paid in advance. Assume next year's issue contains advertising and new issues sell for five dollars plus the actual postage. How do you think this would affect the market?

CHAPTER REFERENCES

ATTWOOD, PETER R.; *Planning a Distribution System* (London: Gower Press, Ltd., 1971).

BEIER, FREDERICK J.; "Information Systems and the Life Cycle of Logistics Departments," *International Journal of Physical Distribution* (Summer, 1973), pp. 312–321.

————; "The Role of the Common Carrier in the Channel of Distribution," *Transportation Journal* (Winter, 1969), pp. 12–21.

BOONE, LOUIS E. and James C. Johnson, (eds.); *Marketing Channels* (2nd ed.; Tulsa, OK: PPC Books, 1977).

BOSWORTH, JANET; "What Does a Traffic Manager Do?," *Distribution Worldwide* (March, 1971).

BOWERSOX, DONALD J.; *Logistical Management* (New York: MacMillan Publishing Co., Inc., 1974).

BROWNE, WILLIAM G.; "Demand Stimulation, Cost Control, and the Logistics System," *Transportation Journal* (Spring, 1973), pp. 46–52.

CHAPMAN, DANIEL K.; "Untangling Industry's Toughest Knot: Physical Distribution Systems in the Seventies," a paper distributed by Robertson Distribution Systems, Inc., Houston, 1973.

DAVIS, GRANT M. and Stephen W. Brown; "Physical Distribution Strategies and Market Structures," *The Logistics and Transportation Review* (Volume 8, Number 1), pp. 89–98.

DENSMORE, MAX L. and John R. Grabner; "The Effect of Returned Goods on Distribution Performance," *International Journal of Physical Distribution* (June, 1972), pp. 135–143.

"FTC Accepts Orders on Plywood Shipment Practices of Two Firms," *The Wall Street Journal* (April 24, 1974).

HARPER, DONALD V.; *Price Policy and Procedure* (New York: Harcourt, Brace & World, Inc., 1965).

JENKINS, CREED H.; *Modern Warehouse Management* (New York: McGraw-Hill, 1968).

JOHNSON, JAMES C. and Louis E. Boone; "How Competitive Is Delivered Pricing," *Journal of Purchasing and Materials Management* (Summer, 1976).

MAGEE, JOHN F.; *Industrial Logistics* (New York: McGraw-Hill, 1968).

MALEY, W. E.; "Facets of Complex Distribution," *Transportation Journal* (Winter, 1967), pp. 60–63.

MEISSNER, ROGER and Paul Nelson; "Where Do We Start?" *Handling and Shipping* (February, 1976).

MILLER, H. G.; "Accounting for Physical Distribution," *Transportation and Distribution Management* (December, 1961).

PERRINE, LOWELL E.; "A Product Protection Program," *Traffic Management* (April, 1973).

"Putting the FAST in Fast Food," *Distribution Worldwide* (June, 1975).

SAMPSON, ROY J. and Martin T. Farris; *Domestic Transportation: Practice Theory and Policy*, 3rd ed. (Boston: Houghton Mifflin Co., 1975).

Schiff, Michael; *Accounting and Control in Physical Distribution Management* (Chicago: National Council of Physical Distribution Management, 1971).

SMITH, GEORGE G.; "Knowing Your P.D. Costs," *Distribution Age* (January, 1966).

SMYKAY, EDWARD W.; *Physical Distribution Management*, 3rd ed. (New York: MacMillan, 1973).

STEINER, HENRY MALCOLM; "Opportunity Cost, Capital Recovery, and Profit Analysis of Logistics Systems," *Transportation Journal* (Fall, 1973), pp. 15–22.

STERN, GEORGE L.; "Traffic: Clear Signals for Higher Profits," *Harvard Business Review* (May-June, 1972).

WASSAMANSDORF, PAUL A.; "Identifying and Controlling the Costs of Physical Distribution," *Management of the Physical Distribution Function*, Management Report No. 49 (New York: American Management Association, 1960).

WITTRIECH, WARREN J.; "Misunderstanding the Retailer," *Harvard Business Review* (May-June, 1962).

An order picker filling a parts order. *Credit:* Demag Material Handling Corporation.

CHAPTER THREE

Customer Service Standards and Order Processing

The business of keeping *customers—which is what customer service is all about—is submerged in the business of* getting *customers.*

Customer service begins when the sale is made. For better or for worse, the customer is delivered into the hands of a small army of people of varying skills, responsibilities, and motivations, and the sum of their activities will ultimately determine not only whether the customer remains a customer, but also whether he remains as a profitable customer.

> —HERBERT W. DAVIS
> *Handling and Shipping*
> November, 1971

We in distribution have recognized that providing a proper level of service to the customer is one of the major objectives of the physical distribution operation. Getting the product to the customer when *he wants it and* where *he wants it is the most important thing that we do. And performing this operation at a reasonable cost is the primary objective of every good distribution operation. I believe that it is going to be the major objective of every successful manufacturer during the balance of the 1970's.*

> —HARVEY N. SHYCON
> 1973 National Council of
> Physical Distribution Annual
> Proceedings

WHAT CUSTOMER SERVICE IS ALL ABOUT

Customer service is the collection of activities performed in filling orders and "keeping customers happy." It is an excellent competitive weapon. It has an advantage over price competition of being difficult to imitate. If a firm cuts its selling price, its competitors can initiate a matching price reduction immediately and the first company's comparative advantage is eliminated. Customer service improvements, which by their very nature take longer to establish, are much more difficult for competitors to emulate.

FIG. 3-1 A Humorous "Solution" to Customer Service Complaints.

PSYCHO

CALENDAR

NEG	FRI	FRI	THU	WED	TUE	MON
8	7	6	5	4	3	2
16	15	14	13	12	11	9
23	22	21	20	19	18	17
31	30	29	28	27	26	24
38	37	36	35	34	33	32

1. Every order is RUSH! Everyone wants his material shipped yesterday. With this calendar a customer can place his order on the 7th and have it delivered on the 3rd.
2. Most customers want their orders shipped by Friday, so there are two Fridays in every week.
3. There are seven extra days at the end of the month to take care of shipments which MUST go before the first of the following month.
4. There are no "first of the month" bills to pay because there isn't any "first." We've omitted the "tenth" and "twenty-fifth" so that you won't have to pay our invoices in accordance with our terms.
5. There are no bothersome non-productive Saturdays and Sundays. In that way we can manufacture your rush orders requiring week-end production without time-and-a-half or double-time overtime charges.
6. There's a new day each week called Negotiation day. Requests for improved delivery can be reviewed and discussed once weekly.

If the firm continues to offer inadequate customer service, the consequences are highly detrimental. Customer "ill-will" can accumulate to the point where the buying firm actually refuses to purchase the products of the vendor who consistently offers unacceptable customer service. The alienated customer is typically reluctant to accept future products from a vendor which is known for "good promises and poor performance." The effect is that customer service failures prevent the firm from being able to sell their products.[1] Customer service controversies have generated a significant quantity of "tongue-in-cheek" humor. Figure 3-1 illustrates an example—the "psycho calendar."

Understanding customer service is important to individuals working in physical distribution because the physical distribution department is often held responsible for meeting the salesperson's commitments. In addition, one objective of customer service is to present the firm's "best" image to customers. PD personnel must coordinate their efforts with those sections responsible for other aspects of customer service such as credit terms offered to buyers, honoring product warranties, stocking repair parts, etc.

This chapter will first examine the basic aspects of customer service standards for which physical distribution personnel are held responsible. In addition, a key aspect of customer service, the order processing system, will be analyzed so that its relationship to customer service standards can be appreciated. This chapter deals with relationships between the PD staff and buyers who are outside the firm. It complements chapter two, which dealt with relationships between the PD staff and other personnel *within* the firm.

CUSTOMER SERVICE STANDARDS DEFINED

Customer service has traditionally been a frustrating area of physical distribution, because of the problems involved in obtaining a specific, all inclusive, statement of objectives. A National Council of Physical Distribution Management task force dealing with customer service noted, "No apparent means exist to specifically measure customer service performance in a total sense. *Therefore, individual 'elements' must be defined and measured.*" (Emphasis added.)[2]

A number of companies distinguish between *goals* and *objectives* in their pursuit of customer service excellence. *Goals* tend to be broader, generalized statements regarding the overall results that the firm is attempting to achieve. *Objectives* are the means by which the goals are

[1] James A. Constantin, *Principles of Logistics Management* (New York: Appleton-Century-Crofts, 1966), p. 407.
[2] NCPDM news release.

achieved. Objectives often start from a base point and the idea is to improve the specific requirements over the given time period.

The E. I. duPont de Nemours & Company has established both *goals* and *objectives* for their firm. They state:

> Our *Primary Goal* is to provide a level of service equal to or better than major competition in select area markets of opportunity, and in other areas, improvements requiring little or no physical system change.
>
> Our *Secondary Goals* (in support of the primary goal)
> —adequate stock available at all times to satisfy customer requirements promptly.
> —dependable shipments and delivery service of products within the established objectives or the date specified by the customer.
> —prompt notification to customer upon any deviation from standard terms.[3]

Their objectives are much more specific in nature. An example of two of them are:

> In 1973 reduce the error rate on shipments from 2/1000 to 1/1000.
> In 1973 reduce ocean order packing time from 5 days to 4 days without error rate change.[4]

While there are many measures that can be used regarding the achievement of specific objectives, the authors believe the following four are especially important.

1. The total elapsed time from when the customer places an order until the customer physically receives the order.

2. The percentage of customer orders which can be filled immediately and completely from stock located in the supplier's warehouse.

3. The total elapsed time from when a supplier receives an order until the shipment is tendered to the transport mode for delivery to the customer.

4. The percentage of customer orders which are both picked and sent correctly to the customer.

CUSTOMER SERVICE OBJECTIVES OR STANDARDS SHOULD BE SPECIFIC

Unfortunately, many firms have customer service goals that are couched in platitudes, and nowhere can there be found any specific objectives regarding how the goals are to be achieved. Why is this a serious problem? The answer is that unless the customer service objectives or standards are stated in specific terms, they may be ignored; or else they are so vague that they offer no real guidance to operating personnel. In addition, the physical distribution department may then become the scapegoat for the marketing department. Assume a new product "flops." The marketing department might state that customer

---

[3] T. R. Elsman, "Export Customer Service," *Annual Proceedings of the National Council of Physical Distribution Management* (1972), p. 172.
[4] *Ibid.*, p. 170.

service levels were not as high as needed, and therefore the new product introduction failed. Without specific guidelines, the customer service staff lacks a base to prove that acceptable levels of customer service were maintained.

The solution to the above quandry is obvious. Customer service objectives or standards must be very specific in nature, as witnessed in the above duPont illustration. When this is done, it becomes easier to determine whether the customer service staff did in fact "drop-the-ball." With specific customer service standards, the customer service department would be in a better position to refute allegations if the established objectives had been met.

Almost everyone who studies the area of customer service standards agrees that they should be stated in writing. In this way, there can be considerably fewer problems involved in determining whether service standards have been met. Nevertheless, the practice of written customer service standards is far from universal. A survey of 124 firms which have stressed the importance of physical distribution was conducted by *Transportation and Distribution Management* magazine. The subject of the survey was customer service. Less than half of the respondents reported that they had written statements regarding any aspect of customer service standards.

Regarding individual aspects of customer service, 49 percent of the respondents noted that they have written statements dealing with the allowable time to process an order. The maximum time to physically pick an order in the warehouse and assemble it for tendering to the carrier was specified by 44 percent of the respondents. Forty percent specified the maximum delivery time which they allowed their carriers. Finally, 32 percent of the companies had written statements regarding the maximum time which the sales department has to report their sales to the order processing department.[5]

Another survey, one involving the textile industry, indicated that approximately one-third of the firms did not have any type of written customer service standards. Of the firms with a written customer service statement, only 15 percent gave their statements to their customers.[6]

THE ORDER CYCLE

The *order cycle* is of great importance in analyzing customer service activities for which a firm's PD section is responsible. From the seller's

---

[5] "Survey: Customer Service," *Transportation and Distribution Management* (May-June, 1974), pp. 46–47. The National Council of Physical Distribution Management established a customer service study task force in 1973. Their findings are scheduled for release in 1977.

[6] Herbert W. Davis, "4 Reasons Why Customer Service Managers Can't Manage Customer Service," *Handling and Shipping* (November, 1971), p. 52.

standpoint, it is defined as the time from when a customer places an order to when he or she receives the goods at the receiving dock. From the *buyer's* standpoint, the order cycle is really the *replenishment cycle* for goods needed on a regular basis. As will be discussed in the inventory chapter, the shorter and more consistent the order or replenishment cycle is, the less inventory one's customers have to maintain themselves.

Herbert W. Davis, a management consultant who has specialized in physical distribution, noted:

> Most managements (there are some notable exceptions) think of customer service as the time it takes an order to reach a customer once it's been shipped. They fail to realize that customer service is not a simple event, but rather a chain of events which, like any chain, is only as good as its weakest link.
>
> Transportation is a key link in that chain of events, to be sure. But the best transportation in the world cannot make up for the typical 2 to 5 week lag between receipt of an order and shipment of the goods to the customer. And even automating the order processing function cannot overcome a stock-out situation that started with inaccurate forecasting and compounded itself with inventory policies and production plans laid down far from the customer service scene.[7]

Many firms define their customer service standards in terms of the time involved in the entire order cycle or in regard to certain aspects of the order cycle. The order cycle is composed of four parts: *order transmittal, order processing, order picking,* and *order delivery.* Each of these subsystems will be examined.

ORDER TRANSMITTAL

Order transmittal is the time from when a customer places an order until the vendor receives the order. This aspect of the order cycle has drawn more attention in recent years. This situation has been caused by two factors. Many firms have calculated that the order transmittal time is from two to five days if the U. S. Postal Service is used to carry the order. (Some feel this is unreasonably long.) The second factor is the unpredictable variations in mail service. One Minneapolis firm reports that orders from St. Paul, about five miles away, take anywhere from one to four days to arrive. Orders mailed from Florida vary from two to seven days. This high degree of variability makes it difficult to provide any sort of overall consistency regarding the time involved in the order cycle. Unfortunately, the buyers assume the vendor receives the order almost immediately after it is mailed.

To correct the above deficiencies, many companies have their salespeople and customers order directly by phone or some other electronic

[7] *Ibid.,* p. 51.

method of order transmittal. Telephone order placement has experienced significant growth in recent years. It has the advantage of being instantaneous, but has the disadvantage of not providing "hard copy" or written information. Because of this disadvantage, there exists the possibility for transcribing errors from the phone to order sheets. This problem can be substantially reduced by having the recipient of the order read it back to the sender in order to verify its accuracy.

Electronic "hard copy" transmission is also becoming increasingly used to correct for telephone voice transcription errors. This includes the use of telephone "hard copy" systems, teletype, and other high speed data transmission programs. In addition, some firms equip their sales offices and large customers with C.R.T. (cathode ray tubes—they look like television screens) units. The sender types the order on the C.R.T., corrects and verifies the accuracy of the order, and then electronically sends it.

Johnson and Parker researched the importance of efficient order transmittal, and concluded that it was often the primary reason why a firm could have an unacceptable order cycle system.[8] For this reason, many firms have initiated a cost "trade-off." The costs of order transmittal have increased by having customers and salespeople use telephone or electronic "hard copy" equipment. On the other hand, this system allowed the firm to use less expensive order processing, order picking, and transportation, and to reduce the number of distribution centers.

ORDER PROCESSING

Order processing is the time from when a firm *receives* an order to when the warehouse *is notified to ship* the order. This time frame typically includes factors such as: (1) the credit department verifying credit, (2) the marketing department crediting the salesperson with the sale, (3) the accounting department recording the transaction, and (4) the inventory department locating the closest warehouse to the customer, telling it to make the shipment, and updating the firm's master inventory controls.

There are some firms in which the order processing subfunction is totally responsible for an excessive overall time in the order cycle. These companies are often noted for their poor levels of customer service.

A fundamental decision is whether to have a centralized or decentralized order processing system. In a *centralized* system all the orders flow into one processing center and then the materials are sent from either that location or other warehouses. With *decentralized* order processing customers send their orders directly to the closest regional order

---

[8] Richard A. Johnson and Donald D. Parker, "Optimizing Customer Delivery Service with Improved Distribution," *Business Review* (October, 1961), pp. 38–45.

processing center. General Foods Corporation, for example, has a decentralized system with 20 order-processing centers in the United States.

The trend appears to be toward centralized order processing systems, especially with the increased usage of "hard copy" electronic data processing. The centralized system allows certain economies-of-scale, such as only having to maintain one master inventory file.* The firm can best decide which location should physically ship the products, which under certain circumstances may not be the warehouse closest to the customer. This would be the case, for example, if there were temporary stock-outs at selected warehouses. Patterns in transportation rates may be such that the shipping point physically closest to the customer may not be the one from which shipping charges are the least.

A major problem area in achieving an efficient order processing system is "bunching." Bunching results from an abnormally high number of customer orders arriving at approximately the same time. Because of the immediate overload on the order processing system, many of the orders are delayed in handling. The result, of course, is that the entire order cycle time is increased and the firm's customer service standards are reduced.

Many companies are taking positive actions to reduce the bunching problems. The solutions generally center around attempts to influence the buying behavior of their customers. Specifically, firms want to control the time when their customers place their orders. If their customer's ordering schedules can be influenced, the firm will then be able to balance them out so that a minimum of peaks and valleys will be found in the order processing work load.

Three techniques are commonly used to control the time when the customer places an order. One involves having the firm's salesperson call on customers for the purpose of taking orders at that time. Most customers would prefer the ease of ordering directly from salespersons because of their extensive knowledge of the product line. Thus, when a customer knows that a firm's salesperson arrives the first Monday of every month, they will typically hold their orders until they can give them personally to the salesperson, (known in this instance as an "order-taker"). A second procedure is that the firm places a phone call to the customer (or the customer can call collect) on a given time(s) during the month to take the customer's order directly by phone. This method, because of its ease of operation, is effective in controlling when orders are received. The final technique is to offer a substantial price discount

---

* A counter-trend appears to be in the embryonic stage. It involves the usage of "mini"-computers. They are located throughout the U.S. and serve all the needs of a region. At night—over leased phone lines—the mini-computers "talk" to one large computer in the firm's home office. The central computer then knows what has happened in each region and home office personnel can make any inter-regional adjustments that appear necessary.

to customers who place their orders on certain dates, such as every fourth Monday.

Order processing is now being recognized, not as a necessary evil, but as an aspect of the order or replenishment cycle which offers significant possibilities for increased overall efficiency. It has proven to be that aspect of the order cycle which has consistently shown significant improvements in efficiency in recent years. As the order processing function becomes further automated and refined, its overall contributions to an efficient and smoothly operating physical distribution system will be further enhanced.

ORDER PICKING

Order picking is the time from when a warehouse receives notification to ship an order until the order has been assembled, packaged, etc. and tendered to the transportation carrier. This function will be discussed in chapter nine.

ORDER DELIVERY

The final subpart of the order or replenishment cycle is *order delivery*, the time from when a carrier picks up the shipment until it is delivered to the customer's receiving dock. The factors that affect the speed and reliability of transportation service will be examined in Chapter Four.

With the above subparts of the order cycle in mind, attention can now be turned to one of the most complex and challenging aspects of customer service—the establishment of specific customer service goals and objectives.

PD'S ROLE IN ESTABLISHING CUSTOMER SERVICE GOALS AND OBJECTIVES

The establishment of customer service goals and objectives is an important senior management decision. Why? Because the firm's customer service goals and objectives can have significant ramifications on a firm's overall sales success. A logical question becomes—what role does the physical distribution department have in the establishment of these goals and objectives?

PHYSICAL DISTRIBUTION: ADVISORS TO MARKETING

The marketing department's recommendations regarding the appropriate levels of customer service are generally very influential to senior

FIG. 3-2 The Relationship Between Inventory Levels and Customer Levels.

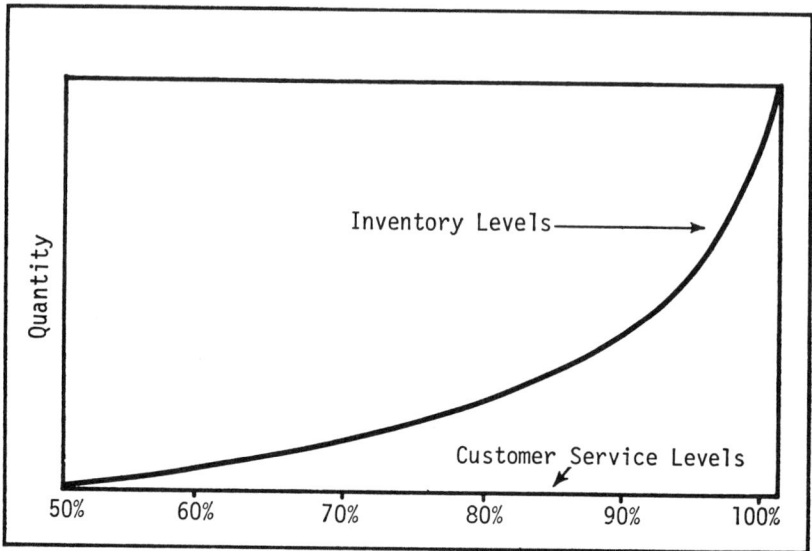

SOURCE: Mason and Dixon Lines, Inc., "Needed: Credible Measures of Customer Service Costs and Penalties," *Procurement/Distribution Ideas and Methods Manual*, p. 101.

management. The specific role of the physical distribution department is to act as an advisor or consultant to the marketing department. Why? Because marketing executives are occasionally guilty of believing that *sales maximization* is the same as *profit maximization*. Some marketing practitioners still believe that the most important objective of the firm is to increase sales. The result of this practice is that customer service goals and objectives are set at unreasonably high levels which ignore the costs incurred to achieve them.

The physical distribution department then must act as marketing's conscience by asking "Are you aware that the goals and objectives you want established are going to cost $$$?" Relatively small increases in the overall level of customer service objectives can substantially increase the costs of maintaining the increased level of customer service. John F. Magee, once noted, "Approximately 80 percent more inventory is needed in a typical business to fill 95 percent of the customers' orders out of stock than to fill only 80 percent."[9]

A study involving the Grocery Manufacturers of America looked at the increased levels of inventory needed to support higher levels of

[9] John F. Magee, "The Logistics of Distribution," *Harvard Business Review* (July-August, 1960), p. 92.

customer service. Customer service was defined as the percentage of orders which could be completely filled without back-ordering. Figure 3-2 illustrates the relationship between higher levels of customer service and inventory levels.

The above examples illustrate the need to consistently point-out the *costs* of the firm's customer service goals and objectives. Most firms have delegated this authority to the physical distribution department. Warren Blanding observed that the physical distribution group must:

> *Help set customer service standards.* Note the word *help*. Physical distribution can outline the alternative means of delivering products to customers and calculate the cost for different levels of customer service: the size of inventories, the number of shipping points, the order-processing requirements, warehousing, and transportation. It can do all this, but it cannot (or at least should not) set actual customer service standards. That is management's job, with sales and marketing helping to determine the levels of customer service that the competitive situation requires—and that pricing policies and profit objects will permit.[10]

Figure 3-3 discusses a situation where it becomes extremely important to carefully analyze costs of serving each customer. As Blanding points out, the obviously good customer upon scrutiny may turn out to be a "loser" and vice versa. Remember that sales maximization is often not compatible with profit maximization. The "devil's advocate" role of consistently pointing out this fallacy often falls upon the physical distribution department. Sam R. Goodman, Controller for the Nestle Company, sums it up by observing:

> It may be that we can go to the sales force and say, "Don't sell to this customer," or "Let's reduce our volume, we will be better off for it." Now, this is a no-no to the accountant and to the marketing man . . . You might make a lot more profit for the company by having a lower volume and fewer customers. It's not very different from having a lovely rose bush growing in your garden. If you want it to be lovelier, you prune it.[11]

Examples of the role of physical distribution as an advisor to the marketing department have been given. The actual establishment of customer service goals and objectives will be examined next.

ESTABLISHMENT OF A CUSTOMER SERVICE PROGRAM

A central element in the establishment of customer service goals and objectives is to determine the customer's viewpoint. This requires ask-

---

10 Warren Blanding, "Yes, There is Such a Thing as Too Much Customer Service," *Sales Management* (October 14, 1974), pp. 41–42.

11 Sam R. Goodman, "Improving Productivity Measurement and Control for Physical Distribution," *Annual Proceedings of the National Council of Physical Distribution Management* (1971), Section X, pages not numbered.

FIG. 3-3 An Analysis of Customer Profitability.

AN ANALYSIS OF CUSTOMER PROFITABILITY

He always orders in carload or truckload lots, always gives you plenty of lead time, and uses a purchase order your customer service personnel can understand. He accepts substitutions and back orders, pays his invoices promptly, and doesn't harass you to trace and expedite when shipments are a few days late. In short, he's a model customer.

Yet you may not even know he exists in those terms. To a sales manager, he may seem to be a moderately attractive account but relatively small potatoes in terms of total volume; certainly far down the priority list for allocating a scarce product. That oversight could be costing you more than you realize.

For today's shortages are largely the result of limited plant capacity, and when you're selling all the product you can get your hands on at sky-high prices, there's only one way to increase profits. That's by systematically identifying and concentrating your sales efforts on the accounts that (individually and in the aggregate) show the greatest margin between what you are paid for the product and what it costs you to get it. Discrete physical distribution costs are often a critical factor in separating the sheep from the goats.

For example, Customer A buys 80,000 lb. of product a year from you, Customer B, 240,000. Obvi- ously, you would term Customer B the "better" customer. But wait a minute. Customer A buys two truckload lots a year—40,000 lb. each—which means you get full use of your truck. Also, he happens to be located only a few miles from one of *your* suppliers, so that further savings can be realized by having the truck stop and backhaul materials ordered by your purchasing department.

Meanwhile, you discover that Customer B's 240,000 lb. are spread over some 30 orders, a few for truckloads, to be sure, but a surprising number for 500 lb. or less. What's more, fully half the total orders required expediting because he simply hadn't given you enough lead time. Customer B's erratic and unpredictable manner of ordering made it virtually impossible to set up backhaul movements for your truck fleet. In fact, there were half a dozen instances when a truck was dispatched with a "rush" order of less than 10,000 lb.—and then had to deadhead home.

By the time you add on the comparative amounts of salesman expense involved in each of the two accounts, plus the relative demands on your customer service personnel, you will start wondering how many more Customer B's you have getting unwarranted red-carpet treatment. You may also decide to upgrade the likes of Customer A.

SOURCE: Warren Blanding, "Sizing Up Customers This Way Can Gain You Nothing But Profits," *Sales Management* (May 27, 1974), p. 31.

ing customers about the importance of the various aspects of customer service. Klass' research has illustrated the importance of customer service to purchasing agents. He found that customer service considerations were second only to product quality as the basic determinants of which vendors to patronize.[12] Perreault and Russ noted that purchasing agents are frequently instructed to consider the physical distribution service offered by suppliers when computing vendor evaluation analysis.[13]

Hutchison and Stolle suggested three basic aspects of customer service that must be ascertained, typically by means of a comprehensive survey.[14] The first factor involves questions asking if additional elements of service are important to the customer. What services would he like to receive that are presently not available? For example, could the method of order transmittal be improved? If yes—how? Would it be helpful to have order shipment notification? If yes—why?

The second factor involves determining the significance to the customer of the various aspects of customer service. Is the present speed of the order or replenishment cycle acceptable? If not—why? A key question for those who indicated that some aspect of the current customer service level is unsatisfactory is: are they willing to pay more to receive a higher level of service?

The third and final factor, and one which the authors believe is of great importance, is, how does the customer evaluate the service levels of competing vendors? Some purchasing agents will release this information.*This information can be helpful in establishing the minimum levels of customer service that must be maintained.

When all the above survey information has been gathered and analyzed, the next job is to establish the firm's customer service goals and objectives. Heskett noted that the survey information can best be analyzed by dividing the information into three basic categories: *economics*, the *nature of the competitive environment*, and the *nature of the product*.[15]

Economic considerations deal with the reality that higher levels of customer service are necessarily more expensive. Rapid order delivery generally requires premium transportation and its higher rates. Or, if all orders are to be picked in the warehouse within 24 hours of receipt,

---

* See college bookstore example in chapter 12.

12 Bertrand Klass, "What Factors Affect Industrial Buying Decisions?" *Industrial Marketing* (May, 1961), pp. 33–35.

13 William D. Perreault, Jr. and Frederick A. Russ, "Physical Distribution Service: A Neglected Aspect of Marketing Management," *MSU Business Topics* (Summer, 1974), p. 38.

14 William M. Hutchison, Jr. and John F. Stolle, "How To Manage Customer Service," *Harvard Business Review* (November-December, 1968), p. 89.

15 James L. Heskett, "Controlling Customer Logistics Service," *International Journal of Physical Distribution* (June, 1971), pp. 140–145.

A COMPREHENSIVE CUSTOMER SERVICE STATEMENT
OF GOALS AND OBJECTIVES

GENERAL STATEMENT

We guarantee our customers service that is timely, dependable, convenient, and understandable. We will devise an individual plan for each customer to guide us in our service to him. Specific levels of individual services are detailed under the following four headings: time, dependability, communication and convenience.

A. *Time*

(1) Order-cycle time (defined as the time taken from the submittal of an order from a customer to receipt of the merchandise) will be developed with each individual customer within prescribed limits. Typically, this will be five days in metropolitan areas and ten days in rural areas.

(2) Emergency orders have priority and will be specially processed so that a minimum amount of time elapses. In most cases this should be same-day or next-day shipment.

(3) Invoices will be mailed one day after merchandise has been shipped.

(4) Credit memoranda will be issued the day after approval has been made. The approval process should not exceed a week and covers damages, return goods, order filling and shipping errors.

B. *Dependability*

(1) The order-cycle times developed for each customer will be met with dependable regularity (95% of the time) with an allowable tolerance of plus or minus a day.

(2) Order filling accuracy should be at the 99.5% level or better.

(3) Stock-outs should not exceed 1% of all items stocked.

(4) Back orders will be handled according to customers' desires (cancel all back orders, ship immediately, ship with next shipment, etc.).

C. *Communication*

(1) A special function has been designated responsible for all customer/company communications on physical distribution services—the sales order service department. Such important topics as order status, complaint handling, notification on delays, etc., will be handled by this department. The customer will be able to depend on getting answers from this contact point. All contacts will be done by courteous, intelligent, knowledgeable and service-oriented individuals.

(2) Salesmen's communications on distribution services will also be handled by the sales order service department.

(3) Invoices, order forms, and other means of written communications will be designed to provide the kind of information customers need and in the form they desire it.

(4) All policies pertinent to customer service will be explained in an easy reference guide given to the customer.

D. *Convenience*

(1) During the course of working out an individual plan for each customer on desired standards for order-cycle time, other services should be determined also. These include order submittal, shipping and loading instructions, delivery instructions, invoicing instructions, back-order procedures, and other pertinent customer considerations.

(2) The only information source on customer services will be the sales order service department. Customer contacts will be courteous, prompt, and made by knowledgeable individuals.

SOURCE: John F. Gustafson and Raymond Richard, "How to Establish Yardsticks for Customer Service," *Transportation and Distribution Management* (July, 1964).

then it is necessary to maintain a larger work force to fill such orders.

The *nature of the environment* refers to the customer service expectations of customers and to the actual customer service standards rendered by competitors. The customer service survey is invaluable in generating information for this section.

The *nature of the product* also affects the level of customer service that should be offered. Substitutability is one aspect. It refers to the number of products that a firm's customers can choose from to meet their needs. If, for some reason, a firm has a near monopoly on an important product, then a high level of customer service is not required. Why? Because if the customer needs the product (which is assumed), he or she will buy it under any reasonable customer service standard. On the other hand, if there are many products which all basically perform the same task, then customer service standards become very important from a competitive marketing point-of-view. Another factor is the products' *physical ability to accept storage*. Some products, by their very nature, cannot be stored very long without deterioration or impotency.

When the above information has been thoroughly analyzed, it is possible to promulgate a written statement regarding customer service goals and objectives. Figure 3-4 illustrates such a comprehensive statement, issued by a firm specializing in parts repair.

It has been said that "talk is cheap and actions dear." In other words, grandiose statements regarding a firm's level of customer service represent little more than rhetoric unless the customer service standards are actually implemented. To accomplish the latter, a systematic program of measurement and control is required.

MEASUREMENT AND CONTROL OF CUSTOMER SERVICE

Measurement and control of customer service determine whether a customer service program is effective or a failure. It is important that companies must not only establish written customer service goals and objectives, but also constantly monitor the level of customer service being received by their customers.

A problem that is encountered in the measuring or monitoring of actual customer service standards is determining what factors are to be measured. A common situation is that firms prefer to measure those aspects of customer service which are the easiest to measure instead of those which may be the most important from the customer's point-of-view. Some firms will not measure the complete order or replenishment cycle, because it is difficult to measure the order transmittal time and the order delivery aspects of the order cycle. Instead, they measure order processing and order picking times, because these order cycle elements are readily available to them. The problem, of course, is that the aspects measured may indicate that all is going well, while in fact the complete order cycle time may be unreasonably slow and driving away good customers from the firm.

Assuming that the firm is committed to measuring those aspects of customer service that are relevant from the *customer's* viewpoint, how can this be accomplished best? One technique that appears to be gaining in popularity is the performance model.[16] The performance model is based on a questionnaire which determines the percentage of times in which the firm is accomplishing its customer service goals and objectives. This can be done on a sampling basis.

A recent survey by *Transportation and Distribution Management* magazine indicated that 68 percent of the respondents made some attempt to determine if their customers were satisfied with their present level of customer service. Forty-three percent conducted their survey by phone and thirty-seven percent used a letter.[17] It is sometimes desirable not to identify the user of the data; respondents will supply more accurate data to an independent research firm. In some trades, respondents may be very willing to comment directly to the supplier regarding its performance.

A difficult measurement problem has been the order delivery segment of the order cycle. John F. Sweers, physical distribution manager for Western Publishing Company, has established a simple and proven method.[18] Using a carefully prepared sampling procedure, the firm places a stamped post card in each selected order. The customer is asked to supply only the date of arrival and the condition of the goods at destination. Sweers found that the customers are willing to return the cards. This technique allowed his firm to build a valuable data base so that carriers who provide good service can be identified.

Another way of measuring performance is by auditing "credit memos," the documents which must be issued to rectify errors in shipping and billing. Comparing them with the volume of error-free activity gives a measure of relative accuracy in performance. This system is not foolproof, however, since customers who receive more than they are billed for may not call that type of error to the shipper's attention.

So far this discussion has dealt almost exclusively with *measurement*

16 See, for example: Peter M. Lynagh, "Measuring Distribution Center Effectiveness," *Transportation Journal* (Winter, 1971), pp. 21–33. See also: James R. Carman, "Depend on the Computer for Dependable Service," *Handling and Shipping* (October, 1974), pp. 54–57.

17 "Survey: Customer Service," *Transportation and Distribution Management* (May-June, 1974), p. 47.

18 John F. Sweers, "A Standard to Beat the Carrier's Clock," *Handling and Shipping* (October, 1973), pp. 54–55.

of customer service goals and objectives and very little on *control*. Control is the process of taking corrective action when the measurements indicate that the goals and objectives are not being achieved. Measurement by itself is merely wasted time and effort if no action is taken based on the feedback received. It is the actions taken after the deficiencies have been noted that makes for a strong and effective customer service program.

Table 3-1 Major Customer Service Problems.

	Total %
Total Companies	100
Meeting delivery dates (general)	42
Transit time; other carrier problems	39
Stockouts, backorders	33
Paperwork problems	29
Personnel problems	28
Warehouse problems	26
Inability to provide fast, accurate information	21
Problems of customer understanding	18
Length of order cycle time	11
Inability to determine customer needs	8
Product problems	8
Forecasting	7
All other problems	10

SOURCE: Herbert W. Davis, "Customer Service: The Connecting Link in Physical Distribution," Memorandum 304 of the William E. Hill and Company, Inc., 1972, p. 7.

CUSTOMERS DEMAND A HIGH LEVEL OF SERVICE

The above discussion has assumed the importance of maintaining reasonably high levels of customer service standards. It is appropriate to examine the reasons *why* customer service has been thrust into such a prominent role. The basic factor for this is that customers have *demanded* higher and higher levels of customer service from their vendors. In addition, the market condition has usually been such that their demands were successful. Table 3-1 illustrates the most serious customer service problem areas that were determined in a recent survey of 71 corporations of various sizes. Not meeting delivery dates was the single most serious customer service problem. This problem was closely followed by delays in transit time caused by carriers.

Firms are demanding higher levels of customer service for a number of reasons. One is that when a customer has a vendor who provides an order cycle which is dependable and reasonable in length, the customer is able to maintain a lower level of inventory, especially safety stocks.* The lower average level of inventory thus allows savings in inventory holding costs.

A second factor which has necessitated higher levels of customer service is the increased usage of *vendor quality control programs.* In recent years many firms, especially retailers and wholesalers, have become more inventory conscious. This emphasis has resulted in computer-assisted analysis to identify vendors who consistently give either good or bad levels of service. In the past, with manual systems, it took repeated and serious customer service errors before a vendor's activities would be singled-out for corrective action. Today, these factors are automatically programmed into the computer and companies are able to constantly monitor the *quality* of service received from each vendor.

Willett and Stephenson attempted to verify the importance of customer service as perceived by purchasing executives. They surveyed 480 drug-store retailers and found that their buyers were able to consistently discriminate between even relatively small differences in the consistency and length of the order cycles offered by their vendors.[19]

The final reason for increasing emphasis on high levels of customer service is that in our automated and computerized world, the relationships between customers and vendors often become *dehumanized.* (See Figure 3-5). This situation is both frustrating and often inefficient from the customer's viewpoint. The firm that can offer a high level of customer service, especially on a personal basis, finds it has a powerful sales advantage in the marketplace. A senior physical distribution practitioner has noted:

> We are right in the middle of another "backlash"—the computer number backlash. Depersonalized mechanization and centralization have the buyer at all levels rebelling. Have you tried to write a letter or telephone a computer system to correct an error? It simply cannot respond. As human overrides have been lessened and lowered in discretionary action, the buyer becomes frustrated. Even the industrial buyer, using tools of value analysis, and—all things being equal, and they are equal to a growing extent for a long list of products—will use the supplier that somehow treats him as a person, not only in the sales contact, but in order entry, tracing, physical delivery, invoicing, and follow-up. These are the coming measures of service.[20]

* Extra inventory carried in stock to fill unexpectedly large orders during a specified time period.

[19] Ronald P. Willett and P. Ronald Stephenson, "Determinants of Buyer Response to Physical Distribution Service," *Journal of Marketing Research* (August, 1969), pp. 279–283.

[20] James R. Davis, "Customer Service—PD's Newest Responsibility," *Annual Proceedings of the National Council of Physical Distribution Management* (1973), p. 447.

FIG. 3-5 Dehumanized Relations Can Be Prevented By Effective Customer Service.

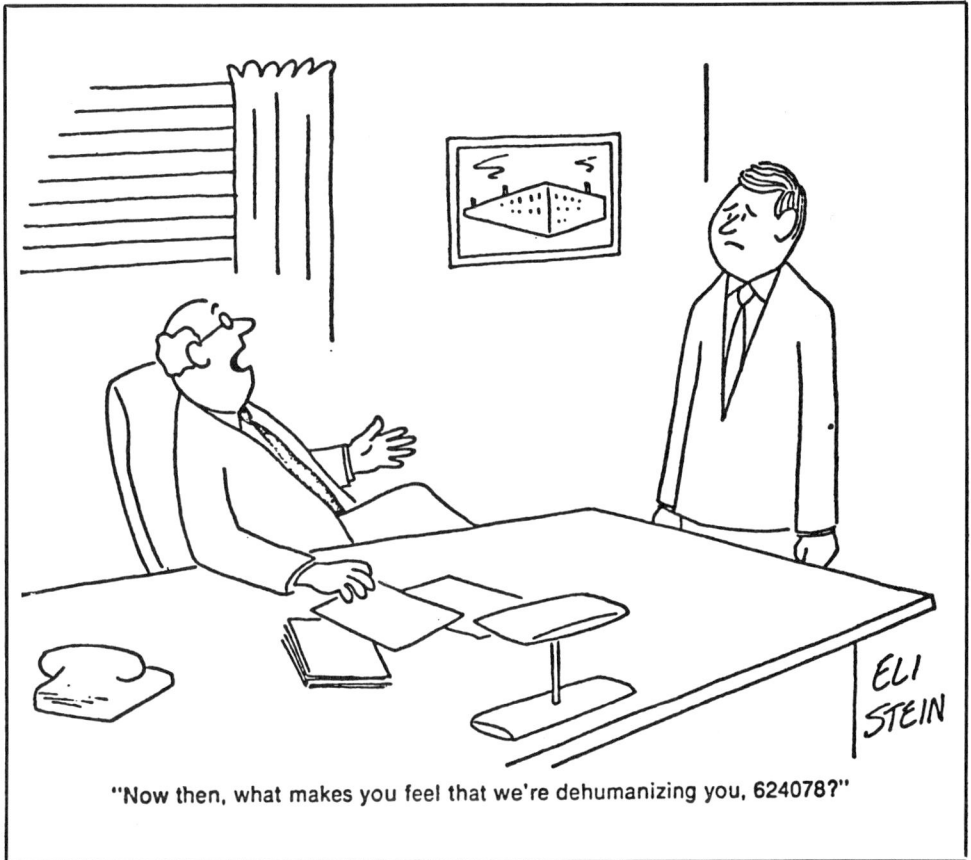

"Now then, what makes you feel that we're dehumanizing you, 624078?"

SOURCE: Reproduced by permission of Eli Stein and *The Wall Street Journal*.

GENERAL MILL'S SHIPMENT STATUS SYSTEM:
AN EXAMPLE OF CUSTOMER SERVICE

Much of this chapter has discussed what customers desire. What follows is a brief description about one supplier's program to improve delivery service in order to meet customers' needs. The Shipment Status System is a freight car control program which has enabled General Mills, Inc. (GMI) to improve its level of service in its use of railroad transportation. The program was initiated in the late 1960s when GMI recognized needs to improve the reliability of railroad service and the utilization of food-quality freight cars. GMI, because of the transportation characteristics of many of its food products, their freight rates, and the location and design of its food production/distribution centers, has a fairly inflexible need to use railroad transportation. GMI cannot easily switch that portion of its rail-based food distribution to truck transportation and therefore it devotes substantial effort to improving the quality of railroad service. Such *quality* includes the reliability of the service, the availability and cleanliness of the freight car, and such an *effort* as Shipment Status System.

The need to improve the reliability of railroad service reflected a mandate from marketing to physical distribution management to improve and maintain high levels of control over the distribution system. Included in the elements of the distribution system were "customer service" and "inventory management."

Simply stated, the problem was—how to maintain required levels of customer service and inventory at a time when most railroad service performance was at inadequate or deteriorating levels? The senior physical distribution managers of GMI met with executives of all the railroads which received substantial quantities of GMI traffic. The purpose of these meetings was to explain GMI's situation and to solicit the cooperation of the railroads to correct the service deficiencies. After these meetings were successfully completed, GMI established an elaborate computer program which established "standard times" for all basic rail transportation runs between the various cities. For example, assume that the railroads involved were taking an average of 11 days for a carload shipment between Minneapolis and Los Angeles. The "standard-time" for this shipment would be 11 days, plus or minus one day. Therefore, "on-time" delivery between these two cities occurred if the shipment arrived between the tenth and twelfth day after departure.

The heart of the Shipment Status System is a massive computer program which determines where the railcar must be each day after departure if the car is going to arrive with an "on-time" status. Assume, for example, that 48 hours after departure, the railcar should have departed Sioux Falls, South Dakota. GMI's computer asks the railroad's computer if the car has departed Sioux Falls. If it has not, the computer is programmed to wait one day and then make the same query. If at this time, the car has still not left Sioux Falls, the computer prints out an *exception* report stating that the car in question is now one day behind schedule. The exception reports are then analyzed by GMI employees and the typical action taken is that the railroad is notified by phone of the situation and asked to take correction action.

The strength of the Shipment Status System is that it allows GMI to take corrective action regarding potentially late shipments *before* they become late shipments. In addition, it allows GMI to notify customers ahead of time if they know that the shipment will not be delivered when expected. Even the ability to forewarn customers of late shipments has been a well received service.*

SUMMARY

This chapter has discussed the interactions of customer service standards with the overall physical distribution system.

Customer service standards are often established in terms of *goals* and *objectives*. In order to determine whether these goals and objectives are being accomplished, it is imperative that they be stated in specific, written, and measurable terms.

The *order cycle*, which is also called the *replenishment* cycle, is the time from when a customer places an order to when the order is received at the customer's freight dock. The order cycle is composed of four separate subparts: order transmittal, order processing, order picking, and order delivery.

The physical distribution department should act as an advisor to the marketing department when establishing the firm's level of customer service. In this capacity, the *costs* of achieving the various levels of customer service are indicated by the physical distribution department.

Customer service goals and objectives are often based on the results of a customer survey which determines the importance of the various elements of customer service. The actual establishment of the customer service "package" is achieved by combining the survey information into three basic categories: economic considerations, the nature of the competitive environment, and the nature of the product.

Once the customer service goals and objectives have been established, it is important that periodic measurement and control be initiated. This will ensure that the firm's customer service standards are being implemented and not reduced to mere rhetoric.

Customer service considerations are becoming increasingly important in recent years because customers are *demanding* higher levels of service. The basic factors responsible for this are: customers are able to reduce their inventory holding costs and "vendor quality control" programs.

QUESTIONS FOR DISCUSSION AND REVIEW

1. Discuss *why* customer service is often considered an important aspect of physical distribution management.

2. Who in the firm should establish the customer service goals and

---

* The authors wish to thank Mr. William K. Smith, vice-president-transportation at General Mills, Inc., for editing the discussion of the Shipment Status System.

objectives? What departments should assist in arriving at this decision? Why?

3. Assuming that a company has an inadequate customer service relationship with its customers, why would this have detrimental effects?

4. Define, in general terms, customer service *goals* and *objectives*. Then give a specific example of each one.

5. What are the most commonly used specific objectives for customer service programs?

6. The text argues that customer service objectives should be as specific as possible. Do you agree? Why?

7. Why should customer service goals and objectives be in writing?

8. Define and discuss the *order cycle*. Why is it considered to be an important aspect of customer service?

9. Discuss fully the four basic subparts which combine to form the order cycle.

10. Which of the four subparts of the order cycle do you believe is the most important? Why?

11. What specific actions have firms taken in recent years to make their order transmittal function more efficient?

12. What activities normally are accomplished during the *order processing* stage of the order cycle?

13. The establishment of the customer service goals and objectives is a basic corporate responsibility. What information should the various departments in the firm provide for making this important decision? Why? Be specific in your answer.

14. The text stated, "The role of the physical distribution department is to act as an advisor to the marketing department regarding customer service standards." Explain the rationale of this statement.

15. Assume that *you* are asked to establish the firm's customer service goals and objectives. What information should you collect and how would you gather it?

16. Does it ever make sense to purposely curtail sales to certain customers? Why?

17. After the customer service survey has been completed, what basic categories of information can be used to analyze the data? Why is this helpful?

18. Discuss fully the importance of *measurement* and *control* in achieving an effective customer service program.

19. A potential weakness in the measurement of customer service standards is that the wrong elements may be measured. Discuss why this could happen.

20. Surveys are commonly administered as part of the customer service department's regular activities. What types of information are the surveys attempting to gather? Why are these data important?

21. It has been said that customers are demanding higher and higher

levels of customer service from their vendors. Discuss fully the reasons that explain this situation.

22. Discuss why General Mills, Inc. established the shipment status system. What is the purpose of this system and how does it actually work?

23. Discuss the advantages and disadvantages of centralized versus decentralized order processing.

24. What is "bunching?" What actions, if any, can the firm take to correct this problem area?

CASE 3-1 "FLUB STUB"

Donna Brown was vice president of Melrose Markets, a chain of 70 food stores in southern Indiana. This year she was legislative vice president of the Indiana Grocers Association, which meant that she had to appear on behalf of the Association in various legislative hearings. The Association's executive secretary kept track of bills and, during periods the legislature was in session, the association's directors met weekly to determine the stand to take on various bills and to assign one or more directors to appear at legislative committee hearings.

Donna's phone rang. It was Welden Gerrard, Melrose's physical distribution manager, who said: "Donna, I just got my weekly traffic newsletter from Indianapolis and it said a bill was introduced in the legislature that would make us give customers a rain check or 'flub stub' in case we ran out of advertised merchandise during a sale. The 'flub stub' would allow them to buy the item at sale price whenever it was restocked."

"I know about the bill, Welden," said Donna. "The Grocer's Association will oppose it. It will be too disruptive at the check out counter."

"I wish you wouldn't oppose it," said Welden. "It would take a lot of heat off distribution because we get blamed if the stores are short of goods and we get stuck with high transportation costs because—as you well know—we're the last ones who know what's going on sale."

"You're right," said Donna. "In fact, I should apologize for not asking your opinion before I went to our association's directors' meeting last Tuesday. Tell you what, hearings on the bill aren't for several weeks. You send me a memo outlining how and why you think the 'flub stub' idea will help you. I'll take it along to the directors meeting next Tuesday and see if I can get them to reverse their stand. They usually will if one director puts up a spirited argument."

Question One: Assume you are Welden Gerrard. How would you go about assembling information needed for the memo?

Question Two: What do you think the memo would say?

CASE 3-2   HANDY ANDY, INC.

Handy Andy Inc. was a subsidiary of a larger company. Handy Andy produced garbage/trash compactors in a plant in St. Louis, Missouri and sold them throughout the United States. Nearly all sales were in large urban areas where trash collection costs were high.

The basic unit was about three feet high, two feet deep, and 1½ feet wide. A deluxe model had the same dimensions but contained more features. Since most of the sales were to go into existing kitchens, a wide number of colors and exterior styles were manufactured, providing a selection which would match almost any kitchen decor. The standard model came in five colors and three different trims for a total of 15 different combinations. The deluxe model came in eight colors and four different trims for a total of 32 different combinations. Retail prices were set by the dealer with the standard model retailing for between $210 and $240 and the deluxe model from between $235 and $315.

Sales were slow until trash collectors in a city raised their rates per can of refuse. Because of the slow sales and wide number of styles and colors available, the retailers usually stocked only a display unit. They also had an expensively-printed full color brochure showing all the styles and colors for the prospective customer to take home in order to choose the style and color which would fit best into his or her kitchen. When the retailer completed the sale, he would take the order and the compactor would be delivered from one central supply source in the city, under the control of a so-called "factory-distributor." The factory distributor was a large appliance dealer who also agreed to stock at least five compactors of each style and color (and more of the more popular ones) and to deliver and install them for all retailers in the metropolitan area. The general agreement between Handy Andy Inc. and the factory distributor was that the factory distributor would deliver and install a compactor within five working days after one of the other dealers informed him of the sale. For performing this service, the factory distributor received nine percent of the compactor's wholesale price, paid by Handy Andy within ten working days after the compactor was delivered and installed. In most areas this arrangement worked well.

Jose Ortega worked in Handy Andy's distribution department and was currently working on a project involving several other departments to determine whether the compactor warranty should be extended from one to two years. Customers who purchased a compactor received a postage-paid post card (exhibit one) along with their instruction booklet. Over 97 percent of the buyers did mail in the cards. The phrase at the bottom that the warranty is good for one year from date of purchase as determined by Handy Andy's records had been inserted to prevent a customer from not mailing the postcard until the compactor malfunctioned. Whether this statement was necessary was not known since almost no customers experienced defects within the compactor's one year warranty. Mr. Ortega was in the process of systematically contacting 500 purchasers who had owned the machines for between one and four years (when they were first introduced) to determine whether the compactors had required repairs at any time after the warranty expired and if so, to learn the details of the repairs.

Through use of special telephone service, Mr. Ortega was able to call purchasers throughout the country. In talking with them, he found that there were remarkably few complaints involving the durability of the Handy Andy compactor. Another form of complaint did arise, however, and that dealt with the initial delivery and installation of the machine. In several major metropolitan areas, it appeared that representatives of the "factory distributor" would contact individuals who had purchased Handy Andy compactors from other (non-factory distributor) dealers and attempt to get the buyer to cancel the order with the non-factory dealer and write a new order with the factory distributor for another model or color/trim combination. The price was usually the same as was charged by the initial selling dealer. The buyer was usually told that the model which had been initially ordered was out of stock but that the factory distributor had a "better" model already in stock which the customer could have installed for the same price. The factory distributors also told buyers that they could expect better service if the compactors were purchased from the factory distributor than from the initial dealer. In one metropolitan area, the factory distributor created the impression that the factory distributor, not Handy Andy Inc., stood behind the one-year warranty.

Mr. Ortega realized that he had uncovered a larger problem than he had anticipated and after talking briefly with his supervisor, decided that he would change the format of his telephone interview to ask a few more questions regarding the compactor's installation. He expanded his sample to include buyers who had purchased compactors within the past 12 months. The only new piece of information he uncovered was that, in nearly all major market areas, the factory distributors did a better job installing compactors they had sold than they did installing compactors which other dealers had sold. The delivery was faster (in terms of elapsed time since date of sale); and more time was spent explaining to customers how the machine worked; and phone calls were made three days and ten days after installation to make certain that the customer had no additional questions regarding the compactor's operation. When a compactor that was sold by another dealer was delivered, it was frequently left in the middle of the kitchen with scarcely a word exchanged between the customer and the "installation" personnel.

Mr. Ortega again met with his supervisor and was surprised to see

Handy Andy's marketing Vice President sitting in on the meeting. The marketing Vice President was clearly perplexed, because if the pattern Mr. Ortega was uncovering was true, it meant that Handy Andy's entire distribution setup might have to be revised. He asked Mr. Ortega this question: "Do you think the pattern holds for the entire U.S.?"

"No," answered Mr. Ortega. "In the 25 major metropolitan areas where I've been talking with buyers, I'd say the pattern holds for sure in six to eight. Three more I'm uncertain about, I get mixed reports— maybe the factory distributor in those cities is trying to torpedo only a few other dealers. In half of the cities, I don't think we have much of a problem. There are some complaints, but not enough to fall into a pattern."

The marketing Vice President then said: "If half the cities are satisfactory, we will not change our entire system. Let's find out the areas where the problems you have described are the worst, and that's where I'll make some changes. We know factory distributorships for Handy Andy compactors are profitable, even when conducted legitimately. We need give only 60 days notice to terminate any factory distributorship, so if we get rid of the bad ones first, the others will soon 'get religion.' "

"It's hard to get concrete data by phone," said Mr. Ortega, "because often I feel I'm leading people on. If my questions get to be too direct, people on the other end of the line clam up. They don't want to get involved. Besides, most of them are happy with their compactors. They're really not mad at anyone."

"That's a valid point," said the marketing Vice President. "Besides, I guess we shouldn't be using these phone calls to undermine confidence in any of our dealers or distributors."

"How about this?" asked Mr. Ortega, holding up one of the postage-paid warranty registration cards, (Exhibit one). We can redesign it and put in a few questions about delivery service."

"Good idea!" responded the marketing Vice President. "You design a postcard with the changes and show it to me tomorrow in my office." He pulled an appointment book out of his suitcoat pocket and looked inside it. "I'm free at 3 P.M. I'll see both of you in my office then."

Question One: What additional questions should be added to the warranty card to obtain the information which the marketing Vice President wants?

Question Two: On a sheet of paper draw a rectangle 4½″ by 7¼″. (This is the same proportions as a postcard although slightly larger). Type or print neatly all the questions you intend to have asked on the postcard in the order and arrangement which seems best.

Question Three: What other procedures or techniques, besides phone and postcard, could be used to obtain the necessary information?

EXHIBIT 1

MAIL WITHIN FIVE DAYS OF INSTALLATION!

Serial Number _____
(the eight-digit number under switch)

Dealer compactor purchased from

Name_____

City_____

Date of Purchase_____/_____/ 197_____
　　　　　　　　　　MONTH　　　DAY　　　YEAR

Your Name_____

Address_____

City_____State_____Zip_____

This card requires no postage. Just fill out and drop in any mailbox. Your warranty is good for one year from date of purchase, as determined by our records. Contact your dealer first with any questions. Thanks.

HANDY ANDY, INC.

CHAPTER REFERENCES

BLANDING, WARREN; "Yes, There is Such a Thing as Too Much Customer Service," *Sales Management* (October, 1974).
————; "Sizing Up Customers This Way Can Gain You Nothing But Profits," *Sales Management* (May, 1974).
CARMAN, JAMES R.; "Depend on the Computer for Dependable Service," *Handling and Shipping* (October, 1974).
CONSTANTIN, JAMES A.; *Principles of Logistics Management* (New York: Appleton-Century-Crofts, 1966).

DAVIS, HERBERT W.; "4 Reasons Why Customer Service Managers Can't Manage Customer Service," *Handling and Shipping* (November, 1971).

———; "Customer Service: The Connecting Link in Physical Distribution," Memorandum 304 of the William E. Hill and Company, Inc. (1972).

DAVIS, JAMES R.; "Customer Service—PD's Newest Responsibility," *Annual Proceedings of the National Council of Physical Distribution Management* (1973).

ELSMAN, T. R.; "Export Customer Service," *Annual Proceedings of the National Council of Physical Distribution Management* (1972).

GOODMAN, SAM R.; "Improving Productivity Measurement and Content for Physical Distribution," *Annual Proceedings of the National Council of Physical Distribution Management* (1971).

GUSTAFSON, JOHN F. and Raymond Richard; "How to Establish Yardsticks for Customer Service," *Transportation and Distribution Management* (July, 1964).

HESKETT, JAMES L.; "Controlling Customer Logistics Service," *International Journal of Physical Distribution* (June, 1971).

HUTCHISON, WILLIAM M., JR. and John F. Stolle; "How to Manage Customer Service," *Harvard Business Review* (November-December, 1968).

JOHNSON, RICHARD A. and Donald D. Parker; "Optimizing Customer Delivery Service with Improved Distribution," *Business Review* (October, 1961).

KLASS, BERTRAND; "What Factors Affect Industrial Buying Decision?," *Industrial Marketing* (May, 1961).

LYNAGH, PETER M.; "Measuring Distribution Center Effectiveness," *Transportation Journal* (Winter, 1971).

MAGEE, JOHN F.; "The Logistics of Distribution," *Harvard Business Review* (July-August, 1960).

"Needed: Credible Measures of Customer Service Costs and Penalties," *Procurement/Distribution Ideas and Methods Manual*, Mason and Dixon Lines, Inc.

PERREAULT, WILLIAM D., JR. and Frederick A. Russ; "Physical Distribution Service: A Neglected Aspect of Marketing Management," *MSU Business Topics* (Summer, 1974).

———; "Physical Distribution Service in Industrial Purchase Decisions," *Journal of Marketing* (April, 1976), pp. 3–10.

SHYCON, HARVEY N. and Christopher R. Sprague; "Put a Price Tag on Your Customer Service Levels," *Harvard Business Review* (July-August, 1975), pp. 71–78.

"Survey: Customer Service," *Transportation and Distribution Management* (May-June, 1974).

SWEERS, JOHN F.; "A Standard to Beat the Carrier's Clock," *Handling and Shipping* (October, 1973).

WAGNER, WILLIAM; "Managing Customer Complaints in Distribution," *International Journal of Physical Distribution* (June, 1972), pp. 126–131.

WILLET, RONALD P. and P. Ronald Stephenson; "Determinants of Buyer Response to Physical Distribution Service," *Journal of Marketing Research* (August, 1969).

Part Two.

The Elements of a Physical Distribution System

Part II presents a detailed examination of each of the individual elements that combine to form the physical distribution department.

Chapter 4 analyzes the transportation system that is available in the United States. Each of the alternative transportation modes—railroads, motor carriers, pipelines, water transportation, and air freight—is examined. Chapter 5 builds upon this analysis by examining the complex regulatory environment that is characteristic of the transportation industry. The subject of freight rate determination is also explored. Chapter 6, the final chapter dealing exclusively with transportation, examines the multifaceted functions of the traffic manager.

Inventory control and analysis is the subject of Chapter 7. Physical distribution, by its very nature, involves spatial differences which are often of considerable magnitude. Chapter 8 examines these locational and geographical considerations which directly interface with the physical distribution department.

Warehousing is discussed from a physical distribution viewpoint in Chapter 9, while the following chapter is devoted to an analysis of the fundamental aspects of materials handling and protective packaging. Chapter 11, the final chapter in Part II, presents a comprehensive discussion of the complexities and challenges inherent in international physical distribution management.

Transferring cement to special truck trailers. *Credit:* Butler Manufacturing Co.

CHAPTER FOUR

The Transportation System

Our transportation system in its present form is an asset without which our peacetime and wartime accomplishments never would have come to pass. Our economic prospects of the future are tied irrevocably to the efficient operations of that system.

—FRANK CUSHMAN
Business Horizons
April, 1974

This inability to earn money in the industry's finest year [1972] is more than a knockdown of traditional wisdom. It raises a serious question about the future viability of the entire railroad industry. Instead of enjoying the most profitable year in history, many railroads are worn out and exhausted.

Business Week
September 8, 1973

THE MOST EXPENSIVE PART OF PD

The transportation system of the United States is large by any measure, and its presence is so pervasive that most people are only vaguely aware of its existence until a segment of it malfunctions. Table 4-1 shows the nation's 1973 estimated freight bill for each of the major modes of transport. The nation's total estimated freight bill accounts for about ten percent of the Gross National Product.

It is imperative that PD practitioners have a working knowledge of all aspects of transportation and traffic management. This chapter and the next two present the fundamentals of this important aspect of PD. Transportation is pivotal to the successful operation of any physical distribution system.

For example:
(a) Transportation costs are directly affected by the location of the firm's plants, warehouses, vendors, and customers.

TABLE 4-1   The Nation's Estimated Freight Bill

	in millions of dollars 1973	Percent of Total
Highway		
Truck-Intercity		
ICC-Regulated	21,000	16.4
Non-ICC Regulated	25,515	19.9
Truck-Local	57,303	44.7
Bus	137	.1
	103,955	81.1
Railroad	14,801	11.5
Water	6,224	4.9
Oil Pipe Line	1,701	1.3
Air	1,591	1.2
GRAND TOTAL	128,272	100.0
GRAND TOTAL % OF GNP	10.07	

SOURCE: Transportation Association of America, *Transportation Facts and Trends*, Eleventh Edition (December, 1974, released in January, 1976), p. 11.

(b) Inventory requirements are influenced by the mode of transport used. High speed, high price transportation systems require smaller amounts of inventories at customer locations.

(c) The transport mode selected has an influence upon the packaging required.

(d) The type of carrier used dictates a manufacturing plant's materials-handling equipment. This involves loading and unloading equipment and the design of the receiving and shipping docks.

(e) An order processing methodology which encourages maximum consolidation of shipments between common points results in larger shipments tendered to the carriers. These shipments will receive volume discounts.

(f) The customer service goals (mentioned in Chapter 3) influence the type of carrier selected.[1]

Neuschel surveyed 26 large companies involved in food processing, chemicals, petroleum, building materials, and metal fabricating to de-

[1] *Feedback* (Chicago: "The Fernstrom Moving System," March-April, 1974), pp. 2–3.

termine their distribution costs. The results in Table 4-2 show that transportation (carrier) costs more than twice as much as the next expense item. The Air Transportation Association also estimated the various PD costs, and the results are in Figure 4-1. Both studies show that the transportation factor of a PD system is the largest single cost item.

TABLE 4-2   Major Elements of Distribution Cost

Item	Percent of total
Carrier charges	44%
Warehousing and handling	20
Inventory carrying cost	18
Shipping room	11
Administrative	7
Total	100%

NOTE: These averages are for the survey sample as a whole, based on available company data and/or author's estimates. Percentages assigned to various items themselves vary as much as ±20% among the 26 individual companies in the sample.

SOURCE: Robert P. Neuschel, "Physical Distribution—Forgotten Frontier," *Harvard Business Review* (March-April, 1967), p. 132.

ALTERNATIVE TRANSPORTATION MODES

The transportation sector of the United States economy is generally competitive, not only among the different modes of transportation but also among the various carriers within each mode. Table 4-3 presents data for 1975 and earlier regarding the ton-mile distribution of freight between the various modes. (A ton-mile is a common unit of measure in the transportation industry; it simply means one ton of freight moved one mile.)

Table 4-1 showed the dollar distribution by mode. Perhaps the most interesting comparison between Tables 4-1 and 4-3 is the relationship between the railroads and the motor carriers. While railroads transported 58 percent more intercity ton-miles than motor carriers in 1975, the motor carriers received 316 percent more revenue than did the railroads. The reason for this disparity is the types of product each mode tends to carry, and the quality of service each carrier offers.

RAILROADS

Figure 4-2 shows the current railroad network. In 1975, there were 200,000 miles of railroad *line* in the United States. Total miles of *track*

FIG. 4-1 Estimated Cost Items of Physical Distribution.

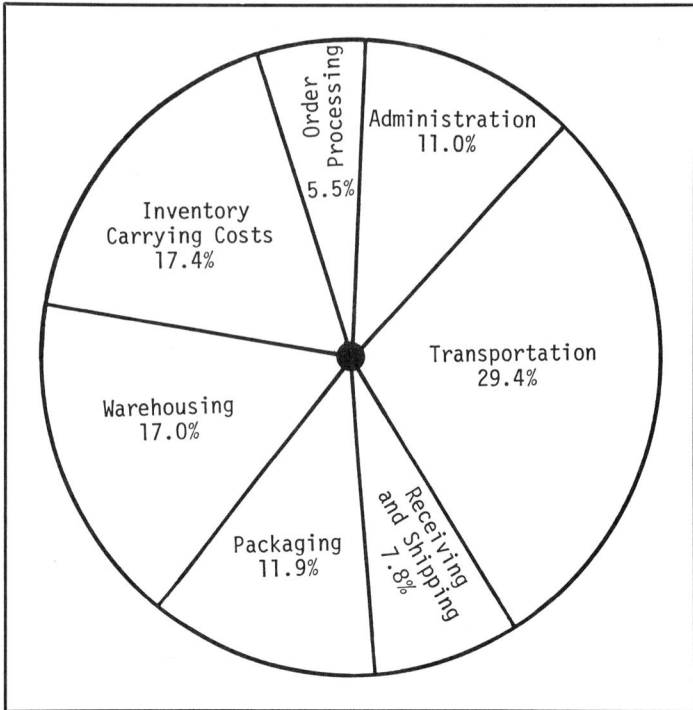

SOURCE: Air Transportation Association, *Air Cargo from A to Z* (1971), p. 5.

is approximately 325,000. This figure is larger because it counts switching yard trackage and situations where there are parallel tracks. The total miles of railroad line has been declining since 1916, the peak year when there were 254,037 line miles. Today the railroads are actively involved in attempting to abandon rail lines. In 1973, more than 2,000 miles of line were discontinued, while only about 200 miles of new line were built. There are two reasons for the abandonment of rail line. First: as industries move and as population shifts, many railroads have lines that are no longer economically feasible to operate. Second: growth in the highway system, especially the Interstate System, has made it very difficult for the rail industry to compete for short-haul traffic.

The railroad industry is dominated by 52 Class I railroads (an Interstate Commerce Commission classification for railroads with greater than $10 million in annual operating revenues). They produce more than 90 percent of the railroad ton-miles. While there is a considerable variation in size among the Class I railroads, the average Class I rail carrier has over 7,500 employees and approximately 3,000 miles of rail line.

TABLE 4-3   Intercity Modal Ton-Mile Distribution

Millions of **Freight Ton-Miles** and Percentage of Total (including mail and express)

Year	Rail-roads	%	Trucks	%	Great Lakes	%	Rivers and canals	%	Oil pipe-lines	%	Air	%	Total
1929	454,800	74.9	19,689	3.3	97,322	16.0	8,661	1.4	26,900	4.4	3	—	607,375
1939	338,850	62.4	52,821	9.7	76,312	14.0	19,937	3.7	55,602	10.2	12	—	543,534
1944	746,912	68.6	58,264	5.4	118,769	10.9	31,386	2.9	132,864	12.2	71	—	1,088,266
1950	596,940	56.2	172,860	16.3	11,687	10.5	51,657	4.9	129,175	12.1	318	—	1,062,637
1960	579,130	44.1	285,483	21.7	99,468	7.6	120,785	9.2	228,626	17.4	778	—	1,314,270
1970	771,168	39.8	412,000	21.3	114,475	5.9	204,085	10.5	431,000	22.3	3,295	0.2	1,936,023
1974	855,700	38.6	495,000	22.3	107,451	4.9	247,431	11.2	506,000	22.8	3,910	0.2	2,215,492
1975	761,000	37.0	441,000	21.4	108,000	5.2	235,000	11.4	510,000	24.8	4,000	0.2	2,059,000

SOURCE: Association of American Railroads, *Yearbook of Railroad Facts* (1976), p. 36.

Railroads specialize in transporting raw materials and unprocessed products in car-load (CL) quantities, which typically implies 30,000 pounds or more per shipment. Less-than-carload (LCL) quantity shipments are less than one percent of all railroad freight car loadings and in many states not handled at all. In 1975, forty-one percent of all CL shipments were products of mines, such as metallic ores, coal, stone, gravel, nonmetallic minerals, clay and coke. Coal is the largest commodity transported by the rails, amounting to 20.2 percent of all shipments in 1975. Unprocessed agricultural products account for nine percent of all shipments, while processed food products shipments equal eight percent. Other products which use the railroad system extensively are: forest products, paper, chemicals, oils, metals, automobiles, and scrap. The average rate charged by the railroads in 1975 per ton-mile was about 2.04 cents. This reflects the efficiency of transporting commodities in bulk movements.

The current financial condition of the railroads is difficult to examine in the aggregate, although, for the most part, it is not good.[2] (See Figure 4-3.) In 1975, all railroads averaged only 1.2 percent return on net invested capital.* The carriers in the South and West did better than this, but those in the Eastern district averaged a deficit. There were a dozen rail carriers in bankruptcy proceedings, mostly in the Northeast region of the country.[3] In an attempt to solve the crisis precipitated by the Penn-Central collapse, Congress passed the *Northeast Regional Rail*

* The railroad industry uses betterment accounting which does not utilize annual depreciation of long-term assets. Therefore, the railroads' actual net invested capital is smaller than reported, which means that their percentage return on invested capital is higher than 1.2 percent.

2 See: Robert P. Neuschel, "How Rail Management Can Boost Revenues and Control Costs," *Railway Age* (January 12, 1976), pp. 34–38.

3 See: James C. Johnson and Donald V. Harper, "The Shipper Views Proposed Solutions to the Northeast Railroad Problem," *Transportation Journal* (Summer, 1974), pp. 5–13.

FIG. 4-2 United States Railroad Network.

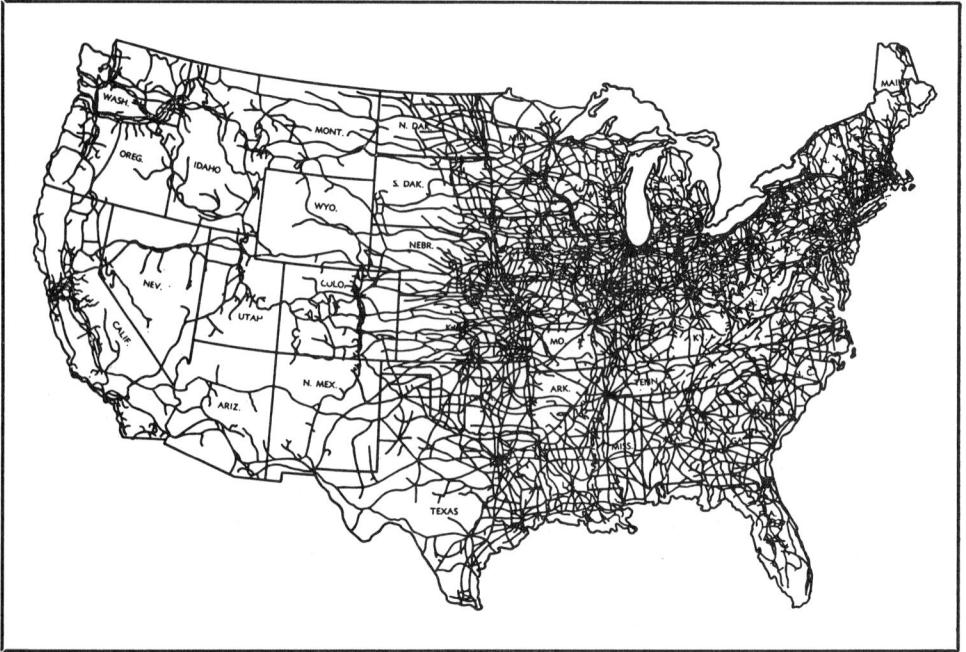

SOURCE: Association of American Railroads.

Reorganization Act of 1973. This controversial legislation provided for more than $2 billion of federal loan guarantees and outright grants. A new government sponsored railroad, the Consolidated Rail Corporation (Conrail), has taken over on April 1, 1976 the essential operations of the Penn-Central and other bankrupt carriers.[4] The implementation of the above legislation has been very sporadic because it has been so widely contested by creditors of the bankrupt lines, the unions, and communities which may lose rail service.[5]

Railroad Operating Problems. During a 1972 Interstate Commerce Commission (ICC) hearing regarding an investigation of railroad freight service, General Mills, Inc. issued a statement which noted that railroad

[4] "Conrail Begins Operations as 2000 Miles of Branch Lines Lose Freight Service," *The Wall Street Journal* (April 1, 1976), p. 9.
[5] See: Frank W. Davis, Jr., Edwin P. Patton, and Robert E. Tuttle, Jr., "Local Participation: The Key to Preserving Adequate Railroad Services," *MSU Business Topics* (Winter, 1976), pp. 40–46.

FIG. 4-3 Some Railroads are Experiencing Financial Problems.

WALL STREET JOURNAL

"I traveled by railroad all through their good years and I think it's only fair to stick with them when the going is tough."

Reproduced by permission of Bob Brown and *The Wall Street Journal*.

freight service is generally "erratic and unreliable."[6] *Distribution Worldwide* surveyed shippers regarding the quality of service they were receiving from the railroads. The article concluded by saying "one notes a constant re-use of a key word: Deterioration. Deterioration of

[6] William K. Smith and David M. Schwartz, *Initial Statement of General Mills, Inc. In the Investigation of Railroad Freight Service,* Ex Parte No. 270 (March 24, 1972), mimeographed, p. 2.

service that once ranged from acceptable to excellent on the railroads seems to be the basic complaint of most shippers interviewed. That deterioration has forced large percentages of traffic onto the highways."[7] The railroads are currently experiencing three basic problem areas: *lack of roadbed maintenance, inadequate car supply* and *poor labor relations.* The first two problems are directly related to the railroads' inadequate return on net invested capital.

The railroad industry, during many years of "lean" earnings, put off maintenance of their tracks and rights-of-way. The common term for this is *deferred maintenance.* The effects of this problem are devastating. From 1972 to 1973, American railroads experienced a 34 percent increase in derailments.[8] Frank E. Barnett, chairman of the Union Pacific Railroad, remarked that certain railroads have 60 percent of the mainline track under *slow orders.*[9] A slow order is a speed restriction necessitated by the track and roadbed's inability to withstand the stress of a train traveling at its normal speed.

The second problem is of inadequate car supply. Railroads, by law, are required to supply cars to their customers on request. In 1929, the railroads had 2.61 million cars, each with an average carrying capacity of 46.3 tons. In 1975, there were only 1.72 million cars available, although their average car capacity had increased to 73.9 tons. (Many of the newer rail cars have carrying capacities of 100–120 tons.) The maximum carrying capacity for the railroad car fleet has remained about the same. However, the problem, according to shippers, is a loss of flexibility. There are two reasons for this. The first is that rail cars are seldom loaded to capacity. The second problem is that the newer cars tend to be specialized and not the general service boxcar. This, again, reduces flexibility.

The car shortage problem has been especially serious in recent years. In late 1973, the ICC stated, ". . . fiscal 1973 was a period of increasingly critical freight car shortages. The problem escalated to the point where the shortage was the most severe in the history of the Commission, becoming so acute at times that it threatened the nation's commerce."[10] In 1974, the ICC ordered the nation's major railroads to purchase a total of nearly 70,000 new cars and to restore another 18,000 cars, all within a two year period.[11]

Railbox, a nationwide fleet of 50-foot, general service boxcars, began operation in 1974. Most Class I railroads belong to a pool which owns

[7] "Shippers Talk About Rail Service," *Distribution Worldwide* (April, 1973), pp. 43–46.

[8] Lewis M. Phelps, "As Railroads Defer More Maintenance, Number of Accidents Increases Sharply," *The Wall Street Journal* (October, 1974), p. 28.

[9] "The Railroad Paradox: A Profitless Boom," *Business Week* (September 8, 1973).

[10] *8th Interstate Commerce Commission Annual Report* (1973), p. 20.

[11] "ICC Orders Rails to Purchase 69,609 New Freight Cars, Restore 18,000 Others," *Traffic World* (July 1, 1974), pp. 29–30.

these 10,000 cars. Since they are not owned by a specific railroad, they do not have to be returned to the owning railroad. This significantly increases their utilization and helps to combat the shortage of general purpose rail cars.[12]

Another operating problem is labor relations. In 1929, there were 1.7 million railroad employees. By 1975, this figure had dropped to 487,789. This declining total railroad employment has made the rail unions unwilling to innovate and compromise with railroad management.[13] The problem areas involve work rules and crew sizes. The majority of today's railroad work rules were developed prior to 1900. An example is the system of pay for line-haul train employees, by which a day's pay is computed as being equivalent to 100 miles traveled. The mileage factor was equitable in 1880, when trains often could not average 15 miles per hour. Now, however, many railroads are able to achieve freight train speeds of 50 miles per hour, and therefore the crew is paid for a full day's work after two hours. One writer noted that "these 'make-work' or 'featherbedding' practices produce a mal-allocation of resources, prevent further innovations, and further exacerbate the deteriorating competitive position of American railroads."[14]

The crew-size controversy has been a perennial problem area for railroad management. On line-haul freight trains, the unions require a four-man crew, while management believes that a three-man crew should be the maximum and that even two employees would be feasible. In general, the unions have adamantly opposed these suggestions to reduce crew size. Recently, however, there has been a break in the unions' position. The Providence and Worcester Railroad signed a contract that provided for a guaranteed annual wage for operating employees, and in turn the union authorized three-man crews.[15]

Railroad Service Innovation. Not all railroads are bankrupt. Many are profitable and through service innovations and aggressive marketing are recapturing lost traffic. The key to the railroads' attempts to increase levels of customer services has been their commitment to capital improvements. There are numerous examples. Because trains are traveling faster with heavier loads, the rail carriers have been replacing their rails with heavier track. Instead of pre-World War II rails, which came in 30-foot sections and weighed 70–90 pounds per yard, today's rail weighs 115–130 pounds per yard and is welded into continuous sections, often a quarter-mile or longer in length. The continuous welding helps

12 "Railroad Technology," *Handling and Shipping* (January, 1975), p. 43.

13 A major problem with the Northeast railroad solution was the uncompromising position of the labor unions. See: Albert R. Karr, "How to Derail a Merger," *The Wall Street Journal* (April 9, 1976), p. 6.

14 Marvin J. Levine, "The Railroad Crew Size Controversy Revisited," *Labor Law Journal* (June, 1969), p. 373.

15 "The Little Railroads That Could," *Distribution Worldwide* (April, 1974), p. 38.

to eliminate a major cause of product loss and damage, which is the vibration caused by the rail cars rolling over joints of the individual sections of rail.

Railroad classification yards are complexes where rail cars are brought into, separated, and then switched to a new train traveling in the direction of the car's destination. Computerized classification yards are speeding up this function. The Burlington Northern recently spent $40 million on its Northtown Yard near Minneapolis. Each rail car entering this facility has its car number "read" by an optical scanner, connected to a computer, which then checks its memory bank to determine the car's destination. The computer then operates the switches to place the car on the proper departing track.

Automatic Car Identification (ACI) is the system that allows the railroads to "read" car numbers. More than 95 percent of the United States and Canada rail car fleets are equipped with the color reflective stripped labels. Scanners at classification yards and other strategic locations on the rail system "read" the car number and report this information to the railroad's central computer facility. This system allows the railroads to achieve better car utilization, because problems and bottlenecks can be more readily spotted and corrective action taken. Also, shippers' inquiries regarding location of specific cars can be accurately answered.[16]

Augmented by the above capital improvements, some railroads have started to offer shippers a number of innovative services. Only a few examples will be mentioned here. One new service is the *unit train*. This is a train of permanently connected cars that carries only one product non-stop from origin to destination. It can be thought of as a conveyor belt. Once the product is delivered, the train returns empty to its origin and makes another non-stop run. The advantage to the railroads of unit trains is that they achieve a very high percentage of car utilization. Shippers appreciate unit trains because their total freight bill is typically slashed and they are given more dependable service. The Association of American Railroads reports that 25 of the 52 Class I railroads offer unit train service. Currently, over 90 percent of all coal movement is via unit trains. General Motors uses a unit train from Chicago to Los Angeles carrying assembled autos and auto parts.

Another new service is the *run-through train*. The emphasis here is upon saving time. These trains typically involve long distance moves, so that two or more railroads will combine to offer this service. These trains bypass most classification yards and hence "run through" from origin to destination. They often only stop for crew changes, or safety checks. The locomotives are not switched either, and generally include

---

[16] Closely associated with ACI is TRAIN II: see: Kenneth Ellsworth, "TRAIN II's Goal: A 10% Increase In Car Utilization," *Railway Age* (September 8, 1975), pp. 66–68.

power units from each of the participating carriers. One such train operates on a 40-hour schedule between Chicago and San Francisco, averaging better than 60 miles per hour. They have helped rails recapture tonnage from truckers.

MOTOR CARRIERS

The highway system of the United States approximates 3.2 million miles. These roads vary from ungraded dirt surfaces to the multi-laned divided highways. The *backbone* of the highway system is the 42,500 miles known officially as the "National System of Interstate and Defense Highways," commonly referred to as the *Interstate System*. Figure 4-4 shows this system, which is about one percent of the total highway mileage, but which carries more than 20 percent of all automobile and truck traffic.

The trucking industry can be broken into two parts, the governmentally-regulated portion and the non-regulated. The distinction between these two carriers will be discussed more in chapter five.

Referring only to the regulated carriers, in 1975 there were 885 Class I truckers (a carrier with annual revenues over three million dollars), 2,670 Class II truckers (operating revenues between $500,000 to $3 million) and 12,450 Class III truckers (operating revenues less than $500,000).

The trucking industry is the major transportation mode for a surprisingly large variety of products. Table 4-4 illustrates that the trucking industry transports large percentages of manufactured products. The importance of trucking to agriculture is detailed in Figure 4-5.

Regulated motor carriers concentrate their activities in transporting "small" shipments. Recently, the average shipment received weighed about 1,600 pounds. More than 70 percent of the shipments for regulated truckers were under 500 pounds and only five percent were more

TABLE 4-4   Manufactured Products Shipped by Truck

Item	*% of Tons Shipped*
Radios, T.V., Phonos & Records	75.3
Carpets & Rugs	81.1
Clothing	82.1
Drugs	68.3
Tires and Inner Tubes	54.7
Engines and Turbines	76.5
Office and Accounting Machines	91.1
Aircraft Parts	82.4

SOURCE: *1967 Census of Transportation,* U. S. Department of Commerce.

FIG. 4-4 The United States' Interstate Highway System.

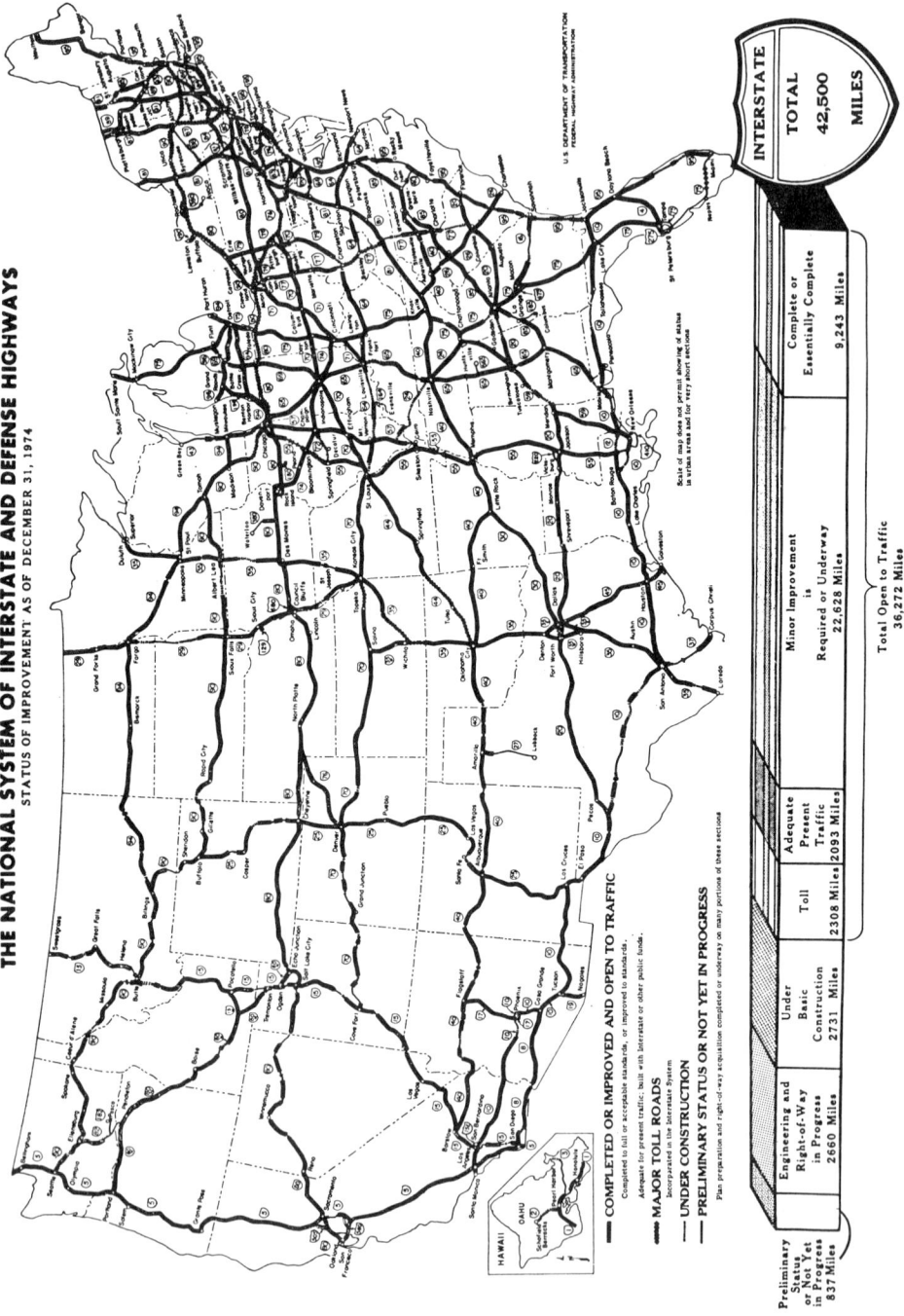

THE NATIONAL SYSTEM OF INTERSTATE AND DEFENSE HIGHWAYS
STATUS OF IMPROVEMENT AS OF DECEMBER 31, 1974

—— COMPLETED OR IMPROVED AND OPEN TO TRAFFIC
  Completed to full or acceptable standards, or improved to standards.
  Adequate for present traffic, built with Interstate or other public funds.

◆◆◆ MAJOR TOLL ROADS
  Incorporated in the Interstate System

——— UNDER CONSTRUCTION

——— PRELIMINARY STATUS OR NOT YET IN PROGRESS
  Plan preparation and right-of-way acquisition completed or underway on many portions of these sections

Scale of map does not permit showing of status
in urban areas and for very short sections

U.S. DEPARTMENT OF TRANSPORTATION
FEDERAL HIGHWAY ADMINISTRATION

| INTERSTATE |
| TOTAL |
| 42,500 |
| MILES |

| Preliminary Status or Not Yet in Progress 837 Miles | Engineering and Right-of-Way in Progress 2660 Miles | Under Basic Construction 2731 Miles | Toll 2308 Miles | Adequate Present Traffic 2093 Miles | Minor Improvement is Required or Underway 22,628 Miles | Complete or Essentially Complete 9,243 Miles |

Total Open to Traffic
36,272 Miles

SOURCE: Federal Highway Administration.

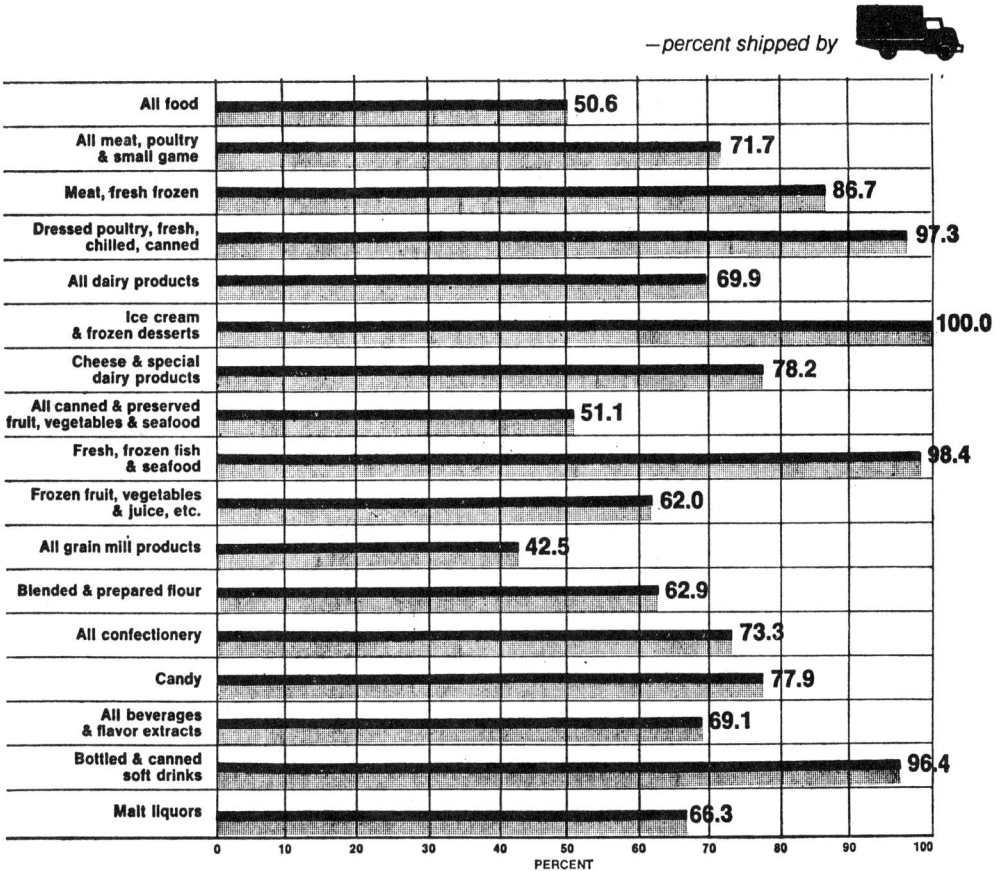

FIG. 4-5 Agricultural Products Shipped by Truck.

—percent shipped by

	PERCENT
All food	50.6
All meat, poultry & small game	71.7
Meat, fresh frozen	86.7
Dressed poultry, fresh, chilled, canned	97.3
All dairy products	69.9
Ice cream & frozen desserts	100.0
Cheese & special dairy products	78.2
All canned & preserved fruit, vegetables & seafood	51.1
Fresh, frozen fish & seafood	98.4
Frozen fruit, vegetables & juice, etc.	62.0
All grain mill products	42.5
Blended & prepared flour	62.9
All confectionery	73.3
Candy	77.9
All beverages & flavor extracts	69.1
Bottled & canned soft drinks	96.4
Malt liquors	66.3

0 10 20 30 40 50 60 70 80 90 100
PERCENT

SOURCE: 1967 Census of Transportation, U. S. Department of Commerce, in *Pacific Traffic* (October, 1973), p. 50.

than 5,000 pounds. Because the regulated truckers have specialized in providing a high level of service, they received 8.0 cents per intercity ton-mile in 1971. This figure can be compared to the 2.04 cents that the railroads receive.

The financial condition of the trucking industry can best be described as healthy, if not prosperous.[17] The 1974 Class I and II operating ratio (found by dividing total expenses by total operating revenue) was 94.5. However, because truckers have relatively little capital investment, they have a high capital turnover ratio (operating revenue divided by

[17] See, for example: Dana L. Thomas, "No Brakes on Growth," *Barron's* (March 29, 1976), pp. 3ff.

capital investment), averaging since 1960 between 4.5–5.0. This allows individual truckers to achieve remarkably high earnings on invested capital, often in the range of 12–19 percent annually.

Motor Carrier Problem Areas. From the shipper's point-of-view, the regulated truckers, while generally offering a high quality service, have not been without service problems. During a recent *Distribution Worldwide* interview, the traffic manager for a large lighting company stated, "Service by motor common carrier has deteriorated over the past five years." Universal Textured Yarns reported that service level declines from 1967 to 1972 forced them to reduce their use of regulated (common carrier) trucks by 66 percent and to compensate for this loss by the use of their own private trucking fleet. The survey indicated that the most serious problems with regulated common carriers were: refusal to pick-up freight promptly, slow delivery schedules, and loss-and-damage problems.[18]

From the regulated truckers' viewpoint, there are a number of basic problems, the three most important of which are: *small-shipments, highway availability,* and *increase in private trucking.* Each will be briefly discussed.

The small-shipments problem involves shipments that weigh less than 500 pounds. The truckers believe that the revenue they receive for each shipment this size does not cover the costs. For example, the president of Ryder Truck Lines reported that for his firm, the average small-shipment weighed 128 pounds and was shipped 480 miles. A typical shipment of this size from Atlanta to Cincinnati (476 miles) involved these costs:

Pick-up cost	$2.47
Dock cost	.73
Terminal rating and billing	.98
Line-haul	.64
Delivery cost	2.47
Collection and administration	2.13
Total Cost	$9.42

On the revenue side, the shipper of this 128 pound shipment paid $4.75.[19]

---

[18] Janet Bosworth Dower, "The Shipper Speaks Out," *Distribution Worldwide* (September, 1973), pp. 36–40, 44–45.

[19] For a complete discussion of the small-shipment problem, including this example, see: James C. Johnson, "An Analysis of the 'Small-Shipments' Problem With Particular Attention To Its Ramifications On A Firm's Logistical System," *ICC Practitioners' Journal* (July-August, 1972), pp. 646–666 and by the same author "The Small-Shipment Problem: Fact or Fiction," *ICC Practitioners' Journal* (March-April, 1973), pp. 291–307.

FIG. 4-6 It is Alleged That Trucks Cause an Excessive Number of Accidents.

Reproduced by permission of the artist and the Masters Agency.

Another problem involves the motor carriers' use of the highway system. There are two issues. The first is size and weight limits on trucks and trailers. The strongest opposition to increasing them comes from the multi-million member American Automobile Association.[20] This group wants to restrict the truckers to using only certain roads, because they believe that the long, large trucks are dangerous on highways. (See Figure 4-6.) A physician who heads the Insurance Institute For Highway Safety noted, "It's obvious that mixing small, fast-stopping vehicles with ponderous, slower-braking ones would create a problem. And it does. It's an inherent safety hazard."[21]

Not all states allow the use of a tractor with two trailers. This is especially true in the Southeast, the Midwest, and New England. Twin trailers, each 27 feet in length, represent an increase of 30 percent in

[20] See, for example, "Little Hope for Truckers' Relief," *Distribution Worldwide* (June, 1974), p. 12.

[21] August Gribbon, "Danger Rides With Big Rigs," *The National Observer* (June 7, 1971), in Martin T. Farris and Paul T. McElhiney, eds., *Modern Transportation: Selected Readings* (Boston: Houghton Mifflin Co., 1973), p. 87.

FIG. 4-7 The Trend is Toward Longer Trucks.

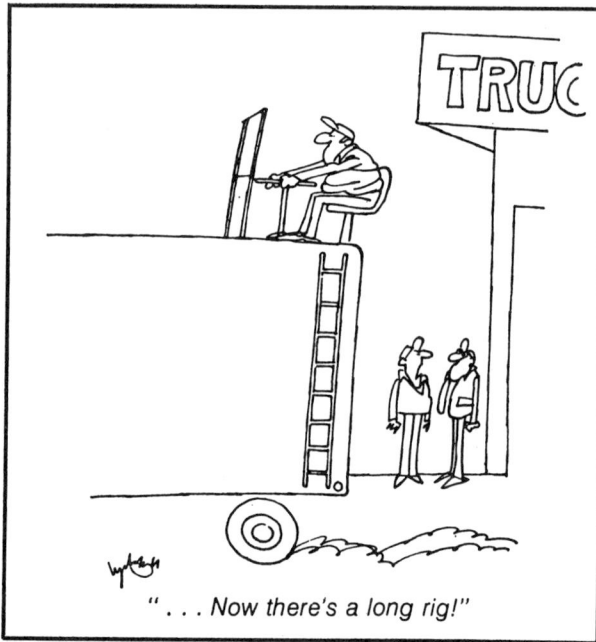

" . . . Now there's a long rig!"

Reproduced by permission of *Heavy Duty Trucking Magazine.*

cubic capacity as opposed to one standard 40 foot trailer. The primary opposition to double-bottoms comes from auto owners and the A.A.A. who stress the safety problems of longer trucks.[22] (See Figure 4-7.) However, during the fuel "crisis" some states relaxed limitations— especially on axle weight.

A third problem for regulated truckers is the increase in private motor carriage, often called *do-it-yourself* trucking. When a company such as Pillsbury stops using the services of a for-hire trucking firm, such as Consolidated Freightways, and starts transporting its own products in its own trucks, it is engaging in private transportation. A recent survey indicated that the use of private trucking has increased 16 percent from 1968 to 1973 on a total tonnage basis. Sixty-one percent of the shippers contacted indicated that their firms currently used a private motor carrier fleet. When asked why, 71.7 percent stated that better service was the primary reason they switched to private trucking and 47.7 percent said that cost savings was another motivation. The traffic

[22] See, for example, Jim Dixon, "The Urgent Need for Double Bottoms," *Distribution Worldwide* (March, 1974), pp. 35–39.

manager of a large Florida firm stated, "Service is declining at a regular rate. I think this is due to a lack of concern by motor carrier personnel. And as a result, increased rates with poor service put us into private carriage."[23] Another motor carrier problem is the increase in "illegal" trucking activities. It will be discussed in chapter six.

Motor Carrier Service Innovations. The Interstate Highway System allowed truckers to perform faster service. In addition, the motor carrier industry is expanding its usage of specialized equipment. Trucks can now transport oxygen and hydrogen in liquid form, using double thermos shells. With this equipment, temperatures can be kept between minus 300 and minus 423 degrees Fahrenheit. Similar trucks haul liquid asphalt at plus 400 degrees Fahrenheit directly to construction sites. Another equipment innovation involves the use of pneumatic systems for rapid loading and unloading of dry-cargo truck trailers. Approximately one hundred flowable commodities, such as cement, chemicals, and grains are now using this truck equipment extensively.[24]

Computer technology is another area that has assisted the motor carrier industry to achieve improved levels of customer service. Consolidated Freightways has established a computer program that is typical of many of the larger regulated truckers. It allows the firm to pinpoint the exact location of all shipments in the system at any time. This is very helpful to customers who are concerned about when a shipment will arrive, when it left certain terminals, etc. Computers also check to make sure that the correct rate has been applied to freight.[25]

PIPELINES

The oil pipeline system of the United States is extensive. There are two types of oil pipelines: *crude-oil* and *product.* Crude-oil lines transport petroleum from the wells to the refineries. There are approximately 150,000 miles of crude-oil pipelines, shown in Figure 4-8. There are two types of crude-oil lines. Somewhat more than half of the crude-oil line mileage is *gathering lines.* These lines start at each well and carry the product to concentration points. Gathering lines are generally 6 inches or smaller in diameter, and are frequently laid on the ground. *Trunklines* are larger diameter pipelines which carry crude-oil from gathering line concentration points to the oil refineries. They vary in diameter from three inches to 48 inches. However, eight to ten inch pipe is the most common size.

23 Dower, *op. cit.*, p. 36.
24 See: "A State-of-the-Art Report on Technology and Highway Transportation," *Handling and Shipping* (January, 1971), pp. 52–55.
25 "The Trucking Industry: Working Behind the Scenes," *Transportation and Distribution Management* (April, 1972), pp. 20–24.

FIG. 4-8 Crude-oil Pipelines.

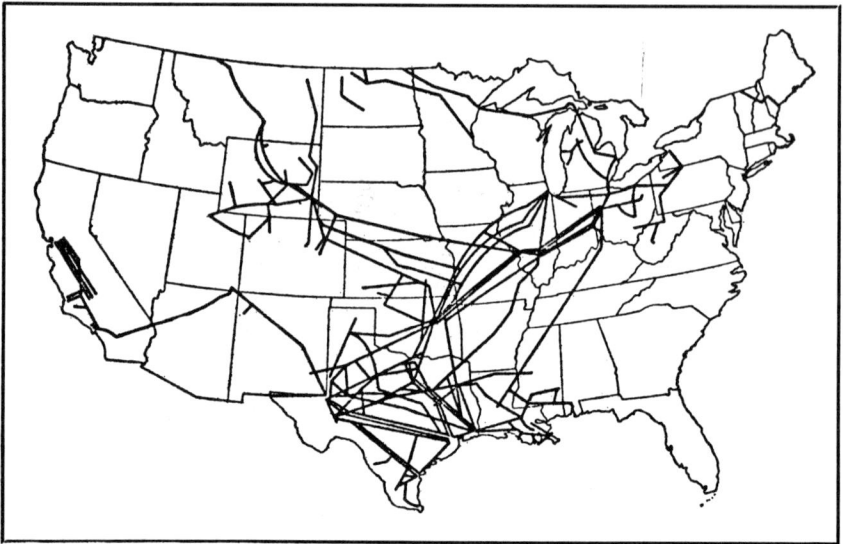

SOURCE: The American Oil Company.

Product lines transport the refined petroleum products from the re-fineries to the population centers. There are approximately 75,000 miles of product line, shown in Figure 4-9. The diameter of product lines is the same size or somewhat smaller than the trunklines.

Figures 4-8 and 4-9 show that the oil pipeline system of the U. S. is *not* evenly dispersed throughout the country. Texas has one-quarter of all the nation's pipeline mileage and Oklahoma, Kansas, and Illinois combined have another quarter.

In 1975 the oil pipeline industry produced 510 billion ton-miles of transportation service. This was 24.8 percent of all intercity ton-miles. In Canada, with the terrain less conducive to other modes of transportation, the pipelines produce 30 percent of all intercity ton-miles. The pipeline is a very efficient means of transporting oil products, and al-most 90 percent of petroleum products are transported this way. An example of this efficiency is that the oil pipelines generate 17 times as many ton-miles per employee as do the railroads. A large pipeline's capacity is also impressive. The 48 inch Trans-Alaska pipeline, which is 789 miles long, will discharge two million barrels (42 gallons each) per day.[26]

There were 104 oil pipeline companies reporting to the ICC in 1975.

26 Pat Gallagher, "A Convoy vs. the Arctic—An Alaskan Passage Report," *Handling and Shipping* (December, 1975), pp. 35–37.

FIG. 4-9 Oil Product Pipelines.

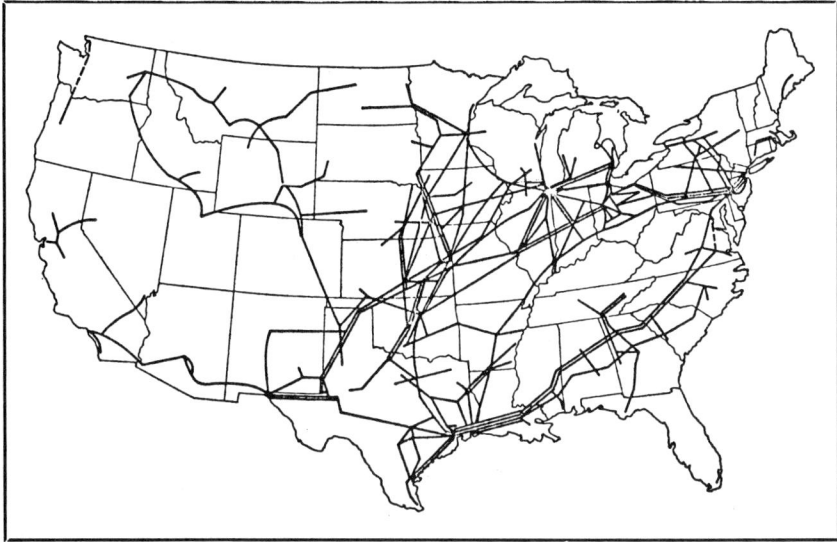

SOURCE: The American Oil Company.

The average petroleum pipeline company had gross revenues of approximately $13.5 million and 150 employees. As these employment figures indicate, pipelines are very capital intensive. Labor costs are 59 percent of total operating expenses for the motor carrier industry, 53 percent for the railroads, and only *10 percent* for the oil pipeline industry. The current financial condition of this industry is sound. In 1972 the industry achieved a 10 percent return on invested capital.

Non-Petroleum Products. A number of other products are also transported by pipelines. Chief among these is natural gas. There are approximately 180,000 miles of intercity natural gas pipelines. This aspect of pipelining is regulated by the Federal Power Commission instead of the ICC which regulates all other surface transportation modes, including oil pipelines.

A non-petroleum pipeline concept that appears to have significant potential is the use of *slurry* pipelines. This involves grinding the product to be transported into a powder and then mixing it in water and then sending it through the pipeline in suspension. At present, the most extensive use of slurry pipelines involves the transport of coal. Additional products that are adaptable to slurry technology include iron ore, limestone, Gilsonite, sulphur, potassium chloride and waste commodities. The largest and longest coal slurry line in operation today is the Black Mesa pipeline, which transports pulverized coal in an 18 inch pipe 273 miles from strip mines in Northern Arizona to an electric generating station on the Colorado River near Davis Dam, Nevada. The $35 million project started operation in 1971 and it is owned by the Southern Pacific Company. The slurry line was constructed because unit-train operation was not feasible over the terrain involved. The 50 percent water, 50 percent coal mixture moves at four miles per hour and makes the trip in three days. The speed of the movement must be carefully maintained because excessive speed makes the coal powder act like sandpaper on the inside of the pipe. Too slow of a movement causes the coal powder to fall out of suspension and build upon the bottom of the pipe. When the slurry solution reaches destination, centrifuges spin out the water and the coal is fed into the furnaces.[27]

A revolutionary concept, now in its infancy, involves sending capsules through pipelines. The Transcontinental Gas Pipe Line Company has proposed a capsule system to the United States Postal Service. The company has two 36 inch prototype pipelines, which are each 800 feet long. By using compressed air, they can transport a 300-pound payload in a capsule at 30 miles per hour.

Pipeline Problem Areas.   While the pipeline industry is healthy and growing, it does have some problem areas. The recent concern for ecology and environmental protection has greatly increased the costs of pipeline construction. It has been estimated the Trans-Alaska Pipeline, which is expected to cost approximately $5 billion, would have cost only $2 billion if it were not for the sophisticated environmental engineering that was required.

A second problem area involves the difficulty of acquiring the rights-of-way for new pipeline construction. Some states do not give pipelines the ability to condemn property for their right-of-way, which is known as the *right of eminent domain*. Without right-of-way, pipelines are forced into circuitous routes. A current coal-slurry pipeline right-of-way controversy involves a projected 1,030 mile pipeline from Wyoming to Arkansas. The coal would be consumed by a number of electric public utilities in the Southeast region of the United States. The builders of the slurry line are attempting to win federal Congressional action in order to secure the interstate right of eminent domain. Without this authorization, which appears doubtful, the construction is stymied because it crosses railroad properties in 44 places. The railroads, because of their dependence on coal tonnage, have refused to grant the slurry

[27] "A Pipeline From Black Mesa," *Transportation and Distribution Management* (October, 1969), p. 50. See also: J. G. Montfort, "Black Mesa System Proves Coal Slurry Technology," *Pipe Line Industry* (May, 1974), pp. 30–31.

pipeline the right of transversing their properties. Louis W. Menk, Chief Executive Officer of the Burlington Northern Railroad, referred to this proposed slurry line as, "a transportation concept that is about as appropriate to the nation's needs as the windup light bulb."[28]

INLAND WATER CARRIERS

This section will discuss water carriage on the inland and coastal waterway system. (Ocean transportation will be covered in chapter 11 dealing with international physical distribution.)

The inland waterway system, not counting the coastal routes, the Great Lakes, or the St. Lawrence Seaway System, approximates 16,000 miles that are dredged to a depth of nine feet, which is the minimum required for most barges. Figure 4-10 illustrates most of this system, which is concentrated in the southeastern region of the United States. In 1975 there were 78 inland and coastal water carriers which had gross revenues of greater than $100,000. They had an *average* freight revenue of $4.3 million and employed 110 people apiece. They earned a healthy 11.7 percent return on net invested capital. Inland water carriers receive only 0.3 cents per ton-mile of transportation, slightly higher than the figure for pipelines.

In general, the domestic water percentage of all intercity ton-miles has not changed significantly from 1929 to 1975. However, there has been a shift in the composition. In 1929, the Great Lakes accounted for 16 percent of the total, while rivers and canals were only 1.4 percent. By 1975, the former was 5.2 percent and the latter registered 11.4 percent of all intercity ton-miles. In 1975 inland water carriers received only 5.7 percent of all freight revenue for transporting about 16.6 percent of all intercity ton-miles.

The domestic water carriers have specialized in transporting bulk products at very low prices and at slow average speeds (six miles per hour). Petroleum and related products account for 36 percent of total barge commerce. Coal is second, with 28 percent. Other products that move extensively in the inland waterway system are: grain and grain products, industrial chemicals, iron and steel products, forestry products, cement, sulphur, fertilizers, paper products, sand and gravel, and limestone. In most cases these products are tendered to the carriers in barge-load lots, which range from minimums of 500 to 2500 tons on the rivers and canals up to 20,000 tons on individual vessels in ocean going, coastal or Great Lakes service.[29]

Towboats, with powerplants from 1,000 to 9,000 horsepower, *push* the loaded barges. The barges are lashed together so that they are in

28 "Coal Slurry Pipelines," *Railway Age* (November 24, 1975), p. 31.
29 See: Jim Dixon, "Traffic's Booming On America's Water Highways," *Distribution Worldwide* (December, 1975), pp. 23–27.

FIG. 4-10 Waterways of the United States.

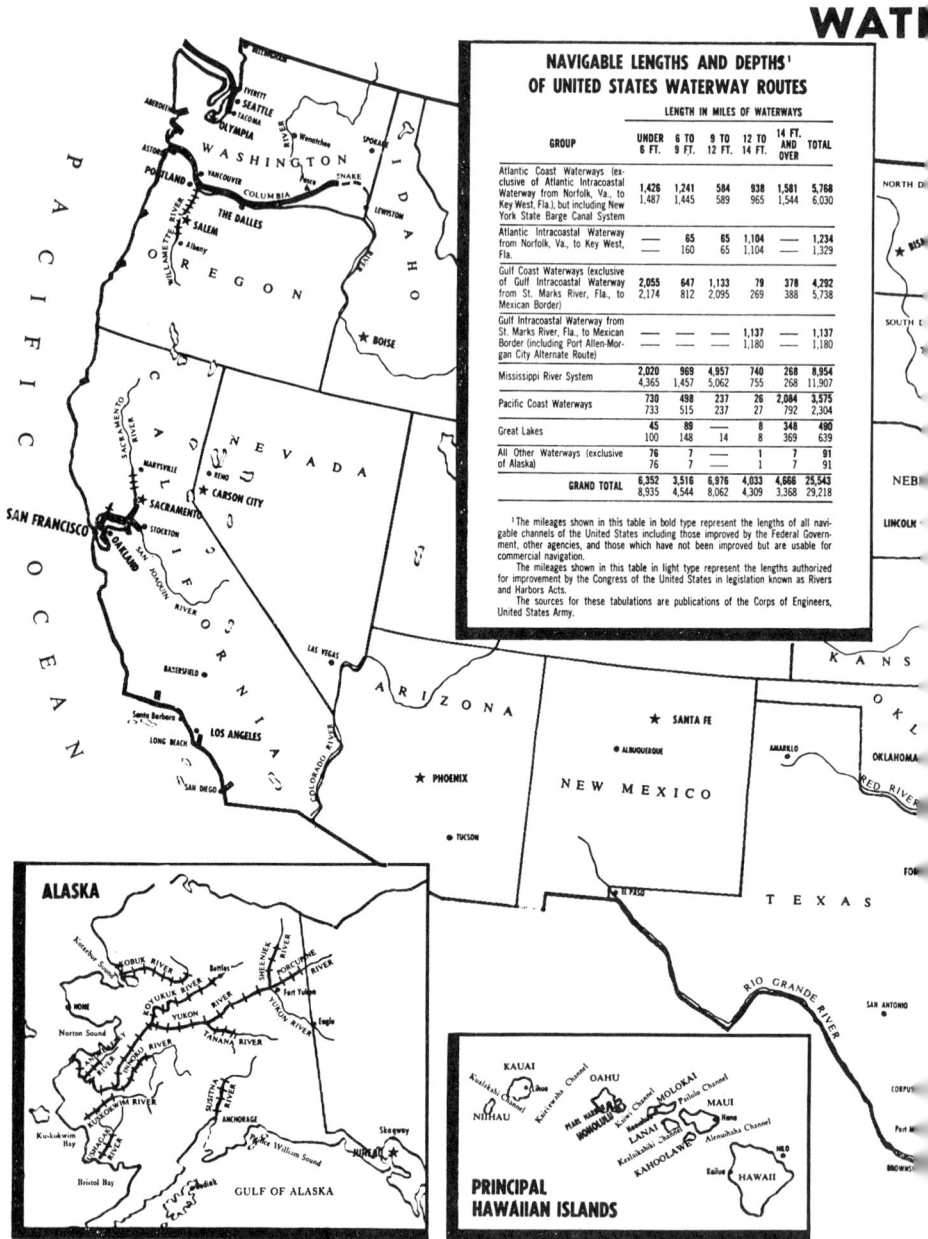

NAVIGABLE LENGTHS AND DEPTHS[1]
OF UNITED STATES WATERWAY ROUTES

GROUP	LENGTH IN MILES OF WATERWAYS					
	UNDER 6 FT.	6 TO 9 FT.	9 TO 12 FT.	12 TO 14 FT.	14 FT. AND OVER	TOTAL
Atlantic Coast Waterways (exclusive of Atlantic Intracoastal Waterway from Norfolk, Va., to Key West, Fla.), but including New York State Barge Canal System	**1,426** 1,487	**1,241** 1,445	**584** 589	**938** 965	**1,581** 1,544	**5,768** 6,030
Atlantic Intracoastal Waterway from Norfolk, Va., to Key West, Fla.	— —	**65** 160	**65** 65	**1,104** 1,104	— —	**1,234** 1,329
Gulf Coast Waterways (exclusive of Gulf Intracoastal Waterway from St. Marks River, Fla., to Mexican Border)	**2,055** 2,174	**647** 812	**1,133** 2,095	**79** 269	**378** 388	**4,292** 5,738
Gulf Intracoastal Waterway from St. Marks River, Fla., to Mexican Border (including Port Allen-Morgan City Alternate Route)	— —	— —	— —	**1,137** 1,180	— —	**1,137** 1,180
Mississippi River System	**2,020** 4,365	**969** 1,457	**4,957** 5,062	**740** 755	**268** 268	**8,954** 11,907
Pacific Coast Waterways	**730** 733	**498** 515	**237** 237	**26** 27	**2,084** 792	**3,575** 2,304
Great Lakes	**45** 100	**89** 148	— 14	**8** 8	**348** 369	**490** 639
All Other Waterways (exclusive of Alaska)	**76** 76	**7** 7	— —	**1** 1	**7** 7	**91** 91
GRAND TOTAL	**6,352** 8,935	**3,516** 4,544	**6,976** 8,062	**4,033** 4,309	**4,666** 3,368	**25,543** 29,218

[1]The mileages shown in this table in bold type represent the lengths of all navigable channels of the United States including those improved by the Federal Government, other agencies, and those which have not been improved but are usable for commercial navigation.

The mileages shown in this table in light type represent the lengths authorized for improvement by the Congress of the United States in legislation known as Rivers and Harbors Acts.

The sources for these tabulations are publications of the Corps of Engineers, United States Army.

SOURCE: The American Waterways Operators, Inc.

AYS OF THE UNITED STATES

COMMERCIALLY NAVIGABLE
WATERWAYS
OF THE
UNITED STATES

CONTROLLING DEPTHS

9 FEET OR MORE
UNDER 9 FEET

AUTHORIZED EXTENSIONS

PUBLISHED 1973 BY
THE AMERICAN WATERWAYS OPERATORS, INC.
1250 CONNECTICUT AVENUE, WASHINGTON, D.C. 20036
Compiled from Information Supplied by
CORPS OF ENGINEERS, U.S. ARMY

effect one large mass of floating freight. As many as 50 barges are secured and operated as one "tow."

Inland Water Carriers Problem Areas. The domestic water carriers, like the other modes of transportation, have their share of problems. One serious quandary is that the environmental groups have taken a strong stand against the expansion of the inland waterway system. The environmentalists believe that the dredging and the disposal of materials dredged from channels will upset the "balance of nature" in the areas affected.[30] For example, environmentalists generated sufficient pressure to bring about a halt in the construction of the cross-Florida segment of the intra-coastal waterway.

Another problem area for the barge carriers is that Congress is seriously considering a user tax on the waterway system. At present, the federal government builds and maintains the inland waterway system and does not charge the barge owners for their usage. Recently, a governmental study group, the National Water Commission, recommended that the water carriers should pay a motor fuel user tax. The water carrier industry is adamant regarding its position against this suggestion. Also, pro-water carrier members of Congress (mostly from the South) are fighting this proposal. Senator J. Bennett Johnston (D.-La.) termed the user tax proposal as "outrageous" and "incredible."[31]

An operational problem plaguing the water carriers is the time delays necessitated by the locks on the waterway system. Many of the older locks are 600 feet long, but with the larger tows often considerably longer than this, the tow must be broken and put through the lock in two parts. Thomas J. Barta, President of the Valley Line Company, reports that because of congestion, tows on the Upper Mississippi at Alton, Illinois sometimes have to wait 24–36 hours to proceed through the locking system.[32]

Inland Water Carrier Service Innovations. The typical carrying capacity of a barge tow has increased from 150,000 to more than three million ton-miles per day while improvements in propulsion, navigation, and control have reduced crew size by 50 percent.[33] Today, barge

[30] See: David P. Garino and Connie S. Harrison, "Railroads Join Environmental Groups to Fight Plan for New River Locks Near Alton, Ill.," *The Wall Street Journal* (December 3, 1975), p. 32.

[31] Carlo J. Salzano, "Barge, Towing Industry Hits NWC Report, Pledges Fight Against River User Charge," *Traffic World* (September 24, 1973), p. 26.

[32] Thomas J. Barta, "Bottlenecks Hindering Productivity in the Water Transportation Industry," in *Transportation Research Forum 13th Annual Proceedings* (Oxford, Ind.: The Richard B. Cross Co., 1972), pp. 219–222. See footnote 30 regarding this lock.

[33] "U.S. Domestic Shipping Cargoes Should Triple by 2000 A.D.," *Commerce Today* (March 4, 1974), p. 5.

carriers are introducing new services made possible by equipment innovations.[34] The Federal Barge Lines offers specially equipped barges that regulate both temperature and humidity for the shipment of anhydrous ammonia and sulphur. This equipment is running between Chicago and Houston on a 17 day schedule. Peter Fanchi, president of Federal Barge, stated that his company will supply the transportation services that their customers demand. "If somebody comes around here tomorrow and says, 'I'm going to move steel at 1,200 degrees,' why we'll build a barge to conform with that man's needs."[35]

An equipment innovation that is revolutionizing much of the inland water transportation system is the *LASH (Lighter Aboard Ship) concept*. (A lighter is a small ship or barge.) *LASH* barges are very similar to typical inland barges. What makes the system so unique is that ocean-going ships are equipped to take these barges directly on board ship via elevator systems. This greatly reduces the cargo transfer costs at the ocean port. Instead of the product having to be unloaded from the barge and then loaded onto the ocean going ship, the loaded barge is loaded into the "mother" ship. For many products bound for export or import, an all water route is now feasible. (*LASH* vessels are also discussed in Chapter 11.)

AIR FREIGHT

Domestic air freight operations today are growing at a healthy rate. Nevertheless, the rate of growth has not been as spectacular as was predicted in the 1960's. T. P. Gallagher, Jr., assistant vice-president-freight sales for American Airlines, observed:

> We look into the future today with a little more caution and understanding than many people had in the sixties. To some, the future of air freight then seemed to have absolutely no horizon. Vast fleets of jet freighters were coming. Every airport would have huge freight terminals, completely automated, of course. . . . Some of those dreams have faded, and some were excessive to start with. It is a cold fact that in 1972 the major U. S. airlines lost money on their all-cargo jet freight operations.[36]

This section will examine the current problems and strengths of domestic air freight operations. Figure 4-11 illustrates the trunk-line

[34] James R. Smith, "Barges Move the Basics," *Transportation and Distribution Management* (March-April, 1976), pp. 24–25.

[35] "Barge Lines: No Trimmings," *Transportation and Distribution Management* (March, 1972), p. 25.

[36] T. P. Gallagher, Jr., "Marketing, Money and Those Empty Bellies," *Transportation and Distribution Management* (November, 1973), p. 1 supplemental section. See also: Leigh B. Boske, "Cost Efficiency in the Domestic Trunk Airline Industry," *Journal of Economics and Business* (Winter, 1976), pp. 128–137 and a special air-freight issue of *Distribution Worldwide* (January, 1976).

Fig. 4-11 Trunk-line air carrier routes.

UNITED STATES AIR T

ROUTES CERTIFICATED

MARCH

Source: Civil Aeronautics Board, Office of Facilities and Operations, March 31, 1974.

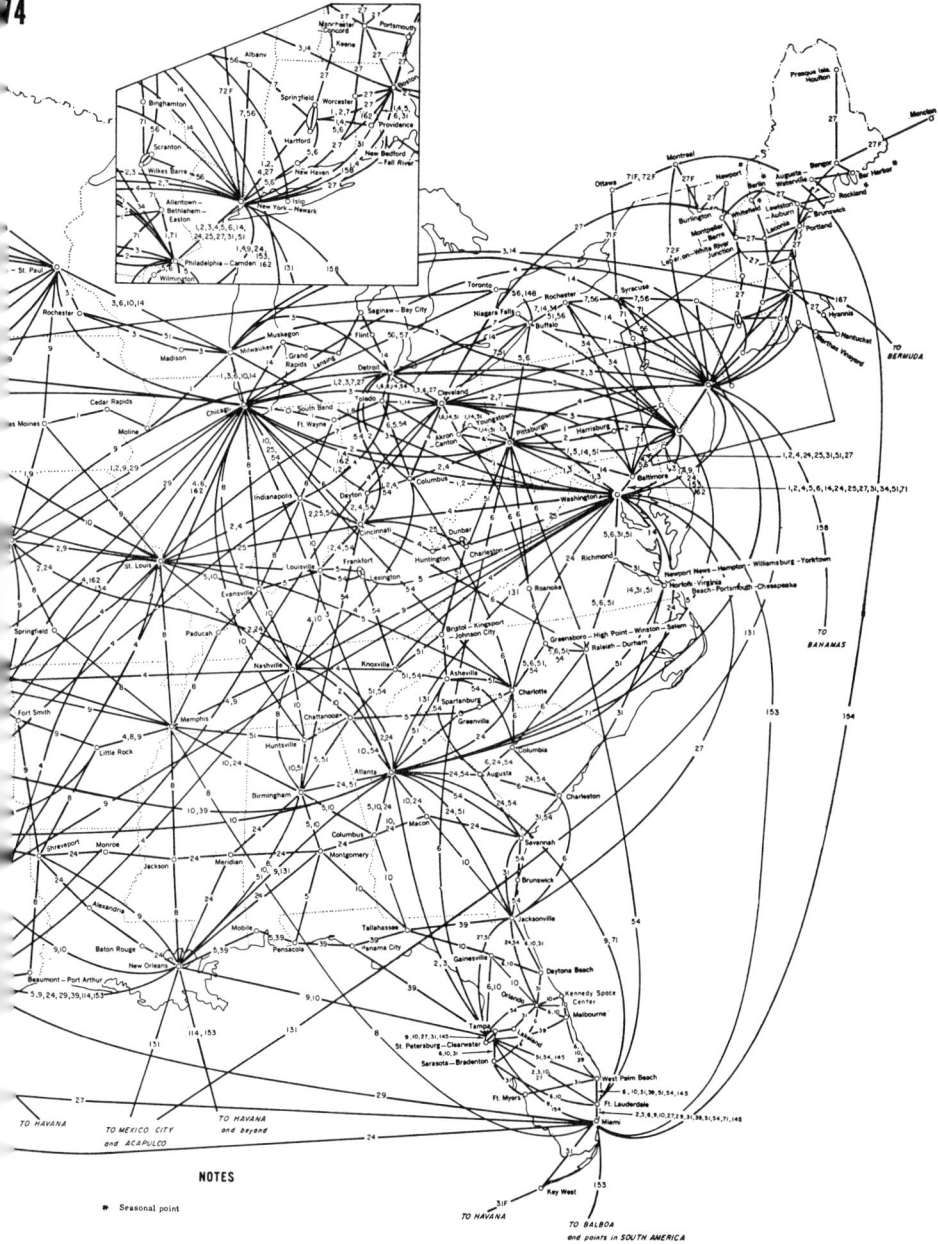

Maynard - Concord · Portsmouth
Albany · Keene
Binghamton · 72 F
Springfield · Worcester
Scranton · Hartford
Wilkes Barre
Allentown - Bethlehem - Easton
New Haven · Providence · New Bedford - Fall River
New York - Newark · Islip
Philadelphia - Camden
Wilmington

St. Paul
Rochester
Madison · Milwaukee · Muskegon
Cedar Rapids · Grand Rapids · Lansing
Moline · Chicago · South Bend · Ft. Wayne
Des Moines
Indianapolis · Dayton · Cincinnati
St. Louis · Louisville · Frankfort · Lexington
Springfield · Evansville · Paducah
Nashville · Knoxville
Fort Smith · Memphis · Chattanooga
Little Rock · Huntsville
Birmingham · Atlanta
Shreveport · Monroe · Meridian · Columbus · Montgomery
Jackson
Alexandria · Mobile · Pensacola · Tallahassee · Panama City
Baton Rouge · New Orleans
Beaumont - Port Arthur

Toronto · Rochester · Syracuse
Niagara Falls · Buffalo
Detroit · Cleveland
Toledo · Youngstown · Pittsburgh · Harrisburg
Akron · Canton
Columbus · Dunbar · Charleston · Richmond
Huntington
Washington · Baltimore
Roanoke
Bristol - Kingsport - Johnson City
Asheville · Greensboro - High Point - Winston Salem · Raleigh - Durham
Spartanburg · Charlotte
Greenville · Columbia
Augusta · Charleston
Macon · Savannah
Brunswick
Jacksonville
Gainesville · Daytona Beach
Orlando · Kennedy Space Center · Melbourne
Tampa · St. Petersburg - Clearwater · Lakeland
Sarasota - Bradenton
Ft. Myers · West Palm Beach
Ft. Lauderdale
Miami
Key West

Montreal · Ottawa
Burlington · Newport
Montpelier - Barre · Whitefield · Lewiston - Auburn
Lebanon - White River Junction · Laconia · Portland
Keene · Rockland
Hyannis · Nantucket
Martha's Vineyard

Presque Isle - Houlton
Moncton
Bangor · Bar Harbor
Augusta · Waterville
Brunswick
Portland

Newport News - Hampton · Williamsburg - Yorktown
Norfolk - Virginia Beach - Portsmouth - Chesapeake

TO BERMUDA
TO BAHAMAS

TO HAVANA
TO MEXICO CITY and ACAPULCO
TO HAVANA and beyond
TO HAVANA
TO BALBOA and points in SOUTH AMERICA

NOTES

* Seasonal point

air carrier routes. All of these carriers offer air freight service. The system is relatively comprehensive and air freight service is available to most cities of over 50,000 population.

The structure of the air freight industry is unusual compared to the other modes of transportation. This is because the great majority of the air freight ton-miles flown are performed by airlines whose primary business is passenger operations. Often, only about ten percent of their revenue comes from air freight. The top 20 U.S. airlines in freight ton-miles included only three all-cargo air carriers. Flying Tiger was third in this list. Seaboard World was sixth and Airlift International was eleventh. The other 17 positions were combination passenger and air freight carriers. The general level of air freight rates is very high compared to the other modes of transportation, averaging 21.5 cents per ton-mile.

The air freight industry transports a remarkable variety of products. (See Figure 4-12.) The following product groups represent the largest users of air freight: wearing apparel; electronic/electrical equipment and parts; printed matter; machinery and parts; cut flowers and nursery stock; auto parts and accessories; phonograph records, tapes, T.V.'s, radios, recorders; fruits and vegetables; metal products; and photographic equipment, parts and film. As this list illustrates, products that are air freighted tend to be high in value, of a perishable nature, or possessing "emergency" characteristics.

Air Freight Problem Areas. The industry is experiencing difficult financial problems. "To put it in the colloquial, ain't nobody making a profit,"[37] stated a senior vice-president for freight marketing at American Airlines. The industry may be starting to reverse this unfavorable financial situation.

For the combination passenger-air freight companies, which dominate the industry, the problems of the past must be avoided. Probably the most serious situation involves *belly cargo.* This is air freight that is flown in freight compartments on scheduled passenger flights. Historically, the airlines priced their air freight relatively low; and the volume of business generated was too extensive to be transported exclusively as belly freight. Therefore, all-cargo freighters were introduced. However, the established air freight rates were so low that an all-cargo aircraft, full of cargo, lost money. Further complicating the picture for the all-cargo aircraft has been the introduction of the wide-body jets. These are the Boeing 747, the McDonnell-Douglas DC-10, and the Lockheed 1011. More than 300 of the planes have been received or are presently on order for United States airlines. Because of the in-

[37] "Air Cargo: Still Cinderella?," *Transportation and Distribution Management* (April, 1973), p. 42.

FIG. 4-12 Airfreight Capabilities.

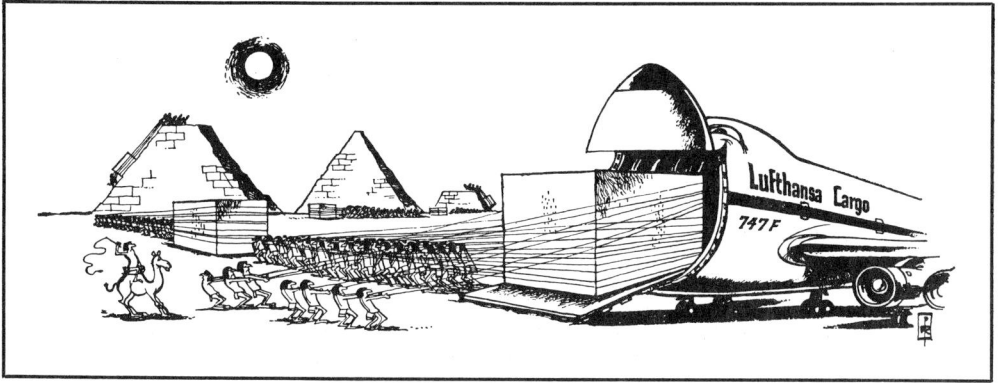

SOURCE: Compliments of Lufthansa German Airlines.

creased size of the wide-body jets, the amount of belly cargo space has significantly grown. This has precipitated major changes in the airfreight economics and profitability.

Since the majority of the air freight firms are combination carriers (i.e., passenger and freight), the air freight end of the business is often neglected relative to the much larger dollar volume passenger segment. Otto Becker, a senior air freight marketing executive for a combination carrier mused, "The whole industry is passenger-oriented. American Airlines became a billion-dollar corporation as a passenger carrier. And you say, here's a $100 million business in cargo, one-tenth of the business, get excited about it! The industry and corporate management generally do not appreciate cargo."[38]

Another air freight problem involves ground terminals. The price of land at airport terminals is very high. It has been estimated that airport property costs two to four times more than similar real estate a half-mile from the airport (and this assumes that new terminal land is available). A serious terminal-related problem is ground handling and sorting equipment. It is a sad fact that in some cases the inherent speed advantage of air freight is badly dissipated by slow, archaic, and costly ground handling operations. *Transportation and Distribution Management* studied this situation and concluded that ground-handling problems remain the primary source of the air freight industry's "profit anemia." These involve terminal and rampside congestion as well as relatively slow manual loading systems.[39]

A quandary is associated with the wide-body passenger jets and their belly cargo freight. Traditionally, all cargo aircraft flew during the

[38] "Air Cargo: Still Cinderella," *op. cit.*, p. 43.
[39] *Ibid.*, p. 45.

night to avoid passenger plane airport congestion and because it worked best from the shippers' point-of-view. With the growth of belly freight capacity in wide-body planes, more and more air cargo is being flown during the *daylight* hours. On the surface, this does not appear to be significant. However, it is! Customers are used to preparing their air freight shipments during regular working hours and tendering them to the carriers late in the day. The airlines sorted them in the early evening and they would be transported later that night and arrive at destination the following morning. Now, with shipments tendered in the same fashion, the freight does not even leave the airport until the following day when the belly cargo is transported on passenger flights. In essence, a day's time is often lost. From a shipper's point-of-view, delivery time has doubled.

The last problem to be discussed here is that the "typical" air freight product shipped "cubes-out" long before it "weighs-out." Commodity's average density is $7\frac{1}{2}$ to $8\frac{1}{2}$ pounds per cubic feet. However, most jets can lift freight that averages 14 to 15 pounds per cubic foot. Since most air cargo rates are based on weight, and were formulated at a time when planes had different carrying characteristics, the carrier often finds its planes "cube out" and each flight is denied additional revenue that would have been generated had the products been of greater density.

Air Freight Equipment Innovations. The air freight industry has been known for its readiness to innovate in the area of equipment.[40] Some industry leaders believe the increased belly capacity of the wide-bodied jets will spell the death of the all-cargo jet freighter. "In the next two or three years I see a phasing out of the freighters. I think that with the capacity and lift capability that we have with the 747's and DC 10's there really won't be any need for the freighter," stated Lee Slay, vice president-cargo sales for Continental Airlines.[41] On the other hand, other observers believe that there will always be a place for the all-cargo aircraft, but only on the major airfreight routes, such as Dallas-Chicago and New York City-Los Angeles. Very recently, a few U. S. airlines acquired 747F (all-freight) aircraft.

Another approach to freight aircraft is the wide-body DC-10CF (convertible freighter). Although this plane is *not* designed to be changed everyday, it is possible, to convert it from primarily passenger service to an all-cargo configuration. This would perhaps be done on a seasonal basis. During the summer months, when tourism is at a high level, the plane would be used as a passenger aircraft, able to accommodate 380 passengers. During periods of slack passenger demand, the DC-10CF can be changed into an all-cargo plane. World Airways has a 747 with

[40] See: "The Next Commercial Jet ... If," *Business Week* (April 12, 1976), pp. 62–65ff.

[41] "An Interview with O. Lee Slay," *Pacific Traffic* (September, 1972), p. 40.

similar conversion capabilities. Perhaps the only *true* innovation in air freight in the future will be the lighter-than-air *airship*. One version would be inflated with 12 million cubic feet of helium and it would have a 300,000 pound lift capacity. It would have a cruising range of 6,000 miles, traveling between 80-90 miles per hour. Either diesel or gas turbine engines would power the airship at approximately 5,000 feet altitude. The designer of the above hypothetical vehicle believes the cost per ton-mile would be in the 6-8 cents range.[42]

A final aircraft equipment innovation had been proposed by the late Edward N. Cole, former president of General Motors. Cole planned to create an air freight company, International Husky, that would use an aircraft he designed. The plane is said to be a flying box, which contains 29,000 cubic feet, compared to the 747F with 23,690 cubic feet. Boeing would produce the aircraft with the initial production run calling for 300 planes at a total cost of $7.5 billion.

Cole believed the Husky airplane, since it was specifically designed for air freight, would be able to substantially reduce the costs of air freight service. He had projected that his freighter would be able to transport bulk commodities and industrial products for about 6 cents per ton-mile. This is less than one-third the average revenue currently being received for such cargo and it is less expensive than truck tariffs. It should be noted that some air freight industry executives do not share Cole's enthusiasm for his rate predictions. Wayne M. Hoffman, chairman of Flying Tiger Airlines, has mused, "Hell will freeze over before we'll see airfreight costs below trucks."[43]

FREIGHT FORWARDERS

Freight forwarders are not "modes," but—from the shipper's viewpoint—they are analogous to other carriers. There are two types of domestic freight forwarders—surface and air—and they both perform the same basic function. Freight forwarders can best be thought of as consolidators of freight. Both surface and air transportation modes give volume discounts to shippers tendering large quantities of freight at one time to the carrier. For example, the motor carrier rate from City A to City B might be $5.00 per 100 pounds for shipments less than 20,000 pounds. This is called an LTL (less than truck load) rate. The TL (truck load) rate might be $2.00 per 100 pounds when 20,000 or more pounds are tendered. The freight forwarder exists by offering his

[42] See: Francis Morse, "Cargo Airships: A Renaissance?" *Handling and Shipping* (June, 1972), pp. 47–50. See also: John F. Pearson, "Don't Sell the Airship Short," *Popular Mechanics* (September, 1974), pp. 112–117ff. and Richard R. Leger, "Interest in Lighter-Than-Air Transport Revives Because of Economic Needs, New Technology," *The Wall Street Journal* (October 2, 1974), p. 32.

[43] "Making Money with Air Freight," *Business Week* (November 2, 1974), p. 106.

service to shippers who must use LTL rates because they do not generate enough volume to use TL rates. Without the freight forwarder, the small shipper has to use the $5.00 LTL rate. The freight forwarder, however, offers the same transportation service for a rate in between the LTL and TL rate, say $4.00. This is possible because the freight forwarder will consolidate all the small-shipments it has and give them to the carrier (a trucker in this case) and hence qualify for the $2.00 TL rate. The forwarder therefore makes his living by charging less than the LTL rate but more than the TL rate. The freight forwarder typically offers pick-up and delivery service but he does not perform the line-haul service. This is done by the motor carrier or railroad involved. Forwarders also function as "traffic departments" for small firms, performing other traffic management functions.

Surface Freight Forwarders, as an industry, in 1975 had 134 class A carriers (forwarders with annual revenues of $100,000 or more), each of which *averaged* 104 employees and gross revenues of $8.0 million. Because they do not perform any line haul transportation, their level of invested capital is not great. The surface freight forwarders do *not* constitute a healthy industry.

There are two reasons for the anemic condition of the surface freight forwarding industry. The first deals with "terminal area" size. The ICC has stated that the forwarders can only make pick-ups and deliveries with their own vehicles within each city's terminal area. These areas were often determined decades ago, before urban "sprawl." Therefore, many suburbs and outlying areas of cities are not included. This means the forwarder must use an independent motor carrier, and the latter are often unwilling to participate with the freight forwarder, because they would rather carry the freight for the entire haul. The solution, according to the forwarders, is to expand the size of the terminal areas to more realistic and modern dimensions.[44]

Another problem of the forwarders is their relation with the rail roads. At present, motor carriers can legally negotiate special rates with the forwarders to handle their over-the-road trailers. However, forwarders are prohibited from receiving special rates from the railroads. The forwarder must pay the same railroad rates as does any other shipper. The rationale for the forwarders to have lower rail rates than other shippers is that it costs the railroads less to deal with them because the forwarders' terminals are typically very near if not within the railroad classification yards. This means that the costs of switching and placing cars at individual shipper locations is not present. The freight forwarding industry and the ICC are actively supporting a bill before Congress to allow the forwarders to achieve exclusive negotiated rates with the railroads.

[44] See: Jim Dixon, "Which Way For Forwarders," *Distribution Worldwide* (June, 1975), pp. 39–42. Note: The ICC did significantly increase terminal areas in early 1977.

Air freight forwarders perform the same consolidation service that surface forwarders do, but their line-haul business is given to air carriers. Presently there are fewer than 100 air freight forwarders and, unlike surface forwarders, this segment of the transportation picture is experiencing an excellent growth record. In 1973, the air forwarders were responsible for 40 percent of the cargo revenues received by the air carriers, and this share is growing every year. Approximately 35–40 percent of all air freight shipments were handled by air forwarders, up from 25 percent ten years before.

The air forwarding industry works with the air carriers and there appears to be no animosity between the two. The air carriers realize that the forwarders consolidate shipments and tender them, typically in containers, which are ready for aircraft loading. This results in significant ground-handling time savings for the airlines.

The only potential problem area for the air forwarders is the decrease in nighttime freight flights discussed earlier. One air forwarder executive, discussing this situation, noted: "The bulk of our business is emergency freight, and we're not looking to change that. We're not looking to convert that to second or third-day deliveries. There is a definite need for overnight service, priority air freight."[45]

Shipper cooperatives perform basically the same function as surface and air freight forwarders, except they do not operate as a profit-making organization. All profits achieved through their consolidation program are returned to members. This type of consolidation program has been well received by shippers. It is estimated that there are now between 300–500 shipper cooperatives. According to railroad figures, in 1970 cooperatives loaded 239,763 rail cars of freight, compared to 271,403 by the freight forwarding industry.

An example of a large surface cooperative is Charter Oak, which serves the Connecticut area. Approximately 400 shippers belong to it and the cooperative in 1969 processed 83,000 shipments, with 50,000 of them less than 500 pounds. Charter Oak was able to save its members an average of 28 percent compared to the LTL and LCL rates their members would have had to pay without the cooperative.[46]

AUXILIARY CARRIERS

The primary transportation alternatives have now been discussed. However, a number of auxiliary services are available, which generally specialize in small shipment transportation. These will now be mentioned.

[45] "Forwarders Evaluate Day Rates," *Distribution Worldwide* (January, 1973), p. 52.
[46] "How Effective Are Shipper Co-ops?," *Distribution Worldwide* (August, 1970), pp. 30–34.

Parcel Post is a service of the United States Postal Service. There are definite size and weight limitations (approximately 70 pounds). Charges are based on weight and distance and are relatively low. In most cases, the parcel must be carried to the post office, but it will be delivered to the receiver.

Bus Package Service is offered by intercity bus companies. The maximum weight per package is 100–150 pounds. The packages travel in special compartments on the intercity buses. The service is fast, reliable, and packages delivered 30 minutes before a bus's departure will be aboard that bus. There is no pick-up or delivery service.

Other Parcel Services include United Parcel Service (UPS), which has specialized in parcels of under 50 pounds. This company has experienced growth because it has earned a reputation for very reliable service at rates that are equal to or less than parcel post. However, it does not serve all areas. In addition, UPS rates include both pick-up and delivery.

Federal Express offers a similar service to UPS, except that it operates its own fleet of small cargo jets. Maximum weight per package is 50 pounds and overnight service is provided. Rates include pick-up and delivery.

INTERMODAL TRANSPORTATION

We have now discussed all the individual transport modes available to the PD practitioner. However, a number of services are available that use a combination of two modes of transport. The most common is piggyback.

Piggyback Service is also called Trailer on Flat Car (TOFC). It is by far the most important intermodal transportation service. It involves the transportation of highway trailers on railroad flatbed cars. Two standard 40-foot highway trailers can be accommodated on each rail car. Containers are also transported and this service is called Container on Flat Car (COFC). The advantage of this intermodal service is that it is less expensive than the all motor carrier movement. In addition, especially in the mountainous western region of the United States, TOFC is faster than truck service.

Piggyback service has enjoyed a very healthy growth, both in absolute terms and as a percentage of rail carloadings. In 1964 there were 890,000 TOFC/COFC carloadings and this was 3.0 percent of all rail carloadings. In 1975, the comparable figures were 1,220,637 and 5.2 percent.

Why has this service been so successful, especially during middle 1970's? One rail executive observed:

> We believe that there will be a substantial return of private trucking to rail piggyback. The rising cost of highway trucking plus the pessimistic outlook

for energy in the long term will necessitate that more companies using private carriage take a new look at their options. More and more traffic will swing to piggyback.[47]

There are at least six basic plans of piggyback service available. Each alternative is known by its respective number.

Plan I: The railroads provide the line-haul service for the regulated motor carriers. The shipment moves under one contract (the bill-of-lading) and it is issued by the trucker. Currently, 11 percent of piggyback carloadings use this plan.

Plan II: The railroads provide a door-to-door service for their customers. In addition, the trailers or containers are supplied by the railroad. Twenty-two percent use this plan.

Plan II½: Here the railroad supplies the containers or trailers, but the shipper delivers the equipment to the railroad and also delivers it at destination. This is by far the most popular plan, being 50 percent of all piggyback carloadings in 1973. It is widely used by freight forwarders.

Plan III: This is a terminal-to-terminal rate which is a flat charge regardless of what is in the trailer or container, which is not furnished by the railroad. There is no pick-up or delivery included. Five percent of TOFC/COFC carloadings participate in this plan.

Plan IV: In this plan, the shipper provides the containers/trailers and also the rail car. The railroads provide only the power and the use of their roadbeds. In 1973, this represented 9 percent of piggyback loadings.

Plan V: This is a joint rail-truck movement. Each mode may solicit this business. It represented 3 percent in 1973.

A recent survey by *Railway Age* asked railroad executives which TOFC/COFC plans had the best growth potential. Plan II½ was the winner by a large margin. Plans III, IV, and V received good support and Plans I and II were in last place.[48]

CRITERIA FOR SELECTING
TRANSPORTATION MODES

We have surveyed the essential operating characteristics of each transportation alternative available to the PD manager. However, the fol-

---

[47] Gus Welty, "For TOFC/COFC, a Brighter-Than-Ever Future—If . . . ," *Railway Age* (June 24, 1974), p. 23. See also a special intermodal issue of *Distribution Worldwide* (March, 1976).

[48] *Ibid.*, p. 23.

lowing three basic characteristics of any transportation service will now be examined: *speed, dependability,* and *capability.*[49]

SPEED

Without question the fastest transport mode from airport to airport is the *jet aircraft,* which often cruise at 550 miles per hour. However, ground-handling delays often significantly reduce this impressive speed.

Motor carriers generally offer the next most rapid service. *Railroads,* especially in the western region of the United States, are able to approach motor carrier service standards, especially on runs of 1,500 to 2,000 miles in length.

Inland water carriers and the *pipelines* are clearly in last place regarding speed. Both average 3–6 miles per hour.

DEPENDABILITY

This refers to a transportation modes' ability to deliver a product *when* it has promised it. Dependability of service, as previously noted, is generally of much greater concern to shippers and consignees (receivers) than is speed.

Pipelines know no equal in this respect. This is because weather has no affect on them and because they require so little labor, that if a strike takes place, supervisory management can continue to operate the system. *Motor Carriers* are the next most dependable. The basic reason for this is the small operating unit involved. Once a truck is loaded for shipment, only the drivers involved can cause the shipment to be late, barring equipment breakdowns and bad weather.

Air carriers have significantly improved their service level regarding dependability. Weather is still a problem, but the jet aircraft has become a very dependable piece of equipment. When ground-handling problems are cleared up, they should achieve a level of dependability equal to the truckers'.

The *railroads* have historically done a lackluster job in respect to dependability. A reason for this was their desire to delay the running of a freight train until a predetermined large number of cars were accumulated. As the train waited for the requisite number of cars to accumulate, service delays for some shipments necessarily increased. The railroads, recognizing their problem, have consistently reduced the average number of cars per freight train since 1968. Another source of delay has been the "bottlenecks" involved at classification yards. Rail-

[49] This section is based on a discussion in Heskett, Glaskowski and Ivie, *op. cit.,* pp. 113–118.

roads are currently spending millions of dollars to correct this deficiency.

The *inland water carriers* are the least dependable mode. This is caused by the vicissitudes of weather and the unpredictable delays encountered at the locks on the waterway system.

Table 4-5 presents the results of a 1974 Department of Transportation survey which dealt with the quality of service offered by the various modes.

CAPABILITY

Capability refers to the size, weight, and variety of products that the mode can physically accommodate. *Barge carriers* clearly are in first place in this respect. The Valley Line Company possesses covered barges that are 200 feet long, 35 feet wide, 12 feet deep and which can transport 80,000 cubic feet of cargo. Barges, for example, have been responsible for transporting the Saturn and other space program rockets to Cape Kennedy.

Railroads are next in capability. Some rail cars can support 150,000–200,000 pounds or more of freight, but they are limited in height by their bridges and tunnels. *Truckers* are basically limited by the state and federal weight restrictions on their highway system. *Air carriers* have recently increased their overall capacity, with such planes as the 747F. It has 23,690 cubic feet of capacity and can lift payloads in excess of 220,000 pounds. *Pipelines* are the least capable of transporting a variety of products. Besides liquids, as we have seen, a number of additional products are currently being transported in slurry pipelines.

SUMMARY

This chapter has surveyed the transportation system available to PD managers. A basic understanding of transportation is vital to PD management. Transportation directly affects the other components of PD and it is the largest single cost category of most PD operations.

The *railroads* transported 37 percent of all ton-miles in 1975. Railroad companies tend to be relatively large compared to the other transport modes, averaging 7,500 employees per Class I railroad. This mode specialized in transporting car-load quantities (greater than 30,000 pounds) of raw materials and bulk products. Their average revenue per ton-mile is 2.04 cents. The three most serious railroad operating problems are: lack of roadbed maintenance, inadequate car supply, and labor relations. Service improvements have resulted from automated classification yards, Automatic Car Identification, and unit trains.

TABLE 4-5 Performance Ratings for Each Mode

Performance factor	Mode	Number and percentage[1] of shippers ascribing each level of performance for each mode									
		Excel-lent		Quite good		Ade-quate		Mini-mally accept-table		Unsatis-factory		Total usable responses
		N	%	N	%	N	%	N	%	N	%	
On-time pickup	Motor	51	27	79	42	47	25	9	5	3	2	189
	Rail	23	23	31	31	19	19	20	20	7	7	100
On-time delivery	Motor	26	15	65	37	70	39	12	7	4	2	177
	Rail	7	7	26	25	33	32	22	22	14	14	102
	Air	32	29	47	42	22	20	8	7	2	2	111
	Water	13	32	12	30	11	27	3	7	1	2	40
Arrivals without loss, short, or damage	Motor	58	31	82	44	33	18	9	5	3	2	185
	Rail	21	20	42	39	25	23	12	11	6	6	106
	Air	55	49	42	37	11	10	2	2	1	1	111
	Water	21	51	12	29	6	15	2	5	0	0	41
Specified equipment availability	Motor	52	31	58	35	41	25	9	5	4	2	164
	Rail	17	16	24	23	25	24	19	18	18	17	103

[1] Percentages calculated on basis of total number of shippers using each mode and rating it for the specific performance factor.

SOURCE: *1974 National Transportation Report, Summary* (Washington, D.C.: U. S. Department of Transportation, December, 1974).

There are approximately 15,000 regulated interstate *motor carriers*. All truckers (regulated and private) produced 21 percent of all intercity ton-miles. The regulated truckers' average revenue per ton-mile is 8.0 cents. The motor carrier industry has specialized in relatively small shipments (less than 10,000 pounds) that are typically high in value manufactured products. The three most serious problem areas are the small-shipments problem, restrictions on equipment size, and the increase in private trucking. In order to improve customer service, the truckers have introduced specialized equipment and computer assisted programs to monitor shipment status in their systems.

The *oil pipelines* are responsible for one-fourth of all intercity ton-miles. There are three basic types of oil pipelines: crude gathering lines, crude trunklines, and product lines. The average revenue per ton-mile was less than 0.3 cents. Pipelines also carry solid products in slurry lines. Problem areas include the public's concern for the environment and the availability of rights-of-way.

The *inland water carriers* produce about 16 percent of intercity ton-miles. They specialize in bulk movements of raw materials. Average revenue per ton-mile was similar to the oil pipelines at 0.3 cents. Proposed user taxes, environmental constraints, and lock delays are problem areas for the inland water carriers.

Air freight continues to grow at a healthy rate. The great majority of air freight is performed by combination passenger-cargo airlines. In 1977, air freight accounted for only 0.2 percent of intercity ton-miles. One reason for this is the expense involved. The average revenue per ton-mile is 21.5 cents. Air freight is currently experiencing some financial difficulties.

The *freight forwarder*, who specializes in the consolidation of small-shipments, is an important transportation intermediary. The shippers' non-profit association and a number of auxiliary carriers also play important roles in the transportation industry.

The final section examined each mode of transportation according to these three modal selection criteria: speed, dependability, and capability.

QUESTIONS FOR DISCUSSION AND REVIEW

1. The initial statement in this chapter by Frank Cushman talked about the tremendous importance of the United States transportation system. Do you believe this statement is valid or does it involve some "puffery"? Defend your answer.

2. It has been said that the transportation segment of the PD system is the most important. Is this true? Why?

3. Discuss briefly the *structure* of the railroad industry. Be sure to include in your answer: the approximate number and size of the carriers, the products that they specialize in, and their current financial condition.

4. It has been indicated that railroad service at times leaves something to be desired. Discuss three basic operating problem areas that have aggravated railroad service levels.

5. Labor relations has historically been a difficult area for rail management. What are the problem areas involved?

6. The United States railroads have achieved very definite service improvements during the last few years. Discuss briefly a number of these service innovations.

7. Discuss briefly the *structure* of the motor carrier industry. Be sure to discuss: the approximate number and size of the carriers, the products that they specialize in, and their current financial condition.

8. Although the trucking industry appears to be basically healthy, it does have a number of problem areas. Discuss them.

9. Examine briefly a number of areas in which the trucking industry

has been able to achieve significant improvements in customer service levels.

10. Discuss the *structure* of the pipeline industry. Your answer should include these points: the approximate number and size of the carriers, the products that they specialize in, their current financial condition, and the basic types of oil pipelines.

11. What is a slurry pipeline? How do they operate and what products are currently being transported in slurry lines? Do you believe slurry pipelines have significant growth potential?

12. Discuss or define briefly each of the following:

(a) The Black Mesa project   (f) Load-factor
(b) A LASH ship   (g) An airship
(c) A user-tax or user-fee   (h) A freight-forwarder
(d) Wide-body jets   (i) A shippers' non-profit association
(e) Belly cargo   (j) TOFC/COFC

13. Discuss briefly the *structure* of the inland waterway system. Be sure to mention: the products that they specialize in and their current financial condition.

14. Discuss briefly the three major problem areas of the inland water carriers.

15. Discuss the *structure* of the air freight industry. Cover these aspects: the types of firms offering air cargo service, the products that they specialize in, their current financial condition, and the future of this industry.

16. What is the basic problem of belly cargo versus the jet freighter?

17. From an air freight point-of-view, discuss the current problem areas.

18. Surface freight forwarders have two major problem areas. Discuss each briefly.

19. In general terms, discuss the various piggyback alternatives. Which plan is by far the most successful?

20. Regarding transportation modal selection criterion, which modes do the *best* and the *worst* for speed, dependability, and capability. Why?

CASE 4-1   SHEBOYGAN PICKLE CO.

Sheboygan Pickle Company was located in Sheboygan, Wisconsin, a small Great Lakes port. The firm was nearly one hundred years old and its location could be considered as "resource oriented" since it was on the eastern edge of one of the largest cucumber-growing areas in the nation. It produced sweet pickles, relish, dill pickles and Kosher dill pickles. It sold nationwide under both its own brand name and under more than fifty different "private" labels of large food chains and buying coops. Nationally, its sales were increasing about three percent a year; sales under private labels were increasing much faster than sales with its own label.

Its best sales area continued to be upstate New York, in the area from Albany to Buffalo. Sheboygan Pickles had never penetrated into the New York City market although some of the large buyers in Albany did ship some pickles to the New York City area, but these usually bore "private" labels, rather than the Sheboygan Pickle label.

The reason Sheboygan pickles sold well in upstate New York is somewhat historic. Many settlers in Wisconsin had originally settled in upstate New York before moving west again. Hence there were many original family and trade ties which still existed. Sheboygan pickles destined for upstate New York had been a major cargo on many Great Lakes "package" freighters through the 1920's, when the freighters dropped out of business. Since then, Sheboygan Pickle Company relied on railroads to reach its upstate New York customers. Indeed, nearly all of its outbound shipments moved by rail. Rates varied, of course, although the average rail rate on a 60,000 lb. carload shipment to points in upstate New York was $450.

The firm purchased labels, bottles, and some spices from nearby Milwaukee. Cucumbers were purchased locally from about 50 growers who would truck them directly to the plant. Each year the pickle factory bought 5000 tons of sugar. Currently the best arrangement was to buy it in New Orleans for $400 per ton and ship to Sheboygan by rail carload. The rail rate was $283 for each 50,000 lb. carload. The sugar was needed during only four months of the year, July, August, September and October, when most of the production occurred.

Sales were spread fairly evenly throughout the year, although they were a bit higher during the summer months and around the Thanksgiving and Christmas holidays. By August 15 of each year, Sheboygan Pickle Company produce buyers would have a good idea of the entire harvest of cucumbers for the season and the remaining production for the season would be scheduled. In most "good" crop years, Sheboygan Pickle Company would start offering "deals" to buyers about September 1, offering them lower prices for larger-than-average orders. The buyer, then, would assume responsibility for warehousing the pickles, rather than Sheboygan Pickle Company.

George Abernathy had been traffic manager of Sheboygan Pickle Co. since 1962. Since the late 1960's he had been troubled by the continual decline in the quality of rail service in the northeast. Buyers tended to blame him, rather than the carriers, when cars were delayed or lost. Additional "lead-times" had been assigned to cars destined to upstate New York markets although, on rare occasions, the car would arrive too early and the consignee would have to unload it before he wanted it just to avoid demurrage charges. Truck transportation from Sheboygan was too expensive. The average common carrier cost would be about $400 for a 40,000 lb. shipment; contract carrier rates would be about 10 percent less.

Several of the large customers in upstate New York, including one firm which had been buying Sheboygan pickles since 1913, indicated they would drop the line from their shelves unless better delivery service could be provided. Top management of Sheboygan Pickle Co. became concerned because the upstate New York market was one where "brand loyalty" to the Sheboygan label still existed. If that market were lost, Sheboygan Pickle would be one large step closer to becoming merely a supplier to chain stores, and all of its products would be sold under chain labels.

Abernathy cancelled his regular Saturday golf game and went into the office to see if he could figure out whether Sheboygan Pickle Co. should locate a distribution center in upstate New York, supply it by rail, and make deliveries by truck. He had just completed tallying 1974 shipments from Sheboygan to upstate New York. They totalled 20,000 tons. The phone rang. He answered it. It was Bob Benson, one of his regular golfing partners. Benson worked for a neighboring shipyard where he was a sales engineer.

"You missed a good game today, George," said Benson. "If we'd played for our usual stakes, you would be three dollars richer this very moment!"

"Playing with you three for money is like plucking chickens," retorted Abernathy, "but you know why I had to work."

"That's why I called," said Benson. "Up in Escanaba, we may have the answer to your problems."

"What do you mean?" asked Abernathy.

"Up there is a converted World War II landing craft which has new adjustable loading ramps on both sides. We were converting it for the Department of Defense for use in southeast Asia when we got a 'stop-work' order. We got paid for our work and then bought it on speculation. We just about had it sold to a paper company for picking up shipments of logs from small Lake Superior islands, when their financing fell through. I thought of you right after you called to cancel out of the golf game because the vessel is small enough to pass through the New York State Barge Canal."

"The what?" asked Abernathy.

Benson answered: "The New York State Barge Canal is the successor to the old Erie Canal. It stretches from Buffalo to Albany and is presently used mostly by pleasure boaters. Its locks are too small to handle conventional barges. I recall you said once that your upstate New York markets were influenced by the location of the old Erie Canal. We

EXHIBIT 1. Great Lakes–St. Lawrence System and New York State Barge Canal.

worked out cost figures for the paper company and I'd be glad to show them to you. How about Monday?"

Benson appeared in Abernathy's office at 9 AM Monday with a map of the Great Lakes and the barge canal (exhibit 1): a batch of marine engineering drawings; photos of the vessel and its new loading ramps; and a packet of cost figures. Benson and Abernathy calculated that the vessel could carry 2,000 tons of pickles which would lower the vessel to its maximum allowable draft of 12 feet. The vessel could travel at 10 knots in open sea. Benson explained that the side loading ramps meant that conventional fork-lift trucks could be used to load and unload pallet-loads of pickle cases. Once the cargo was stowed it would be protected from the weather and from heavy seas.

"Do we have 12 feet of water alongside our plant?" Abernathy wondered. He called the pickle company's plant engineer and asked him. An answer was promised later that day.

Benson said operating costs would be about $700 per day for a 240-day season. (The northern extremities of the Great Lakes are closed to navigation during the period from December to March although studies are underway to determine whether the navigation season could be extended.) These operating costs were exclusive of depreciation. "How much for depreciation?" ask Abernathy.

"That depends what you pay for it and how long you plan on keeping it," said Benson. "For the paper company, we had said the vessel would sell for $150,000 and they could count on its use for 10 years. I'd have to check, but I'm sure you could use the $150,000 figure in your calculations. I've got to go now to a luncheon appointment. I'll leave all this material with you. We should get together before the week's out." He left and Abernathy was alone. The phone rang.

It was the plant engineer who reported that the U. S. Army Corps of Engineers maintained the navigation channel adjacent to the plant at a depth of 18 feet. The area right next to the plant had silted to nine feet and it would be Sheboygan Pickle Company's responsibility to dredge alongside its bulkheading. A contractor had estimated that it would cost $8,000 to perform the dredging and dump the spoil in an approved spill site. The contractor said one dredging would last for several years; he did not think much silt would accumulate at the site, especially if it were being used. He also thought that the bulkheading was in satisfactory condition to accommodate the dredging and any shoreside storage and cargo-handling activity.

During the following week Abernathy and his assistants were busy. They assembled the following facts.

1. Sugar could be purchased in New York for $404 per ton and in Albany for $406 per ton. Costs of loading the sugar aboard the vessel in either port would be $1 per ton.

2. A route could be set up from Sheboygan to Buffalo and then through the Canal to Albany. Pickles could be unloaded at Buffalo, three intermediate points (Rochester, Syracuse, and Utica), and Albany. The trip eastbound, including the loading of a backhaul of sugar at Albany, would take 14 days. The trip from Albany to Sheboygan would take five days. At Sheboygan the sugar would be unloaded in one day and the pickles loaded in one day. Costs of unloading and loading at Sheboygan would be the same as presently experienced for loading and unloading rail cars. Loading and unloading during rainstorms would be an occasional problem. Tarpaulins would have to be thrown over each pallet. Aboard ship, there would be no problem with moisture. In the 14-day trip estimate just given is a one-day delay factor to cover the possibility of inclement weather.

3. During the eight-month season, 11 or 12 round trips could be made. (Two days could be saved when sugar was not a return haul.)

4. Costs for operating longer than the eight-month season climbed swiftly. Wage rates were higher, insurance was higher, and Coast Guard regulations did not allow the vessel to load as heavily. It would increase the time required to move through the Canal.

5. The costs of carrying pickles inland from the five points along the Canal was very low, averaging only $2 per ton. They were low for two reasons. In some instances they represented a desirable "back-haul" for motor carriers. In two instances, large buyers had

their warehouses adjacent to the Canal and could unload the vessel as easily as they could rail cars.

Question One: Based on the information given so far, do you think Abernathy should recommend purchase of the vessel? Give your reasons.

Question Two: If you were Abernathy, what additional information—not given above—would you like to have?

CASE 4-2   BIRMINGHAM STEEL

Susan Boyer graduated from Auburn University in 1947. Her first position with the Birmingham Steel Corporation was in public relations. When a management position in the traffic department opened in 1951, Susan applied and was accepted. Although the only female among more than 40 employees in the traffic department, Susan liked her work and because of her enthusiasm and drive, she was rapidly promoted. In 1959, the company had privately selected her as a candidate for a possible "senior" management position.

In 1960 the company promoted Susan to traffic manager of the $680 million-a-year company. Her operating budget was $32 million. By 1963 she was named transportation manager because the firm had started an extensive private trucking operation.

Because of her interest in transportation law, she had taken and passed the I.C.C. Practitioner's test in 1958. She realized the importance of regulation in traffic, and therefore in 1961 started attending night law school. In 1968, she received her law degree and was admitted to the Alabama Bar. Her employer encouraged her continued education and in fact paid all of Susan's educational expenses. In 1970 she was named vice president-transportation. She was the highest ranking female in the firm. By 1975 the firm had $1.34 billion in sales and her budget was in excess of $80 million.

Attorney Boyer prided herself in her knowledge of complicated transportation issues. She frequently testified at state and federal hearings regarding carrier rates, services and common carrier certificate applications. Also, she frequently journeyed to Washington, D.C. to testify before the ICC, Department of Transportation and Congressional hearings regarding various aspects of National Transportation Policy. Her opinion was well respected by transportation experts both in the government and in private industry.

The issue of inland water carrier user fees was before Congress again in the Spring of 1976. Boyer had been asked by Senator Ackerman to testify at the U.S. Senate sub-committee hearing in Washington, D.C. on Friday morning, April 23. She had accepted the invitation, feeling a duty to represent the interests of the firm at the hearing. While flying to Washington, she contemplated her remarks, and she re-read two letters she had received earlier in the week. They follow.

NATIONAL COMMITTEE FOR FREE WATERWAYS
Office of the Executive Secretary
WASHINGTON, D.C.

April 16, 1976

Mrs. Susan Boyer, Attorney
V. P.—Transportation
Birmingham Steel Corp.
Birmingham, Alabama

Dear Mrs. Boyer,

The National Committee for Free Waterways is dedicated to keeping America's waterways free from user fees. Our records indicate that in 1975 your firm paid over $11 million to common and contract inland water carriers. Because of your significant involvement in water transportation, we thought you would be interested in the following five points regarding the user fee issue.

First, in 1787 the Northwest Ordinance specifically stated that the "waterways shall ever remain free." It appears unreasonable at this point in time to override a Congressional policy that has served our country well for almost two hundred years.

Secondly, we believe that all citizens benefit from a free inland waterway system. If user fees are enacted, the transportation costs of products on the waterways will necessarily be increased. Since the waterways tend to carry bulk, raw material type products—the inputs into countless thousands of products—the user fees would tend to accelerate the present inflationary situation. More specifically, the present low water rates have forced the railroads to lower their rates to be competitive. Without these "water-compelled" rates, industries such as yours would be forced to pay considerably higher freight rates.

The third point involves damage to the environment by the inland waterway system. We know of no serious problems caused by the building, dredging and maintenance of the inland waterway system. In fact, the waterways are an ideal resting area for the nation's mid-continent migratory waterfowl flyway.

The fourth issue is that a gross injustice would be perpetuated on industries—such as yours—that have located near or on the waterway system because of the low water rates and the water-compelled rail rates. It would be totally unfair to these firms to negate the primary reason for their industrial site location.

Finally, all carriers receive some form of federal subsidies. Why choose to single-out the inland water carriers for punitive measure. James R. Smith, President of the American Waterways Operators, Inc. has noted:

> "The myth that the waterways are subsidized and that the railroads pay their own way is equally fallacious. No mention was made of widespread

federal subsidies that railroads receive, such as AMTRAK, to preserve passenger traffic, assumption by the United States of Railroad Retirement Act obligations, elimination of rail grade-crossing expenses, rapid write-off of rolling stock construction costs, the Rail Relocation Act which seeks an additional $2.5 billion in federal money plus uncounted state and local tax benefits granted to lure the railroads along certain routes."[1]

I trust that the above information will be of assistance to you as you contemplate this very important National issue.

Best regards,

Charles L. Good
Executive Director

THE COMMITTEE FOR TRANSPORTATION EQUALITY
WASHINGTON, D.C.

April 18, 1976

Ms. Susan Boyer, J.D.
Vice President—Transportation
Birmingham Steel Corporation
Birmingham, Alabama

Dear Ms. Boyer:

The Committee for Transportation Equality is dedicated to the position that all surface carriers should be treated equally by all governmental units. As you know, Congress will again in the near future hear testimony on inland waterway user fees. Our position is unequivocally in favor of these user fees. Our position is founded on three basic points. First, it is not fair to the railroads and motor carriers to have to compete against a competitor which has its right-of-way supplied *free* by the federal government. The railroads own and maintain their right-of-way. The truckers pay gasoline and oil taxes and special federal user taxes on the gross weight of their vehicles and on tread rubber. These motor carrier user fees pay the truckers "fair-share" of building and maintaining our nation's highway system.

Secondly, without user fees, the primary benefactors of the waterway system are the water carriers themselves and the cities located on the waterways. The benefits are localized and certainly not shared nationally. It is common knowledge that waterway projects are and have always been considered the classic example of Congressional "Pork Barrel" legislation. It is interesting to note that the inland water carriers claim they can't "afford" to pay the proposed user fees. Nevertheless, their industry rate-of-return on invested capital is approximately three times the railroad average.

Finally, the subsidized inland water carriers are sopping the strength of the railroad system. If the railroads continue to earn an inadequate rate-

[1] Actual letter to Mr. Paul Lowenwarter, CBS Producer of "60 Minutes", dated August 28, 1975.

of-return, they will eventually have to be nationalized. I believe you agree that this situation is indeed feasible and would be highly detrimental to the overall transportation industry as well as to our "private enterprise" system.

If I can be of any further assistance, please call me collect.

Sincerely,

Abraham Warner
President

Question One: Draft a statement to be presented by Ms. Boyer to the congressional sub-committee.

Question Two: Ms. Boyer is an important individual whose opinions are widely respected. What if she feels that waterway user fees are good for the country although not good for Birmingham Steel?

CHAPTER REFERENCES

Air Cargo From A to Z; Air Transportation Association (1971).
"Air Cargo: Still Cinderella?" *Transportation and Distribution Management* (April, 1973).
ALTMAN, E. I.; "Predicting Railroad Bankruptcies In America," *The Bell Journal of Economics and Management Science* (Spring, 1973), pp. 184–211.
"An Interview with O. Lee Slay," *Pacific Traffic* (September, 1972).
"A Pipeline From Black Mesa," *Transportation and Distribution Management* (October, 1969).
"A State-of-the-Art Report on Technology and Highway Transportation," *Handling and Shipping* (January, 1971).
"Barge Lines: No Trimmings," *Transportation and Distribution Management* (March, 1972).
BARSNESS, RICHARD W.; "Highways and Motor Vehicles: A New Era In Public Policy," *MSU Business Topics* (Spring, 1973), pp. 15–26.
BARTA, THOMAS J.; "Bottlenecks Hindering Productivity in the Water Transportation Industry," *Transportation Reserch Forum 13th Annual Proceedings* (Oxford, Inc.: The Richard B. Cross Co., 1972).
BLAINE, J. C. D.; "The Dynamics of Transportation," *Transportation Journal* (Summer, 1967), pp. 19–27.
BOSKE, LEIGH B.; "Cost Efficiency in the Domestic Trunk Airline Industry," *Journal of Economics and Business* (Winter, 1976).
BOYLE, LAWRENCE and Stanley Hille; "Railroad Mergers—An Alternative?" *ICC Practitioners' Journal* (March-April, 1967), pp. 405–411.
BREITENBACH, ROBERT B.; "An Analysis of Freight Networks," *Transportation Journal* (Summer, 1973), pp. 54–60.
BROWN, TERENCE A.; "Forwarder—Motor Contract Rates," *Transportation Journal* (Summer, 1974), pp. 19–24.
————; "Freight Forwarder—Motor Carrier Relations," *Transportation Journal* (Winter, 1972), pp. 28–32.

CERWONKA, RONALD; "Planning for Future Air Transportation Facility Needs: A Case Study," *Transportation Journal* (Summer, 1975), pp. 40–47.

"Coal-Slurry Pipelines," *Railway Age* (November 24, 1975).

CONANT, MICHAEL; "Structural Reorganization of the Northeast Railroads," *ICC Practitioners' Journal* (January-February, 1976), pp. 207–223.

"Conrail Begins Operations as 2000 Miles of Branch Lines Lose Freight Service," *The Wall Street Journal* (April 1, 1976).

COVER, VIRGIL D.; "The Rise of Third Level Air Carriers," *Transportation Journal* (Fall, 1971), pp. 41–51.

DAVIS, FRANK W., JR., Edwin P. Patton and Robert E. Tuttle, Jr.; "Local Participation: The Key to Preserving Adequate Railroad Services," *MSU Business Topics* (Winter, 1976).

DEWITT, WILLIAM J., III; "The Railroad Conglomerate: Its Relationship to the Interstate Commerce Commission and National Transportation Policy," *Transportation Journal* (Winter, 1972), pp. 5–14.

DIXON, JIM; "Traffic's Booming on America's Water Highways," *Distribution Worldwide* (December, 1975).

———; "The Urgent Need for Double Bottoms," *Distribution Worldwide* (March, 1974).

———; "Which Way for Forwarders," *Distribution Worldwide* (June, 1975).

DOWER, JANET BOSWORTH; "The Shipper Speaks Out," *Distribution Worldwide* (September, 1973).

EADS, GEORGE; "Airline Capacity Limitation Controls: Public Vice or Public Virtue?" *The American Economic Review* (May, 1974), pp. 365–371.

87th Interstate Commerce Commission Annual Report (1973).

ELLSWORTH, KENNETH; "TRAIN II's Goal: A 10% Increase in Car Utilization," *Railway Age* (September 8, 1975).

FAVILLE, DAVID E.; "This Business of Aviation," *Transportation Journal* (Spring, 1967), pp. 34–36.

Feedback; Chicago: The Fernstrom Moving System (March-April, 1974).

FELTON, JOHN RICHARD; "The Utilization and Adequacy of the Freight Car Fleet," *Land Economics* (Aug., 1971), pp. 267–273.

FISHER, FRANKLIN M. and Gerald Kraft; "The Effect of the Removal of the Firemen on Railroad Accidents, 1962–1967," *The Bell Journal of Economics and Management Science* (Autumn, 1971), pp. 470–494.

"Forwarders Evaluate Day Rates," *Distribution Worldwide* (January, 1973).

FOSTER, JERRY R. and Martin F. Schmidt; "Rail Terminals and the Urban Environment," *Transportation Journal* (Fall, 1975), pp. 21–28.

GALLAGHER, PAT; "A Convoy vs. the Arctic—An Alaskan Passage Report," *Handling and Shipping* (December, 1975).

GALLAGHER, JR., T. P.; "Marketing, Money and Those Empty Bellies," *Transportation and Distribution Management* (November, 1973).

GARINO, DAVID P. and Connie S. Harrison; "Railroads Join Environmental Groups to Fight Plan for New River Locks Near Alton, Ill.," *The Wall Street Journal* (December 3, 1975).

GILL, LYNN E.; "The Transportation Challenge," *Transportation Journal* (Spring, 1972), pp. 39–45.

GRIBBON, AUGUST; "Danger Rides with Big Rigs," *The National Observer* (June 7, 1971).

GRITTA, RICHARD D.; "Risk and the 'Fair Rate of Return' in Air Transportation," *Transportation Journal* (Summer, 1974), pp. 41–45.

HARBESON, ROBERT W.; "Some Policy Implications of Northeastern Railroad Problems," *Transportation Journal* (Fall, 1974), pp. 5–12.

————; "The Rail Passenger Service Act of 1970," *ICC Practitioners' Journal* (March-April, 1971), pp. 330–339.

HARPER, DONALD V.; "The Dilemma of Aircraft Noise at Major Airports," *Transportation Journal* (Spring, 1971), pp. 5–28.

HAZARD, JOHN L.; "The Second Decade of the Seaway," *Transportation Journal* (Summer, 1970), pp. 33–40.

HILLE, S. J., F. T. Paine, A. N. Nash, and G. A. Brunner; "Consumer Transportation Attitude in Baltimore and Philadelphia," *Transportation Journal* (Summer, 1968), pp. 30–47.

HOLDER, JACK J., JR.; "Achieving Goals and Objectives in the Motor Carrier Industry," *Transportation Journal* (Spring, 1971), pp. 51–59.

"How Effective Are Shipper Co-ops," *Distribution Worldwide* (August, 1970).

"ICC Orders Rails to Purchase 69,609 New Freight Cars, Restore 18,000 Others," *Traffic World* (July 1, 1974).

JOHNSON, JAMES C.; "An Analysis of the 'Small-Shipments' Problem with Particular Attention to Its Ramifications on a Firm's Logistical System," *ICC Practitioners' Journal* (July-August, 1972).

————; "The Small-Shipment Problem: Fact or Fiction," *ICC Practitioners' Journal* (March-April, 1973).

JOHNSON, JAMES C. and Donald V. Harper; "The Shipper Views Proposed Solutions to the Northeast Railroad Problem," *Transportation Journal* (Summer, 1974).

JOHNSON, TIMOTHY E.; "Toward Optimality in the Trucklines," *Transportation Journal* (Fall, 1973), pp. 38–50.

KARR, ALBERT R.; "How to Derail a Merger," *The Wall Street Journal* (April 9, 1976).

KRAMER, WALTER; "What's Not Wrong with Railroad Marketing," *Transportation Journal* (Fall, 1967), pp. 21–28.

LEGER, RICHARD R.; "Interest in Lighter-Than-Air Transport Revives Because of Economic Needs, New Technology," *The Wall Street Journal* (October 2, 1974).

LEVINE, MARVIN J.; "The Railroad Crew Size Controversy Revisited," *Labor Law Journal* (June, 1969).

"Little Hope for Truckers' Relief," *Distribution Worldwide* (June, 1974).

LONG, WESLEY H.; "State Trucking Activity Indexes: A Case Study of Maine," *Transportation Journal* (Summer, 1968), pp. 60–64.

"Making Money with Air Freight," *Business Week* (November 2, 1974).

McLAUGHLIN, G. M.; "Applications, Technology and Economics of Slurry Pipelines," *The Logistics and Transportation Review* (Volume 8, Number 3), pp. 69–81.

MELTON, LEE J., JR.; "The Competitive Transportation System: A Myth," *Transportation Journal* (Summer, 1975), pp. 48–55.

MIKLIUS, WALTER; "Estimating Freight Traffic of Competing Transportation Modes: An Application of the Linear Discriminant Function," *Land Economics* (May, 1969), pp. 267–273.

MONTFORT, J. G.; "Black Mesa System Proves Coal Slurry Technology," *Pipe Line Industry* (May, 1974).

MORSE, FRANCIS; "Cargo Airships: A Renaissance?" *Handling and Shipping* (June, 1972).

MORTON, ALEXANDER LYALL; "Northeast Railroads: Restructured or Nationalized?," *The American Economic Review* (May, 1975), pp. 284–288.

NARODICK, KIT G.; "Domestic Air Cargo: Shipper's Delight—Airline's Dilemma," *Handling and Shipping* (April, 1971), pp. 60–63.

NEUSCHEL, ROBERT P.; "How Rail Management Can Boost Revenues and Control Costs," *Railway Age* (January 12, 1976).

———; "Physical Distribution—Forgotten Frontier," *Harvard Business Review* (March-April, 1967).

1974 National Transportation Report, Summary (Washington, D.C.: U.S. Department of Transportation, December, 1974).

"1967 Census of Transportation, U.S. Department of Commerce," *Pacific Traffic* (October, 1973).

NORTON, HUGH S.; "The Wheel: Should We Reinvent It?" *The American Economic Review* (May, 1974), pp. 378–383.

NORTON, HUGH S. and Robert J. Carlsson; "Is AMTRAK the Answer?" *Transportation Journal* (Fall, 1971), pp. 52–59.

OLSON, CHARLES E. and Terence A. Brown; "The Output Unit in Transportation Revisited," *Land Economics* (August, 1972), pp. 280–281.

PATTON, EDWIN P.; "Amtrak in Perspective: Where Goes the Pointless Arrow?" *The American Economic Review* (May, 1974), pp. 372–377.

———; "Implications of Motor Carrier Growth and Size," *Transportation Journal* (Fall, 1970), pp. 34–51.

PEARSON, JOHN F.; "Don't Sell the Airship Short," *Popular Mechanics* (September, 1974).

PFISTER, RICHARD L.; "A Case for the Highway Trust Fund," *Business Horizons* (June, 1973), pp. 31–34.

PHELPS, LEWIS M.; "As Railroads Defer More Maintenance, Number of Accidents Increases Sharply," *The Wall Street Journal* (October, 1974).

PLOWMAN, E. G.; "Transportation Research Foundation Feasibility Report on the Proposed Study to Measure and Evaluate Transportation Capital Requirements and Investment Sources," *ICC Practitioners' Journal* (March-April, 1969), pp. 1496–1523.

QUAST, THEODORE; "The Output Unit in Transportation," *Transportation Journal* (Winter, 1970), pp. 5–7.

"Railroad Technology," *Handling and Shipping* (January, 1975).

RAKOWSKI, JAMES P.; "Characteristics of Private Trucking in the United States," *ICC Practitioners' Journal* (July-August, 1974), pp. 572–576.

———; "Competition Between Railroads and Trucks," *Traffic Quarterly* (April, 1976), pp. 285–301.

———; "Potential Sources of Railway Freight Traffic," *ICC Practitioners' Journal* (July-August, 1973), pp. 576–580.

REEKER, DAVID H.; "Air Freight Has Problems On The Ground," *Business Horizons* (February, 1968), pp. 33–38.

SALZANO, CARLO J.; "Barge, Towing Industry Hits NWC Report, Pledges Fight Against River User Charge," *Traffic World* (September 24, 1973).

SCHARY, PHILIP B.; "Measuring Concentration and Competition in the Regulated Motor Carrier Industry," *Transportation Journal* (Summer, 1973), pp. 49–53.

——— and Robert M. Williams; "Airline Fare Policy and Public Investment," *Transportation Journal* (Fall, 1967), pp. 41–49.

SCHULTZ, RANDALL L.; "Studies of Airline Passenger Demand: A Review," *Transportation Journal* (Summer, 1972), pp. 48–62.

SCOTT, RONALD DEAN and Martin T. Farris; "Airline Subsidies in the United States," *Transportation Journal* (Summer, 1974), pp. 25–33.

"Shippers Talk About Rail Service," *Distribution Worldwide* (April, 1973).

SLOSS, JAMES; "Regulation of Motor Freight Transportation: A Quantitative Evaluation of Policy," *The Bell Journal of Economics and Management Science* (Autumn, 1970), pp. 327–366.

SMERK, GEORGE M.; "Quo Vadis, Highway Trust Fund?" *Business Horizons* (October, 1972), pp. 52–54.

SMITH, JAMES R.; "Barges Move the Basics," *Transportation and Distribution Management* (March-April, 1976).

SMITH, WILLIAM K. and David M. Schwartz; *Initial Statement of General Mills, Inc. In the Investigation of Railroad Freight Service*, Ex Parte No. 270 (March 24, 1972).

SNOW, CHARLES R.; "The Effects of Economic Fluctuations on U. S. Freight Traffic," *Transportation Journal* (Spring, 1973), pp. 29–38.

SPYCHALSKI, JOHN C.; "The Diversion of Motor Vehicle-Related Tax Revenues To Urban Mass Transport: A Critique of Its Economic Tenability," *Transportation Journal* (Spring, 1970), pp. 44–50.

STEPHENSON, P. RONALD and Ronald P. Willett; "Consistency: The Carrier's Ace in the Hole," *Transportation Journal* (Spring, 1969), pp. 28–33.

STRASZHEIM, MAHLON R.; "Airline Profitability, Financing, and Public Regulation," *Transportation Journal* (Summer, 1969), pp. 16–33.

"The Little Railroads That Could," *Distribution Worldwide* (April, 1974).

"The Next Commercial Jet . . . If," *Business Week* (April 12, 1976).

"The Railroad Paradox: A Profitless Boom," *Business Week* (September 8, 1973).

"The Trucking Industry: Working Behind the Scenes," *Transportation and Distribution Management* (April, 1972).

THOMAS, DANA L.; "No Brakes on Growth," *Barron's* (March 29, 1976).

THOMPSON, W. H., and C. P. Baumel; "Impact of Transportation Equipment Shortages on Iowa Country Elevators," *Transportation Journal* (Fall, 1972), pp. 50–57.

Transportation Facts and Trends, 11th ed., Transportation Association of America (January, 1976).

TRIPP, ROBERT S., Norman L. Chervany, and Frederick J. Beier; "An Economic Analysis of the Multi-Modal Transportation Company: A Simulation Approach," *The Logistics and Transportation Review* (Volume 9, Number 1), pp. 69–84.

"U.S. Domestic Shipping Cargoes Should Triple by 2000 A.D.," *Commerce Today* (March 4, 1974).

VENTRE, GERARD G. and Kenneth E. Case; "Control and Abatement of Transportation Noise," *Transportation Journal* (Summer, 1971), pp. 54–59.

VERLEGER, PHILIP K., JR.; "Models of the Demand For Air Transportation," *The Bell Journal of Economics and Management Science* (Autumn, 1972), pp. 437–457.

VICKREY, WILLIAM S.; "Congestion Theory and Transport Investment," *The American Economic Review* (May, 1969), pp. 251–260.

WARNE, CLINTON; "Economic Factors Relating to the Impact of Routes and

Schedules on Subsidy Needs of Local Service Airlines," *Transportation Journal* (Winter, 1967), pp. 5–14.

WEEKS, DALE H.; "Private-Public Enterprise for the Railroad Industry," *Transportation Journal* (Winter, 1969), pp. 5–11.

WELTY, GUS; "For TOFC/COFC, a Brighter-Than-Ever Future—If . . . ," *Railway Age* (June 24, 1974).

WHYBARK, D. CLAY; "Manpower Planning Guidelines for Civil Aviation," *The Logistics and Transportation Review* (Volume 8, Number 1), pp. 21–26.

WILLIAMS, ERNEST W., JR.; "Traffic Composition and Railroad Earning Power." *Transportation Journal* (Fall, 1969), pp. 17–21.

WINDUS, MARGARET L.; "A National Freight Car Information System," *Traffic Quarterly* (January, 1976), pp. 23–39.

WITNEY, FRED; "The Last Chance: An Alternative to Government Domination of Rail Labor Relations," *Transportation Journal* (Winter, 1968), pp. 5–14.

Yearbook of Railroad Facts, Association of American Railroads (1975).

Toyota automobiles imported at Portland, Oregon. *Credit:* Convoy Company, Portland.

CHAPTER FIVE

Transportation Regulation and Rates

*Railroads are the greatest victims of [government] bureaucratic
procedures since the invention of carbon paper.*
> —HENRI F. RUSH
> 1974 American Society of Traffic
> and Transportation Annual Meeting

*We have a serious problem with carriers avoiding our business.
I don't blame the truckers for preferring easier commodities. The
furniture is light, but loads bulky. It is hard to handle, and
damage claims tend to be high. But these guys call themselves
common carriers. It's their business to take my freight.*
> —ROY BAILEY
> *Distribution Worldwide*
> November, 1974

BRIEF HISTORY OF REGULATION

The precedent for governmental regulation of transportation dates
back to England. In 1670, Lord Chief Justice Hale, in his treatise *De
Portibus Maris*, stated that when private property is used in such a
manner that the majority of the public has a vital economic interest
in its usage, then the owner of the property, ". . . grants to the public
an interest in that use, and must submit to be controlled by the public
for the common good." It was felt that the transportation system was
so basic to the efficient operation of the economy that it could be regulated by the court system using the *common law* as opposed to *statutory
law.** During the 1600's and 1700's in England the common law system
of regulation of the transportation systems prevailed with respect to

---

* Common law developed as grievances decided by the court system on a case by
case basis. Over extended periods of time, the courts made similar rulings in cases
that had approximately the same circumstances. This consistency of judicial interpretation and findings is known as common law. The stability and continuity of
this system basically made it unnecessary to establish statute law, which is often nothing more than the common law precedents being written and enacted into law by
legislative bodies.

unreasonable rates and service practices. Statutory laws were not considered necessary, due to the relatively simple business conditions and practices of the time, and because of the prevailing attitudes of *Laissez-faire* (that which governs least governs best).

This system of common law transportation rate and service regulation was adopted in the United States. Since the public's demand for transportation regulation was not acute, this common law methodology worked reasonably well until the 1870's. After the panic of 1873, the United States experienced depression. Farmers, who were at best irritable because of the depressed agricultural prices, became incensed by a number of railroad activities. These railroad practices included:

(1) Rate discrimination, which meant that shippers who had services of competing railroads paid low rates, while shippers served by only one railroad paid high rates.

(2) The farmers were often heavily taxed to pay for gifts that had been formerly pledged to the railroads by local and state governments. When a railroad was being built into an area, it was a matter of life-and-death for communities to be located on the rail line. The railroads knew this and would survey as many as four or five alternative routes from City A to City B. Then the railroads would play the communities along one proposed route against those on the others. The winning communities would be those which pledged to build a free terminal, grant the railroad a number of years of no taxation, and give it the largest cash bonus. These gifts necessitated the subsequent taxation of the farmers and other landowners.

(3) The railroads were the first major industry to extensively sell their stock to the general public. Many farmers had mortgaged their farms to buy the securities, which often turned out to be worthless because the rail management had "watered" their stock, i.e., issued more stock than the firm's assets justified.

(4) The arrogant attitude of railroad management and the ease with which they "bought" legislators enraged the public. This was the era when Commodore Vanderbilt's son, William, uttered his famous statement, "Let the public be damned."[1]

The powerful farmer organization, the Patrons of Husbandry, commonly known as the Grange, pushed for legislative solutions. From 1869 to 1874, Illinois, Wisconsin, Iowa, and Minnesota passed stringent laws regulating railroad activities. This initial state transportation regulation become known as the *Granger Laws*. Many of these laws

[1] See: Stewart H. Holbrook, *The Story of American Railroads* (New York: Crown Publishers, 1947), p. 92.

proved unworkable. However, the key case that developed out of these laws involved grain elevators.

In 1870 Illinois had passed a law regulating the maximum rate that the elevators could charge. The elevator owner claimed that the state was violating the Fourteenth Amendment to the U.S. Constitution, which prohibits a state from depriving any person of his or her property without due process of law. The owner's argument was that since the state set a lower rate than he wanted to charge, the value of his elevator as an income producing asset was diminished. This case, *Munn v. Illinois* (94 U.S. 113) was decided by the U.S. Supreme Court in 1877, which said that, in certain cases, industries that are vital to the efficient functioning of the economy can be regulated by the states. These industries fall into a special category known as those which are "affected with a public interest." The Illinois law was upheld. The significance of this decision was that if grain elevators were affected with a public interest and could be regulated by the states, so could railroads.

The states, after the Munn case, started to cautiously reassert their right to regulate the railroads. All went relatively smoothly until the *Wabash Case* (118 U.S. 557), decided by the Supreme Court in 1886. The state of Illinois had attempted to set interstate rates from Illinois to New York City. The high court agreed with the railroad, which had argued that only the federal government could regulate interstate rates. Hence, there was great agitation to have federal railroad regulation.

THE ACT TO REGULATE COMMERCE

In 1887 Congress passed the *Act to Regulate Commerce*, whose name was changed in 1920 to the *Interstate Commerce Act*. This legislation was designed to control the most serious railroad abuses. While it dealt with many specific areas, the first six sections are still of importance. The section numbers are also important, because the expressions, "Section I discrimination," "Fourth section relief," etc., are commonly used by transportation practitioners.

> *Section I*: All rates must be "just and reasonable." The term *just* implies that the rate must be fair to the shipper in relationship to what other shippers pay for moving similar commodities under approximately the same conditions. *Reasonable* means that the carrier shall be allowed to earn a fair return on his investment.[2]
> *Section II*: Personal discrimination is covered by this section.

[2] See: John Guandolo, *Transportation Law* (Dubuque, Iowa: Wm. C. Brown Co., 1973), Chapter 24.

All shippers were to receive similar rates and services when the transportation is performed under similar conditions.

Section III: The third section is a broad anti-discrimination clause. It prohibits "undue preference or prejudice" to any person, locality, or product.

Section IV: This is the *long-and-short haul* clause, which states that a carrier cannot charge more from City A to City B than it does from City A to City C.* Some exceptions are allowed, and are known as "Fourth Section relief."

Section V: This section prohibited the railroads from pooling or combining their traffic at points where it was not economically feasible for all of them to operate. This provision has subsequently been relaxed.

Section VI: The publication of *all* railroad rates and fares was prescribed by this section. This reduced the opportunity for discrimination since all rates had to be published.

The 1887 act created the Interstate Commerce Commission (ICC) to administer the act on a day-to-day basis. Congress had given the ICC broad overall guidance, and the Commission was expected to interpret and implement these mandates. (This established the pattern for other, subsequent, federal regulatory agencies.) The original Commission had five members, today it has eleven.

Because the 1887 act was a vanguard in government regulation of business, its legislative drafters overlooked a number of "loopholes" that became apparent after its enactment. As a result, Congress, in 1903, passed the *Elkins Act*, also known as the "anti-rebate" act. Prior to the *Elkins Act*, if the government proved that rebates or special concessions had been given to a shipper, only the carrier was penalized. The 1903 act made *both* parties to the illegal act equally guilty. The *Elkins Act* is still enforced and trade publications frequently report penalties for violations.

In 1906, the *Hepburn Act* was enacted. This allowed the ICC to prescribe *maximum* rates if they found that the existing rates were not just and reasonable. Thirty days' notice to shippers was required when a carrier wished to change a rate. The *Hepburn* Act also brought *oil pipelines* under the 1887 act, although they are not regulated as strictly as the railroads. The rationale for this legislation was that the Standard Oil Company appeared to control railroad transportation of all oil products. The rail rates for oil were kept relatively high and Standard Oil negotiated (illegally) to receive rebates both on the oil they tendered the railroads and also on the oil tendered by other, competing oil companies. Furthermore, Standard had a virtual monopoly on all existing oil pipelines and did not allow their competitors to use their

* When AC is farther than AB, such as shown on Fig. 5-8.

system. Congress reacted by declaring in the *Hepburn Act* that all oil pipelines are common carriers and hence they had to accept all oil shipments tendered to them. This legislation broke the Standard Oil monopoly on oil transport.

In 1910 the *Mann-Elkins Act* gave the ICC the power to suspend proposed rate changes so the Commission would have more time to study the changes. The current time period for suspension and investigation is seven months.

The railroads were operated by the government from late 1917 to 1920.[3] They were brought back to private control by the *Transportation Act of 1920*. One of the more important features of this Act was that it gave the ICC power to establish *minimum* rates for the railroads. In addition, the Commission, if it found a rate to be unjust or unreasonable, could even prescribe the *actual* rate.

THE 1935 MOTOR CARRIER ACT

Individual states started to regulate truckers during the early 1920's. This regulation was of three types: to physically protect the highways, to require safe vehicles, and to regulate the carriers' rates and services.[4]

In August, 1935, the *Motor Carrier Act* placed trucking under federal safety and economic regulation. The key aspect of this legislation was *entry control*. Thereafter, anyone who wanted to enter the interstate trucking business as a common carrier had to obtain a *certificate of public convenience and necessity* (commonly called a certificate) from the ICC. The existing truckers in 1935 were able to continue in business under a *grandfather* provision. The existing truckers, in return for this protection from competition, are regulated with respect to both rates and service. The 1935 act recognized three distinct types of trucking companies: *common carriers, contract carriers*, and *private carriers*. The distinction and obligations of each of these carriers will be examined shortly. Common carriers, those who serve the general public, are basically subject to Sections I, II, III and VI of the ICC Act, which also apply to the railroads.

The farm bloc was able to obtain an *agricultural exemption* in the 1935 act. The farmers argued that their need for trucking service differed from that of the rest of the business community. There was relatively little being transported most of the year, but at harvest times, the need for trucking capacity was great. The farmers argued that if agricultural products could only be transported by carriers with certificates

[3] For a brief discussion of this period, see: James C. Johnson, "Government Control of the Railroads in World War I: Was It Really Disastrous?" *Traffic World* (April 9, 1973), pp. 68–69.

[4] For a discussion of the background of federal trucking regulation, see: James C. Johnson, *Trucking Mergers: A Regulatory Viewpoint* (Lexington, Mass.: D. C. Heath and Co., 1973), Chapter 3.

it would be impossible to get the products out of the fields during harvest periods. Congress accepted this argument and created the agricultural exemption. This provision states that agricultural commodities, including ordinary livestock and fish, are exempt from regulation. This means that as long as the agricultural products are unprocessed, anyone who has a truck can legally transport them.[5]

THE 1938 CIVIL AERONAUTICS ACT

Regulation of the domestic air carrier industry, as was the case of motor carriers, was basically sponsored and supported by the industry itself. It was felt that governmental entry control was necessary to stabilize the industry from excessive competition. A feature of the 1938 act was entry control, which required all new carriers to receive a certificate from the regulatory body, now known as the Civil Aeronautics Board (CAB). In general, economic air carrier regulation is similar to and was based on the precedents used for both rail and motor carriers. Safety regulation of the air industry is administered by the Federal Aviation Agency (FAA), which is part of the U.S. Department of Transportation.

THE 1940 TRANSPORTATION ACT

Five years after federal trucking regulation was enacted, Congress again passed another significant piece of transportation legislation. The *Transportation Act of 1940* brought some *inland water carriers* under federal economic regulation. As it turned out, the inland water carriers are at best nominally regulated, because of the extensive exemptions from economic regulation that were allowed. The most important exemptions include all bulk commodities (assuming there are three or less types of bulk products per tow) and all liquid commodities. The ICC has estimated that only ten percent of all tonnage shipped by inland water carriers is subject to federal economic regulation.

The *1940 Transportation Act* also contained a declaration of the *National Transportation Policy*. It was intended to be a broad over-all policy for the ICC to use in regulating the railroads, oil pipelines, motor carriers, and water carriers. It is a relatively brief statement telling the Commission to provide fair and impartial regulation of all modes of transportation and to also recognize and preserve the inherent advantages of each transport mode. The ICC has interpreted this to mean that it must allow each mode to survive, and "cut-throat" competition, whether intra-modal or inter-modal must be prohibited.

---

[5] For a discussion of recent problems involving agricultural products, see: James C. Johnson, "Governmental Undermining of the Common Carrier System," *The Transportation Law Journal* (July, 1975), pp. 209–218.

FREIGHT FORWARDER REGULATION

In 1942 Congress declared that freight forwarders were subject to the Interstate Commerce Act, even though they are supplemental or indirect carriers. The forwarders were subject to most of the regulatory pattern that applies to the railroads, including entry control, rate, and service regulation. Instead of certificates, forwarders need a *permit* from the ICC. A unique feature of this legislation is that freight forwarders cannot own or control any railroad, oil pipeline, motor carrier, or water carrier, but these carriers can own and control forwarders. Also, since forwarders cannot do any line-haul intercity transportation themselves, this segment of the haul must be performed by common carriers. In 1950, freight forwarders were declared by Congress to be common carriers, although they still cannot perform any line-haul intercity transportation service.

THE REED-BULWINKLE ACT (1948)

This act legalized intramodal *rate bureaus*. A rate bureau is a multi-carrier committee that coordinates the joint-rates and through-routes of its carrier members. It also establishes and publishes uniform rates for its member carriers. Each member carrier, however, has the right to establish different rates than the other bureau members, which is known as "flagging-out" a rate, or "taking independent action." * Finally, this legislation provides that bureaus which conform to the ICC's rules will be exempt from the antitrust provisions of other U.S. statutes.

THE TRANSPORTATION ACT OF 1958

This act attempted to strengthen Section 15a of the Interstate Commerce Act which deals with intermodal rate-making, by stating that, "Rates of a carrier shall not be held up to a particular level to protect the traffic of any other mode of transportation, giving due consideration to the objectives of the National Transportation Policy." This Congressional guideline was apparently not as clear as it appears here and in the *Ingot Molds Case*, to be discussed shortly, the U.S. Supreme Court emasculated the meaning or intent of the mandate. The 1958 Act also clarified the definition of the agricultural exemption, generally removing frozen foods from the exempt list.

THE DEPARTMENT OF TRANSPORTATION ACT (1966)

This legislation created the U.S. Department of Transportation (DOT). The DOT was created to consolidate 38 separate governmental

---

* Initially, carriers propose rates which rate bureaus usually accept. Appeals may be made later to the I.C.C. by shippers or other affected carriers.

agencies, all of which dealt with various aspects of transportation. (Ocean shipping programs, however, remained in the Department of Commerce.) It has an annual budget of greater than $8 billion and by this measure, is the third largest cabinet department. The primary objectives of the DOT are to administer governmental programs in three key areas: *research, promotion,* and *safety.* The administration of *economic regulation* was not given to the DOT, but was retained by the ICC, the Civil Aeronautics Board, and the Federal Maritime Commission. However, DOT has the authority to study regulations and to make recommendations regarding the National Transportation Policy.

RAILROAD REVITALIZATION AND REGULATORY REFORM ACT (1976)

In February, 1976, President Ford signed a major law regarding the railroad industry. It made available $2.1 billion for the Consolidated Rail Corporation (Conrail) to function as a for-profit railroad in lieu of the bankrupt railroads in the Northeast and Midwest. In addition, $600 million in government loans to railroads for improvements in plant and equipment was made available, as was an additional $1 billion of loan guarantees for the same purpose.

Railroad rate deregulation was also enacted and it will be discussed later in this chapter.

OCEAN CARRIER REGULATION

The history of ocean water carrier transportation is somewhat complex, due to the multiplicity of agencies that have been involved at one time or another. At present the ICC nominally regulates water transportation on the inland waterway system, the Great Lakes and on the coastwise (i.e., New York City to Norfolk) and intercoastal (i.e., San Francisco to Newark) water systems. The Federal Maritime Commission (FMC) regulates ocean carriers in foreign commerce and between the United States mainland and Alaska, Hawaii, and the United States' possessions. The FMC also attempts to insure that foreign ocean transportation practices and services do not discriminate against United States flag carriers and shippers. The FMC reviews steamship "conference" agreements (discussed in Chapter 11) but because of the sovereign rights involved with international transportation, it cannot regulate the *level* of ocean freight rates.

CONTEMPORARY REGULATORY ISSUES

The importance and pervasiveness of the transportation system make it controversial. Indeed, this subject is rife with issues in search of solutions. Two of the most basic controversies today involve transportation deregulation, and multimodal transportation companies. Each of these will be briefly examined.

The most debated issue in transportation policy during recent years regards *deregulation*. Those who favor deregulation have stated: "The ICC, through its regulation of the transportation industry, has ignored the tenets of the free market."[6]

On the other hand, there are strong and vociferous defenders of the present regulatory situation. They say: "For the public, I believe broad-brush indiscriminate deregulation—especially in ratemaking and free entry—would be disastrous. It would be a path of almost no return."[7] The strongest supporters of deregulation have proposed that the ICC be abolished and that carriers be regulated by the Sherman and Clayton Antitrust Acts.[8] Although bills are annually introduced into Congress to accomplish this objective, they have received little serious attention. There are less drastic proposals which have received widespread industry discussion and often cautious support. A recent survey of non-transportation and transportation (shipper-side) executives indicated that a majority of both groups favored less economic regulation for both railroad and motor carriers. Specifically, they supported less entry control and more ratemaking freedom.[9]

Recall that Congress amended Section 15a of the Interstate Commerce Act in an attempt to allow greater intermodal rate-making freedom. However, Section 15a was emasculated by the ICC decision—subse-

---

[6] *1968 Conference on Mass Transportation—The Government Role* (New York: Popular Library, 1968), p. 23.

[7] Kenneth H. Tuggle, "To Regulate or Not to Regulate," *ICC Practitioners' Journal* (January-February, 1972), p. 168.

[8] See, for example: George W. Hilton, "The Two Things Wrong With The Interstate Commerce Commission," *Transportation Research Forum, Eleventh Annual Proceedings* (Oxford: Richard B. Cross Co., 1970), pp. 299–305.

[9] Donald V. Harper and James C. Johnson, "The Shipper Views Deregulation of Transportation," *ICC Practitioners' Journal* (March-April, 1974), pp. 317–331. See also, "Survey: The Regulators," *Transportation and Distribution Management*, (March-April, 1974), pp. 38–40. For additional discussion of deregulation, see: John A. Creedy, "Competition and Regulation in Transportation," *Traffic World* (March 24, 1975), pp. 75–78; James C. Johnson and Donald V. Harper, "The Potential Consequences of Deregulation of Transportation," *Land Economics* (February, 1975), pp. 58–71; George L. Stern, "Surface Transport: Middle-Of-The-Road Solution," *Harvard Business Review* (November-December, 1975), pp. 80–89; "Survey: The National Transportation Policy Statement," *Transportation and Distribution Management* (November-December, 1975), pp. 39–41; and the issues of *Distribution Worldwide* (September, 1975) and *Traffic Management* (January, 1976) are devoted exclusively to transportation deregulation.

quently upheld by the U.S. Supreme Court—in the well-known *Ingot Molds Case* [326 ICC 77 (1965)]. This case involved the transportation of ingot molds from Pittsburgh, Pennsylvania to Steelton, Kentucky. The barge-truck rate was $5.11 per ton. The railroads, who were not carrying this traffic, reduced their rate from $11.86 to $5.11 per ton. The railroads admitted that their new rate was below their full costs of $7.59 per ton but it was greater than their variable costs* of $4.69 per ton. The barge and truck carriers contested this proposed rate on the theory that the National Transportation Policy demanded that each carrier's "inherent advantage" be protected. Since they were the low-cost carriers on a full-cost basis, they argued that the railroads' proposed rate not be allowed. The ICC decided against the railroads and disallowed the rate decrease, holding that the term "inherent advantage" should be interpreted to mean the lowest full-cost carrier. The railroads appealed this decision to a federal district court, which overruled the ICC. The court reasoned that Section 15a would not have been amended by Congress unless their desire was to literally stop the holding up of one mode's rate to protect another.[10] This lower court decision was appealed to the Supreme Court, which reversed the lower court and thus upheld the ICC. Since the ICC had ruled that the lowest *full-cost* carrier possessed the inherent advantage, the Supreme Court said this interpretation must stand until Congress, if it so desires, passes additional legislation telling the ICC what "inherent advantage" in fact should mean.[11]

Among those who favor deregulation, the infamous *Yak Fat* Case of 1965 is always discussed. Thomas Hilt, a trucker in Nebraska, was sick and tired of the railroads always protesting to the ICC when a motor carrier decreased its rate. (In fairness, the truckers typically took the same action when the railroads proposed to lower a rate.) Therefore, to prove that the railroads *automatically* protested all new rates and downward rate changes, Hilt proposed a $9.00 per ton rate on yak fat from Omaha to Chicago. It should be noted that the nearest yaks in sufficient numbers to yield a substantial quantity of yak fat are in eastern Tibet. Nevertheless, the railroads dutifully protested the rate as

---

* The full cost of production is composed of two sub-parts: variable costs and fixed costs. Variable costs vary directly with volume and are often referred to as "out-of-pocket" costs. For a railroad, examples would be labor and fuel costs. Notice that variable costs are not incurred unless a train actually runs from city A to city B. Fixed costs, on the other hand, do *not* vary with volume. They are constant, regardless of the volume of business. Examples would be a railroad's roadbed and track, tunnels, bridges, terminals, and classification yards.

10 *Louisville & Nashville R. Co. v. United States,* 268 F. Supp. 71 (1967).

11 *American Commercial Lines v. Louisville and Nashville Railroad Co.,* 392 U.S. 571 (1968).

"unjust and unreasonable" and noted that a more equitable rate would be $12.60 per ton of yak fat.[12]

Many individuals have speculated on the magnitude of transportation rate decreases that would be precipitated by reduced entry control and the authorization of all transportation rates that exceed the variable costs of production. James Sloss calculated that deregulation of the motor carrier industry would reduce the overall truck shipping bill to the public by approximately $359 million per year.[13] Williams and Bluestone have stated that the effect of deregulation would be that the annual transport bill would be decreased by several billions of dollars.[14] In addition, the President's Council of Economic Advisors reported that the proposed Regulatory Modernization Act of 1971 was expected to yield an annual savings of approximately $1 billion.[15] An indication of rate reductions precipitated by deregulation occurred in the agricultural industry. As a result of a number of judicial decisions in the early 1950's, a variety of poultry and frozen products were removed from motor carrier economic regulation because they were declared to be "exempt" commodities. The U.S. Department of Agriculture found that truck rates for 1956–1957, the initial years with no regulation, decreased approximately 33 percent for poultry, and between 11 and 29 percent for frozen fruits and vegetables.[16]

In 1976, rate deregulation was enacted by the *Railroad Revitalization and Regulatory Reform Act*. This law stated that rates which are equal to or greater than variable costs shall not be found to be unjust or unreasonable on the basis that they are too low. This legislation specifically stated that the rate of a carrier shall not be held up to a particular level to protect a competitor carrier.

In 1976 the Ford Administration also actively sought to deregulate the motor and air carrier industries. The ICC and the trucking industry were adamant against the deregulatory proposal, while the airline in-

[12] See: John Burby, *The Great American Motion Sickness* (Boston: Little Brown & Co., 1971), Chapter 10.

[13] James Sloss, "Regulation of Motor Freight Transportation: A Quantitative Evaluation of Policy," *The Bell Journal of Economics and Management Science* (Autumn, 1970), p. 351.

[14] Ernest W. Williams, Jr. and David W. Bluestone, *Rationale of Federal Transportation Policy*, U.S. Department of Commerce (Washington, D.C.: Government Printing Office, April, 1960), p. 5.

[15] "The Annual Report of the Council of Economic Advisors," in *Economic Report of the President—1972* (Washington, D.C.: U.S. Government Printing Office, 1972), p. 135.

[16] Walter Miklius, *Economic Performance of Motor Carriers Operating Under the Agricultural Exemption in Interstate Trucking*, U.S. Department of Agriculture, Marketing Research Report No. 838 (Washington, D.C.: U.S. Government Printing Office, January, 1969), pp. 1–5.

dustry and the CAB were more receptive to a trial period of partial deregulation.[17]

THE MULTIMODAL TRANSPORTATION COMPANY

A *transportation company* is defined as a firm which offers *multimodal* transportation service to its customers. It could offer a combined rail-motor carrier movement with one firm owning both modes of transportation. U. S. statutes and regulatory bodies have discouraged transportation companies, because of the belief that if one mode could own a potentially competitive mode, there is the possibility of a decrease in competition. At present, railroads and airlines can run trucks that are used for pick up and delivery within specified distances of their terminals. The railroad industry is the largest supporter of the idea of legalizing transportation companies.

Advocates of transportation companies believe it would offer the shipping public a better quality of service at lower rates because the transportation company would use each mode of transportation where it is economically superior.[18] In addition, one sales representative would be able to offer a shipper a "smorgasbord" of services for each shipment from City A to City B. If speed of delivery was of importance, air freight service would be used exclusively. The next quality level would be truck-air or all truck service, and so on.

Another argument in favor of transportation companies is that they would allow carriers to expand their operations into newer, developing forms of transportation. At present, since this is illegal, carriers often divert their investment capital funds into non-transportation activities.

While transportation companies are basically non-existent in the United States, they are legal in Canada. The Canadian Pacific is a "true" multimodal transportation company, offering all modes of transport service. Because of the significant potential advantages of transportation companies to the shipping public and since they have yielded no apparent detrimental effects in Canada, there is considerable and growing support for legalizing this concept in the United States.[19]

LEGAL OBLIGATIONS OF CARRIERS

We have examined briefly the history of transportation regulation and two contemporary regulatory issues. It is now appropriate to analyze the

[17] "CAB Urges a Sharp Cut In Own Power To Control Airlines Services and Prices," *The Wall Street Journal* (April 9, 1976), p. 10.

[18] See, for example: James E. Suelflow and Stanley J. Hille, "The Transportation Company: An Economic Argument for Intermodal Ownership," *Land Economics* (August, 1970), pp. 275–286.

[19] See, for example: Robert C. Lieb, "A Revised Intermodal Ownership Policy," *Transportation Journal* (Summer, 1971), pp. 48–53.

specific regulatory obligations of the transportation modes. *Common carriers, contract carriers, exempt carriers,* and *private carriers* will be defined and discussed in turn.

COMMON CARRIER OBLIGATIONS

The common carrier system is the backbone of the transportation industry. All railroads are common carriers, and common carriers are also found in trucking, water carriage, air freight, and pipelines. The key factor that separates a common carrier from the other forms of transportation is the specific obligations that the common carrier assumes: to *serve,* to *deliver,* to *charge reasonable rates,* and to *avoid discrimination.*[20]

Service Obligation. Common carriers have a legal obligation to serve *all* customers who request their service. This assumes the requested service is one the carrier has the authority and equipment to serve. For example, a motor common carrier of general commodities may refuse to accept a 10,000 gallon bulk shipment of sulfuric acid if this is a type of commodity that the carrier does not have the proper equipment to handle. Also, a common carrier cannot carry a shipment to a destination it cannot legally serve. A motor common carrier operating exclusively between Dallas and Atlanta cannot carry a shipment from Dallas to Phoenix.

Recently, the common carrier "duty to serve" has become a topic of controversy, because of the "small-shipment" problem. Many motor carriers believe that they experience an out-of-pocket loss (i.e., the revenues received do not cover the variable cost) on these shipments, and they are refusing to pick up this type of shipment. This refusal is illegal, and the ICC has warned carriers that they run the risk of forfeiting their operating rights.[21]

Delivery Obligation. The common carrier has a strict obligation to *deliver* the products entrusted to it to the consignee (the receiver). This delivery must be accomplished with reasonable dispatch and the products must be delivered in the same condition as the carrier received them. It is this obligation under which the *law of loss and damage* (L&D) is founded. It is generally believed that this duty is the oldest common carrier obligation. Writing in 1703 Lord Holt stated:

> The law charges this person thus intrusted to carry goods, against all events, but Acts of God, and the enemies of the King. For though the force

[20] For further information, see: Martin T. Farris, "The Role of the Common Carrier," *Transportation Journal* (Summer, 1967), pp. 28–34.
[21] See, for example: "Commission Adopts New Rule Requiring Motor Carriers to Provide 'Full Service'," *Traffic World* (March 7, 1970), pp. 41–42.

FIG. 5-1 Is This An "Act of God?"

"How we gonna explain *this* one to the boss?"

be ever so great, as if an irresistible multitude of people should rob him, nevertheless, he is chargeable. And this is a politic establishment, contrived by the policy of the law, for the safety of all persons, the necessity of whose affairs oblige them to trust these sorts of persons, that they may be safe in their ways of dealing; for else these carriers might have an opportunity of undoing all persons that had any dealings with them, by combining with thieves, etc., and yet doing it in such clandestine manner as would not be possible to be discovered. And this is the reason the law is founded upon that point.[22]

Today, all a shipper or consignee has to prove to have a valid claim against a common carrier is that: (a) the goods were tendered to the carrier in good condition; and (b) when received by the consignee the product was damaged, or (c) the product was lost. When this occurs, the carrier is liable for a loss and damage claim. The rule of thumb regarding compensation is that the shipper or consignee should be put in the same position as he would have been if the loss or damage did not take place. The carrier, however, is not always liable for a L&D claim, even if the goods are, in fact, lost or damaged while in the possession of the carrier. The carrier has five specific exemptions. The first exemption is an *Act of God*. This is any severe unpredictable condition, such as earthquakes, tornadoes, or floods, (see Figure 5-1). The second exemption, also mentioned by Lord Holt, is *Ememies of the King*, who are soldiers or saboteurs of an enemy country. Three additional exemptions have been added by statute over time. The third is *Acts of the Public Authority*, which involves situations where governmental agencies prevent the carrier from fulfilling its timely delivery obligation. An example of this would be an examination of products, such as Arizona administers, to determine whether horticultural diseases are being brought into the state. If a shipment is suspected of being infested, and it takes the state two weeks to determine whether the shipment is "clean," the carrier is not liable for damage resulting from this delay. A fourth exemption is *Acts of the Shipper*, which involves two situations. The first is when the shipper improperly packages a product. The second is when the shipper improperly loads the transportation vehicle, causing the products to shift and break. The final exemption is *Inherent Nature or Vice of the Goods*. Some products, such as petroleum, shrink or evaporate regardless of any protective actions the carrier takes. Therefore, the carrier is not liable for this product loss. Also, some products are perishable, but if the carrier expedites delivery, it is not liable if the products arrive in a spoiled condition.

Reasonable Rates. Because the number of competitors is limited, it is only logical that the rates of existing carriers be kept at a reason-

[22] Richard R. Sigmon, *Miller's Law of Freight Loss and Damage Claims* (Dubuque, Iowa: Wm. C. Brown, 1961), pp. 2–3.

able level. This is what Section I of the 1887 *Act To Regulate Commerce* dealt with, when it stated that all rates must be "just and reasonable.[23] This is a complex subject and it will be discussed in detail later.

Avoidance of Discrimination. The final common carrier obligation is to treat all customers, products, and geographic locations the same when similar circumstances are present. Sections II and III of the 1887 Act address themselves to this common carrier requirement.

CONTRACT CARRIER OBLIGATIONS

Contract carriers are found extensively in the motor carrier and inland water carrier industries. A contract carrier offers a specialized service to a limited number of clients on a contractual basis. The contracts specify in detail the compensation the carrier will receive, the services it must render, etc. Because of the tailor-made individual nature of the contract between each contract carrier and its customer, this type of service is almost the same as a private transportation system for a company.

An important difference between contract and common carriers involves discrimination. The contract carrier is under no legal obligation to render any service to the public and only has to serve those customers with whom it has contracts. Also, the contract carrier is under no obligation to treat all of its contract customers on an equal basis. Westmeyer explains the rationale for this provision:

> The amount a contract carrier charges any given shipper will vary with the volume of traffic the shipper can offer, the regularity of the traffic, the possibility of obtaining a back haul for trucks which would otherwise have to return to their point of origin without a payload, the cost and practicality of a shipper providing his own motor transport facilities, and possibly other factors which vary from shipper to shipper. To attempt to establish a uniform schedule of rates under such conditions would destroy the peculiar advantage of this type of transportation.[24]

EXEMPT CARRIERS

Exempt carriers can legally transport any commodity that is specifically "exempted" from regulation in the Interstate Commerce Act. Important exempt commodities have already been discussed, these include "unprocessed" agricultural products in trucking and bulk and liquid products transported in barges. In other words, any *trucker* can transport unprocessed agricultural products in interstate commerce. This includes

[23] This subject is discussed in detail in D. Philip Locklin, *Economics of Transportation* (Homewood, Ill.: Richard D. Irwin, Inc., 1972).

[24] Russell E. Westmeyer, *Economics of Transportation* (Englewood Cliffs, N.J.: Prentice-Hall, Inc., 1952), p. 403.

common carriers, contract carriers and private carriers. However, when they haul the exempt commodity, they become for that haul an *exempt carrier*. Exempt carrier rates and services are not regulated—they must be negotiated directly between the carrier and the shipper.

PRIVATE CARRIERS

Private carriage is often called "do-it-yourself" transportation. This involves a company buying (or leasing) its own vehicles and operating them, thus providing its own cartage service. Private carriage is used most extensively in the motor carrier mode, but it is also used in other modes except railroads. There is no economic regulation of private carriage by the ICC. Private carriage is subject to safety regulations. A key point regarding private transportation is that it *cannot* solicit business from other companies. A private carrier can only haul its own products, either inputs to make the good or the finished product itself. A serious problem typically found in private motor carriage is the empty back haul.

The transportation regulatory environment has thus been examined. It is now time to discuss a key aspect of regulation—the logic and determination of just and reasonable freight rates.

FREIGHT RATE DETERMINATION

Freight rate determination is incredibly complex. To the uninitiated, it would appear the height of folly to state that it is very difficult to determine the correct carrier rate for a 30,000 pound shipment of shoes from Norfolk, Virginia to Reno, Nevada.

The complexity of freight rate determination is related to *tariffs*, which are often 1000 pages or more in length, and are used to determine the applicable freight rate. Tariffs are known as "official publications," because when the carriers properly file them with the ICC, CAB or FMC, they take on the force and effect of law. In 1960 one tariff expert estimated that there were 43,000,000,000,000 (that's 43 trillion!) rates on file with the ICC.[25] Another indication of this unbelievable complexity is that there are over 200,000 active tariffs on file with the ICC. The *1975-ICC Annual Report* noted that the Commission receives 4,226 pages of new tariffs every working day.

One veteran observer of transportation noted:

"There are certain things," said a General Attorney for one of the Western Railroads, "spiritual and material, in the presence of which ordinary mortals stand dumb. When I stood at the tomb of Napoleon, first

[25] Herbert O. Whitten, "Why Freight Rates Must Be Computerized," *Distribution Age* (March, 1966), p. 30.

viewed the Washington Monument, gazed into the Grand Canyon, words were superfluous.

"Feeling akin to this arises within me when I contemplate a freight tariff, with its exceptions, items, notes, commodities, distances, proportionals, disproportionals, gateways, basing points, arbitraries, and God knows what. If the thing itself amazes, what must be the feeling when one views from afar the mind that conceived it?

"I can approach a Superintendent, a General Manager, a General Solicitor, or a President, if you will, with a certain amount of assurance, and composure; but when I approach the portals of a Traffic Expert's office, I not only remove my hat, but also my shoes, and like the devout Moslem, chant as I near the throne:

"'Great is Mohammed,' but greater is the man who understands the freight tariff."[26]

An entire profession has developed merely to catch mistakes made in trying to determine the proper freight charge. These individuals are known as *freight bill auditors*. They function as an independent check of the individual company's ability to determine the correct freight rate. After a shipper has paid the freight rate, he turns over the paid bills to the freight bill auditor who checks to make sure the lowest rate has been paid. An auditor who discovers an overpayment generally receives 50 percent of the overcharge, which the shipper recovers from the carrier.

FULL COST VS. VALUE-OF-SERVICE RATE-MAKING

The complexity of the freight rate structure is related to the extensive use of "value-of-service" pricing as opposed to full cost pricing. *Full cost pricing* refers to setting a price that covers both fixed and variable costs plus a margin for profit. *Value-of-service* pricing, which is also called *differential* pricing, *discriminatory* pricing, or *"charging what the traffic will bear"* pricing, involves using variable costs only to establish a floor below which rates will normally not go. The objective is to set rates that will maximize the contribution received over and above the variable costs incurred for carrying each shipment. The result is that a ton of steel, a ton of gravel, a ton of canned goods, a ton of liquor, and a ton of furniture, each moving from City A to City B, pay different rates. In fact, one commodity may just barely cover variable costs involved, while another product pays as much as 100 to 200 percent more than the full costs of carriage.

The extensive use of value-of-service rate-making is a result of the precedent established by the railroads during the 19th century.* The

* This 19th Century pricing structure is at the root of contemporary railroad problems since they have lost "high-value" business to other modes and are left carrying bulk products at rates which sometimes fail to cover full costs.

26 Anonymous quote in Paul T. McElhiney and Charles L. Hilton, *Introduction*

railroads, which had no effective competition during this period, established a pricing structure which called for high rates for relatively high valued commodities (i.e., liquor, manufactured products, etc.) and low charges for products of lower value (sand, gravel, coal, pulp wood, etc.). This pricing system was sanctioned by the ICC. Why? "*The theory behind this method of pricing was to maximize the total movement of goods in the United States,* and profits derived from the transportation of high valued and high rated commodities were expected to offset the carriage of other commodities at less than their full cost." (Emphasis added.)[27]

Value-of-service pricing, which was started by the railroad industry, has been adopted to one degree or another by all of the other modes of transportation. The truckers use it the least because their very high variable cost structure leaves little room to cut prices and still cover variable costs. Rates far above full cost are impractical because this forces shippers into private transportation.

BASIC FREIGHT RATES

The specific rate for shipping a product from City A to City B is determined by the use of tariffs. There are three basic types of freight rates: *class, exception,* and *commodity.*

Class rates can be thought of as standard rates that can be found for almost all products or commodities shipped. These rates are found with the help of a *classification tariff.* This tariff gives each shipment a *rating* or *class* ranging from 400 to 13 in the widely used *Uniform Freight Classification.* It contains 30 separate ratings or classes, and it is used extensively by the railroads and many truckers and water carriers. The other widely used classification tariff is the *National Motor Freight Classification,* which has ratings or classes from 500 to 35, with 23 separate ratings. The higher the rating or class, the greater is the relative charge for transporting the commodity. A multitude of factors are involved in determining a product's specific class or rating. Taff summarizes the important factors below:

1. Weight per cubic foot as packed for shipment.
2. Value per pound as packed per shipment.
3. Liability to loss, damage, waste, or theft in transit.
4. Likelihood of injury to other freight with which it may come in contact.

to Logistics and Traffic Management (Dubuque, Iowa: Wm. C. Brown Co., 1968), p. 229.

27 Paul M. Zeis, "Competitive Rate Making in the United States, *Transportation Journal* (Summer, 1969), p. 36.

5. Risks due to hazards of carriage.

6. Kind of container or package as bearing upon the matter of liability or risk.

7. Expense of, and care in, handling.

8. Ratings of analogous articles.

9. Fair relation of ratings as between all articles.

10. Competition between articles of different description but used for similar purposes.

11. Commercial conditions and units of sales.

12. Trade conditions.

13. Value of service to the shipper.

14. Volume of movement for the entire country.

15. Adaptability to movement in carloads.

16. Carload minimum weights which are fair to carriers and shippers.[28]

Once the commodity rating or class is determined, it is necessary to establish the rate bases number from the applicable tariff. This number is the approximate distance between any two city pairs. With the commodity rating or class and the rate bases number, the specific rate per hundred pounds can be located in another tariff. Finally to establish the specific cost of moving commodity A between City B and City C, the formula—*weight* (in hundred pound units) × *rate* (per hundred pounds) = *charge*—must be used.

An example will help to clarify the situation. Assume a professor of archeology is retiring and moving from Sioux Falls, South Dakota to Hannibal, Missouri. He has collected 30,000 pounds of bones during his long career. The railroad serving his town used the Uniform Freight Classification (UFC). To establish the rating (class), it is necessary to find the commodity in UFC index. Figure 5-2 (page 155) contains the appropriate page from the index which contains human bones. It will be noticed that the letters *noibn* follow human bones. This stands for Not Otherwise Indexed By Name. We are referred to item number 13350. Figure 5-3 (page 156) is the page in the UFC which contains item number 13350. This tariff also specifies how the human bones are to be packaged for presentation to the carrier. On the right hand edge of Figure 5-3 are the appropriate ratings or classes. The first rating of 200 is the less than car-load (LCL) rating. Then it states that if 20,000 or more pounds of bones are tendered to the carrier, then the Car-Load (CL) rating is 100. Since this shipment involves 30,000 pounds, the CL rating of 100 will be used. The next requirement is to determine the rate bases number. Figure 5-4 (page 157) illustrates a typical tariff page containing this information. The appropriate rate bases number between

[28] Charles A. Taff, *Management of Physical Distribution and Transportation* (Homewood, Ill.: Richard D. Irwin, Inc., 1972), p. 297.

FIG. 5-2

INDEX TO ARTICLES

STCC No.	Article	Item	STCC No.	Article	Item
	Hulls₋Concluded:			Huskers₋Concluded:	
20 914 45	Cottonseed,mixed with meal 37130		35 225 23	Corn,and fodder shredders,	
20 914 25	Cottonseed,not ground. . . .31250,†31270			combined,ot hand,	
20 939 46	Fleaseed (psyllium). 33800,80090			SU	3370,†14050
34 412 15	Launch,steel 11690		34 236 79	Corn,hand	
37 329 12	Launch,wooden,in the white,			(husking gloves) 36260	
	KD. 11490		35 225 60	Corn,noibn,ot hand,	
37 329 13	Launch,wooden,in the white,			KD. . . . . .3360,†14050	
	SU. 11490		35 225 59	Corn,noibn,ot hand,SU,	
20 939 55	Nut,noibn. 86140			on wheels. . . . . .3360,†14050	
20 418 30	Oat. 47110			Green corn. 62530	
20 999 25	Peanut,crushed or ground 37530		35 227 30	Husking gloves,corn	
20 939 20	Peanut,not crushed nor ground. . . 37540		34 236 79	(corn huskers) 36260	
20 939 46	Psyllium seed (fleaseed) . . 33800,80090			Husking pins. 36500	
20 449 15	Rice,ground and rice bran,		34 236 80	Husks,corn (shucks) 37350	
	feed. 37580		01 199 30	Hydrants,or sections 29520	
20 449 20	Rice,ground,feed 37590		33 219 16	Hydrastis canadensis (golden seal)	
20 449 25	Rice,unground (rice chaff),		28 311 51	roots,ground or powdered . . 33590,33800	
	feed. 37600		01 915 13	Hydrastis canadensis (golden seal) roots,	
09 131 55	Shrimp . . . . ♂			not ground nor powdered. . . 33620,33800	
20 923 16	Soybean,ground 37640		35 329 10	Hydraulic accumulators,mining,	
20 923 17	Soybean,not ground 37640			ore milling or smelting. 63480	
20 939 56	Sunflower seed 88440		32 411 15	Hydraulic cement. . . . . . .21680,†77130	
20 939 27	Tung nut 52790		35 999 16	Hydraulic cylinders,ot rotary,steel 60780	
20 939 64	Velvet bean,ground 95550		35 691 45	Hydraulic rams. . . . .†61240,64890	
20 939 66	Velvet bean,not ground 95560		35 329 10	Hydraulic rotary swivels,oil,	
28 311 21	Human blood,liquid,frozen or			water or gas well. 72070	
	chilled.. 11355		29 912 10	Hydraulic system fluid,ot,	
39 998 21	Human bones,noibn. 13350			petroleum. 14690	
39 994 10	Human hair 48320			Hydraulic wheel presses . . . . . .†66800	
39 994 20	Human hair goods,noibn. 48390		34 434 38	Hydro-pneumatic tanks,copper,	
39 994 15	Human hair samples,mounted on			cylindrical closed at both ends. . 89040	
	cardboard 48360		34 434 40	Hydro-pneumatic tanks,silicon	
40 291 47	Human hair waste,not stumps nor			bronze,cylindrical,closed at	
	combed hair 95490			both ends. 89050	
	Humidifiers:		34 434 42	Hydro-pneumatic tanks,steel,14	
41 111 10	Air and blowers or fans combined,			gauge or thicker,cylindrical,	
	mounted on freight			closed at both ends. 89060	
	automobile. 73400		38 213 15	Hydrobarometers 32990	
35 857 20	Air and blowers or fans combined,		28 139 92	Hydrocarbon gas,noibn 45630	
	noibn,. 130740,58510		35 599 78	Hydrocarbon recovery systems. . . . ♂	
35 857 45	Air bakers',cast iron. . . .58610,†58720		28 194 50	Hydrochloric (muriatic)	
37 142 12	Coolers and filters,air,			acid 2340,33800	
	automobile,non-electric 8125		28 194 34	Hydrocyanic acid. 2260	
34 336 49	Hot air house heating		28 194 42	Hydrofluoric and sulphuric acid,	
	furnace,automatic 12700			mixed. 2280,33800	
34 299 30	Humidors,ot display. 52800		28 194 38	Hydrofluoric acid 2270,33800	
14 917 15	Humus. 27320		40 251 65	Hydrofluoric acid waste,	
33 992 50	Hungarian nails,noibn,brass,			aqueous. . . . . ♂	
	bronze or copper. . . . . .†49771,50810		28 194 46	Hydrofluosilicic acid 2290,33800	
33 152 25	Hungarian nails,noibn,steel,with		28 139 20	Hydrogen bromide,anhydrous,	
	ot steel or zinc			liquefied. 45410	
	heads . . . .†49781,50820		28 139 22	Hydrogen chloride,anhydrous,	
33 152 30	Hungarian nails,noibn,steel,			liquefied. 45420	
	with steel heads. . . . . .†49781,50830		28 199 31	Hydrogen dioxide. 24020,33800	
33 152 35	Hungarian nails,noibn,steel,		28 134 60	Hydrogen gas. 45640	
	with zinc heads . . . . . .†49781,50840		28 199 31	Hydrogen peroxide 24020,33800	
	Hurdles,track,steel with		28 139 46	Hydrogen sulphide 45650	
	wooden cross bars,		20 469 10	Hydrol (corn,sorghum grain	
	noibn 7580			or wheat sugar final	
	Hurdles,track steel with			molasses). 37360	
	wooden cross bars,uprights		38 219 14	Hydrometers 33000	
	folded to base,or SU nstd,		28 186 20	Hydroxy acetic acid 2300,33800	
	in nests of five or		40 251 62	Hydroxy aldehydes,waste,	
	more. 7580			containing not less than	
22 995 73	Hurds,hemp or ramie. 52810			40% water. 96090	
35 225 29	Huskers and pickers combined,		28 612 20	Hypernic extracts,dry 35860	
	corn. . . . . .3390,†14050		28 612 21	Hypernic extracts,liquid or	
35 225 61	Huskers and shellers,combined,			paste. 35870	
	corn,ot hand. . . . . . . .3380,†14050		40 291 57	Hypo-mud,photo silver 95720	
	Huskers:				
35 225 24	Corn and fodder shredders,				
	combined,ot hand,KD . . . .3370,†14050				

FIG. 5-3

UNIFORM FREIGHT CLASSIFICATION 7   13250–13470

Item	ARTICLES	Less Carload Ratings	Carload Minimum (Pounds)	Carload Ratings
	BOILERS, FURNACES, RADIATORS, STOVES, RELATED ARTICLES OR PARTS NAMED (Subject to Item 11960)—Concluded: **Group No. 1**			
13250	Coal hods (scuttles) or vases, steel; cookers or steamers, stock feed, noibn; furnaces, house heating, hot air, with or without equipment of air conditioning apparatus or thermostats; griddles, kettles, pots, skillets or spiders, sheet steel; holloware, cast iron, as described in Item 49880; house heating furnace casing parts; sugar or syrup evaporator kettles, iron; stove or range cabinets, closets or high shelves, steel; stove or range ovens; stove or range parts, iron or steel, other than castings, noibn; stove pipe drums or drum ovens; stove pipe or elbows, sheet iron, steel or tin plate, side seams closed; stove pipe thimbles, plate or sheet iron or steel or tin plate, side seams closed; stove or range reservoirs or reservoir attachments; tee joints and draft regulators combined, stove pipe.			
	Group No. 2			
13260	Air registers, noibn, including air louvres, iron or steel; andirons, iron; ash scrapers; heating furnace pipe or elbows, sheet iron, steel or tin plate; house heating furnace castings, iron; burners, gas, for coal, oil or wood stoves, see Note 58, Item 13271; oil burning outfits for brooders or coal or wood stoves; pans, baking, dripping or frying, sheet steel; fire pokers, iron; sad irons, with or without stands, other than self-heating; stove boards, iron or metal clad wood or fibreboard; stove cover lifters, iron; stove or range castings, iron; stove pipe, sheet iron, steel or tin plate, side seams not closed, nested; dampers, noibn, iron; stove pipe thimbles, cast iron or plate or sheet iron or tin plate, side seams not closed, nested; stove shovels, sheet steel; water heaters, noibn			
13261	Note 52.—Weight of articles in Group 2, Item 13260, must not exceed 50% of weight upon which charges are assessed.			
13265	Mixed CL of two or more of the following articles, viz.: Stoves or ranges, iron or steel; dampers, noibn, iron; electric logs, see Note 54, Item 13266; fireplace grates or grate baskets, with or without heating units; fireplace grate parts, noibn; gas logs; heaters, gas, with or without clay radiants; andirons (fire dogs); fenders or fireplace guards or screens, brass, see Note 54, Item 13266; fenders or fireplace guards or screens, iron or steel, plain or brass coated or plated, or with brass trimming; fireplace sets (shovels and tongs), with or without hearth brushes, holders or pokers, brass or brass and iron combined, see Note 54, Item 13266; fireplace sets (shovels and tongs), with or without hearth brushes, holders or pokers, iron; lighters, fire, brass or iron, see Note 54, Item 13266; or wood holders or racks, fireplace, see Note 54, Item 13266....		24,000R	45
13266	Note 54.—Aggregate weight of articles subject to this note must not exceed 50% of weight upon which charges are assessed.			
13267	Note 56.—Section 2 of Rule 34 is not applicable.			
13270	Superheaters, other than locomotive: SU, loose or in packages...	70	24,000R	40
	KD, or superheater parts, KD, loose or in packages................................	65	24,000R	40
13271	Note 58.—Ratings apply only on burners for converting coal, oil or wood stoves into gas stoves.			
13272	Note 60.—Weight of articles subject to this note shall not exceed 10% of weight upon which charges are assessed.			
13280	Tanks, oil stove, sheet steel, 26 gauge or thicker, capacity not exceeding 5 gallons, in boxes or crates........	110	16,000R	60
13281	Note 66.—Ratings also apply on stoves or ranges designed for separate permanent installation of oven and surface cooking units.			
13282	Note 68.—CL ratings will include iron or steel garbage or offal incinerators, not exceeding 25% of the weight upon which freight charges are assessed.			
13295	Bolster rolls for beds, couches or lounges, fibreboard with plywood ends and reinforcing ribs, upholstered, in Package 9F..	150	10,000R	100
13300	Bolster rolls for beds, couches or lounges, noibn, in boxes or crates............................	200	10,000R	100
13310	Bone, charred filtering (animal charcoal), other than spent, in bags or barrels....................	70	36,000	35
13320	Bone, charred filtering (animal charcoal), spent, in bags....................................	50	40,000	20
13330	Bone, charred filtering, synthetic, in bags or barrels.......................................	70	36,000	35
13340	Bone ash, in bags, barrels or boxes...	55	36,000	30
13350	Bones, human, noibn, prepaid, in barrels or boxes..	200	20,000R	100
13360	Bones, noibn, ground or not ground, LCL, in bags or barrels, or in barrels with cloth tops; CL, loose or in packages...	50	40,000	22½
13370	Book ends, moulded wood or plaster, in boxes...	85	24,000R	55
13380	Book stacks, library, consisting of iron brackets, floor framing, stairs, railings, standards, and shelves, in packages; also CL, loose..............................	70	36,000	40
13390	Boot or shoe arch supports or arch support insoles, in boxes................................	100	20,000R	70
13400	Boot or shoe forms or trees, in barrels or boxes...	85	20,000R	55
13410	**BOOTS, SHOES, OR BOOT OR SHOE FINDINGS:**			
13420	Boot or shoe findings, noibn, in bales, barrels or boxes, or in barrels with cloth tops..........	100	16,000R	70
13430	Boots or shoes, noibn, see Note 1, item 13431, in boxes; in trunks in crates; in salesmen's sample trunks, locked; in Packages 277 or 1197; also in straight CL in Package 1126....................	100	24,000R	70
13431	Note 1.—Ratings also apply on Huaraches (Mexican leather sandals) in bamboo baskets or hampers, tops securely closed.			
13440	Boots or shoes, old, used, leather, having value other than for reclamation of raw materials, prepaid, see Note 2, Item 13441, in packages; also CL, loose....................	85	36,000	50
13441	Note 2.—Old used shoes rebuilt or repaired, will be rated as shoes, noibn.			
13450	Boots or shoes, plastic, rubber or rubber and canvas, felt or wool combined, in bales or boxes.....	100	15,000R	70
13460	Boots or shoes, wooden or leather with wooden soles, in packages..........................	92½	24,000R	65
13470	Box toe boards, in packages; also CL, loose..	70	36,000	35

Reproduced by permission of tariff publisher.

FIG. 5-4

Freight Tariff No. W-1000

APPLICATION OF RATE BASES

BETWEEN (See Item 100) AND (See Item 100)	Greeley Centre Neb.	Green Bay Wis.	Greenbush Minn.	Grenville S.D.	Grinnell Iowa	Grover Colo.	Hallock Minn.	Hannaford N.D.	Hannibal Mo.	Harvard Ill.	Hawarden Iowa	Hartun Colo.	Hays Kan.	Hasen N.D.	Herington Kan.	Hermansville Mich.	Hermosa S.D.	Herrick S.D.	Hettinger N.D.	Hibbing Minn.
Rugby............N.D.	716	716	233	340	680	944	202	128	855	768	465	914	939	306	824	687	609	714	461	372
Rulo.............Neb.	240	619	712	627	237	546	718	621	251	477	244	438	318	699	179	715	619	347	669	636
Russell..........Kan.	335	844	919	834	479	474	925	828	457	606	451	482	27	906	121	941	695	506	875	868
St. Cloud........Minn.	489	350	262	223	317	828	287	241	495	401	250	737	712	433	596	367	558	487	461	193
St. Francis.......Kan.	309	918	935	850	568	502	941	844	620	809	467	363	363	922	332	985	646	487	892	884
St. Ignace........Mich.	937	256	681	735	619	1277	713	722	659	392	713	1186	1098	914	959	166	1064	935	966	477
St. James.........Minn.	358	380	430	345	220	697	436	363	408	388	133	607	581	488	465	414	498	356	457	314
St. Joseph........Mo.	284	579	737	652	213	587	743	646	207	437	269	479	293	724	154	676	657	383	694	614
St. Louis.........Mo.	583	458	854	812	305	890	880	833	⊕	⊕	545	783	561	983	414	553	940	668	952	719
Sabetha..........Kan.	223	640	740	655	273	524	747	649	267	498	272	414	277	727	155	736	604	349	697	666
Sabula...........Iowa	492	246	639	597	146	832	665	618	⊕	⊕	364	741	625	792	486	343	756	572	762	504
Sac City.........Iowa	250	464	545	460	143	589	552	472	317	362	115	499	462	561	347	540	510	302	530	442
Salem............S.D.	330	539	456	359	313	670	442	304	488	512	76	579	553	383	438	572	340	328	352	437
Salina...........Kan.	258	767	842	757	402	526	848	751	380	619	374	405	104	829	44	864	618	429	798	791
Salisbury.........Mo.	412	515	778	734	201	720	804	757	91	362	383	612	393	838	253	611	771	497	808	649
Sanborn..........Minn.	376	407	396	311	238	715	402	329	427	415	151	625	599	454	483	430	470	374	423	325
Sanish...........N.D.	793	817	368	428	768	962	336	247	942	871	543	933	1016	227	901	815	628	791	447	506
Sargent..........Neb.	102	750	766	681	408	475	773	675	530	641	298	389	406	754	308	816	538	314	723	716
Sauk Centre......Minn.	517	392	234	181	359	857	254	199	537	443	279	766	740	391	625	409	546	515	419	228
Sault Ste Marie...Mich.	955	273	685	739	664	1294	717	726	708	452	730	1203	1144	918	1004	184	1082	953	984	481
Sawyer...........Kan.	405	872	987	903	522	656	994	897	480	719	520	552	210	975	158	968	765	576	944	923
Schley...........Minn.	648	427	146	276	476	988	178	258	654	518	409	897	871	450	756	399	670	646	522	82
Scott City........Kan.	461	959	1044	959	594	437	1051	953	572	811	576	486	241	1032	228	1055	726	632	1001	993
Scottsbluff.......Neb.	365	980	897	804	638	175	883	746	729	871	529	145	565	765	467	1046	222	544	735	946
Sedalia..........Colo.	490	1105	1095	1001	762	130	1081	943	832	996	554	180	361	963	505	1171	420	669	932	1071
Sedalia..........Mo.	413	568	831	787	254	709	857	792	144	415	415	603	371	870	224	664	794	529	840	702
Seney............Mich.	891	210	605	660	601	1231	637	646	641	388	667	1140	1080	838	941	120	1012	889	906	401
Severy...........Kan.	375	757	920	835	410	643	926	829	364	605	452	522	231	907	114	854	735	521	877	811
Sharon Springs....Kan.	355	965	982	897	608	317	988	891	623	851	514	366	140	969	287	1031	606	534	938	931
Shawano..........Wis.	690	38	553	544	403	1030	585	570	447	190	498	939	882	956	743	107	860	721	763	351
Shawnee..........Wyo.	479	1023	864	771	731	165	850	677	843	948	539	259	612	732	581	1056	190	575	702	940
Sheboygan........Wis.	700	63	613	604	356	1040	645	631	397	129	522	949	835	817	696	159	905	745	822	411
Sheldon..........Ill.	653	275	802	760	304	986	828	781	⊕	⊕	533	881	717	962	578	372	925	738	931	601
Sheldon..........Iowa	267	471	464	379	216	607	471	392	395	415	43	516	490	480	375	505	429	265	449	404
Shenandoah.......Iowa	218	571	657	572	189	547	663	566	268	429	189	441	383	644	243	556	577	303	614	562
Sheridan Lake....Colo.	536	1034	1120	1035	669	361	1126	1029	647	886	652	411	319	1107	303	1131	651	707	1077	1069
Sidney...........Neb.	328	943	908	815	601	102	894	757	691	834	492	73	504	776	429	1009	233	507	746	909
Simpson (Johnson Co.)....Ill.	733	552	995	953	446	1040	1021	974	⊕	⊕	686	933	711	1123	564	649	1081	818	1093	835
Sioux City........Iowa	211	527	512	427	236	550	518	421	398	453	44	459	434	499	318	561	444	209	468	461
Sioux Falls.......S.D.	299	499	437	340	273	639	444	337	448	473	46	548	522	422	407	533	380	297	392	397
Sisseton.........S.D.	537	503	318	193	439	831	304	230	627	552	284	786	760	385	645	521	496	535	354	370
Smithboro........Ill.	625	432	858	816	309	932	884	837	⊕	⊕	549	825	604	987	464	528	944	710	956	711
South Beloit.....Ill.	588	150	634	592	242	928	660	613	⊕	⊕	433	837	721	805	581	247	819	653	802	434
Sparta...........Ill.	637	490	908	866	359	944	934	887	⊕	⊕	599	837	607	1036	460	587	994	722	1006	769
Spencer..........Iowa	303	443	500	415	180	643	507	428	359	379	79	552	527	511	411	486	465	302	486	386
Spooner..........Wis.	570	253	353	379	473	909	385	394	510	328	345	818	786	586	659	247	697	568	599	149
Springfield.......Ill.	580	369	794	752	261	894	820	773	⊕	⊕	501	786	584	938	445	486	895	665	908	642
Stafford.........Kan.	360	841	944	858	479	568	949	852	449	688	475	507	165	930	113	937	720	531	899	880
Stanley..........N.D.	795	804	348	419	759	1023	317	214	934	856	544	993	1018	315	903	799	688	793	535	486
Stapleton.........Neb.	212	827	843	759	485	423	850	753	575	718	376	365	411	831	313	893	519	391	800	973
Sterling..........Colo.	343	958	948	855	616	106	934	796	707	849	507	33	460	816	443	1024	273	522	785	924
Stiles Jct........Wis.	727	28	575	575	419	1061	607	602	463	207	530	971	899	788	759	75	892	753	794	371
Stockton.........Kan.	271	838	867	782	481	539	874	776	477	707	399	418	217	854	157	914	630	442	824	817
Strasburg........Colo.	477	1086	1003	1015	730	144	1094	957	779	973	635	194	299	977	443	1153	434	656	949	1053
Stratton.........Neb.	256	866	883	798	516	275	889	792	586	757	415	202	329	870	298	932	442	435	839	832
Streator.........Ill.	583	297	732	690	231	916	758	711	⊕	⊕	460	811	648	888	508	370	852	668	858	556
Streeter.........N.D.	582	630	304	241	547	810	290	134	721	687	332	780	805	257	690	648	475	580	537	411
Studley..........Kan.	330	923	956	871	558	388	963	865	536	775	488	398	157	944	200	1006	677	409	913	906
Sturgeon Bay.....Wis.	762	58	630	621	449	1102	662	648	492	236	570	1011	928	834	180	1063	934	793	839	428
Sublette.........Kan.	479	971	1062	977	606	473	1069	971	580	819	594	523	261	1049	240	1067	763	661	1019	1007

⊕For rates refer to I. F. A. Tariff No. I-1002, I. C. C. No. 757, R. G. Raasch, Agent.

Sioux Falls, South Dakota and Hannibal, Missouri is 448. Finally, it is necessary to establish the specific rate per hundred pounds. Figure 5-5 (page 159) contains a tariff page which uses the rating (class) and rate bases number to determine the rate, which is $3.01 in this example.* The total charge can now be determined using this formula:

Rate (per hundred pounds) × Weight (in hundred pound units) = Charge

$$\$3.01 \times 300 = \$903$$

Exception rates can best be thought of as modified class rates. They are designed to produce a less expensive rate than the class rate. The class rate formula, however, is still used to calculate the freight charge. The exception rate is lower than the class rate by taking "exception" to some aspect of the class rate. Thus, the exception tariff may provide for a lower rating or class than the class tariff, it may provide for less expensive packaging requirements, or it may require a lower minimum weight to qualify for a TL or CL rate. An exception rate, since it produces a lower overall charge, has priority over a class rate. Exceptions are generally the result of competitive factors, either between modes or between individual carriers of the same mode. They also are established because of unusual regional or local operating conditions. Figure 5-6 (page 160) illustrates a page from a typical exception tariff. This particular tariff deals with exceptions to tariff rules.

Commodity rates can be thought of as custom-made economy rates that a carrier makes available because a specific commodity is shipped in large quantities and/or at frequent intervals. These rates, which are found in commodity tariffs, are specific in nature. They state the commodity, the origins and destinations involved and the minimum weight required for the commodity rate. Figure 5-7 (page 161) illustrates the specific nature of commodity rates. Commodity rates are lower than either class or exception rates, and hence should be used whenever they are available.

The railroad industry is very dependent on commodity rates, although all modes use them. One rate authority has noted, "The economy of this country has been built around the commodity rate."[29]

HIERARCHY OF RATES

Class, exception, and commodity rates have been discussed. It is important to note that there is a priority or *hierarchy of rates* regarding which of these rates to use at any given time. The Interstate Commerce Act stated that *commodity* rates have the highest priority. In other words, whenever a shipment is tendered to a carrier, the commodity rate should be used if it is available. If it does not exist, then an *excep-*

[29] Edward A. Starr, *The Interpretation of Freight Tariffs* (Fort Worth, Texas: The Transportation Press, 1961), p. 106.
* Please note that interpolation is *not* used in tariff rate determination.

FIG. 5-5

Tariff W-1000

CLASS RATES IN CENTS PER 100 POUNDS

RATE BASIS NUMBERS	CLASSES																							
	400	300	250	200	175	150	125	110	100	97½	95	92½	90	87½	85	82½	80	77½	75	73½	72½	70	67½	66
5	328	246	205	164	144	123	103	90	82	80	78	76	74	72	70	68	66	64	62	60	59	57	55	54
10	356	267	223	178	156	134	111	98	89	87	85	82	80	78	76	73	71	69	67	65	65	62	60	59
15	384	288	240	192	168	144	120	106	96	94	91	89	86	84	82	79	77	74	72	71	70	67	65	63
20	408	306	255	204	179	153	128	112	102	99	97	94	92	89	87	84	82	79	77	75	74	71	69	67
25	420	315	263	210	184	158	131	116	105	102	100	97	95	92	89	87	84	81	79	77	76	74	71	69
30	448	336	280	224	196	168	140	123	112	109	106	104	101	98	95	92	90	87	84	82	81	78	76	74
35	460	345	288	230	201	173	144	127	115	112	109	106	104	101	98	95	92	89	86	85	83	81	78	76
40	480	360	300	240	210	180	150	132	120	117	114	111	108	105	102	99	96	93	90	88	87	84	81	79
45	492	369	308	246	215	185	154	135	123	120	117	114	111	108	105	101	98	95	92	90	89	86	83	81
50	504	378	315	252	221	189	158	139	126	123	120	117	113	110	107	104	101	98	95	93	91	88	85	83
55	524	393	328	262	229	197	164	144	131	128	124	121	118	115	111	108	105	102	98	96	95	92	88	86
60	536	402	335	268	235	201	168	147	134	131	127	124	121	117	114	111	107	104	101	98	97	94	90	88
65	556	417	348	278	243	209	174	153	139	136	132	129	125	122	118	115	111	108	104	102	101	97	94	92
70	564	423	353	282	247	212	176	155	141	137	134	130	127	123	120	116	113	109	106	104	102	99	95	93
75	572	429	358	286	250	215	179	157	143	139	136	132	129	125	122	118	114	111	107	105	104	100	97	94
80	588	441	368	294	257	221	184	162	147	143	140	136	132	129	125	121	118	114	110	108	107	103	99	97
85	600	450	375	300	263	225	188	165	150	146	143	139	135	131	128	124	120	116	113	110	109	105	101	99
90	616	462	385	308	270	231	193	169	154	150	146	142	139	135	131	127	123	119	116	113	112	108	104	102
95	624	468	390	312	273	234	195	172	156	152	148	144	140	137	133	129	125	121	117	115	113	109	105	103
100	636	477	398	318	278	239	199	175	159	155	151	147	143	139	135	131	127	123	119	117	115	111	107	105
110	656	492	410	328	287	246	205	180	164	160	156	152	148	144	139	135	131	127	123	121	119	115	111	108
120	676	507	423	338	296	254	211	186	169	165	161	156	152	148	144	139	135	131	127	124	123	118	114	112
130	700	525	438	350	306	263	219	193	175	171	166	162	158	153	149	144	140	136	131	129	127	123	118	116
140	720	540	450	360	315	270	225	198	180	176	171	167	162	158	153	149	144	140	135	132	131	126	122	119
150	740	555	463	370	324	278	231	204	185	180	176	171	167	162	157	153	148	143	139	134	134	130	125	122
160	756	567	473	378	331	284	236	208	189	184	180	175	170	165	161	156	151	146	142	139	137	132	128	125
170	784	588	490	392	343	294	245	216	196	191	186	181	176	172	167	162	157	152	147	144	142	137	132	129
180	796	597	498	398	348	299	249	219	199	194	189	184	179	174	169	164	159	154	149	146	144	139	134	131
190	812	609	508	406	355	305	254	223	203	198	193	188	183	178	173	167	162	157	152	149	147	142	137	134
200	828	621	518	414	362	311	259	228	207	202	197	191	186	181	176	171	166	160	155	152	150	145	140	137
210	852	639	533	426	373	320	266	234	213	208	202	197	192	186	181	176	170	165	160	157	154	149	144	141
220	868	651	543	434	380	326	271	239	217	212	206	201	195	190	184	179	174	168	163	159	157	152	146	143
230	884	663	553	442	387	332	276	243	221	215	210	204	199	193	188	182	177	171	166	162	160	155	149	146
240	900	675	563	450	394	338	281	248	225	219	214	208	203	197	191	186	180	174	169	165	163	158	152	149
250	940	705	588	470	411	353	294	259	235	229	223	217	212	206	200	194	188	182	176	173	170	165	159	155
280	964	723	603	482	422	362	301	265	241	235	229	223	217	211	205	199	193	187	181	177	175	169	163	159
300	996	747	623	498	436	374	311	274	249	243	237	230	224	218	212	205	199	193	187	183	181	174	168	164
320	1032	774	645	516	452	387	323	284	258	252	245	239	232	226	219	213	206	200	194	190	187	181	174	170
340	1060	795	663	530	464	398	331	292	265	258	252	245	239	232	225	219	212	205	199	195	192	186	179	175
360	1092	819	683	546	478	410	341	300	273	266	259	253	246	239	232	225	218	212	205	201	198	191	184	180
380	1116	837	698	558	488	419	349	307	279	272	265	258	251	244	237	230	223	216	209	205	202	195	188	184
400	1148	861	718	574	502	431	359	316	287	280	273	265	258	251	244	237	230	222	215	211	208	201	194	189
420	1180	885	738	590	516	443	369	325	295	288	280	273	266	258	251	243	236	229	221	217	214	207	199	195
440	1204	903	753	602	527	452	376	331	301	293	286	278	271	263	256	248	241	233	226	221	218	211	203	199
460	1228	921	768	614	537	461	384	338	307	299	292	284	276	269	261	253	246	238	230	226	223	215	207	203
480	1260	945	788	630	551	473	394	347	315	307	299	291	284	276	268	260	252	244	236	232	228	221	213	208
500	1288	966	805	644	564	483	403	354	322	314	306	298	290	282	274	266	258	250	242	237	233	225	217	213
520	1308	981	818	654	572	491	409	360	327	319	311	302	294	286	278	270	262	253	245	240	237	229	221	216
540	1344	1008	840	672	588	504	420	370	336	328	319	311	302	294	286	277	269	260	252	247	244	235	227	222
560	1368	1026	855	684	599	513	428	376	342	333	325	316	308	299	291	282	274	265	257	251	248	239	231	226
580	1396	1047	873	698	611	524	436	384	349	340	332	323	314	305	297	288	279	270	262	257	253	244	236	230
600	1420	1065	888	710	621	533	444	391	355	346	337	328	320	311	302	293	284	275	266	261	257	249	240	234
620	1448	1086	905	724	634	543	453	398	362	353	344	335	326	317	308	299	290	281	272	266	262	253	244	239
640	1476	1107	923	738	646	554	461	406	369	360	351	341	332	323	314	304	295	286	277	272	267	258	249	244
660	1508	1131	943	754	660	566	471	415	377	368	358	349	339	330	320	311	302	292	283	277	273	264	254	249
680	1532	1149	958	766	670	575	479	421	383	373	364	354	345	335	326	316	306	297	287	282	278	268	259	253
700	1560	1170	975	780	683	585	488	429	390	380	371	361	351	341	332	322	312	302	292	287	283	273	263	257
720	1592	1194	995	796	697	597	498	438	398	388	378	368	358	348	338	328	318	308	299	293	289	279	269	263
740	1616	1212	1010	808	707	606	505	444	404	394	384	374	364	354	343	333	323	313	303	297	293	283	273	267
760	1640	1230	1025	820	718	615	513	451	410	400	390	379	369	359	349	338	328	318	308	301	297	287	277	271
780	1672	1254	1045	836	732	627	523	460	418	408	397	387	376	366	355	345	334	324	313	308	302	293	282	276
800	1700	1275	1063	850	744	638	531	468	425	414	404	393	383	372	361	351	340	329	319	312	308	298	287	281
825	1724	1293	1078	862	754	647	539	474	431	420	409	399	388	377	366	356	345	334	323	317	312	307	291	284
850	1756	1317	1098	878	768	659	548	483	439	428	417	406	395	384	373	362	351	340	329	323	318	307	296	290
875	1784	1338	1115	892	781	669	558	491	446	435	424	413	401	390	379	368	357	346	335	328	323	312	301	294
900	1812	1359	1133	906	793	680	566	498	453	442	430	419	408	396	385	374	362	351	340	333	328	317	306	299
925	1840	1380	1150	920	805	690	575	506	460	449	437	426	414	403	391	380	368	357	345	338	334	322	311	304

Reproduced by permission of tariff publisher.

Fig. 5-6

		SECTION 1
		EXCEPTIONS TO RULES OF UNIFORM CLASSIFICATION
Item	**SUBJECT**	**RULE**
1000	REFRIGERATORS IN TRAP CAR SERVICE	(EXCEPTION TO RULE 5) Ratings applying on Refrigerators,Store Display,as described in Items 30658 and 30690 of UFC 6,when handled in trap car service and shipped as less carload freight from one consignor to one consignee,will apply in Package 998 of UFC in connection with shipments of 6,000 lbs or more.
1020	MIXED CARLOADS	(EXCEPTION TO RULE 10,SECTION 1) Provisions published in Section 2 of Rule 10 of UFC will also apply on the following: Glass,polished prism or wired,as described in Items 45960,45970 or 45980 of UFC 6,or Glass,rolled,as described in Items 46040,46050,46060,46070 or 46071 of UFC 6,in mixed carloads with Glass,laminated,as described in Items 45960, 45970,45980 or 45981 of UFC 6,or Glass,window,as described in Items 46100, 46110,46120 or 46130 of UFC 6. (EXCEPTION TO RULE 10,SECTION 2) Provisions published in Section 1 of Rule 10 of UFC will also apply on the following: Cement,as described in Item 21680 of UFC 6,in mixed carloads with Alumina, calcined or hydrated. Doors,glazed or not glazed; Sash,glazed or not glazed; Frames,door,with or without weather strips attached,KD; Frames,window,with or without pulleys and with or without weather strips attached,KD,and Moulding,carpenters; Plywood and Built-up Wood. Furniture,as described in Items 42535,42900 to 42910 (Steel Filing Cabinets), 43050,43070,43470 (Metallic (not wooden) Desks),43480 (Steel Desks),43950, 43960 (Steel Tables) of UFC 6.
1030	MIXED CARLOADS	(EXCEPTION TO RULE 10) The provisions of Rule 10 of UFC will also be applied subject to the following: Rule 24 of UFC will not apply to mixed carload shipments under the following conditions: When the car carrying the excess exceeds 40 feet 7 inches in length and contains any article which would be subject to Rule 34 of UFC if shipped in straight carloads. (See Note 1). NOTE 1.-Closed cars exceeding 40 feet 7 inches but not exceeding 41 feet 6 inches and not exceeding 3,925 cubic feet capacity will be considered as not exceeding 40 feet 7 inches in length.
1040	MIXED CARLOADS OF ALUMINUM LADDERS WITH WOODENWARE.	(EXCEPTION TO RULE 10) When Aluminum Ladders,as described in Item 55600 of UFC 6 are shipped in mixed carloads with two or more of the articles described in Item 98040 of UFC 6,they will be charged for at the actual weight and straight carload class rate on the weight of the Aluminum Ladders as described in Item 55600 of UFC 6 and at the actual weight and mixed carload commodity rate column,class or exception to the Classification rate on the weight of the other articles in the shipment. The car-load minimum weight will be the highest provided for the Aluminum Ladders or for mixed carload shipments of two or more of the other articles in the mixed carload and any deficit in the minimum weight will be charged for at the highest carload rate as described above.
1060	MIXED CARLOADS OF COOLING OR FREEZING APPARATUS, HEATERS, STOVES,ETC.	(EXCEPTION TO RULE 10) Any or all of the following articles: Air conditioning cabinet sleeves,sheet steel,as described in Item 85920 of UFC 6 Air coolers,heaters,humidifiers,dehumidifiers or washers and blowers or fans combined,noibn,as described in Item 58510 of UFC 6 Broilers,noibn,cookers,noibn or roasters,electric,as described in Item 12250 of UFC 6 Cabinets,air conditioning,without air conditioning equipment,SU,as described in Item 19520 of UFC 6. Cabinets or Lockers,kitchen,noibn,steel,with or without glass,SU Cooling boxes,noibn,as described in Item 30630 of UFC 6 Cooling boxes or refrigerators and cooling or freezing apparatus combined,as described in Item 30650 of UFC 6. Cooling or freezing machines,as described in Item 62750 of UFC 6 Disc heaters,frying pans,griddles,grills or hot plates,as described in Item 13140 of UFC 6 Dish washing machines or dish washing machines and cabinet sinks combined,as described in Item 60910 of UFC 6. Electric Baking Oven Parts,viz.: Automatic Timing Control Devices (Continued on next page)

Reproduced by permission of tariff publisher.

Fig. 5-7

TARIFF 999-N

		SECTION 1 - SPECIFIC COMMODITY RATES			
Item	COMMODITIES	FROM (Except as noted)	TO (Except as noted)	RATES IN CENTS PER 100 LBS (Except as noted)	Route
2530	IRON AND STEEL,viz.: Scrap,as described in Item 480. Min wt 75,000 lbs. RATES IN CENTS PER 2,000 LBS.	BETWEEN Davenport . . . .Iowa	AND Hoopeston . . . .Ill.	541	60,101
2540	IRON AND STEEL,viz.: Scrap,as described in Item 480. Min wt 75,000 lbs. RATES IN CENTS PER 2,000 LBS.	Clinton . . . . .Iowa	Beloit. . . . .Wis. South Beloit. .Ill.	550	1
		Dubuque . . . . .Iowa	Beloit. . . . .Wis. South Beloit. .Ill.	550	1
	+IRON and STEEL,Scrap. Min wt 56,000 lbs. RATES IN CENTS PER 2,240 LBS. + Issued in compliance with order of the Interstate Commerce Commission in Docket 31238 of June 8,1954.	Clinton . . . . .Iowa Fulton. . . . .Ill. Savanna . . . .Ill.	Beloit. . . . .Wis.	625 605 584	1
2550	IRON AND STEEL,viz.: Scrap. Min wt and description as shown in Item 480. RATES IN CENTS PER 2,240 LBS. ① Applies between.	Dubuque . . . . .Iowa	① Davenport . .Iowa	395	1
			① Byron . . . .Ill. De Kalb . . . .Ill. ① East Moline .Ill. ① Freeport. . .Ill. ① Holcomb . . .Ill. Kingston. . . .Ill. ① Moline. . . .Ill. ① Rochelle. . .Ill. ① Rockford. . .Ill. ① Rock Island .Ill.	421	1
2560	IRON OR STEEL,viz.: Scrap. Min wt and description as shown in Item 480,except as noted. RATES IN CENTS PER 2,240 LBS. ① Between Davenport,Iowa and Clinton, Iowa,+321 per 2,240 lbs. ② Min wt 89,600 lbs. + Applies Northbound.	BETWEEN Davenport . . .Iowa East Moline . .Ill. Moline. . . . .Ill. Rock Island . .Ill.	AND Clinton . . . .Iowa Fulton. . . . .Ill.	{ ① 345 +② 297	1
		Savanna . . . .Ill. Mt.Carroll. . .Ill.	Davenport . . .Iowa East Moline . .Ill. Moline. . . . .Ill. Rock Island . .Ill.	382	
		Clinton . . . .Iowa Fulton. . . . .Ill.	De Kalb . . . .Ill.	421	
2570	IRON OR STEEL,viz.: Scrap. Min wt and description as shown in Item 480. RATE IN CENTS PER 2,240 LBS.	Bettendorf. . .Iowa Camanche. . . .Iowa Clinton . . . .Iowa Davenport . . .Iowa East Moline . .Ill. Fulton. . . . .Ill. LeClaire. . . .Iowa Moline. . . . .Ill. Pleasant Valley . . . .Iowa Princeton . . .Iowa Rock Island . .Ill. Savanna . . . .Ill. Thomson . . . .Ill.	Alton . . . . .Ill. Federal . . . .Ill. East St.Louis .Ill. St.Louis. . . . Mo.	691	3,98,123, 124 3,26,35, 57,64, 98,123

Reproduced by permission of tariff publisher.

tion rate should be used. If it is not available, the *class* rate can always be found for any product. This is even true for new products that are not currently located in the class tariffs. A procedure known as the *rule of analogy* is used. This states that if a product is not described in the tariff, then the shipper and carrier will agree to use the rating or class of the most similar existing product in the tariff. Eventually, they will arrange to have the new product placed in the classification tariff. This is why a class rate is sometimes referred to as "the old standby," because it is possible to find a class rate for every product.

ADDITIONAL TYPES OF FREIGHT RATES

Class, exception and commodity rates are the basic transportation freight rates. However, a large number of additional aspects are further used to classify *commodity* freight rates. This section will discuss them.

QUANTITY ORIENTED RATES

Many commodity rates are established on the basis of the quantity or volume of freight that is tendered to the carriers.

Incentive Rates have been primarily used by the railroad industry. Railroads have often had a given rate for car-load (CL) quantities. Assume the CL minimum was 30,000 pounds, yet the rail car itself frequently had the physical capacity to hold 70,000 to 100,000 pounds. Since it costs the railroad very little more to haul a car with 100,000 pounds as opposed to the same car with 30,000 pounds, the railroads initiated rates designed to provide an "incentive" to shippers to load more freight into each car. An incentive rate would be: 103 cents/100 pounds for the first 30,000 pounds; 65 cents/100 pounds from 30,000 pounds to 60,000 pounds; and 51 cents for 60,000 to 100,000 pounds.

Volume Rates are found in the trucking industry. They generally are used for shipments that are larger than the truck-load (TL) minimum and they are designed to compete with railroad CL rates. A major difference between the rail CL rate and volume truck rates is that the latter includes loading and unloading assistance by the truck driver. CL rates provide that all loading and unloading is done by the shipper and consignee.

Multiple-Car Rates are used by railroads. Generally, the rates call for a minimum of five cars and a maximum of 25. The logic for the significant rate reductions found is that by moving cars in blocks, switching costs at terminal areas are reduced. These rates specify the minimum weight that must be loaded into each car. Multiple-trailer rates are also used by the truckers to compete with the railroads' multiple-car rates.

Train-Load Rates are the rail rates used with unit trains, which specialize in entire train-load movements of coal, lumber, etc. The train-load tariffs often specify the minimum tonnage to be transported via each unit train and also the minimum number of trains that will be operated each week, month, or year.

MISCELLANEOUS RATE DEFINITIONS

A *local rate* implies that a transportation service from City A to City B is performed by just one carrier. It has nothing to do with geographical considerations. A local rate on the Burlington Northern Railroad can apply from Chicago to Seattle. On the other hand, a *joint rate* extends over the line of two or more carriers.

A *through rate* is one that applies from origin to destination for a shipment. It can be either a local through rate or a joint through rate. A *through route* is an arrangement between connecting carriers in which a transportation service is offered from origin on one carrier's line to a destination on the other carrier's line. A common description is a *joint-rate* and a *through-route*.

Combination rates exist when there are no joint or local rates from origin to destination. Therefore, the applicable rate is a combination of the local rate or joint rates. The latter is feasible, as shown in Figure 5-8. The shipment originates in City A and is bound for City E. If there are no joint rates, then the applicable rate will be a combination rate made up of local rates number 1, 2, 3 and 4. However, assume a joint rate does exist from City B to City E. Then the applicable rate is also a combination rate, made up of local rate number 1 and joint rate number 1.

The *aggregate of intermediates* rule is important regarding combination rates as opposed to through rates. It states that the through rate should be less expensive than the combination or aggregate of the intermediate rates. If it is found that the combination or aggregate rate is less expensive, then most tariffs specify that the lower rate may be used in lieu of the through rate.

"All-commodity" rates are also known as *"freight, all kinds"* (FAK). These are commodity rates established by the railroads and motor carriers primarily to retard the growth of private truck transportation. These rates are applied only on the basis of weight regardless of the type of freight that is actually transported. The most frequent users of FAK rates are retail chain stores, forwarders, and shippers' cooperatives, all of which transport large shipments containing a variety of unrelated products.

It was noted earlier that common carriers are responsible for the "full actual loss" if they receive a valid loss or damage claim from a shipper or consignee. However, in the case of *released value rates* this is not true. This involves lower rates to the shipper in return for his agreeing to a reduced liability for the common carrier. When released value rates are

FIG. 5-8 Combination rates.

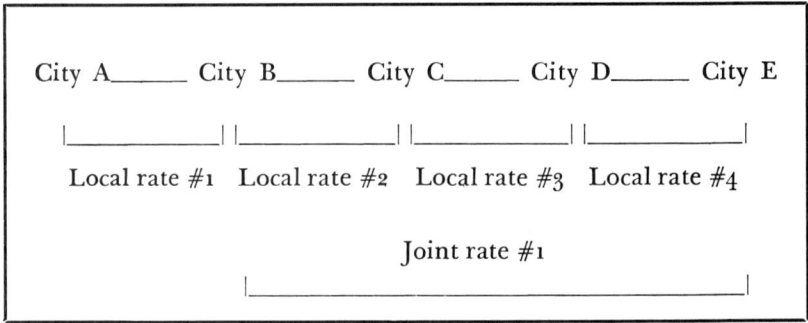

City A_____ City B_____ City C_____ City D_____ City E

|_____| |_____| |_____| |_____|

Local rate #1 Local rate #2 Local rate #3 Local rate #4

Joint rate #1

|_____|

applicable, it is important that the shipper determine whether additional insurance is needed for the goods given to the carrier.

A *"paper rate"* is one which is legally filed in a tariff, but which is seldom if ever, used. That is, it exists on paper, but it has no real-world application. The "yak fat" rate, had it been established, would have been an example.

A *blanket rate* is also known as *group* rate. It involves the same rate from one origin to a destination area in which all points therein pay the same rate. Thus a railroad rate on plywood from Seattle may have one and the same rate for all points east of the Mississippi River and north of the Ohio River to the Pennsylvania state line. Blanket rates are used most extensively in the railroad industry. A primary reason for the existence of blanket rates is that it greatly simplifies tariff preparation, because the various locations in the blanketed area do not have to be individually named. The railroads also use blanket rates to prevent Section 4—long and short haul—violations. This is done by giving the intermediate locations the same rate as the more distant destinations.

Section 22 of the Interstate Commerce Act allows reduced rates for governmental organizations. Reduced rates under Section 22 are extensively used by the United States Government. The Department of Defense uses Section 22 rates for about 70 percent of its traffic by weight. The use of Section 22 rates is a controversial area and the D.O.T. has proposed that these rates only be available to the government during times of national emergency.[30]

A *measurement rate* is very frequently used in ocean carrier transportation. It involves what is commonly called *ship's option*. This indicates that the ship will define a ton of freight as being 2240 pounds or 40 cubic feet, whichever produces the greater revenue.

[30] For further information, see: James C. Johnson, "Section 22: Panacea or Parasite?," *Transportation Journal* (Summer, 1974), pp. 34–40 and Enrico DiGiammarino and Donald F. Wood, "Motor Carrier Section 22 Tenders: Do They Cover Variable Costs?," *The Transportation Law Journal* (July, 1975), pp. 155–176.

Export and import rates will be discussed in chapter eleven. At this point it should be noted that export and import rates have priority over domestic rates and they are also less expensive. For example, the rail rate on grain from Minneapolis to New Orleans bound for overseas is less than the domestic rate for grain between these same two cities. The rationale for lower export and import rates is that without them, the traffic might not move at all because foreign competitors closer to the markets would have price advantage.

SUMMARY

This chapter has presented an overview of transportation regulation and rates. The transportation industry, because of its public nature and importance to commerce, has been regulated since the 1600's in England by the common law. The United States followed this precedent until the 1870's when an agrarian revolt against the railroads led to the enactment of the Granger Laws and eventually the 1887 *Act to Regulate Commerce*. This vanguard legislation was designed to promote "just and reasonable" railroad rates and to eliminate unreasonable personal, place, and commodity discrimination. The law was administered by the Interstate Commerce Commission, an independent regulatory body. The law was subsequently strengthened by legislation as problem-areas developed.

Starting with the railroad industry in 1887, the other modes of transportation were subsequently brought under federal regulation. The 1906 *Hepburn Act* regulated the oil pipeline industry. The trucking industry became regulated under the 1935 *Motor Carrier Act*. Inland water carriers were added with the *Transportation Act of 1940*. Finally, the freight-forwarders became federally controlled in 1942.

The air carriers came under federal regulation with the 1938 *Civil Aeronautics Act*, which created the Civil Aeronautics Board. The intercontinental ocean shipping industry has been subject to various forms of regulation since 1916. This industry is currently regulated by the Federal Maritime Commission.

The Department of Transportation was created in 1966 to coordinate federal programs in transportation research, promotional policy, and safety regulation.

Common carriers can be distinguished from other carriers because of their four fundamental duties: to serve, to deliver, to charge reasonable rates, and to avoid discrimination. *Contract carriers* are also "for-hire" in nature, although they only serve a limited number of customers under specific contracts. *Private transportation* involves a company performing its own transportation in its own vehicles.

Freight rate determination is complex. A primary reason for this situation is that value-of-service pricing is extensively used relative to cost-of-service pricing.

The three basic types of freight rates are: class, exception, and commodity. Additional rates include: incentive, volume, multiple-car and multiple-trailer, train-load, local and joint, through, combination, all commodity, released value, paper, blanket or group, Section 22, measurement, and export and import.

QUESTIONS FOR DISCUSSION AND REVIEW

1. The transportation industry has been subjected to governmental regulation in England since the 1600's. What factors warranted this action during a period where the basic concept of *Laissez-faire* was predominant?

2. The Grange was very active in demanding both state and federal regulation for the railroad industry. Discuss why the Grange took this position.

3. Two basic Supreme Court cases were influential regarding the eventual passage in 1887 of the *Act to Regulate Commerce*. Discuss each completely. Be sure to mention the key point each case established.

4. Discuss briefly the key elements of the 1887 *Act to Regulate Commerce*.

5. What was the basic reason for federal regulation of oil pipelines in 1906?

6. Discuss briefly positive reasons for federal trucking regulation in 1935.

7. What were the negative points regarding federal trucking regulation?

8. What major concession did the agricultural interests obtain in the 1935 Motor Carrier Act? Why?

9. Define or discuss briefly:

(a) rate bureau
(b) the National Transportation Policy
(c) the *Ingot Molds* case
(d) permit

(e) "inherent advantage"
(f) tariff
(g) the rule of analogy
(h) freight bill auditor

10. Why did the airline industry become federally regulated? Discuss.

11. Take a position *for* or *against* transportation deregulation and defend your answer.

12. What is a "transportation company?" Do you believe they should be encouraged in the United States? Why?

13. Common carriers have four basic obligations. Discuss each.

14. Discuss a common carrier's obligation regarding loss and damage claims. Be sure to mention the exemptions that are available to common carriers.

15. Discuss the concept of contract carriage as opposed to common carriage.

16. What is an exempt carrier? What products can they transport?

17. Compare and contrast full-cost versus value-of-service pricing.

18. Discuss the basic factors needed to determine a class rate.

19. What is an exception rate? Why are they used?

20. Discuss briefly why commodity rates are established.

21. What is the hierarchy-of-rates concept?

22. Discuss each of the following:

(a) incentive rates

(b) volume rates

(c) multiple-car and multiple-trailer rates

(d) train-load rates

(e) aggregate of inter-mediates rule

(f) any-quantity rates

(g) minimum rates

(h) local rates

(i) joint rates

(j) through rates

(k) combination rates

(l) all commodity rates

(m) released value rates

(n) paper rates

(o) blanket or group rates

(p) Section 22 rates

(q) measurement rates

(r) export and import rates

CASE 5-1   BOONE SHOE COMPANY

"Red" Boone founded the Boone Shoe Company in St. Joseph, Missouri during the 1930's. Unable to find work as a sheet metal worker, Red started to make moccasins for friends who had always admired the ones he had made for himself. Over time, the reputation of Boone's shoes spread, and Red expanded his product line and hired additional employees.

The real growth of the company took place during World War II. In 1942, almost as a joke, Red submitted a bid to the War Department to produce 100,000 pairs of combat boots. Much to his surprise, the contract was accepted, probably because Red noted in the bid that a sufficient non-combative labor force (females and retirees) existed in the area to produce the boots.

The main production input, leather, was easily obtained at the nearby Kansas City stockyards. After the war, the Boone company expanded its production of civilian shoes and related products and also continued to supply the military services with all types of leather footware.

Red Boone's son, Barry, was in charge of all marketing and distribution activities. Larry Gitman functioned as the firm's warehouse, purchasing and traffic manager. Three years before, he had graduated from Central Methodist College in Fayette, Missouri.

After two years experience as a management trainee with a large motor common carrier, Larry had accepted the position at Boone's Shoe

Company. Because of the firm's steady annual growth rate of 15 percent, Barry Boone had authorized Larry to hire an assistant.

Steve Knapp, although just out of high school, was working part-time from 1:00 to 6:00 p.m. and also attending the local community college. Steve had progressed so rapidly that Larry felt comfortable taking a three-week vacation, his first extended vacation in some years.

During Larry's vacation, Steve assumed Larry's responsibilities. As Steve sat in his office, the intercom buzzed and Barry asked Steve to pick up line #3 and take part in the conversation. The call was from Tom Cook, Boone's salesman for Minnesota and Wisconsin. Tom stated, "I'm calling from the buying office of Lawson department stores in Green Bay. Although they're currently overstocked in shoes, they are interested in buying a sizeable quantity of our 'Light Stride' arch support insoles. They plan on giving them away with their shoes in order to stimulate shoe sales. They want to buy FOB destination. I need to know in the next few minutes the cost of sending 17,000 pounds of the arch supports from St. Joseph to Green Bay."

Steve asked, "Will they accept a rail shipment? It's less expensive and we usually receive fairly good rail service on our northbound shipments."

Tom replied, "The buyer said he expected the shipment to come via rail."

Barry came on the line and asked, "Steve—can you look up this info for Tom?"

Steve said, "No problem, I'll call you back with the answer in 15 minutes or less."

Question One: Assume there are no commodity or exception rates in effect for this shipment. Using Figures 5-3, 5-4, and 5-5, calculate the applicable rate.

Question Two: Steve remembered that he had heard Larry speak of shipping "wind." This involved paying the CL minimum weight in order to receive the CL rate, even if the shipment actually weighed less than the carload minimum weight. Should this technique be used for the shipment? Why or why not?

CASE 5-2 CHIPPY POTATO CHIP COMPANY

Located in Reno, Nevada since 1947, the Chippy Potato Chip Company manufactured potato chips and distributed them within a 100 mile radius of Reno. It used its own trucks for delivery in the Reno, Carson City, and Lake Tahoe area and common carrier trucking for all other outgoing shipments. All of its common carrier shipments were on an LTL (less than truckload) basis. The applicable motor carrier freight rating or classification for LTL potato chips was 200. The classification (200) was high although potato chips are often given as textbook examples of bulky freight which will cause a truck to "cube-out" (reach cubic capacity before weight capacity).

At present, the potato chips were packed in bags containing eight ounces of chips. Twenty four eight-ounce bags were packed in cartons which were 12 inches by 12 inches by 36 inches. The packed carton weighed 14 lbs. The eight-ounce bags of chips wholesaled F.O.B. plant for 40 cents each and retailed at 59 cents (although some chains sold them at 55 or 57 cents).

Recently the Chippy firm acquired rights to produce a new type of chip, made from powdered potatos yielding chips of identical shape which could be packed in tubular shaped containers. A five ounce paper tube of chips would wholesale (F.O.B. plant) at 40 cents and retail for 59 cents. The new chips were much less bulky: 24 five ounce containers could be packed in a carton measuring one cubic foot. The filled carton weighed eight lbs.

(The differences between weight of chips and cartons is because of packaging materials. The carrier is paid on the basis of carton weight.)

Chippy management believed that since the new chips were less bulky, the LTL classification of 200 was too high. They decided to ask the motor carrier tariff and classification bureau for a new, lower classification.

Question One: If you worked for Chippy, what new classification would you ask for? Give your reasons.

Question Two: Classifications are based on *both* cost and value of service. From the carriers' standpoint, how has cost of service changed? How has value of service to the customer changed?

CHAPTER REFERENCES

ALLEN, W. BRUCE; "ICC Behavior on Rail Abandonments," *ICC Practitioners' Journal* (July-August, 1974), pp. 553–571.
———; "On the Use of the 'Burden Study' to Calculate 'Savings' of New Rail Revenue Policies," *ICC Practitioners' Journal* (January-February, 1976), pp. 224–239.
BARRETT, COLIN; "Competition and Controls," *ICC Practitioners' Journal* (July-August, 1973), pp. 551–561.
———; "Deregulation: A Study in Illogic," *ICC Practitioners' Journal* (November-December, 1971), pp. 8–18.
———; "Diversification—'Or Scatteration'," *ICC Practitioners' Journal* (January-February 1970), pp. 198–208.
BENNETT, JAMES W., JR. and William J. DeWitt, III; "The Development of State Departments of Transportation—A Recent Organizational Phenomenon," *Transportation Journal* (Fall, 1972), pp. 5–14.

BROWN, TERENCE A.; "Ex Parte 266 Forwarder–Rail Contract Rates," *ICC Practitioners' Journal* (July-August, 1972), pp. 667–669.

BURBY, JOHN; *The Great American Motion Sickness* (Boston: Little Brown & Co., 1971).

"CAB Urges a Sharp Cut In Own Power To Control Airlines Service and Prices," *The Wall Street Journal* (April 9, 1976).

CALMUS, THOMAS W.; "Full Cost Versus Incremental Cost: Again," *Transportation Journal* (Winter, 1969), pp. 31–36.

"Commission Adopts New Rule Requiring Motor Carriers to Provide 'Full Service'," *Traffic World* (March 7, 1970).

CONANT, MICHAEL; "Merger Valuation of Net Loss Railroads," *ICC Practitioners' Journal* (March-April, 1975), pp. 281–298.

CORSI, THOMAS M.; "The Policy of the ICC in Trucking Merger, Control, and Acquisition of Certificate Cases, 1965–1972," *ICC Practitioners' Journal* (November-December, 1975), pp. 24–38.

COYLE, JOHN J.; "The Compatibility of the Rule of Ratemaking and the National Transportation Policy," *ICC Practitioners' Journal* (March-April, 1971), pp. 340–353.

———; "The Ingot Case and Competitive Ratemaking," *ICC Practitioners' Journal* (May-June, 1969), pp. 1654–1672.

CREEDY, JOHN A.; "Competition and Regulation in Transportation," *Traffic World* (March 24, 1975).

CUTLER, HERSCHEL and Gerald S. Goldman; "New Scrap Rates Should Be Scrapped!" *Transportation and Distribution Management* (February, 1973), pp. 28–32.

DAVIS, GRANT M.; "An Analysis of the Propriety of Transferring Car Service Functions to the U.S. Department of Transportation," *ICC Practitioners' Journal* (May-June, 1970), pp. 554–566.

———; "An Evaluation of the Propriety of Establishing One Consolidated Transportation Regulatory Commission," *ICC Practitioners' Journal* (July-August, 1971), pp. 726–745.

———; "Modifications in the Identifying Characteristics of Several Federal Transportation Activities," *Transportation Journal* (Summer, 1970), pp. 5–15.

———; "The Freight Car Dilemma–A Problem of Contracting Capacity," *ICC Practitioners' Journal* (November-December, 1973), pp. 23–37.

DAVIS, GRANT M. and Linda J. Combs; "Some Observations Regarding Value-of-Service Pricing in Transportation," *Transportation Journal* (Spring, 1975), pp. 49–58.

——— and Martin T. Farris; "Federal Transportation Safety Programs–Misdirected Emphasis and Wasted Resources," *Transportation Journal* (Summer, 1972), pp. 5–17.

——— and Jack J. Holder, Jr.; "Does the United States Have a Cohesive National Transportation Policy?–An Analysis," *ICC Practitioners' Journal* (March-April, 1974), pp. 332–349.

——— and Leon J. Rosenberg; "Physical Distribution and the Regulatory Constraint: An Analysis," *Transportation Journal* (Spring 1976), pp. 87–92.

——— and Charles S. Sherwood; "Transportation Regulation: Another Dimension," *ICC Practitioners' Journal* (January-February, 1975), pp. 164–174.

———, Charles S. Sherwood and Richard W. Jones; "An Estimate of Labor Protection Cost in Selected Railway Consolidations," *ICC Practitioners' Journal* (November-December, 1975), pp. 56–71.

————, and Alvin Swimmer; "A Methodological Approach for Evaluating Transportation Rate Increases," *ICC Practitioners' Journal* (March-April, 1973), pp. 308–325.

DiGIAMMARINO, ENRICO and Donald F. Wood; "Motor Carrier Section 22 Tenders: Do They Cover Variable Costs?," *The Transportation Law Journal* (July, 1975).

DODGE, WILLIAM H.; "The Dilemma of Intermodal Rate Competition," *ICC Practitioners' Journal* (July-August, 1969), pp. 1801–1815.

————; "The Inherent Advantages of Carrier Modes Under the National Transportation Policy," *Land Economics* (November, 1968), pp. 492–502.

————; "Transportation Pricing Innovation to Promote Economic Efficiency," *ICC Practitioners' Journal* (July-August, 1970), pp. 732–745.

DONOHUE, EDWARD J. and Stanley J. Hille; "National Transportation Policy and the Regulatory Agencies," *MSU Business Topics* (Spring, 1971), pp. 67–75.

DOUGLAS, G. W. and J. C. Miller, III; "The CAB's Domesitic Passenger Fare Investigation," *The Bell Journal of Economics and Management Science* (Spring, 1974), pp. 205–222.

DURIEZ, PHILIP; "Rail-Motor Rate Competition—The T. O. F. C. Experience," *Transportation Journal* (Fall, 1967), pp. 35–40.

EADS, G. C.; "Railroad Diversification: Where Lies the Public Interest?" *The Bell Journal of Economics and Management Science* (Autumn, 1974), pp. 595–613.

EDELMAN, MURRAY; "The Public Regulatory Bodies: Economic Functions and Political Functions," *ICC Practitioners' Journal* (July-August, 1968), pp. 747–762.

EDWARDS, FORD K.; "The Role of Transportation Costs and Market Demand In Railroad Ratemaking," *ICC Practitioners' Journal* (March-April, 1970), pp. 420–425.

FARRIS, MARTIN T.; "The Role of the Common Carrier," *Transportation Journal* (Summer, 1967).

————; "Definitional Inconsistencies In The National Transportation Policy," *ICC Practitioners' Journal* (November-December, 1967), pp. 25–33.

————; "Transportation And The Public Utilities Transportation Regulation and Economic Efficiency," *The American Economic Review* (May, 1969), pp. 244–250.

FRITZSCHE, DAVID J.; "Consumer Response Information—A Potential Tool for Regulatory Decision Makers," *Transportation Journal* (Winter, 1974), pp. 22–26.

FRYE, JOSEPH L.; "An Analysis of Rail-Water Coordinate Service," *Transportation Journal* (Spring, 1967), pp. 5–15.

GRILICHES, ZVI; "Cost Allocation In Railroad Regulation," *The Bell Journal of Economics and Management Science* (Spring, 1972), pp. 26–41.

GUANDOLO, JOHN; *Transportation Law* (Dubuque, Iowa: Wm. C. Brown Co., 1973).

HARBESON, ROBERT W.; "Pricing Developments in Transportation and Public Utilities: Comment," *Transportation Journal* (Spring, 1975), pp. 42–48.

————; "Some Transport Policy Implications of Energy Shortages," *Land Economics* (November, 1974), pp. 387–396.

————; "The Supreme Court and Intermodal Rate Competition," *ICC Practitioners' Journal* (March-April, 1969), pp. 1487–1495.

————; "Toward a More Compensatory Rail Rate Structure," *ICC Practitioners' Journal* (January-February, 1973), pp. 145–157.

————; "Transport Regulation: A Centennial Evaluation," *ICC Practitioners' Journal* (July-August, 1972), pp. 628–636.

HARPER, DONALD V.; "Discussion of Papers on 'The End of Economic Regulation?'," *Transportation Journal* (Spring, 1976), pp. 34–39.

———— and James C. Johnson; "The Shipper Views Deregulation of Transportation," *ICC Practitioners' Journal* (March-April, 1974), pp. 317–332.

HEADS, JOHN; "Some Lessons From Transportation Deregulation In Canada," *ICC Practitioners' Journal* (March-April, 1975), pp. 270–280.

HILLE, STANLEY J.; "Comments on 'A Comparative Evaluation of Canadian and U. S. Transport Policy'," *Transportation Journal* (Summer, 1973), pp. 27–29.

HILTON, GEORGE W.; "Competitive Transportation: The Law of The Jungle?" *Business Horizons* (June, 1968), pp. 69–77.

————; "The Hosmer Report: A Decennial Evaluation," *ICC Practitioners' Journal* (March-April, 1969), pp. 1470–1486.

————; "The Two Things Wrong With The Interstate Commerce Commission," *Transportation Research Forum Eleventh Annual Proceedings* (Oxford: Richard B. Cross Co., 1970).

HOLBROOK, STEWART H.; *The Story of American Railroads* (New York: Crown Publishers, 1947).

HYNES, CECIL; "Small Business and Deregulation of the Motor Common Carriers," *Transportation Journal* (Spring, 1976), pp. 74–86.

JOHNSON, JAMES C.; "Government Control of the Railroads in World War I: Was It Really Disastrous?." *Traffic World* (April 9, 1973).

————; "Government Undermining of the Common Carrier System," *The Transportation Law Journal* (July, 1975).

————; "Section 22: Panacea or Parasite?," *Transportation Journal* (Summer, 1974).

————; *Trucking Mergers: A Regulatory Viewpoint* (Lexington, Mass.: D. C. Heath and Co., 1973).

———— and Donald V. Harper; "The Potential Consequences of Deregulation of Transportation," *Land Economics* (February, 1975).

———— and Terry C. Whiteside; "Professor Ripley Revisited: A Current Analysis of Railroad Mergers," *ICC Practitioners' Journal* (May-June, 1975), pp. 419–452.

KEELER, THEODORE E.; "Airline Regulation and Market Performance," *The Bell Journal of Economics and Management Science* (Augumn, 1972), pp. 399–424.

LEVINE, HARVEY A.; "Toward Modernizing the Regulatory Method for Determining Motor Common Carrier Costs," *ICC Practitioners' Journal* (January-February, 1974), pp. 190–203.

———— and Nai Chi Wang; "Motor Carrier Financing and Earnings Regulation: The Other Side of the Coin," *ICC Practitioners' Journal* (November-December, 1974), pp. 26–41.

LEVY, LESTER S.; "A Positive View of Commission Regulation Revisited," *ICC Practitioners' Journal* (May-June, 1974), pp. 430–435.

LIEB, ROBERT C.; "Promoting Change in Transportation Regulation," *Business Horizons* (June, 1975), pp. 91–94.

————; "A Revised Intermodal Ownership Policy," *Transportation Journal* (Summer, 1971).

LOCKLIN, D. PHILIP; *Economics of Transportation* (Homewood, Ill.: Richard D. Irwin, Inc., 1972).

LORCH, ROBERT S.; "Administrative Court Via The Independent Hearing Officer," *ICC Practitioners' Journal* (May-June, 1969), pp. 1673–1679.

LYNAGH, PETER; "Motor Carrier Reparations, A Settled Issue?" *Transportation Journal* (Winter, 1973), pp. 27–33.

McCARNEY, BERNARD J.; "ICC Rate Regulation and Rail-Motor Carrier Pricing Behavior: A Reappraisal," *ICC Practitioners' Journal* (July-August, 1968), pp. 707–719.

————; "The Intermodal Pricing Behavior Expectations Under Reduced Regulations," *ICC Practitioners' Journal* (July-August, 1974), pp. 532–542.

McELHINEY, PAUL T. and Charles L. Hilton; *Introduction to Logistics and Traffic Management* (Dubuque, Iowa: Wm. C. Brown Co., Inc., 1968).

McLACHLAN, D. L.; "Canadian Trucking Regulation," *The Logistics and Transportation Review* (Volume 8, Number 1), pp. 59–81.

MIKLIUS, WALTER; *Economic Performance of Motor Carriers Operating Under the Agricultural Exemption in Interstate Trucking*, U.S. Department of Agriculture, Marketing Research Report No. 838 (Washington, D.C.: U.S. Government Printing Office, January, 1969).

MORTON, ALEXANDER LYALL; "Intermodal Competition for Intercity Transport of Manufacturers," *Land Economics* (November, 1972), pp. 357–366.

MUNRO, JOHN M.; "A Comparative Evaluation of Canadian and U. S. Transport Policy," *Transportation Journal* (Summer, 1973), pp. 5–26.

————; "New Directions on Canadian Transportation Policy," *Transportation Journal* (Winter, 1968), pp. 34–44.

NELSON, JAMES C.; "A Critique of DOT Transport Policy," *Transportation Journal* (Spring, 1972), pp. 5–22.

————; "Marginal Cost Pricing: A Form of Price Discrimination?" *Transportation Journal* (Summer, 1969), pp. 5–15.

————; "Motor Carrier Regulation and the Financing of the Industry," *ICC Practitioners' Journal* (May-June, 1974), pp. 436–457.

NEVEL, R. and W. Miklius; "The Operating Ratio as a Regulatory Standard," *Transportation Journal* (Winter, 1968), pp. 15–18.

1968 Conference on Mass Transportation—The Government Role (New York: Popular Library, 1968).

NORTON, HUGH S.; "Economics and Economists In The Interstate Commerce Commission," *ICC Practitioners' Journal* (May-June, 1969), pp. 1646–1653.

OLSON, CHARLES E.; "Considerations in Pricing the St. Lawrence Seaway," *Transportation Journal* (Fall, 1971), pp. 36–40.

OORT, CONRAD J.; "Bracket Tariffs—The Proposed System of Rate Regulation In The European Economic Community," *Transportation Journal* (Fall, 1967), pp. 29–34.

PALMER, J.; "A Further Analysis of Provincial Trucking Regulation," *The Bell Journal of Economics and Management Science* (Autumn, 1973), pp. 655–664.

PEGRUM, DUDLEY F.; "Should The I.C.C. Be Abolished?" *Transportation Journal* (Fall, 1971), pp. 5–13.

————; "The Chicago and North Western-Chicago, Milwaukee, St. Paul, and Pacific Merger: A Case Study in Transport Economics," *Transportation Journal* (Winter, 1969), pp. 43–50.

POSNER, R. A.; "Theories of Economic Regulation," *The Bell Journal of Economics and Management Science* (Autumn, 1974), pp. 335–358.

RHODES, ROBERT G. and Richard E. Briggs; "The ICC's Rail Carload Waybill Sample," *ICC Practitioners' Journal* (January-February, 1968), pp. 235–251.

ROBERTS, MERRILL J.; "Transport Pricing and Distribution Efficiency," *Land Economics* (May, 1970), pp. 181–190.

ROBERTS, MERRILL J.; "Transport Pricing Reform," *Transportation Journal* (Spring, 1973), pp. 5–15.

RUPPENTHAL, KARL M., Robert R. Piper, and Brendan Quirin; "Some Economic Aspects of the Barge Line Mixing Rule," *Transportation Journal* (Spring, 1970), pp. 5–13.

SENECA, ROSALINA S.; "Inherent Advantage, Costs, and Resource Allocation in the Transportation Industry," *The American Economic Review* (December, 1973), pp. 945–956.

SEQUIN, C. JOSEPH; "A Case Against the ICC," *Business Horizons* (February, 1970), pp. 49–54.

SHERWOOD, CHARLES S.; "The Operational Reality of Independent Rate Making: Some Empirical Findings," *Transportation Journal* (Winter, 1975), pp. 5–12.

SHIRLEY, ROBERT E.; "Analysis of Motor Carrier Cost Formulae Developed by the Interstate Commerce Commission," *Transportation Journal* (Spring, 1969), pp. 21–27.

SIGMON, RICHARD R.; *Miller's Law of Freight Loss and Damage Claims* (Dubuque, Iowa: Wm. C. Brown, 1961).

SLOSS, JAMES; "Regulation of Motor Freight Transportation: A Quantitative Evaluation of Policy," *The Bell Journal of Economics and Management Science* (Autumn, 1970).

SMITH, JAY A., JR.; "Concentration in the Common and Contract Motor Carrier Industry—A Regulatory Dilemma," *Transportation Journal* (Summer, 1973), pp. 30–48.

SPANN, ROBERT M. and Edward W. Erickson; "The Economics of Railroading: The Beginning of Cartelization and Regulation," *The Bell Journal of Economics and Management Science* (Autumn, 1970), pp. 227–244.

SPYCHALSKI, JOHN C.; "A Railway Agricultural Exemption: One Step Toward Greater Efficiency In Transport?" *ICC Practitioners' Journal* (November-December, 1967), pp. 44–56.

———; "Criticisms of Regulated Freight Transport: Do Economists' Perceptions Conform with Institutional Realities?" *Transportation Journal* (Spring, 1975), pp. 5–17.

———; "Imperfections In Railway Line Abandonment Regulation and Suggestions for Their Correction," *ICC Practitioners' Journal* (May-June, 1973), pp. 454–468.

———; "On The Nonutility of Domestic Water Transport Regulation," *ICC Practitioners' Journal* (November-December, 1969), pp. 7–22.

———; "On Transport Deregulation: Some Questions For Messrs. Houthakker, McLaren, et al.," *ICC Practitioners' Journal* (November-December, 1971), pp. 37–52.

———; "Political Considerations in the Formation of Transport Policy: Products of Legislative Compromise," *ICC Practitioners' Journal* (January-February, 1967), pp. 211–220.

———; "Shippers' Views Toward Railway Rate Deregulation: The Case of Agricultural Traffic," *Transportation Journal* (Spring, 1967), pp. 16–25.

STARR, EDWARD A.; *The Interpretation of Freight Tariffs* (Fort Worth, Texas: The Transportation Press, 1961).

STEPHENSON, FREDERICK J., JR.; "Transport Deregulation—The Air Freight

Forwarder Experience," *ICC Practitioners' Journal* (November-December, 1975), pp. 39–55.

STERN, GEORGE L.; "Surface Transport: Middle-of-the-Road Solution," *Harvard Business Review* (November-December, 1975).

SUELFLOW, JAMES E. and Stanley J. Hille; "The Transportation Company: An Economic Argument for Intermodal Ownership," *Land Economics* (August, 1970).

"Survey: The Regulators," *Transportation and Distribution Management* (March-April, 1974).

SWARTZ, THOMAS R.; "Incremental-Cost Analysis—Costs or Benefits?" *Transportation Journal* (Spring, 1969), pp. 5–10.

TAFF, CHARLES A. and David Rodriguez; "An Analysis of Some Aspects of Operating Rights of Irregular Route Motor Common Carriers," *Transportation Journal* (Winter, 1975), pp. 31–42.

———; *Management of Physical Distribution and Transportation* (Homewood, Ill.: Richard D. Irwin, Inc., 1972).

"The Annual Report of the Council of Economic Advisors," *Economic Report of the President—1972* (Washington, D.C.: U.S. Government Printing Office, 1972).

TOSTERUD, ROBERT J.; "Car Allocation in North Dakota Revisited," *ICC Practitioners' Journal* (September-October, 1975), pp. 703–706.

——— and Ronald Q. Nichols; "Rail Car Allocation in North Dakota: Procedure, Problems, and Performance," *ICC Practitioners' Journal* (September-October, 1974), pp. 676–683.

TUGGLE, KENNETH H.; "To Regulate or Not to Regulate," *ICC Practitioners' Journal* (January-February, 1972).

WALLIN, THEODORE O.; "Alternatives in Transport Policy: A Matrix Approach," *Transportation Journal* (Winter, 1975), pp. 43–53.

WASSOM, JOHN C.; "Railroads: An Example of Multiple-Product Price Discriminating Firms," *Transportation Journal* (Summer, 1967), pp. 39–48.

WATERS, L. L.; "Adapting to New Regulatory Regimes," *Transportation Journal* (Spring, 1976), pp. 29–33.

WESTMEYER, RUSSELL E.; *Economics of Transportation* (Englewood Cliffs, N.J.: Prentice-Hall, Inc., 1952).

WHITTEN, HERBERT O.; "Why Freight Rates Must Be Computerized," *Distribution Age* (March, 1966).

———; "Why Not Density Rates?" *ICC Practitioners' Journal* (November-December, 1968), pp. 1149–1178.

WIEDENBAUM, MURRAY L.; "The High Cost of Government Regulation," *Business Horizons* (August, 1975), pp. 43–54.

WILLIAMS, ERNEST W., JR. and David W. Bluestone; *Rationals of Federal Transportation Policy*, U.S. Department of Commerce (Washington, D.C.: Government Printing Office, April, 1960).

WILSON, GEORGE W.; "Regulation, Public Policy, and Efficient Provision of Freight Transportation," *Transportation Journal* (Fall, 1975), pp. 5–20.

———; "Transportation and Price Stability," *The American Economic Review* (May, 1969), pp. 261–269.

ZEIS, PAUL M.; "Competitive Rate Making in the United States," *Transportation Journal* (Summer, 1969).

Transferring a truck/aircraft container. *Credit:* Seaboard World Airlines, Inc.

CHAPTER SIX

The Traffic Management Function

My personal observation based on experience has pretty well convinced me that if management is unable to evaluate the Traffic Manager or does not know what he does, the fault may lie as much or more with the Traffic Manager than with management.

—GERALD J. WERNER
Distribution Worldwide
May, 1973

Many critical decisions concerning inventory buildup, consolidation planning, and so forth, are predicated on the scheduling services offered to us by the various common-carrier modes. As has been repeated by many others many times in the past, I would rather have a carrier give me consistent third-day reliable service than to get 25% overnight, 50% second-morning and 52% third-morning. From a planning standpoint, this is exceedingly difficult to cope with.

—WALTER L. WEART
Railway Age
January 26, 1976

TRAFFIC MANAGEMENT: BACKGROUND AND SCOPE

The field of traffic management is challenging. However, senior executives often view the traffic management function as highly technical, esoteric, and beyond control. A *Harvard Business Review* article commented, "Executives complain, frequently, about freight costs, but the whole area of traffic management is a little like the weather—although people talk about it, no one does anything about it."[1]

Why should senior management even be concerned about traffic management? The answer is that transportation represents a major expense item. In 1973, United States business firms spent more than $128 billion on freight transportation, which represented ten percent

[1] George L. Stern, "Traffic: Clear Signals For Higher Profits," *Harvard Business Review* (May-June, 1972), p. 72.

177

of the nation's Gross National Product. Neuschel's studies indicate that a manufacturing company's traffic bill averages 44 percent of its distribution expenses (including inventory holding costs).[2] Figure 6-1 contains a statement of the traffic department's objectives as established by the Motorola Corporation. Figure 6-1 should be carefully studied, because it contains both an overview of this chapter and a review of the prior two chapters.

Prior to federal transportation regulation of rates and services in 1887, the real job of the traffic manager was to negotiate the largest possible rebates from the railroads. A business using a particular railroad often choose its traffic managers from among people who worked for that railroad. Hence, the newly appointed traffic managers could "negotiate" the best "deals" from their prior cronies. When the *Act To Regulate Commerce* was enacted into law in 1887, the traffic management position fell upon hard times. Since rebates and other discriminatory practices became illegal, the special "services" of the traffic manager were no longer needed. Nor was the job of purchasing transportation service considered to be complex at this time, because the only viable mode of inland transportation was the railroad. Therefore, the traffic manager was replaced by a shipping clerk who notified the railroad when shipments were ready.

After World War I the traffic management function began to grow in stature again. The reason was the growth in competitive transport modes. This included significant federal government funding for the dredging and expansion of the inland waterway system. The truck had proven its dependability in World War I, and a highway system was being built. Oil pipelines and freight-forwarders were emerging as additional alternative choices for traffic managers. The regulatory environment and carrier rate structures started to assume their present day complexity. Firms also had the option of operating their own trucks. These factors all worked together to re-establish the importance of the firm's traffic management function.

Today, riding on the crest of enthusiasm for the physical distribution concept, the traffic management function is considered to be an important member of the physical distribution team. A survey by *Distribution Worldwide* pointed out the multi-faceted activities that most corporations assign to their traffic departments. The specific responsibilities of the traffic manager are shown in Figure 6-2. No longer are the traffic manager's only activities carrier selection and rate determination (although they are still of fundamental importance), but instead he or she must be conversant with and able to solve many more far-reaching problem areas. Dr. E. G. Plowman, former Vice-President of

2 Robert P. Neuschel, "Physical Distribution—Forgotten Frontier," *Harvard Business Review* (March-April, 1967), p. 125.

Fig. 6-1 An example of traffic management corporate objectives.

MOTOROLA'S TRAFFIC OBJECTIVES

1. Direct and control the purchase of adequate domestic and international freight and passenger and employee household goods transportation and public warehouse space at the lowest cost consistent with the overall good of the company.

2. Aid in the elimination of wasteful practices and needless expense such as incurred through loss and damage in transit, car demurrage and truck detention, the use of improper bill of lading descriptions and uneconomical routings, the shipping and receiving of uneconomical quantities, the use of unnecessary premium cost transportation, and the payment of excess duties and Customs penalties.

3. Remain familiar with transportation and Customs laws and. regulations to insure that the company's traffic operations are conducted accordingly and that all benefits to which we may be entitled are secured. Keep company and division management informed of any changes that may affect the company.

4. Operating either independently for Motorola or through our local and national Traffic Committee and Association Memberships, support or oppose carrier and shipper proposals as well as local, state and federal legislation affecting transportation in general or Motorola in particular; also negotiate with carriers, their Freight Rate Making Bureaus, and Classification Committees for adjustment of rates, ratings, rules and regulations to reduce transportation costs and/or improve services.

5. Formulate, standardize, recommend and coordinate corporate traffic and transportation policies regarding public warehousing and the company's movement of materials, supplies, finished goods and personnel. Cooperate and work with all Divisions, departments, and sales areas to make sure that these policies are complied with and that there is no relaxing of control procedures.

6. Assist all Divisions in solving local and field problems involving domestic and international traffic and transportation activities, including Customs problems, and serve as liaison between those Divisions, the carriers, and Customs personnel.

7. Analyze and keep abreast of the constant changes, trends, methods, services, equipment, and technological advances in the domestic and international transportation field and when practical and economical, apply them to the company's operation.

8. Study transportation economies with respect to our domestic and foreign distribution and marketing methods; also with respect to plant, warehouse and distributor locations. Make recommendations based on such studies.

9. Study and develop current and long-range plans and programs involving the organization and functions of the Corporate, Canadian, and Western Area Traffic Departments so that changes can and will be made as needed to be sensitive and responsive to the requirements of all Divisions, and the company overall.

10. Operate the department at minimum cost consistent and compatible with the department's essential space and people requirements if its Objectives and Goals are to be achieved in all areas of the company operations. Includes the necessity to maintain standards as high as our budget permits when hiring personnel to insure a maximum level of proficiency within the department.

11. Encourage personal development and self-improvement; counsel and advise Traffic personnel in the development of their technical and managerial abilities so as to enable them to deal more effectively with associates and others, and to improve their overall capacity for advancement to positions of greater responsibility.

12. Cooperate with traffic and transportation organizations to promote the transportation industry and to make it more attractive to prospective employees.

13. *All things being equal,* use and promote the use of carriers who are customers and/or potential customers of the company; also secure an interest in and promote the use of company products by the carriers.

14. Promote, foster and maintain good relations with all carriers, warehousemen, suppliers, and customers—with the best interests of the company foremost at all times.

SOURCE: Janet Bosworth Dower, "How Top Management Evaluates the Traffic/Distribution Function," *Distribution Worldwide* (May, 1973), p. 56.

FIG. 6-2 The functions that traffic departments perform.

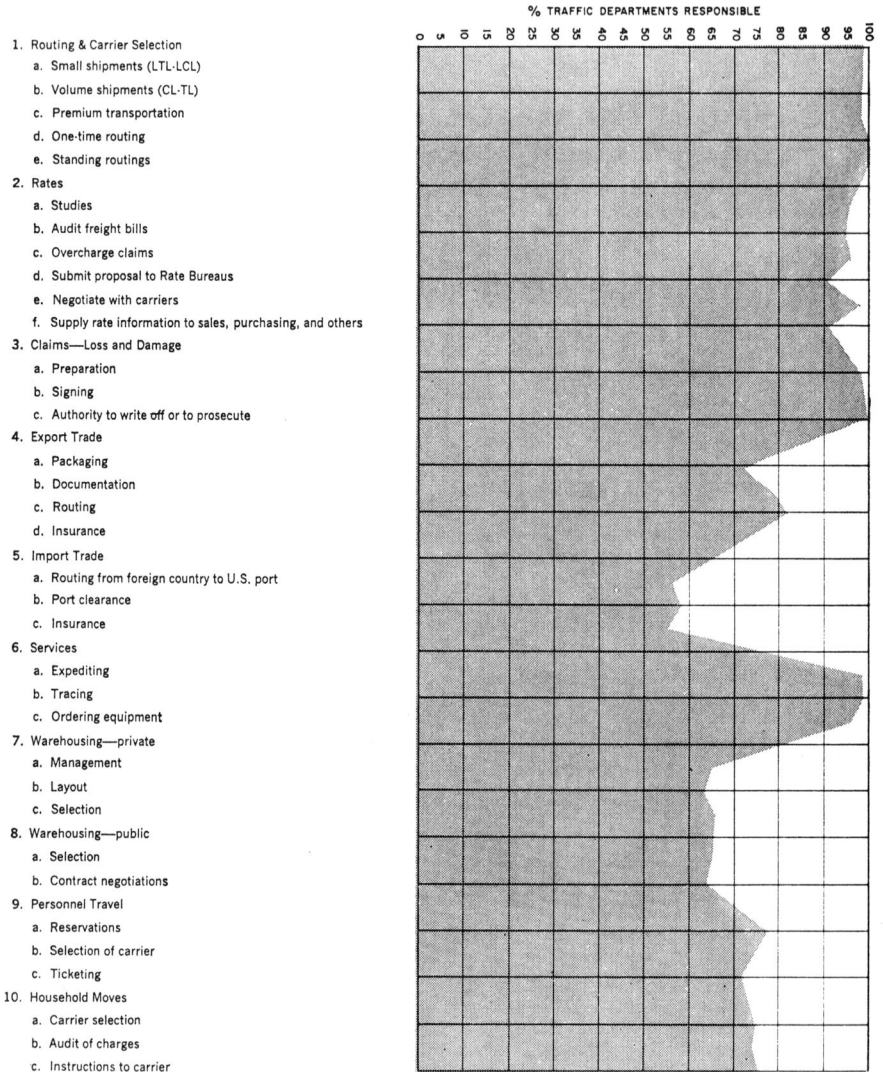

% TRAFFIC DEPARTMENTS RESPONSIBLE
0 5 10 15 20 25 30 35 40 45 50 55 60 65 70 75 80 85 90 95 100

1. Routing & Carrier Selection
  a. Small shipments (LTL-LCL)
  b. Volume shipments (CL-TL)
  c. Premium transportation
  d. One-time routing
  e. Standing routings
2. Rates
  a. Studies
  b. Audit freight bills
  c. Overcharge claims
  d. Submit proposal to Rate Bureaus
  e. Negotiate with carriers
  f. Supply rate information to sales, purchasing, and others
3. Claims—Loss and Damage
  a. Preparation
  b. Signing
  c. Authority to write off or to prosecute
4. Export Trade
  a. Packaging
  b. Documentation
  c. Routing
  d. Insurance
5. Import Trade
  a. Routing from foreign country to U.S. port
  b. Port clearance
  c. Insurance
6. Services
  a. Expediting
  b. Tracing
  c. Ordering equipment
7. Warehousing—private
  a. Management
  b. Layout
  c. Selection
8. Warehousing—public
  a. Selection
  b. Contract negotiations
9. Personnel Travel
  a. Reservations
  b. Selection of carrier
  c. Ticketing
10. Household Moves
  a. Carrier selection
  b. Audit of charges
  c. Instructions to carrier

SOURCE: Janet Bosworth, "What Does a Traffic Manager Do?" *Distribution Worldwide* (March, 1971), p. 34.

Transportation for United States Steel, stated that the position really involved "transport control management." He said:

> Transport control, in its broadest sense, is the central task of present-day traffic management. It is concerned not alone with the price paid to or the service rendered by one or several carriers but also with the entire group of transportation costs and of service aspects that, taken as a whole, move the inbound or outbound product from some origin to a chosen destination. Handling methods, time in transit, packaging costs, disposal of unpackaging debris, warehouse or storage-pile costs, cost of intra-plant movement and the avoidance of wastage or damage, all are part of this transport control task.[3]

The following sections will discuss the primary activities of the traffic department. The order of presentation is arbitrary with the exception of the first two activities, rate determination and negotiation and carrier selection, which are discussed initially because they still are the premier activities of the traffic manager.

RATE DETERMINATION AND NEGOTIATION

The determination of the correct freight rate is extremely difficult, at best. A noted transportation rate consultant has mused:

> The able lawyer who may never have engaged in practice before the Interstate Commerce Commission has learned to approach the freight tariff warily and with distrust. Even the experienced traffic manager has at times found his own tools, the freight tariffs, reaching a state of baffling complexity.[4]

Rate determination is of paramount importance to the traffic manager. This position is often challenged by the neophyte, who says: "Why all the fuss about determining the correct freight rate? Everyone knows the carrier has a legal obligation to determine the correct rate. Why not leave this problem up to the carrier?" The answer to this is that it is a naive method of freight rate determination. Chapter 5 has already examined the complexities of correct freight rate determination. In most situations there are numerous applicable rate which can be found in the tariffs. If the carrier representative is left to determine the correct rate, he or she has no incentive to actively search the tariffs to find the *lowest* applicable rate. Instead, the carrier representative will typically use that rate which is the easiest to find. Based on our consulting experience, we understand that an industry rule-of-thumb is

---

[3] From a speech delivered to the Transportation Club, Toronto, Ontario, as found in Kenneth U. Flood, *Traffic Management* (2nd ed., Dubuque, Iowa: Wm. C. Brown Co., 1965), p. 2.

[4] Edward A. Starr, *The Interpretation of Freight Tariffs* (Fort Worth: The Transportation Press, 1961), p. 1.

that when the carrier calculates the "correct" freight charge, it averages about ten percent higher than the lowest applicable legal rate.

Freight tariffs and rates are not engraved in stone. Given sufficient lead-time and patience, freight rates can be and frequently are altered. This is accomplished initially by negotiations between the carrier and the shipper; then after additional, often routine, procedures have been followed, the rate can be officially changed.

While there are numerous factors that influence the shipper to negotiate lower rates with the carrier, there are three situations in which the shipper's arguments are most likely to prevail. The first, and generally conceded to be the most important situation, is the volume of new business—for both the shipper and the carrier—that would result from a rate change. Assume, for example, that the existing commodity rate on widgets from Knoxville, Tennessee to San Antonio, Texas is $1.80 per CWT and at the current rate the shipper ships 100,000 pounds per year. Assume further that the shipper has determined by market research that if freight costs can be reduced 30 cents per CWT, he can increase sales in San Antonio to 300,000 pounds per year. The carrier would probably see real merit in this lower rate (assuming it covers the variable costs of carriage) because its total revenue would increase from $1,800 to $4,500. Therefore, the carrier undoubtedly would favor the proposed rate change before the appropriate rate bureau.

A second situation which helps in lowering carrier rates is to compare the present rates with the existing rates on similar and often competing products. Assume the railroad commodity rate for apples from Saint Joseph, Michigan, to Greenville, South Carolina is $2.85 per CWT and that you are the traffic manager for a firm which ships pears, and the rate for pears is $3.71 between the same two cities. Since these two products compete, and the value of each is roughly the same (as are costs of carriage), an argument can be made that the rate on pears should be closer to the rate on apples. If the railroad will not support the proposed rate reduction, as traffic manager you can take your case to the ICC, complaining that Sections 1 and 3 of the Interstate Commerce Act have been violated.

The final situation which will bring about carrier rate reductions involves the rates of competing forms of transportation. If another transport mode has a lower rate and it is actively participating in the carriage of freight based on this lower rate, then this factor is often very influential regarding a carrier's decision to lower its existing rate. Related to this is the shipper's threat of using or expanding the usage of private transportation.

Assume that after several meetings with the shipper's traffic manager, a carrier decides to lower its existing rate. The carrier must request that the rate bureau which publishes the applicable rates now consider altering the rate. Sometimes there is a hearing at which both shippers and carriers can argue for or against the proposed rate change. The right of independent action is an alternative available to carriers. Such action, called *flagging-out* a rate, indicates that a carrier chooses to have a different rate from the other members of the rate bureau.

In some rate bureaus the threat of independent action by a carrier is taken seriously. Sometimes a compromise rate—between the present and proposed one—is agreed upon. If shippers or affected carriers remain unhappy, they may have the right to appeal to the ICC.

CARRIER SELECTION

The selection of the mode and then the specific carrier within that mode is another of the fundamental activities of the traffic department. However, the decision regarding which transport mode or modes to actually use may not be exclusively determined by the traffic manager. In many corporations, especially when premium transportation (i.e., air freight) is being considered on a regular basis, the decision to use the more expensive forms of transportation is decided by more senior management. A survey by *Distribution Worldwide* found that the traffic department typically initiated the research on the modal choice and then presented its findings to the vice-president of physical distribution, or materials, or manufacturing, who controlled the modal-choice decision. The same survey found that once the modal decision has been decided, then the traffic department was charged with the responsibility of selecting the specific carriers.[5]

While there are numerous factors to consider when selecting a carrier, the following five tend to be the most important: rates, consistency of service, speed, loss and damage record, and special services available. Three of these factors will be examined here. Loss and damage and special services will be covered later in this chapter.

RATES

While rates charged by alternative modes are of importance when deciding upon a mode, it is of much less consideration when deciding upon a specific carrier. Why? The answer is that activities of rate bureaus result in uniform rates for carriers in a given region. The only situation where there is price competition between common carriers is when one or more carriers decide to "flag-out" a rate and hence have a different rate than the rest of the bureau members. While this situation is not common, the alert traffic manager should always be monitoring the tariffs to detect "flag-outs" on products he or she is trans-

[5] Janet Bosworth Dower, "Will the Real Airfreight Buyer Please Stand Up?" *Distribution Worldwide* (January, 1974), pp. 28–29.

porting. The other situation where price competition takes place is between contract carriers, or between carriers of exempt commodities.

CONSISTENCY OF SERVICE

Inventory holding costs are expensive and, if a high degree of dependability of service is offered by the carrier, smaller inventories would be sufficient at each location. Assume a retailer sells 100 units per day and when reordering, places an order for 1,000 units. Assume that one day delivery is possible and always achieved. Then the retailer would reorder when inventory was at 100 units. The next day the 100 units remaining would sell and the following day the new order of 1,000 units would arrive. Now assume instead of taking the usual one day for the order to arrive, it takes several days more. The retailer would be out of stock and his customers would be unhappy. To avoid this happening again, the retailer would have to maintain, perpetually, a larger *safety stock*—additional inventory designed to prevent an excessive number of stock-out occurrences. This would be expensive. An alternative would be to find a more dependable delivering carrier.[6]

SPEED OF SERVICE

The specific time that it takes to transport a shipment is typically of less importance than the consistency of service that the carrier can offer. Nevertheless, if two competing carriers offer an equally reliable service, then the actual speed or time of delivery is important because less money is invested in goods in transit. Speed is important for any type of perishable good.

DOCUMENTATION

The traffic department is responsible for completion of all documents necessary for the transportation of the firm's products. The most important single document is the *bill-of-lading*.

The bill-of-lading is the basic operating paper in the transportation industry. There are three functions that it performs.

The bill-of-lading functions as a delivery receipt when products are tendered to common carriers. The carrier, upon receipt of the freight, signs the bill-of-lading and gives the original of this document to the shipper. The signed original of the bill-of-lading is the shipper's legal proof that the carrier received the freight.

The second function of the bill-of-lading is that it contains a binding

---

[6] The importance of carrier reliability is emphasized in Camille Thiele, "Reliability—In No Uncertain Terms," *Railway Age* (Jan. 26, 1976), p. 72.

contract specifying the duties and obligations of both the carrier and the shipper. When properly executed and signed by both the carrier and the shipper, the bill-of-lading is a contract. The fact that the bill-of-lading contract for surface carriers is basically standardized by law greatly simplifies the traffic manager's job, because it specifies exactly the duties of the traffic manager as the shipper and the duties of the carrier.

When an *order* bill-of-lading is used, it also serves as evidence of title to the goods. It is necessary to know that there are two types of bills-of-lading, the *order* and the *straight*. On a *straight* bill, which is printed on *white* paper, the name of the consignee is stated in the appropriate place and the carrier is under a strict legal obligation to deliver the freight to the named consignee and to no one else. Ownership of the goods is neither stated nor implied. On the *order* bill-of-lading, which is printed on *yellow* paper, the name of the consignee is not specified. Assume that a lumber company in Seattle has loaded a boxcar of plywood which it had not yet sold. It would use an order bill and tender the shipment to the Burlington Northern Railroad, which would start the car moving toward Chicago. Once a buyer for the plywood is found, the shipper would send via airmail the original copy of the order bill to a bank near the buyer and would also notify the buyer as to which bank had possession of the order bill. The buyer would go to the bank and pay for the plywood, and the bank would surrender the original copy to the buyer. The buyer would take it to the railroad and the railroad would deliver the carload of plywood. (Order bills are used in one other situation, that involving "slow-payers," because they guarantee that the customer must pay for the products prior to receipt.)

An additional classification of bills is the specific form—long, short, and preprinted. The long form bill-of-lading, which may be either an order or straight bill, contains the standard information on the face of the bill (see Figure 6-3) and the reverse side contains the entire contract between the carrier and the shipper. The reverse side is printed in extremely small print. Because of the difficulty of reading the long form contract and because of the printing costs of including the contract on all bills, the railroads and motor carriers in 1949 adopted the short form bill-of-lading. Instead of printing the entire contract on the back of the bill, the short form has the following statement on its face: "Every service to be performed hereunder shall be subject to all the terms and conditions of the Uniform Domestic Straight Bill of Lading. . . ."

Another type of bill, which may be a long, short, order, or straight, is *preprinted*. In theory, the bill-of-lading is prepared and issued by the carrier. In fact, however, many shippers buy their bills and then have them preprinted with a list of the products that they regularly ship. Figure 6-4 illustrates a preprinted, short form, bill-of-lading. Why

Fig. 6-3 A long-form bill-of-lading.

(Uniform Domestic Straight Bill of Lading, adopted by Carriers in Official and Western Classification territories, March 15, 1922, as amended August 1, 1930, and June 15, 1941.)

UNIFORM STRAIGHT BILL OF LADING

Original—Not Negotiable

Shipper's No..........

(To be Printed on "White" Paper)

Agent's No............

Company

RECEIVED, subject to the classifications and tariffs in effect on the date of the issue of this Bill of Lading,

at..., 19...

from...

the property described below, in apparent good order, except as noted (contents and condition of contents of packages unknown), marked, consigned, and destined as indicated below, which said company (the word company being understood throughout this contract as meaning any person or corporation in possession of the property under the contract) agrees to carry to its usual place of delivery at said destination, if on its own road or its own water line, otherwise to deliver to another carrier on the route to said destination. It is mutually agreed, as to each carrier of all or any of said property over all or any portion of said route to destination, and as to each party at any time interested in all or any of said property, that every service to be performed hereunder shall be subject to all the conditions not prohibited by law, whether printed or written, herein contained, including the conditions on back hereof, which are hereby agreed to by the shipper and accepted for himself and his assigns.

(Mail or street address of consignee—For purposes of notification only.)

Consigned to..

Destination...State of.........................County of.....................

Route..

Delivering Carrier.................................Car Initial.....................Car No....................

No. Pack- ages	Description of Articles, Special Marks, and Exceptions	*Weight (Subject to Correction)	Class or Rate	Check Column	Subject to Section 7 of conditions, if this shipment is to be delivered to the consignee without recourse on the consignor, the consignor shall sign the following statement:
....		....	....	....	The carrier shall not make delivery of this shipment without payment of freight and all other lawful charges.
....		....	....	....	
....		....	....	....	
....		....	....	....	
....		....	....	....	
....		....	....	....	(Signature of consignor.)
....		....	....	....	
....		....	....	....	If charges are to be prepaid, write or stamp here, "To be Prepaid."
....		....	....	....	
....		....	....	....	....
....		....	....	....	Received $.......... to apply in prepayment of the charges on the property described hereon.
....		....	....	....	
....		....	....	....	
....		....	....	....	Agent or Cashier.
....		....	....	....	Per.......... (The signature here acknowledges only the amount prepaid.)

*If the shipment moves between two ports by a carrier by water, the law requires that the bill of lading shall state whether it is "carrier's or shipper's weight."

Note.—Where the rate is dependent on value, shippers are required to state specifically in writing the agreed or declared value of the property.

The agreed or declared value of the property is hereby specifically stated by the shipper to be not exceeding

Charges advanced:

....per.................... $....................

....Shipper. ....Agent.

Per.. Per...

Permanent postoffice address of shipper..

Reproduced by permission of tariff publisher.

FIG. 6-4 A preprinted bill-of-lading.

NAME OF CARRIER

STRAIGHT BILL OF LADING — SHORT FORM — Original — Not Negotiable

RECEIVED,* subject to the classifications and tariffs in effect on the date of the issue of this Bill of Lading,

the property described below, in apparent good order, except as noted (contents and condition of contents of packages unknown), marked, consigned, and destined as indicated below, which said carrier (the word carrier being understood throughout this contract as meaning any person or corporation in possession of the property under the contract) agrees to carry to its usual place of delivery at said destination, if on its route, otherwise to deliver to another carrier on the route to said destination. It is mutually agreed, as to each carrier of all or any of said property over all or any portion of said route to destination, and as to each party at any time interested in all or any of said property, that every service to be performed hereunder shall be subject to all the terms and conditions of the Uniform Domestic Straight Bill of Lading set forth (1) in Official, Southern, Western and Illinois Freight Classifications in effect on the date hereof, if this is a rail or rail-water shipment, or (2) in the applicable motor carrier classification or tariff if this is a motor carrier shipment.

Shipper hereby certifies that he is familiar with all the terms and conditions of the said bill of lading set forth in the classification or tariff which governs the transportation of this shipment, and the said terms and conditions are hereby agreed to by the shipper and accepted for himself and his assigns.

CARRIER'S NO.

SHIPPER'S NO.

FROM KILSBY-TUBESUPPLY At TULSA, OKLA.   DATE   19

CONSIGNED TO   (Mail or street address of consignee—For purposes of notification only.)

DESTINATION   STATE   COUNTY

(To be filled in only when shipper desires and governing tariffs provide for delivery thereat.)

DELIVERY ADDRESS

ROUTE		DELIVERING CARRIER		VEHICLE OR CAR INITIAL & NO.			
No. Packages	KIND OF PACKAGE, DESCRIPTION OF ARTICLES, SPECIAL MARKS AND EXCEPTIONS			*Weight (Sub. to Corr.)	Class or Rate	Ck. Col.	FOB POINT
BOXES	PIPE OR TUBING WROUGHT STEEL, N.O.I.	☐ 20 GA. AND THINNER	HEAVIER THAN ☐ 20 GA.				
TUBES	PIPE OR TUBING WROUGHT STEEL, N.O.I.	☐ 20 GA. AND THINNER	HEAVIER THAN ☐ 20 GA.				Subject to Section 7 of Conditions of applicable bill of lading, if this shipment is to be delivered to the consignee without recourse on the consignor, the consignor shall sign the following statement:
PCS	PIPE OR TUBING WROUGHT STEEL, N.O.I.	☐ 20 GA. AND THINNER	HEAVIER THAN ☐ 20 GA.				The carrier shall not make delivery of this shipment without payment of freight and all other lawful charges.
BDLES	PIPE OR TUBING WROUGHT STEEL, N.O.I.	☐ 20 GA. AND THINNER	HEAVIER THAN ☐ 20 GA.				KILSBY - TUBESUPPLY
BOXES	PIPE OR TUBING ALUMINUM	☐ 2" DIA. AND UNDER	OVER ☐ 2" DIA.				(Signature of Consignor) If charges are to be prepaid, write or stamp here, "To be prepaid."
TUBES	PIPE OR TUBING ALUMINUM	☐ 2" DIA. AND UNDER	OVER ☐ 2" DIA.				Rec'd $ to
PCS	PIPE OR TUBING ALUMINUM	☐ 2" DIA. AND UNDER	OVER ☐ 2" DIA.				apply in prepayment of the charges on the property described hereon.
BDLES	PIPE OR TUBING ALUMINUM	☐ 2" DIA. AND UNDER	OVER ☐ 2" DIA.				Per Agent or Cashier (The signature here acknowledges only the amount prepaid.)
							Charges Advanced $
	☐ **PACKING LIST**						"Shipper's imprint in lieu of stamp; not a part of bill of lading approved by the Interstate Commerce Commission."
	☐ SMALL SHIPMENT SERVICE REQUESTED PREPAID/RELEASED VALUE NOT EXCEEDING 50¢ LB. SIGNED BY						The Fibre Boxes used for this shipment conform to the specifications set forth in the box maker's certificate thereon, and all other requirements of Rule 41 of the Consolidated Freight Classification.
							C.O.D.
	CUST. P.O. #						

KILSBY - TUBESUPPLY   SHIPPER, PER_____

Permanent Post Office Address of Shipper

1819 NO. GARNETT ROAD
TULSA, OKLA. 74116

_____AGENT, PER_____

1

do shippers go to the expense of buying and printing their own bills? The answer is that in practice, shippers frequently prepare their own bills prior to calling the carrier. The preprinted bill can be prepared more rapidly, and with less chance for error. The shipper can insert the correct rate rather than letting the carrier determine it.

The other basic document that the traffic manager must be familiar with is the freight bill. It is an invoice, submitted by the carrier, requesting to be paid. Often, the traffic manager must approve each freight bill before it is paid.

ROUTING

The top section of Figures 6-3 and 6-4 has a line entitled *route*. A rail shipper has an absolute right to route shipments to their destinations. This provision was added to the original 1887 Act by the Mann-Elkins Act. The purpose was to give the shipper the ability to patronize rail carriers that were offering good services but which did not serve the origin city.

The Interstate Commerce Act says nothing about the right to route a shipment via motor common carriage. It was always assumed that this privilege did not exist in the trucking industry. In recent years, however, the ICC has ruled that it is an unreasonable motor carrier practice to sign a bill-of-lading that has routing instructions on it and then ignore them. The trucker can refuse to accept a shipment with specific routing instructions. However, if the trucker signs the bill which specifies the routing on a shipment, he must follow the instructions.

Should the traffic manager specify routing instructions on the bill-of-lading? A helpful rule to keep in mind regarding this issue is that in the absence of any shipping directions, the carrier is legally obligated to use the least expensive available route. As a general rule, it is best not to specify routing instructions unless there is a good reason to do so. Railroads, for example, often work out expeditious interchange agreements with other railways at junction points which insure rapid transfer of the freight from one carrier to the next. This is also true of motor carriers.[7]

TRANSIT PRIVILEGES

For many traffic managers, one of the most complex activities involves administering and using transit privileges. Transit privileges are used in the rail industry and, to a limited extent, by truckers and inland water carriers.

It is necessary first to understand the concept of *tapering* rates, used extensively by the railroads. Figure 6-5 illustrates the concept of tapering rates. Notice that the rate for the product in question is $1.60 per CWT for a 200-mile shipment. If the shipment length is doubled to 400 miles, the rate increased to $2.50. Rates do not increase as rapidly as distance because a certain amount of costs occur in terminals and are the same, regardless of distance. Therefore, as the distance of a shipment increases, it is possible to spread the terminal costs over more miles. The result is that the rate increases, but it increases less than proportionally with distance.

[7] Flood, *op. cit.*, pp. 240–241.

Fig. 6-5 Tapering rates.

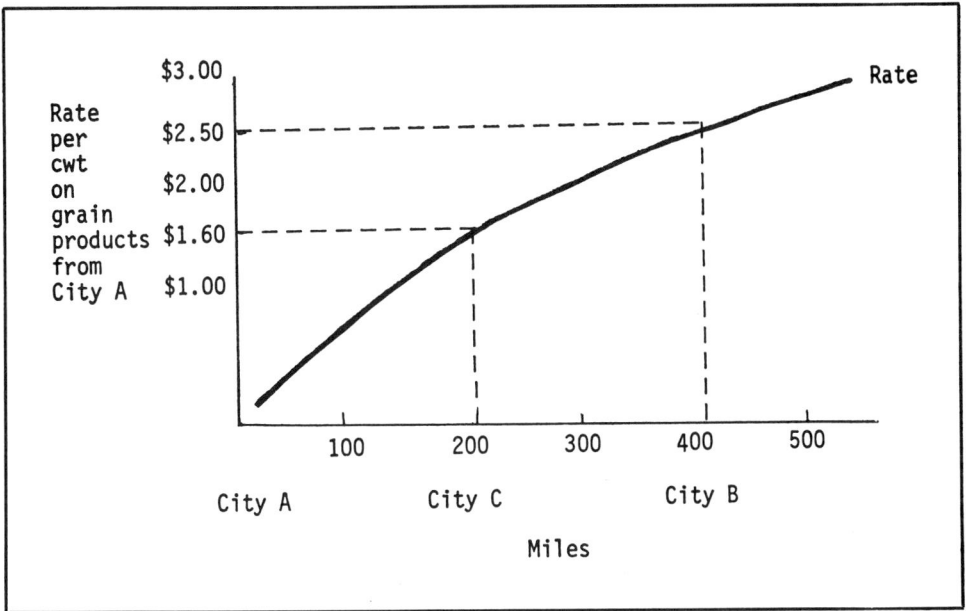

Referring to Figure 6-5 again, assume a grain merchant regularly buys grain in City A and Sells it in City B. He buys the unprocessed grain in the fall at City A, then stores it for several months until it is needed in City B. The question becomes—where to store the grain? Based on Figure 6-5 it is obvious from a transportation cost point-of-view that the storage should be located at either City A or City B but at no city in between. If the grain is stored at City A until needed, then a 400 mile transportation shipment would be involved at a total cost of $2.50 per CWT. Alternatively, immediate shipment to City B for storage would have the same transportation costs. What about intermediate cities between City A and City B, such as City C? Because of the tapering rate situation, grain storage facilities in all intermediate cities are at a disadvantage from a transportation cost point-of-view. If, for example, City C were chosen as the storage point, one would pay $1.60 per CWT to transport the grain from A to C. At the end of the storage period, one would have a 200 mile shipment from C to B, at a cost of $1.60 per CWT, for a total transportation cost of $3.20, rather than $2.50.

The net effect of tapering rates was to prevent economic activity from locating at intermediate locations. Some railroads, in order to correct this situation, initiated the transit privilege. It stated that products could be stopped-off at an intermediate location, and there be stored, blended, mixed, milled, inspected, refined, reconditioned, fabricated, etc. Then, typically up to one year later, the product can be carried to its ultimate destination. The innovative aspect of the transit privilege is the carrier pricing system used in conjunction with it. A common plan calls for the regular rate to be paid to the intermediate location. In Figure 6-5 the rate of $1.60 per CWT would be paid if storage was to be at City C. However, when the remainder of the transportation to City B was accomplished, the shipper gives the railroad a copy of the bill-of-lading proving that the shipment originated in City A less than a year before, and then would pay only 90 cents per CWT for the rest of the trip. The net effect is that a shipment can be stopped at an intermediate point and still pay the rate as if one long-haul had been performed.

LOSS AND DAMAGE

"Cargo loss and damage has been the bane of the transportation industry since the invention of the wheel."[8] A Department of Transportation study noted that a loss or damage claim "... costs the carriers $5.00 to pay out $1.00 and the consignee must spend $3.00 to collect each dollar claimed. Therefore, there is a total outlay of some $2.4 billion per year because shipments of merchandise are lost, stolen, or damaged."[9]

Common carriers traditionally were slow in handling loss and damage claims. Therefore, in 1972 the ICC issued a new regulation,[10] which placed three requirements on all surface common carriers. First, common carriers must acknowledge receipt of each loss and damage claim within 30 days. Secondly, carriers are charged with the responsibility of promptly investigating all new claims. Finally, all claims must be resolved within 120 days of their receipt or else the claimant must be given a written explanation as to the reasons why the carrier has neither paid the claim nor officially rejected it.

Assume that the carrier and the shipper are not able to resolve a dispute regarding a loss and damage claim. What then? Loss and damage claims are handled by the court system and not the ICC. The law states that the claimant has nine months from the date the shipment is delivered to file a claim with a carrier. If the carrier and claimant cannot settle the issue, then the claimant has two years and one day from the date the claim is denied (in whole or in part) to file a claim in the

---

[8] Carlo J. Salzano, *Traffic World* (April 7, 1975).

[9] As reported in "Exorcising Distribution's Demons," *Handling and Shipping* (April, 1973), p. 61.

[10] For further information, see: *Loss and Damage Claims*, 340 ICC 515. See also the *86th ICC Annual Report*, pp. 59–61.

appropriate Federal District Court. If the claim is not filed within this time period, the statute of limitations is binding and no further action can be taken against the carrier.

One of the most difficult and challenging aspects of claim work is the determination of the exact dollar amount of the damage. The law states that the common carrier is responsible for the *full actual loss* sustained by the shipper or consignee. How can this figure be determined? A common rule-of-thumb is the following:

> The basic thought underlying the federal statutes which define the liability and prescribe the measure of damages in cases of this kind is that the owner shall be made whole by receiving the proper money equivalent for what he has actually lost, or, in other words *to restore him to the position he would have occupied, had the carrier performed its contract.* (Emphasis added.) [11]

A key factor in determining the value of the "full actual loss" is the word *earned*. Assume that a retailer owned the products shipped via a common carrier and that they were damaged beyond repair. The question arises, should the retailer recover the wholesale price or the retail price? If the products destroyed were going into a general inventory replacement stock, the retailer would receive only the wholesale price plus freight costs, (if they had been paid) because the retail price had not been *earned*. Assume instead, that a product is ordered especially for a customer. When the product arrives, it is damaged and the retailer's customer states that he will wait no longer and cancels the order. In this situation, the retailer is entitled to the retail price, because the profit would have been *earned* if the carrier had properly performed its service.

Another very difficult area for both shippers and carriers alike involves concealed loss or damage. If a shipment arrives in damaged condition and the damage is detected before the consignee accepts the goods, then the issue is not whether the carrier is liable but the dollar amount of the claim that the carrier must pay. However concealed loss and damage cases are more difficult to handle because the exterior package does not appear to be damaged or tampered with. At a later date, the consignee opens the package and finds that the product is damaged or missing. As can be appreciated, carriers are reluctant to pay concealed loss and damage claims for two reasons. If the package came through the shipment with no exterior damage, then there is a strong possibility that the product was improperly protected on the inside. If this is the case, the carrier is exempted from liability, since improper packaging is a *fault of the shipper*. Secondly, the possibility also exists that the consignee's employees broke or stole the products.

---

[11] *Atlantic Coast Line Ry. Co. v. Roe*, 118 So. 155.

One writer noted that ". . . carriers do not have a monopoly on damaging freight or on employing 'light-fingered' employees."[12]

An important ally of the traffic manager who also wants to reduce freight claims is the carriers themselves. The railroads, for example, have been actively involved in the claim prevention area. Apparently their efforts are paying off, because 1973 represented the lowest loss and damage payout ratio to total revenues in 11 years. In addition, theft claims in 1973 were reduced 13.5 percent over 1972.[13] The railroads are accomplishing these improvements via number of techniques. The Southern Railway analyzes loss and damage claims on a computer for similarity of problem area occurrences and when they are discovered, corrective action is taken. The Bangor & Aroostook railroad uses a radar system to ensure that rail cars do not couple at excessive speeds.[14]

REPARATIONS

The preceding discussion just illustrated the importance of the traffic manager working closely with the carriers to solve mutual problems. In other cases, the traffic manager must be assertive to protect the interests of his or her company, even if it involves alienating the carriers. Such is the case with *reparations*. These are payments made to a shipper by a carrier who has charged illegally high rates in the past.

To understand the procedure involved in securing a reparation payment, it is necessary to distinguish between a *legal* rate and a *lawful* rate. A *legal* rate is any rate that is filed with the ICC and subsequently published in a tariff. If a rate can be located in an official tariff, then by definition it is legal. A *lawful* rate, on the other hand, is a legal rate that does not violate any provision of the Interstate Commerce Act. Since the ICC processes thousands of rate changes daily, it is not possible for the Commission to determine whether each rate change is lawful. Therefore, it is possible to have a legal rate which is not lawful.

Assume that a traffic manager of clay bricks is paying the legal commodity rail rate of $5.17 per CWT from San Diego to Philadelphia. However, he has located in another tariff that concrete bricks transported between the same cities pay only $3.67. The traffic manager believes that since there is no substantial difference between the two products, he—as a shipper—has been discriminated against. Therefore, he files a complaint with the ICC alleging that the $5.17 rate violates

[12] Richard R. Sigmon, *Miller's Law of Freight Loss and Damage Claims* (3rd ed.; Dubuque, Iowa: Wm. C. Brown Co., 1967), p. 141. See also: Colin Barrett, "Myth and Fact About Loss and Damage," *Transportation and Distribution Management* (Jan.-Feb., 1976), pp. 22–25.

[13] Association of American Railroads, "Loss and Damage Payout Ratio Hits 11-Year Low," *Information Letter No. 2121* (May 22, 1974), p. 1.

[14] See the special issue on railroad loss and damage in *Railway Age* (March 25, 1974).

Sections 1 and 3 of the Interstate Commerce Act. Assume further that the ICC rules that the rate in question is unlawful. In this case only, the ICC will determine what the lawful rate should be. Finally, assume that the Commission notes that clay bricks are subject to greater breakage than concrete bricks, and therefore should have a higher rate, say, $3.77 per CWT.

At this point, the traffic manager is eligible to receive a reparation from the railroad, because the carrier has been unlawfully overcharging the shipper in the past. The shipper or consignee can be reimbursed for the difference between the past legal rate and the new lawful rate for all shipments during the past 24 months.

DEMURRAGE AND DETENTION

Demurrage is a penalty payment made by the shipper or consignee to a railroad for keeping a rail car beyond a specific length of time before returning it to the carrier. Demurrage is also collected by inland water carriers if their barges are kept by the shipper or consignee for too long a period. Pipelines are also involved with demurrage if oil stored in tanks at destination is not removed within specified time limits. *Detention* is the same concept, except that it usually has the connotation of referring to the trucking industry. Users of airline-owned containers are subject to similar charges.

For many traffic managers, rail demurrage is an important area of responsibility. Demurrage payments are authorized by the Interstate Commerce Act in order to prevent shippers or consignees from unreasonable delays in returning cars to the railroad.

The rail demurrage tariffs typically state that demurrage payments will start after the expiration of the applicable "free-time." For most cars, the shipper or consignee has 48 hours of free-time past the first 7:00 a.m. to unload the freight car. In June, 1975, the "free-time" for *loading* a car was reduced from 48 hours to 24 hours. The free-time does not count Saturdays, Sundays, or holidays. If a rail car is delivered to the consignee at 10:00 a.m. on Thursday, the first day of free time starts on Friday at 7:00 a.m. Saturday and Sunday are not counted and then the second day starts at 7:00 a.m. on Monday. The consignee must release the car to the carrier by 7:00 a.m. Tuesday morning or else pay demurrage charges. The current ICC authorized payment schedule is $10.00 per day or any part of a day for the first five penalty days. During penalty days, all days including weekends and holidays are counted. For the next five penalty days the payment is $20.00 per day and thereafter it is $30.00 per day.

The ICC is authorized to declare emergency periods of car shortages and to either increase demurrage payments and/or to reduce "free-time." This action was taken to a limited extent during the serious car shortage caused by the 1972–73 Russian grain sale. A more dramatic example took place during the early period of World War II when there was a serious shortage of flat cars, necessary to transport tanks, armoured artillery, etc. The ICC reduced the free-time to six hours starting immediately when the car was delivered and the demurrage payment was $150 per day or any part thereof. As would be expected, this kept the fleet of flat cars moving!

Many traffic managers who are large users of rail cars have found it advantageous to enter into *averaging agreements* with the railroads. An accounting system of debits and credits is established. Every time the shipper or consignee releases a car one full day early, he receives one credit. Each time a car is surrendered to a carrier one day late, a debit is recorded. Debits and credits can only be applied to the loading of the car or to the unloading, but they cannot be cross-used, i.e., credits for rapid loading cannot be applied against debits accrued for slow unloading. At the end of each month the debits and credits are added up. If there is a credit balance, the carrier does not pay the shipper or consignee. If, however, there is a debit balance, the shipper or consignee will pay the carrier the appropriate payment based on the size of the debit balance. Each month the average agreement starts again and credits from the prior month cannot be brought forward.

Detention, as mentioned earlier, is the similar penalty payment assessed by the motor common carriers. In the case where the driver waits with the vehicle, the detention penalty often starts after one or two hours. Similarly, if the trucker delivers a trailer for loading, the "freetime" before detention begins is generally considerably less than the railroads typically offer.

TRACING AND EXPEDITING

Tracing is a procedure which involves attempting to locate lost or late shipments. When the traffic department determines that a shipment has not arrived at destination on time, it may contact the carrier to whom it tendered the shipment and ask them to trace the shipment. This is a no-cost service offered by common carriers. Tracing should be requested only when a shipment is unreasonably late. Many of the airlines, larger trucking companies, and almost all of the railroads have computer systems which monitor the progress of all freight movements throughout their system. This allows the carrier's tracing procedure to be almost instantaneous.

Expediting is another no-cost service of common carriers. It involves notifying the carrier as far in advance as possible of the need to expedite or rapidly move a shipment through the carrier's system. The carrier makes every effort to ensure that the shipment is delivered to destination with maximum speed. The carrier must have sufficient lead time to alert its employees regarding the shipment to be expedited. For the railroads this involves alerting the yardmaster at each relevant classification yard so that the expedited car can be singled-out when it arrives and immediately switched to the proper outbound train. Motor carriers generally notify the operations manager of each freight terminal that the product will be flowing through; in this way, the operations manager can ensure that the product will be quickly placed on the next outbound vehicle.

APPEARANCES BEFORE RATE BUREAUS, REGULATORY BODIES, AND THE COURTS

The traffic manager is often called on to present testimony before rate bureaus, regulatory hearings and, occasionally, courts. Appearances before rate bureaus is a common activity for most traffic managers. This is especially true if the traffic manager is actively trying to lower rates, alter packaging requirements, or lower ratings or classifications. Rate and tariff bureaus hold hearings on most matters and it is at these meetings where the traffic manager will present his argument, as forcefully as possible, as to why the change he wants should be made.

If the proposed change is suspended by the ICC, then the Commission will hold hearings on the issue. Again, the traffic manager will be present to argue for the proposed change. It is very possible that other traffic managers and carrier representatives will also be present arguing against the proposed change. Finally, if the issue is appealed to the federal court system, the traffic manager would likely be called again to present his or her testimony regarding the controversial issue at hand (although this time the traffic manager probably would be accompanied by the firm's legal counsel).

Another situation in which traffic managers typically present testimony is at ICC hearings regarding the issuance of new motor common carrier certificates. The trucker wishing to receive additional operating authority or a totally new certificate will have traffic managers at the hearing testifying as to the need for the proposed service. Truckers in the market would ask friendly traffic managers to testify that existing service was not only adequate but, indeed, of high quality.

OVER AND UNDER CHARGES

The traffic manager is charged with the responsibility of not overpaying freight bills. Likewise, the carriers are legally bound not to undercharge their customers (if they did, this would be discriminatory).

Therefore, both groups attempt to ensure that the correct freight rate is assigned the first time. However, due to the labyrinthine system of rates in the United States, the probability of errors is substantial. The Interstate Commerce Act states that both over and under charge claims must be presented within three years from the delivery of the freight to the consignee.

The primary technique used to determine carrier overcharges (few traffic managers actively look for undercharges) is the freight-bill audit. There are two basic types of freight-bill auditing. The *internal audit*, as the name implies, is conducted by employees of the company involved. The *external audit* is performed by independent companies. Both types of audits are designed to detect current errors which result in the carrier overcharging the firm and also to correct these deficiencies in the future.

BANK PAYMENT PLANS

The ICC requires that rail carriers be paid within five working days of receipt of the freight bill and that motor common carriers be paid within seven working days. Many traffic managers, in an attempt to meet these time limits and for convenience reasons have been participating in what is known as *bank payment plans*. Once the traffic manager initiates this program with the nearest affiliated bank, the carriers submit their freight bills directly to the appropriate bank. The bank treats the freight bills as checks drawn on the shipper's freight account. The bank then pays the carriers by transferring the funds out of the shipper's account into the carrier's account. Each day the bank sends to the shipper the freight bills that were paid that day.

Bank payment plans are experiencing substantial growth because shippers appreciate the convenience of the bank handling the paperwork involved in paying freight bills. Carriers support the concept because of the ease and speed in which they are compensated for their transportation service rendered.

SMALL-SHIPMENTS PROBLEM

The small-shipments problem represents one of the most bewildering situations faced by the traffic manager. Small-shipments are usually defined as those which weigh more than 50 pounds and less than 500 pounds. Shipments under 50 pounds can be handled relatively expeditiously and inexpensively by either the Postal System or by United Parcel Service. Small-shipments, as defined above, are transported almost exclusively by the trucking industry.

There are two problem areas from the shipper's point of view. First, truckers are reluctant to accept certain small-shipments because of their physical characteristics. These products are often light in weight and called "balloon traffic." Typical products in this category are toys, stuffed animals, and furniture. Secondly, motor common carriers have been reluctant to accept small-shipments based purely on the volume of the shipment or shipments tendered by the shipper. These are usually a violation of the common carrier's legal obligation to transport, without discrimination, all traffic that is specified by its certificates and tariffs.[15] As Chapter 4 indicated, the reason motor common carriers dislike small-shipments is that they fail to cover costs.

Because small-shipments frequently receive relatively poor service at high rates, the traffic manager must be innovative in order to correct these deficiencies. While there are numerous solutions, three primary concepts appear to be most readily used. The first involves the use of inter-firm consolidation,[16] or shipper cooperatives, which have already been discussed in Chapter 4. The second type of solution involves *intra-firm consolidation*. In this case, the traffic manager seeks ways to consolidate shipments within his or her own firm. This typically involves a systematic study of the firm's past shipments in order to locate consolidation possibilities.[17] The result of this analysis is that either *make-bulk* or *break-bulk* distribution centers will be utilized. These are facilities through which products move rapidly.

Figure 6-6 illustrates a *break-bulk distribution center*. Assume that a manufacturer of pharmaceutical products in Los Angeles has a number of wholesale customers in the Baltimore, Philadelphia, New York City, and Boston areas. Previously each customer from this overall area would place an LTL order from 300 to 1,000 pounds. The shipments would be sent at relatively high costs with low service levels because many motor common carriers believed that they were losing money on these shipments. To correct this problem, the traffic manager initiated a break-bulk distribution center in Philadelphia. Now, instead of numerous LTL shipments to the East Coast, one TL shipment is consolidated for delivery to the Philadelphia distribution center. Upon arrival of the TL shipment at Philadelphia, the products are distributed to other truckers who make the final delivery. The net result is that substantial transportation savings are achieved, often with a corresponding *decrease* in the total delivery time of the product. This is because TL shipments, unlike LTL, travel to their destination with no intermediate stops.

15 See, for example: "Commission Adopts New Rule Requiring Motor Carriers to Provide 'Full Service,'" *Traffic World* (March 7, 1970), pp. 41–42.

16 Gilbert L. Gifford, "The Small-Shipment Problem," *Transportation Journal* (Fall, 1970), p. 24.

17 See, for example: M. J. Newbourne and Colin Barrett, "Freight Consolidation and the Shipper: The Elements of Consolidation," *Transportation and Distribution Management* (March, 1972), pp. 36–39.

FIG. 6-6 A break-bulk distribution center.

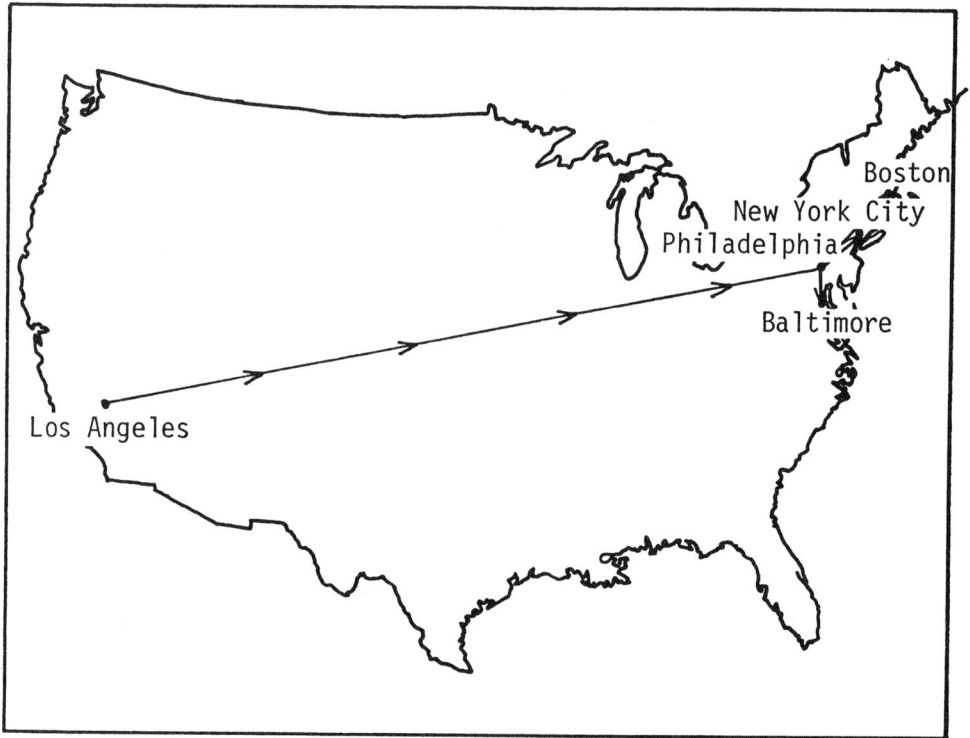

Make-bulk distribution centers are illustrated in Figure 6-7. In this case, a multi-division firm near Seattle has a large customer in Dallas. Historically, each division would process its own orders and send them directly to Dallas, often in LTL quantities. The traffic manager now establishes a make-bulk distribution warehouse in Seattle. Each division now consolidates its shipments in Seattle, so that TL rates and service-levels can be achieved for the Dallas movement.

The final basic solution to the small-shipments problem is the use of private "do-it-yourself" transportation. Traffic managers who become frustrated with the service inconsistencies on small-shipments are often forced into private trucking.

PRIVATE TRANSPORTATION

Private transportation has been experiencing rapid growth. The 1967 U. S. Census of Transportation noted that there were 16.8 million trucks in the United States, and that only 739,000 of them, or 4.4 per-

FIG. 6-7 A make-bulk distribution center.

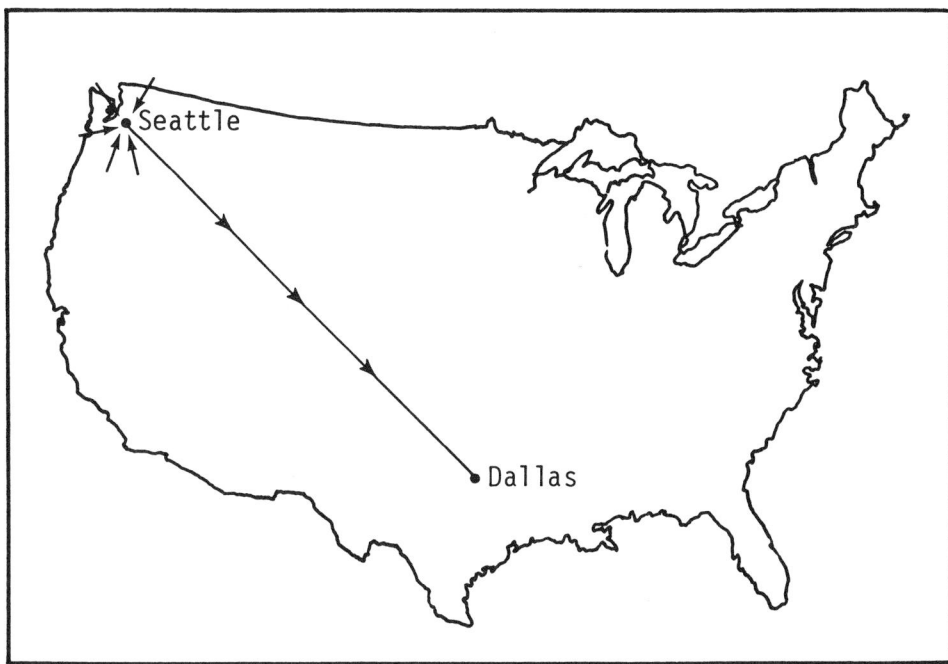

cent, were operated by common or contract motor carriers. Of the remaining 16 million vehicles, an estimated 75 percent were operated as private trucking operations for business firms. A further indication of the importance of private trucking can be seen by looking at the registration of trucks with three or more axles, vehicles that are primarily involved in intercity carriage. Of these trucks, approximately seven out of every ten are registered as private trucking vehicles. Finally, the ICC reports that approximately 60 percent of all motor carrier intercity ton-miles are performed by private trucking operations. With these impressive figures in mind, the following statement by Allen Boyd, the Department of Transportation's first secretary, can be appreciated:

". . . with no advertising, no promotion, no regulation, few constraints and little analysis—the decisions and techniques of private carriage are ubiquitously reflected in today's widespread crisis of common carriage. For the first time, perhaps, the very existence of common carriage itself may be in serious jeopardy."[18]

[18] As quoted in Robert M. Butler, "Private Carriage is Dominant Transport Factor—47.2% of Major Shippers Operate Own Trucks," *Traffic World* (Feb. 11, 1974), p. 78.

The growth of private trucking can be equated to a number of factors. Without a doubt, the most important single factor is the improved level of customer service that private trucking makes feasible. The vice-president for trucking of Burlington Industries, which has a multi-million dollar private trucking operation, said:

> Private carriage was born out of necessity. The primary impetus was *service improvement*. If economies result it is a welcomed gain. We have found, however, that our private truck operations people have the ability to innovate and improvise on a day-to-day, hour-to-hour basis almost beyond imagination, and we are credited with a substantial improvement in sales in many product areas as a result of the service rendered to our customers.[19]

Private trucking, for many companies, also offers the advantage of being less expensive than motor common carriers. This is typically the case when the private trucking operation is able to achieve full loads in both directions, although, it must be remembered that private truck operations cannot legally solicit business from other companies. They can legally carry "exempt" commodities, such as unprocessed agricultural products. For example, a burial vault manufacturer in Minnesota has an extensive private trucking fleet, in which many of the trailers are equipped with "reefers" (refrigeration units). The sight of a burial vault semi-trailer with a refrigeration unit is somewhat unsettling. The logic is that empty burial vaults are transported to the southeastern and western regions of the United States and instead of "deadheading" (running empty) back, the trailers are loaded with vegetables and fruits for the return trip.

Another advantage is that private trucking vehicles can be rolling billboards which advertise the product. This factor can be important, especially if the vehicles look "sharp," have courteous drivers, and create a positive impression to the thousands of viewers who see the vehicles each day.

A final positive factor comes into play if the traffic manager uses both private carriage and common carriage, which is often the case. The traffic manager has a good working knowledge of the costs of using both types of trucking service, and is in a better position to evaluate merits of carrier rate increases. The traffic manager can threaten to take traffic from the common carrier and haul it in the in-house trucking operations.

The decision to enter into a private trucking operation should be very carefully researched and analyzed.[20] One factor is often ignored in the cost calculations is the requirement that the private trucking

---

[19] Statement by George J. Agamemnon, in "PDM Challenged at Seminar," *Handling and Shipping* (July, 1973), p. 57.

[20] See: Thomas R. Henke, "Going Private? Simulate First," *Transportation and Distribution Management* (January-February, 1976), pp. 41–43.

FIG. 6-8 Private truck fleets must be properly maintained.

"No, we're not going to take off. Now get out and see what's wrong."

Reproduced by permission of *Heavy Duty Trucking*.

operation be managed by a professional. All too often, the traffic manager assumes that along with many other duties and responsibilities, he or she will also supervise the private trucking operation. When it becomes obvious that all but the smallest fleets require a full-time manager (who supervises vehicle scheduling, maintenance, labor relations, etc.), the firm finds that a large expense item was not counted in initially. Figures 6-8 illustrates the result of neglected vehicle maintenance. Another factor is that one should consider the effect on the country's common carrier system if the firm opts to use private trucking. Figure 6-9 discusses this point. Every time private carriage usage is increased, the common carrier system is necessarily weakened.[21]

[21] For further recent information on private trucking, see: "Survey Private Carriage," *Transportation and Distribution Management* (July-August, 1974), pp. 52–57; Bart Rawson, "Shipper's Choice—Common vs. Private Carriage," *Distribution Worldwide* (September, 1974), pp. 36–40; and Homer O. Darnall, "Update: Legal Private Carriage," *Distribution Worldwide* (Sept., 1974), pp. 61–64.

FIG. 6-9 Private carriage considerations.

Before You Go Private

If you have thoughts of going into private trucking or are in fact now involved, recognize that you are in the trucking business with all the responsibilities and challenges that go with same. In comparing the cost of private trucking versus for-hire carrier cost, do it honestly on a fully allocated cost basis and use appropriate for-hire carrier costs for comparison purposes. Give your common and contract carrier friends a chance to talk you out of it. When you do this, do it with a relatively high level of carrier management. Too frequently, top carrier management discovers a new private trucking operation too late to do anything about it or doesn't get a chance to compete with one already in existence. Analyze and plan using total cost and optimum mix concepts. Keep in mind that private carriage is not a panacea for all your transportation ills.

—W. J. Mueller
Corporate Director of Traffic and Transportation
The Richardson Co.

SOURCE: *Transportation and Distribution Management* (Sept., 1973), p. 7.

Assuming that the traffic manager and the firm decide on private transportation, they must avoid becoming involved in *illegal trucking*. The most common problem here is the private trucker illegally soliciting business so that the vehicle will not have to be deadheaded back to origin. The ICC and state officials perform roadside checks to detect illegal private trucking.

SUMMARY

Traffic management is an important aspect of most firms, for many reasons but especially because it is typically a large expense item. In 1973 approximately ten percent of the United States' Gross National Product involved freight transportation expenses.

The traffic manager's position involves administering a multifaceted operation. Two aspects, however, can be considered the premier functions of the department. The first involves *rate determination and negotiation*. The traffic manager should not abdicate rate determination to the carriers, because the latter will typically not quote the shipper the lowest legal rate. The three most important factors regarding rate negotiations with carriers are: the projected change in volume after the rate change is initiated, a comparison with rates on similar products, and a comparison with the rate of competing modes of transportation. The role of the rate bureau in rate changes was noted.

Carrier selection is the second pivotal aspect of traffic management. Five factors tend to be of importance: rates, consistency of service, speed, loss and damage record, and special services available.

Documentation involves preparing the bill-of-lading and processing freight bills. The bill-of-lading performs three basic functions: a delivery receipt, a contract for carriage, and in some cases it is documentary evidence of title.

Transit privileges, which are typically offered by railroads, allow intermediate cities between origin and destination locations to attract industrial activities. Because of the tapering principle, one long haul is less costly than two shorter movements. The transit privilege allows the two-part movement to be performed at the same charge as though one long haul had been performed.

The problem of *loss and damage* claims was discussed. Common carriers are subject to pay the claimant the "full actual loss" sustained by either the shipper or consignee. Concealed loss and damage claims are undoubtedly the more difficult aspect of claims work.

Demurrage and *detention* are penalty payments for keeping carrier equipment an excessive length of time. Averaging agreements often are a helpful method of reducing overall demurrage payments.

Two additional activities include *tracing,* which is a procedure to locate late shipments and *expediting,* which involves insuring that a shipment arrives according to a prearranged schedule.

Appearances before rate bureaus, regulatory bodies, and the courts is an activity in which the traffic manager often presents expert witness testimony.

The traffic manager is responsible for detecting all over and under charges from the carriers. These are often detected by means of an internal and/or external audit. Bank payment plans are being extensively used because they greatly simplify the traffic manager's procedure for paying freight bills within the specified legal time frame.

The traffic manager can reduce the seriousness of the small-shipments problem by a program of freight consolidation. This typically involves the usage of shippers' cooperatives, make-bulk distribution centers, and break-bulk distribution centers.

Private transportation is generally started because common carriers cannot provide the quality of service desired by the firm. The traffic manager must be careful to avoid illegal trucking activities with his private trucking fleet.

QUESTIONS FOR DISCUSSION AND REVIEW

1. Discuss briefly the major differences between the responsibilities and objectives of the traffic manager as opposed to the director or vice-president of physical distribution.

2. In recent years, senior corporate management has started increasingly to stress the importance of the traffic management fuction. Discuss briefly the factors that are responsible for this trend.

3. The chapter noted the traffic management objectives that have been established by the Motorola Corporation. Review these objectives and then discuss those which you believe would be the easiest to achieve and also those that would be the most difficult to accomplish.

4. The traffic manager's overall importance to the firm has had its ups and downs since the 1870's. Discuss briefly the reasons for this situation.

5. Discuss briefly the reasons for the complexity of freight rate determination.

6. Why should a traffic manager be concerned with freight rate determination if the carrier is willing to tell him the correct rate? Discuss fully.

7. Discuss briefly the factors that are influential in negotiating with a carrier for a rate reduction. Be as specific as possible in your answer.

8. Discuss briefly each of the following:

(a) a rate "flag-out"
(b) an order bill-of-lading
(c) the short form bill-of-lading
(d) the tapering principle as applied to rates
(e) a "lawful" rate
(f) a per-diem payment
(g) tracing
(h) expediting

9. Assume you are the traffic manager of a large furniture manufacturer. What information would you want to know before making your carrier selection decision?

10. Is consistency-of-service or overall carrier speed more important to traffic managers? Why? Defend your answer.

11. The bill-of-lading is the most important single document in transportation. Discuss the three basic functions of the bill-of-lading.

12. What authority does the Interstate Commerce Act give the traffic manager regarding the routing of freight shipments?

13. Discuss briefly the logic of the transit privilege. Be sure to mention why the railroads established them.

14. What is the basic rule-of-thumb regarding the determination of

the *full actual loss* sustained by the shipper or consignee in a loss or damage claim situation?

15. Discuss completely the basic issues, conflicts, and problems involved in *concealed* loss and damage claims.

16. What procedure is necessary in order to collect *reparations* from a carrier? Be specific in your answer.

17. Discuss the basic idea of demurrage and how an averaging agreement can often be helpful in this area.

18. Discuss the basic types of freight bill auditing. Why is this procedure necessary in the first place?

19. The small-shipments problem is one of the most perplexing quandries in the transportation industry today. Discuss the *reasons* and *possible solutions* to this difficult problem.

20. Private transportation has been experiencing tremendous growth during recent years. Discuss completely the factors that have been responsible for this situation.

CASE 6-1 WINSLOW FURNITURE

The Winslow Furniture Company was located in Nashville, Tennessee. It was privately owned and in 1977 had $400,000 in sales, primarily in Tennessee and Kentucky, although it had one large buyer in Minneapolis. It manufactured only one product—very high quality leather chairs.

Sam Sneed (no relation to the golfer) was the son-in-law of the firm's founder, Joseph Winslow. Since the elder Winslow was nearing retirement, Sam was assuming more and more operational control of the firm. Because of the relative smallness of the firm, the company only had two "white collar" positions. Sam was in charge of production, sales, and distribution. His brother-in-law Harry, was in charge of finance and accounting.

Sam was concerned about the deteriorating LTL (less than truckload) service the firm was receiving. Loss and damage rates were very high, carriers were reluctant to pay claims, they often were tardy regarding product pick-ups, and the rates had increased almost 90 percent from 1972 to 1976. To combat this situation, Bob Collins, a transportation consultant was hired. His recommendation was for Winslow to purchase a tractor-trailer and make its own deliveries. This suggestion proved feasible, and was implemented since the majority of the firm's sales were to retailers in a 300 mile radius of Nashville.

The remaining problem was reaching Minneapolis, Minnesota. A large and established retailer there had been a long-time and high volume customer. Obviously Winslow's private truck-rig could not feasibly provide service for such a far away account.

The Minneapolis firm had just threatened that unless the loss and damage problem cleared up, they would search for a new vendor. Sam discussed this problem at the various furniture trade shows, especially when he was enjoying a few drinks after a long day on the sales floor.

The caller's card said "James Crumply—District Sales Manager—Evans Operating Room Equipment Company,—Edina, Minnesota." Upon being shown into Sam's office, the usual introductions and small talk took place. Then, Crumply stated: "Let's stop beating around the bush. I've heard you need a high quality trucking service to the Minneapolis area. Our company currently runs a load of operating room furniture from Minneapolis to our Atlanta outlet every 10 days and deadheads (runs empty) back. Our padded trailers would be excellent for carrying your chairs back to Minneapolis. We would pick up your chairs every ten days and they would be delivered less than three days later. All loss and damage claims could be subtracted from the next freight charges. All transactions are to be *in cash* and the rate is $7.00 per chair." After further details were discussed, Sam said he would have to think about it.

The present common carrier trucking rate was $15.50 per chair and the delivery time varied between 6–11 days.

Question One: What should Sam do in this situation? Why?

Question Two: Assuming Sam agrees to use the Evans' offer, what potential problems are likely to occur? Why?

CASE 6-2 GREEN MIDGET PEA CO.

Pierre Le Blanc had been appointed as physical distribution manager for the Green Midget Pea Company, located in Mankato, Minnesota. The firm purchased small peas from southern Minnesota and north-central Iowa during the months of July and August. It canned them and sold them under its own label and also under several chain private labels. The peas arrived from various producers via truck. Metal cans arrived by rail car. Almost all outgoing shipments left by rail, except those destined for markets within 100 or 150 miles of Mankato.

Le Blanc's two immediate subordinates had both been with Green Midget for more than ten years. David Tracy was traffic manager and George Van Bemmel was warehousing manager.

One reason Le Blanc had been hired was to reduce Green Midget's warehousing costs. While Van Bemmel—a former warehouse foreman—had kept warehouse operating costs low, he had never understood that a larger cost item to management's viewpoint was the interest on the investment in canned peas. Le Blanc had arrived fifteen months ago and had spent more than half of his time grappling with problems of inventory management. With the help of the controller's staff and an operations analyst from the engineering staff, he and Van Bemmel had carefully calculated costs for each aspect of maintaining the firm's inventory of canned peas, empty cans, and labels. Top management was pleased with this information and the firm's marketing vice president was able to do a better job of pricing the product since he was now aware of the exact costs to the firm of storing each case an additional day. The precise data had also helped Van Bemmel control his warehousing costs even more closely. In the past 12 months, despite an eight percent increase in warehouse employee wages (and many other costs), Van Bemmel had been able to cut warehousing costs—measured in cents per case handled—by three percent.

It was now 3:40 p.m. on a hot September Friday and Le Blanc had cleared his desk and was waiting for 4 o'clock when he would leave. He knew when he got home that he would loosen his tie, take off his shoes, and have a cold beer. Maybe two beers. His blissful thoughts ended abruptly as both Tracy and Van Bemmel stormed into his office. It was difficult to tell which of the two was the angrier. "What's up?" asked Le Blanc, hoping that, whatever the problem was, it could be resolved by 4 p.m.

"We have some out-going boxcars to be loaded tonight or tomorrow, or else we'll have to pay demurrage," shouted Tracy, "Van Bemmel refuses to pay overtime for a crew to load them."

"That's right," said Van Bemmel, "why pay $200 in overtime to save $80 in demurrage. Everyone around here talks about saving money. I assume they want me to practice what they preach."

"Hold it a minute," said Tracy. "Railroads need cars and if they think we're using them for low cost warehouses, we'll have more trouble the next time we need cars."

Question One: Assume you are Le Blanc. Should Van Bemmel be told to pay a crew overtime to load the cars in order to avoid demurrage? Why or why not?

Question Two: Assume Van Bemmel is told to pay a crew overtime (estimated cost: $200) in order to save $80 in demurrage costs. Is this a warehousing cost or a transportation cost? Why?

CHAPTER REFERENCES

AGAMEMNON, GEORGE J.; "PDM Challenged at Seminar," *Handling and Shipping* (July, 1973).

BARDI, EDWARD J.; "Carrier Selection From One Mode," *Transportation Journal* (Fall, 1973), pp. 23–29.

BARRETT, COLIN; "Myth and Fact About Loss and Damage," *Transportation and Distribution Management* (January-February, 1976).

BOSWORTH, JANET; "What Does a Traffic Manager Do?," *Distribution Worldwide* (March, 1971).

BURNS, GEORGE W.; "An Analysis of Common Carrier Liability for Special Damages," *Transportation Journal* (Summer, 1968), pp. 11–22.

BUTLER, ROBERT M.; "Private Carriage is Dominant Transport Factor—47.2% of Major Shippers Operate Own Trucks," *Traffic World* (February 11, 1974).

"Commission Adopts New Rule Requiring Motor Carriers to Provide 'Full Service,'" *Traffic World* (March 7, 1970).

CONSTANTIN, JAMES A.; "Getting to the Heart of the Small Shipment," *Handling and Shipping* (June, 1974), pp. 72–75.

————; "Traffic and Distribution Management In the Hierarchial Structure," *International Journal of Physical Distribution* (June, 1971), pp. 122–125.

COTHAM, JAMES C., III, David W. Cravens, and William M. Hendon; "Measuring the Quality of Transportation Services," *Transportation Journal* (Fall, 1969), pp. 27–32.

DARNALL, HOMER O.; "Update: Legal Private Carriage," *Distribution Worldwide* (September, 1974).

DOWER, JANET BOSWORTH; "How Top Management Evaluates the Traffic/Distribution Function," *Distribution Worldwide* (May, 1973).

————; "Will the Real Airfreight Buyer Please Stand Up?," *Distribution Worldwide* (January, 1974).

ERB, NORMAN H.; "Truckers as Air Forwarders: Economic Implications For Shippers," *Transportation Journal* (Spring, 1970), pp. 51–56.

"Exorcising Distribution's Demons," *Handling and Shipping* (April, 1973).

FLOOD, KENNETH U.; *Traffic Management* (2nd ed., Dubuque, Iowa: Wm. C. Brown Co., 1965).

GIFFORD, GILBERT L.; "The Small-Shipment Problem," *Transportation Journal* (Fall, 1970).

HENKE, THOMAS R.; "Going Private? Simulate First," *Transportation and Distribution Management* (January-February, 1976).

"Loss and Damage Payout Ratio Hits 11-Year Low," *Information Letter No. 2121*, Association of American Railroads (May 22, 1974).

McKINNELL, HENRY A.; "How to Identify Potential Air Freight Users," *Transportation Journal* (Summer, 1968), pp. 5–10.

McPHERSON, W. K. and H. G. Witt; "Feed and Livestock Transport Cost Relationships," *Transportation Journal* (Fall, 1968), pp. 25–36.

MIKLIUS, WALTER and Kenneth L. Casavant; "Estimated and Perceived Variability of Transit Time," *Transportation Journal* (Fall, 1975), pp. 47–51.

NEWBOURNE, M. S. and Colin Barrett; "Freight Consolidation and the Shipper: The Elements of Consolidation," *Transportation and Distribution Management* (March, 1972).

NEUSCHEL, ROBERT P.; "Physical Distribution—Forgotten Frontier," *Harvard Business Review* (March-April, 1967).

OLSON, CHARLES E.; "Risk and the Transportation Investment Decision," *Transportation Journal* (Fall, 1968), pp. 37–42.

POTTER, JOSEPH R., JR.; "An Analysis of The Small Shipments Problem: Scope of Regulation and Policy For Small Shipments," *ICC Practitioners' Journal* (January-February, 1967), pp. 234–242.

RAWSON, BART; "Shipper's Choice—Common vs. Private Carriage," *Distribution Worldwide* (September, 1974).

SALZANO, CARLO J.; *Traffic World* (April 7, 1975).

SHERMAN, ROGER; "A Private Ownership Bias in Transit Choice," *The American Economic Review* (December, 1967), pp. 1211–1217.

SHROCK, DAVID L.; "Motor Carrier Analysis—The Next Step," *ICC Practitioners' Journal* (July-August, 1975), pp. 572–587.

SIGMON, RICHARD R.; *Miller's Law of Freight Loss and Damage Claims* (3rd ed., Dubuque, Iowa: Wm. C. Brown Co., 1967).

SMITH, BILL C.; "What Constitutes a Bona Fide Shippers' Cooperative?" *Transportation Journal* (Winter, 1969), pp. 22–30.

STARR, EDWARD A.; *The Interpretation of Freight Tariffs* (Fort Worth: The Transportation Press, 1961).

STERN, GEORGE L.; "Traffic: Clear Signals for Higher Profits," *Harvard Business Review* (May-June, 1972).

STUESSY, DWIGHT; "Cost Structure of Private and For-Hire Motor Carriage," *Transportation Journal* (Spring, 1976), pp. 40–48.

"Survey Private Carriage," *Transportation and Distribution Management* (July-August, 1974).

THIELE, CAMILLE; "Reliability—In No Uncertain Terms," *Railway Age* (January 26, 1976).

THISTLE, BOYD L.; "Information Flow in a Computer Oriented Industrial Traffic Department," *Transportation Journal* (Spring, 1968), pp. 18–34.

WALTER, C. K.; "Measuring Pick-Up and Delivery Costs For Small Shipments," *Transportation Journal* (Fall, 1974), pp. 51–56.

An electric lift truck in a warehouse. *Credit:* Allis-Chalmers Corporation, Industrial Truck Division.

CHAPTER SEVEN

Inventory Analysis

In many corporations the first officials to become aware of the soaring costs of inventory were the financial officers.

Item in The Wall Street Journal
February 14, 1974

After many months of strong consideration, I decided to professionally restore cars and as a side line sell parts for them. Brother, I was wrong. The parts and running of an inventory business was more challenging and interesting (and difficult).

Excerpt from autobiographical
sketch of operator of Rick's
Antique Auto Parts, appearing
in its Model A Parts Catalog, 1975

. . . Chrysler, the first firm to offer rebates to stimulate sales, estimates that each car in inventory costs the industry $450 a year in lost interest alone.

Item in San Francisco Chronicle
March 2, 1975

Blamed for the inventory debacle. . . , he has been looking for a new job.

Caption under an individual's
picture in Fortune
April 1974

INVENTORY: WHAT? WHO? HOW MUCH?

Inventories are stocks of goods which are maintained for many purposes, such as resale to others, use in further manufacturing or assembling processes, or for the maintenance of existing equipment. From a PD manager's point of view they are the stocks of products between the end of the firm's assembly line and its customers. There are costs of maintaining inventories of any size; and there are costs that occur whenever a desired item is "out of stock." Nearly all of this chapter deals with how to determine the most desirable size of inventory to maintain.

Inventories are carried as assets on a company's balance sheet. However, an increase in inventories cannot be automatically interpreted as desirable. A firm may manufacture much more than it could sell. One well-known U.S. firm expanded too quickly in its European market and, in "achieving such hectic growth, the company committed a number of classic management errors, and so stumbled into that familiar booby trap: an excess of inventories. . . . It required a full year of ever more costly price cutting to dispose of the goods."[1] Carrying costs for the inventories are significant and the return on investment to the firm for its funds tied up in inventory should be as high as the return it can obtain from other, equally risky, uses of the same funds.

BEARING OR SHARING THE BURDEN?

Inventory policy integrates all aspects of physical distribution management because the PD manager must determine the quantity and location of each item to be stored. Recall from Chapter 3 the discussion of rapid and accurate order processing; and from Chapter 6 the importance of carrier dependability. Buyers prefer situations where they can reduce their inventory levels because they are assured of rapid, on-time replenishment as a result of the supplier's and carrier's dependability.

Because of the high costs associated with maintaining inventories, it is usually desirable to have somebody else maintain the inventory. In a situation where one distributor supplies several dealers, the distributor will try to force the dealers to carry larger inventories so he or she can carry a smaller inventory, while the dealers would prefer an opposite policy. The distribution manager of a pharmaceutical company made the following observation in the Spring of 1975: "Inventory management becomes a difficult thing when your customers take the position that they're not going to operate with any more inventory than they possibly have to. Then they push it back to us. We in turn try the same technique with our suppliers."[2]

This phenomenon occurs even within a single firm. A plant's production manager incurs costs every time he or she changes the type, size, or model of product that a production line is making. The manager would prefer to wait until night or the weekend to make the changes on the line necessary to accommodate the next type of product. Until the change is made, the line will continue to manufacture the former product, possibly far in excess of the marketing manager's desires or needs.

This can become even more complex. In the auto industry, as the

1 "When Levi Strauss Burst Its Britches," *Fortune* (April, 1974), p. 131.
2 "Inventories: Which Way Now?" *Transportation and Distribution Management* (May-June, 1975), p. 27.

model year end approaches, the manufacturer has in stock many accessory components for the current year's model which have proven to be unpopular with buyers. Assume that 20,000 autos are still to be built and the following optional items are in inventory: 17,000 vinyl tops; 14,500 right-hand rear-view mirrors; 6,000 radios with rear seat speakers; and 3,000 tinted windshields. If so, then the last 20,000 autos will contain one or more of these slow-moving optional items. The result is that none of the optional items are left when the 20,000th, and last, car rolls off the assembly line. The production manager's problem has been solved, but the marketing manager's problems have become more acute because dealers are reluctant to take autos containing an odd assortment of accessories for which buyers have already shown disdain.

PUSH AND PULL SYSTEM

Inventory order systems are sometimes classified as being either a PULL or PUSH type. In a PULL situation, the channel members (retailers or wholesalers) request or order products as they are needed from the manufacturer. PUSH systems occur when manufacturers force products upon their channel members in an effort to reduce their own inventories.[3] Thus, auto dealers complain that when auto sales are slow, the manufacturer forces them to accept more autos than they want. If they resist, then when auto sales are brisk, the manufacturer favors those dealers who had cooperated during the slack time.

DETERMINING INVENTORY LEVELS

Inventory size determination deals with the amounts, or levels, of inventories one attempts to maintain at each storage site.* There are costs of maintaining inventories and there are costs of being out-of-stock. The PD manager must maintain an inventory level which minimizes the total of both costs.

INVENTORY CARRYING COSTS

Cost of carrying inventories fall into several categories. *Storage* costs are those of occupying space in a storeroom or in a warehouse. Many

---

* This chapter assumes that inventory storage locations have been selected and that the problem is to determine level of stocks to be maintained. In reality, the number of different sites to be used is chosen after deciding what combination yields a desired level of customer service at the lowest transportation and storage costs. This is discussed in Chapters 8 and 12.

[3] See Roger L. Rosenberger, "Push or Pull Distribution?" *Handling and Shipping*, May, 1972, pp. 62–64. Analogous examples of "Push" systems exist in retailing. Some book and record clubs automatically mail their monthly selections to members unless the member has specifically advised the club not to send it.

inventories must be *insured* against fire, flood, theft, and other perils. The phrase *inventory shrinkage* recognizes the fact that more items are recorded entering warehouses than leaving. *Obsolescence* recognizes that items in an inventory gradually become out-of-date. Styles can change for consumer products. A cosmetic company recently reported a great excess of women's hair coloring kits because a trend quickly developed where the "natural-look" was prominent. Related to obsolescence is *depreciation* which is a form of deterioration that is a function of time and not usage. Upholstery in new automobiles that are stored outside may begin to fade. *Interest charges* for the money invested in inventories must be added to take into account the money that is required to maintain the investment in inventory. The actual rate charged will vary with each company and it is often the firm's cost of borrowing money from a financial institution.

Inventories are sometimes taxed; and in localities where the inventory tax base is calculated on the basis of the inventory on hand on a certain date, considerable effort is made to have that day's inventory be as low as possible. Outgoing shipments are speeded up while suppliers are told to delay their deliveries. The inventory tax and most of the costs associated with avoiding or evading the inventory tax are all part of the inventory carrying costs.

Fresh fish or many types of fresh product deteriorate (or depreciate) completely in only a few days. Hence, the depreciation portion of their carrying costs might be 25 percent to 50 percent per day. Dairy products, drugs, bread and camera film are examples of items with a form of expiration date before which they must be sold or used. Their rate of depreciation can easily be calculated since, at the expiration date, the unsold items must be removed from the shelf. (They may have some value remaining. Bread can be sold at "day-old" stores or be recycled into toasted croutons.)

Some inventory items have other types of carrying costs because of their specialized nature. Pets or livestock must be watered and fed. Tropical fish must be fed and have oxygen added to the water in which they are kept. Precious items require additional security measures.

When added together, these costs are known as *inventory carrying charges*. They are usually expressed as a percentage of the inventory's value and sometimes are surprisingly high. One old, but still widely-cited estimate is that carrying costs aproximate 25 percent per year of a product's value. Table 7-1 summarizes the component breakdown of the 25 percent figure.

STOCK-OUT COSTS

At the other extreme is the problem of inventories that are too small. A "stock-out" occurs when the supply of an item is exhausted and a

TABLE 7-1 Inventory Holding Costs

Insurance	0.25 percent
Storage facilities	0.25 percent
Taxes	0.50 percent
Transportation	0.50 percent
Handling costs	2.50 percent
Depreciation	5.00 percent
Interest	6.00 percent
Obsolescence	10.00 percent
TOTAL	25.00 percent

SOURCE: L. P. Alford and John R. Bangs, eds., *Production Handbook* (New York: The Ronald Press Co., 1955), pp. 396–97.

customer wants to buy the out-of-stock item. The determination of stock-out costs is difficult.

Estimating the cost or "penalty" for a stock-out involves an understanding of customers' reaction to a seller being out-of-stock at the time the customer wants to buy an item. Assume the following customers' responses. How should they be evaluated?

A. The customer says "I'll be back" and this proves to be so.
B. The customer says "Call me when it's in."
C. The customer buys a substitute product which bears a higher profit for the seller.
D. The customer buys a less expensive substitute which yields a lower profit.
E. The customer asks to place an order for the item that is out-of-stock (known as a "back-order") and asks to have the item delivered when it arrives.
F. The customer goes to a competitor.

The loss in situation A is negligible; the sale is only slightly delayed. In situation B, the information upon which to make a judgment is incomplete; it is not known whether the customer will, in fact, return. In situation C, the seller is actually better off than if the item the customer initially desired were in stock, the opposite situation is depicted in situation D. Of interest would be the quality of product the same customer requested the next time he comes in. Situation F is most difficult to evaluate because it is unknown whether the customer is lost temporarily or permanently. The competitor may also be out-of-stock. If the customer is lost for good, then it is necessary to know the cost of developing a new customer to replace the lost customer.

For sake of simplicity, assume the responses can be placed into three categories: sale delayed; sale lost; customer lost. The third is the most critical.

Assume further that over time, 300 customers who experienced a stock-out are queried. It was found that the first alternative occurred ten percent of the time, the second, 65 percent of the time, and the third, 25 percent.

These percentages or probabilities of each event taking place can be used to determine the *average* cost of a stock out. Table 7-2 illustrates the procedure. Each cost is multiplied by the likelihood it will occur;

TABLE 7-2   Determination of the Average Cost of a Stock-Out

Alternative	Loss	Probability	Average Cost*
#1 (Brand Loyal Customer)	$ 0.00	.10	$ 0.00
#2 (Switches and Comes Back)	$ 37.00	.65	$ 24.05
#3 (Lost Customer)	$1200.00	.25	$300.00
Average Cost of a Stock Out		1.00	$324.05

* These are hypothetical costs.

and the results are added. A delayed sale has no cost because the customer is brand-loyal and purchases the product when it is again available. The lost sale alternative results in the loss of the profit that would have been made on the customer's purchase. The lost customer situation is the worst. The customer tries the competitor's product and prefers it to the product originally requested. The customer is lost and the cost involved is that of developing a new brand-loyal customer.

SAFETY STOCKS

Safety or "buffer" stocks are designed to prevent an excessive number of out-of-inventory occurrences. They are maintained at a level which minimizes the combined costs of maintaining them and of stock-outs.

Marginal analysis is generally used to determine the optimum level of safety stock to maintain. Table 7-3 illustrates the analysis. Assume goods must be ordered from the wholesaler in multiples of ten. When adding ten additional units of safety stock, the carrying cost of the *additional* or *marginal* ten units is $1200. However, by stocking an additional ten units of safety stock and maintaining it throughout the year, the firm is able to prevent 20 stock-outs. Since the *average* cost of a stock-out has already been determined to be $324.05, then preventing 20 stock-outs saves the firm $6,481.00 ($324.05 × 20). Savings far outweigh costs, and the next alternative is to maintain a safety stock throughout the year of 20 units. This adds $1,200 to the costs but prevents 16 additional stockouts from occurring, thereby saving $5,184.80.

The optimum quantity of safety stock is 60 units. With this quantity carrying cost of 10 additional units was $1200 but $1296.20 was saved.

TABLE 7-3   Determination of Safety Stock Level

# of units of safety stock	Total value of safety stock ($480 per unit)	25% annual carrying cost	Carrying cost of incremental safety stock	Number of additional orders filled	Additional stock out costs avoided
10	$ 4,800	$1,200	$1,200	20	$6,481.00
20	$ 9,600	$2,400	$1,200	16	$5,184.80
30	$14,400	$3,600	$1,200	12	$3,888.60
40	$19,200	$4,800	$1,200	8	$2,592.40
50	$24,000	$6,000	$1,200	6	$1,944.30
60	$28,800	$7,200	$1,200	4	$1,296.20
70	$33,600	$8,400	$1,200	3	$ 972.15

If safety stocks are increased from 60 to 70 units, the additional carrying cost is again $1200 while the savings is only $972.15. Therefore, the firm would be better off by permitting the three stock-outs to occur each year. Note that this determines a *level of customer service.*

ECONOMIC ORDER QUANTITY (EOQ)

The previous section has indicated the safety stock level, a minimum which we always try to have on hand. However, what determines how we maintain this level? How often do we replenish our stocks? How much should we order at each time?

The typical inventory order size problem deals with calculating the proper order size and attempts to minimize the total of two costs: (a) the costs of carrying the inventory which are in direct proportion to the size of the order which will arrive; and (b) the ordering costs, mainly the paperwork associated with handling each order, irrespective of its size.[4] Were there no inventory carrying costs, customers would hold an immense inventory and therefore avoid the details of reordering. If there were no costs associated with ordering, one would place orders continually, and maintain no inventory at all, aside from safety stocks.

Figure 7-1 shows the two costs on a graph and indicates there is a point where their total is minimized. Mathematically, EOQ is determined by using this formula:

[4] In the EOQ model discussed here quantity discounts and transportation rates which vary with volume are not included. For a technical discussion of the EOQ formula, see: James Don Edwards and Roger A. Roemmich, "Scientific Inventory Management," *MSU Business Topics* (Autumn, 1975), pp. 41–45.

FIG. 7-1 Determining EOQ.

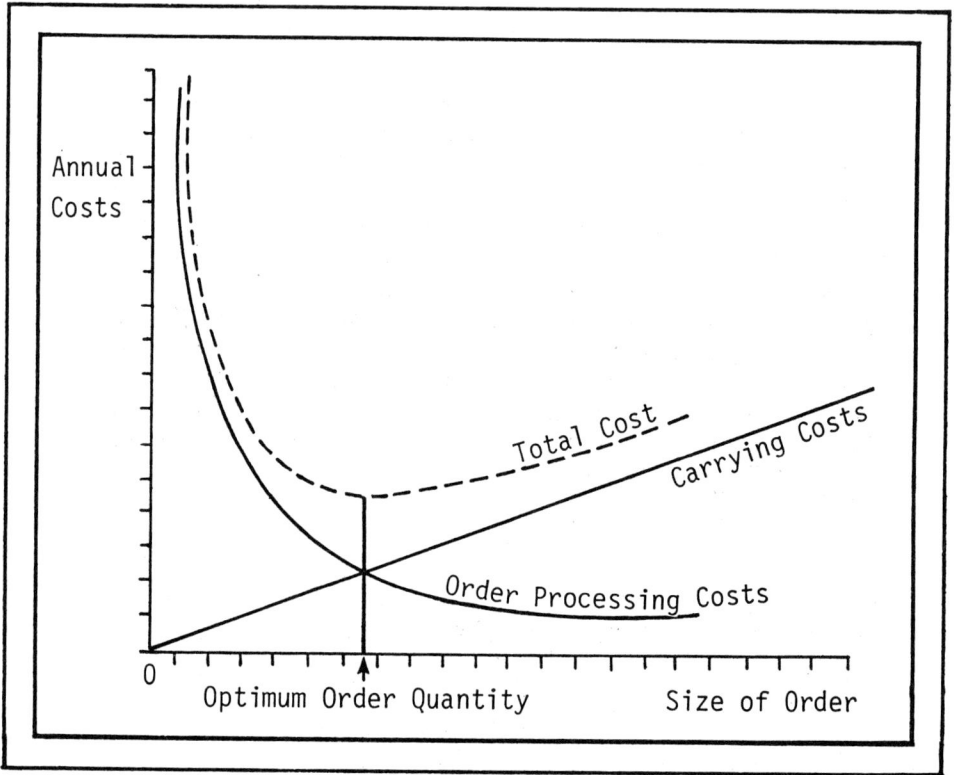

$$EOQ = \sqrt{\frac{2\,A\,B}{I}}$$

where EOQ = the most economical order size in dollars;

A = annual usage in dollars;
B = administrative costs per order of placing the order;
and I = carrying costs of the inventory (expressed as an annual percentage of the inventory's dollar value).

If $1,000 of an item is used each year; if order costs are $25 per order submitted; and if carrying costs are 20 percent, what is the EOQ?

$$EOQ = \sqrt{\frac{2 \times 1000 \times 25}{.20}} = \sqrt{250,000} = \$500 \text{ order size.}$$

One can also see how this answer is reached by using a tabular approach as in Table 7-4. Because of the assumption of even outward flow of goods,

TABLE 7-4   EOQ Calculations

Number of Orders Per Year	Order Size in $	Ordering Costs in $	Carrying Costs on Average Inventory in Stock in $	Total Costs in $
1	1000	25	100	125
2	500	50	50	100
3	333	75	33	108
4	250	100	25	125
5	200	125	20	145

inventory carrying costs are applied to one-half the order size which would be the average inventory on hand. *EOQ's, once calculated, may not be the same as lot sizes in which the product is commonly sold and bought.*

EOQ's can also be calculated in terms of number of units which should be ordered. The formula is:

$$EOQ = \sqrt{\frac{2 \text{ (annual use in number of units) (cost of placing an order)}}{\text{annual carrying cost per item per year}}}$$

Assume that the item employed in the Table 7-4 example cost five dollars. Substituting numbers in the new formula would yield:

$$EOQ = \sqrt{\frac{2 \ (\ 200 \ ) \ (\ 25 \ )}{5 \times .20}} = \sqrt{\frac{10,000}{1}} = 100 \text{ units}$$

The earlier EOQ formula and Table 7-2 showed that $500 was the best order size and, since the product is priced at five dollars per unit, the answer is the same.

INVENTORY FLOWS

It is now possible to integrate the EOQ and the safety stock concepts on an inventory flow diagram. Assume the EOQ in this instance has been determined to be 120 units and the safety stock level is 60 units. Also average demand is 30 units per day and the replenishment or order cycle is two days. Starting on day one (see Figure 7-2) an EOQ of 120 units arrives. Total inventory is at point A which is 180 units (one EOQ plus 60 units of safety stock). Demand is steady at 30 units per day. On day three total inventory has declined to 120 units (point B) and this is the reorder point. Why? Because it takes two days to receive an order and during this time period 60 units would be sold. Since safety stock is *not* to be utilized under normal circumstances, reordering at 120 units means that 60 units (safety stock) will be on hand two days later when

FIG. 7-2 Inventory flow diagram.

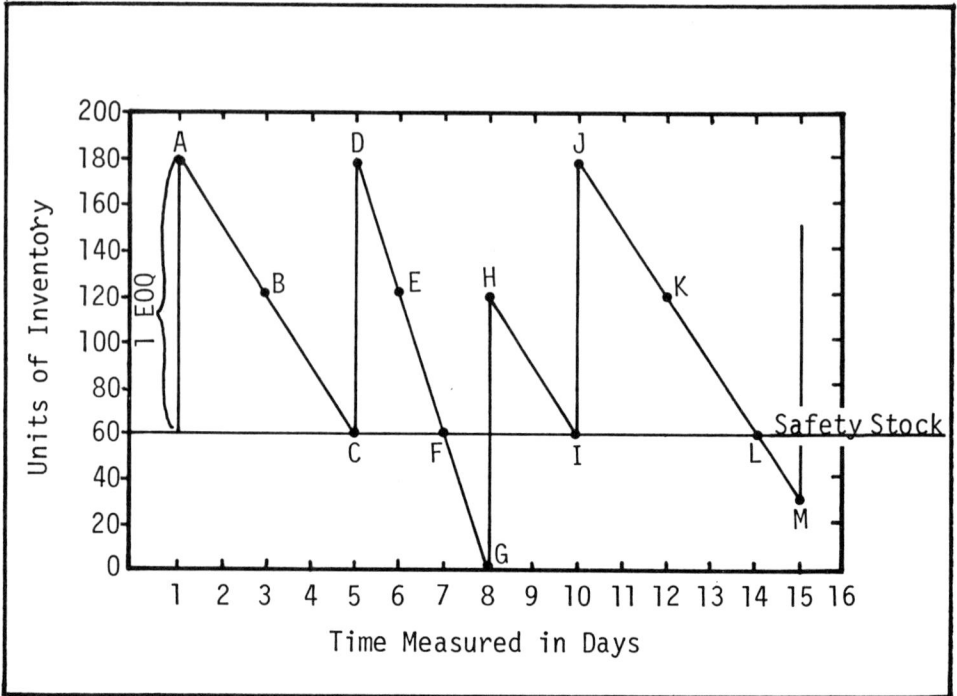

the EOQ arrives. The EOQ of 120 units arrives at point C and then total inventory increases to 180 units at point D.

Now assume that the rate of sales doubles to 60 units per day. At 120 units the reorder point is hit (point E) and an additional EOQ is ordered. However, it will not arrive for two days. A day after the reordering the regular inventory is exhausted and at point F the safety stock is starting to be used. At point G the EOQ arrives just as the safety stock was about to be exhausted. If the EOQ arrived later than day 8, a stock-out would have occurred. The new EOQ boosts the inventory to 120 units which is also the reorder point. Therefore at point H another EOQ is ordered. Starting on day 8 the demand settles back to the old average of 30 units per day. If it appeared that the demand rate of 60 units per day was going to become the average demanded rate, the firm would have to redetermine their EOQ. Recall that a basic input into the EOQ formula is the annual sales of the product. If this figure changes, then the EOQ must be recalculated.

Starting at point H demand is again 30 units per day. The next EOQ arrives on schedule at point I and total inventory increases to 180 units at point J. The reorder point is at 120 units and an EOQ is ordered on day 12. Demand stays constant but the transportation mode delivering the EOQ is delayed one day. Instead of arriving on day 14, it arrives on day 15. Safety stock is entered at point L on day 14. A stock-out is again prevented because the EOQ arrives at point M. Note that safety stock protects against two problem areas—increased rate-of-demand and an increased replenishment cycle.

When an EOQ system is used, such as illustrated in figure 7-2, *the time between orders varies*. The normal time between orders was four days, but when sales doubled the time between orders was only two days. One requirement for the utilization of an EOQ system is that the level of inventory in the system must be constantly monitored. Then, when the reorder point is hit, an EOQ is ordered. With the advent of computerization, many firms have the capability to constantly monitor their inventory and hence have the option of using an EOQ system. A reorder point for each item can be established in the computer's memory so it can indicate when the stock has been depleted to a point where a new order should be placed. Sophisticated computer systems even print the purchase order leaving only the signature space blank so the purchasing agent can sign it.

FIXED ORDER INTERVAL SYSTEM

An alternative inventory concept that is also commonly used is known as the *fixed order interval system*. In this system EOQ's are *NOT* used. Instead, orders are placed at fixed intervals, such as every three days, twice a month, or the like. In the EOQ system, the time interval fluctuated, with order size remaining the same. Under fixed interval systems, the opposite holds, and order sizes may vary each time. Fixed interval systems are used in three situations.

The first is when the firm does *not* maintain automatically updated stock levels. They typically have a clerk manually check the level of all items and determine which stocks are running low. This task is assigned on a regular basis.

A second situation is that vendors may have offered the firm significant discounts if they will place their orders at certain fixed time intervals. Since the discounts are greater than the advantages of using the EOQ system, the fixed order interval ordering system is utilized.

The third and final reason is that the firm buys FOB origin and tries to utilize its own private trucking fleet whenever possible. If one of the firm's trucks currently deadheads (runs empty) from a point near a supply source back to the firm's plant on a regular basis, the firm may decide to buy FOB origin and carry the supplies in its own truck.

The fixed order interval system also involves safety stock. In fact, it requires *more* safety stock than the EOQ system. The reason is that an EOQ system constantly monitors the inventory levels. In an EOQ system, if sales start to increase, the reorder point will be hit earlier and a new order for an EOQ is placed. Stock outs can still take place, but only during the replenishment cycle after the new order has been placed. With the fixed order interval system, since the inventory levels are not monitored, a stock out is feasible during both the order cycle and the time before order placement.

Most fixed interval order systems do borrow one element from EOQ systems. Next to each bin or slot in the warehouse is a card for each product and a minimum product quantity written on the card. When the order pickers note that the stocks have been drawn down to this level, they are to notify their supervisor, who decides whether the reorder should occur immediately, rather than waiting for the next scheduled date.

INVENTORY REORDERING PROCEDURES

Several systems for replenishing inventory stocks exist, and they vary in sophistication. Nearly all inventory systems require some formal sort of stock-level monitoring capability. This section discusses some reorder processes.

A separate listing of what the inventory levels *should be* is usually maintained, and then the actual stock levels are checked against it. A common problem caused by beginning stock clerks is that they assume that when they see the level of some item is low, they will reorder. However, if the stock is exhausted, the clerk forgets completely about the item, especially if adjoining stocks overflow into the empty space. Hence a separate list must be kept and, usually, each bin must be labeled. (However, reserving empty space for an out-of-stock item consumes considerable warehouse space or shelf space.)

In chain grocery stores one frequently sees a code number on the shelves, next to the price listing for each item. Each day, an employee walks up and down each aisle, checking the stocks of several thousand different items the store is supposed to be carrying. The employee pushes along what looks like a grocery cart with a mounted adding machine. Instead of an adding machine, the device punches code numbers in a tape; the first code numbers identify the specific product and the later code numbers indicate the quantity to be ordered. (While performing this task, the clerk also notes the condition of items on the shelves. Misplaced or damaged items are placed in the cart.) The tape containing the punched code numbers can be read by a device attached to a telephone so that the order is transmitted to the firm's warehouse, where the new order is made-up for shipment.

A more complex order system can be shown in this illustration regarding parts for imported autos. The auto is popular and the manufacturer has established and enforces rigid repair parts inventory requirements on all its dealers. The minimum number of each item that must be kept in stock is specified. On a specified day each month (it varies by dealer so that orders reaching the distributor's warehouse are spread out) the dealer must report his inventory to the distributor; and the distributor then determines what parts the dealer needs to bring his stocks up to the minimum levels.

The second type of order is for accessories, sales of which are dependent upon the efforts of new car salespeople (or on other conditions—such as the sudden demand for locking gas caps in early 1974). Since these demands are less predictable, the dealer places a *supplemental* order once a month for accessory items. Parts can also be placed on this order, and it is required to be submitted two weeks after (or before the next) monthly parts order. Note that the dealer has this one chance, midway between his other parts order date, to request parts which are being used quickly. The distributor pays freight charges on both types of orders that have been mentioned.

Two other order systems are available, but the distributor will not pay the freight charges. *Emergency* orders reach the dealer two or three days after being placed (compared with the normal time of two weeks). A *car-down* parts order is handled with even higher priority, and the fastest mode of transportation is used for delivery. Frequently the dealer will phone in the order, then come in and pick it up. For all types of orders except the *car-down* order, the distributor handles the paper work and billing at the same time as processing the order. In the case of the *car-down* order, the part is sent out immediately, then the distributor tends to the paper work.

SUPPLIERS' SYSTEMS

Some order systems are provided by the supplier. In some industries, the supplier employs an "order-taker" who goes on a regular basis to each retail outlet. The order-taker surveys the stocks on the shelves, in the storeroom, and in the warehouse, and writes out a "suggested" order for the retailer to sign. If the retailer has a favorable relationship with the order-taker, he or she will sign the order without questioning it. Sometimes the order-taker will make a small sales pitch for one of the supplier's items and try to get the retailer to order more of that particular item. "Rack-salespeople" operate in a similar manner. A rack-salesperson may maintain the hardware rack in a grocery store and he or she and the retailer agree on the rack's initial inventory. The rack salesperson comes back every other week and replenishes the items which have been removed from the rack and lists the items being replenished on an order form.

REORDER SYSTEM SHORTCOMINGS

While PD thinking has generally held that lower inventory levels were desirable, in 1972 and 1973 there developed in the U.S. a so-called "shortage" economy which meant that certain supplies were in very short supply. Users of these supplies started stockpiling them to avoid both further price increases and stock-out situations. "As vendor backlogs increased, they once again quoted longer lead times. Their customers, in turn, had to order earlier and consequently backlogs increased again."[5] Then, as the economy slowed in 1974, orders dropped and lead times decreased. Buyers—noting the decreased lead times—reduced or delayed their orders. Lead-times decreased further. "In no time at all, those unbelievable backlogs melt[ed] away like the snow in spring."[6] This situation illustrates two shortcomings in inventory replenishment practices of many firms. First, as vendors' quoted delivery time increases, the buyers' order systems (frequently computerized) respond by placing the order for the next needed batch a bit earlier. This increases again the vendors' lead times, and the buyers' systems again respond by placing the order for the next batch even earlier, which further increases the vendors' quoted lead times. Second, in times of shortage, many buyers place identical orders with different vendors, intending to accept only the first order that is delivered, and cancelling the others. This creates a "phony" backlog of orders for many vendors, although they may engage in the same practice when ordering from their own sources of supply. Both practices tend to create bubbles that can easily burst. At this writing, many firms are examining their ordering practices—in relationship to both customers and vendors—to determine whether they can avoid these problems.

KEEPING TRACK OF INVENTORIES

Only in a few instances can an individual look around and see the entire inventory with which he or she must be concerned. A physical distribution manager of a large firm may be responsible for an inventory list of 10,000 or 100,000 different items located at 50 or 100 locations throughout the globe. Much of the "inventory" may not be at a fixed location; it may be aboard a moving ship, a truck, or a rail car. In order to effectively manage an inventory, the PD manager must maintain records that indicate the current quantities of inventory and tell where it is located. These tallies must be adjusted continually to take into account purchases, sales, deliveries, and shrinkage.

[5] Oliver W. Wight, "Where Did All the Backlog Go?," *Modern Materials Management* (May, 1975), p. 17.
[6] *Ibid.*

The simplest record for duplicating an inventory was known as the "scratch-in, scratch-out" method. A sheet of paper, usually on a clipboard, lists all different items down the left-hand margin. Using hatchmarks, a mark is added every time a case is received, and a mark is erased every time a case is removed. The number of hatch-marks on the sheet is the same as the number of cases in the storeroom. On occasion, it is necessary to take the tally sheet into the storeroom and to reconcile the number of hatch-marks with the number of cases.

A modern day example of the same system can be seen in a retail operation selling tires. The inventory is large and is kept near the shop area where the new tires are mounted on vehicles. It is not necessary to display many sizes or styles of tires in the salesroom. A customer who makes a purchase probably wants to have the tires mounted immediately. Thus, the salesperson on the floor must know what tires are in stock. This is done through use of computer punchcards with one card for each tire that is in the storeroom. The cards are printed and key-coded to represent each different type of tire, and the cards are kept in a tray with divider file tabs between each type of tire. If a salesman wants to know whether four tires of a particular style and size are in stock, he checks the tray and if at least four of the cards for that style and size are in the tray, he can assure the customer that four tires are in stock. If the customer then decides to buy, the salesman removes the four cards from the tray and places them in a "re-order" basket. The original tray correctly reflects the depletion of four tires from the stockroom, and the cards in the "re-order" basket can be sent into the wholesaler who will replenish the stock.

MULTIPLE LOCATIONS

More sophisticated systems keep track of inventories that are scattered in many locations. United Air Lines stocks various aircraft repair parts at its maintenance stations throughout the United States. Because it has numerous commercial flights scheduled between these points every day it can easily carry a part from one airport location to another. If a maintenance mechanic in Chicago needs to replace a coffee-warmer in the food galley of an aircraft, he goes to the stock clerk who in turn goes to a computer at the maintenance station and inquires of the computer where the needed replacement item is located in United's repair parts inventory. Even if the part is in Chicago—possibly just on the other side of the wall from where he is standing—it is quicker for the clerk to ask the computer than to go wandering through the parts room. The computer, in seconds, tells him where the part is stocked. If none is in Chicago, he notes where they are located. If the only ones are in Detroit and San Francisco, he can ask the computer when the next United flight from each city will leave for and arrive at Chicago, and then arranges to have the item placed aboard the flight which will result in the earliest delivery to Chicago.

Some items are easier to keep track of because they contain serial numbers. Office equipment, automobiles, cameras, and firearms are examples. In the case of autos or firearms, governmental agencies also keep close control over transfers of the items. Frequently, a governmental agency also has what amounts to a record of each inventory.

Pharmaceutical drugs and some food items must now have "batch" numbers which appear on each carton and on each individual container. In case of product recall, the recall is by batch or lot number, and all such items must be removed from warehouse stocks and from retailers' shelves.

Some items are assigned serial numbers for stock keeping purposes. Figure 7-3 shows a three-part label used by a meat packer for inventory control.

INVENTORIES IN MOTION

Products moving in rail cars, truck trailers, or vessels are considered inventory in motion. For example, rail car diversion and reconsignment privileges are used in the marketing of fresh produce. California lettuce is loaded into rail cars and started moving east. As it moves eastward, the owner sells it by long distance telephone. Once it is sold, the owner notifies the railroad to deliver it to the buyer.

The person who needs the inventory (while never forgetting the adage that "a bird in hand is worth two in the bush") assumes that his or her inventory consists of what is in stock *plus* what is on order. He or she assigns varying probabilities or likelihoods to goods on order showing up in time to avoid stock-outs. The narrowest permissible margin occurs when a salesperson, with a customer out front, discovers the bin empty, but before returning empty-handed to the customer, notices that the stock clerk is coming down the aisle from the receiving dock with goods to replenish the empty bin.

Most common carriers now have computerized systems which shippers can utilize to determine the location of each shipment. Some of these have been referred to in earlier chapters.

An example which shows the flowing nature of an inventory comes from a description of Quaker Oats' computerized system for inventory control. Their computer "prepares a daily stock status report as of 7 a.m. each morning . . . as to goods available, committed and in-transit at all of the distribution centers." The report includes month-to-date experience plus a listing of planned shipments. "It gives those con-

Fig. 7-3 Inventory control labels.

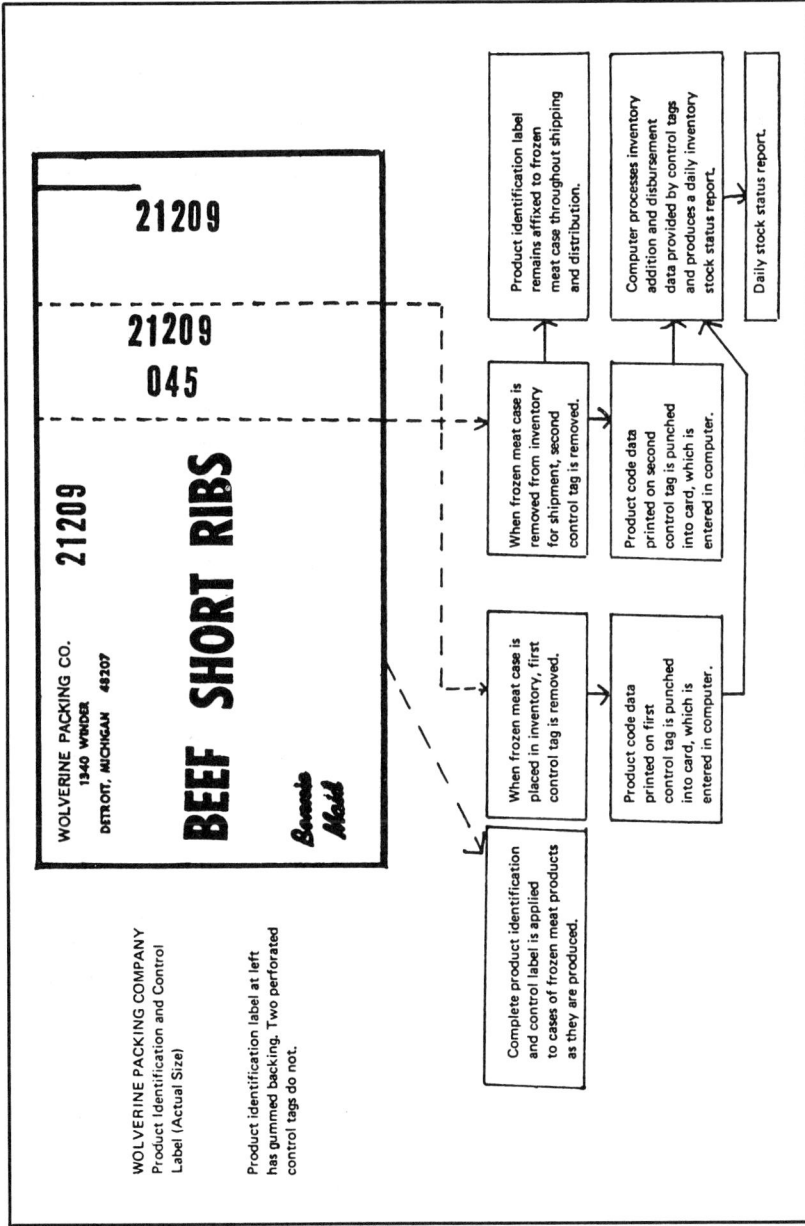

WOLVERINE PACKING COMPANY
Product Identification and Control
Label (Actual Size)

Product identification label at left
has gummed backing. Two perforated
control tags do not.

WOLVERINE PACKING CO.   21209
1340 WINDER
DETROIT, MICHIGAN 48207

BEEF SHORT RIBS

Bonnie
Meli

21209

21209

045

Complete product identification
and control label is applied
to cases of frozen meat products
as they are produced.

When frozen meat case is
placed in inventory, first
control tag is removed.

When frozen meat case is
removed from inventory
for shipment, second
control tag is removed.

Product code data
printed on first
control tag is punched
into card, which is
entered in computer.

Product code data
printed on second
control tag is punched
into card, which is
entered in computer.

Product identification label
remains affixed to frozen
meat case throughout shipping
and distribution.

Computer processes inventory
addition and disbursement
data provided by control tags
and produces a daily inventory
stock status report.

Daily stock status report.

Reproduced through courtesy of Weber Marking Systems, Inc.

cerned with inventory an effective running picture of how things are moving in every line item that the distribution centers handle."[7]

Another example of the "inventories in motion" concept was described by a transportation writer who said: "mobility replaces dead storage" and gave as an example the experience of a southern meat packer who closed several warehouses and substituted in their place truck containers that were continually in motion. The refrigerated containers were fifteen feet long and were equipped with self-contained legs. A larger truck would carry three containers and make individual stops where it would meet smaller trucks, capable of carrying only one container. (Both the large and small trucks have the capability for lifting into place or discharging a container.) At the meeting point between the large and small truck, the small truck unloads an empty container and takes on a full container. This operation is repeated at two other sites with two other small trucks; the small trucks are then making deliveries from the full containers; the large truck is heading back with empty containers to the packing plant. The process is repeated each day.[8]

Legal restrictions may keep an inventory from being in motion. If the goods are kept in a public warehouse, they may also be used as collateral for a loan, and the warehouse manager will not release them without approval of the lender. Liquor or cigarettes in a bonded warehouse may not be released until the owner purchases and affixes various tax stamps. Lastly, where rail transit privileges are being used and the freight is at the intermediate stopping point, there are limitations as to where it can be shipped from the intermediate point, unless the shipper is willing to surrender some of the freight rate savings that were anticipated.

INVENTORY MANAGEMENT—SPECIAL CONCERNS

Generalizations concerning inventory management are often hard to make. One reason is that each commodity has its own handling characteristics. In addition, the framework through which each product is marketed also varies. What follows is a discussion of factors which affect the management of certain but not all inventories.

Many firms stock hundreds or thousands of items and to them the problem is one of determining the relative importance of each item. A rule of thumb which can be applied to most inventories is that 20 per-

[7] "Flexible Inventory Control Fights Shortages and Inflation," *Traffic Management* (January, 1974), pp. 50–52.

[8] James M. Dixon, " 'Distribution in Transit' Comes on Strong," *Distribution Worldwide* (September, 1972), pp. 65–75.

cent of the items account for 80 percent of the sales. The other 80 percent of the items are much less active. This is known as the "20/80" rule.

The term "ABC" is frequently applied when analyzing large inventories. An application of "ABC" analysis might place the top, or fastest selling, ten percent of inventory items in category A; the second fastest-moving group is B; and the slowest is C. Each of the three groups would be handled separately and the system designed would take into account their differing inventory-related characteristics. In a repair parts inventory, an additional consideration would be how "critical" a part might be to customers. Hence, "category A" might include fast-moving repair parts plus a few slow-moving—but extremely important—repair parts. The reason for including both in "category A" is that their stock levels require closer surveillance. A stock clerk might be expected to check "A" category items daily; "B" items weekly; and "C" items every three weeks.

COMPLEMENTARY INVENTORY ITEMS

An example of inventory items with a complementary relationship occurs if they are subject to demand in different seasons. Skis are sold for winter use, scuba equipment is sold during the summer. When goods complement each other in this way, their carrying costs are lower since costs of storage assigned to them is only for a fraction of the year.

Items which are complementary from the retail customer's viewpoint may only intensify the pressures on the retailer or wholesaler concerned with stock maintenance. In the summer, picnic items such as catsup and mustard or weiners and buns, sell together. Almost any time that an item which requires subsequent purchase of a "refill" is sold, the "refills" must be marketed alongside the initial item to demonstrate to buyers that they will not be impossible to find later. Also, the customers want to know the price they will have to pay for refills. An example is filter bags for vacuum cleaners. A store carrying an inventory of vacuums will also carry filters. This is a situation where initial analysis of inventory procedures might lead to the recommendation to drop the line of filters because of high costs involved. Marketing people would then point out that the sale and display of filters is necessary to the sale of new vacuums.

The most frequent complementary relationship between goods in an inventory occurs when incoming goods come from one supplier or outgoing goods go to one receiver or consignee. In these situations, the controlling factors may be the dollar, weight, or cubic volume of the *entire* order. The individual items in the inventories may be of secondary consideration, except to the extent they contribute to totals. A chain food store schedules a truck to go to a specific retail store on

Tuesdays and Fridays. The order to go on Tuesday's truck is small, leaving both cubic and weight capacity of the truck under-utilized. The warehouse will add to the store's order (without consulting the store) and fill the truck, usually with steady-moving, non-perishable items such as paper towels. In this instance the chain owns the inventory, the retail outlet, and the warehouse so its costs of maintaining the inventory do not differ. However, by utilizing the truck's unused carrying capacity, the chain manages to reduce its transport costs.

When using common carriers there are "weight-breaks" which are points in tariffs where the charges per hundred pounds drop as the size of shipment increases. If an inventory manager's order were just under one of these points where the shipping rate per pound would drop, he or she might save money by ordering more and then benefit from the freight savings. Or if the seller pays the freight, a quantity discount may be offered to entice the buyer to purchase a quantity above the weight-break involved.

"DEALS"

Sometimes a manufacturer or wholesaler will have an unbalanced inventory, with too many slow-moving items which have accumulated. To clear the warehouses the manufacturer or wholesaler may offer retailers a "deal" which is a specific lot of merchandise combining desirable and less desirable items. The price is set so that the retailer will buy and does so, realizing that some of the items will be hard to resell, except at a low price. This is offset by the fact that the lot also includes some fast-moving items and that its total price was relatively low. From an inventory management standpoint, when this lot arrived at the retailer's storage facility, it would tend to run counter to the objectives of an inventory management since it would contain some unpopular, slow-moving items which might be the same as the unpopular, slow-moving items already in stock. An example of a "deal" occurred after the introduction of color TV, which proved to be more popular than expected. Manufacturers had many unsold black and white sets, and could get dealers to take them only if they were part of a specially-priced "deal" including color sets.

SUBSTITUTE ITEMS

A more complicated relationship between goods in an inventory occurs when some are substitutes for each other. Because of this, many food stores are relatively unconcerned about temporary stock-outs of food items. They realize that the shopper will not hesitate to substitute a 75 watt light bulb for a 60 watt bulb, or one cut of meat for another. These substitutions could occur in either direction. Sometimes only a one-way relationship exists; an example being that a bolt 7/16 of an inch in diameter could be used in place of a bolt that was one-half inch in diameter, but the reverse may not hold.

The relationships between goods discussed in this section have implications with respect to determining stock-out costs and the sizes of safety stocks to be maintained. If the consumer has no hesitation about making substitutions, it would appear, initially, that there were no penalties for a stock-out. However, a point will be reached where customers become sufficiently annoyed at having to make substitutions that they decide to take their business elsewhere.

INFORMAL ARRANGEMENTS OUTSIDE THE DISTRIBUTION CHANNEL

Competing dealers of the same manufacturer may, in some instances, group their respective inventories for certain purposes. All dealers of a certain make of auto in a city may circulate among themselves a list of each other's inventory of new cars. If one dealer has a ready-buyer for a specific model and color of auto which he himself does not have in stock, he will then check the list of other dealers' inventory to see whether they have the model. If one of them does, he will arrange a "trade" between himself and the other dealer; and then he will have the auto in stock that his buyer wants.

In industries with spirited competition between dealers, there is usually little or no competition between them when it comes to supplying each other with needed repair parts. Both examples are of informal channels of distribution which happen to benefit all parties concerned, including the consumer. They indicate some of the hazards in applying formal inventory analyses to some situations since the informal relationship between dealers may be overlooked.

REPAIR PARTS

Repair part inventories cause many problems. A truck manufacturer with a nationwide market in mind, may advertise that there are one thousand dealers who offer specialized parts and service. This will assure truck buyers that, no matter where in the United States their trucks operate, they will typically be near parts and service. The individual truck dealer sees things differently. To the individual truck dealer the profits come from the sale of new trucks locally, and the dealer feels that the only service customers which must be kept satisfied are those local firms who buy new trucks from him or her. The dealer is less concerned about stocking parts for models of trucks he or she does not sell. If a cross-country trucker experiences a breakdown and must wait several days for the repair part to reach the dealer in question, this makes little difference to the dealer. Hence the manufacturer may *require* the dealer to maintain a certain basic inventory, which often includes items the dealer would typically not choose to carry. This relieves the manufacturer of a portion of the burden of maintaining inventories. In situations where the manufacturer requires dealers to maintain a parts inventory, special incentives are frequently offered. The manufacturer may agree to buy back inventory items at cost in situations where obsolescence or depreciation of the items occurs. The manufacturer may absorb shipping charges on items needed to maintain the dealer's required levels of stock.

Note the problem cited here started out as being one of marketing; i.e., the truck manufacturer wanted to advertise a nationwide network of service and parts. Nearly all inventory policies have a relationship to marketing. Few, if any, decisions are made without speculating as to what customer reaction will be.

RETURN ITEMS—RECYCLED MATERIALS

Inventory systems are designed so goods can flow from the manufacturer to the ultimate consumer. However, in some instances provisions must be made for accommodating a flow, although a lesser flow, in the opposite direction. If a customer is unhappy with an item which is defective and returns it to the store where it was purchased, should the store return it to the wholesaler? Who is authorized to make repairs and then place the item back into stock? If it is not worth returning items, what controls are necessary to avoid fraudulent claims?

Wholesalers who desire to have retailers increase their inventories can offer to buy back unsold items at a later date. A distinction has to be made between returned goods which can be placed back into the wholesaler's stocks and those which are no longer salable. Some products are repackaged or recycled.

In industries where return items are a major consideration, driver/salespeople are sometimes employed. They are paid on a salary plus commission basis and perform more services than the typical delivery personnel. One of these services is to check display cases for dated merchandise, remove soiled items, and collect returnable bottles. Chain food stores frequently rely on driver/salespeople employed by other suppliers to continue to handle items which involve returns. This means that the chain's distribution system need not be concerned with the return flow.

An earlier section described the parts order system used by one foreign automobile manufacturer. There are also return flows within that system. Some automobile parts are considered rebuildable and the customer who buys the rebuilt part must be assured that it meets the manufacturer's factory specifications. The manufacturer rebuilds the motors in its own country, but allows parts such as speedometers to be rebuilt by specific firms in the United States. When a mechanic at the dealer goes to the parts room and asks for a speedometer, the parts clerk notices that the bin containing speedometers has a special-colored tag which makes him request that the mechanic give him the old speedometer in return. If there is no old speedometer to be traded (such as might occur because of an auto accident) the parts clerk charges a higher price to the customer for the new (or rebuilt) speedometer he has just handed to the mechanic. The used speedometers are sent to the distributor who sends them to the plant where they are rebuilt. When finished they are returned to the distributor and become part of his regular inventory. In this instance the distributor has two sources of supply for speedometers: his factory and the rebuilder.

SUMMARY

Inventory policy is affected by the attitude of the other channel members, inventory carrying or holding costs, and the ramifications of a stock-out. The EOQ is a trade-off between inventory holding costs and ordering costs.

Safety stock is extra inventory that is kept to protect against stock-outs. The consequences of a stock-out can be negligible or very serious. The optimum level of safety stock can be calculated using marginal analysis.

Inventory flow is the sequence of events in which inventory arrives and is depleted. Reorder points indicate the time to place an inventory replenishment order. The EOQ system involves varying time between orders but each order is for a fixed quantity indicated by the EOQ formula. An alternative approach is the fixed order interval system, in which the EOQ formula is not utilized; the time between orders is fixed but the quantity varies. "ABC" analysis is often used in conjunction with this approach.

It is important that inventories be physically accounted for, and this can be accomplished using a number of techniques. Inventory ordering procedures involve the methods used to actually place replenishment orders. Both push and pull systems are commonly used and the problem of return items was examined.

Inventories in motion refers to products which have been ordered but have not yet been received. The chapter concluded by examining the key relationships between items in inventory. These included complementary inventory items, "deals," substitute items, informal arrangements outside the distribution channel, repair parts, and recycled materials.

QUESTIONS FOR DISCUSSION AND REVIEW

1. Why should firms consider funds used to purchase items for their inventory as an investment?

2. Why might a production manager and a sales manager have differing opinions as to the "ideal" size of an inventory?

3. What types of products have inventories which fluctuate widely?

4. List the advantages and disadvantages of maintaining large inventories.

5. Give some examples of "complementary" items in an inventory.

6. Assume you own a TV sales and service shop. How would you determine the desirable level of inventory of the following items?

    (a) new sets in your shop

    (b) repair parts in your repair section

    (c) repair parts to be carried aboard each of your six repair trucks

7. What is the concept of "inventories in motion?" Do you agree with it? Why or why not?

8. It is December 1st. How would you determine the rate of obsolescence on the following items?

    A. A new automobile, purchased from the manufacturer on November 1st for $3600. Model changes occur in September.

    B. Christmas trees.

    C. Christmas tree lights.

    D. Snow shovels.

9. Would any of the items listed in Problem 8 also suffer from depreciation—in addition to obsolescence—while waiting to be sold? If so, give examples.

10. Discuss the general concept of inventory carrying costs. Be sure that all elements involved are examined.

11. What is a stock-out? Are they important? Discuss fully.

12. Discuss the basic logic of the EOQ formula.

13. What is safety stock? Discuss the marginal approach to determining the correct level of safety stock. Do you believe the marginal approach is a valid concept? Why?

14. What is the importance of the reorder point? How is it calculated?

15. "Only unsophisticated inventory managers would prefer a fixed order interval system to the EOQ system." Do you agree? Discuss.

16. Discuss the usage of "ABC" analysis.

17. "Sales forecasting is a key input in the fixed order interval system." Do you agree? Why?

18. Discuss the inventory problems associated with return items.

19. The relationship between inventory items was discussed. Outline the key points of this discussion.

PROBLEMS TO WORK OUT

1. Assume you operate a cigar stand. Your customers must request the brand of cigars they want, and you usually sell cigars on a one-at-a-time basis. You sell EL SMOKO's for 15¢ each; they cost you only 10¢ apiece. You are out of El SMOKO's, and on a tally sheet you record the responses of 100 customers who asks for an EL SMOKO and are told that you are out-of-stock.

A. 30 walk away without making a purchase.
B. 20 buy an EL SUPREMO cigar which sells for 25¢ (and costs you 18¢).
C. 40 buy an EL CHEAPO at 10¢ (and which costs you only 8¢).
D. 10 say they can wait and will check with you later in the day to see whether the EL SMOKO's have arrived.

What has it cost you to be out-of-stock of the 100 EL SMOKO cigars you could have sold? What is your best estimate? What other information, if any, do you still need to know?

2. Assume as a retailer you order $5000 worth of SUPER GLO toothpaste per year and it is sold in an even flow. It costs you $40 to place and receive an order of SUPER GLO. Your annual inventory carrying costs are estimated to be 30 percent of the inventory you have on hand. What is your EOQ?

3. You are a retail coal dealer and buy $300,000 worth of coal from the mines each year, and your sales are fairly evenly distributed throughout the year. Order processing costs (including rental of equipment to unload the cars at your yard) are $1000 per order; and carrying costs are 20% per year for the inventory on hand. What is your EOQ?

4. You sell 2000 kegs of nails per year in an even flow and you are trying to determine the most economic order quantity in terms of number of kegs. You are concerned with only two costs: those of order processing and those of warehouse storage. Order processing costs are $60 per order, irrespective of size of order. Warehousing storage costs are $1 per keg and you must rent a constant amount of warehouse space per year, i.e., enough to accumulate the size of your order when it arrives. Your flow of goods outward is so even that you do not have to worry about safety stocks. What is the most economical size of order, in terms of numbers of kegs?

5. (Continuation of the situation in Problem 4) Assume all conditions in Problem 4 hold except that your supplier now offers a quantity

discount in the form of offering to absorb all, or part, of your order processing costs. For orders of 750 or more kegs of nails, he will absorb all of your order processing costs; for orders between 249 and 749 kegs, he will absorb one-half the order processing costs. You still must rent a constant amount of warehouse space per year. What is now the most economical number of nail kegs for you to order?

6. (Alternate continuation of the situation in Problem 4; ignore—temporarily—your work on Problem 5) Instead of the conditions posed in question 5, assume that conditions exist as outlined in question 4 *and* your warehouseman now offers to rent you space on the basis of the *average* number of kegs you have in stock, rather than the maximum amount of space you sometimes require. The storage charge per keg remains the same except it is now based on your average inventory. Does this change the answer to question 4? If it does, what is the new answer?

7. (Continuation of the situation outlined in questions 4, 5 and 6.) Take your original answer to Problem 4 and take into account your supplier's new policy outlined in question 5 *and* your warehouseman's new policy outlined in question 6. How do these two types of quantity discounts affect your most economical order size? What is your new answer?

CASE 7-1 WYOMO GROCERY BUYERS' COOPERATIVE

Located in Billings, Montana, the Wyomo Grocery Buyers' Cooperative served the dry grocery and produce needs of about 150 food stores in the area from Great Falls to Butte in the northwest, to Casper and Cheyenne in the southeast. All dry groceries were shipped out of a 20,000 sq. ft. warehouse in Billings, built by the coop in 1958. Produce was handled out of the Billings warehouse and small rented warehouses in Cheyenne and Great Falls. The coop had its own fleet of 15 tractors, 23 trailers, and several straight trucks. Dry grocery deliveries were made once or twice a week and produce deliveries were made two or three times a week, depending on each store's volume. The stores were responsible for placing orders although a coop representative called on each store weekly and one of his functions was to help some store operators complete their order forms.

The coop was owned by member grocery stores and run by a board of directors elected by the member stores. The directors hired the general manager. Directors were elected with each member store having at least one vote. (The actual number of votes was based on each store's purchases from the coop in the previous year.) Goods were currently sold to the members on the basis of cost to the coop plus eleven percent plus transportation costs. At the year's end, the coop would return 20% of any "profits" to member stores, based on their purchases. The other 80% would be considered as capital and reinvested in the coop. Members received additional "shares" covering this 80% reinvested profit. While not losing money, the coop's volume of business was not growing. This was because its members were generally losing business to chain food stores.

A continual problem facing the board of directors was that some members had small grocery stores, carrying only 1,000–3,000 different products stocked by the coop. Other members had large "check-out" markets and carried 6,000–8,000 different products stocked by the coop. This latter group consisted of the more aggressive merchants, many of whom believed that the coop should forget about its small members and instead help them battle the chains.

The "tissue issue" was a long-standing controversy that was the subject of debate at every annual meeting of coop members. Indeed it had been a problem since the 1950's when tissue manufacturers started manufacturing toilet paper and facial tissues in colors as well as in white. Later they introduced floral patterns for both types of tissue and most recently, "decorator" boxes for facial tissue. The tissue manufacturers did this to capture more shelf space in retail stores. For example, if only white tissue were sold, it could be displayed on a shelf and occupy only 12″ of shelf (measured along the front). If white, pink, yellow, blue, and green tissue were sold, each would require a shelf space of its own and suddenly 60″ of shelf space would be needed. The same held for toilet paper (and for many other products).

From the coop's standpoint, five colors of tissue multiplied the warehouse workload since each color was handled as a separate product, each required a line on order forms, a number slot in the warehouse, etc., and there were five different quantities to be picked. Total volume of tissue handled, however, remained about the same. The volume that was once only white, was now spread over five colors. From the coop warehouse standpoint, the only result had been to raise handling costs as a percent of total volume.

The small member stores, who continued to handle only white tissue and toilet paper, thought it unfair that the coop should raise its warehouse handling charges because some other members now wanted to carry five colors of tissue. The larger members said they had to carry the five colors if they were to compete with the chains. Spokesmen for the smaller stores retorted that they knew something about competing with chains also. The small stores existed in locations some distance from chain stores and admittedly charged more for each item. They survived because their higher charges were not so high as to make it advantageous for customers to drive some distance to shop in a chainstore.

The warehouse built in 1958 had now reached its capacity. It carried 8,200 different items which was the same as the number of available slots for merchandise. If any additional items were to be handled, some changes would be needed. Alternatives were being considered but all involved additional capital expenditures. On the other hand, if the expenditures were not made, some items would have to be "doubled up" in storage slots, and this would increase order picking errors and misplaced stocks.

Of the capital expenditures being considered, the most feasible was a new warehouse. Its estimated size would be 32,000 square feet and—assuming racks and techniques from the present building were transferred—it could accommodate up to 11,000 different items.

At the board of directors meeting, Seth Hardy, who operated a small store at Absarokee, Montana, and who generally spoke for the small members said: "Our warehouse now handles 8,200 difference items. We're told we need a new one, costing God-knows-what so we can handle 11,000 different items. Its the 'tissue issue' again—product proliferation. The manufacturers make the same thing in ten colors and want ten times the shelf space and ten separate bins in our warehouse. Our business volume as a coop is not increasing. Therefore, I offer the following motion: Resolved, that to keep the number of different items our warehouse handles limited to 8,200, all Wyomo buyers are hereby instructed that the number of items for which they are responsible in the warehouse cannot increase. If they want to add an item, they must drop another."

The motion was quickly seconded by Avery Markham of Greybull, Wyoming.

Peter Bright, the coop's general manager, could not vote, but he asked a clarifying question, "What do you mean by 'item'?"

Hardy answered: "It's what you have on each line of your preprinted order form. Fleecy white tissue is one, Fleecy pink tissue is one, Fleecy moon-glow yellow tissue is one, and so on. I think your warehouseman calls them stock-keeping units—he has to keep track of each of them."

Question One: How would you vote on Hardy's motion? Why?

Question Two: Would it make a difference whether you represented a large or small store? Why?

CASE 7-2 SANDY'S CANDY

Sandy Nykerk was an operations analyst for Mannix Model Markets, a food store chain headquartered in Omaha, Nebraska, with fifty-five food stores in an area that extended as far east as Des Moines, Iowa, as far north as Sioux Falls, South Dakota, as far west as North Platte, Nebraska, and as far south as Emporia, Kansas. All of the stores were served by daily deliveries five days a week from a large complex of Mannix warehouses in Omaha. There were two exceptions. Each store's produce department could buy some produce locally, which they usually did during the summer and autumn months. The second exception was that some goods were delivered to the stores by vendors, usually operating through driver/salesmen who would stock the goods on the shelves. Examples of these goods were dairy products, soft drinks, bakery items, "name-brand" snacks, beer, panty hose, candy, and yogurt. Vendors delivered ice cream directly to the stores west of Grand Island; in part this was because Mannix was short of trucks with freezer capacity, especially in summer months.

Mannix Markets was a member of a buying cooperative. The buying cooperative had forced many "name-brand" manufacturers to make their goods available to the cooperative, in which case they would be delivered to each chain's warehouse, and then via chain trucks to individual retail chain stores where chain personnel would place them on the shelves and treat them as any other product. The only goods which could not be purchased through the cooperative was beer. This was because in some states there were stricter regulations regarding the wholesaling of beer (and other alcoholic beverages) initially to insure that the state received all of its beverage tax receipts (although beer wholesalers oppose legislation to relax these regulations).

Sandy knew that most of the vendor-delivered goods were ones that Mannix Markets did not want to handle through its own distribution system. Milk, for example, would be very expensive to handle since it was costly to ship and had a short shelf life. Bakery products had similar characteristics although Mannix Markets did buy some bread from a private bakery and sold it in Omaha stores under the "Mannix" label. Snack foods were also best handled by driver/salesmen working for vendors since they were handled roughly in the Mannix distribution system and by the time pretzels or potato chips reached the shelves, they were mostly broken and filling only the bottom third of each bag.

The buying cooperative had recently entered into an agreement with Schoenecker's Candies, a well-known regional firm that produced eight different types of candies and caramels that were sold in cellophane bags. The experience of Mannix Markets was that Schoenecker's candies sold much better than any competing brand, almost irrespective of price, so Schoenecker's was the only brand that Mannix Markets would carry. Sandy had received a note from her boss saying that Schoenecker's candies could now be purchased directly through the buyers' cooperative and handled through Mannix Markets' regular distribution system. Her boss wanted her to calculate whether Mannix Markets should stop having Schoenecker's candies delivered by driver/salesmen and, instead, purchase through the buying cooperative.

If the cost comparisons were close, Mannix Markets would prefer using its own system for several reasons. The reasons were generalities

PRESENT SYSTEM	ALTERNATE SYSTEM
Schoenecker Candy Co. has driver/salesmen deliver and stock shelves	Purchase Schoenecker's Candies through buying cooperative and distribute to stores through Mannix Markets' own distribution system

BUYING TERMS

Every Friday, the d/s tallies sales for past seven days and store manager approves. Then three days later a bill comes from Schoenecker with 2% discount if paid within ten days (i.e. 13 days after the d/s makes his tally). The entire amount is due within 30 days (or 33 days of d/s tally).	Schoeneker must be paid within seven days after candy is received at Mannix warehouse. No discounts.

WHOLESALE AND RETAIL PRICES OF CANDY

package size	wholesale price paid to Schoenecker	retail price	package size	wholesale price paid to Schoenecker	retail price
3½ oz.	13¢	19¢	4 oz.	10¢	19¢
8 oz.	28¢	39¢	9 oz.	20¢	39¢
12 oz.	42¢	57¢	13 oz.	30¢	57¢

AVERAGE TIME IN INVENTORY

Goods were actually on consignment which meant Schoenecker's owned them and only collected for those which had been sold.	Candy would be in the Mannix warehouse for an average of two weeks and on a retail store shelf for an average of one week.

AVERAGE SALES PER STORE PER WEEK

110 3½ oz. pkgs., 70 8 oz. pkgs., and 40 12 oz. pkgs.	100 4 oz. pkgs., 60 9 oz. pkgs., and 30 13 oz. pkgs. (Sales were somewhat lower because store personnel do not take as good care of merchandise on shelves.)

SHRINKAGE ON STORE SHELF

(unaccounted-for loss): 2 percent per week, paid for by Mannix Markets	2 percent per week, paid for by Mannix Markets

PRESENT SYSTEM	ALTERNATE SYSTEM
SPOILAGE	
(packages torn open on shelf which cannot be sold): 1 percent a week, absorbed by Schoenecker Candy	same rate, paid for by Mannix Markets
ORDERING COSTS	
Absorbed by Schoenecker Candy Co. However store manager or assistant must approve order, twice a week, taking a total of 10 minutes time. Assistant manager makes $16,000 per year plus 15% fringe.	1½¢ per day, 4 days a week, for each of 24 items (8 types of candy in three sizes of package)
SHELF STOCKING	
Absorbed by Schoenecker Candy Co.	20 minute of clerk's time per week. (Clerk's hourly rate is $3.75 plus 10% fringe.) For every 10 stock clerks there is one supervisor paid $13,000 per year plus 15% fringe.
WAREHOUSING COSTS	
Absorbed by Schoenecker Candy Co.	The Mannix warehouse costs $10,000 per day to operate. Its "thru-put" is 750 tons per day, five days a week.
DELIVERY TO STORE COSTS	
Absorbed by Schoenecker Candy Co.	Only available cost figure is 3¢ per ton mile and the average distance from Mannix warehouse to a retail store is 50 miles.
CHECKING IN GOODS AT STORE	
Takes 10 minutes per week of manager's or assistant manager's time.	No check-in necessary; controls are at warehouse, and truck is sealed in between warehouse and store.
BILLING AND BILL PAYING COSTS	
Mannix Markets pays $1.00 per week to process and pay the Schoenecker Candy Co. invoice.	Believed to be less since rather than spot-checking forms from each store, only the Mannix warehouse receipt form need be checked.

regarding driver/salesmen and not specifically referring to the Schoenecker driver/salesmen. The three objections to deliveries by driver/salesmen were:

1. Their deliveries could not be scheduled and sometimes their trucks would tie up an unloading dock which could delay a Mannix truck waiting to discharge ten or twenty tons of groceries.

2. Some driver/salesmen needed space in the stock room and this meant more "unknown" people were wandering an area where pilferage was sometimes a problem.

3. When a driver/salesman appeared, this interrupted the store manager, or assistant manager, who routinely would have to approve the next order and also have to check in the new merchandise and agree on the amount of "returned" merchandise the driver/salesman was removing from the store.

Store clerks disliked some driver/salesmen, claiming that they took shelf-stocking work away from store personnel. Store management discounted this argument because they thought that many store clerks did not like to see how quickly the driver/salesmen worked (the driver/salesmen were mostly non-union and worked on a commission basis). Also, the shelves stocked by driver/salesmen were always neater than those stocked by ordinary store personnel. On occasion, when store clerks disliked a specific driver/salesman, they would sabotage him by rearranging the shelves after he had left, hiding all of his products behind those of a competitor.

Sandy started working on her assignment and found that she was comparing the efficiency of Mannix Markets' distribution system, which handled 10,000 line items, with that of the Schoenecker Candy Co., which handled only eight types of candy in several different sizes of packages. Soon Sandy's project became known as the "Sandy Candy Puzzle" among her fellow workers. Finally, to organize her thoughts and provide a basis for comparison, Sandy took a sheet of paper, drew a line down the middle, and tried to tally as many comparisons as possible. Her analysis is shown on pages 240–241.

Sandy completed her tally sheet and wondered why sales per store should be higher when driver/salesmen service the merchandise. She was told that this was because they did a better job of arranging the goods on the shelves; they kept abreast of changes in demand, such as at Easter and Halloween; and that they sometimes placed posters and other small displays on the candy shelves.

Question One: Given the data that Sandy Nykerk has, do you believe that Mannix Markets should get its Schoenecker Candy through the buying cooperative or continue to rely on direct deliveries by Schoenecker's driver/salesmen? Give your reasons.

Question Two: If you were Ms. Nykerk, what additional information would you like to have before being asked to make such a recommendation?

CHAPTER REFERENCES

DALRYMPLE, DOUGLAS J.; "Sales Forecasting Methods and Accuracy," *Business Horizons* (December, 1975), pp. 69–73.

DIXON, JAMES M.; "'Distribution in Transit' Comes On Strong," *Distribution Worldwide* (September, 1972).

EDWARDS, JAMES DON and Roger A. Roemmich; "Scientific Inventory Management," *MSU Business Topics* (August, 1975).

"Flexible Inventory Control Fights Storages and Inflation," *Traffic Management* (January, 1974).

HOFFMANN, THOMAS R.; "Policy Variables for Lot Size Management," *The Logistics and Transportation Review* (Volume 8, Number 2), pp. 41–48.

HOWARD, KEITH and Philip B. Schary; "Inventory Costs and Product Margins—An Aggregate Approach," *International Journal of Physical Distribution* (October, 1971), pp. 19–24.

"Inventories: Which Way Now?" *Transportation and Distribution Management* (May-June, 1975).

MILLER, JEFFREY G. and Linda G. Sprague; "Behind the Growth in Materials Requirements Planning," *Harvard Business Review* (September-October, 1975), pp. 83–91.

ROSENBERGER, ROGER L.; "Push or Pull Distribution?," *Handling and Shipping* (May, 1972).

SCHARY, PHILIP; "Logistics Strategy and Inventory Decisions," *The International Journal of Physical Distribution* (October, 1970), pp. 31–38.

SCHULZ, ROBERT A.; "Overstock: Definition, Identification, Causes, Costs, Alternatives, and Mathematical Aids," in John R. Grabner, ed., *Perspectives in Logistics Research* (Columbus: The Ohio State University, 1974), pp. 391–400.

"When Levi Strauss Burst Its Britches," *Fortune* (April, 1974).

WIGHT, OLIVER W.; "Where Did All the Backlog Go?," *Modern Materials Management* (May, 1975).

Hopper cars at a prairie grain elevator. *Credit:* Union Tank Car Company.

CHAPTER EIGHT

Warehouse and Plant Location

Transportation specialists speak of a "Second-Morning-Service"
(S-M-S) market as covering a radius of approximately 600 miles. By
this accepted criterion the Dayton S-M-S market is larger than any
of America's top ten business centers. *This is the result of Dayton's*
central location *and* strategic placement *at the crossroads of the*
nation's interstate highway system.

> Brochure published by Dayton,
> Ohio Development Council
> 1973

The use of ZIP codes for rate work by a number of traffic services
attest their growing value and popularity. ZIP codes now define
territories for tariff bureaus, and there are "quick-rate" guides us-
ing primary ZIP codes.

> Frederick Dunn in
> *Handling & Shipping*
> March 1975

LOCATION AFFECTS TRANSPORTATION, COSTS, AND SERVICE

The subject of Chapter Seven was inventories. This chapter deals with
determining where, in geographic terms, to locate the warehouses
which will accommodate these inventories so they can be distributed
to customers. It also will discuss the location of production facilities.

Major factors influencing location decisions are resource availability
and markets. Most facilities are located near one or the other. Also considered to be important are three other factors: labor, taxes, and availability of transport services. Labor is of special analytical significance
because it can be considered as both a necessary resource (in human
form) as well as a market (for final products).

The transportation system examined in Chapter Four moves goods
and materials from their initial origin to the ultimate consumer. This
chapter deals with locating the facilities along the transport routes
where goods are processed, manufactured and stored. The transport

245

system makes the other factors mobile and allows the entrepreneur to combine factors of production which are great distances apart. For example, labor rates are very cheap in Taiwan, and U. S. manufacturers of electrical equipment find it advantageous to manufacture parts in the U. S., ship them in unassembled form to Taiwan where they are assembled, and shipped back to the U. S. for inclusion in a finished product.

While this chapter deals primarily with manufacturing and warehouse sites, similar locational analysis is utilized to locate intermediate facilities used for assembling, mixing or blending. Motorcycle parts may be made near Tokyo, shipped in unassembled form to an assembly point in a foreign country, then from that point distributed to warehouses, and finally shipped to dealers.

This chapter will deal first with the major influences on facility location. Then, it will describe briefly some of the elementary techniques used for choosing general locations. Finally, it will deal with site selection and with facility relocation.

The locational decision process involves several levels of screening or focusing, each step becoming a more detailed analysis of smaller areas or sites. The initial focus is on the region, which for a multi-national company might mean merely to select a nation in which to locate a facility. For a nationwide operation it might mean choosing a state or group of states. The second focus is more precise and usually involves selection of the metropolitan area or community in which the facility will be located. The final analysis is the most detailed and involves selection of a specific parcel of land.

The answer need not always be one site. Sometimes several, or even many sites might be selected at one time. These multiple site selection processes occur, for example, when you are trying to find a combination of distribution warehouses which will allow you to offer a high, specified level of customer service.

FACTORS INFLUENCING LOCATION

Most products are the result of combining raw materials and labor. They are produced for sale in specific markets. Hence, raw materials, labor, and markets all influence the decision to locate a manufacturing or processing facility. Distribution warehouses exist to facilitate the distribution of products. Their location is between, and influenced by, the location of plants whose products they handle and the markets they serve. The discussion which follows covers the location of manufacturing, processing, and distribution facilities. The relative importance of each factor varies with the type of facility, the product being handled, its volume, and the geographic locations being considered.

NATURAL RESOURCES

Natural resources are extracted directly from the earth or from the sea or they are harvested. In some instances, these resources are in locations which are great distances from the point where the materials or their products will be consumed. If the materials must be processed at some point between where they are gathered and where they are needed, their *weight-losing* characteristics become important. For materials that lose no weight in processing, the processing point can be anywhere between the raw material source and the market. If the materials lose considerable weight in processing, then the processing point will be near the point where they are mined or harvested. This results in less transportation effort.

Many products are a combination of several material inputs and labor. Traditional site location theory can be used to show that one (or several) locations exist which minimize the sum of transportation and labor costs.[1] Today, computer programs make similar calculations.

POPULATION CHARACTERISTICS

Population can be viewed in two ways. It represents both markets for consumer goods and a potential source of labor. Distribution planners for consumer products follow shifts in population carefully. Not only are changes in numbers of interest, so are changes in the characteristics of the population—especially when those characteristics can be translated into "buying power." In the United States, a comprehensive census is conducted each decade by the U. S. Bureau of the Census. Between decades, one must rely on data such as estimates made by moving companies as to the numbers of households whose goods are moved from state to state. Figure 8-1 is based on one moving company's 1974 records. State and regional planning bodies possess additional information concerning population within their areas of jurisdiction.

In the United States between 1960 and 1970 three general trends were apparent.[2] The first was from rural areas to urban areas; the second was from the central city to suburbia; the third was to the west coast. The "flight" from the central city was relatively new. The other trends are very old. If you wanted to locate a facility at the center of 1970's population, you would choose Mascoutah, Illinois, near St. Louis. This point is 27 miles west and 9.4 miles south of the pivotal point in 1960.

Population chances are affected by both births and deaths as well as by migration. In the decade of the 1960's the west grew the fastest, fol-

---

[1] C. J. Friedlich (translator), *Alfred Weber's Theory of The Location of Industries* (Chicago: Univ. of Chicago Press, 1929).

[2] This discussion of population is based on E. J. Kahn, Jr., "Who, What, Where, How Much, How Many?" *The New Yorker* (October 15, 1973), pp. 137–157 and (October 22, 1973), pp. 105–132.

Fig. 8-1 States attracting and losing population—1974.

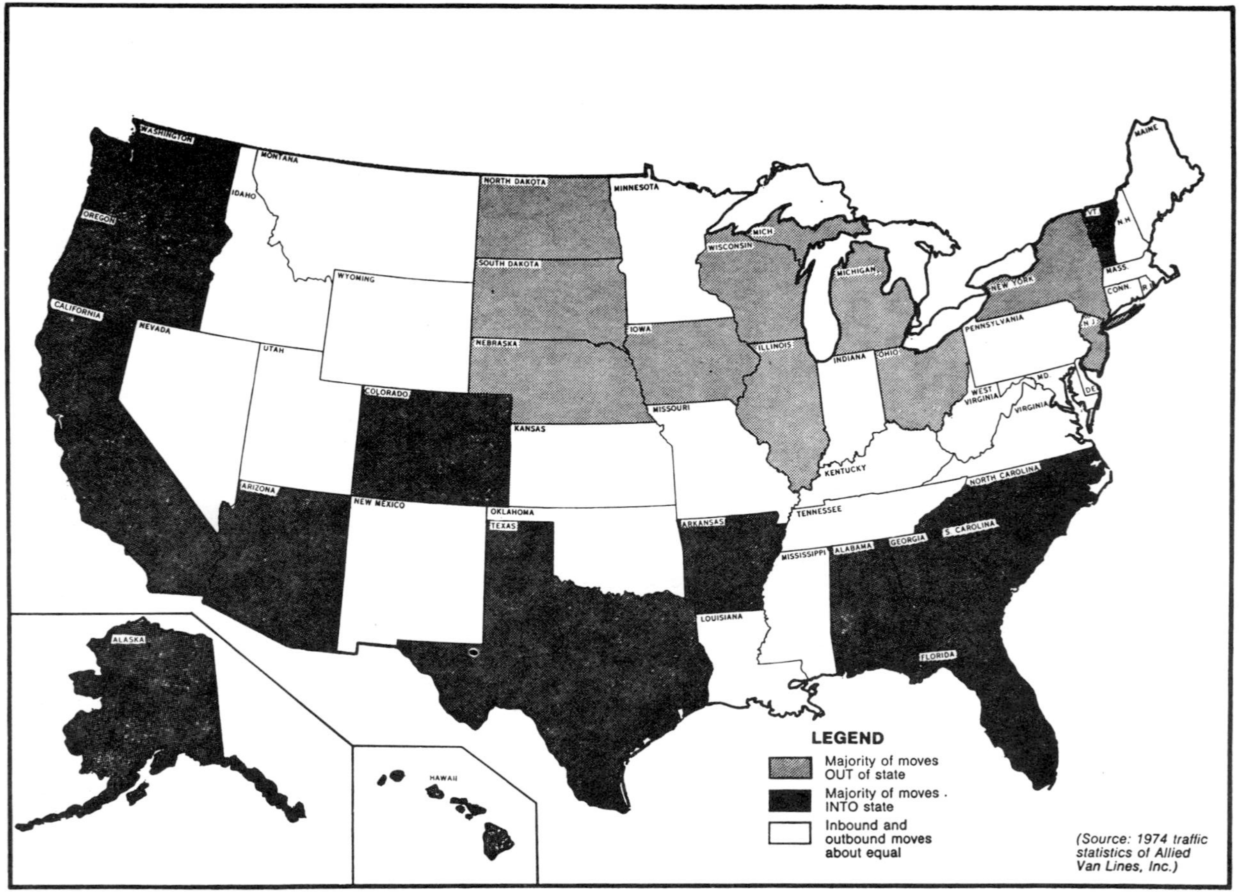

LEGEND

Majority of moves
OUT of state

Majority of moves
INTO state

Inbound and
outbound moves
about equal

(Source: 1974 traffic
statistics of Allied
Van Lines, Inc.)

Courtesy: *Transport Topics.*

lowed by the south; both grew faster than the national average. The midwest and the northeast trailed the national average. Shifts through migration will assume more importance because in recent years the birth rate within the U. S. has dropped to a point where total population remains constant. No longer can marketing and distribution strategy be based on assumptions that population is growing. Many areas will suffer from absolute declines in population.

In suburbs, during the 60's decade, the number of apartments increased by 96 percent compared with an overall increase nationwide of 18 percent in housing units. This surge meant that suburbs no longer were populated solely by families with school-age and younger children. Young childless couples and older couples now live in suburban apartments, rather than apartments in the central city as had formerly been the case. Both the young childless couples and the retired couples represent markets considerably different from the family which is raising children. Retired couples may be more dependent upon retailers who make home deliveries, which means that these retailers would have to adopt the home delivery policies of downtown stores.

Rural population continued to decline and at the same time agricultural production continued to rise. The number of farmers continues to decline, which means rural areas may not be good for products whose markets are calculated solely in per capita terms. Yet, the income of remaining farmers increases, suggesting a smaller number of buyers with more money to spend. Manufacturers of agricultural implements see the same trends; fewer farmers buy equipment, but the size or capacity of each implement sold is increasing because the remaining farmers have larger acreages under cultivation. (In the mid-1970's, there were many reports, although few statistics, regarding a return to rural areas. Not until the 1980 census will we know how significant this movement was.)

From a locational standpoint, this displaced rural population is frequently the source of labor for new or relocated industrial facilities. Census data showed that during the 1960's, communities in rural areas that were both on expressways and had populations of 25,000 or more managed to grow at a rate similar to the national average. This shows two facts of interest. One: the expressways were the arteries which kept the communities connected with larger markets and sources of supply. And two: the 25,000 population figure probably represents the smallest size a city can be and still remain economically viable.

LABOR

Labor availability is of prime concern when selecting a site for manufacturing, assembling and even warehousing. Businesses are concerned with the size of the available work force, its skills, the prevailing wage rates and the extent to which the work force is, or will be, unionized. Individuals seeking sites hope to find a stable, productive work force which will not cost a great deal and which is either non-union or, if unionized, non-militant.

In the United States, the skills of individuals seeking employment are fairly well catalogued. Therefore, someone who is comparing different communities in which to locate should work with representatives of the state employment office. If an existing or prospective employer needed additional workers possessing certain skills, it would be feasible to have state or federal agencies conduct job training courses which would provide the necessary skills. In some areas, unions will agree to supply the necessary labor force. In areas with chronic unemployment, job "re-training" programs are available. Vocational schools and community colleges frequently train individuals to work in various distribution functions; and these educational institutions can be relied upon to train additional personnel. Not all personnel at a new operation will be new employees of the firm. A small number of supervisory staff are frequently transferred from operations at other locations.

When expanding operations into foreign countries there are sometimes limits as to the number of supervisory personnel which can be brought in. The foreign government may insist that its own nationals be trained for and employed in most supervisory posts.

Firms looking for sites often prefer areas where unions are not strong. Some states and communities pride themselves on the fact that unions in their area are not well developed. These states often have "right-to-work" laws which mean an individual cannot be compelled to join a union. At the same time, some unions are expanding their jurisdiction nationwide, and making it more difficult for firms with union contracts to open non-union operations elsewhere. "Industry-wide" bargaining agreements result in fairly uniform wages and work standards.

TAXES

While labor availability and practices are an important consideration in any location decision, taxes are frequently more important, at least insofar as distribution facilities are concerned. The reason is that most distribution facilities, and especially the inventories they contain, are often viewed as "milk cows" by local tax collectors. From the community's standpoint, warehouses are a "desirable" operation to attract because they add to the tax base without requiring much in the way of additional city services.

Tax burdens differ by location, and it is necessary to ask tax consultants to determine the actual tax burden associated with each site. Even when areas have what appear to be identical taxes, there are frequently significant differences in the manner in which assessments are made, or in which collections are enforced. Some localities are so anxious to attract "new" industries that they either formally or informally agree to "go easy" with the tax burden on the new operation for its first several years. While commendable insofar as attracting new industries, it frequently places a burden on existing taxpayers.

While no list of taxes is complete, a partial list would include sales taxes, real estate taxes, corporation franchise taxes, taxes associated with the exchange of real estate, business income taxes, motor fuel taxes, unemployment compensation taxes, and severance taxes (for the removal of natural resources). Of particular interest to physical distribution managers is the *inventory* tax, analogous to the personal property tax paid by individuals. For example, Nevada does not tax goods moving in interstate commerce or consigned to a Nevada warehouse from out-of-state for consignees who also are out-of-state. Goods from the east destined for California—which taxes inventories—are frequently shipped to warehouses in Nevada and held until needed in California. In states with inventory taxes, the assessment date is usually in the spring (chosen by rurally-dominated legislatures as the date for assessing all personal property and which would find farmers' holdings at a minimum). When only one date is used, it is to the advantage of physical distribution managers to have their inventories as low as possible at that time.

Most states have inventory taxes, although frequently they exempt items of political importance. Wisconsin exempts natural cheese in storage for aging; Virginia exempts tobacco still in possession of its producer; Georgia exempts all farm products including cotton; and Maryland exempts imported olive oil and coffee beans. Several states exempt property used for pollution abatement. Other exemptions deal more precisely with distribution functions. Some states exempt goods in public warehouses; one exempts goods brought into the state by water transport so long as they are still stored in the county of the entry port; and some states exempt goods passing through the state on a "storage-in-transit" bill of lading. Many states exempt goods moving on carriers passing through the state and covered by an "active" bill of lading.[3]

As if taxes are not difficult enough to understand, they are but one side of the coin in determining the costs which must be paid to governmental entities. The other is to know the value of services received from these same governmental entities. If water supply is inadequate, or if fire protection is poor, the result will be higher fire insurance rates. If a plant cannot discharge its wastes into a municipal sewage collection and treatment system, it may be forced to install facilities of its own. It may be difficult to attract workers to a community with a poor school system because they are concerned with their children's education. A

---

[3] "Tax Rates/Exemptions," *Distribution Worldwide* (February, 1974), pp. 34–37. See also: "Distribution Know-How," *Traffic Management* (March, 1976), p. 37.

poor school system ultimately places a greater training burden on employers; so the savings in taxes may not be as great as they initially appeared.

TRANSPORTATION SERVICES

When considering a new location, the individual performing the analysis must calculate the transportation costs between sources of supply and each proposed site, and to markets which must be served from the site. Costs are calculated in terms of both money paid to carriers (or for one's own vehicles) as well as the investment in products while they are being carried. Dependability of transport services is also important. Rates are sometimes difficult to analyze if the proposed movement is of a commodity which presently does not move to or from the site in question and therefore no special *commodity* rates exist. Carriers will supply the rate and services in effect and may give an idea as to changes they are willing to make to meet the prospective shipper's needs. The size of the potential shipments is important; larger and frequent shipments have much more influence over carriers than small and sporadic shipments.

Competition among carriers is often important. Some electric utilities located in Great Lakes ports adjacent to deep-draft navigation channels have not installed equipment to unload coal from vessels. However, their waterfront site allows them to obtain a lower "water-compelled" rate from the railroads.[4] Service by several modes also means that a plant is less threatened by strikes in any one mode.

In addition to being served by more than one mode, it is advantageous to have several carriers of the same mode from which to choose. Even if there is no rate competition between carriers, they compete in terms of services. Railroads compete in terms of frequency or scheduling of switching service, or in terms of "finding" boxcars at a time when boxcars are scarce.

CUSTOMERS

The order of presentation thus-far in this chapter has stressed resource, labor, taxes, and transportation factors, rather than customers. Customers are, of course, of great importance. Most distribution facilities are oriented more toward customers than they are toward other factors. Finding and satisfying customers is discussed in basic marketing texts. For consumer products, one usually seeks a population with buying power. The distribution system is then designed so that it carries out the firm's marketing objectives.

4 "Water-compelled" rates are discussed in D. Philip Locklin, *Economics of Transportation* (Homewood, Illinois: Irwin, 1972), 7th Edition, pp. 494–496.

Sellers of industrial products also locate near their buyers. A study of plant location decisions made by firms which located in Greensboro, North Carolina described a specific type of customer orientation referred to as "dovetailing."

> Dovetailing is the process whereby a supplier locates his plant in close proximity to a large customer. The most obvious examples of dovetailing in the United States are the several tin can plants abutting food or beverage packers. For this particular dovetailing situation the tin can conveyor belt is actually extended through a common wall so the finished cans are never touched before they are filled with product. . . . Nonelectrical machinery dominates the dovetailing orientation in Greensboro. These machinery factories were constructed to build machinery for use by the local textile and furniture industry. The other four plants dovetail as follows: the textile plant manufactures woven elastic for the apparel industry; the apparel plant does contract sewing for a large garment manufacturer; the chemical plant manufactures textile chemicals; and the furniture plant does contract upholstering for furniture assemblies.[5]

COMMODITY FLOWS

The previous section discussed shifts in the U.S. population. Firms producing consumers' goods follow the changes in population in order to better orient their distribution systems. There are also shifts in markets for industrial goods. This section discusses general sources of data regarding commodity flows. These data would be studied, much like population figures, to determine changes occurring in the movements of raw materials, semi-processed goods, etc. Government data in these areas are generally complete, but the degree of coverage varies. There may be excellent reports concerning the supply and demand for a specific agricultural commodity, while there may be almost no data at all concerning other, more significant products. Some trade organizations report data concerning their members' activities.

Commodity flow data are related to production. Two vital pieces of information are (1) how much is being produced and (2) where it is being shipped. If you are concerned with a distribution system for an industrial product, this information would tell how the market is functioning, and, in many instances you might be able to identify both the manufacturers and their major customers. At this point, you as the researcher would understand the existing situation and you would ask whether you could find a lower cost production-distribution arrangement. Should your firm join the existing patterns of trade (which is easier to do in an expanding market) or should it set out to produce at a point where no other manufacturers of a similar product are located?

[5] Charles R. Hayes and Norman W. Schul, "Why Do Manufacturers Locate in the Southern Piedmont?" *Land Economics* (February, 1968), pp. 117–121.

Input-output analysis is a device used by economists to describe the inter-relationships (transactions) between various aspects of our economy.[6] Input-output *models* (or series of simultaneous equations) exist which describe the U. S. economy as well as some state and regional economies. The economy is divided into approximately 100 sectors (which are similar to industries) such as coal mining, household furniture, drugs and cosmetics, metal containers, office and computing machines, transportation and warehousing, or state and local government. A large table is constructed, consisting of 100 columns and 100 rows and one row is assigned to each sector and one column is assigned to each sector. Hence, a sector (or industry) shows up twice, as both a row and a column. To read the amounts an industry supplies to other industries, one reads across the table; to read the inputs into (or purchases of) any particular industry, one reads up or down the column. Hence each output is some other industry's input. Where the row and column for the same industry intersect, one sees the industry's consumption of its own product. For example, a small portion of the output of the wooden container industry is used within the industry. Also, inputs and outputs are not always exactly equal; and there are rows and columns to account for imports and exports, depreciation, and changes in inventory levels.

For years, a one percent sample of railroad waybills, (additional copies of the bill-of-lading issued by the railroad for each shipment) were collected and tallied, and reports were prepared showing all state-to-state movements, except in instances where publication of the data would identify one shipper. The Interstate Commerce Commission stopped publishing these reports in the late 1960's due to lack of funds. The sample of waybills was still collected, however, and the Department of Transportation took over the publishing of the data, although in somewhat less detail.[7]

The U. S. Army Corps of Engineers annually publishes data on commodity movements through ports and along waterways. The report series is known as *Waterborne Commerce of the United States.* Less data are available concerning domestic air freight, truck, and pipeline movements although, with searching, one can sometimes discover that data are being recorded and available.[8] Transportation planning agen-

[6] *Input-Output Analysis and Transportation Planning, A Collection of Papers Delivered at an Economics Seminar* (Washington, D.C.: Office of the Secretary of Transportation, 1969).

[7] See: *1972 Carload Waybill Statistics* (Washington, D.C.: Federal Railroad Administration, 1974). These data show movements between and within the five railroad "territories" rather than on a state-to-state basis.

[8] A list of all sources of commodity flow data would be voluminous. One general—and well-documented—source is *Transportation Facts and Trends*, published annually, and revised quarterly, by the Transportation Association of America, 1101 17th Street, N.W. Washington, D.C. An excellent "one-shot" view of all U.S. foreign

cies may conduct detailed studies of movements of goods by trucks within a community, or a state tax agency may collect the tax on petroleum at the point where the petroleum is discharged from the pipeline. Regulatory bodies require that activities be reported on a periodic basis. In proceedings before regulatory bodies, carriers or shippers frequently disclose considerable information regarding their operations.

Most people who deal with commodity flow information are experienced and are able to read more into data. They follow news accounts concerning sales and their own selling force provides information regarding activities of competitors. Having this knowledge gives them some additional insights when they attempt to interpret government statistics.

FINDING THE "LOW COST" LOCATION

Most solutions to locational problems are reached through use of computerized analysis. Frequently, large geographic areas are under consideration and, initially, all possible sites are considered to be "eligible." The problem posed is "where to locate?" A firm exporting into western Europe may decide that it must locate a manufacturing operation inside one of the common market countries so it can avoid the higher tariff barriers facing exports from outside. A U.S. firm, located in Pennsylvania, may decide that the time has come to locate an additional distribution facility west of the Mississippi River. This section illustrates a method for finding the "low-cost" location and discusses the various sources of geographic coding data, available in the United States, which might be needed for any computerized analysis of a locational problem.

CENTER OF GRAVITY APPROACH

The "center-of-gravity" method is frequently used for locating a single facility at a site where the distance to other, existing facilities is minimized. Figure 8-2 shows a "grid" system placed over a map of five existing retail stores. Assuming that each store receives the same tonnage and that straight line (or "as the crow flies") distances are used throughout, the "best" location for a warehouse to serve the five retail stores is determined by taking the average north-south coordinates of the retail stores and the average east-west coordinates. On Figure 8-2, the "grid" system has its lower left (southwest) corner labeled point zero, zero. The vertical (north-south) axis shows distances north of point zero,

trade movements is contained in *Domestic and International Transportation of U.S. Foreign Trade: 1970* published in Washington, D.C. in 1972 by the U.S. Departments of Commerce, Transportation, and Army.

FIG. 8-2 "Center of Gravity" location for warehouse to serve five retail stores.

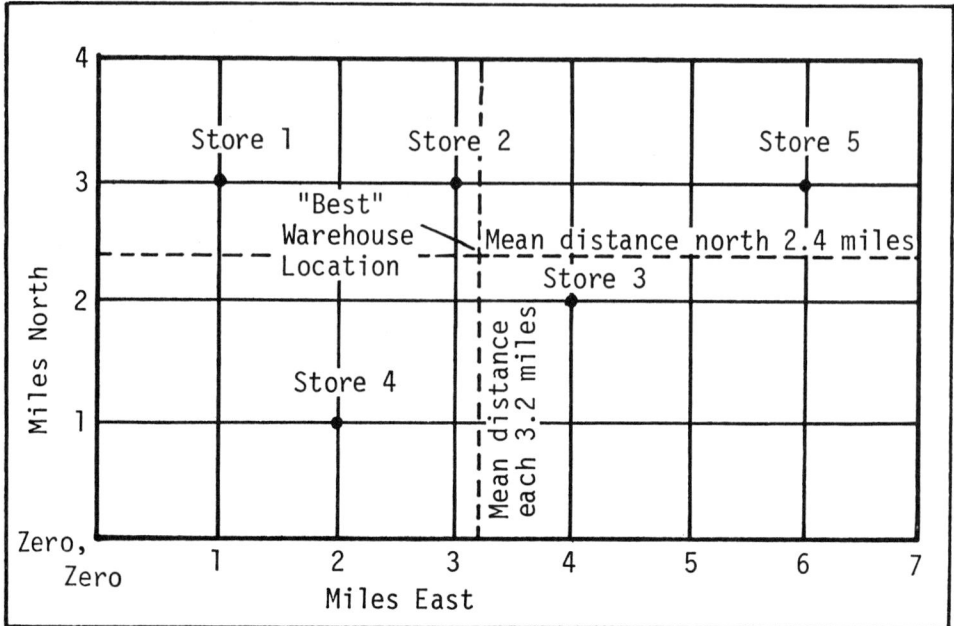

zero; and the horizontal (east-west) axis shows distances to the east. In the example, the average distance north is 3 + 1 + 3 + 2 + 3 divided by the number of stores, or 5, and the answer is 1⅖ or 2.4 miles. The average distance east is 1 + 2 + 3 + 4 + 6 divided by 5 or 3.2 miles. The "best" warehouse location is one with coordinates of 2.4 miles north and 3.2 miles east of point zero. ("Best" has been kept in quote marks because the method described here only approximates the most accurate solution.)[9]

Approaches such as this provide approximate locations of centralized facilities, at least in a transportation sense. However, adjustments have to be made to take into account taxes, wage rates, volume "discounts," the cost and quality of transport services, and the fact that transport rates "taper."

GRID SYSTEMS

"Grid" systems are checker-board patterns placed on a map (such as in Figure 8-2). Squares are numbered in two directions: horizontal and vertical. Recall from geometry that the length of the hypotenuse of a

[9] Ronald H. Ballou, "Potential Error in the Center of Gravity Approach to Facility Location," in *Transportation Journal* (Winter, 1973), pp. 44–50.

right triangle is the square root of the sum of the squared values of each of the right triangle's two legs. It is easy for a computer to calculate the distance between any two points whose grid coordinates are known. Grid systems are placed so they will coincide with north-south and east-west lines on a map (although minor distortion is caused by the fact that east-west lines are parallel while north-south lines converge at both poles). Grid systems are important to locational analysis because they allow one to analyze spatial relationships with relatively simple mathematical tools.

At least one firm has attempted to place varying types of geographic data on one record.[10] Figure 8-3 shows the layout which utilizes 126 digits to record 22 types of information. Some of the types of information require additional explanation. Item 3, unit type, indicates whether the place is a city or a county or some other governmental unit. Items 6 through 8 refer to a numeric code established by Dun and Bradstreet. Items 10 and 11 refer to a Standard Point Location Code developed jointly by the National Motor Freight Tariff Association and the Association of American Railroads for purposes of eventually computerizing tariffs and providing a scheme for identification of transportation activities. Items 15 and 18 are the mean latitudes and longitudes of the counties. Items 19 and 20 refer to a geographic coding system devised by IBM and items 21 and 22 refer to F. I. P. S. or Federal Information Processing Standard, a system devised by the U. S. Bureau of Standards. The firm whose form is pictured lists over 102,000 different "places" in the United States.

The discussion to this point has emphasized transportation data. Marketing data are equally important and a locational researcher might tie into his geographic analysis, statistics concerning the population and buying power of areas for which distribution centers are being considered. This information is available from the U. S. Bureau of the Census or from private services. The marketing and transportation data could be combined and make it possible to search for distribution sites which meet both transportation requirements and are within reach of specified blocs of buying power.

DETERMINING THE NUMBER OF FACILITIES

Very few firms start business on one day and require a nation-wide distribution system the next. Distribution and production facilities are usually added one at a time. *Marginal analysis* is employed to test whether one more (or less) distribution facility is required. The drawback of marginal analysis is that one may miss the "big picture." Very

[10] See: *A Survey of National Geo-Coding Systems* (Washington, D.C.: U.S. Department of Transportation, February, 1972), especially pp. 76–85.

FIG. 8-3 Example of U.S. geographic data layout.

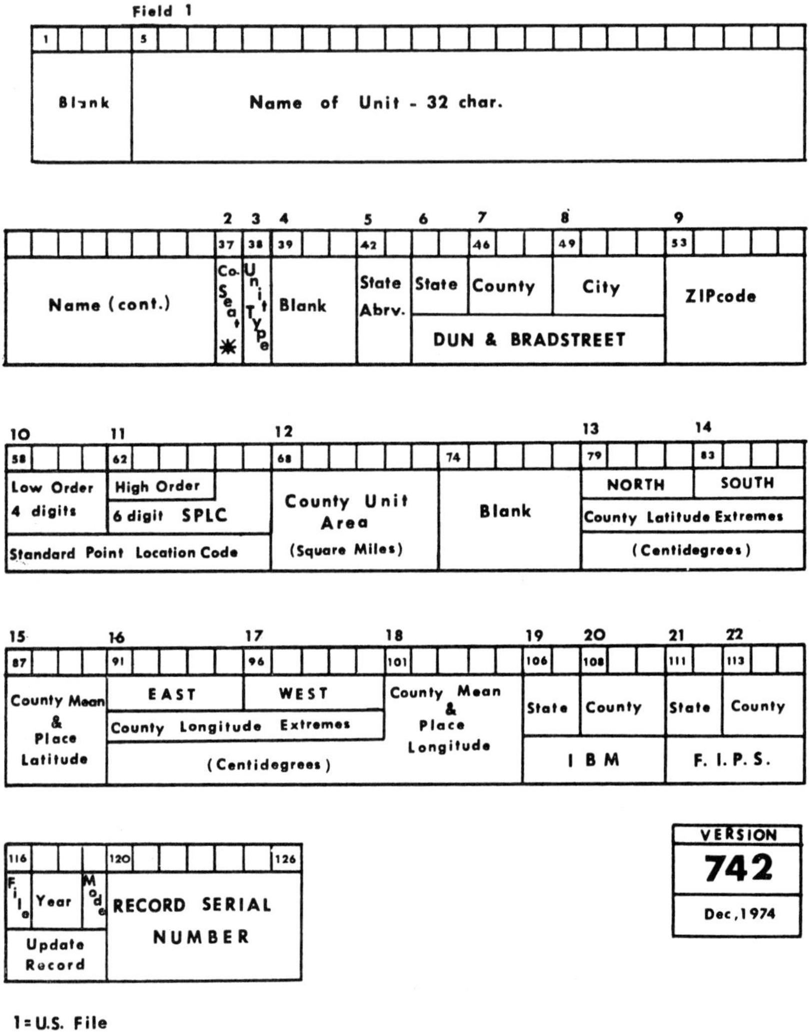

Field 1

| 1 | | | 5 | | | | | | | | | | | | | | | | | | | | | | | | | | | | | | | |

Blank   Name of Unit - 32 char.

| | | | | | | 2 | 3 | 4 | | 5 | | 6 | | 7 | | 8 | | 9 | |
| | | | | | | 37 | 38 | 39 | | 42 | | | | 46 | | 49 | | 53 | |

Name (cont.) | Co. Seat * | Unit Type | Blank | State Abrv. | State | County | City | ZIPcode

DUN & BRADSTREET

| 10 | | 11 | | 12 | | | | 13 | | 14 | |
| 58 | | 62 | | 68 | | 74 | | 79 | | 83 | |

Low Order 4 digits | High Order 6 digit SPLC | County Unit Area | Blank | NORTH | SOUTH
| | | (Square Miles) | | County Latitude Extremes

Standard Point Location Code | | | | (Centidegrees)

| 15 | | 16 | | 17 | | 18 | | 19 | 20 | | 21 | 22 | |
| 87 | | 91 | | 96 | | 101 | | 106 | 108 | | 111 | 113 | |

County Mean & Place Latitude | EAST | WEST | County Mean & Place Longitude | State | County | State | County
| County Longitude Extremes | | | IBM | | F. I. P. S.
| (Centidegrees) | | | |

| 116 | | 120 | | | | 126 | |

Fi le | Year | Mode | RECORD SERIAL NUMBER

Update Record

VERSION

742

Dec, 1974

1 = U.S. File

Courtesy of Centre Mark Co., Elmhurst, Illinois.

painstaking analysis may be applied to the question, "Do we need a 37th distribution facility, and if so, where should it be located?" Instead, the question should have been, "Do we need approximately 35–40 distribution facilities? Is there some other total number which would serve us better?"

An example of this latter type of analysis is Firestone Tire and Rubber Company's "new" system of "45 warehouses. . . . being replaced by only 24 distribution centers."[11] In determining the numbers and locations of the 24 centers, labor attitudes, transportation costs, and inventory levels were all important.

> We developed a sales history for the 2,100 counties in which we sell. From that we built multi-county market zones. Then we started fitting distribution centers arbitrarily into our model. This was a no-strings simulation.

> We began with 12, then 16, then 20, and continued up to 45 locations. Transportation cost curves were made for each location. We also watched the changes in product mix, the average and peak inventory levels, the operating costs per distribution center, and for the whole system. That's basically how we settled on the figure of 24 centers.[12]

Most distribution centers (warehouses) follow markets. A firm trying to establish itself in a new area must first find retailers. These can be served through rented warehouse space, and emergency shipments can be made by air in case demands exceed expectations. There is time to make adjustments. One sporting goods manufacturer, with a product used mainly during the summer, tied into a cigarette promotion scheme whereby a customer, submitting the end of a cigarette carton plus some money, could obtain the sports item at a very advantageous price. Demand far exceeded anyone's dream, and during the first summer, the deliveries of the product lagged behind the planned service standards. However, because of the success of the campaign, it was renewed for a second spring. The sporting goods manufacturer, when asked about physical distribution problems encountered, said, ". . . of course we had a great many last year because of the unexpected volume, but we have learned a great deal. . . . For the current year we have set up distribution centers in eleven warehouses across the country. We will send our product to the warehouse points in carload quantities for redistribution from those points."[13]

Consolidation, from a traffic manager's point-of-view, was discussed in Chapter six. It will be discussed from a warehousing viewpoint in Chapter nine. Economies of freight consolidation often influence the choice of manufacturing, and distribution sites. A goal may be to locate them in a manner that they handle materials on full vehicle-loads both in and out.

In choosing the number of distribution facilities that are needed, an extreme solution is that no distribution facilities are needed, which means one distributes directly from the end of the assembly line. All alternatives are compared with this one extreme and then with each other. Some firms can cover wide areas with only one distribution point.

[11] *Handling and Shipping* (December, 1971), p. 41. Note the old facilities were "warehouses," the new ones, "distribution centers."

[12] *Ibid.*, statement of James F. Davis, Firestone's manager of inventory and distribution research.

[13] Letter to the authors. Firm asked to not be identified.

Sperry Rand's Univac Division established a single repair parts distribution point near Chicago's O'Hare airport, claiming it was capable of supplying computer parts and equipment to any customer anywhere in the world within 24 hours.[14] (It may be that Univac users are located near major airports so this high service level can be achieved.)

Most analytical procedures for determining the number of distribution centers are computerized. This is because of the vast number of alternatives which must be considered. Through simulation techniques (see Chapter 12) varying hypothetical demands are forecast and the ability of each facility, and the entire system, to avoid "stock-outs" and also to provide a specified minimum of service, is tested. The difficulty in testing an entire system is that neighboring distribution centers, while each is designed to serve a specified number of retailers, also serve as "back-up" for each other. Hence, if we test a system for upstate New York and one of the points being considered is Syracuse, we must also measure the ability of Syracuse to "back-up" facilities at Rochester, Binghamton, and Schenectady; and vice-versa. Given these four points; Syracuse is probably the best back-up point because it is located between the other three. However, determining its *value* as a back-up facility is difficult because Rochester could also draw on Buffalo and Binghamton could rely on a facility at Scranton; hence this back-up value must be shared with other locations as well. One can see that the complementary relationship between adjoining distribution facilities makes manual analysis of distribution system design difficult. If, in addition, varying levels of service were being tested, one might find that for each level of service an entirely different series of distribution sites would prove to be ideal. Clearly, these are problems of a scope which only computers can handle.[15]

SPECIALIZED LOCATION CHARACTERISTICS

To this point, the chapter has dealt with many generalized considerations concerning the selection of a site for manufacturing, distributing or assembling. Mathematical techniques may indicate that if a facility is located in a certain spot, transportation costs will be minimized. More sophisticated models take other factors into account and indicate an "ideal" site. This section deals with some specialized considerations which must be recognized before deciding upon a specific area or site. Most of these considerations are "invisible" boundaries which are frequently of great significance.

14 *Transport Topics.* (October 18, 1971.)

15 For a discussion of the mathematical concepts included, see: David M. Smith, *Industrial Location: An Economic Geographical Analysis* (New York: Wiley, 1971).

Within municipalities most lands are "zoned", which means there are limits on the types of uses to which they may be put. Hence a warehouse might be allowed only in areas set aside for wholesale or other specified commercial operations. Restrictions on sites for manufacturing are even more severe, especially if the operation in question is not considered to be a "desirable" neighbor because of the fumes, smoke, dust and noise it creates. Distribution centers are believed to be more desirable, the only complaint against them is the volume of truck traffic they cause on neighboring streets. Zoning classifications can be changed, especially if the community in question is attempting to attract industry. Facilities cannot be placed on vacant land without first checking to see whether and how the land uses for the parcel in question are zoned.[16]

Controls on *environmental pollution* are a matter of increasing concern. While they affect mainly manufacturing and assembling operations, they also can affect distribution operations. Warehouses with incinerators for burning cartons may find an air pollution control inspector insisting that the incinerator chimney be modified. Gasoline distribution operations (including retail service stations) are being required to install devices to capture gasoline vapors which otherwise would escape into the air. The Delaware Coastal Zone Act of 1971 "barred heavy manufacturing industry from locating in a two-mile-wide strip along the state's 115-mile coastline . . . , and prohibited the construction in the bay of marine terminals for the transhipment of liquid and solid bulk materials."[17]

Union locals have areas of jurisdiction. A firm's labor relation manager may have preferences as to which locals he would rather deal with; he should be consulted before any decisions are made. The firm's existing contracts may have some provisions regarding union jurisdiction over new sites. Sometimes unions battle for jurisdiction. For example, stevedores claimed the right to stuff and unstuff containers carrying exports and imports, when the stuffing or unstuffing occurred within 50 miles of a port. Teamsters in the affected area dispute this, because they felt that they should have an equal right to work in the growing container trade.

A very specialized site in which to locate would be a "free trade zone," of which there are about 12 in the United States. "A typical 'free trade zone' is an enclosed facility, under Customs security supervision, situated in or near an international port and into which foreign merchandise . . . may be brought without being subject to formal Customs requirements. The merchandise can usually be stored, exhibited, processed, or used in zone manufacturing operations, without being sub-

---

[16] See William M. Shenkel, "The Economic Consequences of Industrial Zoning," *Land Economics* (August, 1964), pp. 255–265.

[17] "Showdown on Delaware Bay," *Saturday Review* (March 18, 1972), pp. 34–39.

jected to duties and quota unless and until the goods or their products enter the Customs territory of the zone country."[18] The most common advantage of a free trade zone is that the payment of duties can be delayed until the goods are ready to deliver to retailers or customers. For example, liquor purchased in large quantities is stored in a free trade zone until needed. Then import duties are paid and federal and state liquor tax stamps purchased and placed on the bottles. Another distribution function performed in free trade zones is to relabel canned and bottled foods which may be required before they can be sold in U. S. markets.

A SITE'S TRANSPORTATION CHARACTERISTICS

Many "invisible" boundaries exist, the most common being the different rate-making territories of carriers. Railroads operate "switching" districts, in and near large cities, within which rail cars are moved for a fixed charge per car, irrespective of the car's contents. If one were considering a location within a switching district, he would have to use a "switching" tariff to determine charges for reaching other spots within the district. "Commercial" zones are established by the Interstate Commerce Commission or other bodies and delineate the areas in a metropolitan region which is considered to be the same as the region's central city for motor carrier rate-making purposes. Motor carriers with rights to serve the central city can make pick-ups and deliveries at no additional charge within the commercial zone as if it were the central city. The Civil Aeronautics Board usually allows air carriers to offer truck pick-up and delivery service within 25 miles of the airline's airport.[19] Figure 8-4 is an excerpt from a map distributed by the Birmingham, Alabama industrial development agency showing rail facilities including the switching district. Another map, issued by the same agency shows two motor carrier "commercial zones," one recognized by the ICC for interstate hauls, and a slightly different one approved by the state regulatory body for intrastate hauls.

It is believed that shippers benefit from inter-modal competition. One trend is apparent, however, and that is a declining reliance on railroads. Transport users—influenced in part by modern physical distribution thinking—place a higher value on motor carriers' superior level of ser-

[18] John J. Da Ponte, Jr., "Free Trade Zones Around the World and Their Use for Export-Oriented Industrial Operations," a paper delivered at the United Nations Industrial Development Organization workshop in Industrial Free Zones . . . , held at Shannon, Ireland International Free Airport, March, 1972.

[19] Rail, truck and air carrier "zones" are discussed in Charles A. Hedges' "Urban Goods Movements: An Overview," in *Proceedings of the 1971 Transportation Research Forum*, pp. 183–185.

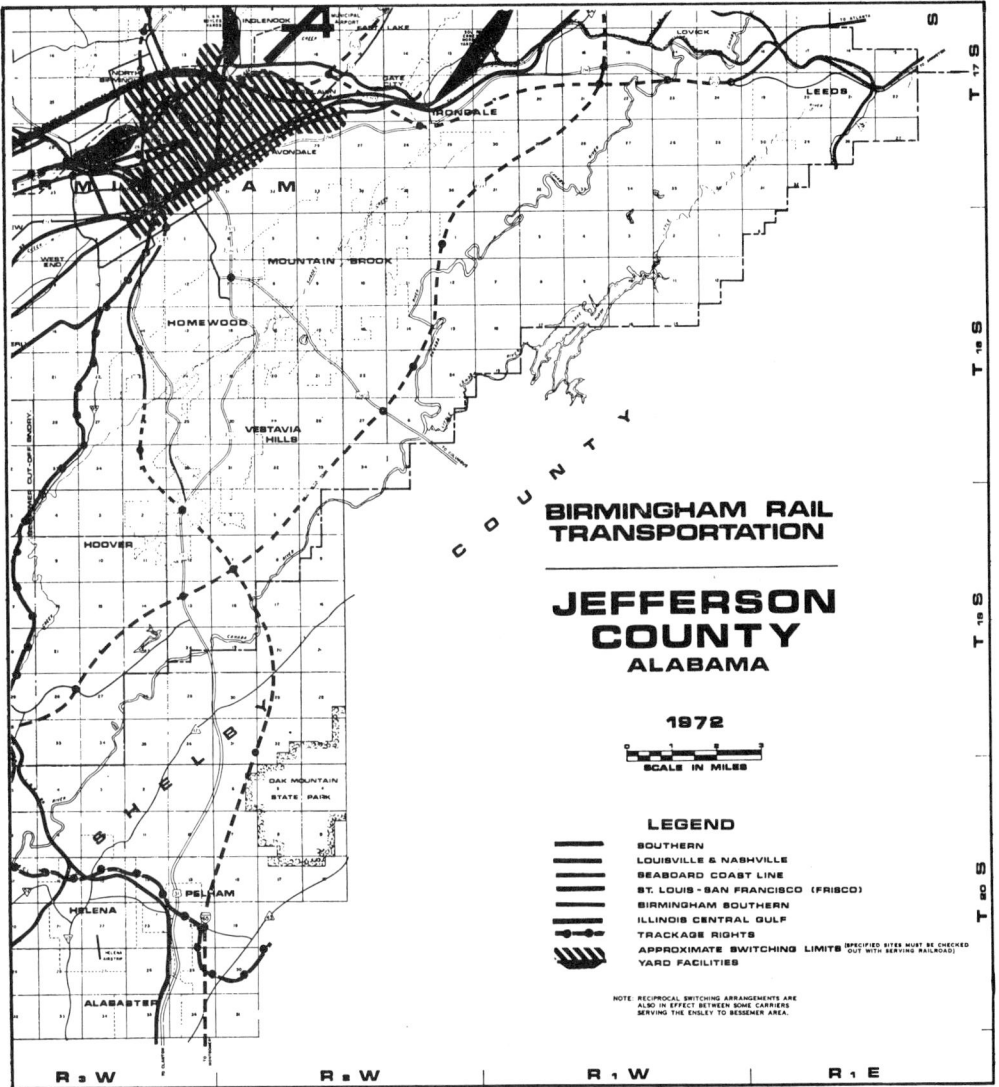

BIRMINGHAM RAIL
TRANSPORTATION

JEFFERSON
COUNTY
ALABAMA

1972

SCALE IN MILES

LEGEND

SOUTHERN
LOUISVILLE & NASHVILLE
SEABOARD COAST LINE
ST. LOUIS - SAN FRANCISCO (FRISCO)
BIRMINGHAM SOUTHERN
ILLINOIS CENTRAL GULF
TRACKAGE RIGHTS
APPROXIMATE SWITCHING LIMITS (SPECIFIED SITES MUST BE CHECKED OUT WITH SERVING RAILROAD)
YARD FACILITIES

NOTE: RECIPROCAL SWITCHING ARRANGEMENTS ARE
ALSO IN EFFECT BETWEEN SOME CARRIERS
SERVING THE ENSLEY TO BESSEMER AREA.

Courtesy: Birmingham Metropolitan Development Board.

vice.[20] It was once thought that waterfront cargo-handling facilities needed rail connections. However, a study completed in the mid-1960's which was based on inventorying 2,000 cargo-handling facilities adjacent to deep water navigation channels in the United States showed that just after World War II, 81 percent of the sites had rail connections. Ten years later this had dropped to 58 percent.[21]

Nonetheless, many new sites are still designed so that they will be adjacent to several modes of transportation. Figure 8-5 shows plans for developing an area just above the mouth of the Houston Ship Channel near Galveston Bay. Note the location of the "Proposed Industrial Park" and its proximity to rail, water, and highway transportation.

OTHER SITE REQUIREMENTS

This chapter has touched on many of the considerations in choosing a location. Once a precise site is under consideration, the title must be searched by attorneys to make certain that the seller can, in fact, sell the parcel and that there are no liens against it. Engineers must examine the site to insure that it will properly drain and to ascertain the load-bearing characteristics of the soil. Architects may indicate what types of buildings can fit on the site and what types of alterations must be accomplished before a building can be started. Even knowledge of the weather is important because it will have some influence on the type of facility which is constructed.[22] One large spice manufacturer/distributor located its facility in Salinas, California because the area is dry and neither heating nor cooling apparatus is required.

Frequently surveys are conducted of firms which have made locational decisions, such as one by the U. S. Department of Commerce entitled, "Survey of Industrial Locational Determinants—1971–75." More than 2,600 respondents indicated that the single most important consideration for both new plant and warehouse locations is *highway access*, defined as a location within 30 minutes of a major highway interchange. Three other factors were of significant importance: scheduled rail service, industrial water supply and natural gas service.[23]

---

[20] See Douglas W. Woods and Thomas A. Domencich, "Competition Between Rail and Truck in Intercity Freight Transportation," in *Proceedings of the 1971 Transportation Research Forum*, pp. 257–288.

[21] *Waterfront Renewal: Technical Supplement* (Madison: Wisconsin Department of Resource Development, 1964), pp. 119–120. (A news item in the May 1974 issue of *Traffic Management* indicated that a number of plant-planning consultants believed that access to railroads was becoming more important because of the energy "crisis" and its adverse impact on trucks.)

[22] For a fairly complete checklist, see: "Site Selection Checklist" in *Distribution Worldwide* (February, 1974), pp. 28–31.

[23] Janet Bosworth Dower, "Choosing an Industrial Site," *Distribution Worldwide* (Feb., 1974), pp. 24–27. See also: T. E. McMillan, "Why Manufacturers Choose Plant Locations vs. Determinants of Plant Locations," *Land Economics* (August, 1965), pp. 239–246.

FIG. 8-5 Development at Morgan's Point, adjacent to Galveston Bay.

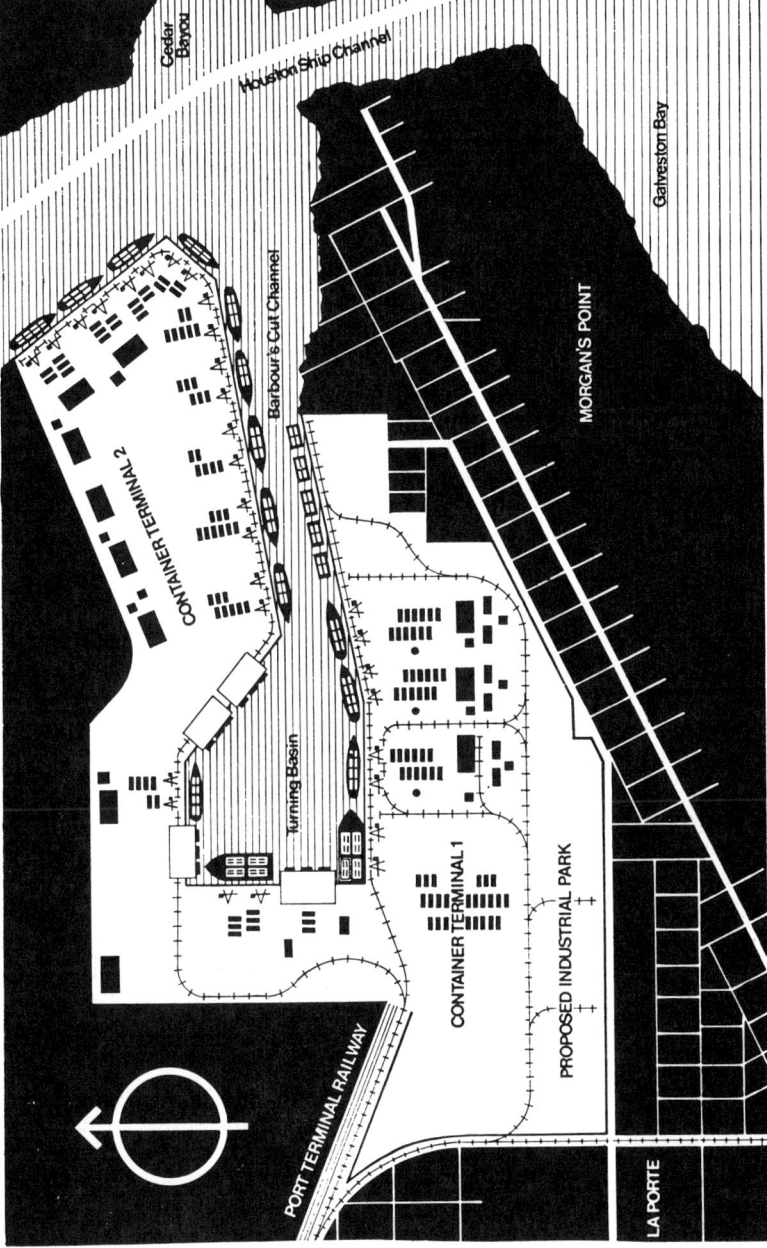

Cedar Bayou

Houston Ship Channel

Galveston Bay

CONTAINER TERMINAL 2

Barbour's Cut Channel

MORGAN'S POINT

Turning Basin

CONTAINER TERMINAL 1

PROPOSED INDUSTRIAL PARK

PORT TERMINAL RAILWAY

LA PORTE

Courtesy *Port of Houston Magazine.*

FACILITY RELOCATION

A specialized, but frequent case of location choice occurs when a firm decides it can no longer continue operations in its present facility and must locate elsewhere. Sometimes the problem is merely lack of room for expansion. A common phenomenon in the United States since World War II has been the relocation of industrial plants and warehouses from the aging and crowded central city to spacious sites in the suburbs. In these instances, the old site could not be expanded and workers who once rode mass transit to and from work, were now demanding private parking facilities for their autos. Trucking firms handling pickups and deliveries at the old site would claim that they could provide better service to suburban sites because there was less traffic congestion.

When relocation is being considered all of the calculations with respect to selecting a new site must be made. In addition, one must compare all proposed alternatives with continuing operations at the existing site. Many existing sites of operation are in satisfactory, if not ideal, locations; and one must choose between expansion at a site which is not ideally located or closing down that site and starting a completely new operation at the "ideal" location.

There are special considerations regarding relocation to distant communities. The first deals with labor. Employees must be kept fully informed of any planned relocations which might affect them. If not, rumors will destroy morale, and workers at the old site will start seeking other employment immediately. Their departure will affect the output capability of the old operation at a time when it is nearly impossible to hire replacements. Policies must be decided and announced with respect to which employees will be asked to relocate to the new facility and have their relocation expenses paid. Others may not have their relocations expenses paid but will have the right to assume comparable positions at the new facility. Older employees may be granted earlier retirement benefits. Employees who are not going to relocate but will agree to stay at the old operation until it ceases operation will be given additional severance benefits.[24]

Difficult decisions must be made regarding equipment. What should be taken to the new site and what should be left behind? This is compounded by the need to maintain production in the old facility as long as possible. Inventories of manufactured products must be expanded at this time to offset the loss in production between the time the old plant or warehouse closes and the new one shifts into operation. There are delays at both sites. At the old site, fewer experienced workers re-

[24] See: Kurt R. Student, "Cost vs. Human Values in Plant Location," *Business Horizons* (April, 1976), pp. 5–14.

main, and those who do, are not happy. At the new site, "bugs" have yet to be discovered.

The physical move of equipment must be timed so as to minimize total "down" time. When General Foods Corporation relocated some of its facilities, it calculated the trade-off between two costs necessary to maintain an adequate inventory of Jell-O's products lines: The first cost was accumulating a larger inventory produced at the older plants by use of overtime. Included in this were the higher (overtime) costs of labor, additional money invested in inventory, and payments for use of public warehouses. The alternative was to pay overtime to the work force installing the new and transferred equipment at the new site. The faster that work was completed, the less would be the "down" time when operations were halted at both the old and new plant. In this instance, use of additional shifts for installing equipment at the new plant was found to be the better alternative.[25]

Another type of problem occurs when it becomes apparent that a firm is over-expanded and must plan an orderly withdrawal from certain markets. The analytical techniques are the same as for location or relocation, except that the new alternatives involve service to a smaller area. While this is not the best situation to be in, it frequently occurs and must be dealt with. In industries with volatile markets, locational decisions are made on a less permanent basis and provisions are made for periodically reviewing performance in each market.

SUMMARY

This chapter dealt with the basic considerations involved in plant and warehouse location decisions. Natural resource locations must be considered, especially if they are a weight-losing product in the manufacturing or processing stage. Another locational consideration is population shifts, because it represents both demand for the firm's product (assuming it's a consumer good) and a potential source of labor. Not only is labor availability significant, the overall skill level and the degree of unionization must be considered.

Taxes are a fundamental locational consideration which vary greatly by status and local taxing authorities. Low tax rates may not be advantageous if the level of public services is substandard.

Other basic considerations involve the availability of transportation, especially motor carriers, and the location of the customers for a firm's

---

[25] Edmund S. Whitman and W. James Schmidt, *Plant Relocation: A Case History of a Move* (New York: American Management Association, 1966), p. 79. The study dealt with General Foods' construction of a new plant at Dover, Delaware which replaced four older plants in the north-eastern United States.

product. Commodity flows help to indicate where products are being produced and when they are being consumed.

The "center of gravity" method of locating a facility was examined. Also, a marginal analysis approach to determining the optimum number of warehouses was mentioned. Once the general area has been determined, specific locational considerations must be taken into account. These include the tax situation, zoning requirements, environmental considerations, union jurisdictions, and transport availability.

The problems involved in relocation of an existing facility were examined. These include employee transfer, equipment relocation and planning to prevent stock-outs during the transition period.

QUESTIONS FOR DISCUSSION AND REVIEW

1. What are the important factors influencing a decision to locate a distribution warehouse or plant?

2. What types of questions should be asked regarding transportation services to and from sites under consideration?

3. When an operating facility is moved from one location to another, what special considerations must be given to the labor force?

4. How do population shifts influence decisions to locate distribution or manufacturing facilities?

5. How do the recent environmental protection programs influence site selection?

6. What are rail switching districts? What are "commercial" zones? How do they affect decisions to locate facilities?

7. Under what circumstances might a firm decide to reduce the number of facilities it operates?

8. What is "input-output" analysis?

9. What are "right-to-work" laws? Do they influence decision locations? How?

10. Why do some states tax inventories? Do you think inventories should be taxed? Why or why not?

11. What mode of transport appears to be most important to firms evaluating new sites? Why do you think this is so?

12. Discuss the basic aspects which should be considered when examining the labor environment of a particular geographical region.

13. Discuss the importance and types of taxes that are involved in a location decision.

14. It was noted that vendors will often "dovetail" their operation into that of their customers. Discuss the rationale for this situation.

15. Discuss the basic considerations involved in a facility relocation decision.

PROBLEMS TO WORK OUT

The figure is a grid, showing miles north and east of point zero, zero.

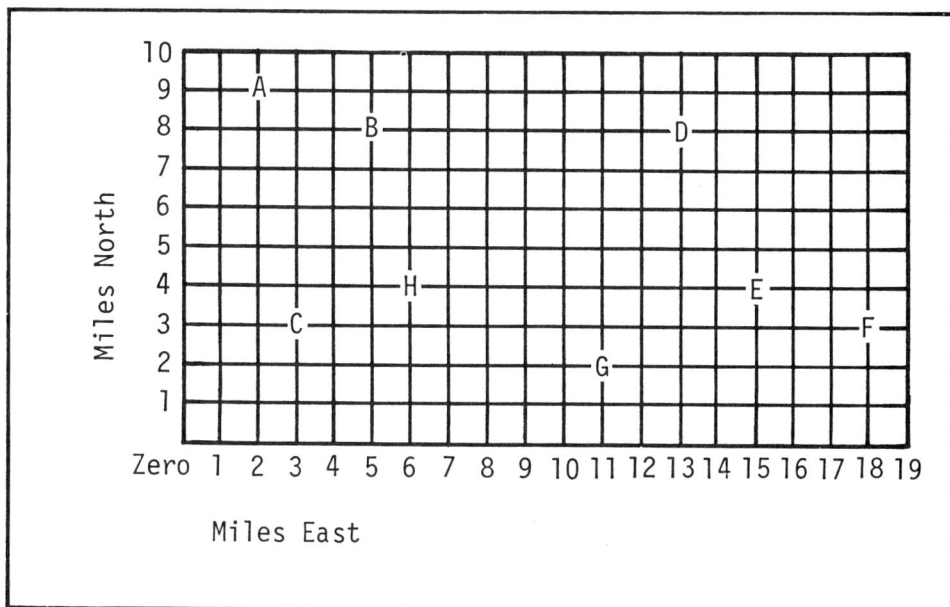

1. Points A, B, C, D, E, F, G, and H are retail stores, receiving equal tonnages. Assume you want to locate a warehouse in the midst of the stores at a location which minimizes the distances your trucks must travel back and forth between the warehouse and each store. Assume straight line distances between the warehouse and each store. What is the best location for your warehouse? (Express your answer in miles, using fractions if necessary, north and east of point zero.)

2. Assume a decision has been made to close store A, and that it is further assumed that after store A closes, store B's volume will double. If this is so, what would be the best site for your warehouse?

CASE 8-1   MOM'S TACOS

Mom's Tacos was a fast-growing food franchise chain. Its motto was "Mom's secret is the sauce" which applied to the sauce served with the tacos. There was no "Mom" as such since the firm was the creation of a group of college-dropouts who had been engaged in communal living and, as a commercial venture, had tried making large batches of tie-dyed shirts. The tie-dye shirt craze passed and that market collapsed. However some of the organic dye ingredients were left over and the group used them in experimental cooking. They managed to produce an excellent-tasting taco sauce and sold the sauce to various restaurants near college campuses. The group then purchased a rundown coffee house, changed its name to "Mom's Tacos" and a legend was born. Within three years the group, now incorporated, of course, had over three hundred franchised restaurants along the west coast, in the southwest, and in the midwest. They were now considering expansion into the south.

Ms. Jenny Wong was logistics manager for the group. She was responsible for purchasing as well. Others supervised the construction and operation of the franchised restaurants. Restaurant operators were governed by very strict rules regarding cleanliness, personnel, amounts of food in each serving, etc. The restaurant operators were allowed to purchase all foods they needed locally, provided that specifications, set forth by Mom's Tacos, were met. The only ingredient the restaurant operators had to purchase from Mom's was the taco sauce itself. It allegedly was a combination of secret ingredients known only to "Mom." The sauce was manufactured at Mom's plant in Del Rio, Texas, where it was shipped by the rail carload, to Mom's distribution points in Los Angeles (for the west coast) and Chicago (for the midwest). There was also a distribution point in Del Rio. After careful market analysis prepared by the well known marketing consultant, Edsel, Tucker and Frazer (E T & F), Mom's was ready to move into the south. E T & F had recommended Savannah, Georgia as the location for Mom's Southern distribution point. Franchise agreements had already been signed for operations in Savannah, Atlanta, and Augusta, Georgia; Tallahassee and Jacksonville, Florida; and Columbia, South Carolina.

The phrase "Mom's secret is the sauce" was not true, at least in its reference to Mom. The rest of the phrase was true, however. The various herbal ingredients were kept secret and some of them were still chemically active. They were added, at the last moment, and under the carefully monitored and guarded conditions, before the sauce left the distribution point bound for the various restaurants. Once mixed, the sauce had a useful life of only ten days, after which the restaurant operations were under the strictest instructions to destroy it. Hence the shipping pattern of the sauce was in the form of a small, steady, move from the distribution point to each restaurant.

The shipping container was a plastic bottle inside a fibreboard box. It was used in one direction only. The cost to Mom's was $46.00 per hundred for the five-gallon size and $81.00 per hundred for the 20-gallon size. When shipped, the five-gallon size of sauce weighed 47 pounds and the 20-gallon size weighed 183 lbs. The exterior dimensions of the five-gallon container were an 18-inch cube. The exterior dimensions of the 20-gallon container were 24 inches square at the base and 48 inches high. The main reason the five-gallon container was used was that in some states, an employee could not be required to lift more than 50 lbs. The 20-gallon container required additional mechanical handling equipment in the restaurant. However, Mom's priced the taco sauce so that the restaurants had a strong incentive to use the 20-gallon container. At first all of them would use the five-gallon container, but within a year of starting operations, over half the restaurants moved to the 20-gallon container.

A small, or beginning restaurant would use a five-gallon container every day or day and a half. The largest, and most successful Mom's Taco restaurant (in Lubbock, Texas) was now using four 20-gallon containers per day.

Because of its interest in maintaining quality and its realization that restaurants would order fewer shipments of larger quantities of sauce in order to benefit from lower per pound shipping rates, Mom's Tacos paid the freight charges on shipments of taco sauce from distribution points to restaurants. Shipments were made to each restaurant twice a week. At any one time, a restaurant would have a three to six day supply on hand. In their weekly report to Mom's Tacos' home office, the restaurant operator would indicate the serial or batch number of each unused can in stock, and would also indicate whether the amount to be shipped in the following week should be increased or decreased.

The present price of the taco sauce, as charged to each restaurant, consisted of three elements: (1) a charge for the sauce, (2) a discount for ordering in 20-gallon containers, and (3) a transportation charge based on "zones", each zone being a certain distance away from the distribution point. The ordinary zone map looked like a "bull's eye" target with the distribution point in the center.

Restaurants that used over 40 gallons of sauce per week had the option of ordering in 20-gallon containers. The price in 20-gallon containers was somewhat lower and was to reflect the lower cost (on a per gallon basis) of the container and (on a weight or gallon basis) of shipping. It was Ms. Wong's assignment to work on a pricing zone system for distribution from the new Savannah facility. She was told to include the price of the sauce at $7 per gallon. In addition to this, she was to add charges for the container (taking into account that larger containers cost less per gallon) and she was to add charges for transportation, using the concentric rings or zone approach. The profits were already in the charge for the sauce, so the charges for the containers and for transportation were to (1) cover costs and (2) reflect the cost differences in reaching each restaurant as accurately as possible. While the initial zone system would apply only to Savannah, Atlanta, Augusta, Tallahassee, Jacksonville and Columbia, it would be in effect for any other new restaurants which were opened in the area. In fact, Mom's Tacos' representatives would use Ms. Wong's cost chart when talking with potential restaurant operators in other southern cities.

Ms. Wong recalled that she had a file folder labelled "Price zone construction" which she had put together after working out the price zones in the southwest from the Del Rio distribution center. In it she found three notes she had written to herself.

> The first note said "use fifty mile rings" and was dated April 3, 1972. She remembered that, after long discussions with both Mom's Tacos' management and with some restaurant operators, it seemed most reasonable to draw circles around the distribution center with radii of fifty miles, one hundred miles, one hundred-fifty miles and so on and then set the same price for deliveries inside each ring.

> The second note said "Remember the Alamo" and it was dated March 31, 1975. Ms. Wong remembered that on that date Alamo Junior College in Brownsville, Texas had won the state basketball tournament. The Mom's Taco restaurant operator in Brownsville had promised free tacos to everyone in case Alamo Junior College won the tournament. That wild night he needed 700 gallons of Mom's taco sauce (his usual weekly usage was 75–80 gallons) and Mom's Tacos had to pay an air freight bill of over $1000. The note was in Ms. Wong's file to warn her that the next time zone prices were set up, some sort of rule would have to be set up so that the home office could avoid the excess freight charges in instances such as "the Alamo."

> The third note said "newer operations cost more to reach" and was dated February 22, 1974. This was after a year-end audit had disclosed that Mom's Tacos was losing money on reaching most of its new restaurants being served out of Del Rio. The reason was that initial franchises were located in large cities to which transport rates from Del Rio were relatively low. However, newer restaurants were in smaller cities, and while still within fifty, one hundred, or one hundred fifty miles of Del Rio, the costs of reaching them was somewhat higher, mainly because they were in areas with poorer transportation service, less carrier competition, and higher rates. The auditor has suggested to Ms. Wong that the next time rates be established, she calculate average rates to a number of points inside each ring, rather than just to points where restaurants were in operation or being planned for.

Ms. Wong then took a map of Georgia and the adjoining areas and, using a compass, drew circles with 50, 100, 150, 200 and 250 radii, from Savannah. (See Exhibit 1.) She then got on the telephone and started tracking down the various carriers who would handle the deliveries from the Savannah distribution point. Some carriers were excluded from consideration because they did not provide both pick-up service and delivery service. Delivery service to restaurants was considered especially important because few restaurant operators had trucks of their own.

Within Savannah, there were several local drayage services who could operate anywhere within the city limits. Their rates were $5.30 per cwt for shipments up to 100 lbs; $4.30 per cwt for shipments between 100 and 499 lbs; and $3.30 per cwt for shipments between 500 and 999 lbs. The minimum charge for any shipment was $5.00 and they would not handle any shipment over 1,000 lbs.

Exhibit 1

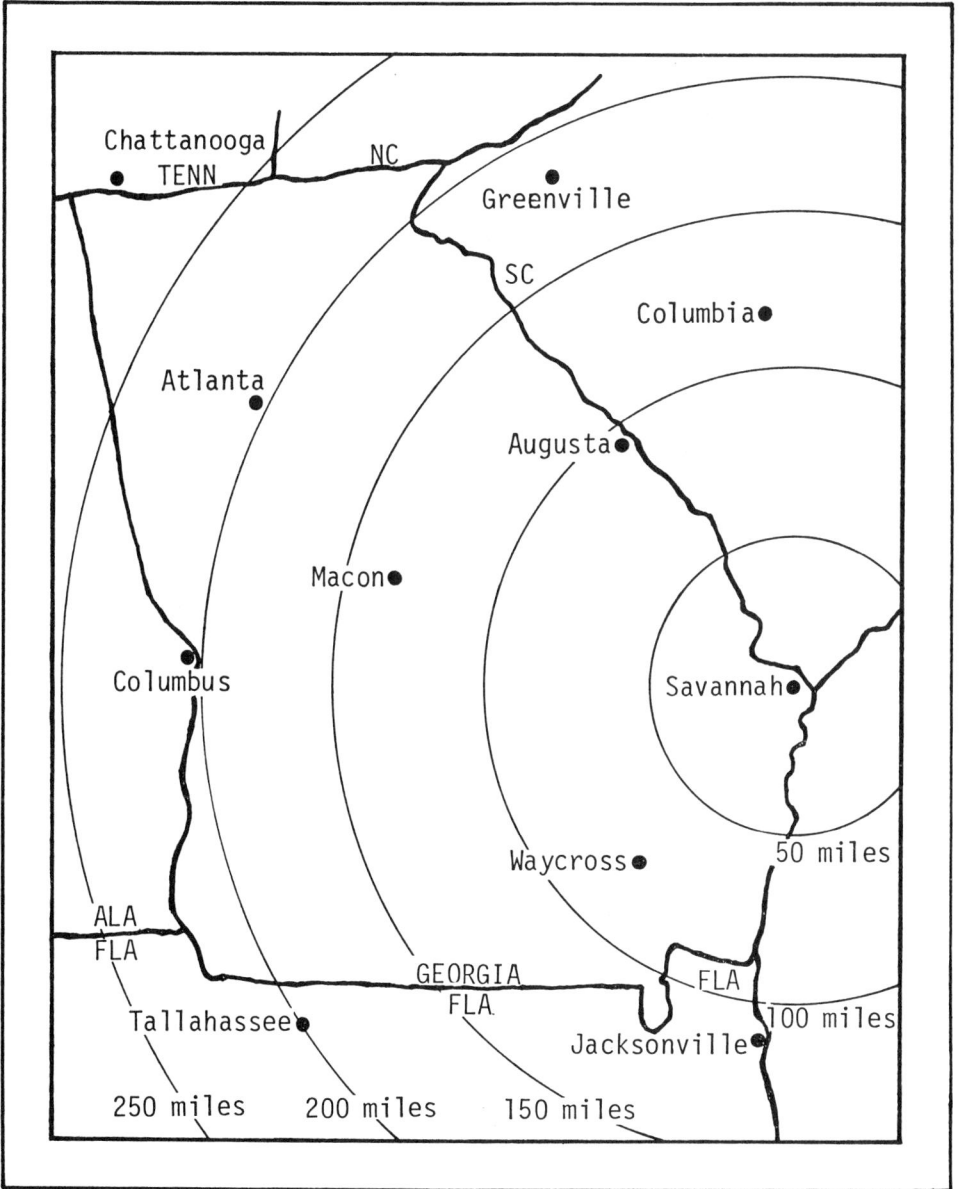

Acme Parcel Service also served most cities in the South. Their rate would be $10 per week (irrespective of volume but which would guarantee that a truck of theirs would stop twice a day at Mom's Tacos' Savannah distribution point to pick up any outgoing orders). Mom's Tacos uses Acme Parcel Service for other shipments and thus already pays the weekly fee. Their rates would be: for deliveries within Savannah, $4.00 per cwt; for deliveries outside Savannah but within fifty miles, $4.50 per cwt; for deliveries within 50–100 miles, $5.75 per cwt; for deliveries within 100–150 miles, $6.50 per cwt; for deliveries within 150–200 miles, $7.50 per cwt; and for deliveries between 200 and 250 miles, $8.00 per cwt. They would not handle any single parcel weighing over 50 lbs, which meant that, say, a 150 lb shipment would have to be made in three separate parcels, each one weighing 50 lbs.

Motor common carrier rates turned out to be: deliveries within Savannah, $5.00 per cwt for shipments under 200 lbs; $4.00 per cwt for shipments between 200 and 999 lbs; and $3.50 per cwt for shipments over 1,000 lbs. The minimum charge on any delivery within Savannah was $6.00. The following table shows their rates for shipments outside Savannah. It was based on the applicable intrastate and interstate motor carrier tariffs in effect.

Rates are in Cents Per Hundred Pounds *

Distance from Savannah in miles	If shipment is between			
	0–99 lbs	100–399 lbs	400–999 lbs	over 1,000 lbs
up to 50	650	600	500	400
50–100	750	700	550	450
100–150	850	800	600	500
150–200	950	850	650	550
200–250	1000	900	700	600
250–300	1100	1000	750	650

* Note one, the minimum charge for any shipment is $6.00.

Question One: Construct a price chart which includes the price of the sauce, the container, and the least costly mode of transportation. The chart should carry out Ms. Wong's instructions, as you understand them.

CASE 8-2   ABC ELECTRONICS CO.

ABC Electronics was a large corporation with its home office in Philadelphia and plants in Lowell, Massachusetts, Atlanta, Georgia, Long Beach, California and Seattle, Washington. Its 1975 sales totalled nearly half a billion dollars. Its principal customer was the U. S. Department of Defense and its other major customers were the military and civilian aerospace manufacturers. About ten percent of its sales were exports, sometimes as part of an "arms sale" to a foreign government.

The ABC Electronics Board of Directors decided to locate a new plant in a specific midwestern city where it would be nearer to several of their large, regular customers. The city had a large black population and the main reason it was chosen for the plant site was that ABC Electronics wanted to increase the percentage of its employees who were female, black, or belonged to other minority groups. They were under considerable pressure to do this because of their numerous government contracts.

ABC Electronics' president established a small task force and sent them to the city where the plant was to be located to select a site which would then be recommended to the firm's executive committee. If the executive committee approved, the site would be purchased and the plant would be constructed. The task force consisted of four individuals who were staying in the Shaw Hotel. Tom Reardon, head of the task force, had rented a suite for himself, and the group used one of his rooms as an office. The other three had rooms elsewhere in the hotel.

Reardon had been with ABC Electronics since the end of the Korean War when he had been a jet fighter pilot. His present title was special assistant to the president, and he functioned effectively as a "troubleshooter." His most frequent assignment was to take over management of some project which was falling behind in time and then, through little more than sheer force of his personality, manage to speed up work and get the project back on schedule. This plant location decision was a minor assignment for him. In two months Reardon was to move to Long Beach where he would become assistant general manager of the Long Beach plant and he would be in line to become general manager when the plant's present one retired in June, 1977.

The second member of the team was Gary Hays, a black, and an aeronautical engineer who had worked for ABC Electronics since 1967. He was one of a handful of minority employees the firm had. It was tacitly understood that one of his functions was to serve as "window dressing" whenever questions were raised about ABC Electronics' minority hiring practices. Hays was a competent engineer, however, and resented the fact that he was always given less challenging work assignments. Reardon had requested that Hays be a part of the task force since they would be dealing with many blacks in their investigations of various plant sites. Hays was happy to get the assignment for two reasons. It was his first chance to work for Reardon and he wanted to impress Reardon with his performance, since Reardon's advice was frequently sought by top management who were looking for individuals to fill certain posts. Secondly, Hays hoped that he would become sufficiently involved in the site selection and construction of the new plant that he might get assigned to a relatively responsible post in the new operation, once it was under way. He thought that since most of the employees would be black, management would have to be black, or mostly black, also. This would give him a chance to do some real work and not just be used for display purposes in the home office.

The third member was Albert Lee, who had worked at the ABC Electronics plant in Atlanta since 1964. He had an M.B.A. degree from a small night college in Atlanta. In 1967–68, he was involved in the construction of an addition to the Atlanta plant and had performed well. At that time he had been promised a role in future construction undertakings of the firm. However, the war in southeast Asia ran down and ended, and the commercial aerospace industry slumped, so ABC Electronics did no new building until just now. The slowdown in construction had been hard on Lee since it deprived him of a chance to show how well he could do. He was not very happy with his present assignment for two reasons. First of all, he had pretty well decided that ABC Electronics future building program would be so slow that it offered no future. Second, he held many prejudices and felt many "minority hiring" programs did little more than discriminate against white males. He was aghast when he was informed that the reason ABC Electronics had to locate in this city was so it could increase its employment of blacks.

The fourth member of the task force was Sandy Northrup, who had worked for ABC Electronics for less than a year. She had a BS degree in marketing and suspected that affirmative action proddings had something to do with her own hiring. She also had yet to be given a challenging assignment. She respected Reardon and got along well with Hays. She and Lee did not get along because he had assumed she was secretary to the group and several times asked her to take dictation or to make coffee. Lee was consistent in his chauvinism, however, at one muddy potential plant site he carried Ms. Northrup 40 feet from the car to a dry board so she would not get her feet dirty. For the next two days, Lee was in bed with a bad cold and a wrenched back.

Reardon had been in the city for two weeks; the other three had been here for a few days less. Reardon had given each of the other three individual assignments. Hays spent most of his time talking with state employment agency representatives to obtain some knowledge regarding the "pool" of minority workers that would be available. He also had contact with several groups in the black ghetto who were interested in improving job opportunities for blacks. Lee spent most of his time investigating various potential sites and the respective building codes, property taxes, zoning regulations, etc., which governed each site. Ms. Northrup evaluated the transportation services available at each site.

Reardon met with each of the three separately for about one-half hour each day. He spent some of his time calling on various ABC Electronics customers and suppliers in the area for two reasons. First, he was letting them know that ABC Electronics was intending to build. Second, he tried to learn from them, their experiences as corporate citizens of the city in question. The firms still located in the central city were unhappy because of urban problems common to many large U. S. cities: high taxes, high crime rates, and the flight of the white middle class away from the city's problems into suburbia. Firms Reardon called upon which were located in the suburbs seemed equally unhappy. Suburban government was no longer a tax bargain. Shoddy streets and utilities built right after World War II were fast deteriorating. The affluent whites were fleeing the suburbs, built right after World War II, which surrounded the city, and moving either back to new luxury apartments in the central city (built on land cleared by urban renewal) or else to newer suburbs even farther away from the central city.

Reardon and his staff had not spent much time together as a group. When they did meet, there was obvious antagonism between Lee and Hays. There was a lesser amount of antagonism between Lee and Ms. Northrup. Hays and Ms. Northrup got along but had little in common except their dislike for Lee and Lee's continual insinuations that neither Hays nor Ms. Northrup would have gotten far on their own merits.

Reardon had initially hoped that he and his staff would meet for supper each evening; he would debrief each one of them and attempt to have a "team" approach develop where each evening the group would see how far they had gotten; what remained to be done; who should do what tomorrow; and then meet again tomorrow night for the same process. Lee and Hays argued, almost violently, at two of the first three supper meetings. Hays then began arranging some of his business appointments with black community groups for the supper hour, saying that most blacks did not have the types of jobs where they could meet during regular daytime hours. Instead, they were available only on their own time which was usually from about 5 PM to 8 PM when those who worked daytime shifts were done working or just before those who were working night-time shift, frequently as janitors, had to report for work. Reardon accepted Hays' reasons and the group no longer met for supper. Reardon was a bit perplexed that relations among his staff were not better. He had, after all, in his many years with ABC Electronics developed a reputation for his ability to create "teams" out of mismatched groups.

Reardon then set aside Thursday afternoon for his staff to meet in the outer room of his suite. Lee came early and taped maps to one of the walls. Hays and Ms. Northrup both showed up on time and appeared to be prepared.

Reardon started by saying that he was both surprised and disappointed that a number of ABC Electronics suppliers and customers in the area on whom he had called had very little praise for either the city or its suburbs as a site for industry. One large customer had even intimated that they were performing only the most necessary maintenance to their factory; it would probably be closed in 1977 unless the firm's overall business picked up so much that it could not be handled at its other plants. Reardon confessed that he (Reardon) had even called his own superior with this news wondering whether the ABC Electronics location decision should be reconsidered. The answer had come back, and it was for Reardon to continue on his original assignment. Reardon then called on Lee.

Lee gave an informative half-hour presentation. There were only two adequate sites available. One, called the "riverfront" site was half a mile from the city's center on a site cleared by federally-assisted urban renewal programs. It consisted of 11.2 acres and would have to be purchased on a bid basis from the city's redevelopment agency. The site had been cleared over three years ago and a suitable redeveloper had not yet been found. Redevelopment agency officials were very anxious for a firm with the national reputation of ABC Electronics to occupy the site. Since the object of the renewal program was to renew the area, the actual price of the land would be quite low (much less than what it had cost the redevelopment agency to buy when it was filled with slums, to clear the slums, to relocate the former slum residents, etc.) ABC Electronics could be a site developer or it could contract with a third party. In any event, a proposal to use the land in a certain manner, an agreement to build a building of certain dimensions, and a bid for the land would have to be presented to the city redevelopment agency. The redevelopment agency would insist on a number of bonds being posted to insure the developer's performance. The redevelopment director had indicated that he would recommend that a bid from ABC Electronics, along with suitable performance guarantees, for $100,000 for the 11.2 acres be accepted. The redevelopment agency would also relocate public streets and utilities in the area in a manner that was most beneficial to the redeveloper.

Lee said the other site was seven miles from downtown, just outside the city limits, in a small suburb of mixed light industry, warehousing, and singe-family housing. The site was known as the "airport site" because it was the remaining 20 acres of what had once been a thriving privately-owned general aviation airport through the 1950's. It had been forced to close down because the airport owner could not afford to buy room for runway expansion, yet the local firms whose business aircraft he cared for were buying larger planes which could no longer operate in and out of his short runways. The airport closed operations in 1964 and the owner (since 1971, his widow) had been selling off blocks of the old airport for industrial and commercial uses. The widow was asking $200,000 for the remaining 20 acres. The price was considered firm, she was in no hurry to sell. She lived in Florida, her interests were represented by attorneys.

"Why are there only two sites?" asked Hays.

"These two are the only ones large enough that are already zoned for industrial uses," answered Lee. "Anything else we would buy would be contingent on a zoning change, and our experience in some cities is that zoning changes cost a lot of money."

Reardon asked: "The airport site is nearly twice as big as the river-front one. How many acres do we really need?"

Lee answered: "In the riverfront site, you'd build a higher building and need less employee parking. The airport site is a bit large but it's 20 acres or nothing. If we didn't need the entire 20 acres, we'd probably lease off a corner of it to some roadside franchise food operation."

"What about building codes," asked Ms. Northrup. "What about requirements that truck pick-up and delivery areas be located sufficiently far away from the street that there is no interference with traffic?" She was trying to show that she had done her homework. Hays grinned and hoped that Lee did not have the answer.

Lee saw the grin and flushed, even though he had the answer. "You're right about the city code," he shot back, "but since the redevelopment agency will locate or relocate streets to serve our site, we should have no trouble meeting the requirement. In our plans, we can move the street, the plant, the loading dock, or all three. The suburban building code has no specific provision although, as any fool would know, one would not lay out a plant on a 20 acre site and create a traffic jam in front since it would foul up the arrival time of each shift."

"Are there other differences in the codes?" asked Reardon.

"Yes," was Lee's reply. "The city code is almost always more stringent. Enforcement is also more stringent because it's going to be part of a large renewal area."

"How much more will it cost to construct a plant to meet the city's code?" asked Reardon.

"We'd need to consult with local architects and contractors," said Lee. "They'd have a general idea. Sometimes other factors prevail. The airport site would not need a sprinkler system or standpipe according to their code, while we need one in the city. But ABC Electronics' insurer insists on a sprinkler and standpipe at all our plants anyway, so the difference between city and suburban codes means nothing in this case."

"Are there many other major cost differences between the two sites that we need to know about?" asked Reardon.

"Well, no offense to minority group members present," answered Lee, "but in the city the minority groups are powerful politically—in the mayor's office, the council, and on the redevelopment agency. I predict they'll force us to use minority group architects and minority group construction firms to design and build the plant."

"So, what's wrong with that?" asked Hays, defensively.

"Our kind of plant is a much more complicated construction problem than many of these minority boys—whoops, wrong word—people have dealt with," answered Lee.

"They should be given a chance!" shouted Hays.

"Hell, no," shouted back Lee, "it's hard enough to build a new plant using experienced architects and contractors."

Reardon took Hays' side and picked up on the argument by saying: "The main reason we're building here is to demonstrate that we're employing minority group personnel. If we don't use minority group architects and contractors, we'll be getting bad publicity right away. The people I talked to in city hall told me as much."

Lee said, "That may be so, but if errors are made in the building's design and construction, its output capability may be adversely affected for its entire life. This will make productivity of all the minority group members we've got working inside look bad, no matter how hard they try."

"From your standpoint, what do you recommend?" Reardon asked Lee.

"That we take the airport site where we'll be under no pressure to use minority group architects or contractors," answered Lee.

"I'd object to that," said Hays.

"We'll get to you in a few minutes," said Reardon, trying to calm things down a bit. "Sandy," he asked, "what have you been discovering?"

Ms. Northrup opened up her notebook and started to speak. "Rates into and out of the area are good because barge transportation, even though we don't use it, has kept the pattern of rail and truck rates low. The riverfront site is served by rail and truck; the airport site by truck only. I called our home office and asked how much we used rail and truck, nationwide. We use rail very little for outbound shipments. In this city we would not use rail at all for outbound shipments since the major customers we're trying to locate near are close enough that truck makes more sense. The fellow at the home office said, if all things were equal, we should pick a site that has rail tracks in case of a teamsters' strike. Secondly, he said that when we build the new plant, it's advantageous to be on a rail line if you're receiving some of the equipment that's used on the assembly line. Some of our presses weigh over 90 tons apiece and they have to be disassembled if they're going to be delivered by truck. Both the airport site and the river site are inside the commercial zone, so rates are the same. Service might be a bit better at the riverfront site because it's close to downtown and most of the carriers are always in the area, usually making deliveries to retail stores. While traffic in the downtown area is congested, at the renewal area it is not because in rebuilding, wider streets were provided. Truck service to and from the airport site is also good. The main advantage there is that it's on a good road to the new airport which means something if we're going to use our own truck to meet certain flights with 'rush' air freight shipments. There is traffic congestion which would affect both sites at the morning and evening rush hours. I don't know that much about our proposed work force or where they'll be living to say much about their commute patterns. Whenever I told people I was talking with that we intended primarily to employ minority group members, they sort of grinned at me."

"The city said they'd put a bus route by our plant if we chose the riverfront site," said Hays. "Some of the neighborhood groups I met with said the present city administration is keeping promises to restructure the city's bus service so it serves the city, not the suburbanites."

"I thought all your kind of people had cars," said Lee to Hays, "that's all I see parked in their neighborhoods."

"Hey, let's cut those references to 'his kind of people,' Lee," said Reardon. "But on the same subject, Hays, tell us a bit about the work force. What have you found for us?"

"The good news is that there's a lot of them out there wanting to work and the bad news is not many of them have skills," answered Hays. "The manpower resource office here can get a combined federal-state grant of up to $5,000 per worker for job training purposes. That's a big investment."

Reardon asked: "How will that work? Will they be ready to start the day the plant opens? Do we open the doors and they walk in, go to their machines, turn 'on' the switches, and start producing?"

"That'll be the day," interrupted Lee, and both Reardon and Hays glared at him.

Hays answered Reardon, "I'm sure there'll be some 'start-up' problems. What we have to do is find our potential supervisors first and, as part of their training, let them see some of our operations in Lowell, Long Beach or Seattle. Then they'll be ready to get the new plant into operation."

"You mean we're going to find our supervisors in the ranks of the unemployed in this city?" exclaimed Lee. "We can't do that! In every other plant of ours we watch a man on the line for one or two years before we decide whether he's of supervisor caliber. I thought we were going to transfer all the supervisors in from our other plants. We make missiles and missile components, you know!"

"If you import a corps of lilly-whites from elsewhere to supervise the blacks and chicanos, it'll only take about a month for some government procurement person to ask 'how come he doesn't see some darker skins amongst your supervisors?' So we'll be back where we started," retorted Hays.

"If we have to locate here," said Lee, "I'm going to bypass channels and write a memo to the executive committee and ask that a copy be placed in my personnel files indicating that I don't think we can start off with minority-group supervisors. This damn plant is going to be a millstone around the neck of everyone involved. What the Hell does Hays know about work quality? It's a widely-known fact that he's never been given a technical engineering assignment of any importance!"

"Knock off these references to Hays!" ordered Reardon, obviously upset himself. "Now, given the two sites, Hayes, for the record, which one do you recommend?"

"It has to be the riverfront," said Hays. "It's closer to the work force. If you make them commute to the airport site, it's surrounded by a lower-class, all-white suburb which won't make them feel welcome at all. If we're seriously trying to employ minority group members who live in ghettos near the center of the city we've got to take the jobs to them. That's why we need the riverfront site!"

"That's what bothers me," said Ms. Northrup, making her first statement in several minutes. "If we take the jobs to them in the central city, aren't we perpetuating the idea of the ghetto? They'll never leave the city and the suburbanites won't enter the city. All we will have done is build the wall a bit higher."

Question One: How well did Hays do on his assigned task? What additional information should Reardon ask him to gather?

Question Two: How well did Ms. Northrup do on her assignment? What types of additional transportation information should she be asked to gather?

Question Three: How well is Lee doing on his assignment? What additional data should he be asked to gather?

Question Four: How well is Reardon's "team" approach working? Should he be doing things differently?

Question Five: Do you think, based on the information given so far, that the riverfront site or the airport site should be chosen? Give your reasons.

CHAPTER REFERENCES

ABERNATHY, WILLIAM J. and John C. Hershey; "Location for Best Service," *The Logistics and Transportation Review* (Volume 8, Number 1), pp. 5–20.

ALLEN, BENJAMIN J.; "The Economic Effects of Rail Abandonment on Communities: A Case Study," *Transportation Journal* (Fall, 1975), pp. 52–61.

A Survey of National Geo-Coding Systems (Washington, D.C.: U.S. Department of Transportation, February, 1972).

BALLOU, RONALD H.; "Potential Error in the Center of Gravity Approach to Facility Location," *Transportation Journal* (Winter, 1973).

BARLOON, MARVIN J.; "The Interrelationship of the Changing Structure of American Transportation and the Changes in Industrial Location," *Land Economics* (May, 1965), pp. 169–179.

CONSTANTIN, JAMES A.; "The Use of Transportation Data in Market Pattern Analysis," *Journal of Marketing* (July, 1964), pp. 74–78.

DA PONTE, JOHN J. JR.; "Free Trade Zones Around the World and Their Use for Export-Oriented Industrial Operations," presentation at the United Nations Industrial Development Organization workshop in Industrial Free Zones . . . , Shannon, Ireland, 1972.

"Distribution Know-How," *Traffic Management* (March, 1976).

Domestic and International Transportation of U.S. Foreign Trade: 1970 (Washington, D.C.: U.S. Department of Commerce, Transportation and Army).

DOWER, JANET BOSWORTH; "Choosing an Industrial Site," *Distribution Worldwide* (February, 1974).

FRIEDLICH, C. S.; *Alfred Weber's Theory of the Location of Industries* (Chicago: University of Chicago Press, 1929).

FULTON, MAURICE; "New Factors in Plant Location," *Harvard Business Review* (May-June, 1971), pp. 4–17.

GARDNER, R. W.; "Real Estate Considerations in Planning New Distribution Facilities," *Warehousing Review* (January-February, 1975), pp. 2–4.

GOLDSTEIN, GERALD S. and Leon N. Moses; "Transportation Controls and the Spatial Structure of Urban Areas," *The American Economic Review* (May, 1975), pp. 289–294.

GREENHUT, M. L.; "When is the Demand Factor of Location Important?" *Land Economics* (May, 1964), pp. 175–184.

GREENWOOD, MICHAEL J.; "Research on Internal Migration in the United States A Survey," *The Journal of Economic Literature* (June, 1975), pp. 307–433.

HARPER, DONALD V.; "The Airport Location Problem: The Case of Minneapolis—St. Paul," *ICC Practitioners' Journal* (May-June, 1971), pp. 550–582.

HAYES, CHARLES R. and Norman W. Schul; "Why Do Manufacturers Locate in the Southern Piedmont?," *Land Economics* (February, 1968).

HEDGES, CHARLES A.; "Urban Goods Movements: An Overview," *Proceedings of the 1971 Transportation Research Forum*.

HOOVER, E. M.; *The Location of Economic Activity* (New York: McGraw-Hill, 1963).

HURST, MICHAEL ELIOT, ed.; *Transportation Geography: Comments and Readings* (New York: McGraw-Hill, 1974). Note especially papers by E. L. Ullman, and J. W. Watson in the introductory section; J. F. Kolars and J. H. Malin in the section on network analysis; R. H. T. Smith and K. R. Cox in the section on flow analysis; P. J. Schwind, S. H. Beaver, J. B. Kenyon, and P. W. Brooks in the section on model systems; R. Borgstrom in the section on interdependencies; and E. J. Taaffe, R. L. Morrill and P. R. Gould, W. R.

Stanley, J. M. Munro, and R. T. Aangeenbrug in the section on development and urban transport.

Input-Output Analysis and Transportation Planning, A Collection of Papers Delivered at an Economics Seminar (Washington, D.C.: Office of the Secretary of Transportation, 1969).

KAHN, E. S., JR.; "Who, What, Where, How Much, How Many?," *The New Yorker* (October 15, 1973).

KHUMAWALA, B. M., and D. C. Whybark; "An Update on Warehouse Location Techniques," *The Logistics and Transportation Review* (1973), pp. 195–206.

KING, GORDON A.; "Effects of Transportation on the Location of Grain and Livestock Activities in the Western Region," *Transportation Journal* (Summer, 1967), pp. 5–18.

LOCKLIN, D. PHILIP; *Economics of Transportation* (7th ed. Homewood, Ill.: Irwin, 1972).

LOGAN, M. I.; "Locational Decisions in Industrial Plants in Wisconsin," *Land Economics* (August, 1970), pp. 325–328.

McDERMOTT, DENNIS R.; "An Alternative Framework for Urban Goods Distribution: Consolidation," *Transportation Journal* (Fall, 1975) pp. 29–39.

McMILLAN, T. E.; "Why Manufacturers Choose Plant Locations vs. Determinants of Plant Locations," *Land Economics* (August, 1965).

MILGRIM, HERBERT; "The Temporal Factor in Spatial Monopoly, *Transportation Journal* (Winter, 1972), pp. 33–38.

NEWBOURNE, M. J. and Colin Barrett; *Guide to Industrial Site Selection,* (Washington, D.C.: The Traffic Service Corporation, 1971).

1972 Carload Waybill Statistics (Washington, D.C.: Federal Railroad Administration, 1974).

PAASWELL, ROBERT E. and Joseph Berechman; "The Urban Disadvantage and the Search for Locational Opportunity," *Traffic Quarterly* (January, 1976), pp. 85–100.

PERSON, MARJORIE and Diane Mitchell; "Distribution Centers: The Fort Wayne Experience," *Business Horizons* (August, 1975), pp. 89–95.

SAZAMA, GERALD W.; "State Industrial Development Loans: A General Analysis," *Land Economics* (May, 1970), pp. 171–180.

SHENKEL, WILLIAM M.; "The Economic Consequences of Industrial Zoning," *Land Economics* (August, 1964).

"Showdown on Delaware Bay," *Saturday Review* (March 18, 1972).

"Site Selection Checklist," *Distribution Worldwide* (February, 1974).

SMERK, GEORGE M.; "An Evaluation of Ten Years of Federal Policy In Urban Mass Transportation," *Transportation Journal* (Winter, 1971), pp. 45–57.

SMITH, DAVID M.; *Industrial Location: An Economic Geographical Analysis* (New York: Wiley, 1971).

STUDENT, KURT R.; "Cost vs Human Values in Plant Location," *Business Horizons* (April, 1976).

TABB, WILLIAM K.; "Government Incentives to Private Industry to Locate in Urban Poverty Areas," *Land Economics* (November, 1969), pp. 392–399.

"Tax Rates/Exemptions," *Distribution Worldwide* (February, 1974).

Transportation Facts and Trends (Washington, D.C.: Transportation Association of America).

Waterfront Renewal: Technical Supplement (Madison, WI.: Department of Resource Development, 1964).

WHITMAN, EDMUND S. and W. James Schmidt; *Plant Relocation: A Case History of a Move* (New York: American Management Association, 1966).

WOODS, DOUGLAS F. and Thomas A. Domencich; "Competition Between Rail and Truck in Intercity Freight Transportation," *Proceedings of the 1971 Transportation Research Forum.*

YASEEN, DAVID W.; "The Interstate Commercial Zone: An Industrial Location Factor," *Land Economics* (February, 1966), pp. 107–112.

Conveyer system at end of a high-rise warehouse. *Credit:* Demag Material Handling Corporation.

CHAPTER NINE

Warehousing and Distribution Centers

The dingy storehouse, a place to keep *things is a thing of the past. Warehousing today is a science of skilled technicians using high-speed machines for the orderly processing of the essential materials of our economy. . . . The change has been accelerated by the physical distribution concept which has focused on inventory costs.*

—CREED JENKINS
In *Handling and Shipping*
May 1973

In one city in the state of Indiana three highly competitive wine and spirits wholesalers consolidated their out-of-town delivery operations. Each company's salesmen call on the out-of-town accounts and write up orders in the traditional way. Although there is no consolidation of inventories under one roof (the out-of-town truck picks up orders at each of the three warehouses), the competitors have recognized the importance of reducing their distribution costs by delivering on a consolidated basis in an unmarked truck to distant points.

—FRANK M. MAGEE
In *Materials Handling in Canada*
1968

STORAGE AND DISTRIBUTION: WHO DOES IT AND HOW?

Chapter 7 dealt with *why* stocks of goods are stored. Chapter 8 discussed *where* they should be located. This chapter deals with the design and operation of the facilities.

Inventory analysis can help individual retailers determine whether or not they should stock all the items in question. Analysis may also have shown that if the items in question were stocked only at the factories where they were manufactured, customer service levels could be inadequate because it might take too long to supply customers. Therefore distribution warehouses represent a compromise. They are justified on the basis of cost analysis which determines that a specified level of customer service can be achieved at minimum cost by locating inventories at certain intermediate locations throughout the country.

The phrase *distribution center* is virtually synonomous with *warehouse* since most goods in a warehouse are in somebody's distribution system. In distribution channels, warehouses are intermediate storage points between the manufacturer and the retailers. A distribution center is a warehouse which places emphasis on the rapid outward distribution of goods.

Donald J. Bowersox, in his thoughtful discussion of distribution channels, defines the *exchange* channel as "consisting of a number of independent firms [which] exists to deliver the specified product assortment to the right location at the right time. A number of functions must be performed jointly by all channel members in the exchange process."[1] The functions are: storage, transfer, handling, communication, and *adjustment* (which consists of choosing a point or points in the exchange channel to concentrate the goods, select from the concentration, and form a new selection of goods to be dispersed to the next level in the exchange channel).[2] The adjustment process occurs at a warehouse. Note that the warehouse is involved in four of the five exchange channel functions: storage, handling, communication and adjustment. Storage and adjustment features are unique to the warehouse. Storage is a somewhat passive function. The *adjustment* function is more dynamic and gets to the basics of physical distribution thinking. In how many places, and at what locations, should goods be concentrated so that new and different selections can be assembled and shipped to the next receiver?

Sometimes warehouses are needed because production and consumption do not coincide; canned fruits and vegetables are typical examples. The warehouses serve to match different rates of flow. When goods are purchased, sometimes larger quantities are bought than can be immediately consumed. This may occur to prevent anticipated scarcity, or to benefit from a seller's advantageously priced "deal." Warehousing space is needed to store the surplus supplies.

Warehouses discussed in a distribution textbook would be thought of as primarily *market* oriented. However, some warehouses are production or raw-material oriented. Manufacturers who stockpile some of the items they need, consider *their* warehouse selection decision as being *production* oriented.

Implicit in many warehouse functions are assembling or light manufacturing processes. Goods are uncrated and tested. Some goods are repackaged prior to distribution to retail outlets. State tax stamps may

---

[1] Donald J. Bowersox, *Logistical Management* (New York: MacMillan, 1974), p. 51. The "firms" need not be independent; they could be logistical components of the same corporation.

[2] *Ibid.*, p. 52.

be affixed. Minor damage to incoming goods may be repaired (and the carrier or party responsible for the damage billed).

SHIPMENT CONSOLIDATION AND POOLING

A warehouse's principal function is to receive goods, store and care for them, and then assemble and ship outgoing orders. They perform the "adjustment" function as has already been defined.

Consolidation is the adjustment function in action and involves arranging one's distribution system so that, insofar as possible, goods arrive and leave in vehicle-load quantities. "Everything in today's distribution environment favors volume shipments for as much of the distance between shipper and receiver as possible. Bear in mind that the carriers are doing whatever they can to avoid individual small shipments themselves, and shippers who want to maintain any semblance of customer service are generally going to be highly motivated —to put it mildly—to plan volume shipments."[3] Thus, one approach to the warehouse number and location choice is to determine what configurations allow for maximum utilization of truckload, rail carload, and barge load lots. Recall the discussion of "break-bulk" and "make-bulk" facilities in chapter six (pages 197–199).

CONSOLIDATION ANALYSIS

Analysis of possible movements which could be consolidated is rather easy to describe, at least in manual terms. A traffic manager sets up tally sheets for each different origin and destination pair. Then, for each day of the week, the manager lists the number of shipments that moved from the origin to the destination and notes the commodity description and weight. Weekly totals are calculated and an attempt is made to determine whether enough weight was involved that a volume truckload or rail carload rate could be used. If the goods are moved on a daily basis, then, of course, this routine is worked out for daily totals.

There are variations to this approach and they are usually more complicated. They would involve learning cyclical patterns in shipments and lead times which were necessary to fill orders. The key is to know what can be done to work up to truckload or carload minima. While transportation savings may be considerable, one must also make certain that other costs—especially those associated with holding inventories— do not increase more. Other changes also occur. Consolidation may be of many small shipments of different types of goods which the firm produces. Once consolidated, they move under an FAK (freight-all kinds)

---

[3] Warren Blanding, "Thirteen Opportunities to Sell Public Warehousing Today," *Warehousing Review* (special issue, 1974), pp. 2–3.

rate, rather than the rate for a specific commodity. However, when moving goods in truckload or carload lots, transit times are reduced considerably because the goods do not have to move through the carriers' own small package terminals.

The vehicle load concept is a very important determinant of warehouse location. A firm looks at its retail outlets and asks, "to and from which points can we most economically serve retail outlets in vehicle-load quantities?" The points selected will then be the sites for renting public warehouse space or, possibly, constructing a private distribution facility. Note that the warehouse sites are between the factory and the retailer; the factory-warehouse links and the warehouse-retail store links must be considered simultaneously. Alternatives would be to look at various arrangements of adjustment points (warehouses) to see if a lower total cost of combined freight rates and inventory changes could be achieved, consistent with some specified level of customer service.

LESS-THAN VEHICLE LOADS

Smaller lots should be considered. Some truck LTL rates have a "break" at 5,000 lbs, which means it costs less per pound for shipments over 5,000 lbs than the cost per pound for shipments which weigh less than 5,000 lbs. Hence, the planning specification for a distribution system may require that warehouses be located so that no outgoing shipment is under 5,000 lbs. In Chapter 10, packaging and material handling will be discussed and the "unit load" concept of using pallet-loads of materials as the materials-handling "building block" will also be mentioned. A firm exploiting that concept could try to locate warehouses in a way that no outgoing shipment be less than a pallet-load. In this instance the objective would be savings in materials-handling costs at both the warehouse and the consignee's receiving dock. Figure 9-1 is a distribution center's tariff showing assembly and distribution charges. Note the incentive for goods on pallets or skids, and for larger shipments.

Carriers also have incentives for consolidation. They offer partial loading or unloading privileges so that a vehicle load can be assembled from several small sources of supply, or a vehicle load can be dispersed among several consignees.

PUBLIC AND PRIVATE WAREHOUSES

A common distinction among warehouses is whether they are public or private. Distribution centers can be either, although they emphasize distributing rather than storing goods.

FIG. 9-1 Excerpt from warehouseman's tariff.

1ST REVISED PAGE 10		*MF-I.C.C. NO. 2
CANCELS ORIGINAL PAGE 10	▲METROPOLITAN WAREHOUSE COMPANY ASSEMBLY AND DISTRIBUTION TARIFF NO. 1	

ASSEMBLY AND DISTRIBUTION RATES — IN CENTS PER 100 POUNDS	ITEM NO.

DESCRIPTION OF COMMODITIES FOR WHICH ASSEMBLY OR DISTRIBUTION RATES ARE PROVIDED HEREIN:
FREIGHT, AS DESCRIBED IN ITEMS 1010 THRU 201080 OF THE GC, EXCEPT THE FOLLOWING, VIZ.: CLASS A OR B EXPLOSIVES OR POISONS; FRESH FRUITS OR FRESH VEGETABLES; LIVE ANIMALS OR POULTRY; MEAT, FRESH; MILK OR CREAM, FRESH; UNCRATED PERSONAL EFFECTS OR HOUSEHOLD GOODS; UNCRATED FURNITURE.
BETWEEN
ASSEMBLER'S OR DISTRIBUTOR'S LOS ANGELES, CALIFORNIA TERMINAL
AND
POINTS WITHIN ASSEMBLER'S OR DISTRIBUTOR'S TERRITORY AS DESCRIBED IN WMTB SCOPE OF OPERATIONS AND PARTICIPATING CARRIER TARIFF NO. 100, MF-I.C.C. NO. 3.

§ 200

CLASS RATES (SUBJECT TO NOTES 1, 2 AND 3)

MINIMUM WEIGHT IN POUNDS		CLASSES					
		100	92.5	85	77.5	70	65
		RATES					
AQ	⊕	311	295	280	264	250	239
	△	286	270	255	239	225	214
5,000	⊕	167	158	151	142	135	128
	△	142	133	126	117	110	103
10,000	⊕	135	128	121	114	108	104
	△	110	103	96	89	83	79
20,000	⊕	112	106	102	95	91	87
	△	87	81	77	70	66	62
30,000	⊕	103	98	93	88	82	79
	△	78	73	68	63	57	54

COMMODITIES RATED CLASS 60 AND LOWER

AQ	MINIMUM WEIGHT IN POUNDS							
	1,000	2,000	5,000	7,500	10,000	15,000	20,000	30,000
	RATES							
	⊕228	⊕179	⊕148	⊕122	⊕111	⊕ 98	• ⊕78	• ⊕72	• ⊕66
	△203	△154	△123	△ 97	△ 86	△ 73	• △53	• △47	• △41

NOTE 1: COMMODITIES TAKING CLASSES IN THE GC LOWER THAN CLASS 60 SHALL BE SUBJECT TO CLASS 60 RATES.
NOTE 2: MINIMUM CHARGE SHALL BE THE CHARGE FOR 300 POUNDS, PER COMPONENT PART.
NOTE 3: WHEN ONE OR MORE SHIPMENTS REQUIRE THE FULL UTILIZATION OF ONE OR MORE UNITS OF EQUIPMENT WHICH IS USED EXCLUSIVELY FOR TRANSPORTATION OF SHIPMENT OR SHIPMENTS ONLY, THE CHARGE SHALL BE ASSESSED BY APPLYING THE APPLICABLE RATE IN THIS ITEM TO EACH SHIPMENT (WHEN MORE THAN ONE SHIPMENT), SUBJECT TO A TOTAL MINIMUM CHARGE OF $80.00 PER UNIT OF EQUIPMENT UTILIZED. (SEE NOTE 4).
NOTE 4: A UNIT OF EQUIPMENT IS ONE TRACTOR AND ONE SEMI TRAILER 35 FEET OR MORE IN LENGTH.

§ RATES IN THIS ITEM WILL NOT APPLY ON SHIPMENTS PICKED UP OR DELIVERED AT STEAMSHIP DOCKS OR WHARVES.
⊕ WILL NOT APPLY FOR WHICH RATES ARE PREFIXED BY REFERENCE ▲▲.
△ APPLIES ONLY ON SHIPMENTS OR PORTIONS THEREOF UNITIZED ON PALLETS OR SKIDS WEIGHING AN AVERAGE OF 1,000 POUNDS PER PALLET OR SKID PER SHIPMENT OR PORTION THEREOF.
* METRO DISTRIBUTION CENTERS, INC., SERIES.
PROVISIONS HEREIN, TO OUR KNOWLEDGE, IF EFFECTIVE, WILL NOT AFFECT HUMAN ENVIRONMENT.

ISSUED: AUGUST 1, 1974	EFFECTIVE: SEPTEMBER 9, 1974
	ISSUED BY: CHARLES S. SHUKEN, VICE PRESIDENT 1340 EAST SIXTH ST. LOS ANGELES, CA 90021
CORRECTION NO. 4 JL/BG-F	- 10 - (LAST PAGE)

Courtesy: Metropolitan Warehouse Company, Charles S. Shuken, Vice President.

PUBLIC WAREHOUSES

Public warehouses are analagous to common carriers in that they serve all legitimate users. Public warehouses are used by firms which cannot justify the costs of having their own facilities. In most analysis of a firm's warehousing needs, public warehouses are considered as the initial alternative. They offer more in the way of flexibility in terms of both space needs and location than would be offered by any system of company-owned facilities. They require no capital investment and space is rented as needed.

Some public warehouses are specialized. They may handle only refrigerated goods, steel or household goods, or even be grain elevators. Maritime general cargo "transit sheds" in ports perform many public warehouse functions although they are more oriented toward *moving cargo through* than they are to storage.

The following is a list of services which many public warehouses provide.

1. *Bonded storage.* This means goods will not be released until U.S. Customs duties or federal or state taxes or other fees are paid. This is important because it is in the interest of the owners to delay paying these governmental fees as long as possible, thereby reducing their investment in inventory until it actually needs to be moved forward in the distribution channel.

2. *Office and display space.* Firms who have large and complex inventory holdings in a warehouse may permanently station one or more of their own staff in the warehouse to perform some of the functions that otherwise would be provided by their warehouseman. Display space would be used by the selling staff in instances where they wanted to show products to prospective buyers.

3. *Data processing equipment* which can be integrated with user's equipment. This allows the user to communicate with public warehouses in the same manner as he communicates with his own.

4. *Inventory level maintenance* for users who specify the inventories they want stocked.

5. *Local delivery* or tendering outgoing movements to carriers. The authority of warehousemen to perform delivery services is regulated, and varies according to the state in which they are located. In any event, they can handle and prepay the outgoing shipment of goods.

6. *Unpacking, testing, assembling, repacking, stenciling, price marking* are additional commonly performed services, as are *break-bulk and assembling functions.*

7. *Securing goods which are being used as collateral for loans.* This can be done either on or off the warehouseman's premises. A *field* warehouse is a warehouse temporarily established at the site

of an inventory of goods, often the premises of the goods' owner. The warehouseman assumes custody of the goods and issues a receipt for them which can then be used as collateral for a loan. Using one's inventory of goods as loan collateral is helpful, although the goods are temporarily "frozen" in the distribution channel.

Many examples could be cited of a public warehouseman's functioning as an integral link in a product distribution channel. In a city with ten dealers for one make of electrical appliance, none of the dealers might stock an inventory. The only models they possess would be on their showroom floors. Once they made a sale, they would notify the public warehouse which would deliver a unit directly to the buyer's residence from the warehouse stock. The warehouse would also notify the factory of the sale and the factory would take steps to replenish the warehouse's stock. In this instance, the stock in the inventory in the warehouse would belong to the manufacturer, a factory distributor or an areawide dealer. The warehouse performs functions that would otherwise have to be performed by the owner of the inventory; the principal advantage is saving dealers from having to maintain large inventories.

PRIVATE WAREHOUSES

Private warehouses are owned or occupied on a long-term lease by the firm using them. They are used by firms who find that their warehouse needs are so stable that they can make long-term commitments to fixed facilities. (Private warehouse operation also requires commitment to a warehouse labor force.) The largest user of private warehouses is retail chain stores. They handle large volumes of merchandise and one of their resulting "economies of scale" comes from integrating the warehousing function with purchasing and distribution to retail outlets.

Manufacturing firms also maintain their own warehouses. Consider a firm manufacturing related products at different locations. Each plant would then ship its items to all of the firm's regional distribution warehouses so that each of them would stock a complete line of products. There are also products with unique handling characteristics such as steel beams, gasoline, etc., which, in some areas, public warehousemen prefer not to handle. In these instances the manufacturer is forced to develop his own facilities.

PLANT WAREHOUSES

A warehouse associated with most manufacturing operations is the plant warehouse, usually located somewhere near the end of the assembly line. Its principal function is to accommodate the differences in production line output and product demand in distribution network.

The second function the plant warehouse performs is to stockpile raw materials needed for the production process. In a "shortage" economy, it is advisable to carry larger inventories of some input items than would otherwise be needed.

The plant warehouse may also be the single location where every line item in the firm's inventory is stocked. This is especially true for repair parts. Dealers may be required to stock certain items. Regional parts depots may be expected to stock a wider assortment. But only the factory may be expected to stock all items. Another centrally-located site could perform this function, but the reason it is performed in the plant warehouse is that part of the stock of repair parts is merely "leftover" components from the assembly process.

Plant warehouses are thought of as being "private," although public warehouses are used for the same function. Public warehouses are used by the auto industry; they feed components to the assembly plants on a daily, and sometimes hourly, basis.

DISTRIBUTION CENTERS

The phrase "distribution center" is applied somewhat loosely. Some public warehouses refer to themselves as "distribution centers," which means they emphasize the distribution aspects of warehousing instead of the storage operations. The emphasis is on fast turn-over of goods. Service to retailers is required to be of such quality that the distribution center is relied upon to maintain the needed levels of inventory, rather than the individual retailers. The distribution center will also house other customer-oriented services such as sales, traffic, and credit.

In some large cities there is concern about the difficulties in delivering and picking up freight, usually in small shipment lots, at downtown points which have inadequate truck-handling facilities. Many different trucks must doublepark to pick up and deliver small parcels to tenants of large office buildings. Each trucker virtually repeats the efforts of the other. Studies are underway now to determine the feasibility of "urban goods consolidation" centers, to be located on the fringes of crowded downtown areas. All goods destined for downtown delivery would move through this consolidation point which would group shipments for each building or block so they could be handled by a smaller number of trucks and drivers.[4] While the studies so far have concentrated on goods being handled by common carrier truckers, they should be viewed with interest by other firms which must distribute within congested portions of a city. It is conceivable that they

[4] See *Goods Transportation in Urban Areas*, Gordon P. Fisher, ed. (New York: The Engineering Foundation Conferences, 1974), 123–148.

could function as distribution centers for the firm's products destined for these specific areas.

WAREHOUSE DESIGN

Public warehouses are usually designed to handle a variety of items, while private warehouses tend to be more specialized. Prior to designing a warehouse, the quantity and character of goods to be handled must be known. Warehouse *"throughput"* is a measure of how much moves *through* a given facility within a specified time.

WAREHOUSE AND DISTRIBUTION CENTER LAYOUT

The relative emphasis placed on the storage function and on the distribution function affect space layout. A storage facility having low rates of turnover is laid out in a manner which maximizes utilization of the cubic capacity of the warehouse devoted to storage. A distribution-oriented facility would attempt to maximize "throughput" rather than storage.

Tradeoffs. Trade-offs must be made between space, labor, and mechanization. Spaciousness may not always be advantageous since the distances that an individual or machine must travel in the storing or retrieving functions are increased. Cramped conditions also lead to inefficiencies. Before layout plans are made, each item that will be handled is studied in terms of its specific physical handling properties, the volume and regularity of movement, the frequency it is "picked," and whether, compared to related items, it is "fast" or "slow" moving.

Many trade-offs are involved in designing both the structure and arranging the equipment inside. Several will be listed here. The trade-offs are often more complex than appear on the list since all factors on the list affect each other.

1. *Fixed vs variable slot locations for merchandise.* Should one slot always be assigned to each product, which results in a "logical" layout but also in low space utilization because many goods have seasonal characteristics? The alternative, which results in higher space utilization, is to assign empty slots in an almost random manner to incoming products.

2. *Horizontal vs "high rise" layout.* The cubic capacity of a warehouse is a function of horizontal area times height. A later section in this chapter discusses "high-rise" storage. The relevant trade-off in utilizing a high-rise operation is between *building costs*, which decline on a cubic foot basis, as one builds higher and *warehouse equipment costs*, which increase.

3. *Order-picking vs stock-replenishing functions.* Should workers who are picking outgoing orders and those who are restocking the warehouse work at the same time? Should they use the same aisles? How much space should be devoted to "active" or "live" stocks, which are stocks the order pickers pick from to fill orders? How much space should be devoted to "reserve" stocks, which are stocks awaiting assignment to the active stock area? If too much space is devoted to active stocks, the bins are larger and the order picker's travel time from bin to bin is increased. If the bins are smaller, the active stocks must be replenished from the reserve stock more frequently.

4. *Two-dock vs single-dock layout.* Conventional warehouses have the receiving dock on one end, the shipping dock on the other end, and goods move through between them. An alternative uses one dock which receives in the morning and ships in the afternoon. Viewed from the top, the goods move in an "U-shaped" rather than a straight configuration. This reduces the space devoted to loading docks but requires carriers to pick up and deliver at more specific times.

5. *Space devoted to aisles vs space devoted to racks.* As aisle space increases, storage capacity decreases. Wider aisles make it easier to operate mechanical equipment but they increase travel distances within the facility.

6. *Labor-intensive vs highly mechanized.* As labor costs increase, many warehouses place an increasing reliance on equipment to perform tasks that had once been performed manually. Union Carbide has a 12-million cubic foot warehouse in West Virginia which can hold 64,000 drums of chemicals. Two persons (one of whom is a computer programmer) handle the entire warehouse.[5]

Three Examples of Layout. Distribution centers have varying layout objectives as the following three examples illustrate.

1. A mens' jeans manufacturer/distributor has only a few products. The main difference is in size of jeans. In laying out this facility, jeans could be arranged by size moving from smallest waist and pants-length through all lengths with that waist, to the next waist size, through all the lengths for that waist size, and so on. This is the way they are displayed in retail stores. Instead, in order to minimize the time of order pickers, the jeans are arranged so that the most popular sizes are in the locations which are the easiest (i.e., least time-consuming) for the order pickers to reach. The less popular sizes are placed on less accessible shelves.

2. A different approach is taken by an auto accessories chain for their distribution center. First, they insist that all of their retail

5 "Automated Storage," *Distribution Worldwide* (February, 1976), pp. 21–27.

outlets have the same physical arrangement of merchandise. Goods in the warehouse are arranged in the same order. Inventory and reorder forms for use at the retail level are laid out in the same order, which is retained when they are converted to the order-picker's form to be used in the warehouse. The warehouse order pickers use metal carts upon which metal baskets can be stacked. The order is picked in the same sequence as it appears in retail shelves which allows the retail clerk to rapidly place the items from the basket/cart onto the shelves.

3. A large food chain continually attempts to encourage its retail outlets to order the "optimum" lot size for a specific item. They may require or encourage the store to order ant poison by the tube, tomato puree by the case of 48 cans, and paper towels by the pallet load. Forms supplied to the retail store allow for orders in only these quantities or multiples thereof. The warehouse is split into three sections: for the individual items; for the items handled in case lots; and for the items handled in pallet lots. When assembling an order for a retail store, a computer separates the three types of orders and assignments are made to order pickers who have different equipment, depending upon the section of ware-house in which they are working. During the course of the year, some items move from one category of minimum lot size to another and the computer is programmed to make the adjustment readily.

Many products experience *seasonal* shifts in demand and this has an affect on their location and the amount of space they require. Fast-moving items sometimes require less of a space allocation than do slow moving items because they are not stored. Layout "flexibility" is im-portant although one warehouse expert has warned that in warehous-ing the word is used "to cover up many bad handling and storing practices" and is considered to be synonymous with "looseness," which it should not be.[6]

Two Working Systems. Figure 9-2 shows a top view and end view of a distribution center. In this example the replenishment and order picking functions are completely separated. Order pickers work in the center aisle. Stock replenishers work in the outer aisles, moving goods from "reserve" to "live" or "active" storage.

Figure 9-3 illustrates a much more complex distribution center which receives pallet loads, breaks them down into carton lots, then reas-sembles the carton lots into new, outgoing pallet loads. In that figure, pallet loads are received at point 2 where a computer-controlled stacker takes each pallet and stores it in one of 17,200 openings in the ten-aisle,

[6] Creed H. Jenkins, *Modern Warehouse Management*, (New York: McGraw-Hill, 1968), p. 68.

9-2 Typical order picking layout.

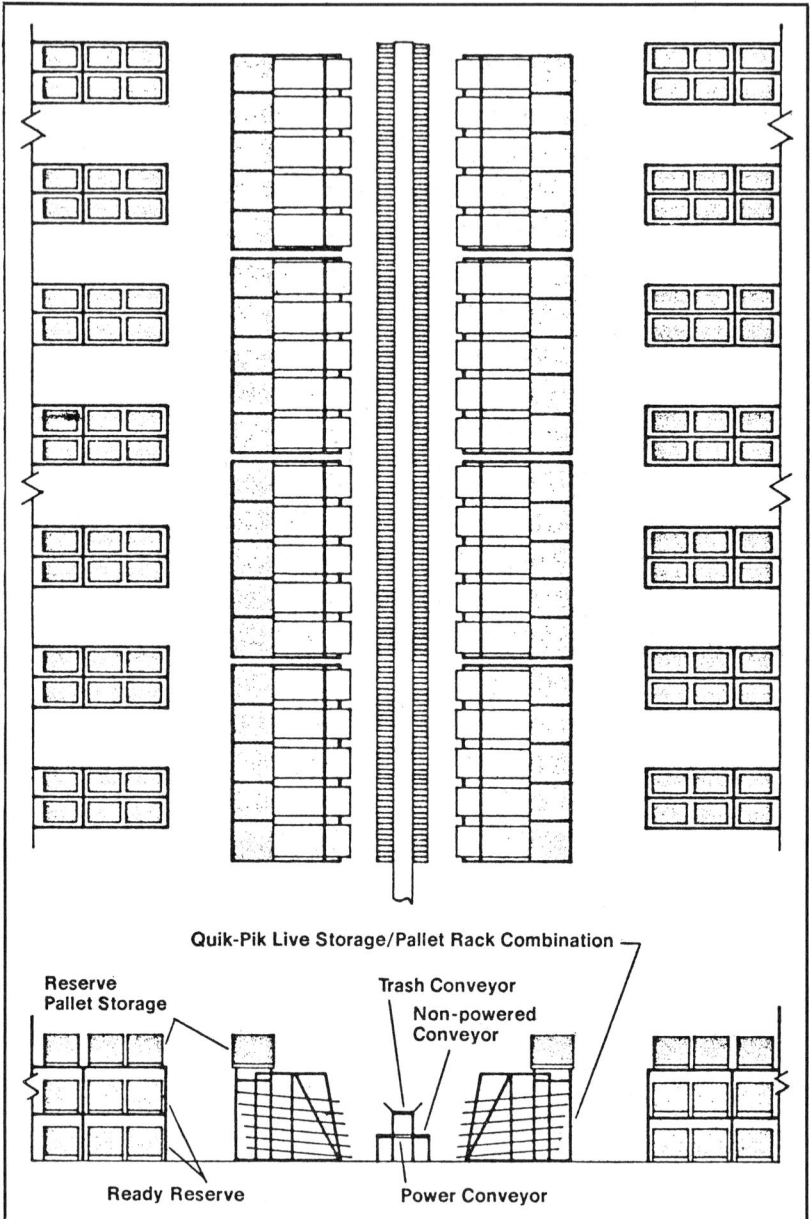

Quik-Pik Live Storage/Pallet Rack Combination

Reserve Pallet Storage

Trash Conveyor

Non-powered Conveyor

Ready Reserve

Power Conveyor

Courtesy: North American Equipment Corp.

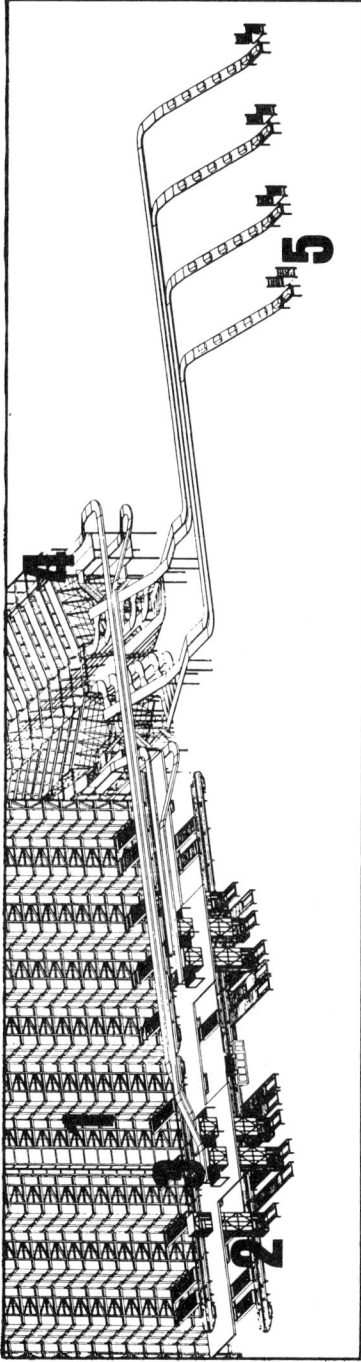

FIG. 9-3 Large automated distribution center.

65-foot high storage area (point 1). As goods are needed to replenish stocks on the lane loaders (point 4—to be discussed shortly), they are retrieved from area 1 and taken by the pallet carrier to one of several de-palletizing stations (point 3). As point 3 the pallets are *manually* unloaded and the cartons placed aboard a conveyor system which takes them to the lane loaders (point 4). At the lane loaders at least one lane is assigned to each product and cartons are loaded into the top of each lane. The bottom of the lane feeds on to a moving conveyor belt which is at right angles to the lanes. The lanes slope downward toward the belt and at the bottom of each lane (near the conveyer belt) is an electrically-triggered escapement device which releases one case at a time on to the conveyer belt. The lane is of sufficient slope that gravity forces the case out on to the conveyer belt. As orders are assembled on the conveyer belt, they move toward point 5 where they are routed to one of four loading stations where they are placed aboard pallets for outgoing shipments. This is also done manually. Hence loading and unloading pallets are the only two manual operations; the other operations are by machine. All operations are computer-controlled.

OTHER SPACE NEEDS

In addition to space for the through-put of merchandise, areas must be set aside for other warehouse activities as well. They require some detailed analysis in terms of space requirements and layout. Examples are:

1. Areas for vehicles waiting to be unloaded or loaded and employee parking.

2. Receiving and loading facilities for each mode of transport serving the facility.

3. Staging, or temporary storage areas, for both incoming and outgoing merchandise.

4. Office space including an area for whatever computer facilities may be involved.

5. Employee washrooms, lunch rooms, etc.

6. Pallet storage and repair facilities. (A large distribution facility which receives unpalletized materials but ships on pallets may require a pallet assembly operation.)

7. An area to store damaged merchandise which is awaiting inspection by the carrier's claim representative.

8. An area to salvage and/or repair damaged merchandise.

9. An area for repacking, labeling, price-marking, etc.

10. A room for accumulating and baling waste and scrap.

11. Area for equipment storage and maintenance. For example, battery-powered lift trucks must be "plugged-in" to battery chargers overnight.

12. Specialized storage areas for hazardous items, high value items, warehouse supplies, or items needing other specialized handling such as freezer or refrigerated space.

RETAIL STOREROOMS

Distribution center design is not an end in itself. It is but one link in the distribution process. The next link is the retail store itself. Some retail stores no longer have storerooms, which means that the goods go from the distribution center directly to the retailer's display shelves. A retail chain will often own two or three times as many trailers as it does tractors. Each time a tractor makes a delivery to a retail store, it will leave a trailer for the store to unload within 24 hours. It will also pick up the trailer which it had left the previous day to be unloaded. Hence, the parked trailer serves as a storeroom and reduces the "truck-to-storeroom" and "storeroom to shelves" movements to only one since the goods will go directly from the parked trailer to the shelves.

This practice does not hold for all industries, however. One successful furniture retail chain utilizes existing warehouses in urban areas. Part of the warehouse is converted to display space and if the customer selects the item, an identical one is given to him from the adjacent storage space.

WAREHOUSE EQUIPMENT

This section will discuss computers, scanners and handling equipment that is used in warehouses. Much of the equipment discussed in this section is more likely to be found in larger warehouses or in specialized distribution centers.

COMPUTERS

Both public and private warehouses utilize computers. In 1973, a sample of public warehouse operators was asked whether and to what extent they used computers.[7] Of the 79 respondents, 30 used computers, including six who used them to link multiple locations. Twelve of the 30 had direct communications links with their customers. The internal functions for which the firms use computers were inventory control, accounting reports, control of slot locations, sales analysis and cost analysis. The customer service functions performed by computer are stock status reports, stock movement reports, and overage, shortage and damage reports.

Computers are used to integrate the operations of facilities located

[7] This survey was summarized in *Warehousing Review* (May, June, 1973).

at different sites. Many large Ford and Lincoln-Mercury dealers are tied into Ford Motor Company's parts distribution center using conventional telephone lines. Special equipment is used at the dealers' sites, involving a keyboard terminal with a cradle to hold the telephone headset. The dealer's computer terminal can then "talk" to the computer in the parts distribution center. The dealer can check on parts availability or place emergency orders. The computer in the parts distribution center has a complete list of substitute parts. It may be that another model of auto uses the same part or part which can be substituted for the part the dealer needs. In this situation, the dealer's terminal will be told the number of the substitute parts so that a check can be made to determine whether they are in stock.[8]

Both buyers and vendors are likely to have computerized inventory control and warehousing systems. In Figure 9-4, which is a food chain purchase order, note that the vendor has an item code. The buyer also has an item code, and a slot number which tells where in the buyer's warehouse the goods should be placed. Some goods even have "batch" numbers telling when and where they were produced.* One reason for assigning "lot" or serial numbers to products or batches or products is that it makes them more identifiable to computer systems. One frozen food warehouse operator stated:

> When we are ready to move goods from storage, the computer performs additional functions. For instance it will only release stock that has been in storage the required number of hours—a duration that varies by product —and it will always select the oldest product in storage, to assure first-in, first-out flow.[9]

The same firm uses computers to print order-picking lists and to assign storage locations. Over 350 different products are handled and those which move in heavier volumes or "turn-over" more rapidly are assigned higher "velocity" figures than the other products. When an incoming shipment is received, the computer assigns each product to the nearest storage opening in its given "velocity" zone.

Figure 9-5 shows computer-printed, adhesive order picking labels. A list of such labels is printed in the sequence that items are arranged in the warehouse. The list is then given to order pickers and, as they select each carton, they affix an adhesive label. The large numbers on the left side of each label are used to sort outgoing shipments.

Warehouses are becoming more automated. In the main Ford parts warehouse, the order pickers ride on lift trucks with the horizontal

---

* Batch numbers are also discussed in Chapter 14.

8 "Dealer Parts Service, Ford's Master Plan," reprint of articles appearing in *Traffic Management* (June, 1973).

9 "What a Computer Can Do for a Ford Truck System," *Modern Materials Handling* (August, 1973), pp. 52–53.

MAIL INVOICE TO →

SAFEWAY STORES, INCORPORATED
P.O. BOX 2093 · SAN FRANCISCO, CALIFORNIA 94119
ACCOUNTING DEPARTMENT

VENDOR'S COPY

	DATE ORDERED			PAGE NO.
	MO.	DAY	YEAR	
	6	04	71	01

SHOW P.O. NUMBER ON INVOICE, BILL OF LADING AND ALL LOADING SHEETS.

PURCHASE ORDER NUMBER
005882

SHIP TO
SAFEWAY STORES, INCORPORATED
GROCERY WAREHOUSE - WHSE #70
2900 HOFFMAN BLVD.
RICHMOND, CALIFORNIA

4201
WAREHOUSE FACILITY

NO BACK ORDERS

6/11/71
DATE TO ARRIVE

SPECIAL INSTRUCTIONS

VENDOR
DOLE CORPORATION
HALL-ROEPKE COMPANY
1450 CHAPIN AVENUE
BURLINGAME, CALIFORNIA 94010

612-01
SELLER # PER BUYER

23-10
CASH DISCOUNT   TRADE DISCOUNT

1/3 OF 1%
SWELL ALLOW (SA) ITEM X

OAKLAND
F.O.B.

OTHER ALLOWANCE
•266.05 PCWT
FREIGHT CHARGE (FC) ITEMS X

PICKUP ADDRESS

BUYER # PER SELLER

TRUCK   OAKLAND
SHIP VIA   SHIPPING POINT

FREIGHT ALLOWANCE (FA) ITEMS X

QUANTITY ORDERED	UNIT	VENDOR ITEM CODE	VENDOR UNIT PACK & SIZE	DESCRIPTION	VENDOR LIST COST	S A	F A	C	VENDOR UNIT ALLOW.	SAFEWAY ITEM CODE	SAFEWAY PALLET PATTERN	SAFEWAY SLOT #	R
95	CS	849	8/6-6 OZ.	DOLE PINEAPPLE JUICE-SLEEVE PAK	3.80	X	X		.485	36604	16X6	15631	
105	CS	824	24/12 OZ.	DOLE PINEAPPLE JUICE	2.40	X	X		.003	36605	21X5	15621	
672	CS	803	12/46 OZ.	DOLE PINEAPPLE JUICE	3.40	X	X		.484	36606	8X7	14751	
105	CS	604	24/13.25 OZ	DOLE CRUSHED PINEAPPLE	5.20	X	X		.007	37825	21X5	17711	
93	CS	143	24/20 OZ.	DOLE SLICED PINEAPPLE-UNSW JCE	7.75	X	X		.01	37829	14X7	17571	
84	CS	613	24/20 OZ	DOLE CRUSHED PINEAPPLE IN JCE	7.75	X	X		.01	37830	14X6	17641	
84	CS	473	24/20 OZ.	DOLE CHUNK PINEAPPLE IN JUICE	7.75	X	X		.01	37831	14X6	17601	

618-01 PER BUYER
SELLER # PER BUYER

TRAFFIC OAKLAND
Special P.O. Distribution

47,193	1,244
Weight	Cases

· ORDER NUMBER MUST BE SHOWN ON INVOICE AND ALL SHIPPING PAPERS

SAFEWAY STORES,
INCORPORATED

BY E. P. CAMERON
BUYER

IMPORTANT NOTICE: This order is expressly conditioned upon acceptance of and compliance with the instructions, terms, and conditions on the face and reverse side hereof.

FORM NO. 622 IMPC (EXPER.) (REV. 5-69) 11-70-113-20

PRINTED IN U.S.A.

FIG. 9-5 Computer-printed order-picking labels.

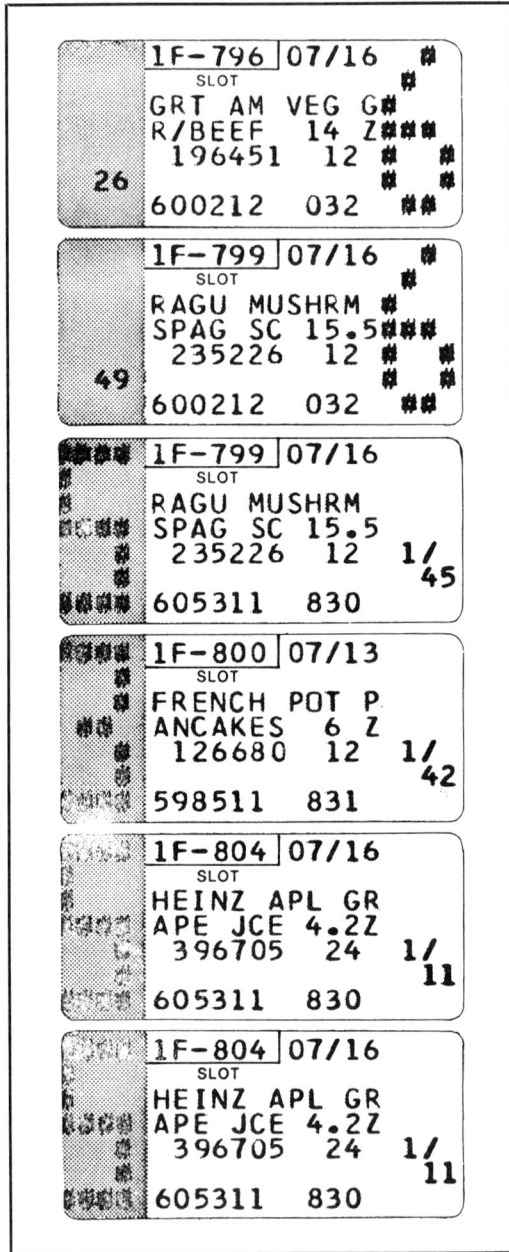

1F-796	07/16
SLOT	

GRT AM VEG G
R/BEEF   14 Z
   196451   12
26
600212   032

1F-799	07/16
SLOT	

RAGU MUSHRM
SPAG SC 15.5
   235226   12
49
600212   032

1F-799	07/16
SLOT	

RAGU MUSHRM
SPAG SC 15.5
   235226   12   1/
                   45
605311   830

1F-800	07/13
SLOT	

FRENCH POT P.
ANCAKES   6 Z
   126680   12   1/
                   42
598511   831

1F-804	07/16
SLOT	

HEINZ APL GR
APE JCE 4.2Z
   396705   24   1/
                   11
605311   830

1F-804	07/16
SLOT	

HEINZ APL GR
APE JCE 4.2Z
   396705   24   1/
                   11
605311   830

Courtesy Acco, Integrated Handling Systems Division.

travel and vertical lift of the picker's platform arc controlled by computer. The picker pushes the "NEXT STOP" button and the lift truck travels to the next location that a needed part is stored. The picker's platform is also lowered or raised (ground level to 20 feet) so that when the truck stops again the picker is in front of the slot where the sought part is stored.

SCANNERS

Optical scanners are possibly the single most important PD technological development in the 1970's. In warehouses, many packages now contain labels which can be "read" by visual scanners. These labels are black-on-white patterns of horizontal bars or circles. Scanners adjacent to conveyer belts recognize and tally each carton as it passes by. The scanner may be tied into a system that sorts each carton with respect to where it should be stored. Once the goods are in storage, inventories can be checked by passing a pen-sized scanner near to each label. The scanner is attached to a decoder which converts the label codes into numeric codes which can be understood by computers.

The use of labels on railcars was discussed in Chapter 4. A sophisticated use of these labels on mail trucks has been designed for the Oakland, California post office, a large structure, with 135 truck docks and space for parking an additional 315 trucks. All trucks enter through one gate and exit through another. At each gate there are scanners, linked to a computer. Mail trucks performing regular, daily tasks must pass through the gates within five minutes, more or less, of a scheduled time. If the trucks arrive at the gate within the ten-minute bloc, the barrier swings open once the scanner identifies the truck's label. If the truck is outside the ten-minute block the barrier remains down and the driver must speak to the control center through an intercom. The control center can then raise the barrier. Another category of truck handled at the facility are larger trucks going to and from other major post offices in the San Francisco Bay area. All these post offices are linked by a communication network and they notify each other of trucks "on their way" and also specify the priority of mail which is on the truck. These trucks also have ACI (Automatic Car Identification) labels as do private trucks of firms which make regular deliveries to the post office.* The monitoring of incoming and outgoing vehicles is a useful control function but it is not an end in itself. It is but one task in the larger framework of assigning workloads throughout the large facility.

---

* In the pre-Christmas rush, trucks without labels are more likely to appear. They belong to contractors who are helping carry the peak load or to private stores delivering large batches of parcels to the post office. These truck drivers must identify themselves through the intercom.

Incoming trucks are told by an electronic visual display board the number of the dock to which they are to proceed. That dock space is known to be empty and in an area of the post office where the workload is comparatively light at that hour.

STORAGE AND HANDLING EQUIPMENT

Conventional single-story warehouses and distribution centers accommodate material at heights up to approximately 20 feet. While it is possible to *store* most materials stacked on top of each other this is inconsistent with the distribution center concept of fast throughput. The oldest pallet would always be on the bottom and the pallet loads above it would have to be removed in order to get at the older pallet load. Hence, steel shelving or pallet racks are used and each pallet sits on an individual shelf and can be stacked or removed without disturbing other pallet-loads. Note that this results in a FIFO (first-in, first-out) flow.

City building codes regulate rack installation. California building codes discourage high storage racks in an effort to minimize earthquake damage.

Within the warehouse, the goods are moved by a variety of manual and mechanical devices. In small warehouses, a wheeled cart may have only a lifting device which must be pushed along the floor. More sophisticated devices are powered for moving along the floor and they may or may not contain accommodations for the user to ride in it. The fork lift truck is the standard "workhorse" in many warehouses.[10]

When outgoing merchandise cannot be handled easily on pallets, an alternative is to use wheeled baskets or carts. The outgoing goods are assembled in one or more baskets and the baskets are rolled directly onto the outgoing truck. The savings from this type of system also come from handling within the retail outlet. The carts are rolled into the retail outlet's aisles and the shelves are restocked directly from the carts. Sometimes the merchandise for sale is displayed on the store floor while still in the cart. The high cost of the system comes from transportation because the baskets or carts are seldom loaded as densely as are pallet-loads or cartons of merchandise. While many distribution systems cannot handle return items easily, one advantage of the baskets is that they can be reloaded with empty soft drink bottles, tires for retreading, auto generators for rebuilding, etc.

Some warehouses have tow lines which are set in the floor. Carts are equipped with gripping devices and pulled along. Carts can be "programmed" to follow different routes within the warehouse.

The photo at the beginning of this chapter shows "high-rise" storage.

[10] The *Modern Materials Handling*, Spring, 1976 issue, is devoted to fork lift truck selection.

Most high-rise warehousing equipment moves up and down narrow aisles and services materials on both sides of the aisle. Aisle widths are narrower than in the case of conventional warehouses. Since equipment can move both horizontally and vertically at the same time, the most efficient layout of goods along any one aisle may be a path of upward and downward undulations. This would consume less time than a path which took the equipment along a horizontal path and stopped; then moved up or down and stopped; then continued along the horizontal path and stopped, and so on.

In addition to highrise systems involving human order pickers, there are also completely automated warehouses. They have automated order picking devices which move along an aisle, stop in front of a bin and with a lateral handling device either store or remove a container.

WAREHOUSE OPERATIONS

Warehouse management is an exacting task. Work force motivation is difficult because of the repetitiveness of the operation. The work is strenuous. Only four aspects of operation will be touched upon here—worker safety, facility cleanliness, inventory controls, and handling of "stock-outs."

EMPLOYEE SAFETY

A 1972 survey showed that nationwide there were 19.2 injuries per hundred public warehouse workers. This compared very unfavorably with the 10.9 per hundred figure for all industries.[11] (See Figure 9-6.) Warehouses are dangerous because of the functions they perform. Goods and workers are in constant motion. A warehouse may receive a pallet that was improperly loaded and this will not become apparent until one attempts to handle it.

A small percentage of all goods a warehouse receives, stores, and ships are damaged, even with the best of practices. Special procedures must be established for handling any broken or damaged item just from the standpoint of employee safety (in addition to assuming or assigning responsibility for the breakage). A broken bottle of household ammonia, for example, results in three hazards: noxious fumes, broken glass, and slippery floors.

Warehouses generate large volumes of waste materials such as empty cartons, steel strapping, broken pallets, or wood and nails used for crating and dunnage.[12] This must be properly handled because it poses

[11] *Warehousing Review*, (September-October 1974), p. 12.
[12] Material used to block and brace products inside carrier equipment in order to prevent the shipment from shifting in transit and becoming damaged.

FIG. 9-6 Warehouse work can be dangerous.

"I said not such a heavy load, Hooper!"

Reproduced by permission of the Masters Agency.

a threat to employee safety and may also be a fire hazard. Large distribution centers may have an overhead conveyer belt system (see Figure 9-2) this is used to remove waste which is then stored, baled, and sold.

OSHA. In 1970, the Federal Occupational Safety and Health Act (OSHA) became law which resulted in increased federal and state supervision of industrial safety practices. Standards have been set for equipment and operations, and inspectors frequently make inspections. They can issue citations and monetary fines may be levied. The enforcement procedures are fairly new and have yet to be completely tested in the courts. In the early 1970's, OSHA was one of the most widely-discussed topics in the warehousing-distribution industry. The OSHA standards are complex and lengthy. What follows are excerpts from an OSHA report of violations at a specific location. In several instances penalties were assessed and they are noted.

1. Failure to maintain passageway, storerooms, and service rooms in a clean and orderly condition.

2. Open sided platform more than four feet above the adjacent floor level was not guarded by standard railings or the equivalent and was not provided with a toeboard.

3. Failure to provide railing on each side of a stairway less than 44 inches wide and having both sides open.

4. Safety shoes were not provided or required to be worn by employees exposed to foot and toe injuries when handling material, equipment, appliances, or similar items, i.e., truck drivers, helpers, and warehouse employees. Penalty $25.

5. Fire extinguishers were obstructed or obscured from view.

6. Failure to install portable fire extinguishers on hangers or brackets or set on shelves.

7. Fork lift trucks did not bear a label or identifying marks or nameplates. Penalty $25.

8. Failure to adjust work rest on a grinding machine to the required maximum of $1/8$ inch.

9. Failure to guard pulleys located less than seven feet from floor level.

10. Failure to guard horizontal belt located less than seven feet above the floor.

11. Failure to provide guards for gears.

12. Failure to legibly mark disconnecting means for motors and appliances.

13. Exposed noncurrent-carrying metal parts of cord and plug connected equipment which was liable to become energized not provided with ground. Penalty $25.[13]

Employee safety is a matter of continual concern. It involves training, motivation, and never-ending supervision.

SANITATION

Warehouse cleanliness is another never-ending concern. The small amount of space devoted to it here does not do justice to its importance. Sanitation is related to both employee safety and to the quality of the products handled.

The U. S. Food and Drug Administration (FDA) is concerned with the sanitation of food and drugs moving in interstate commerce. Its efforts were strengthened in mid-1975, when the U. S. Supreme Court upheld the *criminal* conviction of the *president* of a large food chain (nearly 900 retail outlets) because of unsanitary conditions in one of

[13] *Warehousing Review* (March-April, 1975) p. 19.

the firm's warehouses.[14] This demonstrates that sanitation is a "top management" responsibility.

STOCK CONTROLS

A principal and continuing problem is keeping an accurate count of merchandise moving through the warehouse. If the count is off—either too high or too low—sophisticated handling procedures will be undermined. The initial error occurs when the worker at the receiving dock assumes that all the goods listed on the delivering carrier's bill of lading are, in fact, there. A second type of error occurs when the receiving clerk assumes responsibility for "on the spot" adjustments of overages and shortages. He may note that there is one too many cartons of brown shoe polish and one too few cartons of black shoe polish. Since the price is the same he may accept the shipment without noting the discrepancy. The receiving clerk's single error gets multiplied, because counts for both colors of polish will be off.

Accurate counts of merchandise leaving the warehouse/distribution center are important although there is a partial control in that whoever receives the goods next will, if he or she is doing their job properly, report discrepancies. Shortages will almost always be reported.

One example of checking outgoing shipments is the procedure used in a Levi-Strauss warehouse where separate counts of the same outgoing shipment are made by the order *picker* and the order *packer*. An additional three percent of outgoing shipments are checked by a third individual.[15]

STOCK-OUTS

"Stock-outs" were discussed in Chapter 7 and methods were shown for reducing or eliminating them. Nevertheless they occur. Warehouse/distribution centers must have policies to answer such questions as:

1. Will the customer permit substitutions and, if so, what types of substitution are acceptable?
2. If, because of a partial outage, it is impossible to ship a large enough load to meet minimum load quantities, what should be done?
3. Will the customer accept partial delivery? Will he or she accept back orders? If freight charges are higher because of these split shipments, how shall they be assessed?
4. If shipping dates cannot be met, what actions should be taken?[16]

[14] *Warehousing Review* (July-August, 1975), pp. 2–9.

[15] Interview with Weldon G. Helmus, West Coast Distribution Manager of Levi Strauss & Co., April 16, 1974. Chapter 14 of this book discusses other types of controls in more detail.

[16] Warren Blanding and Howard E. Way, *100 Ways to Improve Warehouse Operations* (Washington, D.C.: Marketing Publications, Inc., 1972), p. 6.

Highly computerized distribution centers have answers to most of these questions programmed into their system and the "answer" can be determined quickly. Unfortunately, not all exceptions can be thought of in advance. Therefore, it is necessary to know to whom the situation should be reported so that a decision can be made.

These examples relate to the customer service element of distribution. Usually a separate report is made to the sales person handling the account whose service is being delayed or altered. It may be preferable to have him or her contact the customer with the reasons for the delay rather than merely leaving the customer waiting for the shipment. If there are some alternative solutions to the problem from which the customer can choose, it may be wise to give the customer the choice. In this case the distribution center's exception policy would be to have the sales person contact the customer.

SUMMARY

In *warehousing* the emphasis is on storage. The emphasis of a *distribution center* is on fast, accurate "throughput" of merchandise. A distribution center assumes some of the inventory maintenance functions of the retail outlets it serves.

Public warehouses are analogous to common carriers. They can be integrated into a firm's distribution system and can perform all of the necessary functions. Their principal advantage is that the user avoids a large investment in fixed facilities and commitment to a warehouse work force.

When arranging a distribution center, the initial goal is to reduce the number of times an item is handled. However, for control purposes it is necessary to have a system of checks and rechecks to make sure accurate tallies are kept of incoming and outgoing materials. Warehouses and distribution centers are being automated.

Warehouses and distribution centers are but one link in the distribution system. They perform the "adjustment" function of receiving, breaking down, reassembling and shipping. They must be located, designed, and operated in a manner which contributes to the overall performance of the firm's physical distribution needs.

QUESTIONS FOR DISCUSSION AND REVIEW

1. Why must an order-picker's order be checked for accuracy?
2. Distinguish between a *warehouse* and a *distribution center*.
3. List the various functions performed by warehouses and distribution centers.

4. What is a *bonded* warehouse?

5. What is OSHA? How does it affect warehousing?

6. What are the functions of a plant warehouse?

7. Why is safety of warehouse employees a problem?

8. What is "high-rise" storage? What limitations, if any, are there on height?

9. Why must accurate counts be kept of merchandise (a) entering, (b) inside, and (c) leaving, a warehouse/distribution center?

10. What are the advantages of public warehouses? When would private warehouses be used?

11. Discuss the *adjustment function*, as defined by Bowersox.

12. How are "consolidation" points selected?

13. Why do warehouses offer incentives for goods loaded on pallets?

14. In a distribution center, which is the more important function— order picking or stock replenishment? Why?

15. Discuss the advantages of *fixed* and *variable* slot locations in distribution centers.

16. Discuss use of computers in warehousing.

17. How are scanners used in warehousing?

18. What is a "FIFO" inventory flow system?

19. Why must distribution centers have developed procedures for handling stock-outs?

CASE 9-1   OBREGON RESTAURANT SUPPLY COMPANY

The Obregon Restaurant Supply Company was a partnership owned by two brothers, Juan and José Obregon, and located in Bakersfield, California. It sold non-food supplies to restaurants. Paper supplies, silverware, and dishes were its three principal lines and accounted for 80 percent of the firm's sales. The other 20 percent were accounted for by a wide range of articles such as napkin dispensers, toothpick dispensers, kitchen pans and utensils, etc. The sales territory included the area bounded by Fresno, San Luis Obispo, Santa Barbara, and Barstow, all in California. The firm did not sell in the Los Angeles area and there was no market to speak of east of Bakersfield. Juan and José took turns staying in the office and selling on the road. Four other full time salesmen were also employed.

The firm's market was the relatively unsophisticated restaurants throughout the entire territory. Salesmen drove small vans in which they stocked the new items they were trying to sell and a variety of small replacement items for which there was frequent demand. Most of the restaurants were regular customers. A salesman would call at a fairly regular time each week and take an order. At the end of the day, the order would be handed in to the Bakersfield office (or phoned in if the salesman were staying away overnight). The next day either Juan or José, whoever's turn it was to be in the office, would tally all of the orders and, in turn, place Obregon's order with about six principal suppliers. These suppliers were located in Bakersfield, Fresno, and in the Los Angeles area. All these goods were bought on an FOB plant or warehouse basis and, late the next afternoon, they would be picked up by an Obregon truck that had finished delivering supplies to restaurants. Obregon trucks would then take them to the small Obregon office/warehouse, where the goods would be unloaded. That night, outgoing orders would be made up and loaded aboard the Obregon trucks.

The truck routes for delivery were fairly regular, as were the pickups of supplies. During the afternoon, one of the Obregon brothers would write out the delivery documents and pickup instructions for each of tomorrow's drivers. That evening, a night crew of two would assemble the next day's outgoing orders, load them—in reverse order of delivery —aboard each truck, and clean and lock up the premises.

About 90 percent of Obregon's business was handled in the manner described. Some kitchen utensils had to be ordered from firms in the East and they would be mailed or sent via parcel service to the Obregon office and then delivered on an Obregon truck. Some of Obregon's outgoing shipments went by motor common carrier. These were usually those destined toward San Luis Obispo and, since there was no backhaul for Obregon trucks from that area, it was cheaper for the Obregons to use common carriers. Common carrier truck service was relatively good despite the small size of the Obregon shipments. The reason was that Obregons had a regular volume of business. Obregon's salesmen also made a few deliveries each week, mainly to restaurants in such isolated locations that no other reasonable alternative existed. In these instances, the salesmen would deliver last week's order while taking the order for delivery next week.

In the past two years, the Obregons had been losing business to a Los Angeles-based competitor who gave "next-day" delivery, which meant that the supplies would be delivered to the restaurant one day after the salesman took the order. (The comparable time for an Obregon order was three to four days after the order was given.) The Los Angeles firm's salesmen just called on larger restaurants on the principal north-south highways between Los Angeles and South San Francisco, where their firm also maintained a warehouse. One day a truck's delivery route would be Los Angeles to South San Francisco and the next day its route would be from South San Francisco to Los Angeles.

The Obregons lost some of their best accounts to this new competitor. The restaurants which switched said that the main reason for switching was improved delivery times. If trends continued, the Obregons would be left serving only two categories of restaurants—small ones in isolated areas that nobody else wanted to serve, and those owned by Americans of Mexican descent who preferred to do business with others of similar origin.

The Obregons decided that in order to remain competitive they would have to maintain an inventory of all supplies in Bakersfield. They also could provide "next-day" delivery along the north-south highways where their competitor was active.

They were somewhat surprised when they calculated that their dollar investment in inventory would not be large. This was because they would be buying in much larger volumes and would enjoy substantial quantity discounts. Some of the suppliers indicated that if the Obregons ordered in rail carload quantities, they could receive goods directly from the factory at even greater savings.

In their investigation, the Obregon brothers talked with several public warehousemen in Bakersfield. In addition, the warehouse foremen in their suppliers' warehouses were helpful, especially with suggestions with respect to handling their own types of product. It was agreed by all, that the Obregons would need about 10,000 square feet of warehouse space. The question then was whether to use a public warehouse or to buy a private warehouse. In addition to the 10,000 square feet of space, they needed: a loading/unloading dock wide enough so that three trucks could be handled simultaneously; parking space for six trucks and six autos; 200 square feet of office space; and, perhaps, a location on a rail siding so that they could receive by rail. Their products were of moderate value and could be handled with relatively unsophisticated warehouse equipment. The suggestion was made that about 1000 square feet of the area be fenced with chicken wire and kept locked most of the time. Inside it would be kept all open cases.

José Obregon investigated the public warehousing available in Bakersfield and found three different firms with which he would be willing to do business. In California, warehousemen's tariffs are regulated by the state public utilities commission, and José believed that if the decision was made to use public warehouse facilities, he would talk with users of all three to determine which offered the best service. José was sold on public warehouses and told Juan of their advantages. "The main advantage is flexibility," he said, "our business may be more volatile than we think and if competition increases we may have a smaller volume of sales and inventory. Then we'll be stuck with empty space. Also, if we're making the right decision, all three public warehouses have rail sidings so we could start receiving paper products by rail. Our only big cash outlay is for inventory. We'd be stretching our credit rating to borrow for a building. Interest rates are high now, we'd be paying 10–12 percent."

"What would monthly charges at a public warehouse be?" asked Juan.

"That depends on what we're handling and the amount of labor.

For our mix of product, renting the space would be about $1400 per month. In addition, we'd need about 300 hours of warehouse labor per month, which is figured at $11 per hour."

"That's high," said Juan.

"You're right," said José, "but we use two men for eight hours every night here."

"Yeah, but they cost us only seven dollars per hour. If we had a private warehouse, one could work the day shift and receive and stock goods and the other could work at night, loading outgoing trucks."

"What would a private warehouse cost us?" José asked his brother.

Juan answered: "There are two private ones we can rent. One is 12,000 square feet which we could have for 10 cents a square foot a month on a five year lease. The second one would be 10,000 feet in a larger structure that a consortium of local investors wants to build. We could get 10,000 square feet at 13 cents a square foot but we'd have to sign a ten year lease. That site has rail siding, the first one doesn't."

"I don't like those long leases," said José. "In a public warehouse we could change the amount of space rented every month. We'd also have to buy equipment, wouldn't we?"

"Yes, but let me finish talking about private warehouses," said Juan. "We could build a 10,000 square-foot structure on a site with plenty of room for expansion for about $85,000, including lot and building. We'd have to pay 40 percent down, and the rest would be paid over 15 years, in annual payments of $7,000 each (which includes 11% of the unpaid balance)."

"What about property taxes?" asked José

"They'd run $1,500 per year for the land and building. We'd also pay an inventory tax but, in this state, it makes no difference whether you're in a public or a private warehouse. As I see it, we'll need only a crew of two for forty hours a week apiece and our wages are only seven dollars per hour."

"Yes, but they need equipment," exclaimed José.

"We won't need much more than we use around here to load and unload trucks," responded Juan. "The only immediate need would be a fork lift truck so we can stack higher. We'd only be using it an hour or so a day and I think we could assume, if we bought a used one, that the cost would be about $1,000 a year."

José asked: "Did the sites you consider have rail sidings?"

Juan said that they were alongside rail tracks and that the Obregon firm would have to pay the cost of the siding on their land. If they generated enough traffic the railroad would not charge them for the costs of the siding that was on railroad property.

Question One: Based on the information given so far, which alternative would you recommend? Why?

Question Two: Before making the decision which the Obregon brothers are going to have to make, what additional information would be useful?

CASE 9-2 SAGINAW AUTO PARTS CO.

Saginaw Auto Parts Co. was located in Saginaw, Michigan. It manufactured and bought automobile replacement parts which it distributed to chain auto supply houses, some service station chains and to two mail order houses. It did wholesale business only. Its principal warehouse was in Saginaw where over 140,000 different parts were stored. One giant conveyor belt, 36 inches off of the floor, moved through the entire warehouse. On either side of the conveyor belt were racks with shelves placed 3", 21", 39", and 52" above the floor.

The warehouse was divided into 15 order-picking zones. Empty baskets left the office with small tabs raised for zones where portions (or all) of the order were to be picked. As the basket reached the zone, the raised tab would activate a mechanism which removed the basket from the belt. There an order picker would fill the basket with whatever parts were located in that zone, release the cocked tab for that zone and place the basket back on the belt where it would travel to the next zone for which a tab was cocked. When a particular zone was especially busy, and accumulated a batch of unfilled baskets, a worker would place some of the unfilled baskets back on the belt without touching the cocking mechanism. The basket would then move to the next station for which a tab was cocked and eventually would return to the station where the temporary overload had existed.

Over 98 percent of all items were handled by the conveyor belt system. The only exceptions were engine blocks, which were too heavy, and tail pipes, which were too long. These items were handled separately out of a room near the loading dock.

Saginaw Auto Parts Company had always been profitable and, in 1968, it had been acquired by a large conglomerate. In 1974, as a gesture to public and governmental pressures, the conglomerate's management promised to increase significantly the employment of females in all of its subsidiaries. When word of this promise reached Saginaw Auto Parts, there was some uncertainty as to how to implement the promise since the entire belt and accompanying storage system had been carefully engineered and designed with the assumption that males would do the order picking. Saginaw's management reported this fact to the conglomerate's board of directors. The directors, whose other agenda item that day dealt with how to handle unfavorable publicity resulting from a recently disclosed 1972 campaign contribution, told Saginaw's management that it would have to change the system so that women could work as order pickers. Saginaw's management was especially unhappy since—within the past six months—they had to rebuild 600 linear feet of rack structure because a Federal O.S.H.A. (Occupational Safety and Health Administration) inspector had said that there were inadequate clearances between the belt and shelving at several locations.

There are many concerns in laying out a warehouse. In the Saginaw warehouse, each of the 15 zones contained a "family" of items such as electrical equipment, transmission parts, etc. A different buyer was responsible for each of the fifteen zones. Within the zones, the goods were located according to two criteria. The fastest moving items were in the shelf 39″ from the floor because that was the quickest location from which to pick. Very heavy items, 35–50 lbs, were also at that level because it was closest to the level of the belt and a higher percent of the work force could handle heavy loads if no vertical change was involved. Fast moving items were also put in the 52″ shelf since most men were tall enough to see and handle items stored at that height. The slowest moving items were in the bottom shelf.

Some items handled weighed 50 pounds or over, but additional lifting equipment was provided to workers handling them. A sample of 20,000 items picked during random days in 1976 showed this weight distribution:

Weight	%
under 1 lb	15
1 to under 5 lbs	20
5 to under 10 lbs	15
10 to under 20 lbs	15
20 to under 30 lbs	10
30 to under 40 lbs	10
40 to under 50 lbs	5
50 lbs and over	10
	100%

Data for each zone varied. In the engine block zone, nearly every item weighed over 50 lbs. In four zones, nothing weighed over 25 lbs.

Table 1 was provided by an insurance company and the portion regarding males had been used in determining shelf level locations in the present warehouse. Items had been placed at heights so that 2/3 of "industrial men" could handle them. (Some of Saginaw's work force, especially older men, could not perform to these standards. They were assigned to zones where none of the items was very heavy.) New employees were given physical examinations before they could become order pickers. During the first two weeks, they were carefully instructed and closely supervised with respect to proper lifting techniques. Workers were expected to meet order picking standards for their zone. Continued failure to do so was a recognized reason for dismissal although,

TABLE 9-1 Percents of Workforce that Can Perform Lift or Various Weights from Specified Heights to the Height of 36 Inches.*

	Lbs.	Industrial Men	Industrial Women	Housewives
From 52″	10	100	100	85
	20	90	85	70
	30	75	70	60
	40	65	60	45
	50	55	45	30
	60	45	35	20
	70	40	25	10
From 39″	10	100	100	90
	20	90	85	75
	30	80	75	65
	40	75	65	50
	50	70	50	35
	60	60	40	25
	70	45	30	15
From 21″	10	100	95	85
	20	90	80	60
	30	75	65	50
	40	60	50	45
	50	50	40	35
	60	45	35	20
From 3″	10	95	90	80
	20	85	75	55
	30	75	60	45
	40	60	45	35
	50	45	35	30

* Figures are hypothetical.

as just noted, older workers who had been with the company for some time were assigned to less demanding tasks.

The center and right columns on Table 1 are for females. Industrial women are experienced industrial laborers. Housewives have less lifting ability, yet they are actively seeking work in the industrial area and presumably represent the individuals whom Saginaw should be attempting to hire.

Question One: Assume you are Saginaw Auto Parts' warehouse engineer and are told to redesign the storage system so that more female workers would qualify as order pickers. How would you go about your task?

Question Two: What additional information, not given in the case, would be useful in answering question one?

CHAPTER REFERENCES

"Automated Storage," *Distribution Worldwide* (February, 1976).

BLANDING, WARREN; "Thirteen Opportunities to Sell Public Warehousing Today," *Warehousing Review* (Special Issue, 1974).

———— and Howard E. Way; *100 Ways to Improve Warehouse Operations* (Washington, D.C.: Marketing Publications, Inc., 1972).

BOWERSOX, DONALD J.; *Logistical Management* (New York: MacMillan, 1974).

CONSTANTIN, JAMES A. and Kung-Mo Kuo; "An Index Screening Approach to the Selection of Commodity Candidates for Regional Warehousing," *Transportation Journal* (Summer, 1975).

"Dealer Parts Service, Ford's Master Plan," *Traffic Management* (June, 1973).

Goods Transportation in Urban Areas, Gordon P. Fisher, ed. (New York: The Engineering Foundation Conferences, 1974).

JENKINS, CREED H.; *Modern Warehouse Management* (New York: McGraw-Hill, 1968).

JONES, J. RICHARD; "Can a Green Graduate from State College USA Find True Happiness in a Public Warehouse?" *Handling and Shipping* (April, 1972), Vol. 13, No. 4, pp. 64–68.

————; "Marketing Attitudes of the Public Warehousing Industry," *The Logistics and Transportation Review* (Volume 8, Number 2), pp. 89–95.

————; "Operational Characteristics Pertaining to Public Warehouses," *Transportation Journal* (Spring, 1972), pp. 23–30.

LYNAGH, PETER M.; Measuring Distribution Center Effectiveness," *Transportation Journal* (Winter, 1971), pp. 21–33.

Modern Materials Handling (Spring, 1976).

Warehousing Review (May-June, 1973; September-October, 1974; March-April, 1975; July-August, 1975).

"What a Computer Can Do for a Fork Truck System," *Modern Materials Handling* (August, 1973).

A loose plastic sheet has been draped over this pallet-load. Heat will be applied to shrink the covering so it is tight. *Credit:* Weldotron Corporation, Piscataway, New Jersey.

CHAPTER TEN

Packaging and Materials Handling

Damage seems to have a mind of its own. We might have shipped 1,000 units of some electronic component and not had a damage. The next one has the damage and that's the one the customer really needed. At that point, all the perfect shipments don't count with the customer.

—JAMES R. STRONG, in
Materials Handling Engineering
1973

Canvas mail sacks—used by the postal service for 200 years—will soon be replaced by fiberboard boxes, the postal service announced last week. The stiff-sided containers promise easier handling and will keep mail in better shape for processing by machine. . . . Currently about 30 percent of the mail suited for machine sorting is bent when it is lugged in sacks or pouches. The bent mail must be sorted by hand. . . .

News item in
San Francisco Chronicle
July 8, 1974

Suppose you're shipping a table, and the regulations say you need a certain amount of packaging for that table. Now if I make that table without gluing the joints and just putting in a couple of staples, you're going to get all kinds of damage unless I go way beyond the carrier's packaging instructions. But if I have a well-constructed table I won't need the carrier's minimum packaging requirements. I think that sometime in the future the carriers will have to accept the guarantees of certified packaging professionals that a particular package will function satisfactorily in shipment for that particular product.

—IRWIN R. GREENE, in
Materials Handling Engineering
1973

THE PRODUCT ITSELF DETERMINES
HOW IT WILL BE HANDLED

This chapter deals with the physical handling of products. The first portion of the chapter deals with packaged goods and the second portion examines products shipped in bulk, i.e., in loose form. This distinction is not absolute. A good may move in bulk form from the manufacturer to a wholesaler, who will package it for retail distribution.

Each product has unique physical properties. For example, density of bulk materials varies. The Great Lakes steamer Richard J. Reiss, when carrying ore, uses only two-thirds of its cubic capacity yet the 15,800 tons of ore will lower the vessel to its maximum allowable draft of 24 feet, 8 inches. When loaded with coal, the vessel "cubes-out," i.e., the cubic capacity is filled and the vessel will lower to only 20 feet, six inches. Grain loads even lighter, and the Richard J. Reiss' draft then is slightly less than 20 feet.[1]

A material's *angle of repose* is the angle size that would be formed by the side of a conical stack. The greater the angle, the higher the pile of materials that can be placed on a specific area. Anthracite coal has an angle of repose of approximately 27 degrees, while for iron ore the figure is 35 degrees. This means more cubic yards of ore can be stockpiled on a certain site and the ore could be carried on a slightly steeper conveyer belt system.

Bulk liquids also have unique handling characteristics. Resistance to flow is measured as *viscosity* and this can be lowered by increasing the temperature of a liquid. Molasses, cooking oils, and many petroleum products are heated before an attempt is made to pump them. Gases also have unique handling properties, although most of them are handled within completely enclosed pipeline systems. An exception is LNG, liquified natural gas, which is cooled and compressed into liquid form which is $\frac{1}{630}$ of its volume in gaseous state. In its liquified, highly pressurized state it is transported by ocean-going vessels in special tanks.

The handling process itself may change the characteristics (or quality) of the product. Rice cannot fall far without the grains being broken. This influences the design of loading and unloading facilities so that the grains never drop more than a few feet at any one time. When sugar is handled, a "dust" is formed because of abrasion between sugar crystals. This dust is also sugar but in much finer form and with different sensitivities to moisture. The dust must be separated from the rest of the sugar, otherwise the quality of the final product in which the sugar is used will be affected.

[1] Correspondence from The Reiss Steamship Company to the authors. These figures are for loads prior to the vessel's conversion to a self-unloader.

The physical characteristics of some goods change while they are moving in the distribution channel. Fresh fruits and vegetables are the best-known example. They are picked before they are ripe and the intention is to have them reach the retail stores as they ripen. Ripening processes can be delayed through the use of lower temperatures or application of gasses. Several years ago, an experiment was conducted to determine whether Colorado and California carnations should be picked and shipped in bud, rather than full-flower form. The buds had better transport characteristics since they were less voluminous (more could be loaded into a carton) and also they weighed less because the stem with the bud contained less water than did a stem with a full flower. An advantage at the receiving end of the shipment was that the buds had a longer shelf-life because ripening could be delayed by keeping the buds at a low temperature. The disadvantages were also at the receiver's end since ripening the carnations required temperature-controlled space and some labor to trim and place the stems into buckets of ripening solutions.[2]

In addition to physical characteristics, products also possess chemical characteristics which affect the manner in which they should be handled. This is especially true for bulk materials since they are not already in containers.

HAZARDOUS CARGO

Under certain conditions, almost any material can possess hazardous qualities. Flour dust will explode, or grain in elevators will self-ignite and burn. Special care is needed to handle these and many other such substances. In the early 1970's there was an increase in governmental regulations involving the movements of so-called "hazardous cargoes." (For a while, commercial airline pilots were refusing to carry certain cargoes aboard their planes.)

The specific requirements differ for each hazardous commodity and the regulations deal with labeling, packaging and repackaging, warnings on shipping documents, advance notification of carrier, etc. A common requirement on transferring flammable materials is that the vehicle and the receiving or discharging device both be electrically grounded. Care must be taken to properly clean tanks, pumps, hoses, etc., to avoid contamination of the next cargo which is handled.

Numerous regulations exist and are issued by all levels of government. Figure 10-1 is a "check-list" from an airline publication and is to be used for hazardous shipments. The requirements posed by this

---

[2] *Transport and Handling of Carnations Cut in the Bud Stage—Potential Advantages*, U. S. Department of Agriculture, Agricultural Research Service, Marketing Research Report No. 899 (Washington, D.C., 1971).

FIG. 10-1 Checklist for airborne hazardous cargo.

SUGGESTED CHECK LIST: Check the regulations indicated by the unshaded areas.
To be used as a guide for packing and documentation of hazardous materials

PROPER DOT NAME OF PRODUCT:_____

(Trade Name: For shipper's use: _____)

REQUIREMENT	FILL IN INFORMATION	CHECK ALL APPLICABLE REFERENCES			
		FAR 103	49 CFR	CAB 82	IATA (for int'l, when more restrictive.)
PROPER SHIPPING NAME					DOT & IATA names may differ. If so, **use both** for int'l.
CLASSIFICATION					
QUANTITY LIMITATIONS: PER OUTSIDE PKG. Passenger Aircraft Cargo Aircraft					
ANY CARRIER EXCEPTIONS?					
REQUIRED LABELS: Class Cargo a/c only? Other?					
OUTSIDE PACKAGING: Exempt from DOT spec? If not, what spec? What markings?					
INSIDE PACKAGING: (type, quantity limits, insulation outage (etc.)					
AIR WAYBILL: Proper Shipping Name Labels req. (class) Cargo only? Passenger—OK? Volume/pkg Other (flash pt, permit #, etc.)					
SHIPPER'S CERTIFICATION: Complete? Authorized sig?					
ANY SPECIAL INSTRUCTIONS?					
ADVANCE NOTICE TO CARRIER					

OK For Release To Carrier _____

Courtesy Flying Tiger Line.

list are in *addition* to normal documentation. Note at the top that four different regulations are applicable.[3]

ENVIRONMENTAL PROTECTION

Public interest in environmental protection has had an impact on physical distribution packaging practices. Use of disposable packing materials is viewed as wasteful. Many of the materials used in packaging can be recycled. This has happened in the case of wooden pallets which tripled in price, creating an incentive for many firms to devise methods for re-using them rather than indiscriminantly disposing of them.

Increased enforcement of water pollution controls has forced some paper and container manufacturers out of business. Higher prices for logs have diverted lumber resources to other uses. Since 1970, there have been shortages of many types of packing and packaging materials. Prices have risen and this has caused some users to recycle their shipping containers. The result is not always without danger, however, since problems arose when goods in re-used containers were contaminated by traces of whatever product had been carried earlier. It was necessary for the U. S. Food and Drug Administration to issue an order restricting the re-use of containers to avoid food contamination. Dressed poultry often carries salmonella organisms (which are killed in cooking) but the organisms survive in the wooden crates and spread to vegetables if they are transported later in the same crate.[4]

Dust and vapors produced during bulk-cargo transfer operations are also being scrutinized more closely by public agencies. Coal dust will blow for several miles from a large coal pile. Some states are requiring those who handle petroleum products, including retail gasoline stations, to install vapor recovery systems. For liquids with vapor-escape problems, the transfer processes are being redesigned so that tanks and other receptacles are loaded from the bottom, rather than the top. This change—when applied to tank truck loading with petroleum—reduces vapor emissions by 80 percent.[5]

METRIC SYSTEM

Adjustment to environmentalists' concerns has been one of the dominant factors influencing the packaging and materials handlings aspect of physical distribution during the 1970's. Adoption of the metric system is the other big change. More and more products will be packaged

[3] The abbreviations stand for: FAR 103; Federal Aviation Regulations, Vol. VI. Part 103; 49 CFR; Code of Federal Regulations, Transportation, Title 49, Parts 170–189; CAB 82; CAB 82, Official Air Transport Restricted Articles Tariff No. 6-D; and IATA: International Air Transport Association Restricted Articles Regulations.

[4] *Transport Topics*, November 21, 1971.

[5] Statement in *Butler Roadrunner*, Minneapolis, Butler Manufacturing Co., 1973.

and sold on a metric measure basis. New packages will be in metric units with the non-metric equivalents printed in smaller type. While the entire change may take several decades in the sense of how long it will take to "forget" the old measures, many of the steps necessary to implement the adoption of the new system must be taken in the next few years.

Eventually package and container dimensions will also be changed. Beverages will be sold in containers measured in liters rather than quarts. (A liter is about five percent larger than a quart.) The pound (453 grams) package would probably give way to the half-kilogram (500 gram) package, and so on.

PACKAGING *

Packaging can be thought of as a system of building blocks. The smallest-size units are the retail or consumer packages or cartons one sees on the shelves of stores. These are usually packed into boxes of one to two cubic feet and light enough in weight so they can be carried by a stock clerk.†

The building-block hierarchy is important to remember because each of the different building blocks is inside another and their total effect must be to protect the product. They function in a complementary sense. If the consumer-size package is very solid, such as the wooden boxes in which salt-codfish are packed, the larger packaging elements require less sturdy packaging materials because the smallest package (the wooden boxes) are themselves sturdy. At the other extreme would be lightbulbs with a retail packing of single face corrugated fiber-board that may protect them from breakage but contributes almost nothing to the internal strength of the larger container.

SALES FUNCTIONS OF BOXES

Boxes are thought primarily to be protective although they may contain features with a sales orientation. Some products are sold in either a consumer-size pack or a larger box or case. Some merchants build displays using box or case lots of goods to create the impression they have made an extra-large purchase of a certain item—presumably at a lower price per unit and this lower price is being passed on to the consumer. In this instance, it would be appropriate to have some adver-

---

* Popular terminology for describing containers differs from that in carrier tariffs. "Boxes" are technically defined as being more rigidly constructed than "cartons" or "packages."

† Later sections in the chapter continue with the "building block" theme. The text refers only to rectangular boxes; the building block concept can be applied to packages of different shapes.

tising on the outside of the box. Some boxes are designed so that they do not have to be unpacked by the stock clerk for stocking on shelves. Instead, the stock clerk cuts away the top two-thirds of the box and places the bottom third with its contents still in place on the shelf. These boxes are designed to indicate the lines along which cuts should be made and they may contain an advertising message on the portion of the box which is placed on the shelf. The advertising objectives and the protective objective of packaging sometimes conflict.

One way to reduce pilferage is to avoid identifying the contents of a box, at least to the casual eye. Code numbers alone are used which means that a potential thief would have to either know the code numbers or else open each carton.

PROTECTIVE FUNCTIONS OF PACKAGING

A protective package must perform the following functions. It must:

1. Enclose the materials, both to protect them and protect other items from them.

2. Restrain them from undesired movements within the container when the container is in transit.

3. Separate the contents to prevent undesired contact, such as through the use of corrugated fiberboard partitions used in the shipment of glassware.

4. Cushion the contents from outside vibrations and shocks.

5. Support the weight of identical containers which will be stacked above it as part of the building block concept. This could mean, in some situations, stacks in a warehouse that are over 20 feet high.

6. Position the contents to provide maximum protection for them. If one were packaging combined sets of waste baskets and lampshades, the package would be designed so that the lampshades were protected by the wastebaskets.

7. Provide for fairly uniform weight distribution within the package since most equipment for the automatic handling of packages is designed for packages whose weight is evenly distributed.

8. Provide sufficient exterior surfaces so that identification and shipping labels can be applied along with specific instructions such as "this side up" or "keep refrigerated."[6]

Figure 10-2 is a checklist prepared by the Fibre Box Association and indicates the range of considerations that go into package choice. Firms which sell packaging material are helpful sources of information to potential users. Often they will provide technical advice. Packaging is

---

[6] List adopted from Richard C. Colton and Edmund S. Ward, *Practical Handbook of Industrial Traffic Management*, 4th edition (Washington, D. C.: The Traffic Services Corporation, 1965), pp. 157–158.

FIG. 10-2 Checklist for box users.

checklist for box users

The corrugated box contains and protects your product, but it can also serve many functions which aid in packing, storage, distribution, marketing and sales. This checklist is a guide to the information you'll want to supply to your box maker. He can then offer suggestions and recommendations to utilize every value-added advantage that corrugated can offer.

your product

	yes	no
1. Have you given your box maker the exact dimensions, weight and physical characteristics of your product?	☐	☐
2. Is the product likely to settle or shift?	☐	☐
3. Is it perishable, fragile, or dangerous in any way?	☐	☐
4. Will it need extra protection against vibration, impact, moisture, air, heat or cold?	☐	☐
5. Will it be shipped fully assembled?	☐	☐
6. Will more than one unit be packed in a box?	☐	☐
7. Will accessories, parts or literature be included with the product?	☐	☐
8. Have you provided your box maker with a complete sample of your product as it will be packed?	☐	☐

your packing operation

	yes	no
1. Is your box inventory adequately geared to re-order lead time?	☐	☐
2. Is your box inventory arranged to efficiently feed your packing lines?	☐	☐
3. Will you be setting up the boxes on automatic equipment? (If so, what type? Size? Method of closure?)	☐	☐
4. Will your product be packed automatically? (If so, with what type of equipment?)	☐	☐
5. If more than one unit or part goes into each box, have you determined the sequence?	☐	☐
6. Will inner packing—shells, liners, pads, partitions—be inserted by hand?	☐	☐
7. Is your closure system—tape, stitches, glue—compatible with the box, packing line speed, customer needs and recycling considerations?	☐	☐
8. Will the box be imprinted or labeled?	☐	☐
9. Will a master pack be used for a multiple of boxes to maintain cleanliness or appearance?	☐	☐

your storage

	yes	no
1. Have you determined the gross weight of the filled box?	☐	☐
2. Does the product itself help support overhead weight in stacking?	☐	☐
3. Will the bottom box have to support the full weight in warehouse stacking?	☐	☐
4. Will boxes be handled by lift trucks which use clamps, finger lifts or special attachments?	☐	☐
5. Will filled boxes be palletized? (The size of pallet and pallet pattern may justify a change in box design or dimensions.)	☐	☐
6. Would a change in box style or size make more efficient use of warehouse space?	☐	☐
7. Will filled boxes be subject to unusual conditions during storage—high humidity, extreme temperatures, etc.?	☐	☐
8. Is the product likely to be stored outdoors at any time during its distribution?	☐	☐
9. Would color coding simplify identification of various packed products?	☐	☐

your shipping

	yes	no
1. Have you reviewed the appropriate rules of the transportation service you intend to use (rail, truck, air, parcel post, etc.)?	☐	☐
2. Is your box approved for shipment of your product?	☐	☐
3. If the package is not authorized, have you requested appropriate test shipment authorization from the carrier?	☐	☐
4. Does your product require any special caution or warning label or legend for shipment?	☐	☐
5. Have you determined how your filled boxes will be stacked or braced in trailers or freight cars?	☐	☐

your customer

	yes	no
1. Does your customer have any special receiving, storage or handling requirements that will affect box design?	☐	☐
2. Will the box be used as part of a mass display?	☐	☐
3. Is the box intended as a display-shipper?	☐	☐
4. Will it contain a separate product display?	☐	☐
5. Will it be used as a carry-home package, requiring a carrying device?	☐	☐
6. Does it need an easy opening feature?	☐	☐
7. Can surface design, symbols or colors relate to promotional materials or to other products of the same corporate family?	☐	☐
8. Should instructions or opening precautions be printed on the box?	☐	☐
9. Can the box be made to better sell your product?	☐	☐

Courtesy Fibre Box Association.

a science and costs can be calculated for various solutions to any packaging problem. Package choice is a concern of physical distribution management since it is related to transportation and storage facilities. It is also related to materials-handling techniques and equipment used in factories, assembly plants, and warehouses.

The list of all packaging materials and all packaging methods would be very long. The biggest change in recent years has been the use of plastic materials replacing wood or paper-based materials.

COMMON CARRIERS' PACKAGING REQUIREMENTS

Chapter 5 discussed common carrier freight classifications and tariffs. The freight classifications influence (if not control) the choice of packaging and packing methods when common carriers are used. In the freight classification documents the type of packaging is specified. The commodity will be listed, followed by a comma, and then by a phrase such as "in machine pressed bales," "in barrels," "in bales compressed to more than 18 lbs. per square foot," "folded flat, in packages," "celluloid covered, in boxes," "SU" (set up), or "KD" (knocked down or disassembled and packed so that it occupies one-third or less of the volume it would occupy in its "set up" state). The carriers have established these different classifications for two main reasons. Packaging specifications determined by product density are to encourage shippers to tender loads in densities which make best use of the equipment's weight and volume capabilities. Specifications that deal with protective packaging are to reduce the likelihood of damage to products while they are being carried, and this, in turn, reduces the amount of loss and damage claims placed against the carrier.

Figure 10-3 shows the type of label that motor carriers and railroads require on any fiber boxes used for shipping freight. This label is the fiber box manufacturer's assurance to the motor carriers and railroads that the boxes will be sturdy enough to meet their handling specifications.

Rail and motor carriers permit shippers to experiment with newer packaging techniques—not currently provided for—so long as the shipper receives permission in advance and complies with various additional rules. Note that these common carrier rules do not apply to goods being shipped by contract or private carriers.

Airlines, express delivery companies, and the postal service also have packaging requirements although they are somewhat less detailed than those used by rail or motor common carriers. Export packing is discussed briefly in Chapter 11. The International Air Transport Association regulates packaging of air shipments; there are fewer requirements regarding ocean shipments. However, exporters nearly always

FIG. 10-3 Box-Maker's guarantee.

NAME OF BOX MAKER GUARANTEEING BOX

BOX CERTIFICATE

THIS
DOUBLEWALL

BOX MEETS ALL CONSTRUCTION
REQUIREMENTS OF APPLICABLE
FREIGHT CLASSIFICATION

BURSTING TEST	200	LBS PER SQ INCH
MIN COMB WT FACINGS	92	LBS PER M SQ FT
SIZE LIMIT	75	INCHES
GROSS WT LT	65	LBS

CITY AND STATE IN HERE

Courtesy Fibre Box Association.

buy additional insurance coverage for their export shipments; and the type of packing influences the insurance rates.

Carrier packaging requirements are becoming more detailed and very complex. At present, carrier classification boards are debating whether to replace detailed specifications with "performance standards." Performance standards would merely state what the packaging was expected to do, i.e. withstand so much vibration, humidity, shock, etc.[7]

PACKAGE TESTING

When new products or new packaging techniques are about to be introduced, it is sometimes advisable to have the packages "pre-tested." Various packaging material manufacturers or their trade organizations provide this service free. Independent testing laboratories can also be used.

[7] "Will It Be Performance Standards or Material Requirements?" *Handling & Shipping* (April, 1975), pp. 41–42.

The packages are subjected to tests which attempt to duplicate all the expected various shipping hazards: vibration, dropping, horizontal impacts, compression (having too much weight loaded on top), over-exposure to extreme temperatures or moisture, and generalized "rough handling." Figure 10-4 shows one testing device, a 14-foot diameter drum which revolves with the packages inside. This is to simulate conditions of "rough handling."

Sometimes specialized tests are devised. The following quotations describe tests conducted on a new type of pallet:

> After bearing a 2,400-lb. load for 48 hours and being checked for deformation, the pallet was again loaded with 2,400-lb. load and run through a series of tests. . . .
>
> > 20 times picked up and set back down on the four by fours in a rough and careless manner.
> >
> > 4 times picked up off the supporting beams with one fork under the center of the pallet only and lifted to a height of 4 feet; then rapidly lowered and raised. This attempt was to crack the pallet in the center.
> >
> > 10 times raised 6 inches by a fork lift that had a fast fork drop rate, and then very rapidly dropped back on its supporting beams.
>
> We then tried to mutilate the loaded pallet by
> 1) Twisting the forks within the pallet-fork openings; i.e. backing up at an angle before disengaging the forks from the pallet. We were able to put a slight tear near the corner of one fork opening.
>
> 2) Roughly, we pushed the pallet to different positions while flat on the floor with one fork. This was done in the attempt to split the outside corners.

In addition to the testing of new products or new packages, shippers should keep detailed records on all loss and damage claims. Statistical tests can be applied to the data to determine whether the damage pattern is randomly distributed. If it is not, then efforts are made toward providing additional protection for areas in the package that are overly vulnerable.

Related to package testing is actual measurement of the environment which the package must pass through. This is done by enclosing recording devices within cartons of the product which are shipped. The measuring devices may be very simple, such as hospital-like thermometers that record only temperature extremes, or springs that are set to snap only if a specified "G" (a measure of force) is exceeded. More sophisticated devices record over time a series of variables, such as temperature, humidity, and acceleration force and duration (in several directions). Acceleration force and duration is usually recorded along three different axes and this makes it possible to calculate the precise direction from which the force originated.

Fig. 10-4 Equipment to simulate "Rough Handling."

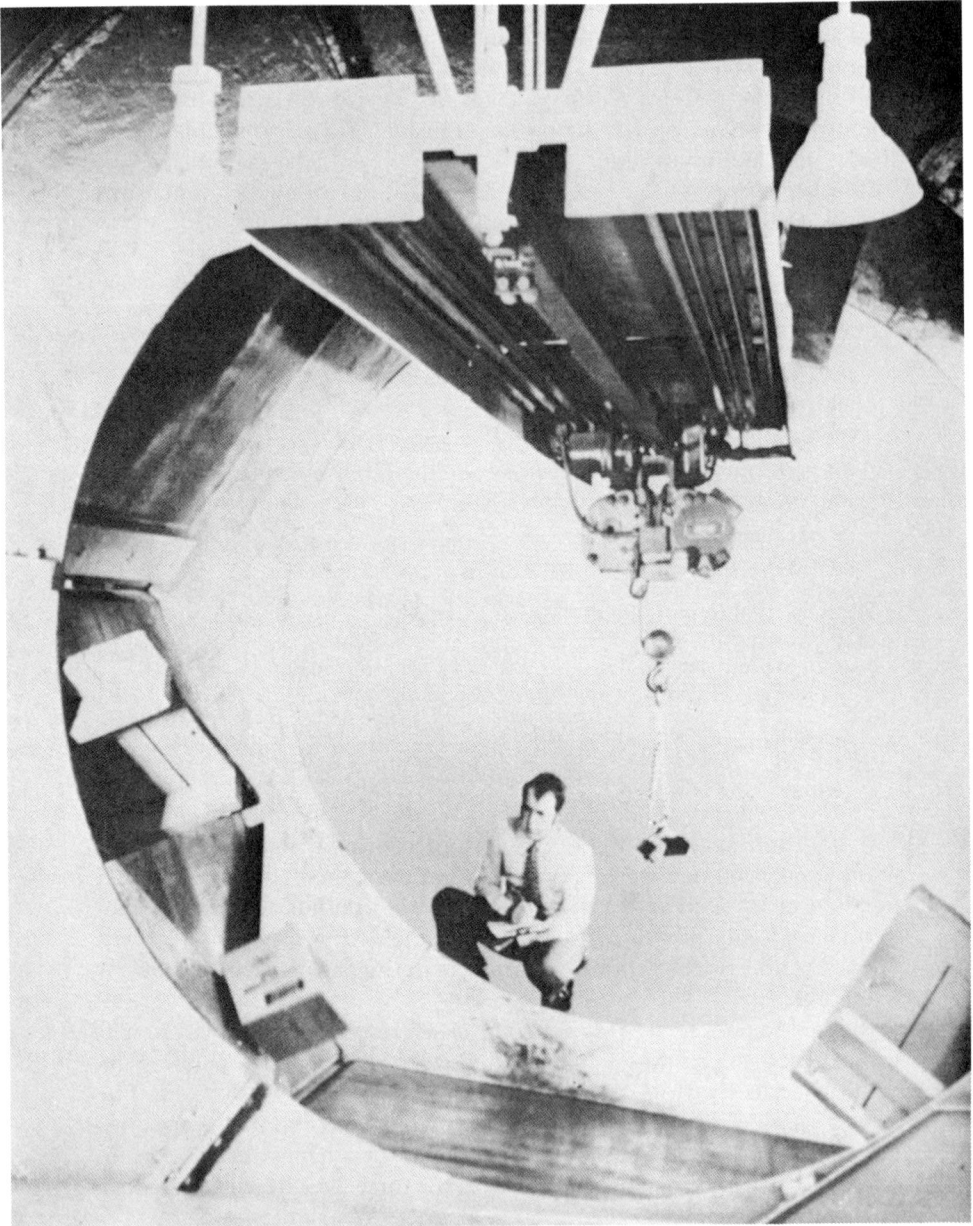

Courtesy Packaging Research Laboratory, Rockaway, N. J.

Sophisticated monitors are expensive. They may be necessary to solve a problem of recurrent in-transit damage. Less complicated devices are used to record temperatures and may or may not be used as the basis for a damage claim against a carrier. They may be used aboard a shipper's own equipment to ensure quality control. A frozen food distributor would want to be certain that his product had not thawed and been refrozen in transit. Large shipments of apples are accompanied by a mechanical temperature recorder, which "provides the receiver with a greater workable knowledge of each load, giving him valuable information on temperature variation that may effect the speed in which he should handle and merchandise its contents."[8]

LABELING AND PRICE-MARKING

Once the material being packaged is placed into the box and the cover is closed, the contents are hidden. At this point it becomes necessary to label the box. Whether it be in words or in code numbers depends upon the nature of the product, its vulnerability to pilferage, etc. Retro-reflective labels that can be "read" by optical scanners may also be applied. "Batch" numbers are frequently assigned to food and drug products.

Packaging is usually accomplished at the end of the assembly line. Package labeling also occurs here, since using this location avoids accumulating an inventory of pre-printed packages. This is also a key point for control since this is where there is an exact measure of what has come off the assembly line. As the packaged goods are moved away from the end of the assembly line they become "stocks of finished goods" and the responsibility of the firm's physical distribution system. (See Figure 10-5.)

For products that are sold off of retailers' shelves, provision must also be made for price-marking. When prices are applied as the goods are placed on the shelves, no special provisions are required. If the price is to be applied at an earlier stage in the distribution process, special package designs are required. A box containing a batch of smaller packages may have a perforated strip which can be removed exposing a small area of each package to which an adhesive label may be attached.

UNIT LOADS IN MATERIAL HANDLING

Mention has already been made of the "building-block" concept for materials handling of package cargo. Unit loading involves the securing of one or more boxes to a pallet or skid so that it can be handled

8 *Transport Topics*, October 14, 1974.

FIG. 10-5 Packaging and shipping occur at end of production line.

I realize you're new here, Mayberry, but would you mind telling me what in hell you think you're doing?

© *Seaway Review*, The Les Strang Publishing Group. Used with permission.

by mechanical means, such as a fork-lift truck. The picture at the beginning of this chapter shows a pallet-load of cartons with a plastic sheet. The load will be moved into an oven where it is subjected to a brief, but intense, application of heat. This draws the plastic taut and the shipment is sealed. The process is known as "shrink-wrap" and can be applied to items of all shapes and sizes. Industrial machinery is frequently attached to pallets and then sealed with shrink-wrap material.*

The boxes or any other containers secured to a pallet are known as a "unit load." The word "unitization" is also used. Computer programs exist which show how to arrange various size boxes in order to maximize the pallet's load.

* "Customized" shrink-wrap applications need not pass through ovens, since portable "heat cannons" can be used. They are devices which blow very hot air which, when directed at the plastic sheet, causes it to pull tight. One of the unanticipated benefits of shrink-wrap for protecting machinery is "it also appears that all who handle the loads, whether employees of the carriers or others, tend to treat the loads more carefully because they see that the cargo is machinery which might be injured by roughness." See *Handling and Shipping*, (May, 1974) p. 71. See also: *Modern Materials Handling* (March, 1976), pp. 58–61.

ADVANTAGES

The unit load has three advantages. It saves labor because it reduces manual handling of individual packages and substitutes mechanical handling. Also, it saves time because the mechanized handling is considerably faster than manually handling each item on a piece-by-piece basis. And it also offers some additional protection to the cargo because the cartons are secured to the pallet by straps, or by shrink-wrap, or by some other bonding device. This provides a sturdier building block. Pilferage is discouraged because it may be more difficult to remove one package or its contents. A pallet can be stacked in such a manner that the cartons containing the more valuable or more fragile items are on the inside of the unit load.

The unit load represents a larger quantity of an item than does a single box—often 30 to 50 times as much. Therefore, it is of limited value to shippers or consignees who wish to deal in small quantities. A pallet load of material may be nowhere near the EOQ amounts calculated through the methods developed in chapter seven. Some shippers recognize this and have a price break at both the "pallet-load" quantity *and* at the "pallet-layer" quantity. All of the distributor's items are in boxes which can be arranged on the conventional 48 inch by 40 inch pallet (although the number of boxes which would cover one layer varies). Nonetheless, the distributor's price break is at the pallet layer quantity, so that the buyer might decide to order one layer (which might be twelve boxes or cases) of canned peaches; two layers (which might be 15 cases each) of catsup; and so on. The distributor, in loading the pallet, would load each layer separately, yet the goods would leave his warehouse as a full pallet, or unit load. He would have given an even lower price if the buyer had purchased a full pallet load of a single item because in that instance the distributor would have avoided manual handling of the product completely; he would have merely shipped out one of the full pallet loads he had received from the canner.

Figure 10-6 shows how quickly products can be accumulated into unit load quantities. A melon picking, grading, and packing trailer unit is pulled by a tractor (at the far right of the picture) through melon fields. Workers on the trailer pick the melons and place them into bins on the side of the trailer. The melons are then sized, labelled, and placed into a box without a cover. When a box is full, a cover is placed on it and the covered box is then placed on a pallet. When the trailer reaches the end of the field where a flat bed truck is parked, a fork lift is used to remove the pallets from the trailer and it places them onto the truck. At the left of the picture, the fork lift is loading blank, or unassembled, boxes to the second story on the trailer. There, a worker uses a machine to assemble bottom halves and top halves. They are fed to the workers on the lower level via a conveyor belt.

FIG. 10-6 Melon picking, sorting and boxing machine.

Courtesy of SWF Machinery.

While somewhat lowly in status, pallets receive considerable attention both in trade journals and at trade meetings. The degree of attention is usually correlated with the price of lumber and pallets are no longer thought of as "free." Shippers are now forcing consignees to return a like number of pallets or else they are billed separately for the pallets which are not returned. On the West Coast, some drivers receive a 25 cent bonus for every pallet they return. Firms are now repairing pallets which several years ago would have been scrapped.

DISADVANTAGES

One disadvantage of the conventional pallet is its height (approximately six inches). When goods are loaded aboard pallets into rail cars, trailers or containers, the space occupied by the pallet is unproductive. A pallet may occupy as much space as a layer of cases of canned soft drinks. The alternative is to strap a heavy flexible material known as a "slip-sheet" under the unit load in place of the pallet and this eliminates the volume occupied by the conventional pallet. The disadvantage is that handling time is increased because the fork lift operator must use the equipment much more carefully to avoid damaging the product. In these instances the goods are placed on conventional wooden pallets once they are unloaded from the vehicle.

While the wooden pallet does occupy space in a vehicle, its construction and physical properties do provide a favorable cushioning effect. The quality of individual pallets has varied widely although several industries are establishing pallet "pools" to provide an orderly mechanism for encouraging the re-use of pallets. This will probably result in an upgrading of pallets in use and standards are being established for the quality of lumber used, construction, identification of manufacturer, and "grading" of used pallets. These steps will increase the utilization of each pallet and spread the concept of unit loading.

Another problem affecting unit loading is that the 48 inch by 40 inch length and width dimension is not universally accepted. One user complained, "It's ironic that we have stacks of pallets from incoming shipments that we have to get rid of—and a shortage of shipping pallets. Dimensions don't match, styles don't match."[9] Aircraft freight containers are of such dimensions that they discourage loading in a 48 inch by 40 inch surface configuration. One west coast fruit grower complained that he "has been forced to use four different pallet sizes for its air cargo movements despite the fact that most produce industry retailers have repeatedly requested standardization on the 48 by 40 inch pallet."[10]

CONTAINERS

For surface cargo, the next-sized block beyond the unit load is the container, which usually is eight feet wide, eight feet high, and 10, 20, 35, or 40 feet long. Containers are widely used in the U. S. foreign trade. Since they are interchangeable between rail, truck, and water carriers they can be used in intermodal applications and reap the advantages offered by each of several modes. Sea-Land is a large container operator moving between U. S. ports and many foreign countries, and it carries some containers in ships between the east and west coasts of the U.S. Figure 10-7 illustrates the intermedal features of containers.

Most containers are dry-cargo boxes. Some are insulated and come with temperature-controlling devices; some contain one large tank; and

[9] Statement of James R. Strong, of Honeywell Inc. in *Material Handling Engineering* (1973 special issue), p. 29.

[10] " 'Standard' Air Pallet for Fruit Still More Fancy than Fact," *Container News* (November, 1973), p. 26.

Fig. 10-7 Containers are intermodal.

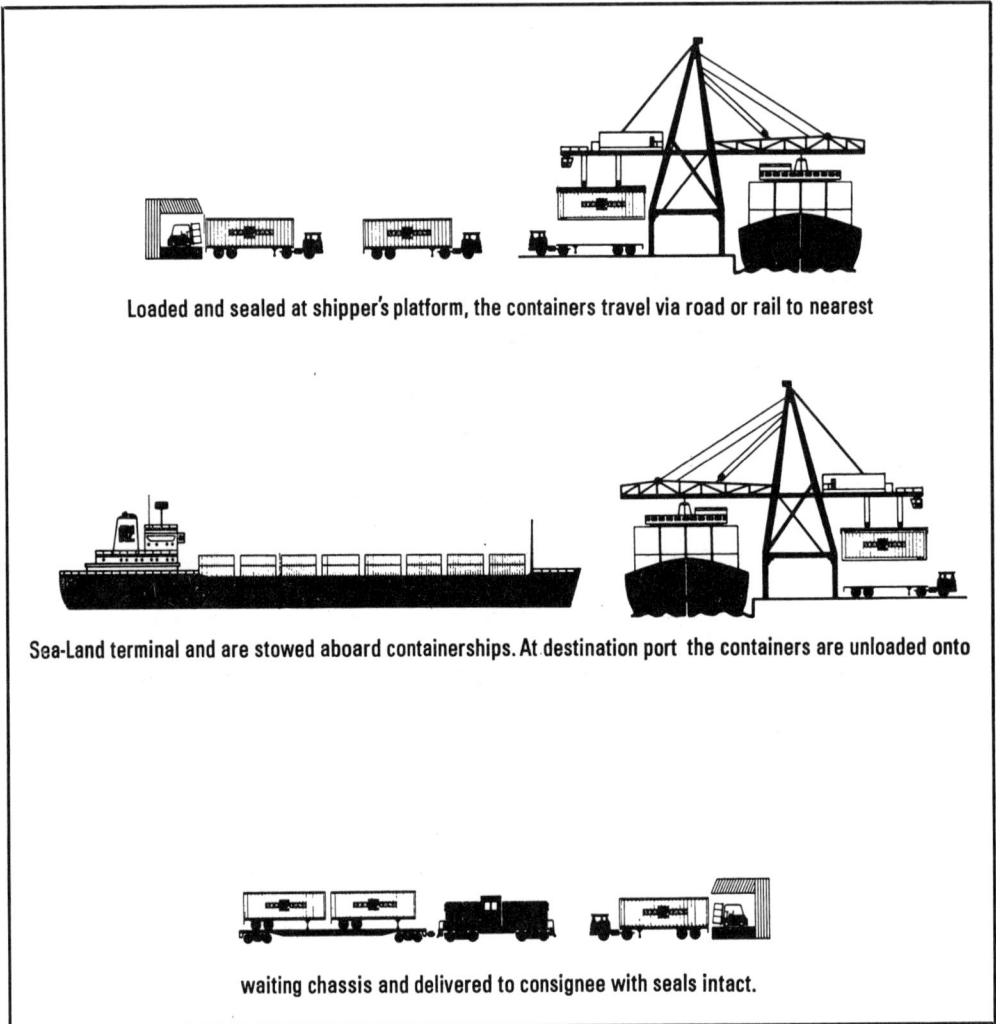

Loaded and sealed at shipper's platform, the containers travel via road or rail to nearest

Sea-Land terminal and are stowed aboard containerships. At destination port the containers are unloaded onto

waiting chassis and delivered to consignee with seals intact.

Courtesy of Sea Land Service, Inc.

some have a flat-bed configuration. There are also specially designed containers for the transport of livestock and for the transport of automobiles.

As the closing statement in the last section indicated, there is a lack of standardization between shipment sizes that fit into air containers and those which are used by surface carriers. Conventional wooden pallets are unlikely to be loaded aboard an airplane because of the waste space they occupy; space on a plane is especially valuable. Containers used aboard aircraft are constructed and loaded to much more exacting specifications than is the case for containers used for surface shipment. The shapes of aircraft containers are dictated by the fuselage contours into which they must fit (see Figures 11-6 and 11-7). Nonetheless, the "building-block" concept holds for air freight although the dimensions of the airline container differs from those of conventional unit loads. In late 1974, one airline introduced Boeing 747 all-cargo flight between Paris and New York and one of the containers used was 8' x 8' x 20' (a size which could be accommodated in either the aircraft or on a truck).[11]

EQUIPMENT LOADING

The last step in the "building block" process is to stow the "unit-load" pallets into a waiting truck trailer, rail car, or container van. Slight clearances must be maintained between pallets to allow for the loading and unloading processes. To fill the voids, bracing or dunnage bags are used. Dunnage bags are inflatable, and are placed in narrow empty spaces. When inflated, they fill the void space and function as both a cushion and a brace.

A problem involved with any bracing or cushioning device is that the load is subjected to forces from all directions. Figure 10-8 shows five of the forces to which a surface-sea load may be subjected. Sea loads are subjected to more forces than the ones illustrated since a vessel in a rolling sea can be subjected to almost any pattern of force. Even when cargoes are properly braced, the various forces can still cause damage. Continued vibrations may loosen screws on machinery. Vibrations can also cause contents of some bags or packages to settle and this could change the nature of support they were offering to materials packed above them. For products where this presents a problem, special preloading vibrators are used to cause the load to settle immediately.

Some goods are so heavy that they utilize the rail car or trailer or container's weight capacity without filling its cubic capacity. These loads, such as heavy machinery, must be carefully braced. The weight must be distributed as evenly as possible. In highway trailers, for example, it would be dangerous to have one side loaded more heavily than the other. In addition, the load should be distributed evenly over the axles.

While protecting the load is important, care should also be exercised to protect the carrier's equipment. A complaint of carriers who provide specialized equipment designed to protect certain types of loads is that shippers abuse or fail to return the protective devices. Indeed, one of

---

[11] *Daily Traffic World*, August 6, 1974.

FIG. 10-8 Various forces to which cargo is subjected.

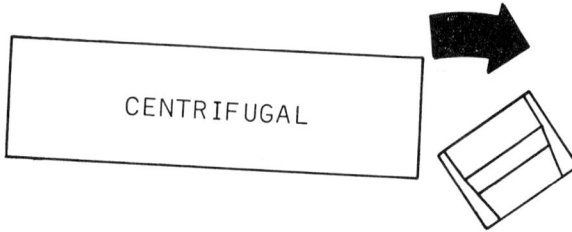

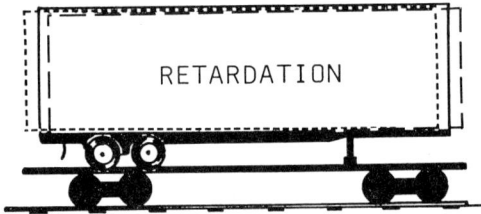

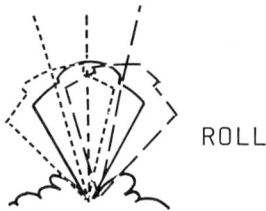

Courtesy of Sea Land Service, Inc.

the problems of common carriers today is that shippers do not treat common carrier equipment as carefully as their own.

This section closes the discussion of the building-block concept. For packaged goods, the vehicle load is usually the largest quantity a PD manager will be concerned with. The only exception is that railroads have multiple carload and unit trainload rates. These are more likely to be used for the shipment of bulk materials, to be discussed in the following section.

BULK MATERIALS

Bulk materials are handled in loose form rather than packaged form, and they are handled by pumps, shovel devices, conveyer belts, or the mere force of gravity. The decision must be made as to where in the distribution system the bulk materials should be placed into smaller containers for further sale or shipment. Figure 10-9 indicates three alternatives for a firm receiving dry bulk materials by rail: the bulk materials can be packaged, transferred to a silo for temporary storage, or transferred directly to specially designed trucks which are capable of delivering them to users. Sometimes bagged and bulk quantities of the same material are part of the same shipments. In vessels, bagged rice is placed on top of bulk rice to provide load stability.

Bulk cargoes have various handling characteristics. An equipment configuration that is "ideal" for one bulk cargo may not be able to handle another. Another consideration is the size of particle of the cargo in question; there are costs involved in pulverizing to a uniform size so it can be handled by pneumatic or slurry devices.

SLURRY SYSTEMS

Slurry systems involve grinding the solid material to a certain particle size, mixing it with water to form a fluid muddy substance, pumping that substance through a pipeline, and then decanting the water and removing it, leaving the solid material. This was discussed in chapter 4. Rail cars can also be used to carry slurry. For example, kaolin (a clay used in paper-making) is mined and separated from the accompanying sand by a water process. The sand-free clay is then subjected to a number of mechanical processes which reduce its moisture content to about 35 percent instead of zero percent. The result is a substance that has the viscosity of heavy cream. This is about the same consistency as is desired by the paper-making plants, so it is shipped in this form, despite the fact that, by weight, a substantial percentage of what is shipped is water. In this instance, the economics are such that it is less costly to

FIG. 10-9 Alternatives for handling dry bulk materials received by rail.

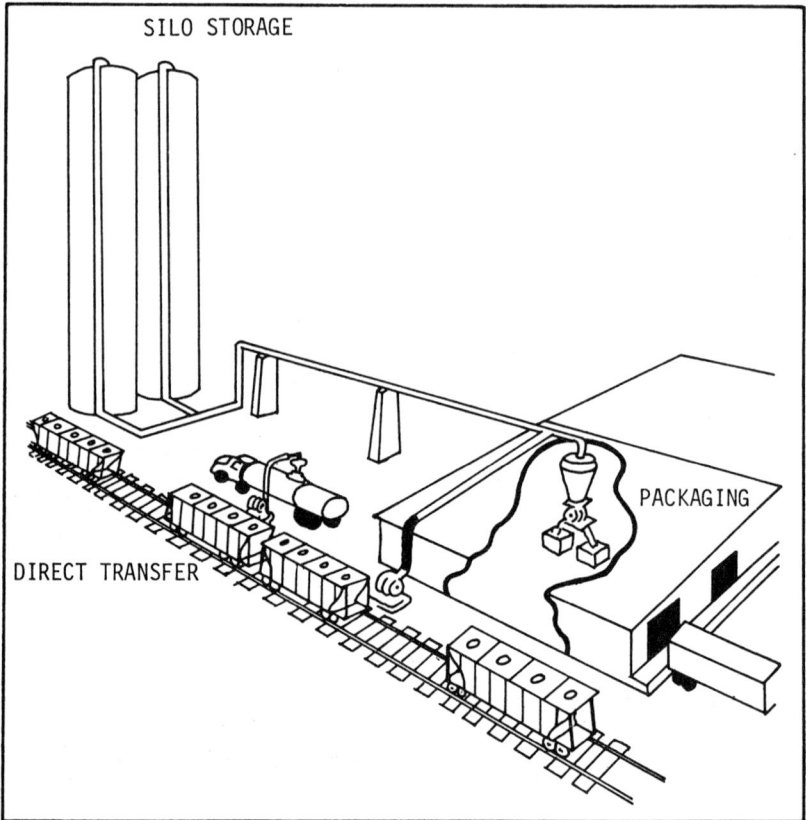

Courtesy Norfolk and Western Railroad Co.

transport the water than it is to remove it near the quarry and add it after shipment at the paper mill.

One slurry operation, known as "Marconaflo", involves the use of specially constructed ocean-going vessels. The ore at the mine is put into slurry form and pumped to the water's edge. A flexible pipeline is used to reach a vessel moored offshore (which avoids both harbor dredging and the need to build shore-side loading facilities). The ore in slurry form is then loaded into the vessel's holds. The cargo is allowed to settle and most of the water rises to the top and it is removed. The remaining ore contains about eight percent moisture and forms into a relatively solid mass. At the unloading port, the vessel can also discharge from an offshore point through a pipeline. At the bottom of each hold is a series of rotating lawn-sprinkler-like devices which are activated, "blasting into the cemented ore from beneath with powerful jets of water. . . , rotating slowly to distribute the water's force evenly. The entire cargo of the hold can be transformed back into slurry and unloaded by pipeline . . . ."[12] The unloading process is illustrated in Figure 10-10.

BULK-HANDLING EQUIPMENT OWNERSHIP

Note in Figure 10-10 that some of the specialized equipment is located aboard the vessel and some is located on land. Ownership of the vessel, the shoreside facility, and the ore is not specified, yet it is safe to assume that a large investment is required. From a distribution standpoint, bulk cargoes require unique, often "'custom-built," handling facilities and there is always uncertainty as to whether the buyer or seller should provide them.

A marketing problem may be that a specialized unloading device will pay for itself only if a specified number of customers install a new type of receiving equipment. What kinds of financial incentives should the seller offer to get his customers to install the new receiving equipment? What types of long-term commitments must each party make to the other to insure a necessary return from the required investment? An example of this situation comes from the food industry where "liquid egg" distributors supply the contents of shelled eggs or egg-base concentrates to food processors, commercial bakeries, and institutional food service industries. Since eggs in the shell have unfavorable transportation characteristics, a truck carrying the eggs' contents after they are shelled can carry about twice as much weight in the same space as a truck carrying eggs in conventional egg cartons. The supplier must invest in an egg-breaking machine located near the egg farms, and also invest in trucks with refrigerated tank trailers which can pump out their own contents. Sanitation is important and this means quality materials must be used and safeguards installed and maintained. The customers' investments are in one or more tanks to receive the yolks, the egg whites, or a mixture of both. Even without knowing the quantities or the costs involved, it is clear that quite a few calculations would have to be made and numerous alternatives would have to be considered. Also, the supplier's investment is much more than that of any one buyer. How can he safeguard it?

EQUIPMENT CHOICE

Many different types of equipment are used to transport bulk materials. Bulk cargo movements are unique in that they almost always

12 "Marconoflo: Engineering, Economics and the Environment," *Transportation and Distribution Management* (November, 1970).

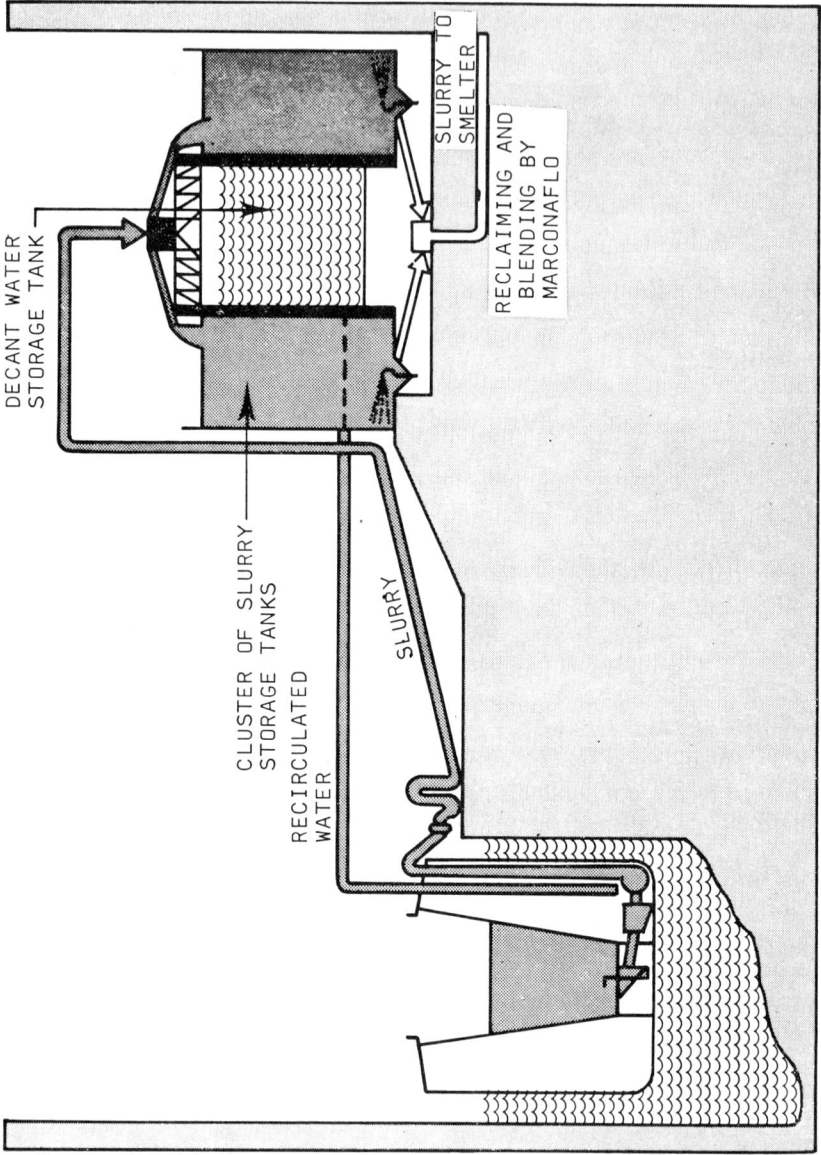

Fig. 10-10 Vessel slurry system.

DECANT WATER
STORAGE TANK

SLURRY TO
SMELTER

RECLAIMING AND
BLENDING BY
MARCONAFLO

CLUSTER OF SLURRY
STORAGE TANKS

RECIRCULATED
WATER

SLURRY

occupy or utilize a vehicle's entire capacity. A bulk cargo shipper thinks in terms of truckloads, barge loads, railcar loads, or ship loads. The shipper is less likely to use common carriers (except for railroads). To the bulk shipper, private carriage and contract carriage are meaningful alternatives, as are pipelines and even long conveyer belts.

Many handbooks and newsletters are published to serve those who are trying to match up cargoes, origins, destinations, and means of carriage. Figure 10-11 shows a page from one such handbook, *Greenwood's Guide to Great Lakes Shipping*. The page deals with self-unloading vessels. The vessel's exterior measurements are important because in some Great Lakes ports there are physical restrictions, such as narrow bridge openings, which limit the size of vessels that can reach certain docks. The vessels have several compartments (holds) which are important in shipping different grades of coal. The boom length and degrees of swing indicate how far inland the vessel can discharge cargo. The farther inland the boom can discharge, the more material can be stockpiled. Note that the vessel's allowable safe draft changes by season; this would be significant if a dense cargo, such as iron ore, were being handled. Greenwood's Guide has similar data for shoreside facilities, indicating how large a vessel they can accommodate and the loading-unloading equipment available.

Choice of equipment is also influenced by the investment the shipper and consignee want to make. Great Lakes coal docks using self-unloaders described on Figure 10-11 do not have to invest in vessel unloading facilities. The vessel owner has made the investment in the conveyer and discharge system. Great Lakes vessel rates for carrying coal on self-unloaders are about ten percent higher than for vessels which the consignee must unload. The consignee can pay that higher rate or invest in his own shore-based unloading equipment.

SPECIAL MOVES

Regularly recurring shipments usually lend themselves to PD analysis that results in either lower cost shipments or a more efficient method of handling the shipment, or both. In some industries, however, each delivery of a new product is so unique and so difficult that a portion of the sales effort involves an engineering study of how to deliver the product. Examples are generators being delivered to dam sites or reinforced concrete forms being delivered to a place where a bridge is being constructed. Sometimes the product has to be assembled at the factory to make sure that it functions. Then it must be disassembled for shipment since its size is too large for any type of carrier to deliver. Then it must be delivered in pieces and reassembled at the site. Clearly, there can be savings if the amount of disassembly and reassembly involved

FIG. 10-11 Page from guide to Great Lakes Vessels.

SELF-UNLOADERS ON THE GREAT LAKES, (cont'd.)

FIRST LINE:
SECOND LINE: Cubic feet per Compartment with coal capacity shown in Net Tons

NOTE: Coal stowage factor 42 C.F. per Net Ton similar to slack coal

Fleet No. / Vessel	Size	Gross Reg. Tons	Net Reg. Tons	Keel	B.P.	O.A.	Beam	Depth	Compartments	Mid-Summer Draft	Summer Draft / Degrees Boom Can Swing Right/Left	Intermediate Draft / Type of Self-Unloader	Winter Draft / Chutes	Capacity at M.S. / Boom Length
6 Hutchinson, John T., B 16-½-24	38x11	9,775	6,964	595'0"	605'0"	620'0"	60'0"	35'0"	4	24'6"	23'11"	23'0"	21'11"	14,650
1) 94,070 C.F. - 2,320; 2) 171,170 C.F. - 3,870; 3) 168,390 C.F. - 3,820; 4) 135,095 C.F. - 3,070 Total: 13,080 N.T.											120	Conveyor	None	250'
2 Jodrey, Roy A. (Can.) 18-24	#1 P & S 12 x 11 #2 2-18 49 x 11	Can. 16,154 U.S. 13,974	11,133	603'3"	619'7"	640'6"	72'0"	40'0"	4	28'6"	27'10"	26'10" At 26'0" -Seaway-	25'7"	23,500 / 20,500
B 1) 229,230 C.F. - 5,470; 2) 179,495 C.F. -4,275; 3) 179,495 C.F. -4,275; 4) 234,885 C.F. -5,580 Total: 19,600 N.T.											100	Conveyor	None	250'
6 Kling, John A. 30-12	38x9	6,829	5,413	538'0"	546'6"	561'3"	56'3"	30'3"	7	21'1"	20'9"	19'11"	19'0"	10,850
B 1) 58,850 C.F. - 1,400; 2) 26,950 C.F. - 670; 3) 52,800 C.F. - 1,250; 4) 64,050 C.F. - 1,500; 5) 47,200 C.F. - 1,130; 6) 58,850 C.F. - 1,400; 7) 65,500 C.F. - 1,540 Total: 8,900 N.T.											100	Conveyor	30'	205'
6 Kyves, Roger M. 20-24	49'6" x 11 5-5-5-5			664'6"	664'6"	680'0"	78'0"	42'0"	4	27'6"	27'6"	27'6"	27'6"	25,650
B 1) 234,545 C.F. -5,600; 2) 227,980 C.F. -5,425; 3) 227,980 C.F. -5,425; 4) 213,930 C.F. -5,100 Total: 21,500 N.T.											96	Conveyor		260'
35 Lakewood B 4-uneven	1-23x12 2-23x64 3-23x84 4-23x14	3,751	2,708	370'0"	377'6"	390'0"	48'0"	28'0"	4	19'5-½"	19'5-½"	19'1-½"	18'7-½"	3,950
1) 12,700 C.F. - 200; 2) 47,000 C.F. - 1,450; 3) 64,000 C.F. - 1,900; 4) 15,600 C.F. - 400 Total: 3,950 G.T. Sand or Stone											100	Conveyor	None	142'
60 Leadale (Can.) 27-12	36x9	7,073	4,701	504'0"	512'0"	524'0"	56'0"	30'0"	6	20'2"	19'9"	19'2"	18'5"	8,950
1) 63,500 C.F. - 1,600; 2) 50,100 C.F. - 1,350; 3) 49,600 C.F. - 1,400; 4) 87,000 C.F. - 2,300; 5) 49,900 C.F. - 1,300; 6) 53,000 C.F. - 1,200 Total: 9,150 N.T.											120	Conveyor	30'	200'

Courtesy: Greenwood's Guide to Great Lakes Shipping, 1975 edition; Freshwater Press, Inc.

can be reduced. Therefore, studies have to be made of shipping routes and procedures which will accommodate the shipment's unusual dimensions.

High weight trucks are sometimes used. Heavy dollies, which are additional axles, are placed under the load and the more dollies that are used the less weight exerted on each axle. When passing over a bridge of limited capacity the dollies must be spaced sufficiently far apart that no more than the allowable weight is on the bridge at any one time. Once the bridge is crossed, the load is stopped and the dollies are placed closer together again to make it easier to negotiate curves. Special permits would be required and police might keep other traffic off of the road. Highway engineers along the route would determine the maximum allowable load. If bituminous pavement were involved, the move might be restricted to cooler times of the year or of the day since the cooler pavement would be less likely to be permanently "marked" by the tires of the dollies. Equipment such as this can carry loads of 500 or more tons—if enough dollies are used.

Weight is only one limitation on the move. There may be height restrictions such as electric wires (which can be moved) or tunnels (which cannot). Curvature of the road or steepness of grade impose other limits. The move must be carefully analyzed by individuals who are both familiar with the transportation complexities as well as with the piece of equipment being moved. Moves such as these are a physical distribution responsibility since the buyer generally purchases on a "delivered" or "installed" basis and the seller who can devise the lowest cost, adequate means of delivery will have an advantage when submitting a bid for the equipment being purchased.

Modular housing (pre-built structures that are transported to home sites) is not especially heavy, but tends to be large. A study regarding industrial sites for manufacturing the modules said:

> Because the housing modules themselves are high and wide, access from the plant to the market areas both by over-the-road and rail, becomes a critical portion of the investigation. Access to the Interstate System is of absolute necessity. And siding needs for outbound shipment from the plants are vastly different than for ordinary industrial sites. When going by rail, the modules will travel on long cars and in trainload lots. Minimum curvatures of about 400 feet and accessible siding lengths of about 250 feet are required.[13]

Figure 10-12 is a portion of an information sheet issued by a railroad which indicates the height and width clearances along its track. This would be used by a shipper with oversized cargo looking for a route which would accommodate it. With advance notice, the railroad in

[13] Carl J. Liba, "The Transportation Market Potential in Modular Housing," in *Proceedings of the Sixty-second annual meeting of the American Railway Development Association, 1971*, pp. 27–32.

Fig. 10-12 Railroad clearances.

TRANSPORTATION DEPARTMENT CIRCULAR NO. 74-13A, Reissued October 2, 1974 **74-13A**
(Previously issued as Circular 74-13, January 1, 1974)

CLEARANCE AND WEIGHT LIMITS.

ST. LOUIS—SAN FRANCISCO RAILWAY.

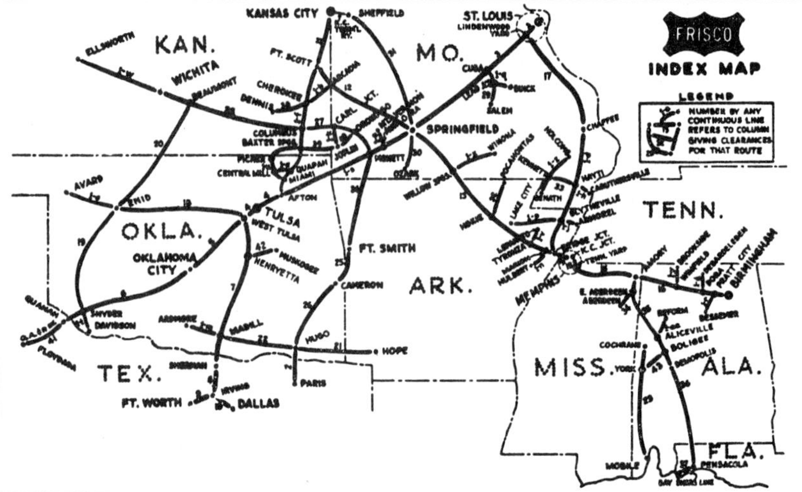

Maximum Gross Weight of Car & Lading.	List of Through Routes. Use figures shown in column indicated by numbers at the right for Points Between.	Refer to Column Numbered.
263,000	St. Louis, Mo.... and Birmingham, Ala..........Notes B, E, F	No. 101
263,000	" .... " Ft. Worth, Tex..................Notes B, F	No. 102
263,000	" .... " Kansas City, Mo..................Notes F, J	No. 103
263,000	" .... " Memphis, Tenn..................Notes B, F	No. 104
263,000	" .... " Oklahoma City, Okla..........Notes F, J	No. 105
263,000	" .... " Pensacola, Fla..................Notes B, F	No. 106
263,000	" .... " Quanah, Tex..................Notes C, F	No. 107
263,000	" .... " Wichita, Kan..................Notes C, F	No. 108
263,000	Kansas City, Mo. " Birmingham, Ala..........Notes B, E, J	No. 109
263,000	" .. " Ft. Worth, Tex..................Note B	No. 110
263,000	" .. " Memphis, Tenn..................Notes B, J	No. 111
263,000	" .. " Oklahoma City, Okla..................Note K	No. 112
263,000	" .. " Pensacola, Fla..................Note B	No. 113
263,000	" .. " Quanah, Tex..................Note C	No. 114

Maximum Gross Weight of Car & Lading.	List of Through Routes—Continued. Use figures shown in column indicated by numbers at the right for Points Between.	Refer to Column Numbered.
263,000	Kansas City, Mo. and Wichita, Kan..................Note C	No. 115
238,000	Tulsa, Okla...... " Birmingham, Ala..........Notes B, E, J	No. 116
250,000	" .... " Hope, Ark., via Madill, Okla..........	No. 117
263,000	" .... " Memphis, Tenn..................Notes B, J	No. 118
263,000	Quanah, Tex.... " Floydada, Tex. (Q. A. & P.)...... Note C	No. 41

GENERAL NOTES

Dimensions in tables apply to single loads, with no overhangs, on cars having 57 ft. coupled length or less. Subtract one inch from permissible width for each two feet of car length over 57 feet. Gross weights listed apply to ordinary four-axle cars with uniformly distributed load.

For loads exceeding these limitations and for protection where advance notice is required, refer to General Superintendent of Transportation, St. Louis-San Francisco Railway, Springfield, Missouri 65802.

THROUGH CLEARANCES.

Heights above Top of Rail. ft. in.	No. 101 Width ft. in.	No. 102 Width ft. in.	No. 103 Width ft. in.	No. 104 Width ft. in.	No. 105 Width ft. in.	No. 106 Width ft. in.	No. 107 Width ft. in.	No. 108 Width ft. in.	No. 109 Width ft. in.	No. 110 Width ft. in.	No. 111 Width ft. in.	No. 112 Width ft. in.	No. 113 Width ft. in.	No. 114 Width ft. in.	No. 115 Width ft. in.	No. 116 Width ft. in.	No. 117 Width ft. in.	No. 118 Width ft. in.	No. 119 Width ft. in.	No. 120 Width ft. in.	No. 121 Width ft. in.	No. 122 Width ft. in.	Heights above Top of Rail. ft. in.
20 0	- -	- -	- -	- -	- -	- -	- -	- -	- -	- -	- -	- -	- -	- -	8 5	- -	- -	- -					20 0
19 9															8 10								19 9
19 6			9 7	5 0		5 0					5 0		5 0		9 2								19 6
19 3		6 0	10 3	9 6	6 0	7 3	6 0			6 0	10 3	6 0	7 3	6 0	9 8		6 0	6 0					19 3
19 0	7 7	9 9	10 7	10 0	11 6	7 7	9 2	1 0	7 7	9 9	10 7	10 7	7 7	9 2	10 1	7 7	8 11	11 0					19 0
18 9	8 0	10 1	11 0	10 0	" "	8 0	9 8	9 0	8 0	10 1	11 0	11 0	8 0	9 8	10 6	8 0	9 6	" "					18 9
18 6	8 5	10 5	11 4	10 3	" "	8 5	10 2	10 10	8 5	10 5	" "	11 4	8 5	10 2	10 10	8 5	10 2	" "					18 6
18 3	8 9	10 9	11 6	10 8	" "	8 9	10 7	11 4	8 9	10 9	" "	11 6	8 9	10 7	11 4	8 9	10 8	" "					18 3
18 0	9 2	11 1	" "	10 11	" "	9 2	10 10	11 6	9 2	11 1	" "	" "	9 2	10 10	11 6	9 2	11 1	" "					18 0
17 9	9 6	11 5	" "	11 0	" "	9 6	11 1	" "	9 6	11 5	" "	" "	9 6	11 6	" "	9 6	11 5	" "					17 9
17 6	9 11	11 6	" "	" "	" "	9 11	11 6	" "	9 11	11 6	" "	" "	9 11	" "	" "	9 11	11 6	" "					17 6
17 3	10 3	" "	" "	" "	" "	10 2	" "	" "	10 3	" "	" "	" "	10 3	" "	" "	10 3	" "	" "					17 3
17 0	10 8	" "	" "	" "	" "	10 8	" "	" "	10 8	" "	" "	" "	10 8	" "	" "	10 8	" "	" "					17 0
16 9	11 0	" "	" "	" "	" "	11 0	" "	" "	11 0	" "	" "	" "	11 0	" "	" "	11 0	" "	" "					16 9
16 6	" "	" "	" "	" "	" "	" "	" "	" "	" "	" "	" "	" "	" "	" "	" "	" "	" "	" "					16 6
16 0	" "	" "	" "	" "	" "	" "	" "	" "	" "	" "	" "	" "	" "	" "	" "	" "	" "	" "					16 0
4 0	" "	" "	" "	" "	" "	" "	" "	" "	" "	" "	" "	" "	" "	" "	" "	" "	11 6	" "					4 0
3 6	" "	" "	" "	" "	" "	" "	" "	11 6	" "	" "	" "	" "	" "	" "	" "	" "	11 4	" "					3 6
3 0	11 0	11 6	11 6	11 0	11 6	11 0	11 6	11 2	11 0	11 6	11 0	11 6	11 0	11 6	11 6	11 0	10 11	11 0					3 0
2 6	10 2	10 2	10 2	10 2	10 2	10 2	10 2	10 2	10 6	10 6	10 6	10 6	10 6	10 6	10 6	10 11	10 7	10 11					2 6
2 0	9 11	9 11	9 11	9 11	9 11	9 11	9 11	9 11	10 2	10 2	10 2	10 2	10 2	10 2	10 2	10 11	10 2	10 11					2 0
1 6	9 7	9 7	9 7	9 7	9 7	9 7	9 7	9 7	10 2	10 2	10 2	10 2	10 2	10 2	10 2	10 4	9 9	10 4					1 6
A①																							

"THROUGH ROUTE" NOTES.

Note A①Maximum gross weight of car and lading will be found in List of Through Routes.
" B—Maximum gross weight of car and lading limited to 220,000 pounds for cars shorter than 45 feet coupled length.
" C—Maximum gross weight of car and lading limited to 220,000 pounds for cars shorter than 38 feet coupled length.
" E—Loads over 17 ft. 3 in. in height above top of rail must not move over 9th Avenue in Birmingham, Ala. between 22nd and 30th Streets.

"THROUGH ROUTE" Notes Continued on following page.

Courtesy of St. Louis-San Francisco Railroad Co.

question can handle wider loads but this imposes restrictions on the train's speed and may involve stopping passing trains.

Some of the more challenging specialized moves in recent years have involved oil field and pipeline equipment to Alaska where the transportation system is relatively undeveloped. Figure 10-13 is an advertisement by Canadian National Railways indicating that they offer several routes to the North Slopes.

One concluding point should be made and that is the size of vehicle used in each mode of transport is increasing. This is of significance to both the specialized shipments mentioned in this section and to the more routine shipments mentioned.

SUMMARY

This chapter has dealt with the physical handling of cargo. The "building-block" concept means building up the packages of each item into palletized, "unit loads", which can be handled by mechanized equipment. Whether these "unit loads" sizes happen to be the same as a buyer's EOQ is not known. If they differ, how much should be offered to the buyer in terms of price concessions to force him to think in terms of "'unit loads"?

The largest sizes in the "building-block" concept are containers and transport vehicle bodies. They must be properly loaded to avoid in-transit damage to cargo.

Carrier tariffs frequently control the type of packaging which must be used. Nevertheless, buyers may blame the seller—rather than the carrier—for any damaged products.

Bulk cargo is usually handled by the rail carload, barge load, or the like. Bulk handling equipment is very expensive and calls for long-term financial commitments by its users. A new development in handling dry bulk materials is to add water, creating a slurry, and then apply fluid-handling methods to the mass of materials.

Sometimes the product being moved is so large that special transportation routes with extra large clearances must be laid out. Buyers of these products often buy on a "delivered" basis so the seller must determine the lowest-cost way to install them.

QUESTIONS FOR DISCUSSION AND REVIEW

1. What is the difference between the *selling* function of packaging and the *protective* function of packaging? Are the two functions related?

2. Describe the function of conventional pallets. What are their disadvantages?

Fig. 10-13 Some routes to the North.

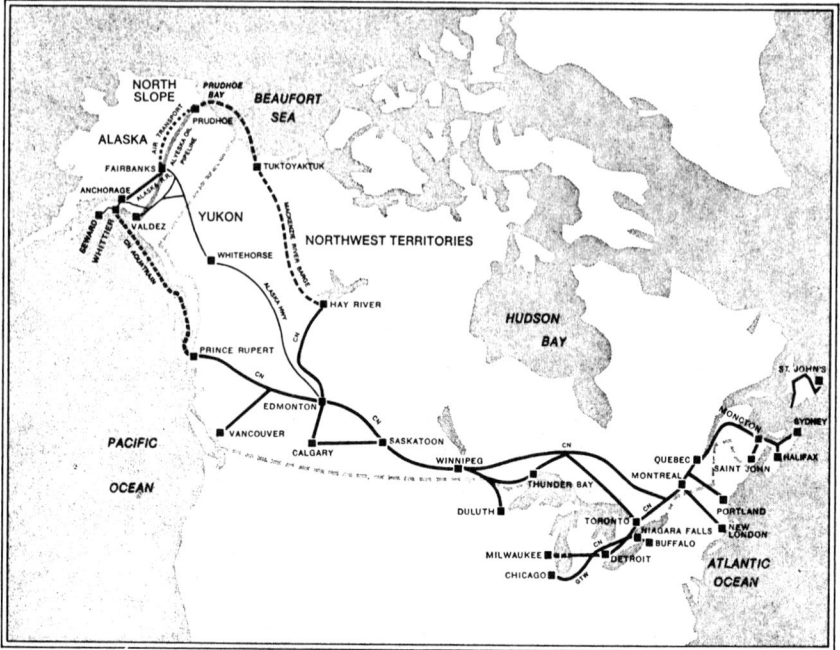

CanadianNational shows you how to ship the heavy stuff to Alaska.

At last the Alyeska Pipeline is on the move. Drilling operations are speeding up. The need for heavy equipment and materials grows daily.

If you want to be sure of getting there on time, with everything intact, Canada's largest transportation system is ready to help.

Space permitting, we can give you a choice of 3 different routes to Alaska and the Canadian Arctic.

1. The coastal route. The CN Aquatrain, a year-round rail-barge service holding 30 railway cars, loads off CN's transcontinental system at Prince Rupert, B.C., northernmost terminal on the Pacific Coast. CN trains arrive there daily; the freight cars travel on by barge to Whittier, Alaska; thence to Anchorage, Fairbanks, and other inland points via the Alaska Railway. (Freight priorities are assigned on the Aquatrain

under a CN permit system. As soon as you're ready, contact CN for a permit number.)

2. The river route. Three times weekly during the summer barging season, CN delivers heavy freight shipments to the Hay River terminal in the Northwest Territories. Transferred to river barges, the freight flows down the Mackenzie River to the delta, then on to Prudhoe Bay and the Western Arctic.

3. The highway route. A rail-truck system operates all year round via CN and connecting trucking companies on the Alaska Highway. From the U.S., freight moves directly onto CN feeder lines, then through Canada to Edmonton, Alberta. From there it's trucked north to Alaska—Anchorage on the West Coast, Fairbanks for air transport on to the North Slope, or Valdez at the southern terminal of the trans-Alaska pipeline.

Whichever way you go, you benefit from CN's experienced, dependable north-to-Alaska service. Quick connections. Reliable, efficient deliveries.

For further information, call the CN Sales Representative in your area, or contact: R. E. Lawless, Vice-President—Freight Marketing, P.O. Box 8100, Montreal, Quebec, Canada H3C 3N4

CN Distribution Systems

Courtesy of Canadian National Railways.

3. How can the handling of cargo pollute the environment?

4. How do slurry systems work?

5. Are there reasons why a liquor distributor should not print his cartons' contents in plain English?

6. How do self-unloading vessels function? What are their advantages and disadvantages?

7. What are the various physical forces to which a package in transit might be subjected? What other hazards might it encounter?

8. What is "shrink-wrap" packaging?

9. What is "unit loading"?

10. Why should a load's weight be distributed evenly inside a truck trailer?

11. What is "angle of repose"? What is its significance to the handling of bulk materials?

12. What are the advantages of "pre-testing" a package prior to its introduction?

13. There is great popular interest in "recycling." How does or should this affect packaging? Discuss.

14. What is the "building-block" concept that is applied to handling of packaged goods?

15. Why is the U. S. postal service giving up use of their traditional canvas mail sacks?

16. What agencies regulate air transportation of hazardous materials?

17. What does it mean when someone says a vehicle has "'cubed-out"?

18. How does viscosity influence the handling of liquids?

19. Will the metric system affect packaging? If so, how?

20. What are the protective functions of packaging?

CASE 10-1   HANVEY SCHOOL FURNITURE CO.

The Hanvey School Furniture Company had one plant, located in Knoxville, Tennessee. It sold school desks and tables throughout the southern and eastern United States. It operated through distributors, with exclusive marketing areas, and used rail carloads for outbound shipments. The usual method of selling was through a distributor who would bid on supplying a school district with several hundred desks of various sizes. There were few "rush" shipments involved since most bids allowed delivery anywhere from 60 to 120 days after the successful bid was selected.

The Hanvey line consisted of a chair with writing table attached on the right side (or on the left side if so specified). Eight different sizes were available, one size for each of the primary grades (1–6), a junior high size, and a senior high size. Desks were manufactured, assembled, and finished in the plant. The four smaller sizes were packed two to a corrugated fiberboard box, and the larger ones were packed one to a box. Damage in shipment was not a problem. This was because the desks themselves were sturdy and the carton was designed to provide additional protection to the writing surface on the desk. The average price of a desk was $47 and the average shipping cost per desk (in 10,000 lb. rail carload quantities) was $9.

Rich Nelson was the distribution manager for Hanvey School Furniture, and he was attending a special staff meeting in the marketing manager's office. The marketing manager explained why he had called the meeting by saying: "For years we've sold only a set-up, finished desk. In part, this is because wage rates around here are relatively low, and we never thought it would be cheaper to assemble and finish them elsewhere. However, up in the Northeast, several large school districts are using some new governmental program to increase employment, and they are toying with the idea of buying desks unassembled, and assembling and finishing them themselves. Personally, I don't think the idea will go very far, but some of our distributors are being asked to submit bids on unassembled, unfinished, desks. I've had my secretary xerox the bid specifications. They differ slightly from each other, but in general they have the following points in common:

1. The orders are large, ranging from 1,000 to 2,200 desks.
2. They require the unassembled desk to consist of no more than 20 separate pieces, exclusive of hardware.
3. Solid glue construction is required and the supplier should, as part of the bid, indicate sale price and rental prices for various glue clamps or other types of hardware or equipment needed to assemble the desks.
4. There should be no more than twelve unassembled desks in each separate carton. They want to assemble each small batch separately and don't want thousands of parts lying around.

The marketing manager then asked for questions. Carlos Ramirez, from the production department spoke up: "What about quality control? What if they use cheap glue and the desks fall apart? Do we want our labels on them?"

"I don't know," answered the marketing manager. "You check with your people and come up with recommendations."

Nelson said: "Carload rates are important to us. Can we keep the minimum order size so large that we can fill up carloads?"

"I think so," answered the marketing manager. "Will you please calculate the costs for unassembled desks in carload quantities?"

Ramirez asked: "Should we offer to have an engineer available to supervise the assembling?"

The marketing manager answered: "It would be a sales help, but we'd have to be careful regarding costs. Who will pay for it? What if the problems are lack of supervision for the untrained work force?"

David Campbell who was in the marketing department, spoke up: "Maybe the distributor should pay this cost. We could supply the engineer, and the distributor could reimburse us. The distributor would be a better judge of how much of our help would be needed."

"Any other questions?" asked the marketing manager and paused, "hearing none, I want you three to work together. Dave can report to me every day. We will need cost estimates to quote our distributors by the week's end."

Nelson returned to his office and took out the railroad freight classification. It flopped open to the page he used most, in the furniture section. The entry is exhibit 1. Nelson then looked up the definitions of packages which he had nearly forgotten since Hanvey furniture had been purchasing package type 3F, a double-faced corrugated fibreboard container. For each desk, the *average* cost of containers and packing material was $2, taking into account some desks were packed one to a carton; others, two to a carton.

Nelson then phoned Tom Bates who supplied Hanvey School furniture with corrugated fiberboard containers. Nelson explained to Bates as much as he knew and told Bates to phone Ramirez directly to get details of how the unassembled desks might be packaged. Nelson hung up and a few minutes later Ramirez phoned to say that Bates was visiting the next morning to discuss packing methods.

The next morning Nelson, Campbell, Ramirez, and Bates met in a conference room. Ramirez had several unassembled desks lying on a table. He had dimensions of all pieces of all desks. The three talked for a while and then Bates said "Give me all the dimensions and I'll go back to my office to see what kind of containers you need. One thing would help: Can you tell me now how many unassembled desks you want in a carton?"

Campbell responded, "Nearly all bids I know of are in multiples of ten."

Ramirez said, "That's OK for a start, Tom. Unless anyone here objects, let's figure on ten unassembled desks per carton."

There were no objections and the meeting broke up. Later that day, Bates phoned Ramirez and said: "Package 7F will meet all your needs, so far as I can tell. The material is not as strong as the one you're using but the packages' contents will provide more internal strength. The average cost for a carton to hold ten unassembled desks will be three dollars. You'll need some internal wrapping material, especially for the writing surfaces. For ten desks per carton, the material would be ten cents per desk. Labor costs also have to be calculated. You know those better than I." Ramirez relayed this information to Nelson.

Nelson had been figuring new densitites and calculated that ten un-assembled desks in a carton would occupy 0.4 times as much space per desk as when the desks were assembled. This would allow them to load carloads with shipments weighing an average of 25,000 lbs.

The last piece of information needed was cost of packing each carton. Ramirez called in the shipping room foreman and the two of them spent some time experimenting with how long it would take to pack a carton containing parts for the ten desks. Their "guesstimate" was that the cost per unassembled desk would be 25 cents; this was less than the cost when desks were set up and finished, which was 50 cents. The main reason for the higher costs for the set up desks was they were finished and, because of this, they required more careful handling.

Question One: Based on the information given, what are the average packing and packaging costs per unassembled desk? What are the average transportation costs per unassembled desk?

Question Two: What additional information would be useful for making more accurate estimates?

EXHIBIT 1

ARTICLE	Less Carload Ratings	Carload Minimum (Pounds)	Carload Ratings
Furniture			
Desks, school			
Wooden, set up and finished, in packages 3F or 6F, packed no more than two to a package	200	10,000	70
Wooden, knocked down, finished or unfinished, in packages 4F or 7F, packed no more than twenty to a package	150	20,000	60

CASE 10-2 BENJAMIN FRANKLIN BICENTENNIAL PLATE

Located in Hartford, Connecticut, the Hamilton Silverplate Company produced a series of ornamental silver plated and pewter dishes and bowls. Most were sold through small gift shops or through firms with mail order catalogs. Between 15 and 20 percent were sold directly through the mail in response to small advertisements placed in various homemakers' magazines. In anticipation of the bicentennial, the company designed and began producing a "Benjamin Franklin bicentennial" plate which had a profile of Franklin in the center and was surrounded by inscriptions of several of Franklin's better-known sayings. The plates had been successfully test-marketed, and regular buyers had placed large orders.

Because of these large orders, Hamilton's had decided to stop producing several other patterns and devote the facilities to Franklin plates. Since a large portion of the firm's output was to be a standardized product, it appeared that some changes could also be made in packaging.

Walt Drummond was Hamilton's executive vice president. He had called a meeting in his office of three subordinates, Amanda Carter, the sales manager, Jerry Stevens, the production manager, and Harry Epstein, the distribution manager. At present, at the end of the assembly line, three workers wrapped each plate in crumpled newspapers and then placed each wrapped plate in a corrugated container. A packaging consultant, Martin Bauer, had been retained to evaluate the present packaging system and make recommendations for a new system. Bauer was also present.

After the group had been seated and Stevens had finally gotten the right mixture of sugar in his coffee, Drummond started the meeting by saying that Bauer's report was ready and he wanted the group to hear it. Bauer stood up and placed a large chart (exhibit 1) on the wall. Bauer said, "I've costed out wrapping your Bicentennial plates. Along the left, I listed the various work and material item costs. At the top I listed your present method on the left. The second column shows changes in costs of placing each plate in a plastic bag and sealing it."

"Why that operation?" asked Stevens. "We don't do it now."

"You're right," said Bauer, "but for what you're asking for the plates, it adds a little more class."

Carter added: "Protection from tarnish is important to the shops handling the plates because they won't have to polish the plate. Right now, they have to polish those plates which have been in stock for a while."

"Maybe they'll order in larger quantities," said Drummond, "if they don't worry about tarnish."

"I hope so," said Epstein.

"Let's continue with Bauer's presentation," said Drummond.

Bauer continued: "The next column shows what happens if we substitute bubble wrap for crumpled newspaper. The main savings comes from use of smaller corrugated cartons. That's because a small thickness of bubble wrap gives much more protection than the newspaper. Note how these costs carry all the way through the handling system."

Carter said: "We and some of our mail order outlets sell plates by mail C.O.D. This should lower the customer's price. That's good."

Bauer continued: "Since you'll have a new corrugated carton, I thought you should consider a one color printing showing a small profile of Franklin and an advertising message." Bauer noted that Epstein was fretting, but he continued: "I know this will be controversial. Amanda wants the message in because she thinks it helps retail sales in small shops where only one plate is on display but the customers want one that's still in a box. If the boxed plates are displayed nearby, the customer may pick up a box and carry it to the cashier. Unfortunately, Harry thinks the advertising message will encourage pilferage of those cartons shipped by mail. So, we added 15 cents for wrapping each mailed carton in plain brown paper."

"Like mailing stag films," snickered Stevens.

"I wouldn't know," retorted Drummond. "What I do want to know is this: Assume Bauer's cost calculations are correct—and I think they're pretty close—how do we allocate them between production, sales, and distribution? You represent three different divisions and I know none of you is going to volunteer to absorb all these costs. What's a fair way for us to allocate these costs?"

Question One: Assume you are Amanda Carter. What do you think is the sales department's "fair" share? From a bargaining standpoint, Amanda will claim a minimum of benefit from the proposed charges. What is this minimum?

Question Two: Answer one from the standpoint of Jerry Stevens and his department. (Note that the production department will package each bowl at the assembly line; they are then turned over to the distribution department.)

Question Three: Read questions one and two. Answer from the standpoint of Harry Epstein and his distribution department.

Question Four: You are Drummond. What would you decide? How would you allocate costs? Why?

Question Five: Evaluate Bauer's presentation.

EXHIBIT 1

	Cost of newspaper-wrapped dish in carton with number only in carton	Change in cost if dish placed in sealed bag	Change in cost if bubblewrap used	Change in cost if advertising on carton
Packing time	.20	+.08	−.05	
Carton cost	.10		−.20	+.10
Sealed bag cost		+.02		
Cushioning mat'l.				
cost	.02	−.01	+.10	
w/h space	.06		−.02	
w/h handling	.12		−.02	−.02
shipping costs				
to warehouses	.10		−.01	
shipping cost				
from warehouse	.20		−.10 *	+.15 **

* average figure. (For individual C.O.D. mail orders, depending on postal zone, price reductions ranged from 25 to 80 cents.)

** for individual carton shipments, wrapping in plain paper required to mask carton's contents.

CHAPTER REFERENCES

AMMER, DEAN S.; *Materials Management* (Homewood, Ill.: Richard D. Irwin, 1974, 3rd ed.).

BARDI, EDWARD J. and Larry G. Kelly; "Organizing for Effective Packaging Management," *Transportation Journal* (Winter, 1974), pp. 53–57.

Butler Roadrunner (Minneapolis, Butler Manufacturing Co., 1973).

COLTON, RICHARD C. and Edmund S. Ward; *Practical Handbook of Industrial Traffic Management*, 4th ed. (Washington, D.C.: The Traffic Services Corporation, 1965).

Daily Traffic World (August 6, 1974).

Handling and Shipping (May, 1974).

LIBA, CARL J.; "The Transportation Market Potential in Modular Housing," *Proceedings of the Sixty-second Annual Meeting of the American Railway Association* (1971).

"Marconflo: Engineering, Economics and the Environment," *Transportation and Distribution Management* (November, 1970).

" 'Standard' Air Pallet for Fruit Still More Fancy Than Fact," *Container News* (November, 1973).

STRONG, JAMES R.; *Material Handling Engineering* (Special Issue, 1973).

Transport and Handling of Carnations Cut in the Bud Stage—Potential Advantages (Washington, D.C.: U.S. Department of Agriculture, 1971).

Transport Topics (November 21, 1971; October 14, 1974).

"Will It be Performance Standards or Material Requirements? *Handling and Shipping* (April, 1975).

Tractors waiting to be loaded aboard a roll on/roll off (Ro-Ro) vessel. Credit: Atlantic Container Line.

CHAPTER ELEVEN

International Physical Distribution

International Distribution is truly an octopus.
> —HENRY WEGNER at
> National Council of Physical
> Distribution Management annual
> meeting, 1972

The Guatemala Chamber of Commerce has so far waged a success-ful campaign to keep Sears, Roebuck out of Guatemala, claiming that a Sears invasion would put three to four thousand Guatemalan shopkeepers out of business.
> —RICHARD BARNET and RONALD MÜLLER, in
> *The New Yorker,* 1974

Mercedes began exporting trucks to America five years ago with a small dealer in New Jersey. Trucks were then brought in from the West German parent firm, Daimler-Benz, the largest diesel truck manufacturer in the world and Europe's largest heavy truck producer.

But in 1973, when the value of the dollar fell in relation to the deutschmark, German-built trucks had difficulty competing in the U.S. from a price standpoint. Mercedes-Benz of North America then turned to Mercedes-Benz do Brazil for its import supplies.
> *Transport Topics*
> 1975

BACKGROUND AND OVERVIEW

International distribution will be defined as the distribution of goods across national boundaries. International distribution would occur un-der any of the following situations:

1. The firm exports a portion of the product made or grown. Examples are paper making machinery moving to Sweden, wheat sales to Russia, and coal shipments to Japan.

2. The firm imports raw materials, such as pulpwood from Cana-

da, or manufactured products, such as motorcycles from Italy or Japan.

3. Goods are partially assembled in one country and then shipped to another where they are further assembled or processed. For example, Burroughs stamps electronic components in the U.S., ships them to a free trade zone in the Far East where low-cost labor assembles them, and then the assembled components are returned to the U.S. where they become part of a finished product.

4. Products are assembled in foreign countries for distribution in those foreign countries and the firm's home country. Some autos sold in the U.S. are assembled in Canada. (Because of a special Canadian-U.S. trade agreement, the U.S. auto manufacturer who relies on Canadian plants to supply a part of its U.S. markets can export to Canada—with little or no tariff restrictions—an equal volume of other models assembled in the U.S.).

Until World War II, concepts of international trade were simple. Industrialized powers maintained political and economic colonies. Colonies were sources of raw materials and markets for manufactured products. When dealing with colonies, manufacturers in the mother country allegedly bought low and sold high. World War II brought an end to the colonial system, as such, and since then "emerging" nations have attempted to develop their own political and economic systems with varying degrees of success.

From a distribution standpoint, the old patterns frequently remain. An emerging nation may discover that its rail and port system—both representing heavy fixed investments—function only to carry raw materials from mines to the sea. Its local airline, which had been carefully developed by the mother nation's own prestigious international carrier may have an airport and route structure that functions only to feed passengers into the international carrier rather than aid in developing the new nation's economy. The local merchants, often the only source of native private capital and entrepreneurial talent, see themselves as agents for trading companies headquartered in the former mother country. Factors such as these make it difficult for the new nation to achieve economic "independence." In addition, a lack of political stability discourages private investment from either national or outside sources. Investors may fear that a change in governments will result in expropriation of foreign firms.

Developing nations insist that an increasing proportion of assembling and manufacturing be conducted within their own borders. Because the role of these governments in their own economies is substantial, they are able to exert considerable influence over outside firms desiring to do business within their borders. Local labor must be utilized whenever possible. Demands are also made that supervisory and managerial talent be recruited from native ranks and trained to replace the managers from the U.S. or other outside country.

The post-World War II experience of a Milwaukee manufacturer of heavy-duty construction equipment is illustrative. Immediately after the war, the manufacturer exported completely equipped machines, including tires and engines. Later, they shipped the machines without tires and without engines and the foreign buyers acquired these components from local sources. Later, even less was exported from Milwaukee, since the importers could now rely on local sources to supply the more common sizes and shapes of steel beams. Finally, by the mid-1960's, all that was exported from Milwaukee was a small crate of the firm's patented machinery control devices. All of the unpatented components of the construction machine were being supplied by local sources in the importing nations. Assembly was completed in the importing nation, but this was done under supervision of the Milwaukee firm, primarily because they wished to maintain quality control.

Firms with annual model changes, such as automobile manufacturers, frequently ship their last year's dies to assembly plants in foreign nations. Parts are frequently interchangeable between model years and price classes of autos. Hence, travelers abroad may see autos which look like the results of "mating" two different American models. "Refrigerators and washing machines from the nineteen fifties are standard items in Bankok and Accra department stores. Distributing last generation's technology is a good way to prolong its marketable life."[1]

International trade is, of course, closely related to international relations. In a peaceful world, most disagreements between nations regard terms and conditions of trade. In the mid-1970's, the most publicized foreign trade activities of the United States involved communist nations: Russia, China, and Cuba.

INTERNATIONAL MARKETING

Marketing overseas is often different from marketing in the United States.[2] Therefore generalizations are difficult since each country of the world possesses unique characteristics when viewed as a market. Conventional marketing analysis is applied, although it must take into account a wider range of differences. In many countries, the size or scale of firms used in the distribution operation is much smaller than would be the case in the U.S. Street vendors, merchants operating out of "holes-in-the-wall" and small shopkeepers may be the rule. Customers

[1] Richard Barnet and Ronald Müller, "Global Reach," *The New Yorker* (December 2, 1974), p. 96. This excellent article is critical of the global corporation's role in technology transfer because "what most of the world needs is not gas-devouring four-wheel tractors. . . , but better hoes and ox plows," (p. 99).

[2] See: Lynn E. Gill, "Beware of Booby Traps in Multinational Distribution," *Handling and Shipping* (March, 1976), pp. 44–46.

shop on a daily basis and buy small amounts. Retailers are more likely to pull the requested good from the shelf behind the counter so there is less need for the type of packaging used in U.S. self-service markets. (There are countries that have retail stores similar to those in the United States.)

If U.S. exporters think that a certain foreign nation will be a promising market for its export products, so will exporters located in other developed nations. They may even use these new markets to test the competitive effectiveness of their products against those produced in the United States.

Firms selling products under their own brand names are concerned about maintaining a reputation for quality in all markets. This can pose problems with respect to customer service. For example, how many parts depots should be located throughout the world? What kinds of guarantees can a U.S. firm make to foreign buyers? How enforceable are they?

In Chapter 7 "push or pull" inventory systems were discussed. In international distribution, "push" systems are rare and the reason is that the international credit system is not as well developed as is the credit system within the United States or other similarly developed economic areas. In international business, if "the buyer or borrower be unwilling or unable to pay, collection of the debt can prove difficult or even impossible in foreign courts. Furthermore, even though the buyer or borrower may be willing and able to pay, he may not be permitted to do so because of foreign-exchange restrictions, expropriation, or political upheavals."[3] If the supplier is a bit uncertain about receiving his payments, he is unlikely to "push" unwanted goods onto his overseas distributors. One of the ways a supplier can be assured of payment is to insist on payment in advance or else to operate through "irrevocable letters of credit" which means a bank guarantees payment provided the supplier meets certain conditions. (See Figure 11-1 for a sample copy. Note the terms.)

TRANSACTION AND EXCHANGE CHANNELS

Chapter 2 discussed transaction channels and exchange channels; transaction channels are the channels through which the ownership of goods passes and exchange channels are the chain of physical moves. This distinction is useful in discussing international distribution.[4]

The next section of the chapter will deal primarily with the transaction function. Most of the discussion will deal with governments' role

[3] Laurence P. Dowd, *Principles of World Business* (Boston: Allyn & Bacon, 1965), p. 393.
[4] See: Bruce Mallen, "Marketing Channels and Economic Development: A Literature Overview," *International Journal of Physical Distribution* (1975), pp. 230–237.

Fig. 11-1 Letter of credit.

IRREVOCABLE COMMERCIAL LETTER OF CREDIT

WELLS FARGO BANK, N.A.

FORMERLY WELLS FARGO BANK AMERICAN TRUST COMPANY
HEAD OFFICE: 464 CALIFORNIA STREET, SAN FRANCISCO, CALIFORNIA 94104

| INTERNATIONAL DIVISION | COMMERCIAL L/C DEPARTMENT | CABLE ADDRESS: WELLS |

OUR LETTER OF CREDIT NO. 27724   AMOUNT: US$12,288.00   DATE: April 1, 1974

THIS NUMBER MUST BE MENTIONED ON ALL DRAFTS AND CORRESPONDENCE

- The Japan Co.
- Box X 25
- Tokyo, Japan
-

S P E C I M E N

- Wells Fargo Bank N.A.
- Fuji Bldg., 2-3, 3-chome
- Marunouchi, Chiyoda-ku
- Tokyo, Japan

GENTLEMEN:

BY ORDER OF   Wards, Oakland, California

AND FOR ACCOUNT OF   same

WE HEREBY AUTHORIZE YOU TO DRAW ON   us

UP TO AN AGGREGATE AMOUNT OF   Twelve Thousand Two Hundred Eighty Eight
and No/100 U.S. Dollars

AVAILABLE BY YOUR DRAFTS AT   sight

ACCOMPANIED BY

Commercial Invoice and two copies certifying merchandise is in accordance
with Purchase Order No. 08142.
Signed Special Customs Invoice in duplicate.
Certificate of Origin in duplicate.
Packing List in duplicate.
Full set clean ocean bills of lading to order shipper, blank endorsed,
freight collect, notify Wards, Oakland, California, dated on
board not later than May 25, 1974.

Relating to: Transistor Radios from FOB vessel Japanese Port to
San Francisco Bay Port.

Partial shipments permitted.   Insurance to be effected by buyers
Transhipment is not permitted.

Negotiating bank is to forward all documents attached to the
original draft in one airmail envelope.

Courtesy Wells Fargo Bank

DRAFTS MUST BE DRAWN AND NEGOTIATED NOT LATER THAN   June 5, 1974
ALL DRAFTS DRAWN UNDER THIS CREDIT MUST BEAR ITS DATE AND NUMBER AND THE AMOUNTS MUST
BE ENDORSED ON THE REVERSE SIDE OF THIS LETTER OF CREDIT BY THE NEGOTIATING BANK.
WE HEREBY AGREE WITH THE DRAWERS, ENDORSERS AND BONA FIDE HOLDERS OF ALL DRAFTS
DRAWN UNDER AND IN COMPLIANCE WITH THE TERMS OF THIS CREDIT, THAT SUCH DRAFTS WILL
BE DULY HONORED UPON PRESENTATION TO THE DRAWEE.
THIS CREDIT IS SUBJECT TO THE UNIFORM CUSTOMS AND PRACTICE FOR DOCUMENTARY CREDITS
(1962 REVISION), INTERNATIONAL CHAMBER OF COMMERCE BROCHURE NO. 222.

W/ SPECIMEN
AUTHORIZED SIGNATURE

Courtesy Wells Fargo Bank.

in international commerce, and how this requires an additional set of facilitating agents who aid in the transaction activities. International forwarders will also be discussed.

Later sections of the chapter will deal with the exchange channel, and how it differs from that used for domestic transactions. International air and ocean shipping will be the principal topics.

GOVERNMENTAL INFLUENCES ON FOREIGN TRADE

Businesses involved in foreign trade find that the government's role is more significant than in domestic transactions. In part, this is because most firms developed in domestic markets first and took all existing governmental controls as a "given" factor. As a firm expands into foreign markets, it finds requirements that differ for each nation with which the firm wishes to trade. The U.S. government also places restrictions and paperwork requirements on U.S. firms which buy or sell abroad.

These restrictions tend to make more difficult the functioning of the transaction channel. In domestic marketing the flows of the transactions and exchange channels are concurrent. In international distribution this is less likely to be so. The seller usually wants to be certain the payment is guaranteed before shipping the goods. Hence, for a single sale, the activities in the transaction channel must be nearly completed before the goods are placed into the exchange channel.

GOVERNMENTAL CONTROLS ON FLOW OF INTERNATIONAL TRADE

National governments play a more significant role in international transactions than they do in domestic transactions for several reasons. The main reason is that governments tax the importation of many items. These taxes are called customs or duties. (At one time, customs collections represented the major source of revenue for the United States government.) Goods, including baggage accompanying travelers, are inspected as they cross borders. If any customs are due, they must be paid before the goods can be transported farther.

Customs or duty rates are set high on many goods to "protect" local manufacturers, producers, or growers. The local interests must possess some political power to achieve protective tariffs. They will argue that theirs are "infant" industries and need protection for only a few years in order to prevent foreign-based competitors from "dumping" goods in the country at prices which are below cost. Once tariff barriers are built, they are not easily torn down. Rather than the infant outgrowing the crib, the walls of the crib are built higher. The results are that local consumers pay more for goods than would otherwise be the case. In addition, the national resources may be allocated in a wasteful manner since they are being used for a production process which is inefficient when viewed from a worldwide perspective.

Related to tariffs are *import quotas*; they are physical limits on the amount that may be imported from any one country during a period of time. They are often used for commodities where no tariffs exist and they serve to protect local producers in years when local prices are high but foreign prices are low. In 1974, both the U.S. and Canada placed quotas on the number of cattle and pigs which could be imported from the other. The quotas were imposed at different times, but when prices in the foreign country were lower.

Many nations are concerned with stopping the spread of plant and animal diseases and will inspect various commodities or products to make certain that they do not contain these problems. If material is found to be infested, it cannot enter a country until it is cleaned.

Entry of other products may be prohibited because they do not meet safety standards. An example is electrical appliances which have different voltage requirements throughout the world. Products that do not meet a country's voltage specifications will not be imported by that country. Another situation is the Japanese restriction on imported foods containing two preservatives—benzoic acid and sorbic acid. "The reason for this is that these two preservatives, if permitted for open use in Japan would be used extensively on all types of fish. Since fish forms a more important part of the Japanese diet than the diets of other nations, there is a clear danger of overconsumption of these two preservatives. . . ."[5] Because of the danger of earthquakes in Japan, upright refrigerators must be built so that they will remain upright even when tilted as much as ten degrees.[6]

Products can be modified so that they meet each nation's requirements. Conversion costs per unit are high in instances where only small batches are involved. From an inventory control standpoint, slight variations in acceptable standards mean that products become less homogeneous. Parts are less likely to be interchangeable, and stocks in one country may not be substitutes for stocks of similar products in an adjoining country.

Some nations restrict the outflow of currency. This is because a nation's economy will suffer if it imports more than it exports over a long term. These regulations are not concerned with specific commodities; they are concerned with restricting the outflow of currency. All imports require advance approval, and goods that arrive without prior approval may not be allowed to enter.

[5] Japan External Trade Organization, *Japan's Import and Export Regulations* (Tokyo, 1974), p. 10.
[6] *Ibid.*, p. 17.

FIG. 11-2 Examples of restrictions on exporting to other nations.

SENEGAL

GOVERNMENT REPRESENTATION

The Republic of Senegal is represented in the United States by an Embassy at 2112 Wyoming Ave., N.W., Washington, D.C. and a United Nations Mission at 51 East 42nd St., New York. Both also act for Canadian affairs.

GENERAL INFORMATION

Customs Airports: Dakar, Saint Louis and Ziguinchor.
Collect Service acceptable to Dakar and Saint Louis only.
COD Service not acceptable.
Free House Delivery not acceptable.

DOCUMENTATION

Commercial consignments—2 commercial invoices containing the following declaration: "Nous certifions que les marchandises denommees dans cette facture sont de fabrication et d'origine (country of origin) et que les prix indiques ci-dessus s'accordent avec les prix courants sur le marche d'exportation."
Sample consignments—Without commercial value: No documents. With commercial value: same as for commercial consignments.
Gift consignments—no documentary requirements.

RESTRICTIONS

Live animals: Health certificate.
Dogs and other domestic animals: Health certificates issued not later than 3 days before shipment and stating that the animals originate from an area free from contagious diseases of the species for the preceding 6 weeks, and in case of cats and dogs, that no rabies has been detected for the same period.
PROHIBITED: Hares and rabbits.
Live plants and plant material: Health certificate.
Arms and ammunition: Special import permit.

PROHIBITIONS

All goods of Portuguese or South African origin; skins of hares and rabbits; beetroot sugar; blankets; cloth of textile fibers; cotton cloth; fibres; flower pots, stoneware, pottery, clay products, matches, ornamental bricks and other clay products for building purposes; outwear, shirts, except shirts over CFA 1700. value; shoes, except fashionable shoes over CFA 400. value; trousers under CFA 1900. value; sisal carpets and rugs; sugar cane, yarn and thread; cotton, apéritifs of alcohol or wine basis; digestives.

IMPORT AND EXCHANGE REGULATIONS

Liberalized items may be imported without quantitative restrictions on the basis of an import certificate, which is made out by the importer, endorsed by the Customs on clearance of the merchandise and delivered to an authorized bank for visa by the Exchange Control Office.
Non-liberalized goods require an import license, issued by the Director General for Economic Services and visaed by the Exchange Control Office. Validity of certificate and license is 6 months.
The currency exchange is obtained through the authorized banks on strength of import certificate or import license. No tolerance in value or quantity shown on import certificate or import license is permitted.
The importation of goods competitive with locally produced items may be prohibited from time to time.
Rate of exchange: 247 C.F.A. Francs = $1.00

SIERRA LEONE

GOVERNMENT REPRESENTATION

Sierra Leone is represented in the United States by an Embassy at 1701 19th Street, N.W., Washington, D.C. and a United Nations Mission at 30 East 42nd St., New York. Both also act for Canadian affairs.

GENERAL INFORMATION

Customs Airport: Freetown.
Collect Service acceptable.
COD Service not acceptable.
Free House Delivery not acceptable.

DOCUMENTATION

Commercial consignments—4 combined certificates of value and origin in English bearing the supplier's letterhead and his seal or stamp against his signature or that of his representative. In case of occasional shipment, when overprinting of the letterhead is prohibitive, the combined certificate must be accompanied with the supplier's own invoice duly signed against his seal or stamp, and containing the certification: "We hereby declare that this commercial invoice is in support of the attached certificate invoice No. . . . and that the particulars shown on the certified invoice are true and correct in every detail."

RESTRICTIONS

Live animals: Import authorization from Veterinary Dept.
Dogs: Additional health and rabies vaccination certificate in English.
Live plants and plant material: Import authorization from Agricultural Department.
PROHIBITED: Aniseed and Indian hemp.
Medicines and narcotics: Import license from Director of Medical services.

PROHIBITIONS

Arms and ammunition from Liberia, obscene photographs, shaving brushes from Japan, traps for night hunting.

IMPORT AND EXCHANGE REGULATIONS

Most goods may be freely imported under "Open General License." Specific import license required for a short list of specified items only . . . issued by the Import Licensing Authority of the Ministry of Commerce and Industry; the validity is generally 12 months.

Exporters should avoid overshipment of goods covered by specific import licenses. No tolerances are permitted.

The currency exchange is obtained through authorized banks. No exchange permit is required. An import license, whether specific or open, automatically entitles the importer to buy the relative foreign exchange.

Rate of exchange: 1 Leone = $1.20

Courtesy Sabena Belgian World Airlines.

Figure 11-2 is from a guidebook prepared by an international airline which outlines the various restrictions that apply when shipping to African nations. From the example of the two nations listed, you can see that exporting involves complications. Note that their embassy locations in the U.S. are listed. Most nations maintain consular offices in major U.S. port cities and these offices—for a fee—prepare a "consular invoice," a document which contains approximately the same information as a commercial invoice. The importing nation uses it as the basis for levying applicable import duties. Consular offices are current sources of information regarding their nation's import and currency exchange regulations.

POLITICAL RESTRICTIONS ON TRADE

For political or military reasons, nations ban certain types of shipments. The United States does not ship military equipment or certain "strategic" materials to Communist Bloc nations. Trade with Cuba is also banned. (Although, at this writing, the ban is being lifted.) Israel and Arab nations do not trade with each other and frequently do not even allow carriers of third countries to fly or sail directly between Israel and the Arab nations. Many African nations are boycotting Rhodesia.

GOVERNMENTS' ROLE IN INTERNATIONAL TRANSPORT

Governments are also more involved in international transportation than they are in domestic transportation. One reason for this is that ocean vessels or international airline aircraft operate as "extensions" of a nation's economy and most revenues they receive flow into that nation's economy. To that nation, international carriage functions as an "export" with favorable effects on the nation's balance of payments. However, to the nation on the other end of the shipment, the effect is the opposite since they must "import" the transport service and this has an adverse impact on their balance of payments position. Some nations with very weak balance of payments positions will issue an import license or permit on the condition that the goods move on a vessel or plane flying that nation's flag (which means they are importing only the goods, *not* the transportation service required to carry them).[7] Situations such as this dictate carrier choice.

In the past decade, the Russian merchant fleet has grown immensely and is making inroads into most shipping routes. By communist state

[7] As used here "flying a nation's flag" is meant to be synonomous with being owned by private or public entities in that nation. "Flags of convenience" are issued by nations with relatively lax maritime safety and work standards to investors of other nations who want to avoid their home nation's control.

accounting techniques, the merchant marine investment has proven to be profitable.[8] The fleet is earning scarce foreign exchange while keeping purchases from foreign countries to a minimum. Russian flag vessels on Pacific trade routes are fueled in the mid-Pacific by Russian tankers rather than buying fuel at non-communist ports.

In order to develop international fleets and air lines, most nations provide subsidies. Many nations train merchant marine officers, absorb portions of the costs of building commercial vessels, etc. Some own—in total or in part—ocean carriers. International scheduled airlines, except those of the United States, are owned, at least partially, by governments and they receive subsidies. International air and vessel rates are frequently established by carrier cartels. Nations rely on carriers they subsidize to represent national interests as they vote on international rate and service issues.

INTERNATIONAL TRADE SPECIALISTS

Few companies involved in international distribution rely solely on "in-house" personnel to manage all of the shipping operations. Specialist firms have developed and are known as international freight forwarders (who generally handle exports) and customs house or import brokers. Sometimes the same firm provides both services and has offices in different countries.

INTERNATIONAL FREIGHT FORWARDERS

International forwarders usually specialize in handling either vessel shipments or air shipments. Yet their functions are generally the same. The following is list and explanation of their functions.

1. *Booking space on carriers.* Space is frequently more difficult to obtain on international carriers than domestic ones. The reasons are: vessel or aircraft departures are less frequent; capacity of the plane or ship is strictly limited; connections with other carriers are more difficult to arrange; and the relative bargaining strength of any one shipper, *vis-a-vis* an international carrier, is usually less than it is with respect to domestic carriers. Forwarders are experienced at keeping tabs on available carrier space and, because they represent more business to the carrier than does an individual shipper, they have more success when finding space is difficult.

2. *Preparing Export Declaration.* This document is required by the U.S. government for statistical and "control" purposes and must be prepared and filed for nearly every shipment.

[8] See Robert E. Athay, *The Economics of Soviet Merchant-Shipping Policy* (Chapel Hill: University of North Carolina Press, 1971).

3. *Preparing Air Waybill or Bill of Lading.* The international air waybill is a fairly standardized document; the ocean bill of lading is not. The latter may differ between ocean lines, coastal areas through which the shipments are moving, etc. Ocean bills of lading are frequently negotiable which means whoever legally holds the document may take delivery of the shipment. Since nearly every ocean vessel line has its own bill of lading, a forwarder's expertise is necessary to fill it out accurately.

4. *Obtaining consular documents.* These were discussed briefly in the previous section. This process involves obtaining permission from the importing country for the goods to enter. Documents are prepared which the importing country will use to determine duties to be levied on the shipment as it passes through their customs.

5. *Arranging for insurance.* Unlike domestic shipments, international shipments must be insured. Either the individual shipment must be insured or else the shipper (or forwarder) has a blanket policy covering all of his shipments. International airlines offer insurance at nominal rates. Rates on vessel shipments are higher and the entire process is complex because of certain practices which are acceptable at sea. For example, if the vessel is in peril of sinking, the captain may have some cargo jettisoned (thrown overboard) to keep the vessel afloat. The owners of the surviving cargo and the vessel owner must then share the costs of reimbursing the shippers whose cargo was thrown overboard. When goods are sold on a "delivered overseas" basis, the shipper needs insurance coverage from the port or airport to the point where the consignee takes possession.

6. *Preparing and sending shipping notices and documents.* The financial transaction involving the sale of goods is carefully coordinated with their physical movement, and rather elaborate customs and procedures have evolved which assure that the seller is paid when the goods are delivered. The export forwarder handles the shipper's role in the document preparation and exchange stages. (The forwarder serves to coordinate the exchange channel and the transaction channel.)

7. *Serving as general consultant on export matters.* New questions continually arise dealing with new products, new markets, or new regulations. The forwarder knows the answers or how to find them. A conscientious forwarder will also advise a shipper as to when certain procedures, such as similar shipments to the same market, become so repetitive that the shipper can handle the procedures in his or her own export department at a lower cost than the fees charged by the forwarder.

Export forwarders' income comes from three sources. Similar to domestic forwarders, they "buy space wholesale and sell it retail" meaning that by consolidating shipments they benefit from a lower rate per pound. Second, most carriers allow the forwarders a commission on shipping revenues they generate for the carriers. Third, forwarders charge fees for preparing documents, performing research, etc.

CUSTOMS HOUSE BROKERS

An opposite, but similar, function is performed by import or customs house brokers. They oversee the efficient movement of an importer's goods through customs and also stand ready to argue for a lower rate in case one of two commodity descriptions apply. They handle the physical and paperwork processes of moving the goods through customs and other inspection points.

Very few firms attempt to handle this complex process by themselves. In 1974, the Japanese manufacturer of Toyota automobiles contracted with Harper Robinson & Company—a worldwide freight forwarder and customs-house broker based in the U.S.—to handle the imports of all Toyota parts into the United States. Some 50,000 different part numbers are involved. "Processing this vast array of parts through customs will involve complex entry procedures to keep parts moving into Toyota's U.S. distribution channels. Harper Robinson will also co-ordinate pickup and delivery to nine parts depots across the country. . . ."[9] Chrysler Corporation of Detroit also relies on the same firm. They contracted with Harper Robinson to be their ocean freight forwarder for both auto components for assembly overseas and vehicles completed in the U.S. for shipment overseas. The contract covered all Chrysler traffic to South Africa, Australia, Greece, Peru, Lebanon, Japan and Guam.[10]

EXPORT MANAGEMENT COMPANIES

An "export management company" specializes in handling overseas transactions. They represent U.S. manufacturers and help them find overseas firms which can be licensed to manufacture the product.[11] They handle sales correspondence in foreign languages, ensure that foreign labeling requirements are met, etc. When handling the overseas sales for a U.S. firm, the export management firm either buys and sells on its own account or else provides credit information regarding each potential buyer to the U.S. manufacturer who can judge whether or not to take the risk.

Export management companies and international freight forwarders are closely related because between them they can offer a complete overseas sales and distribution service to the domestic manufacturer who would like to export but just doesn't know how. Sometimes international forwarders and export management firms work out of the

9 *Pacific Traffic* (November, 1974), p. 26.
10 *Distriubtion Worldwide* (October, 1973), p. 40.

same office with the only apparent distinction being which one of the two phones they answer. Export management companies are also retained by very large firms which have exported for many years, because they can perform their very specialized service at less expense than can the principal firm itself. There are approximately 1,000 export management firms in the U.S., and it is estimated that nearly half of the manufacturers who export utilize export management companies for at least some segments of their export business.[11]

EXPORT PACKERS

As with the other export functions discussed to this point, there is a specialized industry called "export packing" performed by firms typically located in port cities. They will custom-pack shipments in instances where the exporter may lack the equipment or the expertise. However, when exporters have "repeat" business, they usually perform their own export packing.

Export packaging involves packaging for two distinct purposes (in addition to the "sales" function of some packaging).*

The first is to allow goods to move through customs easily. For a country assessing duties on the weight of both the item and its container, this would mean selection of light-weight packing materials. For items moving through the mail, it might mean construction of an envelope with an additional small flap that a customs inspector could open and look inside without having to open the entire envelope. For crated machinery, this might involve using open slats rather than completely closed construction. The customs inspectors could probably satisfy their curiosity by peering and probing through the openings between the slats.

The second purpose of export packing is to protect the products in what almost always is a more difficult journey than they would experience if they were destined for domestic consignees. For many firms, the traditional ocean packaging method was to take the product in its domestic pack and then enclose it in a wooden container. Ocean shipments are subjected to more moisture damage than would be the case for domestic moves. Variations in temperatures are also more extreme. Canned goods moving through hot areas "sweat," causing the can to rust and the label to become unglued.

Recent transportation equipment innovations have helped overcome these climatic problems. International air freight, a post World War II development, has made it possible to reach major cities throughout the

---

[11] See: Howard Grossman, "Almost Everything You Should Know About International Distribution," *Handling and Shipping* (March, 1976), pp. 42–43.

* Packaging for export also has a promotional thrust. In many nations, consumers value reusable containers.

world within 24 or 48 hours, avoiding the long sea voyage. Packaging for international air freight is sometimes no different than packaging for domestic markets. Containerships and LASH (lighter-aboard-ship) are discussed later in the chapter. These vessels are able to provide better care for cargo since shipments are in individual containers which come equipped with freezing, refrigerating, or air circulating equipment in case the cargo demands. Each container can be handled differently, and the ship's personnel are detailed to check temperature gauges outside containers several times daily.

Goods sold in foreign markets require additional labels. The metric system is widely used outside the United States and most measurements of products must be expressed in metric terms. Figure 11-3 shows some simple metric equivalents.

For goods moving in foreign trade, it is not safe to assume that the handlers can read English. Hence, cautionary symbols must be used. (See Figures 11-4 and 11-5.) Cargo moving aboard ocean vessels contains a distinct mark which identifies the shipper, the consignee, the destination point, and piece number (in multi-piece shipments). As with domestic cargo, care must be taken so that pilferable items are not identified. This may include changing the symbols every few months.

EXCHANGE CHANNELS IN INTERNATIONAL DISTRIBUTION

To this point, the chapter has dealt with the international transactions channels. The remainder of the chapter deals with the exchange channel which handles the physical movement of the goods. The entire export process is complicated. The following chapter contains an application of network analysis to an export shipment.

Most of this section deals with transportation. The first part deals with the landward move to the port or airport. The second and third sections deal with international air and ocean shipping. The last section deals with the landward leg in the foreign country.

MOVEMENT TO PORT OR AIRPORT

For air shipments, or products moving by rail or truck to Canada or Mexico, the movement from the manufacturer's plant is similar to that for domestic sales. About the only difference is that more paperwork accompanies each shipment.

Most U.S. rail and motor carrier rate-making bodies have lower rates, known as "export" or "import" rates, for the landward leg of export and import shipments. The U.S.-based shipper or consignee must have documentary proof that the shipment will or did connect with an ocean

FIG. 11-3 Metric equivalents.

weights and measures

metric equivalents

weight

one kilo =   2.2 pounds
pounds ×   0.454 = kilos
ounces ×   0.028 = kilos
cwt. ×   45.4   = kilos
tons × 907.2   = kilos

length

one inch = 25.4 millimeters
inches × 25.4   = millimeters
inches × 2.54   = centimeters
feet × 0.305 = meters
miles × 1.609 = kilometers

capacity

one imperial gallon = 1.2 U.S. gallons
U.S. gallon × 0.833 = imperial gallon
U.S. gallon × 3.78 = liters
liters × 0.264 = U.S. gallon

Courtesy Air France Cargo.

vessel and that the party on the other end of the entire haul is located in another country. Usually a copy of the ocean bill of lading is suffi-ient proof.

The export or import rate for the surface haul within the U.S. is less than it would be for a comparable shipment which terminated in the port city. Two rail carloads of tractors might leave Peoria, Illinois

FIG. 11-4 Some symbols used for packing export shipments.

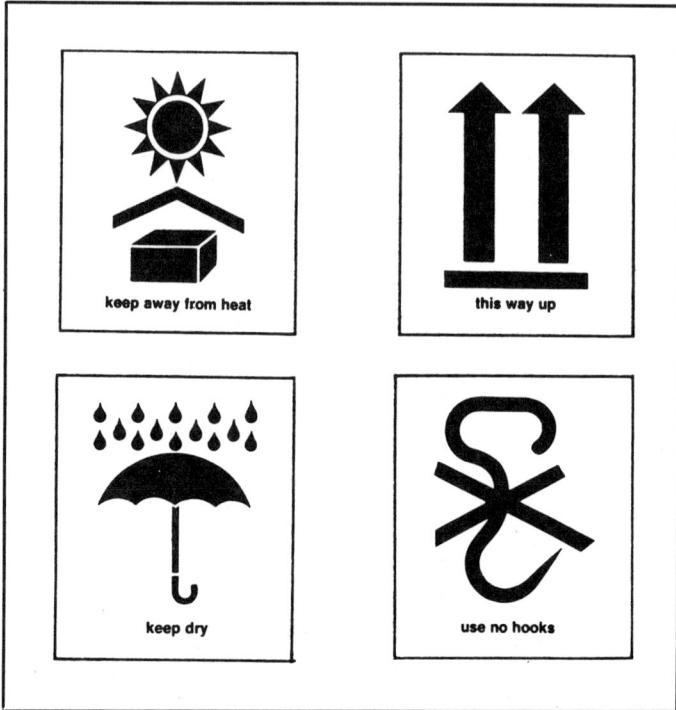

keep away from heat

this way up

keep dry

use no hooks

Courtesy Air France Cargo.

for Charleston, South Carolina, one being consigned to a local implement dealer in Charleston and the other to be loaded aboard ship for export to Brazil. From an operational standpoint, the railroad might handle the two carloads of tractors in an identical manner, yet they would charge less for the carload destined for export. In addition, the firm unloading the export tractors from the rail cars would have more days of "free time" before they would be assessed demurrage charges. Railroads justify the lower rates for export and import traffic on their "value of service" rationale. Goods moving in foreign trade are vulnerable to competition from so many sources that they would be more sensitive to high freight rates.

Ports that handle export or import trade are frequently "grouped" for rate making purposes by both the land and water carriers. Ports on the western bank of Lake Michigan, which handle foreign trade moving through the St. Lawrence Seaway, are grouped in the sense that a firm in Des Moines, Iowa, shipping to or from Copenhagen, is con-

Fig. 11-5 International shipments must be clearly labeled.

They're a heck of a nice outfit to do business with!

© *Seaway Review*, the Les Strang Publishing Group, used with permission.

fronted with the same rail rate (on the import or export commodity) between Des Moines and Chicago, Milwaukee or Green Bay. Also, the vessel rate between Chicago or Milwaukee or Green Bay and Copenhagen would be the same. Hence the choice of port would be based on the quality of service or the specific carriers serving each port as well as the quality of the stevedoring operation in each port.* (Stevedoring charges are also frequently the same in different ports although productivity varies.)

Not only are ports along any one shore grouped for rate-making purposes, even "groups" are grouped. The Des Moines shipper may find that if his shipment moved through ports on Lake Erie the rail charges would be more, the vessel charges less, but the total charges the same. If he considered Baltimore or Philadelphia, he would find the rail charges even higher but the vessel charges correspondingly less

* Stevedores are the labor force used to load and unload ships.

with the total again being the same. In such a situation, the individual controlling the shipment would choose the port which was most advantageous from his *time* standpoint.

Vessel lines operating between U.S. Pacific Coast ports and western Europe frequently find it cheaper to discharge and load their containerized cargo at east coast ports and have it move by rail across the U.S. The vessel line pays for the rail haul but saves the voyage through the Panama Canal. The shipper or consignee pays the same freight rate but benefits because time in transit is reduced about four days. Similar service is available for east coast firms doing business with the Orient. This type of container-rail-ship operation is called "mini-land bridge" and means a unit-train of containers connecting with an ocean-going containership.*

INTERNATIONAL AIR FREIGHT

In relative terms, air freight has probably had a more profound effect on international distribution than on domestic distribution. This is because the airplane has reduced worldwide distances. While transit times between the two U.S. coasts have shrunk from five days to less than one, some international transit times have shrunk from as much as 30 days down to one or two.

There are two types of international air freight operations. The first involves chartering an entire aircraft; the second involves use of scheduled air carriers. Chartering an entire aircraft is, of course, expensive. An example of chartered aircraft moving international commerce, which shows the aircraft's unique advantage, is the carriage of planeloads of livestock which are sold for breeding purposes. In 1969, one charter airline carried 7,000 cattle from Texas to southern Chile. Nineteen flights were involved, each lasting 15 hours. The comparable time by sea was 20 days and past experience showed the sea journey had been difficult on the cattle, causing either lung damage or else long delays before the animal could be bred. The cost of the chartered aircraft was justified by the reduction in time that the breeding stock was nonproductive. The aircraft were specially equipped with light-weight flooring, gates, and kick-panels (an animal's sharp hoof could pierce the side of the plane). Prior to being loaded aboard the plane, the livestock were kept in feedlots and given a transitional diet which combined both the food to which they were accustomed and the food they would be getting at their destination.

The schedules and routes of international air carriers are established

---

* "Land-bridge" means a unit train carrying containers across the country which were unloaded from a vessel on one side of the country and will be loaded aboard another vessel on the other side. Some land bridge trains operate across both the U.S. and Canada although to date the idea has not been very widely implemented.

by negotiations between the nations involved. Rates are established by the International Air Transport Association (IATA), a large cartel consisting of all the western world's scheduled airlines (with one or two exceptions).[12] The principal function of international airlines is to carry passengers. Freight is a secondary product although a few scheduled airlines use some all-freight aircraft in certain markets. Lufthansa, the German airline, was the first airline in the world to use an all-cargo Boeing 747. It was used in trans-Atlantic service and connected Germany with the northeastern United States. It replaced several smaller planes. Compared with earlier jets, the 747 has enormous capacity. Figure 11-6 shows the difference in capacities of several all-freight configurations and compares them with passenger/freight configurations of the 747 and the McDonnell-Douglas DC-10. Note that the 747 in a passenger/cargo configuration can carry more cargo than the all-cargo versions of the smaller planes. In 1974 several other international (and domestic) airlines acquired some all-cargo 747's although it is difficult to ascertain whether they are being placed into air cargo service because of the demands of the cargo market or because of the lack of demands in the passenger market.

Because of the differences in aircraft cargo compartment shapes, more than 20 different container types are in use, although IATA is reducing the number of different containers styles its members will accept from shippers. Figure 11-7 shows some of the large containers which are in use.

Many containers used by international air lines are smaller; some hold as little as 20 cubic feet. They have several special features required by IATA such as a solid floor (to distribute the weight of the contents evenly), and an air flow device allowing air to flow into and out of the container so that air pressure is not trapped when the plane climbs. Use of these IATA-approved containers reduces charges in three ways. First, they take the place of fiberboard boxes which otherwise would have to be used. Second, the weight of the container is *subtracted* from the weight of the shipment so that the container itself travels free. Third, a rebate—approximately the cost of the container—is given to the shipper; the rebate is subtracted from the freight charges.

For shippers of large quantities, the international airlines offer a "unit-load" incentive in conjunction with some FAK (freight-all-kinds) rates. The airline supplies large pallets and, if necessary, the igloos (a fiberglass pallet cover placed over the load, both to protect it and to insure that it does not exceed the allowable dimensions). To obtain the lower rates from IATA carriers, the shipper must tender the pallet loaded to airline specifications and, at the other end of the journey, the entire pallet must be destined to one consignee. A special charge

[12] See: Richard F. Jansen, "The Airlines' Shaky Cartel," *The Wall Street Journal* (October 15, 1975), p. 22.

Fig. 11-6 Aircraft freight capacity.

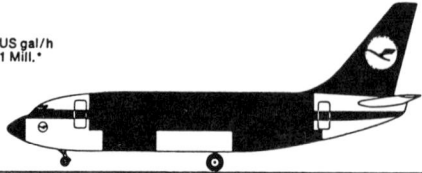

Payload	33 070 lbs
Cargo Volume	3 072 cbft
Cargo Door	86˝ x 134˝
Pallets (88˝ x 125˝)	7 with igloos
Speed	559 m.p.h.
Wing-span	93´-0˝
Length	100´-2˝
Height	37´-0˝

Fuel consumption	865 US gal/h
Basic price	$4.31 Mill. *

737C

Payload	39 903 lbs
Cargo Volume	3 567 cbft
Cargo Door	86˝ x 134˝
Pallets (88˝ x 125˝)	8 with igloos
Speed	578 m.p.h.
Wing-span	108´-8˝
Length	133´-2˝
Height	34´-0˝

Fuel consumption	1110 US gal/h
Basic price	$5.26 Mill. *

727C

Payload	73 276 lbs
Cargo Volume	6 590 cbft
Cargo Door	90˝ x 134˝
Pallets (88˝ x 125˝)	13 with net or igloo
Speed	559 m.p.h.
Wing-span	145´-9˝
Length	145´-6˝
Height	42´-5,5˝

Fuel consumption	1790 US gal/h
Basic price	$7.58 Mill. *

707C

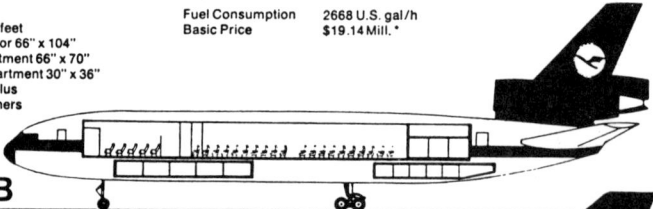

Payload	74,295 lbs
Cargo Volume	3,655 cubic feet
Cargo Door	Forward Door 66˝ x 104˝
	Aft Compartment 66˝ x 70˝
	Bulk Compartment 30˝ x 36˝
Pallets	125˝ x 88˝ plus
	LD3 Containers
Speed	577 mph
Wingspan	161´ 3˝
Length	182´ 0˝
Height	58´ 0˝

Fuel Consumption	2668 U.S. gal/h
Basic Price	$19.14 Mill. *

DC-10MDB

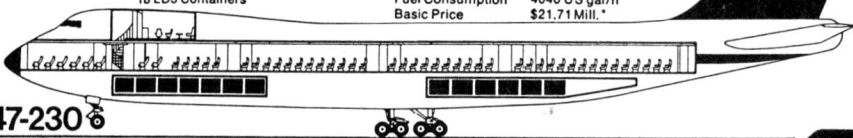

Payload	112,500 lbs.
Cargo Volume	5,550 cubic feet
Cargo Door	8´ 8˝ x 5´ 6˝
Pallets	4 125˝ x 88˝ plus
	18 LD3 Containers

Speed	583 mph
Wingspan	195´ 7˝
Length	231´ 3˝
Height	63´ 4˝
Fuel Consumption	4040 US gal/h
Basic Price	$21.71 Mill. *

747-230

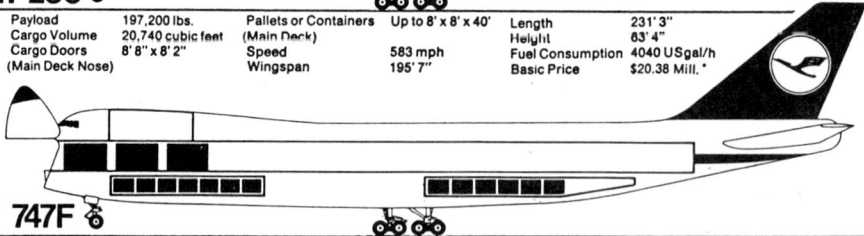

Payload	197,200 lbs.
Cargo Volume	20,740 cubic feet
Cargo Doors	8´ 8˝ x 8´ 2˝
(Main Deck Nose)	

Pallets or Containers (Main Deck)	Up to 8´ x 8´ x 40´
Speed	583 mph
Wingspan	195´ 7˝

Length	231´ 3˝
Height	63´ 4˝
Fuel Consumption	4040 US gal/h
Basic Price	$20.38 Mill. *

747F

*Excluding spare parts.

Courtesy Lufthansa Airlines.

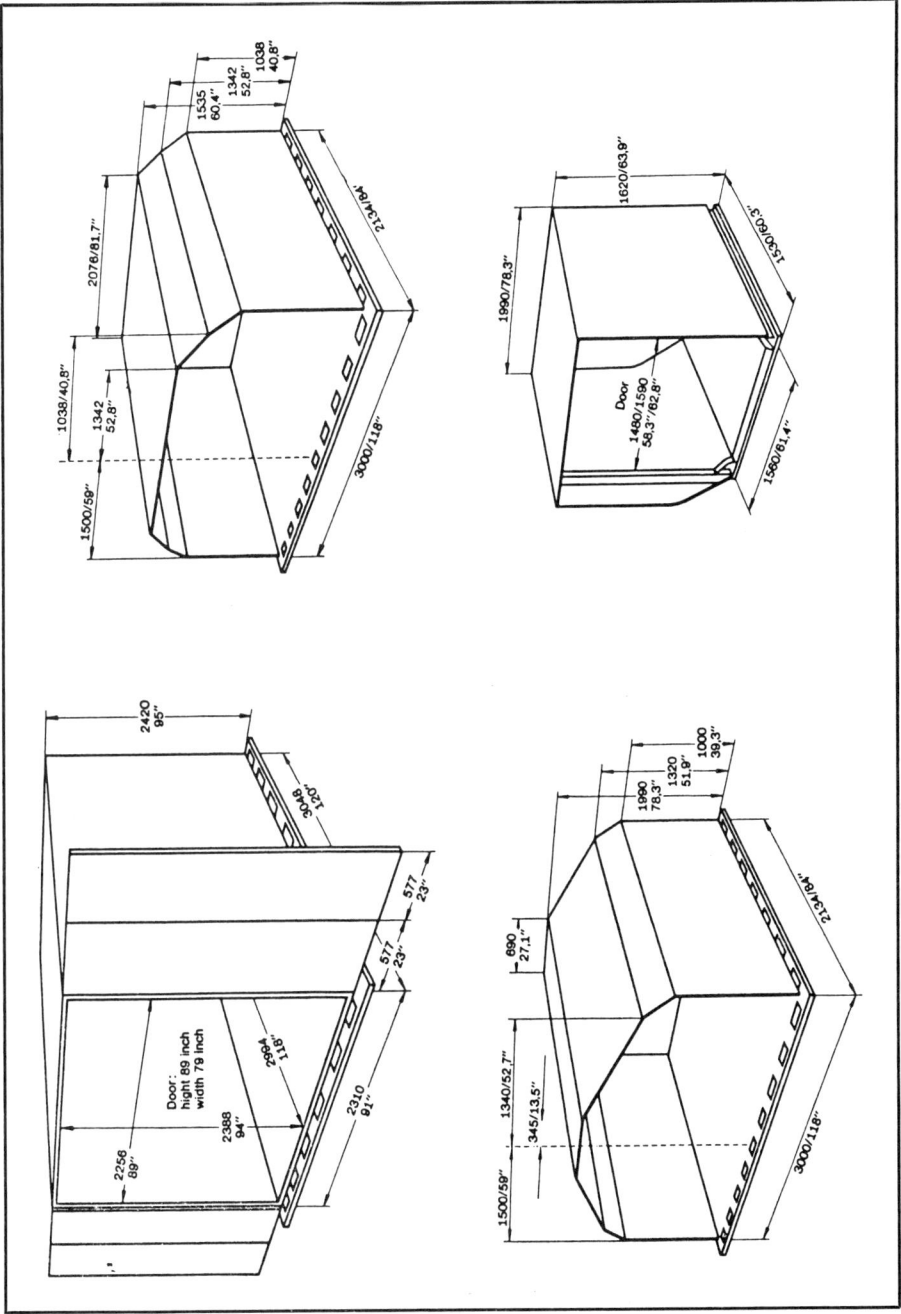

Fig. 11-7 Large airfreight containers.

Courtesy Lufthansa German Airlines.

is made if it is necessary to unload or partially unload the pallet for customs inspection. Both the shipper and the consignee may have the pallet for 48 hours each before demurrage charges are assessed.

The results of the IATA incentives to use containers and unit loads has been to increase the average size of shipments handled by the airlines. This has reduced the number of individual packages each airline terminal must handle. Air freight forwarders have benefitted since they are frequently in a better position than individual shippers to take advantage of incentives offered to larger shipments.*

International air freight forwarders utilize a document entitled "shipper's letter of instructions" which is frequently the only document the shipper need execute. Shippers not utilizing forwarders would need to have their own air waybill prepared. Figure 11-8 shows the air waybill form. Twelve copies of each waybill are prepared.

International air cargo rates are published in tariffs, available from the airlines. There are both general cargo rates and lower specific commodity rates. Rate "breaks" encourage heavier shipments.

OCEAN SHIPPING

In the past decades there have been two significant advances in shipping technology. The first has been much larger vessels. Tankers are now being built which have 30 to 40 times the capacity of the World War II-vintage T-2 tanker! The second change has been in cargo-handling techniques, especially of break-bulk general cargo, which for centuries has been loaded or unloaded on a piece-by-piece basis after being lifted by the ship's boom and tackle.

Types of Ocean Cargoes. Much of the world's shipping tonnage is used for carrying petroleum. Tankers are either owned by the oil companies or else leased (chartered) by them from individuals who invest in ships. Vessels are chartered for either specific voyages or for large blocs of time. The charter market fluctuates widely, especially after events such as the Suez Canal closure or the announcement of U.S. wheat sales to Russia. (Tankers can carry dry cargo, although the reverse is not always true; however, dry cargo and tanker charter rates tend to follow each other.) International commodity traders follow the vessel charter market very closely because they know the differences in commodity prices in different world markets. Whenever the charter rate between these two markets drops to a point where it is less than the spread in the commodity prices, a vessel will be chartered to carry the commodity.

---

* Another alternative for small international shipments is parcel post, by either air or vessel.

FIG. 11-8 International airway bill.

AIR WAYBILL NUMBER		AIRPORT OF DEPARTURE	EXECUTION DATE DAY/MTH/YR	TC	CHGS CODE	CUR'CY CODE	FOR CARRIER USE ONLY	
AIRLINE PREFIX	SERIAL NO.						FLIGHT/DAY	FLIGHT/DAY

131-   131-

AIRPORT OF DEPARTURE (ADDRESS OF FIRST CARRIER) AND REQUESTED ROUTING   AIRPORT OF DESTINATION   FLIGHT/DAY   FLIGHT/DAY

BOOKED

ROUTING AND DESTINATION

1/ TO   BY FIRST CARRIER   TO   BY   TO   BY   TO   BY

NOT NEGOTIABLE
AIR WAYBILL
(AIR CONSIGNMENT NOTE)
ISSUED BY

2/ CONSIGNEE'S ACCOUNT NUMBER   CONSIGNEE'S NAME AND ADDRESS

AIR LINES
MEMBER OF INTERNATIONAL AIR TRANSPORT ASSOCIATION

If the carriage involves an ultimate destination or stop in a country other than the country of departure, the Warsaw Convention may be applicable and the Convention governs and in most cases limits the liability of carriers in respect of loss of or damage to cargo. Agreed stopping places are those places (other than the places of departure and destination) shown under requested routing and/or those places shown in carriers' timetables as scheduled stopping places for the route. Address of first carrier is the airport of departure.
SEE CONDITIONS ON REVERSE HEREOF.

3/ SHIPPER'S ACCOUNT NUMBER   SHIPPER'S NAME AND ADDRESS

The shipper certifies that the particulars on the face hereof are correct and agrees to the CONDITIONS ON REVERSE HEREOF.

SIGNATURE OF SHIPPER

BY BROKER/AGENT

Carrier certifies goods described below were received for carriage subject to the CONDITIONS ON REVERSE HEREOF, the goods then being in apparent good order and condition except as noted hereon.

PHONE:

4/ ISSUING CARRIER'S AGENT, ACCOUNT NO.   ISSUING CARRIER'S AGENT, NAME AND CITY

EXECUTED ON   (Date)   AT   (Place)

AGENT'S IATA CODE

SIGNATURE OF ISSUING CARRIER OR ITS AGENT

Copies 1, 2 and 3 of this Air Waybill are originals and have the same validity.

	CURRENCY	DECLARED VALUE FOR CARRIAGE	DECLARED VALUE FOR CUSTOMS	AMOUNT OF INSURANCE
5/		V	B	E

INSURANCE—If shipper requests insurance in accordance with conditions on reverse hereof, indicate amount to be insured in figures in box marked 'amount of insurance'.

WEIGHT CHARGE AND VALUATION CHARGE   ALL OTHER CHARGES AT ORIGIN

PREPD   COLLECT   PREPD   COLLECT

ACCOUNTING INFORMATION

No. OF PACKAGES RCP	ACTUAL GROSS WEIGHT	kg/ lb.	RATE CLASS	COMMODITY ITEM NO.	CHARGEABLE WEIGHT	RATE/CHARGE	TOTAL	NATURE AND QUANTITY OF GOODS (INCL. DIMENSIONS OR VOLUME)
6/								

THESE COMMODITIES LICENCED BY U.S. FOR ULTIMATE DESTINATION _____ DIVERSION CONTRARY TO U.S. LAW PROHIBITED.

PRE- PAID 7/	PREPAID WEIGHT CHARGE	V	PREPAID VALUATION CHARGE	C	TOTAL OTHER PREPAID CHARGES DUE CARRIER	A	DUE AGENT	P	TOTAL PREPAID

FOR CARRIER'S USE ONLY AT DESTINATION

R   OTHER CHARGES (EXCEPT WEIGHT CHARGE AND VALUATION CHARGE)

COLLECT CHARGES IN DESTINATION CURRENCY

S   COD AMOUNT

T   TOTAL CHARGES

COL- LECT 8/	COLLECT WEIGHT CHARGE	V	COLLECT VALUATION CHARGE	C	TOTAL OTHER COLLECT CHARGES DUE CARRIER	A	DUE AGENT	Z	COD AMOUNT	TOTAL COLLECT

9/

HANDLING INFORMATION

Dry bulk cargoes, such as grain, ores, sulfur, sugar, scrap iron, coal, lumber and logs also usually move in complete vessel-load lots on chartered vessels. Brokers exist who match shippers of large fractional shiploads so they can pool their cargo and fill an entire ship. There are also large specialized dry cargo ships, usually owned by the shipper. Nissan Motor Company of Japan (which manufacturers Datsuns) has eight auto-carrying ships, four of which carry 1,200 Datsuns apiece, the other four can carry 1,900. Most of these vessels carry autos to the U.S. and they load with soybeans for their return voyage. Vessels in general cargo service also carry bulk cargo. A common practice is to "top off" with grain at the last port-of-call. A vessel bound for Europe which has called at various St. Lawrence Seaway ports may be only half-loaded with general cargo. At Montreal, the last port-of-call in North America, the vessel will take whatever general cargo is available and then fill up unused capacity with grain.

Shipping Conferences. Ocean general cargo (or "break-bulk" liner) rates are set by conferences, which are cartels of all vessel operators operating between certain trade areas. Conferences provide stability in markets where cargo offerings fluctuate. They agree to provide relatively regular service and if a shipper agrees to use them exclusively, the shipper pays a rate which is less than will be charged to shippers who do not agree to use the conference regularly. Over 100 different conferences serve U.S. ports. Examples are: the Gulf/UK Conference which handles trade from U.S. Gulf Coast ports to England, Ireland, Scotland, and Wales; and the Israel/U.S. North Atlantic Westbound Conference which handles trade from Israel's Mediterranean ports to U.S. ports from Portland, Maine, to Hampton Roads, Virginia. Some conferences are very stable and well-disciplined, others are not. In the Pacific, for example, a Russian-flag containership operation is not a conference member and is setting rates at levels considerably below those charged by the conference and offering large rebates to forwarders. Some large U.S. firms now use the Russian line.

Tariffs and Rates. Each Conference issues its own tariff. Figure 11-9 is a page from the Pacific Westbound Conference tariff. At the top is the note that rates apply to 2,000 lb. tons (known as a short ton) or 40 cubic feet. The 40 cubic feet is sometimes called a "measurement" ton. However, on this particular sheet, all of the commodities move on a weight basis. The "LT" for baled hay refers to long ton (2240 pounds), which is the measurement used in the trade. There are some "open" and some "open with specified minimum" rates. These are for commodities where the conference is in actual competition with "tramp" or independent vessel operators. The rate is negotiable with shippers, although it cannot go below the specified minimum. The distinction

FIG. 11-9 Page from Ocean Conference tariff.

RATES ON THIS PAGE ARE NOT SUBJECT TO SUPPLEMENT NO. 1	Orig./Rev.	Page
PACIFIC WESTBOUND CONFERENCE LOCAL FREIGHT TARIFF NO. 4 - FMC- 12	7th	158

	Cancels	Page
FROM: Pacific Coast Ports TO: Japan Base Ports (Yokohama, Kobe, Osaka, Nagoya, Tokyo), Manila, Hong Kong, Kaohsiung/Keelung, Busan, Saigon and Bangkok	6th	158
For applicable surcharges see Rule No. 12 and for rates to other ports see Page Nos. 7 through 11	Effective Date	
	August 14, 1975	

Rates are quoted in U.S. Dollars ($). Except as otherwise provided rates apply per 2,000 pounds or 40 cubic feet whichever produces the greater revenue   Corr. No. 1325

COMMODITY	RATE BASIS	JAPAN BASE PORTS	MANILA	HONG KONG	KAOHSIUNG /KEELUNG	BUSAN	SAIGON	BANGKOK	COMMODITY ITEM
		$	$	$	$	$	$	$	
Cereal Straw Cubes	WT C	94.50	86.75	88.25	93.75	88.75	90.25	93.75	081 1100 31
Bulk	WT NC	108.75	99.75	101.50	107.75	102.00	103.75	107.75	
Cereal Straw Cubes in Bulk, in Containers	WT	OPEN MIN. 28.25							081 1100 33
Cereal Straw, Baled	WT	OPEN MIN. 32.00							081 1100 50
Rye Grass Cubes and/or Blocks Bulk	WT	OPEN MIN. 28.25							081 1100 71
SPECIAL RATE (Exp 12/31/75) (R)(R) Rye Grass Cubes and/or Block, In Bulk (R)(R) effective 8/15/75	WT	OPEN MIN. 16.25							081 1100 83
Rye Grass Cubes and/or Blocks Bagged	WT	OPEN MIN. 28.25							081 1100 75
SPECIAL RATE (Exp 12/31/75) (R) Rye Grass Cubes and/or Blocks, Bagged, in Containers Subject to 36,000 lb. min. wt. (R) effective 8/14/75	WT	OPEN MIN. 16.25							081 1100 86
Alfalfa Hay Cubes	WT C	81.25	74.75	76.00	81.75	76.75	78.00	81.50	081 1210 00
	WT C	93.50	86.00	87.50	94.00	88.25	89.75	93.75	
Alfalfa Hay Cubes. Bulk	WT C	OPEN	86.75	88.25	93.75	88.75	90.25	93.75	081 1210 01
	WT NC		99.75	101.75	107.75	102.00	103.75	107.75	
Alfalfa Hay Cubes In Bulk in Containers	WT	OPEN MIN. 24.00							081 1210 23
Hay, Fodder, Roots, Lupines, Vetches & Similar Forage Products, except Alfalfa Hay Cubes, N.O.S.	WT C	63.25	69.00	75.00	76.50	71.00	64.50	80.50	081 1250 00
	WT C	72.75	79.25	86.25	88.00	81.75	74.25	92.50	
SPECIAL RATES (C) (Exp 12/31/75)	WT C			53.25					081 1250 20
	WT NC			61.25					
SPECIAL RATES (C) (Exp 12/31/75) In Bulk in Containers	WT C	58.50							081 1250 63
	WT NC	67.25							
Hay, Baled	LT	OPEN MIN. 41.50							081 1250 50
Applies on shipments compressed to less than 19# per cubic feet									

Courtesy Pacific Westbound Conference.

between "C" and "NC" is that the former rate is paid by shippers who have signed contracts to regularly use the conference. The "NC" rate is higher. Lastly, for "Hay, Fodder, Roots. . .," to Japan, note that the rate is lower if the shipment is containerized. A container is easier for the vessel to load and discharge.

The rates on Figure 11-9 are for cargo originating in Montana, Wyoming, Utah, Arizona and points west, and from Canadian points west of the Manitoba-Saskatschewan boundary. *Ocean* rates on westbound cargo originating from points farther east are *less*. The reason rates from inland points are lower is because of competition from Gulf ports—and Gulf-Pacific conferences—for the same exports.

It is often necessary to "book" space in advance for cargo. A shipper or forwarder looks through listings of vessel sailings or arrivals, such as shown on Figure 11-10, to find the scheduled sailings which is closest to his needs. He then contacts the steamship company or the agent to reserve space. On Figure 11-10, note the phrase "on inducement." It means the vessel will make that call only if a sufficient amount of cargo is involved which will render a profit to the carrier.

Containers. Today, operators of general cargo vessels may never handle, or even see, cargo on a piece-by-piece basis. Their ships are fully containerized which means the only way they can load or unload cargo is to have the cargo stowed inside containers. Shippers or forwarders tender full containers, and if a shipper tenders a less-than-container lot, the vessel operator must load all the less-than-container lots into containers so that the cargo can be loaded aboard the containership. Modern containership technology is less than 20 years old, yet use of containers has grown rapidly. A spokesman for the Port of New York said in 1974: "Already almost 40 percent of the general cargo trade of the Port of New York-New Jersey is moving in containerships or roll-on roll-off ships, and by 1980 the percentage will be substantially higher (possibly over 80%). New, full and partial containerships are on order which will link our port with Singapore and the Straits, with Yugoslavia, the Soviet Union and Poland, and eventually with Brazil and South and East Africa."[13]

In 1973, the New York-New Jersey port handled 899,398 containers, the largest number of any port in the world. Other U.S. ports handling large numbers of containers were San Juan (621,000), Oakland (436,590), Long Beach (361,201), and Seattle (271,428). Ports outside the U.S. which handled more than 250,000 containers apiece in 1973 were Belfast, Bremen/Bremerhaven, Helsingborg, London and Yokohama.[14]

[13] Clifford B. O'Hara, "International Container Movements: Problems and Opportunities, 1974–1980," in *American Society of Traffic and Transportation 1794 Annual Meeting Papers*, p. 131.
[14] *Intermodal World* (July, 1974).

FIG. 11-10 "Sailings" schedule.

Pacific Far East Line
LASH
The Complete American Flag System

EXECUTIVE OFFICES:
One Embarcadero Center,
San Francisco 94111
(415) 576-4000
Cable Address "PACFAREAST"

MINI BULK AND UNITIZED GENERAL CARGO BARGE SERVICE · REEFER AND DRY CONTAINERS · DEEP TANKS · PASSENGERS.

ORIENT SERVICE — OUTBOUND

SAILS: TACOMA, SAN FRANCISCO, LOS ANGELES · ARRIVES: YOKOHAMA … DUBAI

VESSEL / VOY	TACOMA (Loads Arabian Persian Gulf Cargo Only)	SAN FRANCISCO (and Bay Area Ports)	LOS ANGELES	YOKOHAMA (Feeder to Tokyo Bay Ports)	KOBE (Feeder to Osaka Moji Nagoya)	BUSAN (Feeder to Incheon)	KEELUNG	KAOHSIUNG	HONG KONG (Feeder to Bangkok Indonesia Ports)	MANILA (Feeder to Philippine Island Ports)	SINGAPORE (Via Sultan Shoal)	BANDAR ABBAS (And or Bandar Shahpour)	BUSHIRE (On Inducement)	BASRAH	KUWAIT	DAMMAM (Bahrain On Inducement)	DUBAI
THOMAS E. CUFFE ⊕ 28 .●..		3/16	3/14	3/27	....	3/29	4/8	4/7	4/5	4/3	4/22	4/29	4/30	5/3	5/2	5/4	5/5
PACIFIC BEAR ●▲ 26	....	3/26	3/28	4/9	4/11	4/12	4/14	4/15	4/16	4/19	4/22	4/29	4/30	5/3	5/2	5/4	5/5
JAPAN BEAR ⊕ 27	4/9	4/12	4/15	4/27	....	4/29	5/1	5/2	5/3	5/6	5/26	6/2	6/3	6/6	6/5	6/7	6/8
THOMAS E. CUFFE ● 29	4/24	5/2	4/27	5/13	5/15	5/16	5/18	5/19	5/20	5/23	5/26	6/2	6/3	6/6	6/5	6/7	6/8
GOLDEN BEAR ⊕ 26	5/5	5/8	5/10	5/22	....	5/24	5/26	5/27	5/28	5/31	6/24	7/1	7/2	7/5	7/4	7/6	7/7

* VESSELS CALL PORT KELANG, PENANG, BASRAH, BAHREIN ON INDUCEMENT.
⊕ CARGO FOR MALAYSIA & ARABIAN PERSIAN GULF PORTS WILL BE RELAYED AT MANILA.
● CALLS TACOMA ON INDUCEMENT. ▲ CALLS VANCOUVER MAR 23.

ORIENT SERVICE — INBOUND

SAILS: BANDAR ABBAS … TACOMA · ARRIVES: SAN FRANCISCO, LOS ANGELES

VESSEL / VOY	BANDAR ABBAS (And or Bandar Shahpour)	BUSHIRE (On Inducement)	BASRAH	KUWAIT	DAMMAM (Bahrain On Inducement)	DUBAI	SINGAPORE (Via Sultan Shoal)	MANILA (Feeder From Philippine Island Ports)	HONG KONG (Feeder From Bangkok Indonesia Ports)	KAOHSIUNG	KEELUNG	BUSAN (Feeder From Incheon)	KOBE (Feeder From Osaka Moji Nagoya)	YOKOHAMA (Feeder From Shimizu Tokyo Bay Ports)	TACOMA (Discharges Arabian Persian Gulf Cargo Only)	SAN FRANCISCO (and Bay Area Ports)	LOS ANGELES
THOMAS E. CUFFE 569	2/18	2/9	....	2/13	2/17	....	....	....	2/29	....	....	.●..	3/3	3/4	.△..	3/15	3/13
PACIFIC BEAR 25	....	....	....	....	....	....	....	3/5	3/7	3/9	3/10	.●..	3/13	3/15	.▲..	3/25	3/27
JAPAN BEAR ⊕ 26	3/6	3/7	3/10	3/10	3/12	3/13	3/21	3/24	3/26	3/27	3/29	.●..	3/30	4/1	4/9	4/11	4/13
THOMAS E. CUFFE 28	....	....	....	....	....	....	....	4/4	4/6	4/7	4/9	.●..	4/11	4/13	4/21	4/28	4/26
GOLDEN BEAR ⊕ 25	3/29	3/31	3/31	4/2	4/3	4/4	4/15	4/18	4/20	4/21	4/23	.●..	4/25	4/27	5/5	5/8	5/10

* VIA FEEDER SERVICE FOR CONNECTION AT KOBE.
⊕ CALLS PENANG & PORT KELANG ON INDUCEMENT.
△ ON INDUCEMENT. ▲ CALLS VANCOUVER MAR 23.

THROUGH BILLS OF LADING
TO INDONESIA,
INDIA, PAKISTAN, AND
SOUTHEAST ASIA PORTS.

Courtesy Pacific Far East Line.

As is the case of international air shipments, forwarders have benefited from containerization since sometimes only they can consolidate sufficient cargo to enjoy the full advantages of container usage. Containerization is not developing evenly since many small ports are unable to afford the large investment in shoreside handling facilities, or else because the economy served by the port does not handle cargo of the volume or type which is suitable for containers. One example is the string of U.S. and Canadian Great Lakes ports served by the St. Lawrence Seaway. Relatively small ocean vessels call at numerous ports, discharging or taking on very small tonnages of cargo at each one. The same traffic patterns exist at port areas on the other end of the journey. The entire scale of operations is too small to benefit from containerships. Container facilities are also slow in being adopted by less-developed nations.

LASH vessels handle floating containers and can be used most advantageously in areas where the central port is connected to inland areas by shallow waterways. Similar conditions must exist on both ends of the voyage, and this limits somewhat the applicability of the system. LASH barges are approximately 60 feet long, 30 feet wide, and 13 feet deep, or about 20,000 cubic feet. They carry about 400 short tons. The LASH concept is relatively new, and its success is still being evaluated.

Other Handling Methods. The picture at the beginning of this chapter shows farm tractors lined up to be loaded aboard a RO-RO (Roll-on Roll-off) vessel. RO-RO vessels have large doors in the stern through which trailers and equipment on wheels can be moved. Very little is needed in terms of shoreside handling equipment.

Because of the difference in shoreside handling facilities some vessel operators are building "combo" ships with facilities for both vertical lift on and off of cargo as well as horizontal RO-RO facilities. "Considered something of a freak only five years ago, these hybrid ships are now being delivered from shipyards all over the world. And many owners see the Combo as a panacea for all the great differences in the standard of facilities at individual ports. A typical outfit of access equipment for such a ship may include stern door/ramp, internal hoistable ramps, car decks, elevator, weather and 'tweendeck hatch covers, bulkhead doors, and side doors."[15]

SURFACE TRANSPORT IN OTHER COUNTRIES

The quality of transport facilities in foreign nations varies. Some are as well developed as they are in the United States. Two rather uni-

---

[15] "Shipboard Access Equipment," *Fairplay International Shipping Weekly* (July 18, 1974), p. 45.

versal differences should be pointed out. First, few foreign nations have as wide a range of modes from which to choose. The reason is that in the United States an effort is made to allow all modes of transportation to exist.[16] Second, the degree of nationalization of transportation is higher in most foreign countries than in the U.S. In the Republic of South Africa, the "railroad, which is the government, won't permit anything to move by road that could be brought by rail . . . . Not only does a shipper or consignee have to submit documentary proof that his freight could not be moved by rail in order to use a for-hire trucker —he has to do the same thing if he wants to operate the private carriage!"[17]

The widespread use of seaborne containers has brought about hopes of standardizing land vehicles for carrying containers on the landward legs of their journey. The European Common Market has been making progress in its attempt to standardize truck dimensions within all its member countries. Rail equipment sizes vary throughout the world with most nations using equipment much smaller than is used in the U.S. Frequently containers which can be loaded "two-to-a-railcar" in the U.S. are carried on individual rail cars elsewhere.

One of the difficulties in implementing international transport technological improvements is that fairly identical handling equipment must be in place at each end of the trip. In some parts of the world, grain and sugar are still stowed or unloaded by stevedores carrying individual bags on their shoulders and walking up and down gangplanks.

The incidence (or burden) of costs is also significant. "RO-RO" shipping involves the use of trailers rather than containers to be carried aboard ship. The trailers (or other wheeled vehicles) are driven aboard the ship as though it were a large ferry boat. Once loaded, there is considerable waste space—essentially the height of each trailer box above the deck floor. Hence, a vessel cannot carry as much cargo within a given amount of space. Yet, the required port facilities are relatively inexpensive; there need only be a ramp for driving the trailers on or off the ship. The trailers can be hitched to tractors and hauled directly to or from their landward destination. So, while more is spent per ton of cargo on vessel operation, less is spent for port operations. For the system to work, there must be similar facilities at both ends of the voyage. Vessel lines can sometimes force a port to add cargo-handling equipment by placing a surcharge against the port for all shipments until such equipment is installed.

[16] The U.S. Transportation Act of 1940 requires The Interstate Commerce Commission "to recognize and preserve the inherent advantages of each" mode of transport.

[17] John T. McCullough, "Africa," *Distribution Worldwide* (October 1973), pp. 69–70.

INTERNATIONAL TRADE INVENTORIES

Under the best of conditions, the flow of products in an international distribution channel will never be as smooth as a comparable domestic flow. There will always be additional uncertainties, misunderstandings, and delays. Safety stocks must be larger. Montgomery Ward's domestic warehouses turn their inventories about five times per year while their two coastal warehouses, which handle only imported products, turn their inventories three times per year. The main reason they cannot achieve a faster flow is the wider variance in the performance of their overseas suppliers.[18]

Most nations represent smaller potential marketing areas than will be found in the United States; hence, the inventory necessary to serve any one of them will be smaller. One cannot assume that an inventory held in one nation can serve the needs of markets in neighboring nations because there may be minor, but significant variations in the specifications of the product that can be sold in each country. Duties may have to be paid each time a product crosses a national boundary, although frequently there is a provision for "duty-drawbacks" which means that all (or nearly all) of a duty will be rebated if the imported product is exported, usually within a specified time period of its initial entry. Recall from the discussion concerning free trade zones that one of their advantages is that duties do not have to be paid until the goods leave the zone and enter into the importing nation's economy. Goods in a free trade zone could be shipped to a third nation with less involved paperwork than if they had already passed through the customs of the second nation.

Warehouses in many nations are as sophisticated as they are in the United States. In some countries, mechanized, high-rise storage systems are more common than in the U.S. because land values are much higher, forcing the upward development. Warehousing service for articles moving in foreign trade are handled by "total distribution" companies which are a combination of "public warehousemen, multi-mode carriers, freight forwarders, consolidators, insurance brokers and customs agents. Our regulatory and anti-trust laws do not allow such full-service companies to exist in the United States."[19]

"Return" items are virtually impossible to accommodate in an international distribution operation, especially if the return involves movement of the goods across a national boundary. This has some implications to a firm which is trying to achieve a high level of customer service standards on an international basis since it may be unreasonable to tell buyers to return a defective item to the factory where it was

[18] Interview with W.E. Scholz, Traffic Manager, Wards Import Center, Oakland, September 25, 1974.

[19] "Warehousing Overseas," *Distribution Worldwide* (October 1974), pp. 59–65.

built. One U.S. retail chain tells its stores to deal directly with domestic producers with questions regarding product defects. However, for imported products, there is no recourse. The stores are told to either destroy them or sell them at "salvage" prices.

Inventory valuation is difficult on an international scale since the relative values of various currencies continue to change. Import and export quotas affect values of inventories. The value of wheat held in a nation's grain elevators may be the world market price until the government places an embargo on wheat exports (or imports). The value of the wheat within the nation then becomes the domestic price. In times when a nation's (or the world's) currency is unstable, investments in inventories rise because they are believed to be less risky than holding cash or securities.

SUMMARY

International physical distribution is sufficiently complicated that most firms rely on outside "specialists" to assist them. A prime reason is the paperwork involved and also because of changing rules and regulations of every nation with which trade is conducted. Examples of specialists are international freight forwarders and custom-house brokers.

Many nations have physical distribution systems which are as sophisticated as found in the United States. However, transfer of goods between any two countries is difficult and one cannot assume that an inventory in one nation can be shifted to meet the needs of a neighboring market.

Aside from trade with Canada and Mexico, U.S. foreign trade moves aboard ocean vessels or aircraft. Both types of carriers are increasing their use of containers, making it more necessary for shippers to deal in container-size lots. The carriers' insistence on container-size lots has helped the international freight forwarders since they are often in a better position to assemble larger lots of cargo.

Air freight has had a profound effect on international commerce since it has shrunk time distances around the globe. International air freight rates are established by a cartel, the International Air Transport Association (IATA).

Vessel rates on general cargo are also set by cartels, known as shipping conferences. Shippers who agree to use a conference exclusively receive lower rates.

QUESTIONS FOR DISCUSSION AND REVIEW

1. At the beginning of the chapter, Henry Wegner is quoted as saying "international distribution is truly an octopus." Do you agree with him? Why or why not?

2. What are some documents which are required in international trade but are not required for domestic transactions?

3. Why are international freight forwarders needed? What functions do they perform?

4. How are transportation rates for international shipments set?

5. Why are international air carriers and vessel operators using more containers? What impact does this have on the individual shipper?

6. What is a land bridge? a mini-land bridge?

7. What is the measurement ton? How is it used?

8. How are international freight forwarders compensated?

9. Why do developing nations prefer that their own citizens rather than foreigners be employed in new industries?

10. Why should international shipments be insured? What is especially unique about the need for insuring cargo on vessels?

11. What services do export management firms perform?

12. What are the differences between managing an inventory of goods for *domestic* consumption and goods destined for *international* consumption?

13. What functions do import brokers perform?

14. How are "irrevocable letters of credit" used in international transactions?

15. Why do governments exert considerable control over international trade?

16. How does the Russian merchant fleet serve the Russian economy?

17. How does export packing differ from packing for domestic shipment?

18. What are "export" and "import" rates charged by U.S. railroads and truckers? How and why do they differ from domestic rates?

19. What is IATA?

CASE 11-1   JOYFUL LAMP COMPANY

Located in Woodstock, New York where it was founded in the late 1960's by several individuals who had attended the Woodstock festival, Joyful Lamp Company made glass lamp globes. In 1973 it introduced a new style of lamp globe which was shaped like a cube, ten inches on each side. They called it the "cubic globe." Sales of the cubic globe went slowly until 1975 when three different architectural magazines showed the interiors of new buildings which were decorated with the lamps. Inquiries then came in from architects, designers, and decorators throughout the world.

An order for 1800 cubic globes accompanied by a large certified check was received from a well-known European construction firm which was building a new governmental palace for an oil-rich middle-east nation.

A letter accompanying the order said that the purchaser would charter a 747 all-freight airplane to carry various materials that were being purchased in the New York area for use in the palace. The 747 would load at a New York airport in about 25 days.

The letter continued, in part, "from pictures it appears that your globes are perfect cubes and are approximately ten inches along an edge. We need to know how many airline type AQA containers (interior dimensions: 244 centimeters wide by 318 centimeters long by 244 centimeters high) will be required. Please inform our New York office as to the number of containers which will be needed."

The lamp globes were packed in cartons and the cartons would be stored in the AQA container. Each carton was one cubic foot.

Question One: How many AQA containers will be required to hold the 1800 cartons of the cubic globes?

CASE 11-2 HDT TRUCK COMPANY

HDT Truck Company is a small firm located in Crown Point, Indiana, and its only product is large trucks, built to individual customer specifications. HDT had been located in Crown Point since 1910. The firm once produced automobiles and light trucks as well, but dropped out of the auto business in 1924 and out of the light truck business in 1937. The firm nearly went completely out of business at that time but by 1940 its fortunes were buoyed by receipt of several military contracts for "tank retrievers," large wheeled vehicles that could pull a disabled tank onto a low trailer and haul it to a location where it could be repaired.

Since World War II, HDT manufactured only large "off-the-road" vehicles, including airport snowplows, airport crash trucks, oil field drilling equipment and the like. HDT purchased all components from small manufacturers who were still clustered in the Milwaukee-Detroit-Toledo-Cleveland area. Essentially, all HDT did was assemble the components into a specialized vehicle containing the combination of frame, power plant, transmission, axles, cab, etc., which was necessary to do the job.

The "assembly" line was relatively slow moving. After wheels were attached to the frame and axles, the night shift labor force would push the chassis along to its next "station" on the line so it would be in place for the next day's shift. By using one shift, two trucks could be assembled each day. If large orders for identical trucks were involved, it was possible to assemble three trucks per day. Quality declined whenever the pace became quicker. HDT officials had decided they could not grow and became satisfied with their niche in the very heavy truck market. With only two exceptions, since 1960 they had always had at least a four-month backlog of orders. In the 1960's, their best market had been airports, but since 1970 their best market had been for oil field equipment, first for the North Slope in Alaska and then for the Middle East.

In late 1975, HDT received an order for 50 heavy trucks to be used in the oil fields of Iraq. The terms of sale were delivery on or before July 1, 1976, at the port of Al Basrah, Iraq. Specifically, HDT would receive $52,000 per truck in U. S. funds F.A.S. (free along side) the discharging vessel in Al Basrah, which meant HDT was responsible for all transportation costs up until the time and point the trucks were discharged from the ship's tackle at Al Basrah. Once each truck was unloaded, HDT would be paid for it.

Chris Reynolds, production manager at HDT, estimated that production could start approximately April 1, 1976, and the order would take 18 working days to complete. Since weekends were involved, the entire 50 trucks would be completed by April 20–25. Reynolds thought that May 1, 1976, was a more realistic completion date because he had always found it difficult to restrict the assembly line to constructing trucks for only one account. The reason for this was that Vic Guillou, HDT's sales manager, liked to have trucks being built for as many accounts as possible on the assembly line at any one time. Prospective buyers frequently visited the plant and were always more impressed when they could see a diverse collection of models being built for a wide range of uses.

Norman Pon, HDT's treasurer, always wanted to give priority to building trucks that were being sold on an F.O.B. plant basis since that would improve his cash flow position. At the time the $52,000 price had been set on the truck sale to Iraq, Pon had argued (unsuccessfully) that the price was too low. Guillou, on the other hand, argued that the sale was necessary since the Arab world represented a "growth market" by anyone's definition and he wanted HDT trucks there. HDT's president, Gordon Robertson, had sided with Guillou. Robertson thought that Pon was a good treasurer but too much of a "worrier" when it came to making important decisions. Pon, in turn, thought that Robertson had yet to shed the "playboy" image he had acquired in the 1960's when his late father was president of HDT. Pon had lost count of the number of times the elder Robertson had needed cash in order to buy his son's way out of some embarrassing situation. Guillou was young Robertson's fraternity roommate in college and Pon thought the two of them shared similar defects in character.

At the time the order was signed in 1975, Guillou argued that the F.A.S. destination port represented the best terms of sale since ocean charter rates were declining in 1975. This was because of an oversupply of tanker tonnage and the reopening of the Suez Canal. Guillou predicted that by mid-1976, charter rates would be so low that the cheapest method of transport would be to load all 50 trucks on one vessel. Pon countered that HDT should try to make a profit only from the manufacture of trucks since nobody in the firm knew much about ocean shipping. Robertson, who was a gambler at heart, of course, disagreed.

It was now March, 1976, and Reynolds had the fifty truck order scheduled to be on the line from April 2 to April 29 which represented 2½ trucks per working day. Other work was scheduled for the assembly line at the same time so the production schedule was considered to be "firm." Component parts for the oil field trucks and for the other trucks were already arriving. Right now, orders were backlogged for over seven months, the highest figure since 1967. This was due, almost in total, to Guillou's additional sales of oil field equipment to Arab producers. Three separate orders were involved and totalled 115 trucks.

Robertson and Guillou left Crown Point for an industry convention in San Diego. Robertson phoned from San Diego that he and Guillou had decided to vacation in Mexico for a while before returning to Crown Point. Robertson knew that HDT could function in his absence and knew that with Pon "watching the store," the company's assets would be safe. Several days later, a Mexican postcard postmarked "Tijuana" arrived saying that both were enjoying Mexico and might stay longer than initially planned.

Pon was relieved to learn that Guillou and Robertson would be gone for a longer time and immediately began wondering what types of bills they were accumulating in Mexico and for which ones they would want company reimbursement. Both had several credit cards belonging to the company. Based on experience, Pon also expected Robertson to phone for cash about once a week. As usual, Pon started wondering how paying for the Robertson/Guillou vacation venture would affect HDT's cash flow. Pon looked at his cash flow projections, which were always made up for six weeks in advance, in this case through the first of April when some of the bills for components of the oil-field trucks would come due. In fact, if Reynolds' schedule were adhered to, all the components would be on hand by April 10 and, if HDT were to receive the customary discounts, all of the components would have to be paid for in the period between April 8 and April 20 (HDT received a one percent discount for goods paid for within 10 days of actual or requested receipt, whichever came later). For a moment, Pon thought that the worst might happen, i.e., the component bills would be due the same time as Robertson's and Guillou's travel bill, so he called the Crown Point Bank and Trust Company, where HDT had a line of credit, and found that the current rate was 10 percent per annum. He then asked Bob Vanderpool, who was HDT's traffic manager, when the oil field trucks would arrive in Iraq.

"I don't know," was Vanderpool's reply. "I assumed Guillou had arranged for transportation at the time you decided to charge $52,000 per truck. But I'll check further." He did and phoned back to tell **Pon** that Guillou's secretary could find nothing in the files to indicate that Guillou had checked out charter rates.

"That figures," muttered Pon, "would you mind doing some checking?"

Vanderpool said yes he would mind doing some checking. Pon then suggested to him that there were several other newer orders also destined for the Arab countries, so Vanderpool should start thinking about widening his area of expertise. Vanderpool reluctantly agreed and **Pon** heard nothing from him for a few days until Vanderpool passed him in the hall and said the assignment was much more time-consuming than he had imagined.

One week later, Vanderpool said he had done as much as he could and would turn the figures over to Pon. He also said that he (Vanderpool) did not have the authority to charter a ship and suggested that Pon determine who could, in Robertson's absence. Later that day, Vanderpool came to Pon's office with a thick file. "It looks like you've been doing a lot of figuring," said Pon.

"No, not me," said Vanderpool, "but two outsiders. One is Bob Guider, an international freight forwarder in Chicago who we use for our export parts shipments. And he put me in touch with Eddie Quan, a New York ship broker who is on top of the charter market. We have two alternatives."

"What are they?" asked Pon.

"Well," answered Vanderpool, "the St. Lawrence Seaway will open in mid-April so we could use it. The problem is that the Seaway route is circuitous, especially to reach the Arab countries. Also, there aren't many scheduled Seaway sailings to that area, and since the Seaway will just be opening again, cargo space is hard to come by. Therefore, if we're not going to charter a ship, the best bet is to use Baltimore."

"What about chartering a ship?" asked Pon, "why not use Baltimore for that?"

"In theory, we could," answered Vanderpool, "but Quan says the size ship we want is rather small and not likely to be sailing into Baltimore. We could arrange to 'share' a ship with another party but many bulk cargos are pretty dusty and might not be compatible with our machinery. Quan says there is one foreign vessel entering into the Great Lakes in April which is still looking for an outbound charter. Seaway vessels, you know, are somewhat smaller because of the lock restrictions. If we want to charter that vessel, we'll have to move quickly, because if somebody else charters her, she's gone."

"What kind of vessel is it?" asked Pon.

"The vessel's name is the NOLA PINO, the same name as a French movie actress in the 1960's. You may recall that some Greek shipping magnate named the vessel after her but later his wife made him give up both Nola Pino the actress and Nola Pino the ship. At present, she's scheduled to be in Chicago the last week in April with a load of cocoa beans and ready for outbound loading May 1. Quan thinks we could charter her for $1,200 per day for 30 days which would be enough time for her to load, transit the Seaway, reach Al Basrah, and discharge the trucks by May 29th or 30th."

"Tell me about the alternative," said Pon.

"Baltimore has fairly frequent sailings to the area we want to reach," said Vanderpool. "We could load two trucks per day on rail cars here and send them to Baltimore. There are two ships a week scheduled from Baltimore to Al Basrah. It would take the trucks an average of four days to reach Baltimore where they would wait an average of three days to be loaded aboard ship. The figure should be $3\frac{1}{2}$ days but the railroad will hustle if they know we're trying to connect with an outgoing sailing. Sailing time to Al Basrah averages 15 days, a little more, a little less, depending on the amount of cargo to be handled at ports in between."

"That averages to 22 days per truck," stated Pon who had been putting the figures in his new pocket calculator. "What are the charges?"

Vanderpool answered: "It costs $60 to load and block two trucks on a flatcar, which is, of course, $30 apiece as long as they move in pairs. Sticking to pairs, the rail rate for two on a flatcar totals $896 to Baltimore. Handling at Baltimore is $100 per truck and the ocean freight rate from Baltimore to Al Basrah is $720 per truck. We also have to buy insurance which is about $75 per truck."

"That totals $1,395," said Pon, after consulting his calculator, "what are the costs if we charter the NOLA PINO? You said it would be $36,000 for the vessel. What else is involved?"

"There are two ways of getting the trucks to port," said Vanderpool. "There are no 'export' rates to Chicago but the domestic ones aren't so bad. The loading and blocking would be only $20 per truck because we'd be doing all 50 at one time. The rail rate per truck would average out to $90 each and it would take one day for them to reach Chicago and another day to be loaded. We'd be tying up a wharf for one day and the wharfage charge runs $1 per foot and the NOLA PINO is 535 feet long. We'd be responsible for loading and stowing the cargo and this would cost $4,000 for all 50 trucks. The Seaway tolls are 90 cents per ton or, in our case, $27 per truck. At Al Basrah, the unloading costs will be $2,100 for the entire vessel. Marine insurance will be $105 per truck."

"Are there any other alternatives?" asked Pon.

"The only other one that came close was to drive the trucks from here to Chicago," answered Vanderpool. "We would have needed temporary licenses and a convoy permit and pay to have the fuel tank on each truck drained before it was loaded. The problem was that the

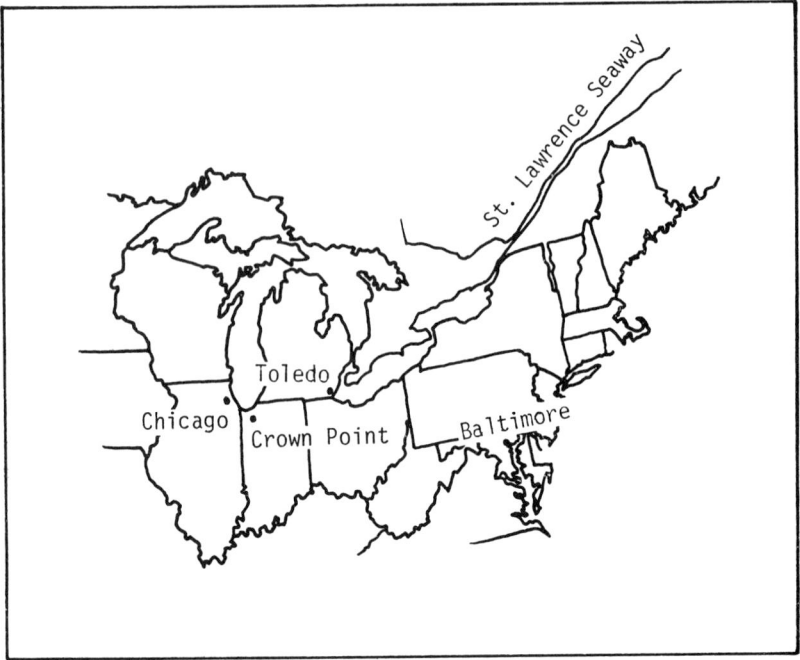

convoy would cross state lines and we would have needed temporary licenses and permits in Illinois as well."

"Do me one favor," said Pon. "Please call Frank Wood, our outside counsel, and ask him what steps we have to go through to charter a ship. Tell him I'm especially concerned about liability. Give him Quan's phone number. I want to make sure there are no more costs involved. Secondly, if Robertson's fooling around is on schedule, he'll be phoning me asking that I cable cash. I'd really appreciate it if you would summarize what you've told me in two columns, with the charter costs on the left and the overland-Baltimore cost column on the right. Then when Robertson calls, I can ask him to decide."

"One question," asked Vanderpool.

"Shoot," responded Pon.

"Why should the charter figures be on the left?"

"Because on a map, Chicago is to the left of Baltimore and that's the only way I'll keep them straight when I'm talking on the phone."

Question One: Assume you are Vanderpool. Draft out the comparison Pon just asked for.

Question Two: Which routing of the two would you recommend? Why?

CHAPTER REFERENCES

AGAPOS, A. M.; "Government Legislation and the Shipbuilding Industry," *Journal of Business Research* (July, 1974), pp. 311–324.

ATHAY, ROBERT E.; *The Economics of Soviet Merchant-Shipping Policy* (Chapel Hill, University of North Carolina Press, 1971).

BARNET, RICHARD and Ronald Muller; "Global Reach," *The New Yorker* (December 2, 1974).

BUSH, WILLIAM L.; "Steamship Conference Contract Rate Agreements and the Dual Rate System," *ICC Practitioners' Journal* (November-December, 1972), pp. 14–27.

DENSMORE, MAX L., and Wesley E. Patton; III, *A Selected and Annotated Bibliography on International Physical Distribution* (University, Ala.: University of Alabama Graduate School of Business, 1973).

DICER, GARY N.; *International Logistics: Elements of a Firm's Physical Distribution System* (Knoxville, Tenn.: University of Tennessee College of Business Administration, 1971).

Distribution Worldwide (October, 1973).

DOWD, LAURENCE P.; *Principles of World Business* (Boston: Allyn and Bacon, 1965).

GILL, LYNN E.; "Beware of Booby Traps in Multinational Distribution," *Handling and Shipping* (March, 1976).

GROSSMAN, HOWARD; "Almost Everything You Should Know About International Distribution," *Handling and Shipping* (March, 1976).

HEAVER, TREVOR D.; "Trans-Pacific Trade, Liner Shipping, and Conference Rates," *The Logistics and Transportation Review* (Volume 8, Number 2), pp. 3–28.

Intermodal World (July, 1974).

JANSEN, RICHARD F.; "The Airlines' Shakey Cartel," *The Wall Street Journal* (October 15, 1975).

Japan's Import and Export Regulations, Japan External Trade Organization (Tokyo, 1974).

KILGOUR, JOHN G.; "The Cargo Preference Program and the Cabotage Restrictions: Effectiveness and Cost," *Transportation Journal* (Spring, 1976), pp. 63–73.

McCULLOUGH, JOHN T.; "Africa," *Distribution Worldwide* (October, 1973).

MALLEN, BRUCE; "Marketing Channels and Economic Development: A Literature Overview," *International Journal of Physical Distribution* (1975).

MOYER, R. CHARLES and Harold Handerson; "A Critique of the Rationales for Present U. S. Maritime Programs," *Transportation Journal* (Winter, 1974), pp. 5–16.

O'HARA, CLIFFORD B.; "International Container Movements: Problems and Opportunities, 1974–1980," *American Society of Traffic and Transportation 1974 Annual Meeting Papers.*

Pacific Traffic (November, 1974).

"Shipboard Access Equipment," *Fairplay International Shipping Weekly* (July 18, 1974).

"Warehousing Overseas," *Distribution Worldwide* (October, 1974).

WATERS, L. L.; "Complications of Common and Charter Operations by U. S. Shipping Lines," *Transportation Journal* (Fall, 1971), pp. 29–35.

WATERS, ROBERT C.; "Role Crisis in America's Ports?" *Transportation Journal* (Winter, 1974), pp. 37–40.

WEBB, CAROL D.; "Rail Export-Import Rates and Steamship Overland Rates Via the Pacific Coast," *Transportation Journal* (Winter, 1970), pp. 8–19.

Part Three.

Analyzing, Designing, and Implementing a Physical Distribution System

The previous eleven chapters presented an overview of physical distribution and focused upon the various individual components of the physical distribution department. Part III will examine methods of analyzing and implementing the physical distribution concept in a firm.

Chapter 12 focuses upon the techniques involved in physical distribution system analysis and design. These techniques are designed to isolate inefficiencies in a firm's physical distribution activities, in order that corrective action can be taken.

Among the most frustrating and challenging aspects of physical distribution management are the problems inherent in the organization and implementation of an integrated physical distribution department. Chapter 13 discusses the various alternative organizational strategies and the circumstances under which each should be implemented.

Chapter 14 examines physical distribution control systems designed to insure that established efficiency standards are being maintained. The final chapter speculates on the many problems and opportunities that are likely to confront the physical distribution manager in the future.

Leaving this container unit on the floor of the supermarket where customers will pick out their cartons of soft drinks saves an entire shelf-stocking operation. *Credit:* Interthor Inc., Broadview, Illinois.

CHAPTER TWELVE

Physical Distribution System Analysis and Design

Although I cannot say that except for this lost . . . tonnage, Third Army might have reached the Rhine early in September, it is fair to assume that Patton would have gone farther than he did. With it he might possibly have pushed on past Metz and into the Saar. Three months and many casualties later we were to be forcefully reminded that in war, opportunity once forsaken is opportunity lost forever.

—GENERAL OF THE ARMY OMAR BRADLEY
A Soldier's Story, 1951

The distribution audit is a continuing measure of performance of products, personnel, profits, and potentials. The rewards for this kind of management effectiveness range from sheer company survival to increasing a share of the market.

—J. H. MINER
Handling and Shipping
April, 1971

WHY ANALYSIS IS NECESSARY

Analysis of physical distribution activity is used to determine whether improvements can be made. Since few things in the business world are static, a system that optimized yesterday's situation may be less than optimal today. For example, changes in the price of fuel have changed the relative transportation costs paid out by distribution operations. Markets are constantly shifting; even public utilities do not consider their demand patterns to be fixed.

As used here, the phrase "systems analysis" means an orderly and planned observation of one or more segments in the physical distribution network to determine how well each segment and, ultimately, the entire system is functioning. The observations provide data which will be subjected to statistical analysis. In some situations, the next step would be to incorporate the data into programmed "models" of the physical distribution network. A model *simulates* some "real-world" condition to determine how well the present system, or a contemplated system, would respond to various happenings. Based on the simulation and other analytical analysis performed, the final procedure may involve redesigning the entire physical distribution system. "Return on Investment" analysis might also be used to determine how well each existing (and proposed) investment in distribution facilities would pay off.

Many firms have staff personnel who conduct "systems analysis" projects anywhere in the firm. Other firms prefer to use outside consultants because this is the type of problem where outside help may be more objective. While consultants vary in quality, they can bring outside viewpoints and broader perspectives to bear on most problems.

Analysis can be a simple operation, such as a "time and motion" study of individuals who handle incoming freight at a receiving dock. Or, it can be nationwide, or even worldwide, in scope, with the idea of completely redesigning a firm's physical distribution system. Such a study would be expensive.

PROBLEMS INVOLVED IN SYSTEMS ANALYSIS

Focusing on a physical distribution system analysis or audit is difficult. What should be the focus of the analysis? The work practices at the receiving dock, or the dock's location in the building, or the building's location in the system? Are the products being handled properly? Are customer service standards adequate, or should the order processing function be automated? The types of analyses which could be performed are limited only by the analyst's imagination and the amount of money his firm or client is willing to spend for the analysis.

Another problem of focus deals with the time-span over which possible improvement proposals will be implemented. Some improvements might deal only with specific adjustments within the network without altering the network itself. Ordering procedures or packaging may be changed, or a decision might be made to link all warehouses by computers. More basic changes, such as changes in the number and location of distribution centers and warehouses, take more time to implement. There might be a period of overlap when the old system is being phased out while the new one is being phased in. Maintaining levels of customer service in such a period may be difficult. Long-range changes (taking from two to five years to implement) would result from decisions to overhaul and redesign a firm's entire distribution system.

Friction is inherent in any attempt to analyze and/or redesign a distribution system. Operations managers are typically performing as well as they can. Systems analysts, whether employees of the firm or outside consultants, cannot continue in business by telling every client that all aspects of his or her present operation are perfect. If analysts did so, they could no longer justify their own retention. Hence their goals and the goals of operating personnel and operating managers differ. Labor may view with suspicion any suggestion that appears to be a "speed-up" or which reduces the hours or numbers of workers needed, or hints that existing facilities might be closed.

EXAMPLES OF PARTIAL DISTRIBUTION SYSTEM ANALYSIS

It is not always necessary or feasible to examine all functioning aspects of a system. What follows are some examples of analysis focused on only a single aspect of distribution. Sometimes, for the purposes intended, such "partial" analysis is sufficient. However, its confined focus is also a limitation, because whatever findings are developed are also somewhat narrow. They cannot be used to improve an entire system. A situation of sub-optimization, such as discussed in chapter 1, may occur if improvements are made in a sub-system without understanding their impact on the total system.

With these caveats in mind, partial analysis is useful and commonly administered. It is not always feasible to continually audit an entire distribution system's performance. Partial analysis is one of the building blocks of total analysis because it is difficult to measure a system's overall performance without measuring and understanding the performance of the various components which make up the entire system. Partial analysis almost always contributes toward understanding how an entire system functions.

Three examples will be cited. An explanation of "why" the partial analysis was performed will also be offered.

FREIGHT RATE DETERMINATION

The first example is of a large shipper who regularly asks carriers what the best rates currently are. The carrier representative who said this, reported: ". . . when I was in Texas, we used to regularly get an inquiry from U. S. Steel about shipping costs via barges—not because Steel's traffic department didn't know how to get the rates. Actually, they were shipping at the time. They just wanted to see if we had discovered anything new."[1] This example is straightforward. The shipper had worked out an efficient system based on known rates and then routinely checked with carriers to determine whether a lower rate had been established or if some other shipper or carrier had determined that a lower rate applied.

VENDOR QUALITY CONTROL REPORT

The second example was from a university bookstore which was caught between professors' tardiness in placing textbook orders and publishers' lack of speed in filling orders. The bookstore compiled and published their listing of publisher performance. The principal criterion was delivery time and the following scale was used:

Excellent	14 days or less
Very good	20 days or less
Good	20–25 days
Fair	25–30 days
Slow	30 days
Very slow	30–40 days
Extremely slow	40–45 days
Poor	45 days plus
Very Poor	Practically no response at all.[2]

Some publishers were rated on their ability to respond in case of problems delaying the order, such as sending notices that the distribution facility is out of stock or that the book is out of print. Personal contact between the publishers' representatives and both bookstore personnel and faculty was considered to be an asset, for two reasons. First, problems could be worked out more quickly in person than by mail. Second, the bookstore was relieved of a portion of the burden of transmitting messages between the faculty members and the publishers.

This report served several purposes: It may have prodded some professors to speed up their own textbook ordering practices. It would have been read with interest by any publisher attempting to maintain or improve a "customer service" image. It may have affected some professors' choice of textbooks. (This would occur in a situation where they wanted

[1] Richard L. Schultz, "Water Carrier Contribution to Improving Cost and Profit," in *Improving Transportation Cost and Corporate Profit, Proceedings of the Second Annual Seminar of the Ohio Chapter of the American Society of Traffic and Transportation* (Akron: The University of Akron, 1970), p. 37.

[2] This discussion is based on a memorandum from the bookstore manager at San Francisco State University, dated 5 November, 1973.

to make their choice later than usual and still wanted to make certain the books would be available at the start of school.) And also, the report may have helped reduce the number of professors' complaints regarding bookstore operations. The report may have functioned as a "lightning rod" and transmitted some of the professors' anger directly to the publishers.

CUSTOMER PROFITABILITY ANALYSIS

The third example deals with a "route-analysis" system that a large dairy chain used to help its delivery personnel analyze the profitability of each stop on their routes. The dairy employs driver/salesmen who are paid on a salary plus commission basis. One of the objectives of the analysis was to show who were the unprofitable customers. The frequency of deliveries to them would be reduced, which would result in either larger sales per delivery or, the customer might discontinue receiving home delivery service altogether. Either result would free some of the driver/salesman's time and he was to use this time for soliciting new customers. The driver/salesmen's route supervisors received more detailed instructions; they were to assist each driver/salesman in performing the analysis. Figure 12-1 was a tally sheet to be completed by the supervisor on a day he accompanied the driver/salesman on his route.[3] The time measurements were made with a stop-watch. While the form is unsophisticated at first glance, note that it does force the individual into focusing upon what makes a profitable or unprofitable stop.

The data which are collected on the form shown in Figure 12-1 and from the driver/salesman's monthly records were then transferred to several other forms so that they could be analyzed more critically. Figure 12-2 uses the same data and points out which customers are "overserviced." It is a tally sheet which shows each customer's dollar volume across the top and the number of deliveries the customer receives along the vertical axis. High dollar volume combined with a low number of deliveries per month is the "goal." Hence, entries toward the upper right-hand corner of the chart show more desirable stops. Entries in the lower left corner of the chart represent less desirable stops. A step downward diagonal line is drawn between the upper left and lower right-hand corners. The inference drawn is that entries below the diagonal should be shifted either upward or to the right or both.

One of the reasons these forms are relatively unsophisticated is that the driver/salesman is an independent or semi-independent operator.

[3] The dairy supplying these forms asked to not be identified. See also Donald F. Wood, "The Driver/Salesman and His Changing Role," *Proceedings, Transportation Research Forum, 1973* (Oxford, Indiana: Richard B. Cross Co., 1973), pp. 631–637.

FIG. 12-1 Home delivery route management growth program—Time review chart.

AM Starting Time, Load a/o Unload_____ Time _4:10_ Salesman _Clure N_
Starting Mileage (at plant)_____568___ Time _4:15_ Route # _9_
Mileage at First Stop_____569___ Time _4:18_ Super. _Alon B._
Mileage at Last Stop_____590___ Time _11:45_
Ending Mileage (at plant)_____513___ Time _11:54_
PM Ending Time, Load a/o Unload _45 min_ Time _12:41_
Check In (Finish Day)_____ _12 min_ Time _12:56_
                    Total Time: Hours _8_ Minutes _46_

	Front Porch			Back Porch	Inside or Ask		Solicitations		
Time 1st hour: _5:18_	45	35	30	85			Hour _6 th_	Time _:51_	
	55	30	35	75			Hour _6 th_	Time _5:03_	
Miles 1st hour: _574_	90	110	120	85			Hour _6 th_	Time _1:01_	
	63	55	34	103	NONE		Hour____	Time____	
Dollars Sold: _30.31 ave 1.13_	88	35		50			Hour____	Time____	
	50	55					Hour____	Time____	
Accounts Served: _20 1 5 10_	45	51					Hour____	Time____	
	45	30							
Time 2nd hour: _6:18_	20	35	42 30	75			Collections from Customers not receiving delivery:		
	23	81	38 30	120					
Miles 2nd hour: _577_	35	60	28 50	60			Hour _3 RD_	Time _3 0_	
	30	30	25 70	61			Hour _7 TH_	Time _33_	
Dollars Sold: _75 ave 111_	182	38	48 60	60	NONE		Hour____	Time____	
	30	108	70				Hour____	Time____	
Accounts Served: _72 1 5 10_	23	64	82				Hour____	Time___	
	45	44	37				Hour____	Time____	
Time 3rd hour: _7:18_	20	30	40		120		Hour____	Time____	
	25	38	23				Hour____	Time____	
Miles 3rd hour: _580_	42	41					Hour____	Time____	
	55	41		NONE			Hour____	Time____	
Dollars Sold: _33 ¾ ave 133_	70	28					Total → _3 33 ½_		
	72	65							
Accounts Served: _18 1 0 11_	22	45		53	85	195	Rest/Eating Stops:		
	-5			56	128	240	Hour _3 RD_	Time _30 0_	
Time 4:__	44			120	95		Hour _4 TH_	Time _11: 8_	
Dollars Sold: _31 ¾ ave 100_	30			55	98		Hour _7 TH_	Time _31: 4_	
	17			50	97		Hour____	Time____	
Accounts Served: _10 1 7 19_	20			60	120		Hour____	Time____	
	21			35	20		Hour____	Time____	
							Total → _58 min 12 Sec_		
Time 6th hour: _10:18_	20			73	170		REMARKS:		
	31			73	110		MARK UP Book 1 ST. _7.00_		
Miles 6th hour: _586_ •	10			90	85		" " " 2 ND _5.20_		
	75			45	60		" " " 3 RD _3:00_		
Dollars Sold: _3401 ave 1 48_	55			75	180		" " " 4 TH _4:00_		
	58			75	120		STRAIGHTEN TRUCK OUT _6.00_		
Accounts Served: _71 8 18_	30			126	120		MARK UP Book 6 TH _3:50_		
				117	126		Total → _28 min 50 SEC_		
c 7th hour: _11:18_	30			65	77		BROKE UP 2 TIMES BECAUSE OF		
	48			60	240		DEAD END STREET Took = 30 SEC		
Miles 7th hour: _589_	23			63	97				
	47			40	85		DELIVERIES	170	
Dollars Sold: _14.49 ave 104_	42				90		DOLLAR SALES	191.53	
Accounts Served: _5 1 4 15._							COMMISSION	37.92	
							SALES PER Stop	1.13	

FIG. 12-2 Home delivery route management growth program—Time review chart.

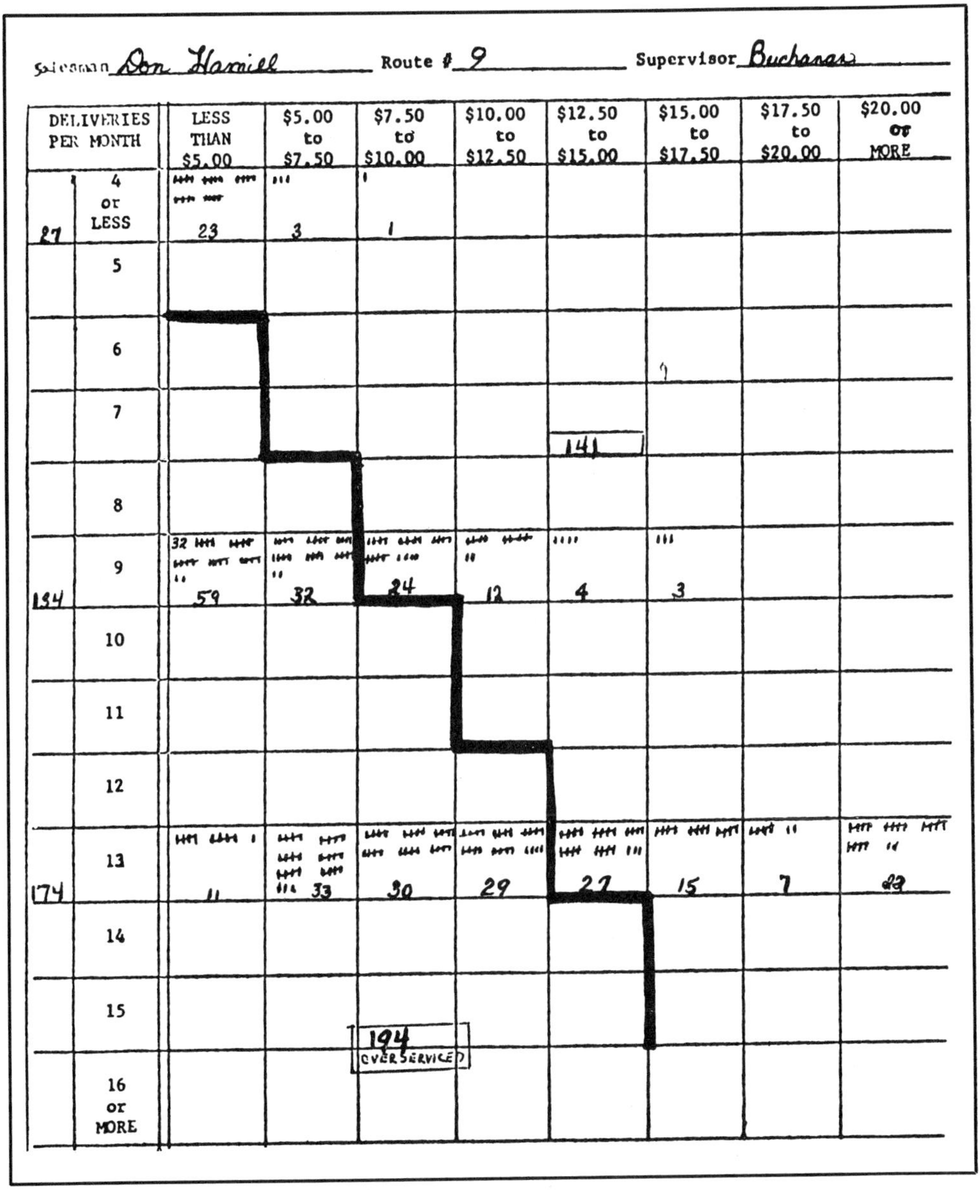

He both sells and delivers and decides who should and who should not receive what type of service. Since he is paid a salary plus commission, the commission portion of his pay is an incentive not to waste time. However, the dairy is interested in his time utilization since they pay the salary part of his wages. Rather than tell him who he can and cannot serve, they have to use an approach such as the one just shown to demonstrate to him how his time can be reallocated in a more productive manner.

INDUSTRY STANDARDS

A type of analysis that is not performed directly by the firm itself, is an industry-wide study. In this case, the firm's role is to cooperate in supplying data concerning its own operations to a centralized research body. Other, competing firms do the same. The research body then compiles data for the entire industry and reports it in a manner which guarantees (hopefully) anonymity for each individual firm. The firms which contributed data then look at the industry-wide tabulation and can tell how they compare with industry-wide performance.

One example of such a study is a periodic tabulation regarding the operations of grocery chain distribution centers.[4] Respondents who were responsible for operating 50 different distribution centers supplied the data. The researchers who compiled and analyzed the data felt that there were six key measures. They, and their medians, are:

Tons per man-hour of direct labor	2.12
Cases per man-hour of direct labor	152.
Tons per man-hour of total labor	1.30
Cases per man-hour of total labor	93.0
Cases unloaded per hour from R.R. cars	231.
Cases selected per man-hour	161.

Ranges and quartiles were also given for the data, and data were also presented over time. The median tons per man-hour of direct labor in 1969 was 2.08; this increased to 2.12 in 1973. Not all of the indices showed improvement over the same period. In part, this may have resulted from a changing mix of unit loads, case lots, and less-than case lots. The figure "cases selected per man-hour" dropped from 1969 to 1973, while the figure for "pieces selected per man-hour" increased.

4 Wendell Earle and Willard Hunt, *Grocery Distribution Center Efficiency Report*, (Ithaca, New York: Cornell University in cooperation with the National Association of Food Chains, 1973).

Data were also given for rates of unloading trucks; picking orders by use of tow trains, chain tows, hand trucks, and pallet jacks; and in loading outgoing trucks with cargo which is unitized or in baskets or cages.

Good performance by some criteria must sometimes be paid for by poorer performance by other criteria. The direction for improvement is usually apparent after examining data for all 50 distribution centers. In one instance, however, the direction for improvement was not apparent. That statistic was the one for number of employees per supervisor. Distribution centers with the largest number of employees per supervisor and distribution centers with the smallest number of emploees per supervisor appeared to be more efficient by most criteria than did firms with the median, or near median, number of employees per supervisor.

PHYSICAL DISTRIBUTION SYSTEM DESIGN

System design in physical distribution is a complex undertaking. The difficulty results from the multiplicity of activities that PD encompasses. Because the various functional areas of physical distribution interact, the establishment of a PD system design necessitates using sophisticated analytical techniques. Two of the more commonly used procedures— PERT and simulation—will be examined, although no attempt will be made to present an "exhaustive" discussion of either.[5]

Figure 12-3 illustrates a logical procedure for designing a physical distribution system. The discussion that follows will be based on this sequence of events.

ESTABLISHMENT OF OBJECTIVES AND CONSTRAINTS

Before a physical distribution system can be designed or redesigned, it is imperative that the goals and objectives of the analysis be delineated. Is cost cutting the objective? What about profits or return-on-investment as goals? Must customer service standards be improved? Are the goals long or short term in nature? An example of a clearly stated objective would be the following:

> Eighteen months from the start of this study, the objectives stated below will be achieved at the lowest possible cost.

[5] Students interested in the quantitative approach to physical distribution analysis should consult the following: Ronald H. Ballou, *Business Logistics Management* (Englewood Cliffs, N.J.: Prentice-Hall, Inc., 1973); M. S. Makower and E. Williamson, *Operational Research* (London: St. Paul's House, 1967); and John F. Magee, *Physical-Distribution Systems* (New York: McGraw-Hill, Inc., 1967).

FIG. 12-3 Steps in designing a physical distribution system.

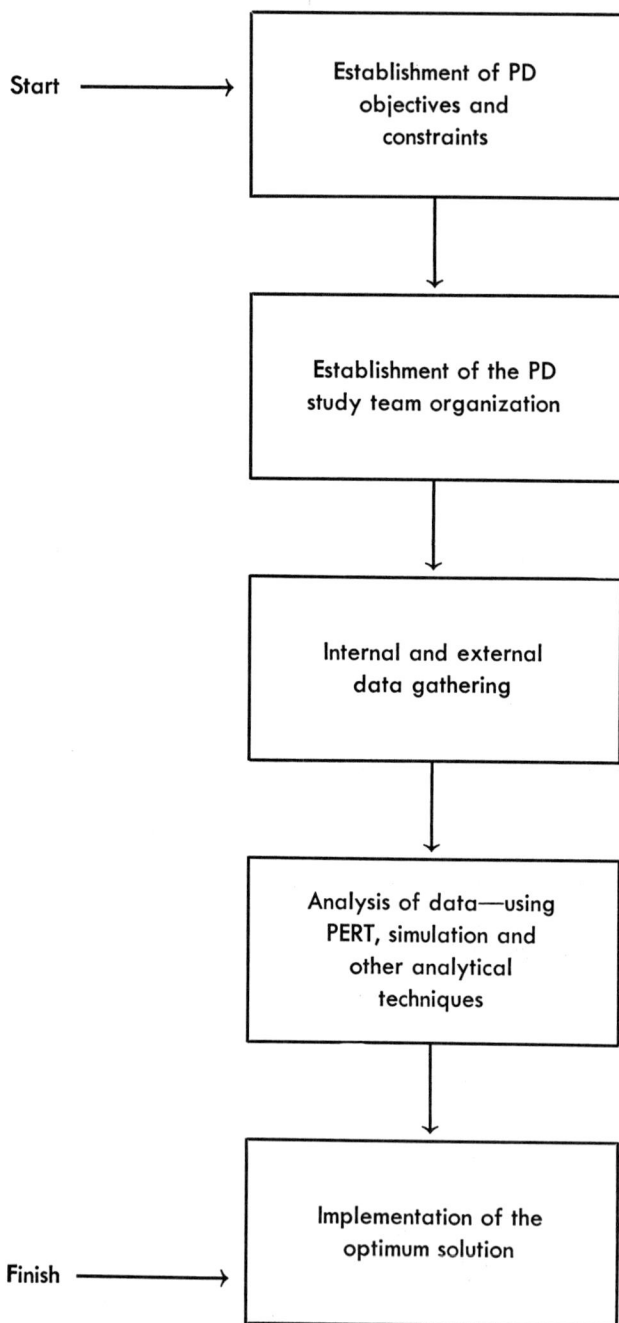

Start ⟶

Establishment of PD
objectives and
constraints

↓

Establishment of the PD
study team organization

↓

Internal and external
data gathering

↓

Analysis of data—using
PERT, simulation and
other analytical
techniques

↓

Implementation of the
optimum solution

Finish ⟶

Objectives

(a) Order transmittal time for our customers will be less than 24 hours.

(b) Orders will be processed within 16 working hours of receipt.

(c) Eighty percent of orders will be completely assembled within 16 working hours. All orders will be assembled within 24 working hours.

(d) Order delivery time from our dock will be no longer than 96 hours for 85 percent of all customers. All domestic orders must be delivered within six days of tendering to the carrier.

(e) Stock-outs will not be accepted for greater than seven percent of units requested. Customers experiencing a stock-out will be immediately advised by phone. The out-of-stock product will be replaced within ten days and expedited transportation will be used to reach the customer.

Notice that the above statement has objectives that are *measurable*. This is important, because when the study has been completed and the new system implemented, it is then possible to determine if the goals are being met. This is also a psychological stimulus to the managers, because it can be determined whether their efforts achieved success.

Before the system design can be initiated, not only must management specify measurable objectives, but also system *constraints*, if any, must be specified. Constraints involve factors in the system that cannot be changed for one reason or another. Examples are the following:

1. The distribution center at Detroit will not be closed nor its employment decreased because the firm has publicly pledged to support the downtown area of this city.

2. The order-transmittal will continue to be based on a telephone system because this equipment was purchased just six months ago at a cost of $2½ million.

3. The Jones common-carrier trucking company will be utilized whenever it has competitive trucking rates and proper operating authority.*

Each constraint simplifies the situation because constraints *reduce* the alternatives available and hence the complexity of the analysis.

ORGANIZATION OF THE PD STUDY TEAM

Once measurable objectives have been established and the constraints outlined, the next step is to organize the firm's personnel for the analysis. John F. Magee, a management consultant, found that it is preferable

---

* This carrier is owned by our president's son, and if it fails, junior will be back working for us, possibly in the PD department!

to have two separate groups working on the analysis. One group is the *working analysis team*. This group involves the managers of the functional areas involved and other staff and quantitative specialists. The customer service director, traffic manager, warehousing manager, et al, are members of this team. If outside management consultants are utilized, they would work with these team members on a day-by-day basis. This team is responsible for the actual analysis performed, and the testing, designing, and implementing of the new system.

The other group is the *management supervisory committee*. This group works with the working analysis team. They represent a broader perspective, the multifaceted viewpoints of the firm. Marketing, law, finance, production, personnel, and accounting executives are represented on this committee. This group is on call to clarify and amplify on the system objectives. It also plays the role of the "devil's advocate" and occasionally probes the working analysis team on *why* they took the action they did.

Magee states that meetings between the two groups should be regularly scheduled. In many cases, a monthly meeting seems appropriate.[6]

DATA COLLECTION

The third and perhaps the most important stage in designing a PD system involves data collection. Obviously the validity of the study can be no stronger than the accuracy of the data base. Four comprehensive audits must be performed. They include: product, existing facilities, customers and competitors. Each will be examined.

The *product audit* involves a comprehensive analysis of both the existing product line and new product trends. Specific information which must be determined for each product would include: (a) annual sales volume, (b) seasonality, (c) packaging, (d) transportation and warehouse information, (e) present manufacturing or assembly facilities, (f) warehouse stocking locations, (g) present transport modes utilized, (h) sales by regions, (i) complementary products which are often sold at the same time as the product under consideration, and (j) product profitability. This list is *not* exhaustive, it is illustrative of the type of product information needed. The majority of the information needed to perform this audit is available in existing company records.

The *existing facilities audit* comes next. Every distribution system is unique and the working analysis team must have a comprehensive audit of its facilities. This would include the following: (a) the location and capacity of production plants, (b) the location and capacity of storage warehouses and distribution centers, (c) the location of the order

---

[6] Magee, *Physical-Distribution Systems, op. cit.,* p. 95.

processing function, and (d) the transport modes utilized (especially when the firm is somewhat "locked" into their usage). When constraints are used, they typically involve aspects of existing facilities which are not to be changed. This audit tells where the firm is now utilizing facilities and it is essential data when contemplating changes in the system.

The *customer audit* focuses on characteristics of current customers. Potential new customers are also analyzed. The following information must be collected: (a) the location of present and potential customers, (b) the products that each customer orders, (c) the seasonality of their orders, (d) do they buy F.O.B. origin or destination?, (e) the importance of customer service, (f) special services they require, and (g) the volume and profitability of sales for each customer.

The customer audit provides a key input for system analysis, because in the end, the system is designed to satisfy the needs and requirements of the firm's customers.

The *competition audit* outlines the competitive environment within which the firm is selling. The following information should be ascertained: (a) the order transmittal methods of competitors, (b) the accuracy and speed of their order processing, (c) the speed and consistency of carrier movements utilized by competitors, (d) the ratio of orders given to competitors that could not be filled because of a product stock-out, (e) the competitor's experience with loss and damage claims, and (f) a narrative statement regarding customers' perception of the customer service strengths and weaknesses of the firm and its competitors.

Unlike the previous three audits, the information required for the competition audit is generally not available within a company, although salespeople can often provide some of it. Also, outside marketing research firms are used to survey competitors to gather the required data. Outside research firms can usually design the questionnaire in such a manner as to disguise the ultimate recipient of the information.

ANALYSIS OF THE DATA

When the information from the four audits has been assembled, the next step is to "massage" it, in the vernacular of the analyst. This can be accomplished using relatively unsophisticated techniques or complex methodologies. Recall in a prior section of this chapter on partial analysis the relatively simple but effective techniques utilized by the dairy driver/salesmen. When systemwide analysis is desired, the quantity of data to be analyzed is usually so massive that more sophisticated techniques must be utilized. Two methodologies will be examined here—PERT and simulation. PERT (an acronym for Project Evaluation and Review Technique) is of value when the analyst is attempting to determine the relationship between all tasks which must be performed. Simulation assumes that the relationships are known; it is used to determine how well a system—actual or proposed—will perform under varying stresses.

PERT. This is a form of network analysis which places all component tasks in the sequence they are to be performed. It recognizes that some tasks can be performed only in a certain simultaneous order, while for others no such relationship exists. There is a period when either, neither, or both can be performed. What follows is an example of how PERT can be applied to the export process, where some 21 different steps are involved.[7] They are listed here and assigned identifying letters. Letters early in the alphabet are assigned to tasks that must be performed first. However, there is no absolute relationship between the letter assigned to a task and when—in comparison to other tasks—it must be performed. While the word *"task"* is implied, the word *event* will be used. *Event* means that the task has been completed.

Event A An order from a foreign customer is received.
Event B Applicable governmental controls concerning the export transaction are determined.
Event C Transportation mode, carrier, and routing are selected.
Event D The goods needed to fill the export order are made available.
Event E The export declaration is prepared.
Event F Space is reserved on the carrier.
Event G Insurance coverage for the shipment is obtained.
Event H Packaging requirements for the export shipment are established.
Event I The delivery permit for the export shipment is obtained.
Event J The commercial invoice covering the shipment is prepared.
Event K The shipment is packed, marked and weighed.
Event L Inland transportation to point of exportation is arranged.
Event M The certificate of origin covering the goods in the shipment is obtained.
Event N The bill of lading or airwaybill for the shipment is prepared.
Event O The consular invoice is obtained from the government representative of the importing country.
Event P Any special certificates required for importation are obtained.
Event Q The shipment is onloaded aboard inland carrier for transport to point of exportation.

---

[7] See James W. Tatterson and Donald F. Wood, "PERT, CPM and the Export Process," *OMEGA, The International Journal of Management Science* (Vol. 2, No. 3, 1974), pp. 421–426.

Event R The shipment arrives at point of exportation and receipt for the goods is issued.

Event S The shipment is loaded aboard the international carrier; the bill of lading or airwaybill is issued.

Event T The shipment arrives at the designated point of entry.

Event U The consignee receives the shipment.

In order to perform the analysis, it is necessary to have some real figures as input data. The example used is a 2,000 pound shipment from an exporter in the San Francisco area destined to a consignee in Manila. The shipment quotation is C.I.F. (Cost-Insurance-Freight) Manila; this means that the exporter is responsible for the performance of all export process events until the shipment is offloaded in Manila. In addition to the regular documentation required, the shipper must obtain a delivery permit from the steamship company. Shipment value is $36,000. The exporter purchases the merchandise at Event A; he receives payment from the customer at Event T. No mode, route, or time limit is specified. Because of the high value and small size of this shipment, the shipper is uncertain whether to ship by sea or air, or whether to expedite the shipment.

Estimates of cost and time must be made for each of the 21 tasks, or events. Instances where one event has a sequential relationship with

FIG. 12-4 Network for example export shipment.

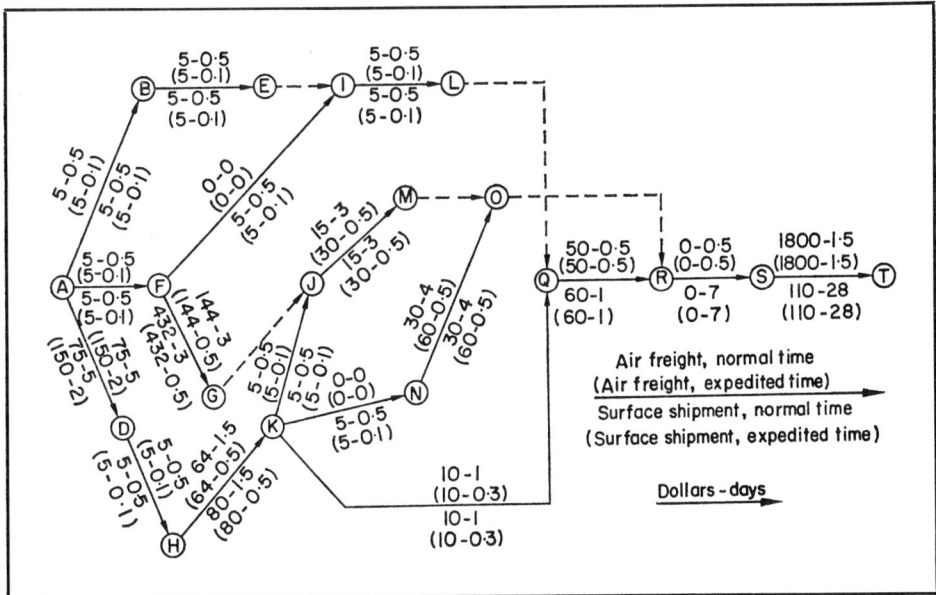

This chart first appeared in OMEGA, vol. 2, no. 3, p. 424.

others must be recognized. Figure 12-4 depicts all of these relationships in network form. Tasks that must be performed in sequence follow along the same line. Tasks which can be performed simultaneously are shown on parallel lines. Cost figures, in dollars, are represented by the first number, the second number represents time, in days. Four alternatives types of shipment are involved. Each line between event A and event T is a path.* The time to travel along each path is then added, giving these results:

Network Path	Total Days Required to Traverse Path
ADHKQRST	44.0
ADHKNORST	46.5 (critical path)
ADHKJMORST	45.5
AFGJMORST	41.5
AFILQRST	37.5
ABEILQRST	37.5

These figures are for the normal shipment via water. While all paths must be traversed, one path ADHKNORST has been designated as the *critical path* because it takes the longest amount of time to traverse. The reason it is considered as *critical* is that if one wishes to speed up the normal surface process, the time-saving improvement *must* be made on one or more events that occur on this path. It would do no good to speed up task J, because even if J is accomplished in less time than originally estimated, it won't affect the total time of the tasks on the critical path.

In fact, you could allot more time to task J than it presently takes without slowing down the export process. The question is "how much?" This is where the path concept is useful. Note that event J appears on several other paths, although not on the critical one. Path ADHKJ-MORST contains task J and is closest in time value to the critical path. It takes 45.5 days to complete while the critical path takes 46.5 days. Hence one could add one more day on to the time to complete task J without affecting overall delivery time. Other tasks not on the critical path could be analyzed in a similar manner. If you did not want to improve delivery time, you could reduce costs by allowing more time for the completion of tasks that are off of the critical path.

Figure 12-4 could also show how to improve delivery time. Using the normal surface transport figures you would concentrate on tasks which are on the critical path since only by reducing their required times can you reduce overall time. Task D (or event D) appears on the

* In this example, the shipper is responsible only for events A through T because of the selling terms. When task T is complete, the consignee has the merchandise and the shipper has the payment.

critical path. Any reduction in time to complete D will reduce the time required to traverse the critical path by the same amount. At present, D takes five days. If the event could be completed in, say, .5 days, this would reduce the critical path from 46.5 days to 42.0 days. There is a limit to improvements that can be made on the critical path, however. Saving time on events D, H, and K, for example, is useful up to a total savings of five days. At that point, path AFGJMORST becomes the controlling, or *critical* path, and D, H, and K are no longer "critical."

The PERT chart suggests how you should go about making adjustments in the time allocations for each task. Costs of altering the time spent on each task should also be known. For events off the critical path, time allowances could be extended if cost reductions will occur. For events on the critical path, any change in time allowance has a direct impact on system performance. This holds until the time saving becomes so great that the path itself is no longer critical.

The discussion so far has dealt with the normal water shipment. In this case it happens to be the least expensive way to ship. The expedited water shipment costs slightly more, even though there are savings from having the investment in inventory reduced, because the total process is speeded up. Air freight is considerably more expensive, despite reduction in the amount of time, money is invested in inventory, packaging costs, and insurance.

Note the usefulness of the PERT chart in evaluating a complete distribution process. It allows you to relate tasks. You can focus attention on any task without losing sight of where it fits in the "big" picture.

Simulation. The computer technique that offers the most potential for physical distribution planning is *simulation*. Simulation usually involves a computer model which is a series of mathematical relationships.[8] Simulation reliability is achieved by making the model as close to the "real world" as possible. Such factors as transport mode availability, transportation rates, warehouse locations, customer locations, customer service requirements, and plant locations, must all be accurately reflected in the model. Although physical distribution simulation models may require many programmers working together for long periods, they allow the firm to have the capability of asking "what if?" questions, such as:

If we reduced the average order cycle time for our customers from 12 days to 7 days, what would be the additional cost involved? Would sales increase?

[8] See: Charles W. Gross and Robin T. Peterson, *Business Forecasting* (Boston: Houghton Mifflin Co., 1976), Chap. 8.

If we started to use railroad service instead of motor common carrier, what would be the ramifications on customer service and on overall costs?

If we reduced the number of distribution warehouses from 32 to 19, what would be the effect on customer service standards? What about costs?

If the minimum order accepted were increased from $20 to $100, what would be the effect on total sales?

If private carriage were substituted for motor common carriage, what would be the changes in total physical distribution costs and what effect would this have on customer service standards?

The primary advantage of simulation is that it allows the firm to "test" the feasibility of a proposed change at relatively little expense. In addition, it prevents firms from experiencing the public embarrassment of making a major change in their physical distribution system which might result in a deterioration of customer service levels or an increase in total operating expense.

Simulation models have been successfully used by the H. J. Heinz Company,[9] the Johnson and Johnson Domestic Operating Company,[10] and the railroad industry,[11] to name a few. Career physical distribution people should familiarize themselves with computer simulations because they are important to physical distribution planning and will become more important.

To grasp the possibilities of a simulation study, the H. J. Heinz study will be outlined. Although this project was not completed recently, it shows the capabilities of a simulation study.[12] The H. J. Heinz Company was concerned with the configuration of their warehouse network. Specific questions involved the following issues: (a) how many warehouses should be utilized?, (b) where should they be located?, and (c) which customers should be served from each warehouse? Due to the size and complexity of the problem, PD consultants Harvey N. Shycon and Richard B. Maffei decided that a simulation model would be the best analysis technique.

When the study was initiated, Heinz had 68 warehouses in the United States. Over time, Heinz officials had noticed that the "Mom and Pop"

[9] Harvey N. Shycon and Richard B. Maffei, "Simulation—Tool for Better Distribution," *Harvard Business Review* (November-December, 1960), pp. 65–75.

[10] Donald J. Bowersox, "Planning Physical Distribution Operations With Dynamic Simulation," *Journal of Marketing* (January, 1972), pp. 17–25 and O. Keith Helferich and Lloyd B. Mitchell, "Planning For Customer Service with Computer Simulation," *Transportation and Distribution Management* (January-February, 1975), pp. 17–21.

[11] "Railroad Technology: The Computer Age," *Background on Transportation* (Washington, D.C.: Association of American Railroads, 1971).

[12] See references to Donald Bowersox in footnote 10, *supra*.

retailers were becoming less important in grocery distribution. Chain stores were the dominant factor and they received their products in fewer locations and in much larger quantities. It was obvious that Heinz had too many warehouses.

Once the objective of the study had been determined and the working analysis and management supervisory groups established, the product, existing facility, customer, and competition audits were completed. Shycon and Maffei determined that there were three alternative distribution methods which could be utilized. First, products could be shipped directly from the production plant to the customer. Second, products could be transported from the factory to other production facilities where consolidation with other products would occur and the consolidated shipment would then be transported immediately to the customer. Or, third, the products could flow from the factory to a storage warehouse and then to the customer. The first two alternatives do *not* utilize warehousing facilities. Warehouses are needed for customers who do not order in large enough quantities to warrant direct shipments, and for those who require relatively short order cycles.

The computer was told to try various numbers and locations of warehouses for shipments which required intermediate warehousing. For each configuration, a year's worth of sales data were simulated and the costs and customer service levels were determined for each alternative. Each alternative configuration required approximately 75 million mathematical calculations by the computer. (See Figure 12-5.)

When each alternative was tested, the results indicated that the optimum number of warehouses was about forty. With this number of warehouses, the customer service standards were achieved and total distribution costs were minimized.

DESIGN IMPLEMENTATION

The final activity in system design is the implementation of the findings. It is a rare situation in which an operating physical distribution system is completely revised at one time. The one-time "across-the-board" revisions are typically too traumatic for most firms to tolerate, because they inevitably result in a breakdown of customer service functions. Orders are lost, incorrect quantities are shipped, stock-outs are frequent —these are the typical problems when a system is changed too radically in a short period of time. In addition, personnel may resist the changes.

Most firms prefer to use their simulation and PERT analysis as indications of the areas of PD which should be changed first, because these functions are the greatest bottlenecks to efficiency. Also, the pay-offs may be greater.

Fig. 12-5 Computers Are Commonly Utilized In Simulation.

"It can't actually think, but when it makes a mistake,
it can put the blame on some other computer."

Reproduced by permission of the artist and the Masters Agency.

SUMMARY

This chapter dealt with various types of system analysis. The purpose of the analysis is to determine if improvements can be made in the physical distribution system.

Systems analysis is difficult because it is hard to determine which aspects or functional area should be subjected to the analysis.

Industry standards are available in selected areas of business and these standards allow each firm to compare their own operating ratios to the industry averages.

Effective system design involves five basic steps: (1) establishment of objectives and constraints, (2) establishment of the study team organization, (3) internal and external data gathering, (4) analysis of the data, and (5) implementation of the findings. Physical distribution system design is often based on complex systems analysis using simulation or PERT techniques.

QUESTIONS FOR DISCUSSION AND REVIEW

1. Note the quotation from General Bradley at the beginning of the chapter. What similarities and differences would there be between a civilian and a military distribution system? Why?

2. What is the purpose of systems analysis in physical distribution? What are its strengths and weaknesses?

3. "Systems analysis is the most important activity supervised by senior physical distribution management." Do you agree? Why or why not?

4. Why are outside consultants frequently employed to analyze a firm's distribution practices?

5. Discuss the problems that are often encountered in physical distribution systems analysis.

6. Why is partial systems analysis so commonly used?

7. What is your reaction to the customer profitability analysis utilized by the dairy driver/salesman? Could it be improved? Discuss.

8. What are the advantages of having a trade group collect and then distribute data concerning the relative efficiency of its various members' operations?

9. Discuss the basic procedure that is used in system design. Does this procedure appear logical to you? Discuss.

10. Why is it important to clearly specify the objectives of a study?

11. What are system constraints? Are they important? Why?

12. "Design objectives should *not* be measurable, because if they are they tend to make the systems analysis inflexible and difficult to implement." Do you agree? Defend your answer.

13. Discuss the duties and responsibilities of the working analysis team and the management supervisory committee. Which group is more important? Why?

14. Discuss the information that should be contained in each of the following audits: product, existing facilities, customers, and competitors.

15. Of the above four audits, which is the *most* and *least* important? Why?

16. What is PERT? What types of problems can be solved using this technique?

17. What is the *critical path*? Why is it important? Discuss.

18. What is simulation? What are its strengths and weaknesses?

19. Outline the problems and procedures used in the H. J. Heinz simulation. Did the analysis used appear logical to you? Discuss.

20. "Design implementation is often accomplished in stages rather than all at once." Is this logical? What are the strengths and weaknesses of the gradual approach?

CASE 12-1   DONELLY METAL STAMPINGS CO.

Donelly Metal Stamping Company was located in East St. Louis, Illinois, where it had been since its founding in 1887. In its relatively small plant it operated 20 punch presses of varying sizes. Punch presses cut and shaped metal parts such as the metal boxes used to contain electrical outlets, or metal bases for scaffolding, etc. Donelly's principal customers were in the St. Louis area although a number were scattered through Missouri, southern Illinois, southern Indiana, and even northern Kentucky. In years when auto sales were good, Donelly even received some orders from the auto industry.

The outgoing product was usually delivered by truck. Sometimes the stamped items could be "nested" (placed one inside the other) in which case the shipment would be densely packed and very heavy. When the products could not be nested, the outbound shipments would be bulky. Donelly operated its own fleet of seven trucks for making deliveries and was able to provide a high level of customer service. Richard Ritter was in charge of all deliveries and the truck fleet. He reported to the marketing manager, worked closely with the production force and sales personnel and was highly regarded by customers.

The principal input was sheet steel and, sometimes, sheet aluminum. Steel was purchased in St. Louis and from mills in the Chicago-Gary-Hammond area. All the steel producers quoted identical prices at various "basing points" plus rail freight charges between the basing point and Donelly's plant. In reality, the steel producers did compete by absorbing part or all of the freight charges. Obtaining these concessions required astute bargaining on the part of Donelly's purchasing department. Herb Wiggins was assistant director of purchasing and specialized in transportation aspects of purchase contracts. He was an I.C.C. practitioner and had, over the years, been able to negotiate very favorable rail rates for inbound steel from the Gary-Hammond mills.

There was little coordination between Donelly's inbound and outbound shipments. For example:

1. Wiggins and Ritter did not get along personally. The firm never designated one as traffic manager for fear of offending the other. Mail or phone calls for the "traffic manager" caused difficulties for the receptionist since, invariably, either Wiggins or Ritter would be offended if the other was given the letter or call.

2. Attempts to use Donelly's private truck fleet to carry inbound shipments of steel as a backhaul never worked out satisfactorily. In part this was because steel was better suited for rail, although neither Ritter nor Wiggins tried to make the backhaul system work.

3. Because of the lack of coordination between inbound and outbound shipments, inventory management problems arose; the main one being shortage of warehouse space. If too much sheet steel were delivered at a time when the warehouse was stocked with outgoing materials, it was necessary to use a public warehouse.

4. During a wildcat rail strike in Illinois, Donelly had attempted to induce motor common carriers to bring steel from the Chicago area. Because of the rail strike, truckers were unusually busy and—while not refusing to carry the steel—indicated that it would receive very low priority. Shipments to the Donelly plant were delayed and the plant had to shut down for two days. Four Donelly trucks were then assigned to drive empty to the Chicago area to pick up steel. Before they left, however, the rail workers ended their strike and the next day three rail carloads of sheet steel—which had been stopped near Springfield—were delivered. Donelly's competitors had not shut down during the strike. They had been able to receive steel which was carried by motor common carriers. Investigation showed that these two competing metal stamping firms did not own and operate their own fleets. They were able to get common carriers, (whom they utilized for outbound shipments) to carry sheet steel from the Chicago area. Donelly, which usually did not use motor common carriers, had no such leverage and, therefore, received no service.

The wildcat rail strike brought traffic problems at Donelly to a head. The two competitors who had not been forced to shut down gained a competitive advantage with several important customers. Wiggins blamed Ritter for not making the company's trucks available earlier to pick up sheet steel. Ritter argued that the trucks had been committed to making deliveries and if they had been withdrawn earlier, some customers would have been seriously inconvenienced. Ritter's boss backed him.

Wiggins and his boss, the director of purchasing, took this opportunity to press for Wiggins' appointment to a new post they proposed be created—director of traffic. The director of traffic would be responsible for both inbound and outbound movements. Ritter was to be named as assistant director.

Ritter and his boss agreed that the new post was needed. However, they wanted Ritter to be the director of traffic with Wiggins to be his assistant.

Within a week, Donelly's management was divided into two camps, those who wanted Ritter to be Wiggins's boss and those who felt the reverse was preferable. Surprisingly, there was complete agreement that the traffic activities had to be under the direction of one individual.

Harold Donelly III, president of Donelly Metal Stamping Company, realized he would have to make a controversial decision. If he named either Ritter or Wiggins to the new post, he would alienate about half his management. The firm's management force was not large and he couldn't easily create a face-saving post for the person who was not selected to be director of traffic. To complicate the situation, neither Wiggins nor Ritter was considered to be very flexible or able to perform well in a non-transport-oriented post. Donelly toyed with the idea of bringing in an outsider and having him supervise both Ritter and Wiggins. Unfortunately, this would be a costly decision. The firm was too small to afford a three-man traffic department.

On Thursday afternoons, Donelly had a standing golf date with Sid Burroughs, president of the East St. Louis bank which handled most of Donelly's business. As Donelly and Burroughs were waiting in the club-house bar for the other two of their foursome to arrive, Donelly told Burroughs of his problem. Burroughs thought for a moment and then said: "Why do you need a traffic department at all? Why not buy at a delivered price basis and sell F.O.B. plant? Let your suppliers worry about reaching you and let your buyers pick up their own goods. If you get rid of your seven trucks, you could reduce your prices quite a bit."

Question One: Comment on Burroughs' suggestion. Do you agree with it? Why or why not?

Question Two: What do you think Donelly should do?

Question Three: Burroughs' suggestion contains a certain simplistic logic. Ignoring the specifics of the Donelly case, note that most firms have both inbound and outbound traffic. Some choose to control both (as Donelly Metal Stamping did); some choose to control neither (as Burroughs suggests). An alternative course is to control inbound or outbound shipments but not both. What kinds of firms would choose to control outbound shipments only? Or inbound shipments only?

CASE 12-2   ALBERTA HIGHWAY DEPARTMENT REGION VI

Region VI of the Alberta Highway Department was responsible for highway maintenance in Alberta in an area west of Lethbridge, Calgary, and Red Deer. One of their most important responsibilities, in the public's mind, was to keep open Canadian Route Number 1 which went across all of Canada. At the very west of Region VI were the Rocky Mountains and in a six mile stretch between Lake Louise and the British Columbia border, the highway climbed from 3000 to 6000 feet. The climb in this stretch was uniform, the road's elevation increased 500 feet each mile as it moved to the west.

At present, a highway maintenance station was near Lake Louise, one mile to the east of the six mile section. At this station were based several heavy duty dump trucks, (manufactured by HDT trucking company) which, in the winter, were mounted with snow plows in the front and sand spreading devices in the rear.

Sanding was used after frosts or freezing rains or in the spring when melting snows would refreeze at night. The higher elevations required more sanding because they were subjected to more freezing temperatures. For the past ten years, since the highway was opened, records were kept for the amount of maintenance required by each mile of highway. (See map.) In terms of sanding, here is the average number of days per year that each mile required sanding:

Mile 1	3000'–3500' elevation	40 days
Mile 2	3500'–4000' elevation	48 days
Mile 3	4000'–4500' elevation	53 days
Mile 4	4500'–5000' elevation	58 days
Mile 5	5000'–5500' elevation	65 days
Mile 6	5500'–6000' elevation	70 days

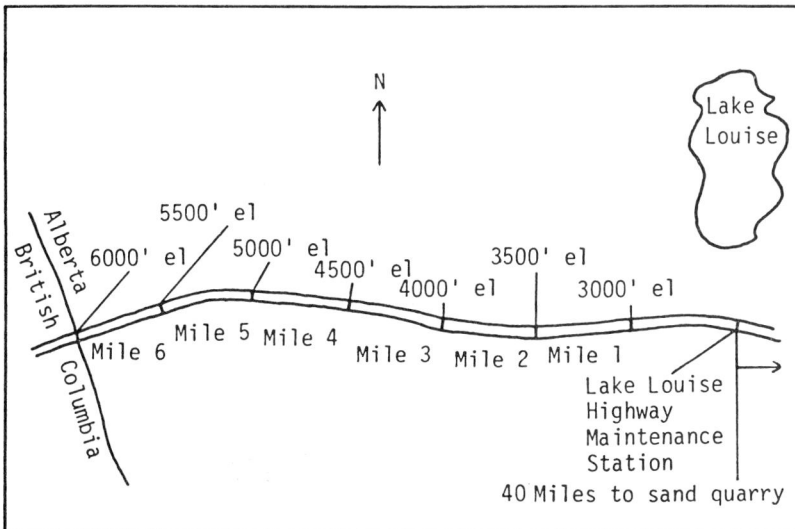

The HDT dump trucks could carry ten tons of sand, which was enough to spread over one mile of highway in both the eastbound and westbound lanes.

Spreading sand was a slow process because, under slippery conditions, highway traffic moved slowly. Several trucks were needed because when sanding was needed, it was needed quickly.

At the Lake Louise maintenance station were large silos for holding the salt-treated sand. At present, the silos could hold nearly 6,000 tons of sand, some of which was used for lower stretches of highway. During summer months, the silos were filled by special trailer dump trucks which carried the sand up from a quarry near Bow Valley, 40 miles to the east on the Lake Louise maintenance station. Then the silo was of such design that it could be split into two. Split segments of the silo could hold different capacities or they could hold equal capacities of sand. However, their total capacity would be 6,000 tons.

Through a departmental program for encouraging employee suggestions, a proposal had been received from a sander truck driver that a portion of the Lake Louise sand silos be moved west toward the higher elevation where more frequent sandings were needed.

The highway was constructed so that at one-mile distances (in this case at elevations of 3000, 3500, 4000, 4500, 5000, 5500, and 6000 feet), it was possible for maintenance trucks to turn around. The shoulders were also wide enough at these points so that the silos could be placed alongside. The silo relocation could be performed during summer months using regular maintenance crews and equipment.

The principal reason for splitting and relocating a portion of the silos would be to place sand closer to where it was needed, and reducing travel time of maintenance trucks to and from the silos. The work crews were paid a constant rate for a fixed number of hours, and if they were not sanding they were performing other tasks. Hence, the only relevant costs were those of truck operation.

The facts and assumptions to be used in the analysis are:

1. Costs of trucking sand from the quarry to the Lake Louise silos or to the relocated silos would be three cents per ton-mile for the length of the full haul in one direction. (Empty backhaul costs are taken into account with these calculations.)

2. Some sand silo capacity must be kept at the Lake Louise maintenance station.

3. Spreader dump trucks are more costly to operate to carry sand between silos and where it is needed. The cost is ten cents per ton-mile (which also takes empty backhauls into account).

4. There are no costs assigned for spreader trucks to initially reach silos. The reason for this is that they are randomly located on

the highway at the time the decision is made to spread sand. Truck crews are then dispatched by radio.

5. If a new silo is located, it must be at one of the turn-around sites between each of the miles.

6. If a new silo is located an even number of miles from the Lake Louise station, a midpoint will be established halfway between the two silos and sanders will load at the silo nearest the mile of road needing sand.

7. If a new silo is located an odd number of miles from the Lake Louise maintenance station, a determination must be made as to which silo will provide sand for the middle mile. (This is because maintenance trucks cannot turn at the middle of mile sections.)

8. No costs are assigned to operating the spreaders within a mile on either side of the silo. This is because they start spreading sand immediately upon leaving the silo. However, for sanding a stretch that was between two to three miles from the silo, the cost of reaching the area would be two dollars (10 tons × 10 cents × 2 miles.)

Question One: Should one portion of sand silos at the Lake Louise maintenance station be relocated to a point to the west, at higher elevation? If "yes," where should it be relocated, how much capacity should it have and what are the projected annual savings in truck operating costs? Show your work.

Question Two: What other information would be helpful for solving this case?

CHAPTER REFERENCES

ADAMS, TOM H., "Use of Linear Programming in the Selection of Optimal Shipping Points," *Transportation Journal* (Spring, 1969), pp. 11–20.

BALLOU, RONALD H.; *Business Logistics Management* (Engelwood Cliffs, N.J.: Prentice-Hill, Inc., 1973).

BOWERSOX, D. J., O. K. Helferich, and E. J. Marien; "Physical Distribution Planning with Simulation," *International Journal of Physical Distribution* (October, 1971), pp. 38–42.

BOWERSOX, DONALD J., *et al*; *Dynamic Simulation of Physical Distribution Systems* (East Lansing, Mich.: Division of Research, Graduate School of Business Administration, Michigan State University, 1972).

————; "Planning Physical Distribution Operations with Dynamic Simulation," *Journal of Marketing* (January, 1972).

CHING, C. T. K.; "An Iterative Procedure for Solving Physical Distribution Problems," *Transportation Journal* (Spring, 1971), pp. 47–50.

DeHAYES, DANIEL W., JR. and Robert G. House; "The Recursive Use of Activity

Analysis and Simulation as a Methodology for Modelling the Logistics System," *The Logistics and Transportation Review* (Volume 8, Number 3), pp. 83–92.

EARLE, WENDELL and Willard Hunt; *Grocery Distribution Center Efficiency Report* (Ithaca, N.Y.: Cornell University, 1973).

GRABNER, JOHN R. and William S. Sargent, eds.; *Distribution System Costing: Concepts and Procedures*, proceedings of the fourth annual James R. Riley symposium on business logistics, (Columbus: Transportation and Logistics Foundation at The Ohio State University, 1972). Note especially papers by Wilbur S. Wayman, M. J. Barrett and F. J. Beier, and Robert M. Sutton.

GROSS, CHARLES W. and Robin T. Peterson; *Business Forecasting* (Boston: Houghton Mifflin Co., 1976).

HELFERICH, O. KEITH and Lloyd B. Mitchell; "Planning For Customer Service with Computer Simulation," *Transportation and Distribution Management* (January-February, 1975).

HESKETT, JAMES L.; "A Missing Link in Physical Distribution System Design," in Donald J. Bowersox, *et al.*, *Readings in Physical Distribution* (New York: The MacMillan Co., 1969), pp. 137–143.

HILLE, STANLEY J.; "An Approach to Analyzing a Large Urban Freight Market for Transportation Companies," *Transportation Journal* (Summer, 1972), pp. 18–25.

LITTLE, WALLACE I.; "A Model for Systems Management of Distribution Functions," *Transportation Journal* (Summer, 1968), pp. 48–59.

————; "Systems Planning in Physical Distribution: A Pre-Production Application," *International Journal of Physical Distribution* (Oct., 1970), pp. 39–42.

MAGEE, JOHN F.; *Physical-Distribution Systems* (New York: McGraw-Hill, Inc., 1967).

MAKOWER, M. S. and E. Williamson; *Operational Research* (London: St. Paul's House, 1967).

MOLLOY, WILLIAM T.; "Evaluating the Need for Automatic Data Processing Equipment in Transportation and Traffic Management," *Transportation Journal* (Summer, 1969), pp. 43–56.

PLOWMAN, E. GROSVENOR; "The Intermodality and Cybernetics Keys to Profitable Computerization in Transportation," *Transportation Journal* (Spring, 1969), pp. 51–55.

POIST, RICHARD F.; "The Total Cost vs. Total Profit Approach to Logistics Systems Design," *Transportation Journal* (Fall, 1974), pp. 13–24.

"Railroad Technology: The Computer Age," *Background on Transportation* (Washington, D.C.: Association of American Railroads, 1971).

SASTRY, M V. RAMA; "Systems Approach to Cost-Benefit Analysis of Urban Transportation," *Transportation Journal* (Spring, 1973), pp. 39–45.

SCHARY, PHILIP B., Robert E. Shirley and Linn Soule; "Analysis and Simulation of a Distribution Channel: A Case Study in Sea Food Marketing," *International Journal of Physical Distribution* (June, 1972), pp. 110–120.

SCHULTZ, RICHARD L.; "Water Carrier Contribution to Improving Cost and Profit," *Improving Transportation Cost and Corporate Profit, Proceedings of the Second Annual Seminar of the Ohio Chapter of the American Society of Traffic and Transportation* (Akron: The University of Akron, 1970).

SHYCON, HARVEY N. and Richard B. Maffei; "Simulation—Tool for Better Distribution," *Harvard Business Review* (November-December, 1960).

STEINER, HENRY M.; "Opportunity Cost, Capital Recovery, and Profit Analysis of Logistics Systems," *Transportation Journal* (Fall, 1973), Vol. 13, No. 1, pp. 15–22.

TATTERSON, JAMES W. and Donald F. Wood; "PERT, CPM and the Export Process," *OMEGA, The International Journal of Management Science* (Vol. 2, No. 3, 1974).

WOOD, DONALD F.; "The Driver/Salesman and His Changing Role," *Proceedings, Transportation Research Forum, 1973* (Oxford, In.: Richard B. Cross Co., 1973).

A laker carries raw materials for an industrial plant in the heart of Cleveland. Downtown office buildings are in background. *Credit:* The Cleveland-Cliffs Iron Company.

CHAPTER THIRTEEN

Organization for Physical Distribution

There is no ideal organization pattern or model for physical distribution.

—Louis S. Goldberg
1974 National Council of Physical
Distribution Management Annual
Meeting

Line executives are a happily blessed race who radiate confidence and power. They stride confidently. They can develop a new pathway to greater profits merely by using decisive words and gestures. However, each line executive usually has one or more logisticians riding on his back. He knows that, at any moment, the logisticians may lean forward and whisper, "No, you can't do that." (An anonymous comment attributed to a military logistics officer)

—E. Grosvenor Plowman
Lectures on Elements of Business Logistics

A RELATIVELY NEW CONCEPT

This chapter deals with the placement of the physical distribution function within the framework of a firm's organizational structure. Examples are drawn from larger firms, although the same issues exist for organizing the PD function within a smaller firm. Organizational decisions, of the type described here, are made by the firm's top management. The PD practitioner is affected by them and, while the practitioner cannot make the decisions, he or she can provide valuable inputs to the organizational (or reorganizational) decision-making process.

Physical distribution organizational problems are bewildering. There are two major reasons for this. The first involves the organizational location of the various PD functions. These activities are scattered throughout the firm's organizational structure. This leads to many communication and coordination problems.

The second complication is that there are no norms or standards regarding an "ideal" PD organization. LaLonde noted: "Other corporate functions, such as production, marketing, and accounting, have had from three decades to more than three centuries to develop appropriate organizational formats and operating procedures. The corporate PD function has been in existence for less than 10 years in most firms and as a result there remains much uncertainty and 'trial and error'."[1]

One reason for the organizational problems is that PD itself is faddish today, and many firms want to have a PD department. Often, the traffic manager receives a new title, *Director of Physical Distribution*, but in effect does little more than previously. The firm, in name at least, has a physical distribution department. But little has changed.

Other firms are attempting to reorganize in order to successfully implement the PD concept. The driving force behind this is the growing recognition by top management that PD can be and is of monumental importance to the overall welfare of the firm. Professor Michael Schiff has noted a growing tendency for top management to view PD activities as important as manufacturing and marketing.[2]

DISPERSION IS PAR FOR THE COURSE

The organizational difficulties of PD are magnified because the existing PD functional areas are already located within various divisions of the company.[3] Figure 13-1 illustrates this situation. For many companies, transportation and traffic, warehousing, and plant location choice are the responsibility of the *manufacturing department*. The *finance and accounting* staff handles inventory control and order processing, while the marketing department is in control of warehouse location and customer service standards.

The problem is one of coordination. John F. Stolle noted that many companies are unsuccessful in their PD activities because:

> Their distribution activities were interrelated in a complex way, and responsibility for them was scattered throughout each organization. No one individual was responsible for distribution, and no one had the authority to coordinate the various distribution tasks. In short, while these companies had developed the ability to make an advanced total distribution analysis, they were not organized to do a total distribution job.[4]

1 Bernard J. LaLonde, "Strategies for Organizing Physical Distribution," *Transportation and Distribution Management* (January-February, 1974), p. 21.

2 Michael Schiff, "Accounting and Control in Physical Distribution," *Proceedings of the NCPDM* (1971), p. 6.

3 Milton Alexander, "Organizational Theory and Practice in Physical Distribution Management," in Jerry Schorr, Milton Alexander, and Robert J. Franco, eds., *Logistics in Marketing* (New York: Pitman Publishing Co., 1969), p. 23.

4 John F. Stolle, "How To Manage Physical Distribution," *Harvard Business Review* (July-August, 1967), p. 94.

Many firms are recognizing the above problems and also the need to consolidate the various PD activities into a single department. Table 13-1 shows the various functional areas of business for which PD departments have been given responsibility.

TABLE 13-1 Responsibility Assigned to the Physical Distribution Department

Activity	Percent of Firms Indicating Responsibility for Activity by Date of Study			
	1962[1]	*1966*[2]	*1968*[3]	*1971*[4]
Transportation	90%	89%	100%	100%
Warehousing	66	70	98	98
Inventory Management	72	55	85	90
Customer Service	N.A.[5]	36	93	93
Order Processing	12	43	89	88
Protective Packaging	40	9[6]	85	73
Production Planning	36	38	61	60
Market Forecasting	N.A.	25	43	40
Number of Firms Interviewed	50	47	87	N.A.

[1] "Profile of P.D.M.," *Transportation and Distribution Management*, June, 1962, pp. 13–17.

[2] John F. Spencer, "Physical Distribution Management Finds Its Level," *Handling & Shipping*, November, 1966, pp. 67–69.

[3] The Mason and Dixon Lines, "Physical Distribution Management: State of the Art."

[4] Herbert W. Davis, "Organization and Management of the Logistics Function in Industry," *Logistics Spectrum*, Fall, 1972, pp. 9–13.

[5] N.A. = Not Available.

[6] This activity was called "Packaging" in the 1966 survey. Such a broader term may be partially responsible for the low percent acknowledging this activity to be in physical distribution.

SOURCE: Daniel W. DeHayes, Jr. and Robert L. Taylor, "Moving Beyond the Physical Distribution Organization," *Transportation Journal* (Spring 1974), p. 34.

THE INHERENT PROBLEMS OF CHANGE

"It must be remembered that there is nothing more difficult to plan, more doubtful of success, nor more dangerous to manage, than the creation of a new system. For the initiator has the enmity of all who would profit by the preservation of the old institutions and merely lukewarm defenders in those who would gain by the new ones."[5] Machiavelli's warning concerning the problems of change are as applicable today as they were in 1513. It is human nature for the vice-president of

[5] As cited by James L. Heskett, Nicholas A. Glaskowsky, Jr., and Robert M. Ivie, *Business Logistics* (2nd ed., New York: The Ronald Press Co., 1973), p. 669.

FIG. 13-1 Physical distribution activities, responsibilities and objectives.

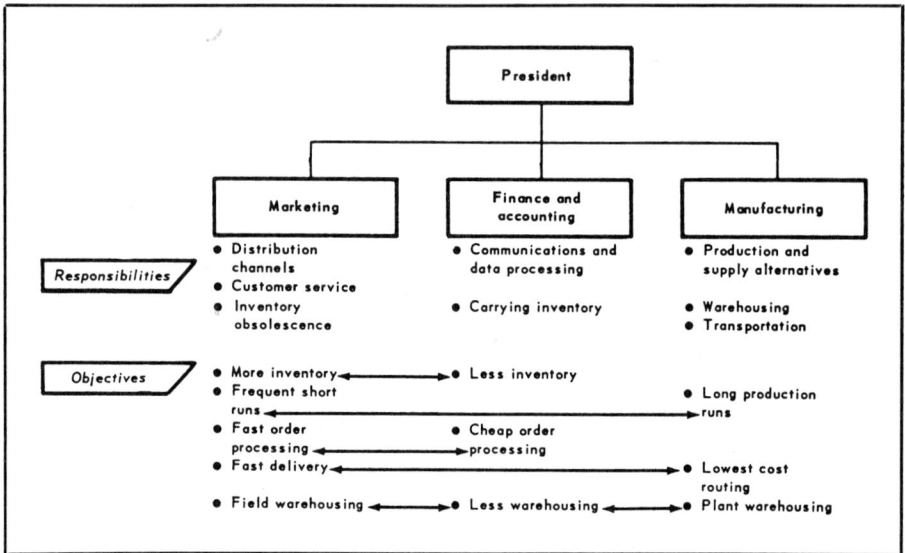

SOURCE: John F. Stolle, "How to Manage Physical Distribution," *Harvard Business Review* (Nov.-Dec., 1960).

manufacturing to oppose the reduction of his operations by moving the traffic and transportation and warehousing functions to a new PD department. Vincent A. Sarni, VP of Marketing for Pittsburgh Plate Glass Industries, noted that one of the difficulties of achieving a smoothly functioning PD operation is the ". . . ability to break down people barriers within your companies and dissipate the latent, and sometimes overt, suspicion of many managers to do things differently."[6] (See Figure 13-2.) Ward A. Fredericks, senior vice president of Massey Ferguson, Inc., noted that many firms got caughtup in the "fad" of having a PD department and therefore the prior traffic or warehouse manager was appointed the VP of Physical Distribution. The new "instant" prince was put in charge of functional areas that were previously in marketing, manufacturing, and finance. This alienated the VP's of each of these areas. Fredericks' scenarios of events is enlightening. He stated that the VP's of these other areas:

> . . . if not mad at him [the VP of PD] . . . at least were displaying lot of passive resistance to whatever he was going to do.
>
> This new *Vice President* was so anxious to make some of the cost saving promises come true (to make his mark on the corporation hierarchy) that

[6] Vincent A. Sarni, "PD in the Near Future," *Proceedings of the NCPDM* (1973), p. 47.

FIG. 13-2 Executives often resist changes in organizational structure.

"Umm ... Mr. Gaffney ..."

SOURCE: Reproduced by permission of the artist and the Masters Agency.

he started questioning some of the requirements registered on his group by the marketing and manufacturing people, respectively.

Now can you think of any better way to torpedo a guy than having the vice presidents respectively of marketing, manufacturing and finance shooting at him? [See Figure 13-3.] Of course the function failed in most of the companies where the organizational solution preceded the thinking behind what the process was all about.[7]

[7] "PDM Challenged at Seminar," *Handling and Shipping* (July, 1973), p. 54.

FIG. 13-3 Physical distribution executives may receive animosity from other corporate officers.

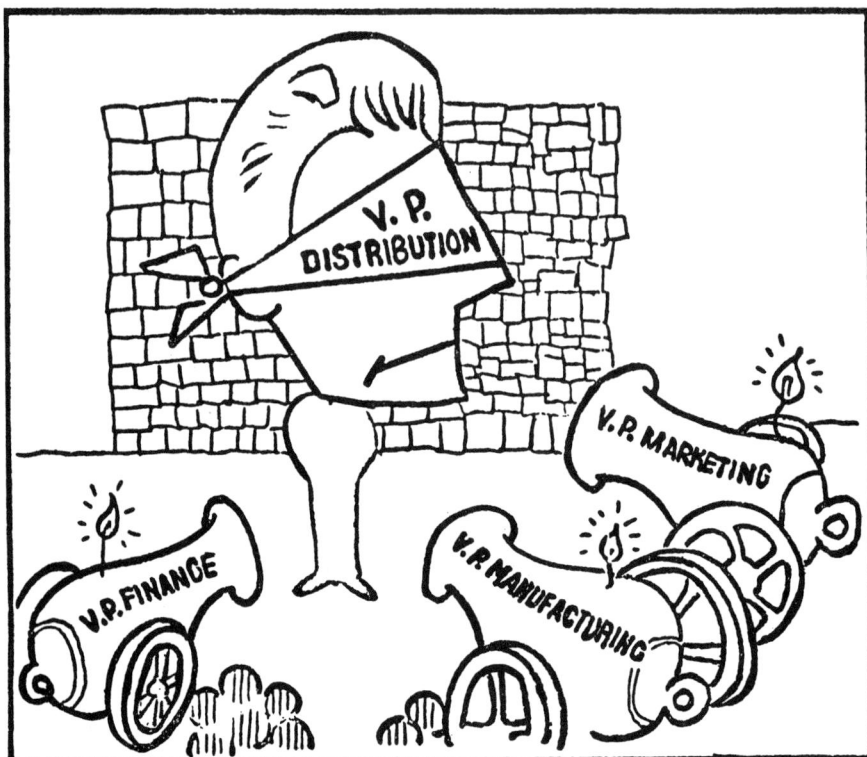

SOURCE: Reproduced by permission of *Distribution Worldwide*.

CAN REORGANIZATION BE AVOIDED?

The above discussion illustrates the potential problems involved in organizing a PD department. A very basic question then becomes, should all firms go through the trauma required of establishing a PD organization? The answer is *NO*.

Three basic factors determine whether the firm needs to recognize and establish a PD department: the *size of the PD bill*, the importance of *customer service standards*, and the *position of top management regarding PD's importance*.

THE COSTS OF PD

A key factor influencing the need to establish a PD department is the overall costs associated with PD activities. U. S. Steel with greater than 30 percent of its sales dollar involved in physical distribution activities is a much better candidate for a PD department than Merrill Lynch, Pierce, Fenner and Smith, Inc., with less than one percent of its costs involved in PD activities. Since corporations have limited managerial resources, they must stress the activities in which potentially high savings or other rewards are possible.

THE IMPORTANCE OF CUSTOMER SERVICE

The second factor determining the need for PD reorganization is the importance of rendering good customer service. As a general statement, excellence in customer service can be enhanced by a smoothly functioning PD department. A sales manager for a major distiller recently commented about what he liked best about the new PD department: " 'Buckpassing' has been reduced 300 percent. We now know who to go to about our distribution problems."[8] An executive in order processing for a paper firm made the following remark after his firm established a PD department: "Now we can pinpoint who is responsible for a service failure. Sales used to always blame me, and I would in turn blame production scheduling or warehousing. With someone in charge of the whole order and shipping cycle, we can set standards and reporting controls that identify when and where something goes haywire."[9]

TOP MANAGEMENT SUPPORT OF PD

The final consideration regarding the establishment of a PD department deals with its support and encouragement from top management. A PD department must start with full and continued support from the "top-down," as contrasted with support from only the "bottom-up." A PD department is doomed if it has only lower and middle management support. Only the senior executives of the firm can implement necessary organizational shifts and, assuming they are less than excited about the PD concept, they will be jealous about protecting their "empires" from encroachment from a new physical distribution department.

This explains why it is generally imperative that the chief executive officer of the firm be a staunch supporter and defender of the proposed PD department. When this is the case, he or she can say to others in top management something like: "You may not like the fact that we are establishing a PD department and that I am taking certain functional areas away from each of you and placing them in it. Nevertheless, it is being done for the best interests of our company. I am committed to the

---

[8] Daniel W. DeHayes, Jr. and Robert L. Taylor, "Moving Beyond the Physical Distribution Organization," *Transportation Journal* (Spring, 1974), p. 35.
[9] *Ibid.*

PD concept and it will succeed. I do not want to hear of any attempts to sabotage it."

Bowersox has stressed that care should be taken to prevent the newly created PD department from becoming a political football. He also believes that the best environment for the new organization is to receive top management support and encouragement.[10]

ACHIEVING COORDINATION

The key to effective PD operations is a high level of coordination between the functional areas. George A. Gecowets, executive director of the National Council of Physical Distribution Management, commented that the key to implementing PD is *coordination*, which may be nothing more than a continuing exchange of information among the traditional functions that combine to form the PD department.[11]

To achieve a high level of coordination, a firm can choose one of three organizational strategies. These include making no change in the present system, experimentation with unique ways of coordination with the existing system, or reorganization of the functional areas of PD into a newly established PD department.

THE STATUS QUO

For some companies it is feasible to obtain the required coordination between the functional areas of PD without any formal change in the organizational structure. This is accomplished by both formal and informal operating procedures which guarantee that the various areas will coordinate and discuss their various problems, proposals, etc. This concept of coordination is generally most feasible when the overall size of the firm and the number of employees trying to coordinate across departmental lines, is not large. For many firms, this is a viable alternative, and it avoids the problems associated with actually transferring and reassigning functional areas.

There are two major drawbacks to this arrangement. The first is that it may not work well in larger firms because of the coordination complexities encountered. This situation recently occurred when the distribution manager (who possessed limited functional authority) of a large firm spent several months developing a plan for a semiautomated warehouse at one of the firm's plants. He presented the study to top management and was chagrined by their response. He was informed

---

[10] Donald J. Bowersox, "Emerging Patterns of Physical Distribution Organization," *Transportation and Distribution Management* (May, 1968), p. 55.

[11] George A. Gecowets, "PDM—Pro and Con," *Distribution Worldwide* (March, 1973), p. 39.

that two years before, a decision was made that no additional capital improvements would be spent at the plant in question because it was considered obsolete. Unfortunately, when this decision was made, only senior management people were informed. It never occurred to top management that the distribution manager should be on the "need to know" list.

The second problem of maintaining the status quo organizational structure is that the influence of PD thinking never gets an opportunity to express itself. PD activities, since they are scattered throughout the firm, always remain subservient to the objectives of the senior department (i.e., marketing, manufacturing, finance) in which they are housed.

THE LINKING-PIN CONCEPT

The second alternative organizational structure is similar to the status quo option. In this case, certain individuals would be assigned the responsibility for ensuring coordination between PD activities. They would be known as "linking-pins," and would be assigned to work in two or three functional areas. An individual may simultaneously be assigned to the traffic department (which is a part of production) and to the warehousing department (which is a part of marketing). The advantage of this system is that the linking-pin members of each workgroup are able to coordinate and express the problems and concerns of each decision as it relates to the respective departments within which the linking-pin person operates.

There are serious problems with this concept. The most basic is that it violates the classic organizational principle of unity-of-command. Since the linking-pin in effect belongs to two or more departments, who is his or her boss? Who evaluates job performance? Who decides about promotions? Linking-pins may find themselves in the position of having no "home." It is possible for the linking-pin member to alienate all the departments for whom he or she works. They may feel that the linking-pin members are becoming too "global" in outlook, and no longer a member of that department's "team."[12]

A UNIFIED PD DEPARTMENT

The final alternative is to combine all the functional areas of PD into one department. This solution is intuitively the best, since coordination between traffic, warehousing, inventory control, and the other functional areas is facilitated when they are combined into one

---

12 See: Rensis Likert, *New Patterns of Management* (New York: McGraw-Hill Book Co., 1961) and by the same author, *The Human Organization* (New York: McGraw-Hill Book Co., 1967).

operating department. This alternative has worked well for many companies and appears to be the preferred solution to successfully overcoming the coordination problems in a physical distribution system.[13]

THE PD DEPARTMENT: INDEPENDENT OR SUBSERVIENT?

Most PD experts agree that in general it is best to unify all PD activities. The key issue is whether the PD department should be on an equal level with manufacturing, marketing, or finance or whether it should report to one of these activities.

ARGUMENTS IN FAVOR OF EQUAL STATUS

The current trend developing is to place the PD department in equal status with the other major functional areas of the firm. The major reason is that it places PD in the best position to implement cost trade-offs and the other aspects of the PD concept. Bowersox, Smykay, and LaLonde have noted:

> The fact remains that, when retained in traditional departmental groupings, the line activities of physical distribution remain secondary activities to the primary mission of their parent organization. Establishment of a line physical distribution organization eliminates the problems of secondary status as long as the responsible executive reports at an equal level with top managers of sales, finance, and manufacturing.[14]

Crown Zellerbach, which in 1974 had over $1.5 billion in sales of paper and other forest products, recently reorganized their physical distribution system. In 1972, with the help of an outside consulting firm, the firm created the position of vice-president of logistics management and positioned it as an equal to the vice-presidents of manufacturing and marketing.[15]

ARGUMENTS IN FAVOR OF A SUBSERVIENT STATUS

A survey indicated that many firms are having their PD departments report to the vice-president of marketing. A number of factors may be responsible for this organizational situation. Professor Alexander argues that there are three basic reasons why the PD department ought to re-

---

13 For a contrary point-of-view, see: Robert S. Jeffries, Jr., "Distribution Management—Failures and Solutions," *Business Horizons* (April, 1974), pp. 55–66.

14 Donald J. Bowersox, Edward W. Smykay, and Bernard J. LaLonde, *Physical Distribution Management* (2nd ed., New York: The MacMillan Co., 1968), p. 378.

15 E. L. Weinthaler, Jr., "Controlling Distribution Costs," *Distribution Worldwide* (December, 1974), pp. 36–40.

port to the marketing department. First, since survival of the firm is the first and foremost corporate goal, the company must be marketing oriented. Why? Because a marketing oriented firm stresses the importance of customer satisfaction and the need to exploit the firm's market potential. Since many of the activities of PD directly interact with marketing, it is only logical that PD should be a subpart of marketing. Another reason is that PD and channels of distribution are closely related. The physical flow of products is intimately tied to the flow of the title, information, and promotion in the marketing channel. Finally, a number of specific segments of PD interface directly with marketing activities. These include packaging (silent selling), inventory control (merchandising) and warehouse location (market penetration).[16]

Another argument for including PD in the marketing department is that it may not work well to have a co-equal PD department vis-a-vis marketing, manufacturing, and finance. This line of reason generally states that PD is still in its infancy, and senior management still does not basically "trust" its capabilities. Jeffries cites a case in which a very able vice-president of PD was not listened to by top management when he came into conflict with the VP of marketing. Jeffries noted, "It is not realistic to expect this vice-president of PD to be accepted readily in a top management role. A new marketing vice-president immediately assumes the inherent prestige of his function, but a new distribution vice-president normally does not have any prestige to inherit."[17] A distribution vice-president would still be less than equal, despite his title.

CENTRALIZATION VS DECENTRALIZATION

Another issue in PD organization strategy is whether the PD department should be centralized or decentralized. A centralized PD department implies that the corporation will have one PD organization which will administer the PD activities for the entire company. Decentralization results in PD activity decisions being made separately at the divisional or product group level, or in different geographic regions.

ARGUMENTS IN FAVOR OF A CENTRALIZED PD DEPARTMENT

Two factors argue for a centralized PD system. The first centers around the *firm's computer facility*. The PD department is a significant user of the company's computer system. For many firms, PD is the second largest user of computer time, next to the accounting department. Why

---

[16] Milton Alexander, "Organization Theory and Practice In Physical Distribution Management," in Jerry Schorr, et. al., eds., *Logistics In Marketing* (New York: Pitman Publishing Corp., 1969), pp. 17–30.

[17] Jeffries. *op. cit.*, p. 58.

is this? Because the PD function, by its very nature, involves keeping track of thousands of details and bits of information. The PD department is dependent on its daily computer print-outs which spell out the current logistical situation and also indicate future problem areas. Because of PD's dependence on computer reports, many companies have found it best to have their PD department in proximity to the corporation's main computer facility.

The second reason for a centralized management structure is the *ability to most effectively consolidate shipments.* A firm can significantly reduce its transportation costs on a per unit basis if it can ship in large quantities and qualify for the TL, CL, or incentive rates. It may also make better use of its own truck fleet. In addition, with greater volume being tendered to the carriers, it becomes more feasible to have a company wide system of make-bulk and break-bulk distribution center warehouses, which were discussed in Chapter 6. The J. I. Case Company of Racine, Wisconsin exemplifies a firm using a centralized physical distribution department. *Traffic Management* magazine noted the basic reason for this organizational structure: "Logistics centralization gains a new momentum these days as sharp cost increases force managements to learn afresh the basic economic law underlying freight transport: maximum point-to-point movement at regular intervals yields lowest cost."[18]

ARGUMENTS IN FAVOR OF A DECENTRALIZED PD DEPARTMENT

Two arguments are generally made for a decentralized PD department. The first stresses the unmanageability of a centralized system in large, multi-divisional firms. Stolle noted that in highly decentralized firms, it is often preferable that the line distribution functions remain in each autonomous division. This organizational system appears to function best when the various product lines of each division have very little in common.[19]

The second factor questions the ability of a centralized PD department to provide the required levels of customer service standards. If customers are willing to wait 30 to 60 days to receive their orders, then a centralized PD department would not prove a handicap to a multidivisional firm. If customers require 24 to 48 hour service, the centralized PD function may not be responsive enough to yield this high level of service. This type of customer service standard may require an "inhouse" (i.e., within the division) PD department that is attuned with the specific physical distribution requirements of the division.

[18] "A Case For Corporate Traffic," *Traffic Management* (December, 1975), p. 30.
[19] Stolle, *op. cit.*, p. 99.

IMPLEMENTATION OF THE PD DEPARTMENT

Assume that top management has decided that the PD concept is a viable idea and will support the creation of a unified PD department. How is this best achieved? Two approaches have been successfully used. These are the *"staff-first: line-later"* approach and the *"gradualism"* method.

THE "STAFF-FIRST, LINE-LATER" APPROACH

One approach to the implementation of the PD department is the "staff-first, line-later" method. This assumes that the establishment of a PD department will be difficult. It requires careful planning prior to consolidating the PD line activities (traffic, warehousing, etc.) into the PD department. To accomplish both this prior planning and the analysis stage of implementation, the staff employees from each functional area break-off from their line counterparts and form the combined PD *staff* for the entire firm. This combined staff section, in effect, become "in-house" consultants and they perform the basic PD concept analysis of cost-trade offs, total cost analysis, and the avoidance of functional area suboptimization. This prior planning stage may take from three months to two years or longer. Once the staff planning stage is completed, the line functions are then consolidated into a new PD department. The final conversion should proceed relatively smoothly since the prior analysis should have predicted most trouble spots.

THE "GRADUALISM" METHOD

An alternative method for implementing the PD department has been recently described by Professor LaLonde. He stated that over the past decade, there has been a tendency for firms to gradually work towards their goal of a PD department encompassing all of its functional areas. In fact, three distinct stages have been observed. The first is termed *primary integration.* Here only traffic and warehousing are combined. Assuming it is successful, the next stage is *functional integration.* Order processing and finished goods inventory are added to traffic and warehousing. At this stage the top PD executive finds himself coming into direct personal contact with the senior officers from marketing, production, and finance. The final stage of implementation is *total integration,* where all of the functional areas of PD are brought into one department. For the first time, the PD director is in a position to implement all aspects and ramifications of the PD concept.[20]

[20] LaLonde, "Strategies For Organizing PD," *op. cit.,* p. 22.

FIG. 13-4 Implementation of physical distribution at the Massey-Ferguson Corporation.

Physical distribution, like any other modern business concept, needs to start off with a group of successes which can
be proved to pretty pragmatic businessmen. They have to be able
to see that the application of the concept addresses itself to
real problems of the enterprise and that it can, in fact, be
profitable to the enterprise to adopt the whole concept.

It has to be started somewhere. . .so pick your spot,
form a small project group to come up with your recommendations,
do a good job of staff work, get the recommendation adopted
and installed.

If that's well thought out, it will be successful. . .Try to
put yourself mentally in the president's chair. Take a look
at the enterprise, take a look at what his problems are and
see to what extent the perspective that the physical distribution
approach gives you can be useful in solving that problem. Then
come up with another project. Again, aim at installing it in
the organization through the organizational structure in existence.

After the successful second installation of a recommendation based on physical distribution thinking and the physical
distribution approach, the receptivity of the corporation in
total towards an organizational realignment to accommodate the
day-by-day application of the approach will be much more
favorable.

This may sound like the hard way to get the job done and
it certainly requires a good deal more thought and planning
than the organizational approach, but I can assure you it's a
good deal better approach to assure job security for whomever
becomes the Vice President of Distribution of your company.
The speed of implementation, once you get rolling in this kind
of approach, can truly surprise you. In two to five years we
have made major changes in the $1.5 billion worldwide enterprise
that is Massey-Ferguson by taking this one-step-at-a-time tactical
approach.

There has been truly an explosion in the development of
thought about physical distribution as an art and an emerging
science. But--large corporations are not normally equipped to
deal with explosions--so implementation had better reflect
the speed of digestion which the corporation can accept. There
are alliances to be made to speed implementation--the finance
people may be easiest to convince--the systems and EDP people
also might provide a key. Above all, the first steps have to work.

SOURCE: Ward A. Fredericks, "PDM's Practicality," in "PDM Challenged at Seminar," *Handling and Shipping* (July, 1973), p. 54.

FIG. 13-5 Dracket's organizational structure.

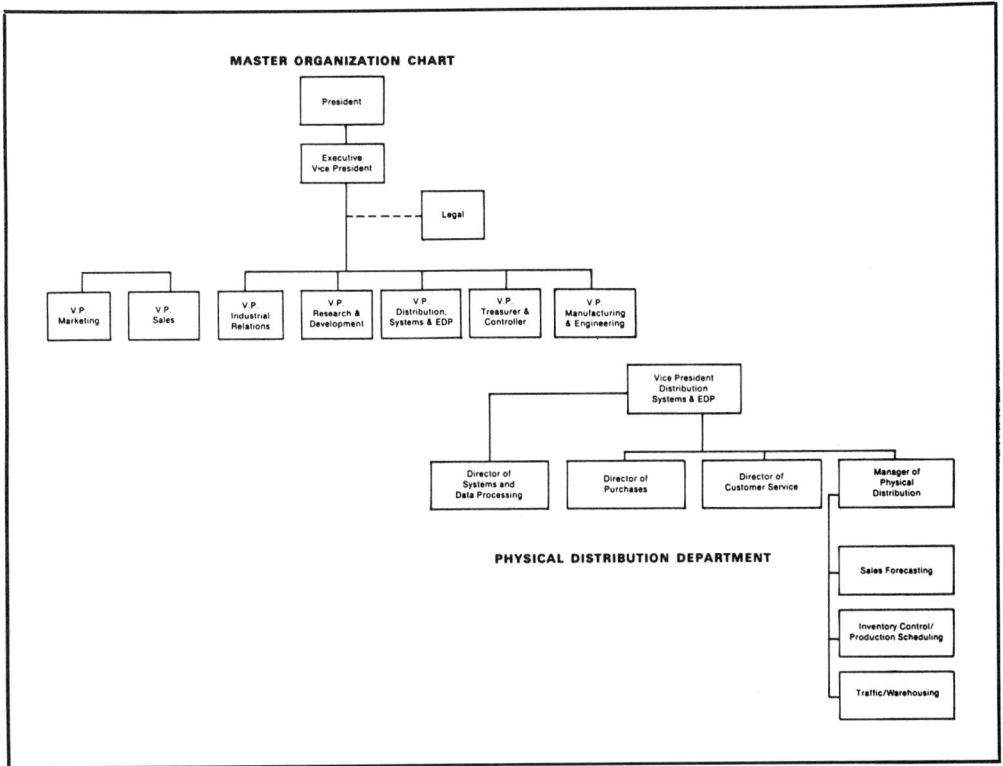

MASTER ORGANIZATION CHART

President

Executive Vice President

Legal

V.P. Marketing — V.P. Sales — V.P. Industrial Relations — V.P. Research & Development — V.P. Distribution, Systems & EDP — V.P. Treasurer & Controller — V.P. Manufacturing & Engineering

Vice President Distribution Systems & EDP

Director of Systems and Data Processing — Director of Purchases — Director of Customer Service — Manager of Physical Distribution

PHYSICAL DISTRIBUTION DEPARTMENT

Sales Forecasting

Inventory Control/ Production Scheduling

Traffic/Warehousing

SOURCE: "Company PD Profile: The Dracket Company," *Transportation and Distribution Management* (March-April, 1974), p. 46.

Another believer in the "gradualism" approach to PD implementation is Ward A. Fredericks, senior vice-president of Massey-Ferguson, Inc. Figure 13-4 presents his reasoning.

EXAMPLES OF SUCCESSFUL PD ORGANIZATION SYSTEMS

The final section of this chapter will examine the PD organizational structure of two major American corporations: The Dracket Company and the Gillette Company.

THE DRACKET COMPANY

The Dracket Company is a subsidiary of Bristol-Myers, Inc. Dracket's 2,000 employees produce approximately $200 million in annual sales. Some of their better known products include: Draino, Windex, Twinkle and Metrecal. Figure 13-5 illustrates Dracket's organization chart and their PD department organizational system. As can be seen, Dracket has a vice president in charge of distribution and electronic data processing. This officer is in charge of EDP, purchasing, customer service, order processing, sales forecasting, inventory control, production scheduling, traffic, and warehousing. Carl J. Stringer, distribution VP at Dracket, stated that there is a clear trend in the consumer products industry toward consolidating the PD functions and then appointing a senior executive to head-up the consolidated department. The reason for this trend, according to Stringer, is primarily to act as a means of effective coordination, both between PD and marketing-production and also to ensure that suboptimization does not become a problem.[21]

THE GILLETTE COMPANY

The Gillette Company, with 8,200 employees in North America, has annual sales of $545 million. Its products include shaving products, toiletry products, Toni cosmetics, Cricket cigarette lighters, Paper Mate and Flair pens and pencils. Figure 13-6 shows Gillette's organization chart and their PD organization structure.

Prior to 1969, several of Gillette's divisions had autonomous traffic and distribution departments. A comprehensive study was conducted in 1969 to determine how the company could improve its performance in the areas of customer service and product availability. Attention was also directed to reducing the overall costs of distribution. Based on this analysis, the traffic and distribution warehousing functions of all divisions were centralized. This consolidation allowed the firm to effectively achieve company-wide consolidation of shipments. In addition, improved transportation scheduling (with both common carriers and their private motor carrier fleet) allowed an overall increased level of customer service and made feasible the closing of a large number of warehouses.[22]

SUMMARY

This chapter has dealt with one of the most difficult aspects of PD— how to achieve an effective organizational structure. Because PD is still

21 "Company PD Profile—The Dracket Company," *Transportation and Distribution Management* (March/April, 1974), p. 47.

22 "Company PD Profile—The Gillette Company," *Transportation and Distribution Management* (March/April, 1974), p. 49.

FIG. 13-6 Gillette's organizational structure.

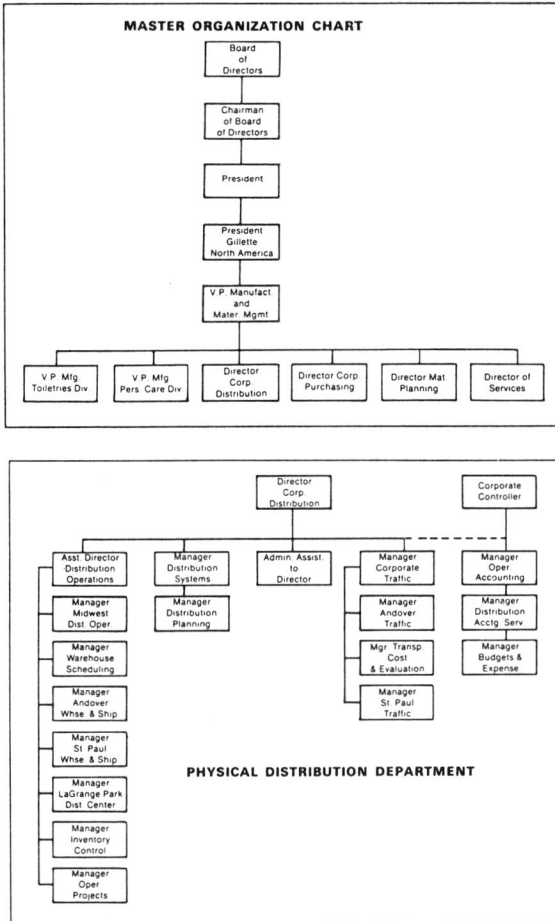

MASTER ORGANIZATION CHART

PHYSICAL DISTRIBUTION DEPARTMENT

SOURCE: "Company PD Profile: The Gillette Company," *Transportation and Distribution Management* (March-April, 1974), p. 49.

a relatively new area of analysis, there are often no right or wrong answers to the organizational issue.

One reason for the organizational problems of PD is that the functional areas of PD (traffic, warehousing, inventory control, etc.) are scattered throughout the firm. Because of this, coordination of the functional areas becomes difficult. Many companies have established PD departments to consolidate the functional areas of PD. This proposal typically encounters resistance from the existing vice-presidents of marketing, production and finance, because they do not want to see their respective operations diminished.

Because of the inherent problems of change in most firms, the issue of the necessity for a PD organization was raised. PD should be stressed if: (1) PD expenses are a significant cost item, or (2) customer service standards are an important part of the firm's marketing effort. In addition, senior management of the firm must be committed to the PD concept.

To achieve the required coordination between the functional areas of PD, there are three alternatives. The first is to leave the functional areas in their present locations and have a system of mandatory coordination. Second, "linking-pin" employees can achieve coordination by being members of more than one work-team. And, third, a unified and consolidated PD department can be organized.

The PD function can report to manufacturing, marketing, or some other department or it can be an autonomous co-equal department.

Another issue examined was whether the PD department should be centralized or decentralized. The arguments favoring centralization dealt with the need to have the computer facility nearby and also the ability to consolidate shipments on a system-wide basis.

The actual techniques of establishing the PD department were examined. It was noted that often the staff PD employees begin the change and they are followed by their line counterparts at a later date.

QUESTIONS FOR DISCUSSION AND REVIEW

1. The management consultant, John F. Magee, has stated, "Logistical system management poses some puzzling organizational problems to the typical, functionally organized firm." Discuss this statement fully.

2. "Luckily, PD organization structure has been subjected to so much study and analysis that the ideal organizational set-up can now be easily predetermined for all firms." Comment critically on this statement.

3. One of the sections of this chapter was entitled, "Dispersion is Par for the Course." What is scattered and why does this make the organizational issues more difficult?

4. The problem of "empires" being cut or diminished was discussed. What is the basic concept here and why does it make organizational problems more difficult?

5. In some cases, it is not necessary for the firm to go through the "trauma" of a PD reorganization. Under what circumstances should PD *not* be emphasized?

6. It has been said that effective PD can be a great assistance to the accomplishment of a high level of good customer service. Why is this true?

7. Why is the support of top management necessary to effectively establish a PD department?

8. Effective coordination is often thought to be one of the important aspects of PD. This chapter suggests three basic methods that can be used to achieve this objective. Discuss briefly each of the three basic alternatives. Which one do you feel is the best? Defend your answer.

9. Who is a "linking-pin" person? What problems and opportunities does this organizational alternative present?

10. Discuss briefly the *pros* and *cons* of an independent PD department that is equal to marketing, manufacturing, and finance.

11. "The PD function logically should be a subpart of the marketing department." Discuss this statement.

12. What is the difference between a centralized and a decentralized PD department? Which is more desirable? Why?

13. Present carefully an argument for the centralization of PD departments.

14. The actual implementation of the PD department is difficult. Suggest a number of solutions to the problem of actually starting a PD department.

15. Compare and contrast the actual PD organizational systems at the Dracket and Gillette companies.

CASE 13-1   ADAMS PLUMBING FIXTURE COMPANY

Located in Cincinnati, Ohio since 1923, the Adams Plumbing Fixture Company had become a well-known regional manufacturer of simple plumbing fixtures such as faucets, threaded joints, short lengths of threaded pipe, and lawn sprinklers. Its principal customers were large plumbing contractors and plumbing supply houses. The reason its sales continued to grow was that the high wage rates enjoyed by plumbers made it increasingly attractive to rely more on joints and pipe that had been cut and threaded at a factory (rather than have each plumber cut and thread the pipes "on the job"). The Adams firm sold in an area bounded by, and including, Indianapolis, Fort Wayne, Toledo, Cleveland, Youngstown, Wheeling, Winston-Salem, Atlanta, Birmingham, and Memphis. It operated a fleet of five trucks that made deliveries to about 200 regular customers. Deliveries were made on a fairly regular basis and routes were laid out so that deliveries would end in either Birmingham, Cleveland, or Youngstown, at which point the trucks would load up with steel pipe and take it to the Adams plant. On the average, each truck made 65 round trips per year.

Because of the weight of the product, the trucks in the fleet were never "cubed out," i.e., their weight capacity was reached before the trailers were full. Highway weight limitations of each of the states were carefully observed. The Adams firm had built into their computerized truck routing program a weight constraint so that the trucks would not be overloaded. In the backhaul carrying pipe, the amount of pipe purchased and loaded was always just within each truck's legal capacity.

The Adams truck fleet operated within the firm as a "profit center", which meant that it billed the marketing department for carrying all outgoing shipments, and the production department for all incoming shipments. The truck fleet covered all its expenditures—both capital and operating—and, in most years earned a small profit. This profit was compared with similar profits earned by all the other functions within the Adams firm which were also considered to be profit centers. The Christmas bonus for the manager of each profit center was based on the profit performance of his department or section.

Since inbound and outbound tonnages were evenly balanced, the same rate was charged for all company carriage. The rate was $25.00 per 2,000 lb. ton, either in or outbound. The routes were already laid out, and the farthest point was the steel plant where pipe was picked up. The $25.00 per ton rate, irrespective of distance, was easy to administer for both inbound and outbound shipments. (Note these were charges to other departments in the firm.) The trucks always arrived and left loaded to weight capacity. The $25.00 per ton figure had been calculated in mid-1972 as an average cost, including profit, of operating the fleet. The total cost was divided by the total of inbound and outbound tonnage carried.

In late 1973, fuel costs increased. Each month, the "rate" charged by Adams' fleet to the marketing and production departments increased. By mid-1974, the rate increased $40.00 per ton, either in or out. At the same time, the firm's sales slumped because high interest rates had resulted in fewer new homes being constructed.

Craig Adams, grandson of the founder, had managed the truck fleet since 1971. Because of the sales slump in 1974, he saw that the $40.00 per ton rate was not going to cover costs. In part, this was because the Adams sales force, in an effort to boost sales, had been making sales outside the traditional market area described earlier. This increased the routes some of the Adams trucks had to travel. So truck mileage was increasing while tonnages, upon which Craig Adams' charges were based, were decreasing.

Three of the five tractor-trailer combinations were in need of replacement. They were each six years old. New trucks were in short supply and one truck salesman had boasted "you can get delivery on a new 747 tomorrow, but if you want one of our new trucks, you'll have to wait six months." Other truck salesmen spoke of similar delays. The most helpful one, however, told Craig that he should not replace the old trucks with newer versions of the same thing. Fuel costs were bound to continue higher and since the Adams' trucks were nearly always

Exhibit 1, Case 13-1

Justifiable First Cost Premiums—Nomograph

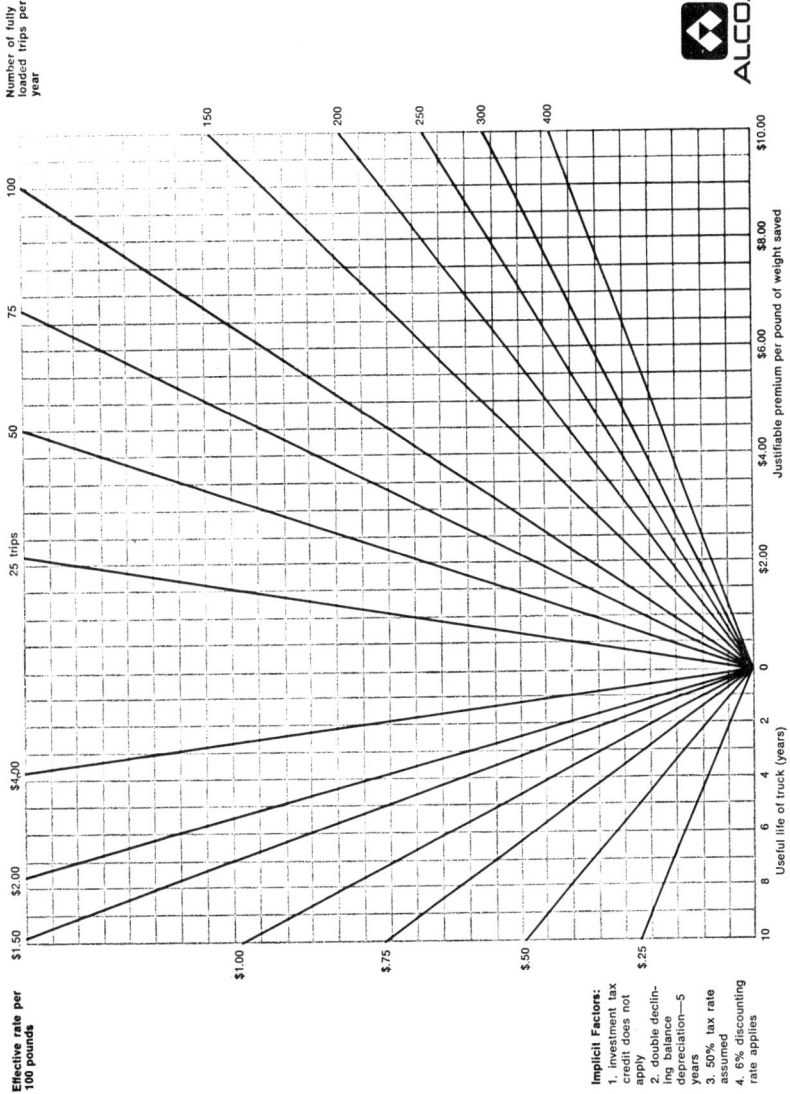

Number of fully loaded trips per year

Effective rate per 100 pounds

Useful life of truck (years)

Justifiable premium per pound of weight saved

Implicit Factors:
1. investment tax credit does not apply
2. double declining balance depreciation—5 years
3. 50% tax rate assumed
4. 6% discounting rate applies

ALCOA

loaded to their weight capacity, Craig should be thinking of a lighter weight vehicle which, given state weight regulations, could carry a heavier payload. The salesman suggested that Craig think of ordering a tractor-trailer combination that used more aluminum and less steel. The lighter weight vehicle components cost more, but the salesman gave Craig a nomograph which indicated how vehicle weight savings could be justified. The nomograph (see Exhibit 1) was used in this way:

1. on the left side of the bottom axis find the figure corresponding to the truck's useful life.

2. From that point, draw a vertical line upward until it (being drawn) intersects the heavy line on the nomograph representing the rate charged per 100 lbs. carried.

3. From that point, draw a horizontal line toward the right to the heavy line representing the number of trips per year.

4. From that point, draw a vertical line downward. It intersects the bottom right axis at the point showing the additional investment the user should be willing to make to reduce one pound of the truck's tare (empty) weight.

Question One: Using the nomograph, how much is a pound of weight-saving in a new truck worth to the Adams firm?

Question Two: At present, the Adams truck fleet charges $40.00 per ton for either outgoing or incoming shipments, irrespective of distance. How might this practice lead to the purchasing department or the marketing department making decisions, which from the entire firm's standpoint, are *suboptimal*? How might the system of charges be altered so that chances of *suboptimalization* are reduced?

CASE 13-2   COLUMBIA LUMBER PRODUCTS COMPANY

The Columbia Lumber Products Company (CLPC) had been head-quartered in Portland, Oregon, where it was founded in 1899. For many years, its principal product had been only lumber; in the 1940's it began producing plywood; and in 1960, particle board. The first two products, lumber and plywood, were produced at various sites in Oregon and marketed on the West Coast and as far east as Chicago.

Particle board was produced in Duluth, Minnesota, at a plant built with a U. S. Area Redevelopment Administration Loan in 1962. Initially, the input to the plant was trimmings and other "scrap" from CLPC's Oregon operations. Particle board sales increased so quickly that the Duluth operation consumed not only all of the former waste from CLPC's Oregon plant but also waste purchased from various lumber and wood products operations in Minnesota and Northern Wisconsin.

CLPC's sales doubled between 1960 and 1975. However, nearly all the growth had been in particle board; lumber and plywood sales remained relatively constant (although varying with changes in the home construction industry). In 1975, exports accounted for nine percent of CLPC's sales. Nearly all of this was plywood sold to Japan. Fifteen percent of CLPC's 1975 purchases were from foreign sources, 5 percent was mahogany from the Philippines used for plywood veneer; and 10 percent was wood scrap purchased from Ontario, Canada, for use in CLPC's Duluth plant.

Particle board produced in Duluth was marketed in all states east of the Rocky Mountains, although sales in the southern United States were somewhat less than spectacular.

The slowdown in home production in the mid-1970's and restrictions on lumber exports to Japan had resulted in three consecutive low-profit years for CLPC. Stockholders, the outside directors, and various lending institutions were becoming increasingly unhappy. After a long, angry board of directors' meeting, agreement was reached only with respect to what some of the organizational problems were. A partial list was:

1. The corporate headquarters was in Portland although the growth was in the Midwest. Possibly the headquarters, or at least more functions, should be shifted to an office in Duluth where the plant was, or to Chicago, where the largest sales office was.

2. There were too many vice presidents (see figure). Since four vice presidents—engineering, finance, personnel and purchasing—would reach mandatory retirement age by 1980, the number of vice presidents should be reduced from nine to no more than six (plus one executive vice president).

3. Logistics and distribution costs were higher than industry averages. Also, the majority of customer complaints dealt with poor deliveries. On the figure, a **T** shows where a traffic management function was located. Geographically, the traffic manager for overseas operations was located in Seattle, which was a foreign trade center for the Pacific Northwest. The Chicago sales office had a traffic manager who handled all fiberboard distribution, and lumber and plywood distribution east of the Rockies. Production and purchasing shared a traffic manager who was headquartered in Portland and whose principal duty was overseeing shipments of "waste" products from Oregon to Minnesota. The traffic manager who reported to the sales vice president was acknowledged to be the firm's "senior" traffic manager and more or less coordinated the efforts of the other three. He was the only one authorized to initiate action

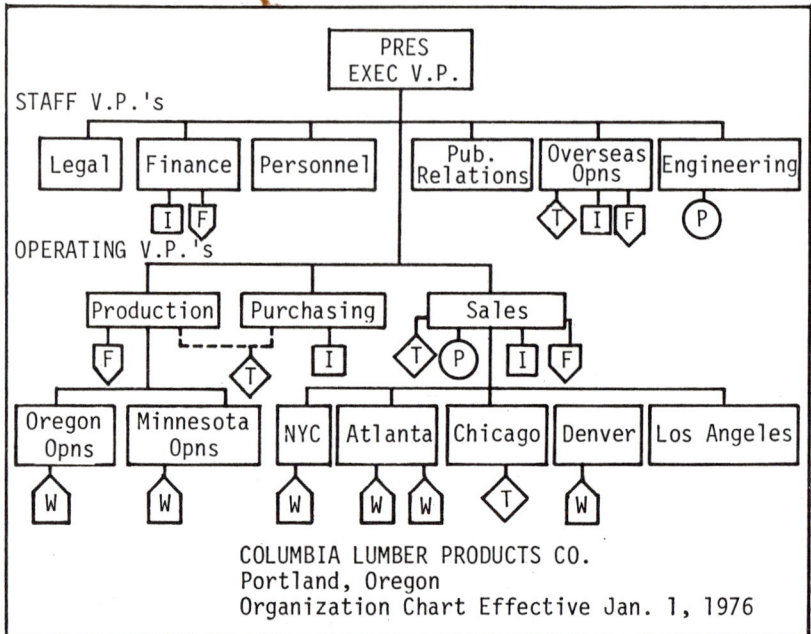

COLUMBIA LUMBER PRODUCTS CO.
Portland, Oregon
Organization Chart Effective Jan. 1, 1976

before regulatory bodies and also handled the serious negotiations with carrier rate-making bodies.

4. **P** on the figure shows two packaging engineering functions. The one under engineering was located in Portland and dealt with plywood products. The one under sales was located in Chicago and handled particle board products. **W** on the figure shows where there are company-owned warehouses. Numerous public warehouses were also used, although not continually. **I** shows locations of individuals concerned with inventory levels. All four individuals were located in Portland. **F** indicates where sales forecasting took place. Only sales and production devoted much staff effort to forecasting. Each quarter, however, the financial vice president's office coordinated all forecasts to insure comparability. Computer operations were under control of the engineering division.

Question One: Draw a new organization chart for Columbia Lumber Products Company which seems to you to overcome best the directors' criticisms of CLPC's present (January 1, 1976) organization. Indicate the geographic location of all operations shown on the new chart. Explain why you established the organization chart the way you did.

CHAPTER REFERENCES

"A Case for Corporate Traffic," *Traffic Management* (December, 1975).

ALEXANDER, MILTON; "Organizational Theory and Practice in Physical Distribution Management," *Logistics in Marketing*, Jerry Schorr, Milton Alexander, and Robert J. Franco, eds., *Logistics in Marketing* (New York: Pitman Publishing Co., 1969).

BOWERSOX, DONALD J.; "Emerging Patterns of Physical Distribution Organization," *Transportation and Distribution Management* (May, 1968).

BOWERSOX, DONALD J., Edward W. Smykay and Bernard J. LaLonde; *Physical Distribution Management* (2nd ed., New York: The MacMillan Co., 1968).

"Company PD Profile: The Dracket Company," *Transportation and Distribution Management* (March-April, 1974).

"Company PD Profile: The Gillette Company," *Transportation and Distribution Management* (March-April, 1974).

DeHAYES, DANIEL W., JR., and Robert L. Taylor; "Moving Beyond the Physical Distribution Organization," *Transportation Journal* (Spring, 1974).

FREDERICKS, WARD A.; "PDM's Practicality," in "PDM Challenged at Seminar," *Handling and Shipping* (July, 1973).

GECOWETS, GEORGE A.; "PDM—Pro and Con," *Distribution Worldwide* (March, 1973).

HESKETT, JAMES L., Nicholas A. Glaskowsky, Jr., and Robert M. Ivie; *Business Logistics* (2nd ed., New York: The Ronald Press Co., 1973).

JEFFRIES, JR., ROBERT S.; "Distribution Management—Failures and Solutions," *Business Horizons* (April, 1974).

LaLONDE, BERNARD J.; "Strategies for Organizing Physical Distribution," *Transportation and Distribution Management* (January-February, 1974).

LANCIONI, RICHARD and John Grashof; "Physical Distribution Organization and Information Systems Development," *International Journal of Physical Distribution* (Spring, 1973), pp. 183–190.

LIKERT, RENSIS; *New Patterns of Management* (New York: McGraw-Hill Book Co., 1961).

————; *The Human Organization* (New York: McGraw-Hill Book Co., 1967).

"PDM Challenged at Seminar," *Handling and Shipping* (July, 1973).

SARNI, VINCENT A.; "PD in the Near Future," *Proceedings of the NCPDM* (1973).

SCHIFF, MICHAEL; "Accounting and Control in Physical Distribution," *Proceedings of the NCPDM* (1971).

SHORT, LARRY E.; "Planned Organizational Change," *MSU Business Topics* (Autumn, 1973), pp. 53–62.

STOLLE, JOHN F.; "How to Manage Physical Distribution," *Harvard Business Review* (July-August, 1967).

WEINTHALER, E. L., JR.; "Controlling Distribution Costs," *Distribution Worldwide* (December, 1974).

This warehouse contains a variety of products. *Credit*: Allis-Chalmers Corporation, Industrial Truck Division.

CHAPTER FOURTEEN

Physical Distribution System Controls

It should appear quite evident that, until decision-makers in Marketing (and this goes down to field salesmen) are evaluated and rewarded on their profit contribution determined after deducting relevant P.D. costs, P.D. costs will continue to increase despite the best efforts of P.D. management.

—MICHAEL SCHIFF
Accounting & Control in
Physical Distribution Management
1972

Hence, the most potent thief—the enemy we really face—is not the armed hijacker, dangerous as he may be, but the dishonest employee, . . . who somehow evades security, and steals a few cartons, a box of shoes, some dresses or television sets. He may make use of these items himself, or, as so often happens, he begins to work up his own personal disposal system for monetary profit.

—FBI DIRECTOR CLARENCE M. KELLEY
Speaking at Transportation Association
of America's 1973 Cargo Security
Conference

The company estimates 600,000 to 720,000 boxes of cereal are affected by the recall but 240,000 to 300,000 are in its own warehouses.

Item in *San Francisco Chronicle*
January 13, 1975

A driver brings home a new percolator, cheerfully announces it was a freight overage and his wife gratefully accepts it as though it were a legitimate gift.

GO, *Transport Time of the West*
November, 1974

The witness told the committee that today a truck dispatcher, "the key man," often makes the initial approach in arranging a theft to a truck driver. The dispatcher knows what goods are moving where. . . . On a load of whiskey worth $100,000, the dispatcher would make between $5,000 and $7,500 for his part, the witness said.

Item in *Journal of Commerce*
May 3, 1973

ANTICIPATE AND MONITOR, PREVENT OR CORRECT

Many textbook authors assume that if all the lessons they teach are followed, all will go well. Unfortunately, this is not so. In the "real world" many things can and do go wrong. This chapter deals with *controlling* the physical distribution system in order to prevent, or at least reduce the likelihood of, things going wrong. No list of potential hazards confronting the physical distribution manager would be complete. This chapter deals with only a few separate topics ranging from the rather mundane problem of costs getting out of control to the more exciting problem of protecting shipments from thefts.

This chapter is especially important to individuals training for entry level positions in physical distribution management. Much of their initial performance with their new employer will be evaluated on the basis of how well they exercise *control* responsibilities. Inability to carry out control functions is easily spotted at the beginning levels of management. This is because the responsibilities are somewhat limited in nature and there are others in the firm with similar tasks with whom comparisons can be made.

This discussion deals more with those controlling functions which are somewhat *protective* in nature. They must be employed to keep a firm's position from worsening. In a competitive world with small, and sometimes shrinking profit margins, application of tight controls may allow a firm to maintain its position while competitors fall behind.

A person with a career in physical distribution management will confront the issues and problems presented in this chapter many times during the course of his or her career. The problems discussed here cannot be eliminated, they can just be controlled. Hence, the title and purpose of this chapter.

ACCOUNTING CONTROLS

In the early 1970's, a number of firms belonging to the National Council of Physical Distribution Management funded a study conducted by Professor Michael Schiff, which dealt with accounting controls in physical distribution management.[1] In his report, Schiff was critical of two industry practices, both of which dealt with what he felt was improper cost allocation. He believed that physical distribution costs should be considered as selling costs insofar as determining sales strategies and incentives. Goals were set for salesmen. But the goals ignored physical

---

[1] Michael Schiff, *Accounting and Cost Control in Physical Distribution Management* (Chicago: The National Council of Physical Distribution Management, Inc., 1972). This study is the same one as cited elsewhere in this book.

distribution costs and therefore sales personnel ignored this expense item.[2]

Schiff also felt that decisions to increase inventory should be subjected to the same amount of management scrutiny as decisions to commit a like amount of funds to any other undertaking. He found this problem would be overcome by assigning an imputed interest charge on the additional investment in inventory to the unit or individual responsible for the decision to increase inventory size.[3]

Schiff devoted a chapter to methods of controlling physical distribution costs and described four methods.[4] They were:

1. *Control using a budget* meant that a conventional budget was set up once a year in advance, based on historic costs applied to anticipated volumes. During the course of the year, monthly performance reports are prepared, comparing costs to date with costs for the same period one year ago and with the budget for the current year. Each month a "budget variance report" is prepared which explains why the amounts spent differed from the figures which had been budgeted.

2. *Control using standard costs* involved calculating "standard" (sometimes "average") costs for performing various functions. Detailed analysis might show that it costs $42.59 to move a pallet load of products through a warehouse. Reporting techniques would be established that would constantly monitor these costs of moving the pallet through the warehouse and variances, especially costs on the high side, would be noted.

3. *Freight cost control* was used by firms spending a large proportion of their distribution budgets on transportation. A large computer stored freight routing and tariff data for the firm's most repetitive shipments. Data from actual shipments are then compared with information in the computer's memory.

4. *Customer service control* involved the establishment of service standards for reaching major customers. The reporting system indicates instances when and reasons why the established standards had not been met.[5]

Accounting is a powerful management tool and is a common denominator used throughout the firm. Schiff's work is of high quality and useful to those interested in the interaction between two management

[2] Schiff, pp. 1–16.

[3] Schiff, pp. 1–18. He said that a similar example of a decision which may ignore investment considerations is the decision to increase the amount of accounts receivable.

[4] Schiff's chapter 4 is devoted to controlling physical distribution costs.

[5] Customer service standards were discussed in Chapter 3. Note that they can be so formalized that control-type measures can be applied to determine whether they are being met.

goals—physical distribution "efficiency" and accounting "controls." Schiff's book is also of value to those who are attempting to understand why the physical distribution concept is (or is not) being adopted by top management.

An example of one firm's efforts at controlling distribution costs comes from the Crown Zellerbach Corporation.[6] They are: (1) identified physical distribution costs; (2) established standards, including customer service standards, by which performance could be measured; (3) took specific actions to reduce costs or improve performance; and (4) undertook long-range distribution planning which would allow for more orderly facility expansion and market development. As an illustration of their analysis, they scrutinized private truck operating costs at one of their distribution centers. Through accurate methods of cost determination and allocation, they determined that they should not be operating their own trucks for hauls with a radius over 150 miles. Longer hauls were turned over to common carriers.

Lanes. Crown Zellerback also developed "lanes" which are linked origins and destinations over which large volumes of the firm's traffic move. Each month a report is prepared for each lane, giving details on the type of product shipped, the volume in each shipment, the mode, and the cost. This makes it possible to determine after each month that some loads should have been consolidated or that some lower cost carrier mode should have been used. The resulting information suggests what actions should be taken in the future to improve performance on any lane in question. This information is also useful when conducting rate and service negotiations with carriers. However, the principal value of the monthly "lane" report is that it serves as a control document because it enables management to review performance and make suggestions for improvements.

WORKER PRODUCTIVITY

Labor is expensive, and its efficient utilization is necessary for a profitable operation. The two most frequent uses of labor in physical distribution are in warehousing and in transport of goods. Both warehousing and trucking involve heavy investments in capital equipment (which frequently reduces the need for workers). The workers and the equipment must be used in a manner which achieves the lowest-cost for a given volume of output. In most areas, warehouse workers, drivers, and helpers, are unionized, and work-rule provisions influence productivity. In areas where warehouse workers' unions resist changes in work rules,

6 This discussion is adapted from a paper by E. L. Weinthaler, Jr. of Crown Zellerbach, delivered at the N.C.P.D.M. annual conference in October, 1974.

a warehouse may become prematurely obsolete, not because of its structure or equipment, but because of high-cost work practices which the union insists on continuing. Firms faced with such a situation can improve warehouse efficiency by locating a new warehouse in an area outside the original union's jurisdiction. The new warehouse would be either non-union or, if unionized, the union should be one that accepted the new work practices.

Efficient use of labor is usually accomplished by scheduling work in advance. In a warehouse the time for performing each task, such as opening a truck door, stacking a pallet, or "picking" a case of outgoing goods, is calculated. Precise time breakdowns—to the number of seconds —are used. The location of the pallet-load in the warehouse or its height above the floor makes a difference. Outgoing cases being picked also require different amounts of time, again depending on their location, volume and weight. "Picking" and assembling an outgoing order comprising cases of different dimensions is more time-consuming than if all cases are of the same or similar size. These data are used in two ways. First, they indicate that the goods within the warehouse should be arranged so that the more popular, or faster-moving, items are located in slots where they will require less time for storage and retrieval. Second, through use of computer programs, an order picker's travel sequence can be arranged in a manner which minimizes time that he or she (and whatever equipment is being used) will require.

SHORT INTERVAL SCHEDULING

One method of analysis is "short interval scheduling," which means looking at each worker's activity (or inactivity) in small time segments. An amount of time is assigned to each unit of work and then the individual's work is scheduled in a manner which (1) utilizes as much of each worker's time as possible and (2) maximizes output for each worker. This scheduling technique is useful to supervisory personnel. It indicates how workers are performing in relation to "standards." Surprisingly, perhaps, some workers regard comparison with computer-established standards as being more equitable than sole reliance on the foreman's judgment of who is a "hard worker." Each day's work for the operation is plotted out and is, in essence, a summation of each worker's tasks. For a warehouse, the scheduling may also be tied into departure times for delivery trucks (also controlled by computerized scheduling) and arrival of trucks with incoming freight. (Large buyers frequently require suppliers' trucks to arrive within rather limited time-blocks, say, 30 minutes or an hour, because this reduces congestion at the receiving dock and spreads the arrival time of trucks throughout the working day.) Because an operation's entire work day can be pre-scheduled, the supervisor can tell as the day progresses how the actual progress compares to the schedule. If at the end of the first hour in an eight-hour shift, less than 1/8th of the work has been accomplished, the supervisor must take steps to catch up within the second hour (or at least to fall no further behind).[7] Short interval scheduling can also be used by intermediate management to assess the effectiveness of supervision. One firm has a "test time review" report to be filled out by the immediate supervisor on a daily basis. In case the immediate supervisor fails to note or explain the lost time, the information appears on a form entitled "unexplained lost time," which intermediate management prepares to cover instances when more time was spent on a job than had been assigned *and* the immediate supervisor failed to report it.[8]

DRIVER SUPERVISION

When discussing supervision of physical distribution labor, a distinction has to be made between warehousing and trucking. In warehousing, the supervisor or foreman is physically present and expected to be "on top" of any situation. Truck drivers, however, once on the road are removed from immediate supervision. In addition, they are in day-to-day contact with customers. Both of these factors indicate different types of supervision, as well as different types of workers, are required. Later in this chapter, in the section entitled "vehicle control," there is a description of devices used to monitor the performance and operation of trucks. They also monitor the performance of the truck driver.

When a worker in a warehouse falls behind schedule, the fact is noticed almost immediately and corrective action can be taken. A foreman can choose from a range of supervisory techniques to provide an incentive for the worker to improve performance. The work of a truck driver is more difficult to evaluate. If he falls behind schedule, it may be because of traffic conditions or the consignee's loading dock was occupied when he arrived, and it was necessary to wait.

Initially, all that a supervisor can do is to accept the driver's word. On the other hand, it is necessary to have a control mechanism so that drivers who continually encounter delays can be distinguished from those who do not. Figure 14-1 is a computer printout showing the monthly delivery performance. Shown are the number of cases and weight handled; the amount of time spent waiting, unloading, and driving; and the truck's average speed. The "P" indicates that pallets are utilized and that the receiver uses a fork-lift truck to unload the trailer. "C" means specialized wheeled carts are used instead of pallets. Various

---

[7] For a discussion of analyzing labor operations in a warehouse, see Arthur S. Graham, "Evaluating and Controlling Manpower Effectiveness," a paper delivered at the N.C.P.D.M. annual conference in October, 1974.

[8] Roland T. Fisher, "Short Interval Scheduling," (a paper presented at N.C.P.D.M. San Francisco Roundtable Workshop, April 29, 1975).

FIG. 14-1 Delivery performance.

ASSOCIATED FOOD STORES, INC.

PAGE NO. 2

DELIVERY PERFORMANCE ANALYSIS
WEEK ENDING 11/01/74

REPORT NO. 2 -STORE-

DRIVER	P	STORE	CASES	WEIGHT	WAIT	UNLD	CS/HR	ADJ CS/HR
B	,D.	P BEL AIR MARKET #7	467		.1	.3	1,556	1,167
D	,P.	P BEL AIR MARKET #7	1,055	30,699	.1	.5	2,110	1,758
F	,J.	P BEL AIR MARKET #7	242	6,000	.1	.4	605	484
M	,J.	P BEL AIR MARKET #7	120		.2	.3	400	240
		TOTAL	1,884	36,699	.5	1.5	1,256	942
F	,J.	C BELL MARKET #1	1,038	24,525	.1	1.1	943	865
F	;J.	C BELL MARKET #1	446	14,306	.1	.9	495	446
F	,J.	P BELL MARKET #1	50	2,000	.1	.2	250	166
		TOTAL	1,534	40,831	.3	2.2	697	613
F	,J.	C BELL MARKET #2	300	12,000	.1	.7	428	375
M		C BELL MARKET #2	729		1.2	1.5	486	270
M	,B.	C BELL MARKET #2	1,242	30,420	.1	1.8	690	653
V		BELL MARKET #2	1		.1	.1	10	5
		TOTAL	2,272	42,420	1.5	4.1	554	405
G	A.	C BELL MARKET #3	913	23,049	.2	1.0	913	760
M		C BELL MARKET #3	1,200	30,601	.3	1.0	1,200	923
		TOTAL	2,113	53,650	.5	2.0	1,056	845
M		C BELL MARKET #4	408	10,392	.2	.9	453	370
M	,J.	C BELL MARKET #4	671	15,109	.2	.9	745	610
		TOTAL	1,079	25,501	.4	1.8	599	490

Courtesy Associated Food Stores.

comparisons are made including the average cost per ton and the average cost per case. "Adjusted cases per hour" takes into account both waiting time and unloading time.

This arrangement of data can be used, for example, to support a driver's contention that his relatively poor performance is caused by delays at the customer's receiving dock. This allegation could be verified by having a different driver make the deliveries to determine whether the delays still happen. If they did, the supplier would approach the customer with these printouts and indicate that some improvements are needed in his receiving procedures.

If it is determined that the cause of the problem is an inadequacy of the customer's receiving ability, care would have to be used in informing the customer. The supplier's marketing staff would have to be made aware of the problem and calculations would have to be made of how profitable the account was at the present time, given the unloading handicaps. If it were determined that the unloading delays made servicing the account unprofitable, then the supplier might threaten to discontinue service or raise prices. If it were found that servicing the account was profitable in spite of the unloading delays, a more tactful approach would be employed.

This illustrates an interface between marketing and distribution in that care has to be used when establishing customer service standards to insure that they do not become a drain on profits. In this example, one does not know what his competitors would do; they are probably handicapped by the same inefficiencies at the customer's receiving dock. The buyer might respond that the problem is not at his dock, but that he runs a friendly and relaxed operation, and if delivery drivers want to have a cup of coffee and chat for a few minutes before unloading their trucks, he doesn't mind. What he does mind, however, is having this friendly atmosphere labeled as "inefficient" by some supplier's computer. In this situation, the customer has indicated that he likes the supplier's drivers but he does not like the supplier's computer.

The point of this example is that supervision of the driver could be related to a firm's selling efforts.

IMPROVING PERFORMANCE

Knowledge of supervisory techniques is important to college students studying physical distribution because a common first position in physical distribution involves supervising a number of people. This section has dealt with measuring performance. However, the goal should be to improve performance (see Figure 14-2). Emery Air Freight Corporation uses a three-pronged approach, consisting of performance audit, feedback, and positive reinforcement. After a worker's performance is measured, it is important that this information be "fed" back to him,

FIG. 14-2   The objective of supervision is to improve performance.

"That new man may bear watching."

so he knows his relative performance. According to a spokesman for Emery, there are several clues which will indicate that lack of "feedback" is a cause of poor performance. They are:

    1. When asked, a worker does not accurately and immediately know his level of performance.

    2. When asked, a worker does not know a performance standard exists.

    3. Whenever a specific performance is consistently below standard.

    4. When an employee says he does not know what he is supposed to do.[9]

Once performance information is made available to the worker, the next step is to continually reinforce his or her instances of good performance with some form of reward which may be anything from an approving nod to a large Christmas bonus. The Emery spokesman asked the question as to which of the following is the better use of an available reward:

    a. "John, would you agree to take the day shift starting Monday?"

    b. "John, your order processing performance for the past three months has been ten percent above our goal. That's an outstanding accomplishment. As a result, you may choose your shift assignment. Starting Monday, which shift would you like?"[10]

Previously it was noted that union work rules are usually inflexible and impossible to change. This is not always true. Sometimes, as part of the bargaining transaction, it is possible for management to get unions to agree to alter some work practices.[11] Usually management would have to demonstrate that neither the union as a group nor its members as individuals would be adversely affected. Hence, when performance standards are measured, some attention should be paid to those standards which are influenced or controlled by contractual work rules. It will be necessary to calculate the savings from eliminating or altering a work rule. This information is necessary to management. As it goes into collective bargaining sessions because it establishes a "value" to management of each contemplated change.

Performance standards, as such, may not be included in the contract. However, provisions have to be made giving management the right to establish them and to use them. The union would want protection from "unreasonable" standards. Mutually agreed-upon procedures are

9 Paul F. Hammond (of Emery Air Freight Corporation), "Increasing Productivity Through Performance Audit, Feedback, and Positive Reinforcement," in *1974 Papers of the American Society of Traffic and Transportation,* p. 31.

10 Hammond, p. 31.

11 See "Productivity Bargaining," *Warehousing Review* (June-July, 1972), pp. 3–7.

also necessary for handling new or continuing employees who consistently fall below the established standards.

PRODUCT RECALLS

A vexing physical distribution problem, one which has cost several physical distribution or product-line managers their jobs, involves the inability to cope with a product recall crisis. Product recall occurs when a hazard or defect is discovered in a manufactured item which is already in the distribution channels. This necessitates a reversal in the usual outward flow of merchandise. One manufacturer who undertook a product recall instructed all his retailers to ship the goods in question back to his plant. To his dismay, he discovered that many of his retailers did not know how to write a bill of lading or to take any of the other necessary steps to accomplish the movement.[12]

In recent years there have been well-publicized recalls involving soups, drugs, toys, and autos. From the manufacturer's standpoint, the publicity is undesirable. This is an instance where the saying "There's no such thing as bad publicity" does not hold. If the manufacturer plays down the amount of publicity, he runs the risk that a user will be harmed by the defective product, after the defect has been known to exist by the manufacturer. In a subsequent lawsuit, the injured consumer might allege that the manufacturer failed to devote sufficient effort and publicity to his recall campaign.

Once a recall campaign is completed (or underway, depending how it is conducted), the manufacturer and his distributors must take immediate steps to refill the retailer's shelves with either uncontaminated or defect-free batches of the same product or with a substitute product. While this step is not as important as the recall, it must be undertaken to minimize losses. Otherwise, competitors will take the opportunity to suggest that the retailer use their own product to fill his empty shelf spaces.

Sometimes products are recalled through different channels than they are distributed. The National Wholesale Druggist Association favors a policy which eliminates the wholesaler in product recalls. Therefore the manufacturer must deal directly with the retail pharmacist, rather than through a wholesaler.

Goods are returned to the manufacturer even though he may simply destroy them after he receives them. In theory, it would be easier to authorize retailers or wholesalers to destroy them. However, if the goods are, in fact, hazardous, it may be desirable for the manufacturer to supervise their destruction. There is always a risk that the defective

[12] Individual being interviewed asked to not be identified.

goods may not be properly disposed of, and individuals will be injured. Accounting controls are necessary to insure that individuals returning the recalled materials are reimbursed for the goods they return and for no more.

Sometimes the problem can be overcome by merely changing the product's label or adding a warning label. A lamp manufacturer might be required to add a sticker to each lamp, saying, "Do not use light bulbs larger than 100 watts in this lamp." In this instance, the manufacturer could have the stickers attached at some intermediate point between the place of manufacture and the retail outlet. In a report released by the National Highway Traffic Safety Administration regarding defective automobile jacks, is the statement:

> The manufacturer of the [defective] models has assured NHTSA that corrective measures have been taken in production procedures to prevent recurrence of this defect. He has also offered present owners new labels to replace the old labels with the old ratings. The new label will contain the lower rating and a new list of safety precautions.[13]

Product recall takes many forms. The differences depend upon the type of product. The responsible government agency (including state and local, as well as foreign governments) all have their own procedures. The degree of danger posed by the defect also differs. The worst defects are those which are discovered to be life-threatening on a direct "cause and effect" basis. Less serious are the defects which are discovered to be *possible* threats to life, such as being linked to causes of cancer if exposure is over a long period of time. Even less of a serious problem is posed by products which are discovered to be merely mislabeled such as saying "contents 16 ounces" when, in fact, the label should read "contents 12 ounces." In this last situation there is no hazard to potential users; however, the manufacturer, and possibly the distributors, would be guilty of violating statutes dealing with consumer fraud.

FEDERAL AGENCIES INVOLVED WITH RECALLS

Federal agencies have various responsibilities. The Food and Drug Administration (F.D.A.) is concerned with food, drugs and cosmetics. In what they consider to be a "Class I Recall," i.e. the most serious of hazards, such as botulism toxin in foods, they will insist that the product be recalled at the consumer level and all intermediate levels, and that 100 percent effectiveness checks be made of all distribution points. They will also cause a public warning to be issued.

Another involved federal agency is the Consumer Product Safety

---

[13] Excerpt from National Highway Traffic Safety Administration, *Consumer Protection Bulletin*, December 17, 1974. He did not specify how present jack owners would learn about the new labels.

Commission. They are less concerned with recall procedures as such, since their approach is to *ban* the sale of products they deem to be hazardous, thereby making it an offense for a retailer, wholesaler, or other distributor to sell a banned product. If that agency bans the sale of a specific item, it becomes "frozen" in all distribution channels since it cannot be sold. Manufacturers and distributors are required to *re-purchase* the banned items. In such a situation, the manufacturer can decide whether he wants the banned items returned to him for correction. The Consumer Product Safety Commission does not concern itself with the items handled by the F.D.A., although it may concern itself with how the items are packaged. The Consumer Product Safety Commission is a much newer agency and has taken over product safety functions of several older federal agencies, and administers some new programs such as those dealing with flammable fabrics. From a distribution control standpoint, note that the F.D.A. has procedures for *recall* which result in a reverse flow of the defective products from the consumer back to the manufacturer. The Consumer Product Safety Commission merely bans sale of the product and halts it in its place in the distribution network.

A third federal agency is the National Highway Traffic Safety Administration which is concerned with motor vehicles and their accessory parts. They do not engage in recalls; they are responsible only for causing the manufacturer to *notify* each purchaser that a defect has been discovered. In practice, the buyer is told to take his auto to the nearest dealer who will correct the defect at no cost to the buyer. The method of notification is registered mail to the first purchaser of record. Sometimes it is not necessary for the owner to take the vehicle back to the dealer. In one instance, the manufacturer had to issue a corrected sticker showing different tire pressures; the owners were instructed to place that decal over the original one (and to see a dealer if they had difficulty following the instructions).

PUBLICITY, LIABILITY AND "FIRE DRILLS"

Product recall, in whatever form it takes, is an extremely serious matter for the manufacturer and all parties in the distribution network. Adverse publicity and large lawsuits can be devastating. Top management must be involved in any recall activity. Other involved staff would be from the firm's legal, controller, public relations, quality control, product engineering, and marketing staffs. Management, who may never have known how the firm's physical distribution system functioned, will be anxiously examining its effectiveness in handling a product recall. Usually a firm designates one individual to be responsible for handling recall activity. Some firms even have practice or "fire drill" recalls to determine their speed and degree of coverage. All actions that a firm takes to prepare for a hypothetical recall are important for two reasons. First, they will allow better performance when the real emergency arises. Second, in case the recall is not completely successful and lawsuits result, a portion of the firm's defense might be the precautionary measures it had undertaken.

BATCH NUMBERS

The possibility of defective products and product recalls increases the need for positively identifying each product or batch as it leaves the assembly line. If a defect is detected, it is easier to "zero in" on the group or batch of items produced at about the same time (which should, at least, be inspected to assure that they are not also defective). Items such as office machines contain serial numbers and their entire move through a distribution system is recorded by that number. In a recall, they would be relatively easy to trace. For items that do not contain serial numbers, a "batch" number is commonly used. An example would be 33 C 7 B 2 5 where

> 33 was day of the year (February 2)
> C was plant
> 7 was year 1977
> B was production line B
> 2 was second shift
> 5 was fifth hour of that shift

A computerized inventory control system might record the batch number that was stencilled on each carton. (This information would also be used to insure that the inventory was being "turned" in proper sequence.) If the batch numbers were recorded as the goods moved through the distribution system, in a recall it would be possible to trace each carton to a warehouse or to a retailer. The problem, and the accompanying adverse publicity, could then be more regionalized than if the manufacturer had to undertake a nationwide search campaign.

PILFERAGE

This section deals with pilferage, the following section, with theft. Pilferage is, of course, one form of theft. Pilferage is usually thought of as theft by one's own employees on a somewhat casual, although generally repetitive basis. The materials stolen are usually for the employee's own use. Theft is more likely to be conducted by outsiders, although one's employees may be involved. It is conducted on an organized basis and the stolen goods are likely to be sold. An East Coast importer made the distinction this way: "Theft we consider as individual packages, or the loss of the whole package; pilferage is where packages are opened and a certain portion . . . taken."[14]

Since pilferage involves one's own employes, this indicates that controls must begin with the hiring process and they must continue with supervisory practices. This is an area where double standards exist. A warehouse employee caught carrying a can of the company's gasoline out of the warehouse and placing it in his private auto would be subjected to disciplinary action or perhaps fired. Yet the warehouse superintendant may use the company car, with company gasoline, to run personal errands. At executive levels an effort may be made to provide executives with an opportunity to travel to professional meetings in Florida, California, or Hawaii, while on the company expense account. This is a form of disguised compensation since the executive will not have to pay taxes on the expense reimbursement payments he receives for these vacation-like "business" trips.

Employees at lower levels tend to view pilferage as their opportunity to obtain comparable disguised (and non-taxable) income. Pilferage is widespread and usually cannot be completely eliminated. Most firms find it less expensive to tolerate a small amount of pilferage than it is to impose a system of "total" control. The principal cost of total control is in employee turnover; many individuals choose not to work under such close scrutiny and supervision.

A toll bridge authority installed an elaborate toll collection monitoring system that made it virtually impossible for toll collectors to cheat. Turnover among toll-takers increased drastically for two reasons: The total income of most toll-takers was apparently reduced. And, without a chance to attempt to "beat" the supervisory system, the tedious job of toll collection became even more tedious. Costs of increased employee turnover soon exceeded the savings from the "cheat-proof" system. The bridge authority then decided to adopt an unannounced policy of letting each collector "pilfer" up to ten dollars per week. That is, even though they knew exactly what a toll collector should have collected, they would say nothing to him until the losses for which he was responsible exceeded ten dollars per week.

> The toll-collection manager has an informal system to signal to the collector that he is under suspicion. A brightly painted authority police car parks right in front of the malefactor's toll booth. The toll taker gets the message. Theft drops back to a tolerable level.[15]

[14] Statement of Edwin A. Elbert before U.S. Senate Committee on Commerce considering cargo security legislation (S. 3595 and S.J. Res. 222), September 29 and 30, 1970, p. 85.
[15] Lawrence R. Zeitlin, "A Little Larceny Can Do a Lot for Employee Morale," *Psychology Today* (June, 1971), p. 64.

ORGANIZED THEFT

Organized theft is more than employee pilferage. It is the organized efforts of outsiders to steal merchandise while it is in the firm's distribution channels. Sometimes thefts, or for that matter, the pilferage, occur while the merchandise is within the custody of a common carrier or a warehouseman. The common carrier or the warehouseman is then liable. However, the incident may still be disadvantageous to the shipper, and for several reasons:

1. The planned flow of the goods in the channel has been interrupted and this may result in a stock-out at some distributors.
2. The carrier's or warehouseman's liability may not cover the entire value of the shipment.
3. Time, telephone, and paperwork costs are not covered.
4. Employees who had knowledge of the shipment's route and timing may come under suspicion.
5. The stolen products may reappear on the market at a low price to compete with goods which moved through legitimate channels.

Another serious problem area is cargo theft. Professional thieves have learned that thefts from carriers are much less risky and often more profitable than the traditional targets—banks, armored cars, etc. The Insurance Information Institute estimated that in 1972, the retail value of cargo theft was $2.8 billion.[16] Motor carriers are a primary target. The six principal cargos stolen from trucks are: clothing, food items (especially meat), tobacco, liquor, appliances and textiles.[17] In the first half of 1974, one motor carrier paid out $51,930 in 39 separate claims resulting from losses in shipments of small hand calculators. The 39 shipments represented only $2,678 in receipts.[18]

BUILDING SECURITY

In recent years, there has been increased interest in providing security for warehouses and other distribution facilities. Figure 14-3 shows some of the measures that can be built into a warehouse. Electronic devices are available to perform three different security functions. First, surveillance equipment is a form of closed-circuit TV with cameras viewing different areas and with the picture being shown on a monitor screen constantly observed by a guard. For areas where there should be no movements, it is possible to have monitoring devices "remember" the image which contained no movement and convert this video infor-

[16] James M. Dixon, "The Billion-Dollar Rip-off," *Distribution Worldwide* (June, 1973), p. 32.
[17] *Transport Topics* (June 18, 1973).
[18] *Transport Topics* (November 4, 1974).

FIG. 14-3 How to plan a "thief resistant" warehouse.

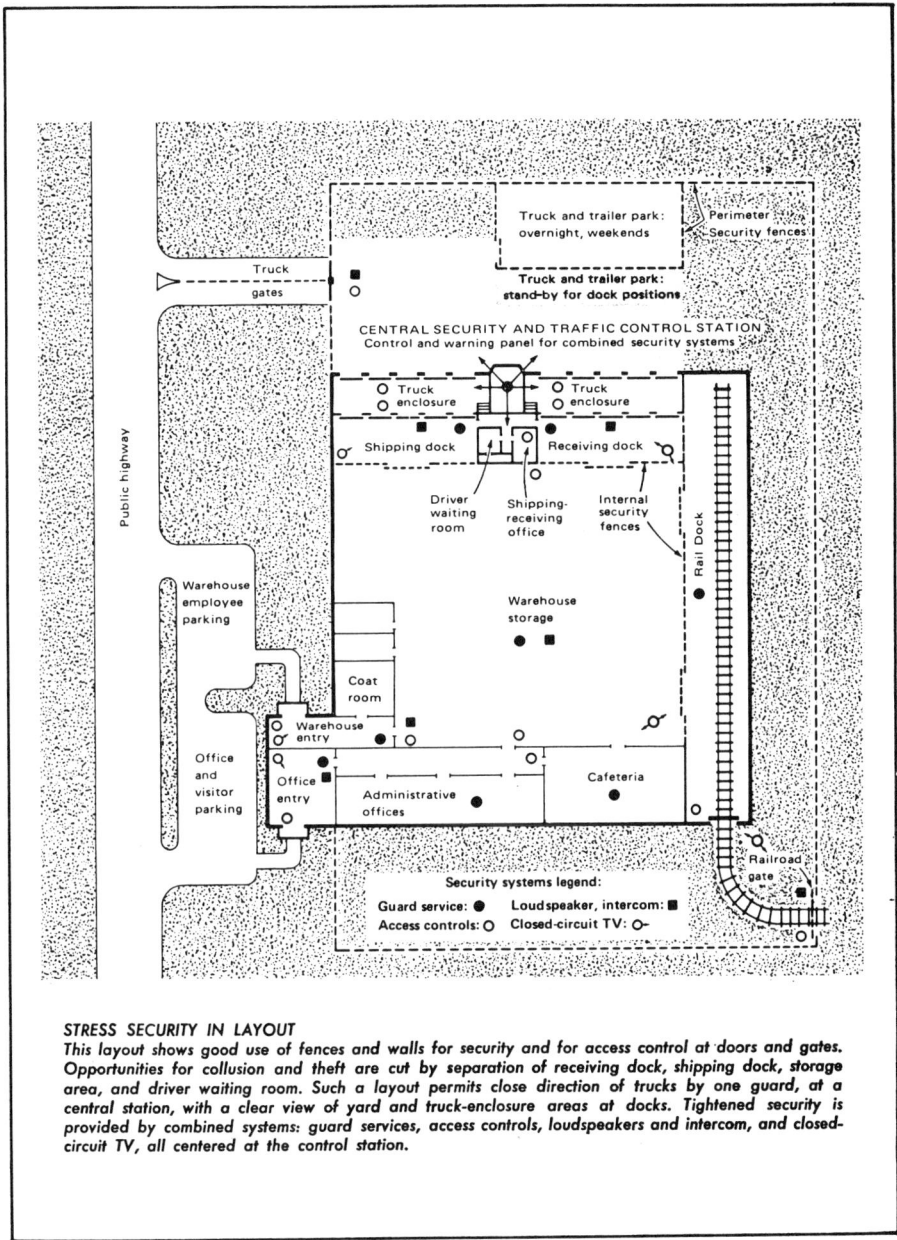

Truck and trailer park:
overnight, weekends

Perimeter
Security fences

Truck
gates

Truck and trailer park:
stand-by for dock positions

CENTRAL SECURITY AND TRAFFIC CONTROL STATION
Control and warning panel for combined security systems

Truck
enclosure

Truck
enclosure

Shipping dock

Receiving dock

Driver
waiting
room

Shipping-
receiving
office

Internal
security
fences

Rail Dock

Public highway

Warehouse
employee
parking

Warehouse
storage

Coat
room

Warehouse
entry

Office
and
visitor
parking

Office
entry

Administrative
offices

Cafeteria

Railroad
gate

Security systems legend:

Guard service: ●   Loudspeaker, intercom: ■
Access controls: ○   Closed-circuit TV: ○–

STRESS SECURITY IN LAYOUT
This layout shows good use of fences and walls for security and for access control at doors and gates.
Opportunities for collusion and theft are cut by separation of receiving dock, shipping dock, storage
area, and driver waiting room. Such a layout permits close direction of trucks by one guard, at a
central station, with a clear view of yard and truck-enclosure areas at docks. Tightened security is
provided by combined systems: guard services, access controls, loudspeakers and intercom, and closed-
circuit TV, all centered at the control station.

Courtesy: *Modern Materials Handling.*

mation to a "binary format and store it in a digital memory and, when a change in the image occurs—such as would be caused by an intruder in a freight storage area—initiate an alarm. . . ." [19] The second form of electronic devices are used for access control. An example is an encoded tag which each employee must insert into a "sensing" device which would both record the event and determine whether the door or gate should be unlocked. The third category and the most common are continuous wire circuits on all doors, windows, and other openings which cannot be broken without triggering an alarm. There are also "invisible" photo-electric beams and many types of "listening" devices which can record unauthorized movements. Within a warehouse, heavier security may be placed around areas where higher-value material is kept. There is no limit to the sophistication or cost of the security devices that can be employed. It is, unfortunately, another cost of doing business.

TRUCK SECURITY

Methods and equipment are also being developed to discourage thefts from (or of) trucks. Numbers can be painted on top of truck trailers to make them easier to spot from the air in case they are stolen. An alternative is to place a transponder (a small device that will respond to radio signals from an outside source) aboard trailers that are likely to be hijacked. Even better locking devices are helpful because thieves have been known to climb onto the rear of a truck waiting at a traffic signal and then force their way inside the vehicle.

SYSTEM SECURITY

One of the best methods of protecting goods is to keep them moving through the system. Goods waiting in warehouses, terminals, or to clear customs, are more vulnerable to theft than goods that are moving.

Methods of improving security have been discussed. No list is complete, and a determined thief could overcome almost any hindrance or barrier placed in his way. However, a few suggestions are offered, mainly to reflect the breadth of measures which might be taken.

—A shoe manufacturer was plagued with thefts from trucks until he decided to ship left shoes in one truck and right shoes in a different truck. They were matched (hopefully) and boxed at their destination.

—In most (but not all) states it is permissible to fingerprint, photograph, and apply lie-detector tests to potential employees. Where this is possible, it has been helpful to employers.

[19] Miklos Korodi, "Stop Thief!" *Distribution Worldwide* (December, 1974), p. 47.

—Decals are required for autos in employee parking lots.

—Fork-lift trucks in warehouses are locked at night, making it difficult to reach high items or to move heavy items.

—Seals (small wire-like devices that once closed cannot be opened without breaking) are used more and more with dispatchers, drivers, and receiving personnel, all being made responsible for recording the seal number and inspecting its condition.

—Some companies have a "continuous" receipt system, so that an employee is considered responsible for each item until he can pass the item on and have the receiver sign a receipt. While somewhat cumbersome, it has been helpful because it enhances the employee's sense of personal responsibility and he views any effort to steal or tamper with the goods as an assault on his own integrity.

PRODUCT IDENTIFICATION NUMBER SECURITY

Mention has been made of inventory control systems based on product serial or product batch numbers. These numbers also have certain advantages with respect to discouraging theft and pilferage. If items are discovered to be missing, it is possible to identify them by number. This makes it possible to reclaim the goods if they are recovered and facilitates prosecution of the people in possession of these goods. These facts are also known to pilferers, thieves, and "fences" and tend to make the "hot" merchandise somewhat less valuable. Altering or destroying the serial or batch numbers is time-consuming and arouses the suspicions of legitimate buyers.

VEHICLE CONTROL

An immediate distinction must be made between vehicles operated by others, such as common carriers, and those operated by the firm itself. Many large operations now work with suppliers, customers, and motor carriers to establish pick-up and delivery time allotments. If a warehouse normally receives 20 truck deliveries a day from fairly regular supply sources, the suppliers are assigned one-hour intervals within which the truck must arrive. These would be spread out evenly over the working day.

The carriers insist on extra compensation if they show up at the scheduled time but cannot be accommodated. Motor carrier tariffs contain "detention" provisions which penalize users who cause trucks to wait beyond a specified amount of time.[20] Many tariffs also contain

[20] Leonard C. Schaffel, "How to Minimize Detention," a paper delivered at the N.C.P.D.M. annual conference in October, 1974.

surcharges for pick-ups and deliveries in congested areas which may, in the long run, influence some users to handle or route small shipments to their facilities in outlying areas where surcharges do not apply. There, they consolidate the small shipments and deliver full loads to facilities in the more congested urban areas.

Railroad service is, as might be imagined, more difficult for the user to control. An exception are large shippers using one railroad and who are so important to the carrier that they are sometimes able to get rail service of such quality and dependability that it becomes virtually an integral part of their production or distribution scheduling. The majority of rail users are less fortunate and one of the reasons for the railroads declining share of freight traffic has been their reputation for mediocre to poor service. One grocery firm recorded the length of time it took 25 different rail cars to move from its Atlanta facility to Jacksonville. One car made the trip in two days, seven took three days; seven took four days; four took five days; one took six days; two took seven days; and the other cars each took eight days, nine days, and ten days. If the user wanted to be "80 percent certain" that a car would arrive, he would have to plan on six days in transit. This would also mean that thirty-two percent of the cars (eight out of twenty-five) would arrive within three days and would have to be unloaded within 48 hours to avoid demurrage charges.[21] Hence, thirty-two percent of the inbound cars would have to be unloaded at least one day before their contents were scheduled to be placed into the next step of the distribution system. Twenty percent of the cars (five out of twenty-five) would be at least a day late. If the Jacksonville operation tried to develop a "flow" system that depended on a rail car from Atlanta arriving on a certain day, 52 percent of the time they would be wrong, the car would either be late or else so early that it would have to be unloaded before needed to avoid demurrage charges.

Some large companies have computerized systems for controlling rail shipments. Their computers develop standard times and then, based on railroad car location reports, the shipper can tell whether the car is about where it should be. This was discussed in previous chapters.

When a firm uses private trucking, it has control over its drivers. A commonly-used device is the *tachograph*, a precision recording instrument which is installed inside the vehicle and produces a continuous written record of the operations of the truck, and presumably, the driver. Figure 14-4 shows a used tachograph chart and the data which were recorded. The nomenclature and graduation of the chart are as follows. (Letter references are to Figure 14-4):

21 Benedict G. Janson, "How Can Demurrage be Minimized?" a paper delivered at the N.C.P.D.M. annual conference in October, 1974. Demurrage charges do not apply on weekends, which would have a slight effect on the calculations in the text.

FIG. 14-4 Tachograph chart.

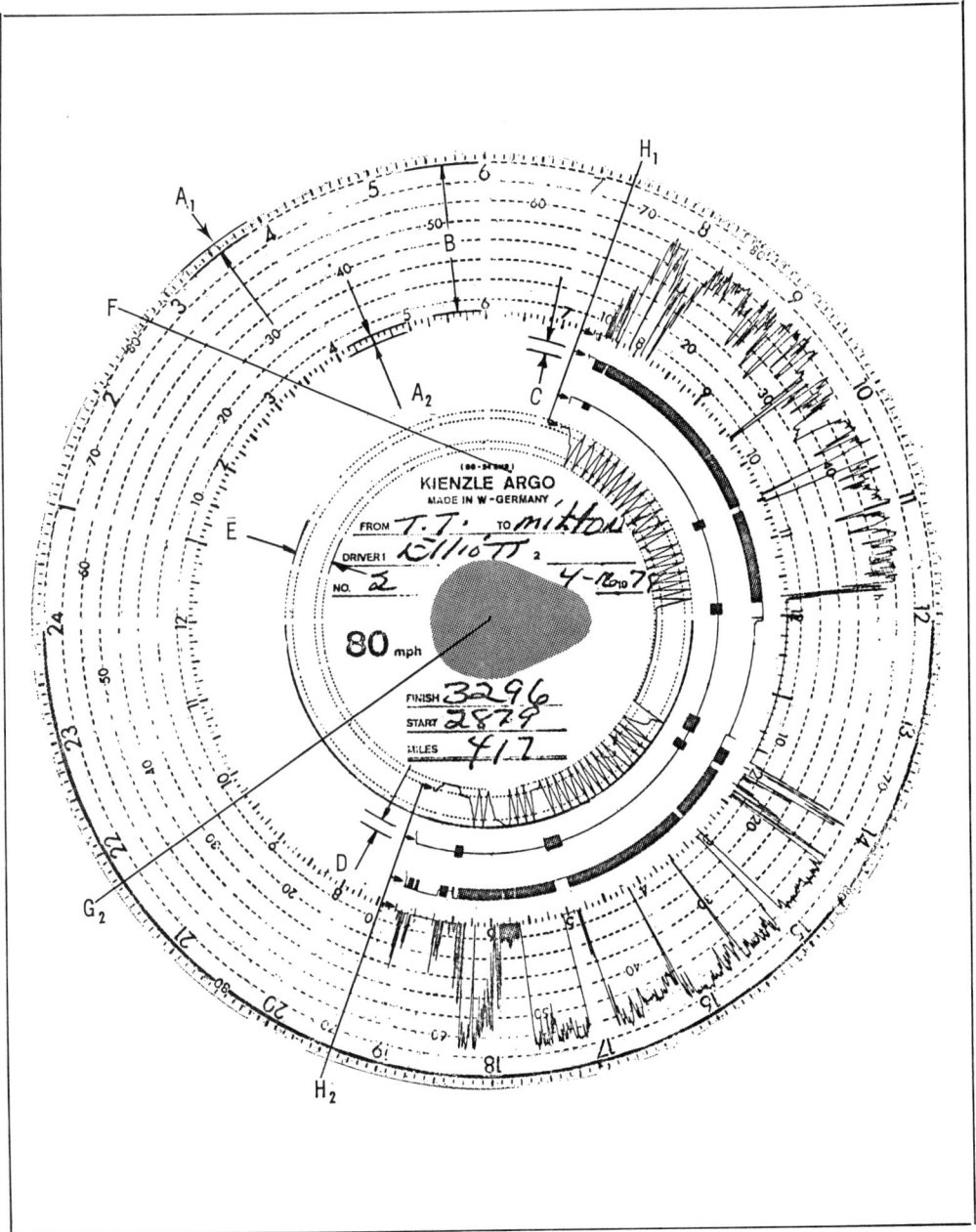

SOURCE: Argo Instruments Corp., Long Island City, New York.

A₁, Outer Time Scale | 0:00 to 24:00 hrs. (Military)

GRADUATION: Single line at 5 min. intervals, full hrs., in wider line also printed out in numbers in 70 to 80 MPH circle. PM time (12 to 24) identified by continuous wider beam.

B, Speed Range
(next inner circle from A₁) | 0 to 80 MPH

GRADUATION: Every 10 miles also by dotted concentric lines at 50 min. intervals except at full hrs. 10 to 80 printed out equally spaced and staggered from bottom to top over periods (four times repeated).

A₂, Inner Time Scale
(next inner circle from B) | 2 times—1 to 12 hrs. (consecutive)

GRADUATION: As A₁
Full hrs. printed in numbers between "o" line and 10 MPH field.

C, Stop and Go Range
(next inner circle from A₂) | Blank space, recording for go periods is a wide beam, for stop periods a thin line.

D, Engine Idling Range | Blank, recording for engine idling is a wide beam. At other times a thin line.

E, Distance Scale
(next inner circle from D) | Between two upper and two lower circles, also, concentric lines at 5 min. intervals.

GRADUATION: One mile each between two upper and lower circles. Total of 5 miles for full band.

F, Center Field | For entries such as date, vehicle number, driver's name, destination, mileage at start and finish, total trip mileage, also manufacturer's name and order number.

G, Cut-out | For proper fastening and synchronizing on instrument.

H₁₋₂, Beginning (1) and
Ending (2) of
Recording Periods | Whenever the stylii are engaged, are disengaged from the chart, a comma-like marking is made.

An individual experienced in working with these charts can tell quickly how efficiently the truck and driver are being utilized. If the driver works on a regular route, it may be possible to rearrange his stops so he can avoid areas of traffic congestion. Bad driving habits such as high highway speeds, or excessive engine idling, are also obvious. In case of an accident, the chart is invaluable in reporting, and perhaps explaining, what had occurred just prior to impact. Courts have recognized the recordings as acceptable evidence.

SUMMARY

This chapter has gone into some detail, explaining types of controls that might be employed to reduce poor performance. The topics covered were: accounting controls, employee work standards, product recalls, pilferage, theft, and vehicle operations control. Accounting controls stressed that many selling strategies overlook distribution costs and may, in fact, cost more than they are worth. The discussion of employee productivity included samples of computer print-outs showing a truck driver's performance. The next section described different types of product recall operations. Pilferage and theft were examined, the latter being the logical extention of the first and likely to occur if no controls were imposed. The final section described a tachograph, a recording device which is placed in many trucks.

The types of problems which this chapter has indicated as needing controls, are continuous. They could occur any day and in most businesses, are occurring right now.

QUESTIONS FOR DISCUSSION AND REVIEW

1. What is the difference between pilferage and theft? From a management standpoint, which would you consider to be more significant? Why?

2. Describe how tachographs function. What bad driving habits can they detect?

3. What steps can be taken to discourage thefts from trucks and truck hijackings?

4. What steps can be taken against pilferage?

5. Do you think that job applicants should be subjected to lie detector tests? Why or why not?

6. What steps should a firm take to prepare for a product recall?

7. Why are serial numbers or batch numbers important?

8. What kind of accounting controls are used in physical distribution?

9. What is shrinkage? How is it measured?

10. Why do larger shippers have more influence over the quality of service offered by carriers?

11. What is "short interval scheduling"? How is it used?

12. What questions might you ask an employe to find out if he knows his relative level of performance?

13. How are "standard" costs calculated? How are they used to monitor performance?

14. List the similarities and differences in controlling outbound shipments moving on one's own vehicles and on common carriers.

CASE 14-1   CALDRAN PLASTICS COMPANY

Jack Kimberly managed Caldran Plastics Company's Denver warehouse. The warehouse covered 50,000 square feet and was responsible for distribution of plastic products over a ten-state area. Kimberly, warehouse foreman Sam Stewart, and three office employees did not belong to the unions. Eight truck drivers belonged to the Teamsters' Union and 23 warehouse laborers belonged to a warehouse and storeroom workers' union.

Three months ago, after a one-week strike, a two-year contract had been signed covering the 23 members of the warehouse and storeroom workers' union. It provided for a 32 cent per hour increase in wages at that time, additions to "fringe" benefits which averaged about 52 cents per hour per employee, and provisions for "cost-of-living" adjustments which were tied into quarterly changes in the consumer price index. Also a part of the new contract was a section dealing with employees who failed to measure up to work standards.

Actual work standards were not specified since management wanted the right to change them at a later date in case more mechanized equipment was installed or if a different character of product was handled. The phrase "reasonable work standards" was in the contract with provisions for hiring a "third-party" arbitrator to decide what constituted "reasonable" in case a disagreement arose. Management also agreed to assign employees who were both (a) over 50 years of age and (b) employed by Caldran Plastics for over 15 years, to the less physically-demanding tasks in the warehouse.

After the contract was signed, Kimberly and Stewart began establishing written standards for worker productivity. They differed little from existing productivity and often were set at the existing 80 percentile which meant that four fifths of the work force was currently meeting or exceeding that standard. In addition, ten percent leeway was allowed which meant that 88 percent (80 percent plus ten percent of 80 percent) of the work was considered as adequate. In human terms, two workers consistently fell below standards. Three others met standards, but only marginally.

The contract provided that workers who were performing below management standards "for a period of at least six consecutive working days shall be verbally informed of the fact by their foreman or other representative of Caldran Plastics. A notice of the warning shall also be given to the union's business agent." The contract then provided a period of twenty more working days during which management was bound "to carefully instruct, supervise, and otherwise counsel the employee in an effort to bring his or her performance up to standards." The contract continued that "if, after the 20 days period, the employee's work continues to be unsatisfactory, management shall provide *in writing* a notice to both the worker and to the union that unless the employee's work improved within the next 20 working day period, the employee would be subjected to immediate dismissal. . . ."

The two employees in question received their oral warnings one month ago and had just finished their first 20-day review period. Their work was still unsatisfactory and written warnings, signed by Kimberly, had been sent via registered mail to their respective homes two days ago.

Yesterday afternoon, Kimberly's secretary informed him that Max Brandt, the union's business agent, wanted to see him. Brandt said that two union members had a grievance against management. Brandt wanted the meeting with Kimberly so he could orally inform Kimberly of the grievance and if he and Kimberly could not work the matter out, Brandt had other, more forceful actions which he could take.

At 3:45 Brandt marched in. Kimberly and Stewart were waiting. Brandt sat down, and refused an offer of coffee. Kimberly said, "This is the first grievance under the new contract, Max. I'm surprised. I thought we had everything worked out."

Brandt responded: "Don't quote me, but I was a bit surprised myself. But you know I'm elected only if I perform."

"Well, what's the grievance?" asked Stewart.

Brandt responded, consulting his notes, "In our contract, Section IV, paragraph B dealing with failure to meet established work standards is the statement 'that if his work continues to be unsatisfactory after the first 20 day period, management shall provide in writing a notice to both the worker and the union. . . .' Well, you clowns went and sent them to the workers' homes by registered mail. Both of their wives opened the letters and now my two men are really in trouble at home. It is *not* their wives' business!"

Stewart responded: "Ho, ho, ho, I saw those two at work today. They were really hustling. I'll bet their old ladies put a fear of God into 'em."

"That may be," said Brandt, "but the contract doesn't say you'll inform workers' wives."

"The letters were addressed to the men," said Kimberly. "It's not our fault if their wives open them. Tell your men to take their complaint to the post office."

"It's unreasonable to expect a wife not to open a registered letter. You two know that. My membership says you're being unfair. From now on, the written warnings are *not* to be sent to the workers' homes."

Kimberly said, "Hold on there, Max. In any other contract I know of, when a written notice is called for, you need something like registered mail. Otherwise, the man says he never got it. What should we do instead, put a notice in the newspaper?"

Question One: Assume you are Kimberly. What are the advantages and disadvantages to Caldran Plastics of giving in to Brandt's demand? What would you do?

CASE 14-2   RED SPOT MARKETS COMPANY

The Red Spot Markets Company operates a chain of grocery stores in New England. It has a grocery distribution center in Providence, Rhode Island, from which deliveries are made to stores as far north as Lowell, Massachusetts, as far west as Waterbury, Connecticut, and as far northwest as Springfield, Massachusetts. There are no stores beyond the two northernmost points in Massachusetts. There are stores to the west, but they are supplied by a grocery warehouse located in Newburgh, New York. The Providence grocery distribution center supplies forty-two Red Spot retail stores.

Robert Easter is Red Spot's distribution manager and responsible for operations at the Newburgh and Providence distribution centers. By industry standards, both were fairly efficient. However, of the two, the Providence center lagged in two important areas of control: worker productivity and shrinkage. Warehouse equipment and work rules were the same for both the Newburgh and Providence centers; yet the throughput per manhour was four percent higher for the Newburgh facility. Shrinkage, expressed as a percentage of the wholesale value of goods handled annually was 0.36 percent for the Newburgh center and 0.59 percent for the Providence center. Jarvis Jason had been manager of the Providence distribution center for the past three years and, at great effort, managed to narrow the gap between the performance of the two Red Spot facilities. Last week, he requested an immediate reassignment and Easter arranged for him to become the marketing manager for the Boston area which would involve supervising the operations of eleven Red Spot markets. The transfer involved no increase in pay.

Easter needed a new manager for the Providence distribution center, and he decided to pick Fred Fosdick for the task. Fosdick graduated from a lessor Ivy League college where he majored in business with a concentration in physical distribution. He had been with Red Spot for two years and rearranged the entire delivery route structure so that two fewer trucks were needed. As part of this assignment, he also converted the entire system to one of "unit loads," which meant everything loaded on or unloaded from a Red Spot truck was on a pallet. Fosdick was familiar with the operations of both the Providence and Newburgh centers. He has been in each facility at least 50 different times. In addition, he spent two weeks at the Providence center when the loading docks were redesigned to accommodate pallet loading. Fosdick was surprised that Jason requested reassignment to a slot that did not involve an upward promotion. That was his first question to Easter, after Easter asked whether he was interested in the Providence assignment.

"I'm sorry you started with that question," said Easter to Fosdick. "Now we'll have to talk about the troublesome aspects of the assignment first, rather than the positive ones. To be frank, Fred, one of the union employees there made so much trouble for Jason, he couldn't stand it."

"Who's the trouble-maker?" asked Fosdick.

"Tom Bigelow," was Easter's answer.

Fosdick remembered Bigelow from the times he had been at the Providence center. Thomas D. Bigelow was nicknamed T. D. since his days as a local Providence high school football star. Fosdick recalled that during work-breaks on the loading dock, Bigelow and some of the other workers would toss around melons as though they were footballs. Only once did they drop a melon. Fosdick recalled hearing the story that Bigelow had received several offers of athletic scholarships when he graduated from high school. His best offer was from a southern school and he accepted it. Despite the fact that the college provided a special tutor for each class, Bigelow flunked out at the end of his first semester and came back to Providence where he got a job in the Red Spot warehouse.

In the warehouse Bigelow was a natural leader. He would have been a foreman except for his inability to count and his spotty attendance record on Monday mornings. On Mondays he was groggy, tired, and irritable. On Mondays he would even hide by loading a forklift truck with three pallets, backing into an empty bay, lowering the pallets in position (which hid the lift truck from view) and fall asleep. The rest of the week Bigelow was happy, enthusiastic, and hard-working. Indeed, it was he who set the pace of work in the warehouse. When he felt good, things hummed; when he was not feeling well, or was absent, work dragged.

"What did Bigelow do to Jason?" Fosdick asked Easter.

"Well, as I understand it," responded Easter, "about two weeks ago Jason decided that he had had it with Bigelow and so he suspended him on a Monday morning after Bigelow showed up late, still badly hungover. It was nearly noon and he told Bigelow to stay off the premises and to file a grievance with his union shop steward. He also told Bigelow that he had been documenting Bigelow's Monday performance—or non-performance—for the past six months and that Red Spot had grounds enough to fire Bigelow if they cared to. He told Bigelow to go home, sober up, and come back on Tuesday when they would discuss the length of his suspension. Bigelow walked through the distribution center on his way out and I'm sure Jason felt he had control of the matter."

"However," continued Easter, "by about one o'clock, Jason realized he had a work slow down on his hands. Pallet loads of bottled goods were being dropped, two forklift trucks collided, and one lift truck pulled over the corner of a tubular steel rack. At 4 PM quitting time, there were still three trucks to be loaded; usually they would have departed by 3:30. Rather than pay overtime, Jason let the work force go home, and he and the foreman loaded the last three trucks."

"On Tuesday, Bigelow did not show up and the slow down got worse. In addition, retail stores were phoning with complaints about all the errors in their orders. To top it off, at the Roxbury store, when the trailer door was opened, the trailer contained nothing but empty pallets. Tuesday night somebody turned off the switches on the battery chargers for all the lift trucks so on Wednesday, the lift truck batteries were dying all day. I got involved because of all the complaints from the stores. On Wednesday, Jason got my permission to pay overtime and the last outgoing truck did not leave until 7 PM. In addition, we had to pay overtime at some of our retail stores because the workers there were waiting for the trucks to arrive. While I was talking to Jason that afternoon, he indicated that he had fired Bigelow."

Easter lit his cigar and continued: "On Wednesday, I decided to go to Providence myself, mainly to talk with Jason and to determine whether we should close down the Providence center and try to serve all our stores out of Newburgh. This would have been expensive, but Providence was becoming too unreliable. In addition, we had a weekend coming up. When I showed up at Providence, Jason and I had breakfast together in my hotel room Thursday morning and he told me pretty much the same thing I've been telling you. He said he knew Bigelow was behind all the disruption and that today (meaning Thursday) would be crucial. I'd never seen Jason looking so nervous. Then we drove to the distribution center. Even from a distance, I could tell things were moving slowly. The first echelon of outgoing trucks, which should have been on the road, were still there. Another twenty of our trucks were waiting to be loaded. On the other end of the building you could see a long line of arriving trucks waiting to be unloaded; usually there was no line at all. I knew that our suppliers would start complaining because we had established scheduled unloading times. However, I decided not to ask Jason whether he had begun receiving phone calls from them.

"Inside the center, the slowdown was in effect. Lift truck operators who usually zipped by each other would now stop, turn off their engines, dismount, and carefully walk around each other's truck to ensure there was proper clearance. Satisfied of this, they would then mount, start their engines, and spend an inordinate amount of time motioning to each other to pass. This was only one example. When we got to Jason's office, he had a message to phone Ed Meyers, our local attorney in Providence who handles much of our labor relations work there. He called Meyers and was upset by the discussion. After he hung up he told me that Meyers had been served papers by the union's attorney, charging that Wednesday's firing of Bigelow was unjustified, mainly because there existed no provable grounds that Bigelow was behind the slowdown. Meyers was angry because, in firing Bigelow on Wednesday, he (Jason) may have also blown the suspension of Bigelow on Monday. Jason and I started talking, even arguing. I talked so much that my cigar went out," said Easter, "so I asked Jason, who was sitting behind his desk, for a match. He didn't carry matches but looked inside his center desk drawer for one. He gasped and I didn't know what was the matter. He got up, looking sick, and walked away from his desk. He said that a dead rat had been left in his desk drawer and he wanted a transfer. He was in bad shape and the distribution center was in bad shape, so I had the opening in the Boston area and I let him have it. Actually right now he and his family are vacationing somewhere in Eastern Canada. He needs the rest."

Fosdick was beginning to feel sorry that he knew all the details, but he persisted. "Then what?" he asked Easter.

"Well, I took over running the distribution center. I phoned Meyers again, and he and I had lunch. He thought that Jason had blown the case against Bigelow and that we should take him back. So on Friday, Meyers, Bigelow, the union attorney, the shop steward, Bigelow's foreman and I met. Jason, of course, was not there. It was a pleasant meeting. Everything got blamed on poor Jason. I did tell Bigelow that we would be documenting his performance and wanted him to know that Jason's successor, meaning you, was under my instructions to tolerate no nonsense from him (Bigelow). Bigelow was so pleasant that day, I could not imagine him in the role of a trouble maker. The amazing thing was when he went out into the center to resume work, a loud cheer went up and all the drivers started blowing their lift truck horns. For a moment, I was afraid all the batteries would run down again. But I was wrong. They were plain happy to see Bigelow back. You know, the slowdown was still in effect when Bigelow walked onto the floor. I'd say it was 10 AM and they were an hour behind. Well, let me tell you what happened. They went to work! By noon we were back on schedule and by the end of the shift we were a half hour ahead of schedule. In fact, the last half hour was spent straightening up many of the bins that had been deliberately disarranged during the slowdown. I tell you, Tom Bigelow does set the work pace in that warehouse!"

"So what do you suggest I do at the center?" asked Fosdick.

"Well, the key is getting along with Bigelow. Talk to Meyers about the kind of records you should keep in case you decide to move against Bigelow. Be sure to consult with Meyers before you do anything irreversible. Frankly, I don't know whether Bigelow will be a problem. We never had trouble with him that I knew about before Jason was there. According to Bigelow and the union attorney, Jason had it in for Bigelow. If I were you, I'd take it easy with Bigelow and other labor problems. See what you can do instead about the inventory shrinkage."

On the next Monday morning, Fosdick showed up at the Providence distribution center. After gingerly looking in all his desk drawers, he had a brief meeting with his foremen and then walked out to meet the entire work force on a one-to-one basis. Many remembered Fosdick from his earlier visits to the facility. Since it was a Monday morning, he had not expected to encounter Bigelow. But Bigelow was present, clear eyed, alert, and enthusiastic. He was happy to see Fosdick and shook his hand warmly. Bigelow then excused himself saying he had to return to work. The truck dispatcher said that the work force was ahead of schedule again, it was 11 AM and they were about 15 minutes ahead. Fosdick returned to his office and there was a phone message from Ed Meyers. Meyers asked to postpone luncheon for that day until Tuesday noon. Then Robert Easter called to ask how things were going on Fosdick's first day. Easter was pleased things were going smoothly.

It was lunch time. Fosdick decided to walk to a small cafe which he had eaten at other times. It was two blocks from the distribution center and on the side away from the office. So he walked through the center which was quiet since it was closed for lunch. He walked by the empolyees' lunch room where there were the normal sounds of fifty people eating and talking. Just outside the lunchroom was one lift truck with an empty wooden pallet on it. As Fosdick watched, one of the new stock clerks came out of the lunch room with an opened case of sweet pickles and from which three jars had been taken. Next came another new stock clerk with an opened carton of mustard and from which two bottles had been removed. One of the clerks suddenly saw Fosdick and said weakly, "We take these opened cases to the damaged merchandise room." Fosdick went into the lunch room. There, on the center table were cases of cold meat, cheese, soft drinks, catsup, and bread. All had been opened and partially emptied to provide the workers' lunch.

Bigelow was making himself a large sandwich when he saw Fosdick approach. "Don't get uptight, man," he said to Fosdick. "You've just come across one of the non-contract fringe benefits of working at the Red Spot Providence distribution center. Can I make you a sandwich?"

Question One: How should Fosdick respond to the immediate situation?

Question Two: What long-term steps should Fosdick take to improve the Providence distribution center's worker productivity and reduce its high rates of shrinkage?

CHAPTER REFERENCES

Consumer Protection Bulletin, National Highway Traffic Safety Administration (December 17, 1974).

DIXON, JAMES M.; "The Billion-Dollar Rip-Off," *Distribution Worldwide* (June, 1973).

FISHER, ROLAND T.; "Short Interval Scheduling," presented at NCPDM San Francisco Roundtable Workshop (April 29, 1975).

GRABNER, JOHN R. and William S. Sargent, eds.; *Distribution System Costing: Concepts and Procedures*, proceedings of the fourth annual James R. Riley symposium on business logistics (Columbus: Transportation and Logistics Foundation at The Ohio State University, 1972). Note especially papers by Richard L. Lewis and Leo G. Erickson, and by H. George Miller.

GRAHAM, ARTHUR S.; "Evaluating and Controlling Manpower Effectiveness," presented at NCPDM Annual Conference (October, 1974).

HAMMOND, PAUL F.; "Increasing Productivity Through Performance Audit, Feedback and Positive Reinforcement," *1974 Papers of the American Society of Traffic and Transportation*.

HILL, RICHARD D.; "How to Thwart a Thief," *Handling and Shipping* (November, 1973), pp. 58–61.

JANSON, BENEDICT G.; "How Can Demurrage be Minimized?," presented at NCPDM Auunal Conference (October, 1974).

KERIN, ROGER A. and Michael Harvey; "Contingency Planning for Product Recall," *MSU Business Topics* (Summer, 1975), pp. 5–12.

KORODI, MIKLOS; "Stop Thief!" *Distribution Worldwide* (December, 1974).

LYNAGH, PETER M.; "Measuring Distribution Center Effectiveness," *Transportation Journal* (Winter, 1971), Vol. 11, No. 2, pp. 21–33.

"Productivity Bargaining," *Warehousing Review* (June-July, 1972).

SCHAFFEL, LEONARD C.; "How to Minimize Detention," presented at the NCPDM Annual Conference (October, 1974).

SCHIFF, MICHAEL; *Accounting and Cost Control in Physical Distribution Management* (Chicago: The National Council of Physical Distribution Management, Inc., 1972).

Transportation Topics (June 18, 1973; November 4, 1974).

ZEITLIN, LAWRENCE R.; "A Little Larceny Can Do a Lot for Employee Morales," *Psychology Today* (June, 1971).

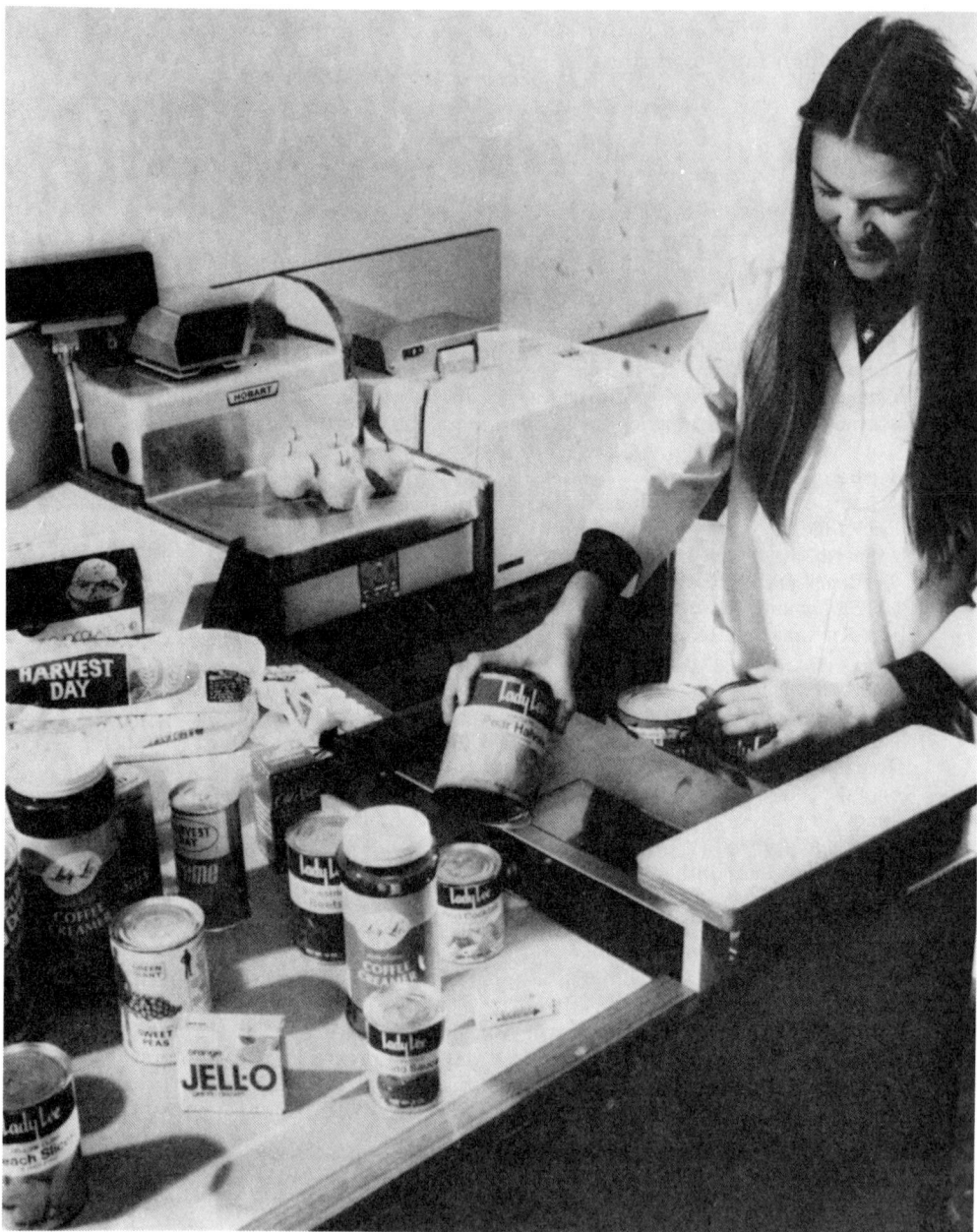

A store clerk passes the bar code on the can over an optical scanner at a check-out counter.

CHAPTER FIFTEEN

Physical Distribution: Future Directions

Only so many straws may be piled on the camel's back; beyond that point, either further progress must be stopped or a new and stronger beast of burden must be found. This is the nature of today's technological outburst in transportation: an accumulation of small changes that are evoking, in their aggregate, big changes in the industry's structure.

—Colin Barrett
Transportation and Distribution Management
August, 1971

What's important to General Motors usually winds up being important to the Republic. That's why G.M.'s announcement that its 1977 standard-size cars will have metric measurements gives the metric conversion movement a big push.

—Nick Thimmesch
Tulsa World
April 11, 1976

What we need most today is a balanced multi-modal approach to maintaining and improving the nation's transportation system.

—Jimmy Carter
Responding to the
American Society of Mechanical Engineers
Presidential Questionnaire
September 1, 1976

WHAT MAY CHANGE, WHY, AND HOW?

The fundamentals of physical distribution have been examined. The purpose of this chapter is to speculate about the future directions physical distribution will take. Because of the spectrum of activities in physical distribution, the authors have chosen a limited number to examine. Any discussion of this sort is subject to the criticism that it tends to be subjective. Nevertheless, it is important for students of physical distribution to take time to contemplate future changes of the discipline.

The following pages will start with the broader, "macro" viewpoint and then progress to the more specific, "micro" issues.

489

INCREASED GOVERNMENTAL INTERVENTION

If history yields any indication of the future, federal and state governmental activities will continue to become more important to physical distribution managers.[1] The reader is already familiar with the formidable amount of regulation involved in the transportation sector of physical distribution. However, governmental activites and regulations also impinge on almost all the other aspects of physical distribution. OSHA (The Occupational Safety and Health Administration) regulations, for example, set forth stringent requirements for warehouse layout and safety features. Material handling equipment is subjected to specific safety requirements, including such factors as overhead guards on forklift trucks, fuel handling procedures, gasoline and fuel storage techniques, etc.

In the area of labor relations, the federal government is actively involved in "Affirmative Action" programs designed to insure that minorities are fully represented in both white- and blue-collar positions. Recently, 349 large motor common carriers were charged by the Justice Department for having violated the Civil Rights Act by not having enough minority drivers. A number of the carriers involved signed a consent decree in which they agreed to hire minorities on a quota basis until a specified percentage of all employees are minorities.[2]

Based on these and many similar situations, Colin Barrett, vice president of the Transportation Association of America, remarked:

> . . . the outlook for labor, from the management viewpoint, appears to be one of the increased pressures in the areas of wages, benefits and working conditions, and a growing level of governmental intervention in the personnel management field. I think it is safe to say that the job of personnel management is not going to get any easier through the 1970's, and that both the law and its administration will continue to impose sharp restrictions on the freedom of business to deal with its labor problems.[3]

A trend that well illustrates the developing interrelationship between government and business involves product recalls, which were examined in the last chapter. They are becoming a very major concern to both industry and government. *U.S. News and World Report* found that in 1974, approximately 25 percent of the country's largest consumer-goods manufacturers were involved in product recall programs. These recalls

---

[1] See: William F. Martin and George Cabot Lodge, "Our Society in 1985—Business May Not Like It," *Harvard Business Review* (November-December, 1975), pp. 143–152.

[2] "Justice Department Files Class Action Civil Rights Suit Against Trucking Industry," *Traffic World* (March 25, 1974), p. 7.

[3] Colin Barrett, "Statutory Implications for Labor to 1980," *Annual Proceeding of the American Society of Traffic and Transportation* (1974), p. 79.

involved about 25 million units.[4] In the present era of consumerism, product recall situations will become much more common. Product recalls, by their very nature, require a sophisticated effort by the physical distribution department in order to retrieve the defective products quickly.

INCREASED GROWTH OF MULTINATIONAL SALES

There is every indication that the trend towards increased foreign sales by American firms will continue unabated. Vincent A. Sarni, vice president for marketing of Pittsburgh Plate Glass Industries, noted:

> Another high profile topic affecting physical distribution's future is multi-nationalism. The effect of the devaluation of the dollar combined with the effect of the long term prospect of a slowing U.S. economy versus the quantum jump experienced by many overseas economies motivates many corporations toward international expansion. On the surface, this may appear to be a financial thrust. But its impact on marketing and procurement will force physical distribution to deal with expanded control problems.[5]

Most Americans are currently unaware of the vast importance of foreign sales by United States domiciled corporations. A casual glance through *The Value Line Investment Survey* indicates this situation. Table 15-1 shows a number of major American corporations and their percentage of foreign sales to total sales. Many businesspeople are ignorant of the fact that almost half of IBM's total sales are in foreign markets.

TABLE 15-1   Foreign Sales by American Firms

	Foreign Sales as a Percent of Total Sales
1. International Business Machines	47%
2. H. J. Heinz	41%
3. Honeywell	41%
4. Sperry Rand	41%
5. Minnesota Mining and Manufacturing	40%
6. Xerox	40%
7. Upjohn	38%
8. Boeing	35%
9. Union Carbide	34%

[4] "A Flood of Shoddy Products—What's Being Done To Stem It," *U.S. News and World Report* (February 24, 1975), p. 39.

[5] Vincent A. Sarni, "PD in the Near Future," *Annual Proceedings of the National Council of Physical Distribution Management* (1973), p. 62.

American-based multinational companies contribute significantly to offsetting our balance-of-payments deficit by repatriation of dividends, royalties, technical assistance fees, and interest and repayments of loans by their foreign subsidiaries. Most important, however, is the direct influx of funds as United States products are sold in foreign commerce.

Chapter 11 discussed the complexities of international physical distribution. The astute physical distribution managers of the future must adjust themselves to the "cultural shock" that is often inherent in dealing with foreign physical distribution operations. The decade of the 1970's has been and will continue to be one of developing trade with communist nations. They will be markets primarily for producers' goods, since their political/economic system does not especially motivate creating and satisfying demands for consumer goods.

Suddenly wealthy oil producing nations are developing markets for U.S. goods. How they will spend their newfound wealth remains to be seen. As this book is being written (1976/1977), there are many reports of Arab ports being clogged by vessels waiting to unload Arab purchases.

U.S. imports are also increasing. Lazer observed that one reason for this trend is that, "Travel, affluence and leisure will foster more cosmopolitan tastes and life styles. The effect will be that our life styles will reflect the tastes and products of the world. Broader exposure of consumers will result in even more favorable images of international products."[6] Importation of products also has significant ramifications on a firm's physical distribution system. Many smaller foreign exporters do not understand the technicalities of international transportation and therefore quote their products F.O.B. origin to U. S. buyers. The U. S. firm must therefore arrange for transportation and insurance of the foreign product to the United States.

METRIC CONVERSION

The United States is the only major industrialized country in the world which is not using the metric system of weights and measures. Most business executives now recognize the inevitability of the United States conversion to the metric system. A survey of physical distribution practitioners asked, "Are you in favor of the United States converting to the metric system?" Fifty-five percent of the respondents answered "yes." Assuming the change to the metric system is inevitable, 68 percent of the respondents thought the change should be mandatory by government edict.[7] (See Figure 15-1.) Many large multinational firms which

6 William Lazer, "Dimensions of Change: 1980 and Beyond," *Annual Proceedings of the NCPDM* (1972), p. 268.

7 "Survey: Converting to Metric," *Transportation and Distribution Management* (July-August, 1975), p. 47.

FIG. 15-1 The metric system will bring changes.

"I'm sure glad your Pa ain't alive to see this."

Reproduced by permission of the artist and *The Wall Street Journal*.

necessarily deal in countries using the metric system have already metri-
cated their operations without much fanfare.[8]

It was generally assumed that if the United States decided to convert
to the metric system, a relatively long conversion period would be beneficial in order to make the transition as smooth as possible. During the
first half of the 1970's, the metrication bills before Congress called for
a 10-year conversion period. A compromise metrication bill was signed
into law on December 23, 1975. The *Metric Conversion Act* creates a
17 member U.S. Metric Board whose job is to plan the conversion and
to educate the public regarding the benefits of the metric system. The
Board has no enforcement power, and no time limits for complete
conversion are established. The softening of the ten-year deadline for
conversion came at the insistence of organized labor. The Board can
recommend to Congress if any federal subsidies are required to help

[8] See: D. M. Kladstrap, "Metrication and PDM," *Handling and Shipping* (December, 1975), p. 46.

meet conversion costs, especially for workers required to purchase metri-cally-dimensioned hand tools.

The majority of multinational firms are already involved in metric conversion plans. One reason for this trend is that the European Com-mon Market has announced that starting in 1978, all products exported into their member countries must move in metric measurements. If this regulation is not compiled with, substantial non-compliance penalties are mandated. Other foreign countries have similar laws; for example, Kenya requires all imported products to be in metric measurements.[9]

The American Warehousemen's Association has stated that conver-sion to the metric standard would not have an unduly severe impact on their operational efficiency. In fact, some members stated that the change would probably produce only a minimum of problems. This is because the versatile fork lift truck now successfully handles a large variety of pallet sizes, and the addition of one or a few more metric pallet sizes would not complicate the situation.[10]

INCREASED COMPUTER ASSISTANCE

There is perhaps no trend in physical distribution development which is more predictable than the increased usage of computers to assist physi-cal distribution practitioners.

CARRIER APPLICATIONS

Common, contract, and private carriers, of all transport modes, will continue in the future to utilize computer technology in their search for greater operating efficiency. Common carriers are realizing that basically, the only distinguishing factor between carriers of the same mode is *service*. "Since a truck is a truck and a driver a driver, the country's top motor common carriers are working more or less behind the scenes on service improvements that benefit the shipper, who may only see the end result—a truck backing up to his dock when expected, the freight inside that truck intact and undamaged."[11]

Many common, contract, and private carriers of all modes use their computers to assist in the following areas: equipment monitoring and

[9] "The Standards Shell Game," *Transportation and Distribution Management* (February, 1973), p. 21. For additional information on the metric system, see: Charles T. Golden, "Ducking into Metrics," *Handling and Shipping* (October, 1974), pp. 51–53 and "The Metric System is Creeping in on U.S.," *U.S. News and World Report* (March 3, 1975), p. 54.

[10] Fred R. Keith, Jr., "Metric Warehousing: A Minimum Impact?," *Transportation and Distribution Management* (February, 1973), pp. 23–25.

[11] "The Trucking Industry: Working Behind the Scenes," *Transportation and Distribution Management* (April, 1972), p. 20.

scheduling, tracing, expediting, rate checking, billing, bill-of-lading preparation, claim prevention analysis, and OS&D (over, short, and damaged) system wide reports. Computers in the future will be used more extensively for route simulation studies to improve equipment scheduling procedures. Profitability analysis of various specific products, customers, routes, etc., will become a standard industry practice.[12]

Carrier and shipper groups are working together to bring about more computerization of shipping documents. Industrial groups are attempting to standardize product descriptions so they can be used by buyer, sellers, and carriers. Figure 8-3 previously showed how standardized location descriptions were being developed which could be used by carriers. As might be expected, the most difficult aspect is the carrier tariffs. Once the correct charges are calculated, a further calculation for many shipments is to divide the freight revenues between the originating, terminating and intermediate carriers.[13]

WAREHOUSE APPLICATIONS

Both public and private warehouses are currently experiencing revolutionary operating changes based on computer technology. In 1964, Dr. E. Grosvenor Plowman made a prophetic prediction regarding warehouses in the future. He stated that future warehouses had the potential of being completely automated. The facilities' central computer would control all product inflow and outflow, and it would maintain totally updated inventory records at all times.[14] Just six years later, in 1970, the Aerojet-General Industrial Systems Division was operating such a warehouse in Frederick, Maryland.

The most spectacular wedding of computer and warehouse technology is the Hallmark Card's distribution center in Liberty, Missouri. This facility processes up to 250,000 orders per day, which results in millions of individual items being shipped to thousands of destinations. The facility stores 22,000 separate products, each of which must be received, recorded, stored, picked, sorted, and shipped. The Hallmark facility is the world's largest high rise warehouse and it is the largest computer-operated warehouse. The storage areas are 65 feet high. It covers more than 36 acres under one roof. The pallet-racks in the storage area contain 163,000 separate pallet locations. The computer controlled system allowed Hallmark to achieve a 20 percent increase in order-filling efficiency. Order-processing and order-picking now averages less than two days, and order-picking is typically only one-half day. The

[12] See a special issue devoted to computer application in the transportation industry—*Traffic Management* (September, 1975).

[13] See Transportation Data Coordinating Committee, *Proceedings, 1974 Forum* (available from the Committee, 1101 17th St., N.W. Washington, D.C. 20036).

[14] E. Grosvenor Plowman, *Elements of Business Logistics* (Stanford, Cal.: Stanford University, 1964), pp. 99–100.

order-picking process is accomplished with stacker-cranes which are completely unattended and directed solely by the central computer. The computer not only "runs" the present facility, but it also was instrumental in originally designing the distribution center. Don Moran, general manager for data processing and order distribution, stated, "Actually the computer began pumping life into the facility before the steel skeleton was finished. Simulations were run long before ground was broken. Every knotty problem we could think of was put into the simulations." [15]

INVENTORY APPLICATIONS

The computer is currently deeply entrenched in the day-to-day operations of both order-processing and inventory control. A 1972 survey of selected members of the National Council of Physical Distribution Management found that over 75 percent indicated that computers were an integral part of their order-processing and inventory control systems. [16]

One of the most important applications of computer technology to inventory control involves the usage of the Universal Product Code (UPC), which was adopted by the grocery industry in 1973. The practically ubiquitous black and white vertical stripe label is now found on almost all grocery products.

The UPC was designed to increase the overall efficiency of grocery stores at the retail level. IBM, NCR, Sperry Univac, and other computer firms are manufacturing computer check-out systems at grocery stores. McKinsey and Company, which has consulted extensively with the grocery industry, predicts that by 1979 approximately 7,800 stores will have installed one of the computer check-out systems.

The system involves passing the UPC label on each product over an optical scanner at the check-out counter. The UPC is "read" and recorded in a computer which supplies such information as the product's price, tax, if food stamps can be used, and whether it can be legally sold on Sundays. The specific price of each product and its description is then flashed onto a television-type screen which is positioned near the counter. When all the products have been recorded, the customer receives a tape which is a list of the products purchased, the price of each article, and the total bill.

An advantage of the computer check-out system is that it substantially reduces clerical error and it is much faster than manually ringing up each product on a cash register. A Kroger store in Cincinnati was able

15 "Hallmark's Distribution Center: A Handling Spectacular," *Modern Materials Handling* (January, 1974), p. 32.

16 B. J. LaLonde and Karl Auker, "A Survey of Computer Applications and Practices in Transportation and Distribution, "*Annual Proceedings of the National Council of Physical Distribution Management* (1972), p. 234.

to increase the number of customers processed per hour from 15.7 to 23.1. Customer waiting time was reduced 40 percent and clerical errors were reduced 75 percent. The store is now able to maintain a minute-by-minute perpetual inventory.[17]

The Universal Product Code is used only at the retail level. Larger, although similar, labels are used in warehousing. Figure 15-2 shows two such examples. Figure 15-3 shows a scanner mounted on a truck used to inventory container yards. As these several examples show, scanners are used on all sizes of containers. They represent the single most important development in inventory and product flow control in the 1970's.[18]

STRATEGIC PLANNING APPLICATIONS

A trend which promises to become more important is the use of computers to perform short and long range planning. LaLonde and Auker said:

> ... the computer is becoming a fact of life for modern distribution management. In order to get the most out of new data processing technology and develop an effective, efficient and responsive distribution system, the distribution manager of the 1970's will require increasing levels of understanding of the power and flexibility of the "magic black box" in solving his distribution problem.[19]

ADVANCES IN EQUIPMENT TECHNOLOGY

In the past, physical distribution management has always benefitted from a steady and uninterrupted flow of new equipment technology. This has allowed the overall physical distribution operation to become more efficient. There are numerous examples of this situation: containerization, stacker-cranes which allow higher warehouse storage, jumbo jets, computerized railroad classification yards, etc.

Can physical distribution management assume that equipment technology will continue to develop at the same pace as in the past? This technological development issue must be considered, because without this important stimulus to efficiency, physical distribution management would have to look into other areas if improvements in physical distribution's efficiency are to be continued.

---

17 "Brave New Checkout," *Newsweek* (February 17, 1975), p. 79. See also: Willard R. Bishop, Jr., "New Approaches to Improving Social Productivity in Food Distribution," *1974 Combined Proceedings: American Marketing Association* (Chicago, 1975), pp. 299–303.

18 See: "For Incoming Materials Flow: A Quantum Jump In Control," *Modern Materials Handling* (March, 1976), pp. 40–44.

19 LaLonde and Auker, *op. cit.*, p. 236.

FIG. 15-2 Warehousing applications of scanners.

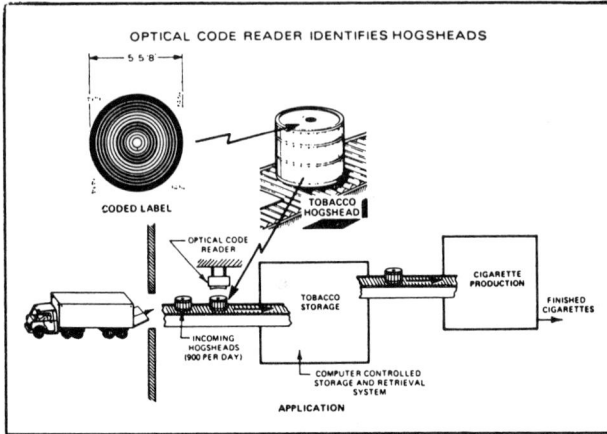

OPTICAL CODE READER IDENTIFIES HOGSHEADS

A circular code pattern utilizing overhead readers identifies and counts hogsheads of tobacco entering a large tobacco plant in Virginia.

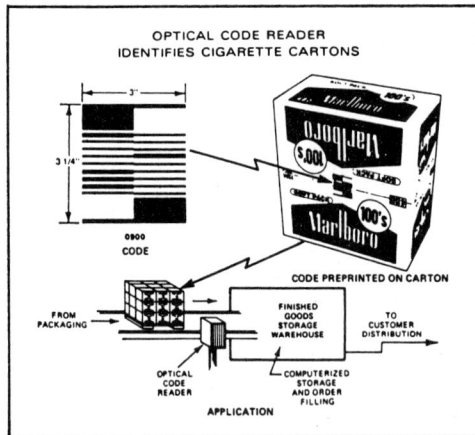

OPTICAL CODE READER IDENTIFIES CIGARETTE CARTONS

Vertically mounted readers are utilized to read and identify the preprinted bar code on corrugated cartons.

© The Materials Handling Institute, Inc., 1975.

FIG. 15-3 Truck-mounted scanner for inventorying container yards.

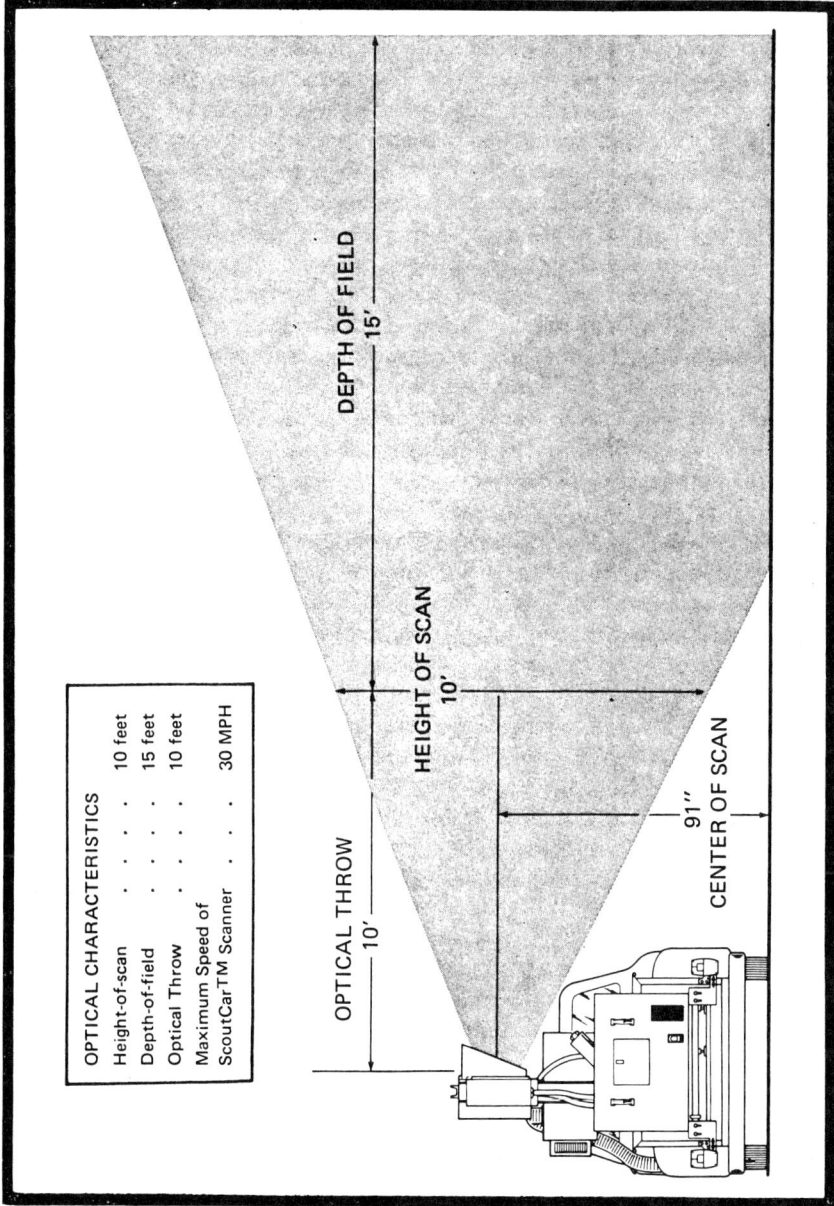

OPTICAL CHARACTERISTICS

Height-of-scan . . . . 10 feet
Depth-of-field . . . . 15 feet
Optical Throw . . . . 10 feet
Maximum Speed of
ScoutCarTM Scanner . . . 30 MPH

DEPTH OF FIELD
15'

HEIGHT OF SCAN
10'

OPTICAL THROW
10'

91"

CENTER OF SCAN

DECREASING RATE OF TECHNOLOGICAL DEVELOPMENT

Professor James L. Heskett has argued that the pace of technological development is waning. He states that there are a number of reasons for this.[20] First, there are certain physical constraints on technology.[21] Rail cars, for example, cannot be substantially increased in height because of the restrictions imposed by the size of tunnels and highway over- and underpasses. Trucks cannot become substantially wider (the industry is lobbying for a six inch increase in width) because of the standard size of highways. Trucks on Interstate highways of up to 80,000 pounds (from 73,280 pounds) were authorized by the federal government with state approval in December, 1974, the first increase since 1956.[22]

A second factor involves a lack of significant economies-of-scale as larger transportation equipment is contemplated. The 747 aircraft was predicted in the late 1960's to "revolutionize" air freight transportation. In fact, it has not substantially reduced air freight rates. A few ocean tankers are presently operating in the 300,000-ton to 500,000-ton category. Although marine architects are confident that ships with a 1,000,000-ton gross weight carrying capacity are technologically feasible, they probably will not be built in the near future because diseconomies-of-scale are present in both the construction and operation of these mammoth ships. Indeed, in 1975, tanker charter rates dropped, and construction of several of the behemoths was halted.

Another factor suggested by Heskett is that at present, physical distribution departments have been overwhelmed by the increasing sophistication of technological developments. The result has been that a significant amount of present technology has yet to be incorporated into daily operations. Most firms are still not fully utilizing existing technology. Therefore, there may be less demand for new physical distribution technological advances because many firms have yet to use what is currently available.

It is interesting to note the conclusions of an international symposium that attempted to predict the future of transportation in the decade from 1980 to 1990. They forecasted that "one should not expect any introduction or rapid expansion of new transport techniques between 1980 and 1990."[23] This statement was based on three basic premises. First, since transport equipment must frequently be interchanged inter-

[20] James L. Heskett, "Sweeping Changes in Distribution," *Harvard Business Review* (March-April, 1973), pp. 123–132.

[21] See: Todd Fandell and Charles Camp, "Transportation in 2000 To Rely on Equipment Much Like Today's," *The Wall Street Journal* (April 1, 1976), p. 1.

[22] Albert R. Karr, "Whoosh! Here Comes the Big Rigs," *The Wall Street Journal* (December 17, 1974), p. 14.

[23] J. P. Baumgartner, *Summary of the Discussion: Fifth International Symposium on Theory and Practice in Transport Economics—Transport in the 1980–1990 Decade* (Paris: European Conference of Ministers of Transport, 1973), p. 25.

nationally, the probability of change is reduced because many countries do not currently or in the foreseeable future have any desire to alter their existing transportation and support equipment. Second, new transportation techniques and equipment tend to be very capital intensive and many countries do not have the ability to fund these types of projects. The current problems that the supersonic passenger plane, the Concorde, is experiencing, illustrate this situation. Developmental costs of this aircraft are many times higher than originally projected and current demand for the plane is substantially lower than the original world-wide forecasts. Finally, the report noted, "The discounted future costs of new transport techniques exceed those of existing modes of transport. In other words, all existing modes of transport offer the advantage of *existing*. This is not a mere philosophical concept but a fact."[24]

FASTER TECHNOLOGICAL ADVANCEMENT

While the above discussion argues that technological development will decline in importance over the coming years, there are many indications that the forecasted decline has not yet materialized. Toffler believes that the increasing rate of technological advancement will continue. He noted that each new machine has the effect of changing all the existing machines, because the old and the new can be combined to produce even more efficient machines. The result is that while new equipment increases at an arithmetic rate, the number of potential combinations of old and new machines increases exponentially.[25]

Examples of continued technological sophistication, which are typically computer assisted, are numerous. Recent computer innovations involve an order-processing system for the S.S. Kresge distribution center in Reno in which products are examined visually by an operator who then literally tells the cartons where to "get-off." The operator's voice activates a mini-computer which "understands" the voice command and performs the requested sorting by having the package transferred to the applicable conveyor belt.[26]

Another computer application which promises to become commonplace by 1980 is one computer "talking" directly to the computer system of a vendor, warehouseman, carrier, or customer. Illustrative of this is the computer of Mobile Chemical Plastic Division in Macedon, New York, which communicates directly with their public warehouse in Indianapolis. Jack H. Larman, President of the AAA Warehouse Corporation, describes the computer interface:

[24] *Ibid.*
[25] Alvin Toffler, *Future Shock* (New York: Bantam Books, Inc., 1970), pp. 28–29.
[26] "Tell Your Cartons Where To Get Off," *Traffic Management* (February, 1975), pp. 24–27.

For almost two years now, our computer at AAA Warehouse has been "talking" twice a day with Mobil Chemical Plastic Division's computer in Macedon, New York. Each day at 11:15 AM, via telecommunications which, in our case is dataphone, we send them all their warehouse receipts for any merchandise we have received in the previous 24 hours, plus information on all shipments, adjustments, back orders for the same period, including an up-to-date stock status.

At the same time, we prepare our own shipping analysis and open order report. Therefore, both management teams know the status of all orders. As this information is being transmitted, it automatically raises the inventory in our computer and in their computer in Macedon at the same time. Each day at 4:15 PM, again over dataphone, we receive orders from Mobil, which then produces a print-out on our printer, on Mobil's bills of lading. At the same time we are receiving these orders for shipments, it is reducing our inventory in our computer and their inventory in their computer simultaneously, and in many instances, it is using inventory that we had transmitted that morning at 11:15 AM. These orders come to us pre-routed and pre-truckline assigned, which again saves a lot of time.[27]

The authors believe that technological growth will continue to expand in the future at an ever increasing rate. The development will not affect each functional area of physical distribution equally. Some aspects, such as transportation, which are very capital intensive, will experience only evolutionary rather than revolutionary changes. On the other hand, areas such as warehousing, inventory control, order processing and use of optical scanners will continue to experience dynamic breakthroughs in technology based on advanced computer applications. Most firms today are already extensively involved in using computer applications in their physical distribution system. As newer computer techniques become available, the marginal costs of applying them are not substantial because the computer hardware is already in place.

PROJECTED MARKETING CHANGES

Throughout this book the close relationship between marketing and physical distribution has been stressed. This section will examine a number of probable marketing changes in the future and how they will interact with the physical distribution department.

INCREASED PRODUCT VARIETY

One of the marketing trends that will continue at an increased rate is the proliferation of the firm's product line. It was noted in chapter 1 that businesses in general have been greatly expanding their variety of product offerings. Revlon alone offers some 33,000 items to satisfy

27 Jack H. Larman, "Computers and Warehousing," *Annual Proceedings of National Council of Physical Distribution Management* (1972), pp. 248–249.

specific customer needs. This trend will continue because customers are demanding a greater variety of products in order to more completely fulfill more exacting requirements. Business firms are finding this trend more palatable because the economies of long production runs can now be achieved in shorter manaufacturing schedules. "When automated electronic production reaches full production, it will be just about as cheap to turn out a million different objects as a million exact duplicates. The only limits on production and consumption will be the human imagination.[28] Many production engineers believe that the day soon approaches when diversity of products will cost no more to manufacture than standardized products.

The trend to increased product variety has the potential to cause significant complexities for the physical distribution department. However, this is not necessarily the case. Remember that there are basically two reasons why production takes place. "Made-to-order" production runs, which are common in the auto industry, involve producing a product which has already been sold. The customer has specified exactly what he or she wants on the car and then it is manufactured to meet those requirements. Made-to-order production runs do *not* cause any significant problems for the physical distribution department, because once the product is manufactured it is transported directly to the waiting customer.

The second type of production is "speculative." Products are manufactured first and then the marketing department attempts to locate buyers. This is the more common type of production. It is in this situation that the increased variety of products can cause massive problems in the area of inventory control. Each new product variation available to consumers is an entirely *separate* and *unique* product from an inventory viewpoint. As the number of product variations increases, the required level of inventory at local, regional, or national distribution centers to support a satisfactory level of customer service grows. One writer cited the example of product varieties, x, y, and z replacing product J. Assuming that sales do not increase with the added variety, the firm still must maintain an increase in overall inventory of 60 percent at field warehouses to maintain the same level of customer service.

SHORTENED PRODUCT LIFE CYCLES

A product life cycle is the time between when a product is introduced in the marketplace to when its sales have declined to the point where it is withdrawn. Toffler has argued that product life cycles will be shortened in the future because of rapid technological advances which will render the current products obsolete.

[28] Marshall McLuhan and George B. Leonard, "The Future of Education: The Class of 1989," *Look* (February 21, 1967), p. 24.

A well-oiled machinery for the creation and diffusion of fads is now an entrenched part of the modern economy. Its methods will increasingly be adopted by others as they recognize the inevitability of the ever-shorter product cycle. The line betwen "fad" and ordinary product will progressively blur. We are moving swiftly into the era of the temporary product, made by temporary methods, to serve temporary needs.[29]

As product life cycles decrease in time, the need for effective physical distribution is highlighted. Time is of the essence for faddish-type products.

REDUCED LEVELS OF CUSTOMER SERVICE

The days of inexpensive energy are over. The three-fold increase in petroleum prices during 1973–1974 was reflected in increased transportation rates. Because of the significantly higher transport rates now in effect, many firms are decreasing their levels of customer service. Another factor that is also pressuring firms into reducing field inventory levels is high interest rates. If the firm's inventories are financed by borrowed funds, this expense item becomes significantly higher.

Because of these two cost escalations, many firms have implemented reductions in customer service levels. This objective can be accomplished in a number of ways. One alternative is to encourage customers to place larger orders, which should decrease the usage of the relatively expensive LTL (less than truckload) and LCL (less than carload) rates. Another method is to lengthen the average time of the customer's order cycle. Customers will experience a longer waiting time from when an order is placed until it is received.

INCREASED CHANNEL AND COMPETITOR COOPERATION

The trend toward increased channel coordination and cooperation will continue to become more important. Companies are realizing that they often cannot operate in a vacuum. There are numerous examples of this type of industry cooperation which are beneficial to all of their members. The Grocery Manufacturers Association established the Universal Product Code, which greatly assists both inventory control and significantly improves the efficiency of grocery check-out systems. This group also established a standard pallet size, 48 by 40 inches. Besides establishing the physical dimensions, the GMA specified such requirements as the types of wood, the shape of the fork lift arm receiving holes, etc. A GMA pallet trading program has been established so that participating firms can exchange pallets. This reduces the need to backhaul empty pallets.

[29] Toffler, *op. cit.*, p. 73.

Channel cooperation has proven to be especially helpful in achieving transportation economies-of-scale. The Supermarket Institute is currently testing the feasibility of consolidating shipments into large urban areas. Competing grocery firms would establish a joint venture distribution system into which all products would initially flow. This would reduce the congestion at each grocer's receiving dock because only fully loaded trucks would make deliveries.[30]

The Canadian Grocery Manufacturers Association established a distribution center in Vancouver which is shared jointly by a number of leading manufacturers and their customers. The result has been a consolidation of shipments destined for urban customers which has resulted in a savings of at least ten percent to the manufacturers involved. Based on this initial success, the concept has been recently utilized in two other Canadian provinces.

W. F. Wendler, vice-president distribution of the Noxell Corporation, has proposed a program of drug manufacturer "cooperative warehouses." He proposed that the drug industry select common distribution points and each firm would then ship full vehicle loads to these warehouses. From the common warehouses, the shipments of all producers would be consolidated to common customers on a single bill-of-lading in order to achieve maximum freight savings. Wendler acknowledged that his plan would involve "a horrendous clerical effort" and suggested that the solution to this quandry would be an on-site shared computer installation. This plan, according to Wendler's sample analysis of shipments from his company would generate savings of 15 to 20 percent.[31]

Recycling of solid waste materials is another area that requires an increased level of channel cooperation. Zikmund and Stanton have noted, "Recycling waste materials is essentially a 'reverse-distribution' process. Reverse distribution is facilitated by a 'backward' channel which returns the reusable packaging and other waste products from the consumer to the producer; it reverses the traditional physical flow of the product."[32]

Because of the socially desirable aspects of recycling, many middlemen and especially retailers are participating in recycling programs even though they are not enthusiastic. Retailers believe that they are not adequately compensated in the recycling of returnable bottles. Empty bottles take up an abnormally large amount of floor space that could be better utilized for selling additional merchandise.

[30] As reported in "Sweeping Changes in Distribution," *op. cit.*, p. 127. See also: "The Transportation Facilitation Center," *Transportation and Distribution Management* (January-February, 1975), pp. 22–26.

[31] "Drug Shippers Join In Drive To Exempt Small Shipments From Rate Regulation," *Traffic World* (March 22, 1969), p. 20.

[32] William G. Zikmund and William J. Stanton, "Recycling Solid Wastes: A Channels-of-Distribution Problem," *Journal of Marketing* (July, 1971), p. 35.

The trend towards increased recycling will continue. Manufacturers who are able to assist other channel members in this activity will benefit from increased good-will. If the manufacturer assumes total responsibility for recycling activities, a very positive advantage can accrue to the firm who relieves the other channel members from participating in the recycling program. The Reynolds Metals Company has been involved in establishing aluminum recycling programs in a number of large urban areas. Their permanent reclamation centers have encouraged individuals to bring used aluminum containers directly to the center for cash payments. In 1972, this program alone collected more than 800 million all-aluminum beverage cans, which is approximately 36 million pounds of scrap aluminum.[33]

NEEDED: MORE QUALIFIED MANAGERIAL PERSONNEL

American firms have generally accepted the logic of the physical distribution concept—the total-cost concept, the usage of cost trade-offs and the avoidance of functional suboptimization. Nevertheless, physical distribution can only continue to make its appropriate contribution to the firm if it has highly capable and knowledgeable management.

It is encouraging to note the continually increasing number of physical distribution courses that are being taught in graduate schools, four-year and two-year colleges. The need for thoroughly educated physical distribution managers is apparent. Ohio State University delved into demographic data of senior level physical distribution executives. It was found that 92 percent possessed an under-graduate degree and that more than one in four had earned a graduate degree.[34]

Future physical distribution executives will have to be both *generalists* and *specialists*. The former is basic because, as early chapters indicated, the physical distribution manager does not operate in a vacuum. He or she is continually interacting with the other functional areas of the firm—marketing, production, finance and accounting. In addition, the physical distribution manager must have a high degree of specialized knowledge in transportation, warehousing, inventory analysis, customer service and order processing. A senior corporate executive summed it up this way:

> This acceptance (of physical distribution) will become easier, I believe, by decade's end as more physical distribution personnel, buttressed by a firmer background in management science skills and a broader knowledge of busi-

[33] Donald Boyes, "Distribution Ecology—An Industry Approach to the Problem," *Annual Proceedings of the National Council of Physical Distribution Management* (1973), p. 280.

[34] Bernard J. LaLonde and James F. Robeson, "Career Patterns in Distribution: 1973," *Annual Proceedings of the National Council of Physical Distribution Management* (1973), pp. 1–28.

ness and its management, move into general executive roles. More broadly based talents, rather than the narrower technical abilities, will increasingly become the hallmark of the successful physical distribution practitioner.[35]

Alvin Toffler in his best selling book, *Future Shock*, predicted that the usage of *task-force* or *project management* will become a very common organizational structure in the future. This involves teams of specialists and generalists who are assembled to solve a specific problem. When their task is accomplished, the task-force is disassembled and each person returns to his or her original functional area. Toffler noted that the Lockheed Aircraft Corporation created a giant task-force to create and produce the C5A military air transport aircraft. The task-force accomplished its mission of manufacturing 58 planes and then was disbanded.

Task-force management structures appear to be the wave of the future. By their very nature, the persons assigned to these groups must not only possess special skills, but they must also be able to appreciate and comprehend where their specialization fits into the "big picture." They must have excellent communication skills in order to efficiently express their particular viewpoint. Toffler concluded:

> Despite much loose talk about the need for "generalists," there is little evidence that the technology of tomorrow can be run without armies of highly trained specialists. We are rapidly changing the types of expertise needed. We are demanding more "multi-specialists" (men who know one field deeply, but who can cross over into another as well) rather than rigid, "mono-specialists."[36]

Future physical distribution managers would do well to "broaden" their horizons as much as possible during their college career. While many of the specialties of physical distribution can be learned on the job, it is difficult to obtain in this manner a feeling for the other functional and environmental aspects of the areas. Besides physical distribution courses, the authors suggest that students should take as many courses as possible in these disciplines; marketing, accounting, economics, public speaking (both large and small group), international business, management science with emphasis on computer applications, and governmental relations with the business community. These courses will provide the student with the ability to grasp both the "micro" and "macro" aspects of physical distribution management.

SUMMARY

This chapter has presented a view of the future development of physical distribution. Its purpose is to stimulate the reader into thinking critically about the material discussed.

[35] Sarni, *op. cit.*, p. 48.
[36] Alvin Toffler, *Future Shock* (New York: Bantum Books, Inc., 1970), p. 288.

It is assumed that physical distribution managers will be subjected to increased governmental intervention in almost every aspect of the discipline, with the possible exception of the transportation sector. This is already evident in OSHA regulations, labor relations and product recalls.

Most marketing observers believe that multinational sales by United States based firms will continue to grow in importance. This trend will place additional demanding requirements on the firm's physical distribution department. Imports will also increase.

The United States will convert to the metric system of weights and measures. Many multinational companies have already converted their products and relatively few difficulties have been encountered.

There is no trend in physical distribution development which is more predictable than the increased usage of computers. Computer technology has been and can be extremely beneficial in the following areas: carrier operations, warehouse operations, inventory planning and control, strategic planning, and forecasting.

Since marketing and physical distribution necessarily interface so frequently, it is imperative to be aware of any basic strategy changes in the area of marketing. The following trends will undoubtedly become more important: increased product variety, shortened product life cycles, reduced levels of customer service, and increased control and competitor cooperation.

Finally, because physical distribution is becoming a readily accepted and respected part of the American business structure, there is a constant need for better trained and more sophisticated managers. Physical distribution executives must have the ability to be both generalists and specialists.

QUESTIONS FOR DISCUSSION AND REVIEW

1. Do you believe that a discussion of possible future trends in physical distribution is worthwhile, or is it too speculative to be of any real value? Defend your answer.

2. In what areas of physical distribution do you believe there should be *increased* federal governmental intervention? Why?

3. In what areas of physical distribution should there be *decreased* federal governmental intervention? Why?

4. Discuss the present areas of federal governmental regulations which interface with physical distribution.

5. Do you believe that the importance of multinational sales will continue to increase? Why?

6. Are multinational sales in the best interests of the United States? Why?

7. Why is the United States one of the few countries which is not currently using the metric system?

8. Take a position *for* or *against* the United States converting to the metric system.

9. Discuss fully the current trends which are appearing that may hasten the conversion to the metric system.

10. It is often said that physical distribution managers must be both *generalists* and *specialists*. Discuss fully why this tends to be a valid statement.

11. Discuss briefly the concept of *task-force* or *project management*. Do you believe it will become more important in the future? Why?

12. Based on your understanding of physical distribution management, what specific areas of expertise should aspiring executives in physical distribution attempt to master? Why? Be specific in your answer.

13. Discuss briefly a number of computer applications in physical distribution which, to the best of your knowledge, are not currently being used but which you believe have real potential.

14. Discuss briefly a number of computer applications in the carrier operations field.

15. What is the UPC? Discuss briefly the advantages of using this system.

16. Does the computer offer any real advantages when attempting strategic corporate planing? Discuss fully.

17. Do you believe that equipment technology will continue to provide a source of increased physical distribution efficiency in the future? Defend your answer carefully.

18. Toffler argues that the pace of technological development will continue to accelerate. Take a position in favor of this premise and present your argument.

19. Discuss the projected changes that may take place in marketing during next decade or two.

20. Why is the trend towards increased product variety likely to occur in the future?

21. What is speculative production? Is it a common or rare occurrence? Why?

22. Why would shortened product life cycles place more importance on effective physical distribution?

23. Some physical distribution prognosticators have predicted that customer service levels will decline in the future. What rationale is there for this position?

24. Why is it predicted that channel members and competitors will experience increased cooperation in the future?

25. Discuss the impact of recycling from a physical distribution viewpoint.

CASE 15-1   ACE GROCERIES CO.

Ms. Ellen Scott was in charge of customer relations for Ace Groceries Co., a chain store operation in the Pacific Northwest. It operated over 100 stores under its own name, and 20 grocery-only sections in large discount stores with other names. In Spokane, they operated the grocery section in a "Discount King" discount store. While the ordinary Ace Store carried 12,000 to 14,000 different items (including many non-grocery items), the grocery section in the Spokane "Discount King" carried only 7,200 different items. This smaller number of items was due to two reasons. First, other sections in the discount store, outside the Ace section, handled many of the non-grocery items. Second, because of Discount Kings' interest in low prices, the number of product line offerings was kept intentionally low.

Because of the smaller number of different items handled, the grocery section of the Spokane Discount King was chosen to test a "check-out" system employing the Universal Product Code (UPC). The UPC is the black bar symbols appearing on the labels of many grocery items. A 10-digit number is involved; the first five identify the manufacturer, the second five are assigned by the manufacturer to specific items. Many, but not all of the grocery manufacturers, had incorporated the UPC symbol on their container or container label. At the check-out counter, the clerk passes each item over an optical scanner which is tied into a computer. The computer retrieves the price of each item and lists each item and its price on the receipt. The price of each item is also shown temporarily on a small screen.

In the receiving area of the store, Ace personnel had their own UPC label-making machine, so they could attach labels to grocery items whose manufacturers had not done so. Ace personnel also supplied UPC codes to driver/salesmen who delivered name-brand soft drinks, bread, and dairy products. The driver/salesmen then placed the label on each package before placing the package on the shelf. (Prior to the UPC, the driver/salesmen had put the price tags on their own merchandise.) The Ace personnel also affixed UPC labels to packaged meats; this was done in conjunction with the wrapping and weighing operation.

From Ace Groceries' standpoint, the UPC offered several advantages:

1. It improved speed and accuracy at the check-out counter.
2. It improved inventory control because sales of each item were recorded and this information was almost immediately available to Ace's buyers. Under the former system, Ace buyers' only data were orders received from retail stores.

3. Store personnel no longer needed to price mark each item. The only visible price was on each shelf.

4. The check-out computer could be tied into Ace's headquarters, from which point all prices could be controlled. This was important since some stores failed to keep up with price changes and there would be discrepancies between their prices and prices listed in advertising.

A 30 day training period had been used to prepare receiving personnel, shelf-stocking clerks, butchers, produce clerks, and check-out clerks for the new system. Some resistance was anticipated from both shelf stocking and check-out personnel because potentially their work hours would be reduced. None materialized, although union officers indicated that automation would be an issue in the next contract negotiation.

On July 7, the system was scheduled to go into operation. On June 15, Ms. Scott had printed two flyers which were inserted in each shopper's bagged-groceries (exhibits 1 & 2). On June 22, a booth was set up near the checkout stands. The booth was staffed from 11 AM to 7 PM daily and contained a UPC check-out machine. Customers were shown how it worked and were allowed to pass various grocery items over the scanners to see how the system would operate.

Ms. Scott handled public relations and each of the local newspapers ran a large feature story on the Discount King's UPC system. T.V. stations gave it some coverage although not as much. Ms. Scott surmised this was because Discount King was a much more important newspaper advertiser than it was a T.V. advertiser.

On July 7, the system was put into operation. There were few mishaps. A few customers complained that the prices charged differed from the price shown on the shelf. (Prices were no longer placed on each item, the UPC had to be connected with a computer which would retrieve the price.) The customers were right. The computer had been fed incorrect price information and corrections were made. Reporters from local papers and TV stopped in during the day and wrote favorable reports concerning the new system in operation. Several Ace Groceries officials had come in for the opening and they were pleased. On July 8, they left Spokane and flew back to the Ace home office. Ms. Scott drove them to the airport and they told her they were pleased with the system and were happy with the large amount of favorable publicity it was apparently generating. Ms. Scott was instructed to stay in Spokane until July 14, then return to the home office herself. Since she had been working long hours, Ms. Scott decided she owed herself a morning off so, as she went to bed that evening in her motel, she did not set her alarm clock.

YOUR RECEIPT LISTS THE ITEM AND THE AMOUNT OF MONEY YOU SPENT.

Description of the Item

Taxable Item

Produce Item

Weight

Price Per Pound

Multiple Purchase

Beverage Purchase with Deposit

Meat Item

Tax is computed automatically

Cash Tender

Change is Computed Automatically

Store

Date

Time

Checkout Lane

```
*  *  *            *  *  *

        DM GRN BEANS    .36
        GUM             .12
        DIAL SOAP       .35 T
        INST COFFEE    2.79
1.72# BANANA3 .14       .24
        BEEF HASH       .79
      6 CELERY SOUP    1.38
        SLICED BEETS    .46
   .60D 7 UP           1.83 T
        T-BONE STEAK   1.99
        TAX DUE         .10

        TOTAL         10.41

        CSH PAID      11.00
        CHG DUE         .59

1/14/75  10:17  002/13
        THANK  YOU
```

"Universal Product Code" — What Is It?

The Universal Product Code (UPC) has been developed after ten years of food industry research. Each item bears a different symbol consisting of a bar code and a corresponding ten digit code. The first five digits identify the manufacturer and the second five digits identify the actual product and size. The bar code represents these numbers in a language which a computer-driven scanner can read and understand.

"Electronic Checkout" — How Does It Work?

The scanner reads the bar code on the package and transmits the information to this store's computer which knows the current price for the item. The computer then transmits the price and description of the item to the display screen and causes them to be printed on the receipt tape. The UPC and the Electronic Checkout system eliminates the need for price marking each package. The current price of each item is clearly marked on the shelf molding and on your receipt tape. All this will mean a faster and more accurate checkout each time you shop.

It's a completely new checkout experience.

She was awakened the next morning by a ringing telephone. It was Craig Jones, Manager of Ace's food section in the Spokane Discount King store. "Ellen," he said, breathlessly, "you'd better get down here p.d.q.* There are television cameras all over!"

"We're getting more publicity?" asked Ms. Scott, still half asleep.

"Yeah, but bad," was Jones' response. "We're being picketed by every consumer group in Spokane!"

"Why?"

"Because of the UPC. They don't like it. Please get down here, pronto!"

"All right, already, I'm on my way," said Ms. Scott. She quickly dressed, skipped breakfast, and drove to the store.

As she approached the store her heart sank. There were four police cars parked at various locations, with policemen trying to keep traffic moving. Two large TV station vans were present. On top of one a cameraperson was taking some large panoramic shots of about 300 pickets in front of the store. Ellen Scott estimated two-thirds of the crowd were women. Many were apparently housewives and accompanied by small children. At least 50 pickets carried placards saying such things as "STOP COMPUTERED CHECKOUTS," "UPC, NON–ITEM PRICEMARKING, OUI," "END UPC," "UPC HURTS CONSUMERS." The pickets were chanting: "One, two, three, four, toss UPC out the door." Leaders of the pickets were aware of TV coverage and told sign carriers to hold them so they faced the TV camera.

Ms. Scott parked her car and went into the store through a side door where Craig Jones was waiting. The store was open, although there were not many customers. "What do you think of the demonstration, Ellen?" he asked. "This is the biggest one we had since the grape boycott."

"I don't know, Craig," answered Ellen. "The only one I've ever seen was in Salem, Oregon, where about 50 pickets wanted us to package our meats in 'see-through' plastic trays. How long do you think this one will last?"

"All day," was the answer. "It won't hurt business much either. There's the old saying about 'no such thing as bad publicity.'"

Just then one of the TV reporters walked up to Jones and Ms. Scott. He was the one who had interviewed Ms. Scott on two previous occasions. "Ellen," he said, "we want to make the noon news. Can I interview you outside?"

"OK," said Ms. Scott, "but what's the issue?" They walked out of the store.

"The issue is the consumers group doesn't like your new coding system. Tell you what, I'll interview their leader first and then ask you

* Pretty damn quick.

to respond," said the TV newsman as he motioned a camera crew into place.

Ellen was a bit uncertain, but could think of no easy way out. She watched as the leader of the consumer group walked over to a spot in front of the camera. The TV newsman motioned Ellen to do likewise. She did and the two ladies were introduced. The other's name was Selma Lopez, a well-known consumer activist. She glared at Ellen.

The TV camera was in place. The TV newsman waited until the red light under the lens lit, showing that the camera was on. He said in a rapid voice: "Selma Lopez is a familiar face on our action news program. Selma, why don't you tell us what you and the others here have against the new Universal Product Code?"

Ms. Lopez reached into a shopping bag and pulled out two cans and held them up in front of the camera and said loudly. "Here's what we've got against the codes. No price marks on the can. Only some funny black lines. The price is shown only on the shelves. You can't expect to take a can of tomato sauce from the vegetable section to the ethnic food section to compare it with spaghetti sauce and remember the price on the original tomato sauce that you saw marked on the shelf. Especially if you got a couple of kids in-tow."

The TV newsman turned to Ellen and the camera pointed at the newsman. The red light was on; the newsman said, ". . . and here for Ace Foods which operates the Discount King food section is Ellen Scott. Ellen, what do you think about the demonstration here today?" The camera pointed at Ellen, the red light was on, and Ellen was on T.V.

Question One: What do you think Ms. Scott's response should be?

Question Two: Assuming Ace Groceries decides to introduce UPC checkout operations in other stores, what changes, if any, should be made to avoid the type of consumer protest they were encountering today?

CASE 15-2 HIJAX SPARKLING COLA

Bradley Gilpin was Vice President and General Manager of Hijax Sparkling Cola Company, located in Colorado Springs, Colorado, where it bottled several flavors of carbonated beverages and sold them under the Hijax label. They also bottled one nationally-known brand of soft drink. They distributed within Colorado Springs and an area within 50 miles, including Pueblo. They did not sell their product in the Denver area. Their largest single customer was a nearby military base. Their second largest customer was the U. S. Air Force Academy.

Hijax Sparkling Cola's 1976 sales, by type of account, are shown below. The percentages are of volume, measured in cases.

1. Military bases (including USAF Academy)   18%
2. Retail chain stores (deliveries to distribution centers)   23%
3. Institutional sales (hotels, hospitals)   8%
4. Retail stores (delivery to stores and placing on shelves)   36%
5. Bars and vending machines   15%

                                                                          ─────
                                                                          100%

Sales had been increasing about four percent each year and the distribution between categories had not changed very much. The method for servicing the five categories of accounts was: Categories 1, 2 and 3 received "drop shipments" performed by Hijax drivers who were paid on a straight salary basis of $4.46 per hour. For these accounts, a marketing representative had already made the sale and the driver merely delivered the purchased goods. Categories 4 and 5 were serviced by driver/salesmen who were paid $3.95 per hour plus five cents per case of 24 bottles or cans. Driver/salesmen received the same fringe benefits as the regular drivers; the fringe benefits cost 63 cents per hour.

Hijax Cola produced and sold 400,000 cases of 24 bottles or cans per year. Half of this volume was from June through September.

The bottling equipment in the Hijax plant was 17 years old, and according to the plant engineer, Robert Lynch, would have to be replaced within two years. The can-filling machine was much newer.

Gilpin was concerned about the metric system's adoption and wanted any new equipment to handle cans or bottles of the slightly different metric sizes. Lynch assured him that either machine could handle different sizes of containers. The only problem would be returnable bottles. Those in the old size would have to be destroyed and replaced by returnable bottles in the new size.

Gilpin did not like having to use three types of containers: cans, returnable bottles, and non-returnable bottles. Frequently, a retail store would want all three types on the shelf. The new cost of a 12 oz can was seven cents; a 12 oz non-returnable bottle cost six cents; and a 12 oz reusable bottle cost 13 cents. The reason that all three types of containers were used was caused by vending machine operators; some of their machines dispensed cans and some dispensed bottles. Where there was some supervision over return of empties, such as in auto service stations, returnable bottles would be used.

Ecology groups favored returnable bottles and had picketed two Colorado Springs retail stores that had stopped carrying them. Colorado people were presently very interested in resource protection and Gilpin knew of one other state which, by law, had prohibited the sale of soft drinks in non-returnable containers. Right now, several ecology groups were lobbying for a similar law in Colorado. In newspaper ads they were showing pictures of discarded bottles and cans and of wildlife that had been killed because of swallowing the "fliptops" off of cans.

Consumers, however, preferred the disposable cans and continually paid about five cents more for a disposable can than for a returnable bottle. (The cola in a returnable bottle actually retailed for five cents more, but ten cents of this was a refundable deposit.)

Gilpin, and nearly all beverage bottlers, also used both glass and metal containers to avoid being dependent on only one type of container. Metal containers sometimes became almost impossible to buy. Glass bottle shortages were less frequent. Returnable bottles were used an average of 15 times each, so a decrease in supply of new ones had almost no affect.

Lynch had calculated that costs of filling the 12 oz cans or bottles were about the same. It cost one cent per bottle to wash, sterilize, and inspect returnable bottles before they were reused. The average delivery cost per case of 24 bottles was more than the cost for a case of 24 cans. The lower cost for the cans was because they could be packed more densely than the bottles.

There were costs associated with returnable bottles. Many of these costs were borne by the merchants who had to administer the refund program. Several retail grocers had tried dropping the returnable bottle line but, as stated earlier, they were then picketed by the ecology groups, and the merchants capitulated. Merchants had to provide storage space for empty bottles. Hijax's driver/salesmen also had to administer the returnable deposits on a wholesale level and they had to load the empty bottles aboard the truck. Gilpin had recently calculated that a driver/salesman handling non-returnable cans could deliver 200 cases per day; non-returnable bottles, 180 cases per day; and returnable bottles, 140 cases per day (including the return of about 130 cases of empties). Drivers who delivered to military bases, chain store distribution centers, or to institutions, could handle about 300 cases of cans, 250 cases of non-returnable bottles or 200 cases of returnable bottles (including return of 185 cases of empties). The average cost of operating any of the beverage delivery trucks was $20 a day.

Gilpin then asked Marcia Mellow, who worked in the accounting office, to calculate the amount and volume of returnable bottles, non-returnable bottles, and cans that driver/salesmen delivered, the amount and volume of each item that straight drivers delivered. This was difficult to do because can sales were higher in the summer due to picnics. Marcia's best guess was that a driver/salesman's load consisted of 60 percent returnable bottles, 20 percent non-returnable bottles, and 20 percent cans. Straight drivers carried 35 percent returnable bottles, 30 percent non-returnable bottles and 35 percent cans.

Question One: Assuming that the wholesale price of each 12 ounces of cola was 10 cents, what price should be set to cover and reflect the differences in cost of non-returnable cans, non-returnable bottles, and returnable bottles?

Question Two: Do you think Hijax Sparkling Cola should continue to distribute its product in all three types of containers? Why or why not?

CHAPTER REFERENCES

"A Flood of Shoddy Products—What's Being Done To Stem It," *United States News and World Report* (February 24, 1975).

ALDERSON, V. RAY; "Adaption of the Motor Carrier Industry to Present and Prospective Supplies of Fuel," *Transportation Journal* (Spring, 1974), pp. 20–23.

BALLOU, RONALD H. and James E. Piercy; "A Survey of Current Status and Trends in Transportation and Logistics Education," *Transportation Journal* (Winter, 1974), pp. 27–36.

BARRETT, COLIN; "Statutory Implications for Labor to 1980," *Annual Proceedings of the American Society of Traffic and Transportation* (1974).

———; "The Trouble With Separatism," *ICC Practitioners' Journal* (July-August, 1970), pp. 721–731.

BAUMGARTNER, J. P.; "*Summary of the Discussion*," *Fifth International Symposium of Theory and Practice in Transport Economics—Transport in the 1980–1990 Decade* (Paris: European Conference of Minister of Transport, 1973).

BEIER, FREDERICK, JR.; "The Educational Challenge Facing Logistics and Physical Distribution Management," *Transportation Journal* (Summer, 1972), pp. 40–47.

BISHOP, WILLARD R., JR.; 'New Approaches to Improving Social Productivity in Food Distribution," *1974 Combined Proceedings: American Marketing Association* (Chicago: 1975).

BOYES, DONALD; "Distribution Ecology—An Industry Approach to the Problem," *Annual Proceedings of the National Council of Physical Distribution Management* (1973).

BRANNAN, TED R.; "Problems of Tomorrow's World," *Transportation Journal* (Winter, 1969), pp. 37–42.

"Brave New Checkout," *Newsweek* (February 17, 1975).

CAMPBELL, THOMAS C.; "Transport and Its Impact in Developing Countries," *Transportation Journal* (Fall, 1972), pp. 15–22.

CAVINATO, JOSEPH L. and Alan L. Stenger; "Energy Consciousness—A Transportation Perspective: Without Emotion, Please!" *Transportation Issues* (May, 1975), pp. 10–13.

CLAYTON, JOHN E.; "Approaches, Opportunities, and the Transport Job Ahead," *Transportation Journal* (Winter, 1967), pp. 15–18.

CLAYTON, W. GRAHAM, JR.; "A Single Intermodal Transportation Company," *Transportation Journal* (Spring, 1972), pp. 31–38.

CREEDY, JOHN A.; "Intermodal Ownership and Voluntary Coordination," *Transportation Journal* (Winter, 1972), pp. 39–45.

"Drug Shippers Join in Drive to Exempt Small Shipments From Rate Regulation," *Traffic World* (March 22, 1969).

FANDELL, TODD and Charles Camp; "Transportation in 2000 To Rely on Equipment Much Like Today's," *The Wall Street Journal* (April 1, 1976).

FARRIS, MARTIN T.; Gilbert L. Gifford, Donald V. Harper, Warren Rose, Hugh S. Norton, and James W. Bennett, Jr.; "Transportation Education: An Evaluation," *Transportation Journal* (Summer, 1972), pp. 26–39.

"For Incoming Material Flow: A Quantum Jump in Control," *Modern Materials Handling* (March, 1976).

GARSON, HELEN S.; "Transportation and Fiction," *ICC Practitioners' Journal* (May-June, 1970), pp. 576–580.

GOLDEN, CHARLES T.; "Ducking into Metrics," *Handling and Shipping* (October, 1974).

"Hallmark's Distribution Center: A Handling Spectacular," *Modern Materials Handling* (January, 1974).

HEAVER, TREVOR D.; "Multi-Modal Ownership—The Canadian Experience," *Transportation Journal* (Fall, 1971), pp. 14–28.

HESKETT, JAMES L.; "Sweeping Changes in Distribution," *Harvard Business Review* (March-April, 1973).

IULO, WILLIAM; "Supply and Demand for Energy: Largely Domestic," *Transportation Journal* (Spring, 1974), pp. 9–14.

"Justice Department Files First Class Action Civil Rights Suit Against Trucking Industry," *Traffic World* (March 25, 1974).

KAPLAN, N. M.; "The Growth of Output and Inputs in Soviet Transport and Communications," *The American Economic Review* (December, 1967), pp. 1154–1167.

KARR, ALBERT R.; "Whoosh! Here Come the Big Rigs," *The Wall Street Journal* (December 17, 1974).

KEITH, FRED R., JR.; "Metric Warehousing: A Minimum Impact?," *Transportation and Distribution Management* (February, 1973).

KLADSTRAP, D. M.; "Metrication and PDM," *Handling and Shipping* (December, 1975).

KNEAFSEY, JAMES T. and Matthew L. Edelman; "A Market-Oriented Solution to the Northeast Railroad Dilemma," *ICC Practitioners' Journal* (January-February, 1974), pp. 174–189.

LACKMAN, CONWAY L.; "Implication of Conglomerates for Transportation in the 1970's," *Transportation Journal* (Fall, 1974), pp. 30–45.

LADD, RICHARD A.; "Joint Demand For Transportation Systems And Recreation Systems," *Transportation Journal* (Summer, 1971), pp. 5–22.

LALONDE, B. J. and Karl Auker; "A Survey of Computer Applications and Practices in Transportation and Distribution," *Annual Proceedings of the National Council of Physical Distribution Management* (1972).

—— and James F. Robeson; "Career Patterns in Distribution: 1973," *Annual Proceedings of the National Council of Physical Distribution Management* (1973).

LANCIONI, RICHARD A.; "Facing the Energy Crisis," *Distribution Worldwide* (December, 1973), pp. 46–49.

——; "Profile of a Crisis," *Distribution Worldwide* (April, 1974), pp. 53–56.

LARMAN, JACK H.; "Computers and Warehousing," *Annual Proceedings of the National Council of Physical Distribution Management* (1972).

LIEB, ROBERT C.; "A Revised Intermodal Ownership Policy," *Transportation Journal* (Summer, 1971), pp. 48–53.

————; "Intermodal Ownership: Experience and Evaluation," *ICC Practitioners' Journal* (July-August, 1971), pp. 746–759.

LYNAGH, PETER M., and Richard F. Poist; "Rational Regulatory Re-evaluation," *Transportation Issues* (May, 1975), pp. 14–16.

MARTIN, WILLIAM F. and George Cabot Lodge; "Our Society in 1985—Business May not Like It," *Harvard Business Review* (November-December, 1975).

McKIE, JAMES F.; "A Commentary on World Petroleum," *Transportation Journal* (Spring, 1974), pp. 5–8.

McLUHAN, MARSHALL and George B. Leonard; "The Future of Education," *Look* (February 21, 1967).

MELLICHAMP, JOSEPH M. and James L. Fillmer; "Simulation and the Superjets," *Transportation Journal* (Winter, 1973), pp. 51–55.

O'NEIL, BRIAN F. and David H. Hinds; "PDM and Ph.D.'s: The Research Gap," *Transportation and Distribution Management* (Nov., 1973), pp. 36–38.

OWEN, WILFRED; "The World Without Automobiles: A Fable," *Transportation Journal* (Spring, 1971), pp. 60–63.

PLOWMAN, E. GROSVENOR; *Elements of Business Logistics* (Stanford, Cal.: Stanford University, 1964).

Proceedings, 1974 Forum (Washington, D.C.: Transportation Data Coordinating Committee).

ROSE, WARREN; "Does the Silver Need Polishing? A Challenge to the Profession," *Transportation Journal* (Summer, 1971), pp. 37–42.

SARNI, VINCENT A.; "PD in the Near Future," *Annual Proceedings of the National Council of Physical Distribution Management* (1973).

SEGUIN, V. C.; "The Impact of the Petroleum Energy Crisis on Intercity Freight Transportation," *ICC Practitioners' Journal* (March-April, 1974), pp. 306–316.

SMERK, GEORGE M.; "The Environment and Transportation," *Transportation Journal* (Fall, 1972), pp. 40–49.

SPYCHALSKI, JOHN C.; "Nuclear Steam-Generation of Electricity: Its Implications for the Future of Coal Transport by Railway and Waterway," *ICC Practitioners' Journal* (July-August, 1967), pp. 736–748.

"Survey: Converting to Metric," *Transportation and Distribution Management* (July-August, 1975).

"Tell Your Cartons Where To Get Off," *Traffic Management* (February, 1975).

"The Metric System is Creeping in on United States," *United States News and World Report* (March 3, 1975).

"The Standards Shell Game," *Transportation and Distribution Management* (February, 1973).

"The Transportation Facilitation Center," *Transportation and Distribution Management* (January-February, 1975).

"The Trucking Industry: Working Behind the Scenes," *Transportation and Distribution Management* (April, 1972).

Traffic Management (September, 1975).

TOFFLER, ALVIN; *Future Shock* (New York: Bantum Books, Inc., 1970).

WILLEY, WILLIAM E.; "Transportation Planning and the Energy Crisis," *Traffic Quarterly* (April, 1975), pp. 273–283.

ZIKMUND, WILLIAM G. and William J. Stanton, "Recycling Solid Wastes: A Channels-of-Distribution Problem," *Journal of Marketing* (July, 1971).

Appendix

QUANTITATIVE TECHNIQUES IN PHYSICAL DISTRIBUTION

This section will examine four quantitative techniques that are commonly used in physical distribution. Each one has many applications in the various functional areas of physical distribution. The four techniques are: the transportation linear program, routing techniques, capital budgeting techniques, and queueing theory.

THE TRANSPORTATION LINEAR PROGRAM

A linear program assumes that all the fundamental aspects of a problem have a linear or straight-line relationship. Thus it is assumed that transportation rates increase at a constant rate as distance increases. Because this assumption is frequently not true (transportation rates taper as distance increases), the solutions from a linear program should be viewed as "ball park" answers which will require additional refinement.

The transportation linear program is one of the most common analytical techniques used by physical distribution managers. Why? Because it helps to solve a common problem—*allocation* of resources to where they are needed at the least cost. Assume a traffic manager has to decide how to utilize the firm's fleet of private trucks. In other words, at what plant should each vehicle pick-up the product and to what customer should it be delivered? Assume that the Jenkins Corporation only produces one product and it has four production plants. The plant locations and maximum monthly output are: Minneapolis, 500 units; Chicago, 300 units; Dallas, 600 units; and Los Angeles, 400 units. Because the product is very specialized, there are only four customers. Their locations and monthly purchases are as follows: San Diego, 200 units; Houston, 400 units; Cleveland, 900 units; and Boston, 200 units. Figure 1 presents a summary of above information with production plants along the top and customer locations down the left hand margin.

The transportation problem requires that the quantity available to be allocated (production capacity) equal the quantity desired (customer

THE TRANSPORTATION MATRIX
Plant Locations

	Minneapolis	Chicago	Dallas	Los Angeles	
San Diego	40	48	49	44	200
Houston	46	41	49	50	400
Cleveland	43	47	45	46	900
Boston	48	42	45	47	200
Dummy	100	100	100	100	100
	500	300	600	400	1800

Consumer Locations (vertical label on left side)

Figure 1

demand). Since total customer demand is 100 units less than total productive capacity, a *dummy* customer is added. Of course, nothing will
be actually shipped to the dummy customer after the optimum allocation has been determined. It could represent goods going into the producer's inventory.

The number in the upper left hand box represents a summation of
three factors in this example. One of the factors represents the production cost of each unit, which often varies among plants based on the
age of the production equipment. Also, because of labor union jurisdictional disputes, a second factor represents a penalty payment that

NORTHWEST CORNER INITIAL ALLOCATION

Plant Locations

Consumer Locations	Minneapolis	Chicago	Dallas	Los Angeles	
San Diego	40 200	48	49	44	~~-200-~~ 0
Houston	46 300	41 100	49	50	~~-400-~~ 0
Cleveland	43	47 200	45 600	46 100	~~-900-~~ ~~-700-~~ ~~-100-~~ 0
Boston	48	42	45	47 200	~~-700-~~ 0
Dummy	100	100	100	100 100	~~-100-~~ 0
	~~-500-~~ ~~-300-~~ 0	~~-300-~~ ~~-200-~~ 0	~~-600-~~ 0	~~-400-~~ ~~-200-~~ ~~-100-~~ 0	1800

Figure 2

must be paid to the union in some cases if products are shipped from certain plants to certain destinations. Finally, a third factor represents the transportation costs of shipping a unit from each plant to each customer. Usually, when all plants have the same production costs and when there are no labor jurisdictional problems, the number in the box just represents the transportation cost between each plant and customer. Note that for the "dummy" row an arbitrarily high production and transportation cost is utilized. This figure (100 in the example) is set very high so that it will have a minimal effect on the allocation procedure.

The problem involves deciding the quantities and plants which should be utilized to satisfy customer requirements.

Northwest Corner Initial Allocation. One procedure to establish the initial allocation is the Northwest Corner technique. Figure 2 illustrates an initial allocation using this procedure. The idea is to start in the Northwest corner of the chart and place as large a quantity of product in it as possible. Either completely fill the customer's demand or exhaust the productive capacity available. In the example, the San Diego customer required 200 units and the Minneapolis plant had 500 units available. Therefore, the customer's total demand of 200 was filled. Notice that the Minneapolis plant still had 300 available for allocation. These units are assigned to the next customer, in this case located in Houston. Houston required 400 units, but only 300 were available from the Minneapolis plant. Therefore, 100 additional had to be supplied from the Chicago plant. Chicago still has 200 units available and they are allocated to the next customer located in Cleveland. The same procedure is continued, moving from the Northwest corner to the Southeast corner.

The Northwest Corner method, while yielding an initial allocation, is not commonly used because it completely ignores the production and other costs in the upper left-hand corner box. To correct this deficiency, another initial allocation procedure can be utilized.

Vogel's Approximation. A technique designed to yield a better initial allocation is Vogel's Approximation. Professor Vogel argued that the initial allocations should not necessarily be where the costs (upper left hand corner box) are the lowest, but where the *penalty* is the greatest for not achieving an allocation at the lowest cost.

To get an idea of what this means, assume that a customer can be supplied by an allocation from either of two plants, one having costs of $41 and the other having costs of $44. Now assume that same customer can be supplied by an alternative allocation from two other plants, one having costs of $44 and the other having costs of $50. In the first allocation, if the lowest cost, $41 could not be used, the next lowest cost, $44, would have to be used. The penalty for not using the lowest cost in this allocation would be $3, ($44 −$41). In the second allocation, the penalty for not using the lowest cost would be $6, ($50 −$44). Vogel would make initial allocations, not where the cost was the lowest, but where the penalty was the highest for not using the lowest cost.[1] Therefore, in this simple example, Vogel would use the second allocation, not the first.

1 For further detail, see: Nyles V. Reinfield and William R. Vogel, *Mathematical Programming* (Englewood Cliffs, N.J.: Prentice-Hall, Inc., 1958) and Thomas M. Cook

VOGEL'S APPROXIMATION INITIAL ALLOCATION

		3	1	0	2	
1		Minneapolis	Chicago	Dallas⑥	Los Angeles④	
4	San Diego	40 ② 200	48	49	44	-2̶0̶0̶- 0
1 ß̶ 5̶	Houston	46	41 ① 300	49	50 ⑦ (100)	-4̶0̶0̶- -1̶0̶0̶- 0
1 2̶	Cleveland	43 ③ 300	47	45 ⑤ 400	46 ⑥ 200	-9̶0̶0̶- -6̶0̶0̶- -2̶0̶0̶- 0
2 ß̶	Boston	48	42	45 200 ④	47	-2̶0̶0̶- 0
0	Dummy	100	100	100	100 ⑧ 100	-1̶0̶0̶- 0
		-5̶0̶0̶- -3̶0̶0̶- 0	-3̶0̶0̶- 0	-6̶0̶0̶- -4̶0̶0̶- 0	-4̶0̶0̶- -2̶0̶0̶- -1̶0̶0̶- 0	1800

Figure 3

Figure 3 illustrates an initial allocation using Vogel's Approximation. The procedure is laborious, yet worthwhile, because it yields an
initial allocation which is commonly very close to the optimum solution.
To start, calculate the penalty for not taking the lowest cost for *each
row* and *each column*. In the Minneapolis column it is $3, ($43 −40);
for Dallas $0 ($45 −$45); for Chicago $1, ($42 −$41); for Houston $5,
($46 −$41); and so on. The penalty costs should be written in small
numbers near the row or column involved. When all the penalty costs

and Robert A. Russell, *Introduction to Management Science* (Englewood Cliffs, N.J.:
Prentice-Hall, Inc., 1977), Chapter 7.

have been written down, find the *highest one*. In this example, it is Houston with a penalty cost of $5. This tells us that the first allocation will be in the Houston row. Next, check the costs from each plant in the Houston row and find the *lowest* plant cost. It is Chicago with a $41 cost. When the lowest is determined, make as large an allocation as possible to that square. Since Houston requires 400 units, but Chicago can only supply 300 units, then 300 units is the maximum that can be allocated from Chicago. Next, *update* the plant output and customer needs. The Chicago plant goes from 300 units to 0 units because all of its production capacity will be shipped to Houston. For simplicity's sake, draw a line completely through the Chicago column, because we can now forget about it. Why? Because all of its output has been allocated. Now update Houston's needs. They were 400 units, but it now has 300 from Chicago, so it only needs 100 additional units.

(What if there would have been a *tie* after checking all the penalties? Assume there were two rows or columns with a $5 value. Then each row or column is checked to find the lowest cost and that's where the initial allocation is made. If two or more locations tie for the lowest cost, select at random one of these and make the initial allocation.)

After the first allocation (300 units) and the updates, the procedure is repeated. But, any row or column that has been satisfied is completely disregarded when calculating the penalties. In this example the Chicago plant has been completely allocated and a line has been drawn through it to remind us to ignore this column. The penalties are updated and again written in small numbers next to the row or column involved. The second allocation goes to San Diego, because its penalty value of $4 is now the highest. This row is checked and the lowest cost is $40 and therefore an allocation is made in this square. The allocation is always as much as possible. San Diego requires 200 units and Minneapolis can supply 500 units. Hence, all of San Diego's 200 units are allocated from Minneapolis. The update results in Minneapolis still having 300 units to allocate, and a line is drawn through San Diego because its requirements have been satisfied. The same procedure is again followed, now ignoring both Chicago and San Diego. The circled numbers in the allocated squares indicate the order in which the allocations were made.

Vogel's approximation yields a significantly improved first allocation relative to the Northwest Corner method. Figure 4 compares the total costs of each allocation.

Optimization Check. When the initial allocation is completed, the next step in the transportation linear program is to check the solution to see if it is the best answer. To simplify the procedure, transfer the initial allocation to a clean matrix which has all the cost information, such as Figure 5.

FIGURE 4   Comparison of Northwest Corner to Vogel's Approximation

Northwest Corner Initial Allocation Cost

$40	×	200 units	=	$ 8,000
46	×	300 units	=	13,800
41	×	100 units	=	4,100
47	×	200 units	=	9,400
45	×	600 units	=	27,000
46	×	100 units	=	4,600
47	×	200 units	=	9,400
(Dummy row is ignored)				$76,300

Vogel's Approximation Initial Allocation Cost

$40	×	200 units	=	$ 8,000
41	×	300 units	=	12,300
50	×	100 units	=	5,000
43	×	300 units	=	12,900
45	×	400 units	=	18,000
46	×	200 units	=	9,200
45	×	200 units	=	9,000
(Dummy row is ignored)				$74,400

On this clean matrix, we will begin the optimization check by assigning check figures to the rows and columns that have squares with allocations in them. The idea behind a check figure will become clear as the discussion progresses. The first step is to assign a value of "o" to the first row, which in the example is San Diego and which has a square with an allocation in its row. This value of "o" is the check figure for the first row. Now how do we assign check figures to the other rows and columns? Consider the following statement, and then we will be able to assign check figures to the other rows and columns.

For each allocated square, the sum of the check figures for the row and the column it occupies, must equal the cost in that square.

Thus, if the San Diego row has a check figure of "o," and the Minneapolis column has an allocation, then the Minneapolis column has a check figure of 40. Why? Because the cost in the Minneapolis-San Diego square is 40, the San Diego row check figure is o, therefore, the Minneapolis column check figure must be 40. (Expressed algebraically, o + X = 40, therefore, X = 40.)

Let's take this a step further. Notice that the Minneapolis-Cleveland square has an allocation. We now know the check figure for the Min-

OPTIMIZATION CHECK

	Minneapolis 1 40	Chicago 34	Dallas 42	Los Angeles 43	
0 San Diego	40 200	48 +	49 +	44 +	200
7 Houston	46 -1 (+100)	41 300	49 0	50 (-100) 100	400
3 Cleveland	43 (-100) 300	47	45 400	46 (+100) 200	900
3 Boston	48 +	42 +	45 200	47 +	200
57 Dummy	100 +	100 +	100 +	100 100	100
	500	300	600	400	1800

Figure 5

neapolis column. Therefore, we can find the check figure for the Cleveland row. The cost in the Minneapolis-Cleveland square is 43, and the Minneapolis column check figure is 40, thus, the Cleveland row check figure is 3, $(40 + X = 43$, therefore $X = 3)$.

Moving along a bit faster now: The Cleveland-Dallas square has an allocation and the cost associated with it is 45; the Cleveland row has a check figure of 3, therefore the Dallas column has a check figure of 42. This procedure is followed until all the rows and columns have check figures.

Occasionally, a problem presents itself when it comes to assigning check figures. There will be no problem if the total number of allocated squares equals the sum of number of rows plus the number of columns, minus one. In our example, there are 8 allocated squares; and also, there are 5 rows plus 4 columns, minus 1, which equals 8. Therefore, no problem and check figures can be assigned to all rows and columns. When the number of allocated squares is less than the sum of the number of columns minus one, this is called a *degeneracy*, and there will be a deficiency of one check figure.

Degeneracy results when simultaneously a row and a column are satisfied. For example, if Cleveland needed 300 units and Chicago had 300 units, then both the Cleveland row and the Chicago column would be satisfied through a single allocation. The result would be that the initial allocations as represented on the matrix would have one less allocated square.

Degeneracy can be solved by finding a square that does not have an allocation and assigning it an allocation of "o" units. The specific square you should use can be found when assigning the row and column check figures. As you proceed in assigning check figures, you will notice a number of unallocated squares, which, if they had allocations, would allow you to assign check figures to all rows and columns. Among all the squares that will allow completion of the check figures, choose the one that has the lowest cost figure and allocate to that square a quantity of "o" units. Treat this square with "o" units as you would any other allocated square, and the degeneracy will be solved.

The next step is to examine all squares that do not have allocations in them. In Figure 5, notice that the San Diego-Chicago square is unallocated. Add the row value (0) to the column value (34) and subtract this figure from the cost figure of the square (48). The answer is 14. Notice the square is marked with a plus sign (+) meaning that the answer was positive. The same procedure is repeated for *all unallocated squares*. One of three answers is possible for each unallocated square. First, a positive answer, which indicates that the square in question will *not* have an allocation when the optimum solution is found. Secondly, a zero is possible, which means that the square may or may not be used in obtaining the optimum answer. A zero indicates that more than one optimum solution exists for the problem. In other words, an allocation can be made in the square, but it will only yield another answer of *equal value*—it will not be any less expensive than the previous solution. Finally, a negative number is possible. When it is found, it indicates that the optimum solution has not been found. In our example, a negative number was found in the Minneapolis-Houston square. If two or more negative numbers are found, the square that is the most negative is used. In our example, the only negative square is Minneapolis-Houston. When a negative square is found, the optimum solution requires allocating as much as possible into the square with the negative number.

Reallocation. The reallocation procedure involves using only the allocated squares. To determine which allocated squares to use, remember that if an allocation is made in the Minneapolis-Houston square, it must also be subtracted from somewhere else because the row and column total unit quantities must remain the same after the reallocation. Minneapolis still must produce 500 units and must allocate them somewhere and Houston still requires 400 units which must be supplied somewhere. Notice the box drawn in Figure 5. This indicates where the additions and subtractions will be made. For every addition, there must be a subtraction, but to keep the matrix in balance, notice that two additions are necessary and two subtractions. The goal is to place as large an allocation as possible in the square with a negative check value. What if we decide to do this by taking 300 units from the Cleveland-Minneapolis square? We would add it to the Houston-Minneapolis square, but that means we would have to subtract 300 units from the Houston-Los Angeles square. This cannot be accomplished because it only has 100 units in it, and no square can logically have a negative allocation. Therefore, the largest quantity to be transferred is limited by the *smallest* number of units in an allocated square from which a quantity will be subtracted. In the example, the limiting square is Los Angeles-Houston. Notice that 100 units is added to the Houston-Minneapolis square; 100 is subtracted from Houston-Los Angeles; 100 is added to Cleveland-Los Angeles; and 100 is subtracted from Cleveland-Minneapolis.

It is important that after a new allocated square has been added (Houston-Minneapolis) that a former allocated square be completely eliminated (Houston-Los Angeles). Why? Because the check figures only work if the allocated squares follow the formula—rows plus columns minus one. Also, after the allocation, all the plant outputs must be the same as well as the customer total requirements.

Figure 6 illustrates the new allocation. New check numbers were assigned for this new allocation and this time there were no negative numbers in the unallocated squares. This indicates that the allocation in Figure 6 is the optimum allocation. Figure 7 shows that the optimum allocation is $100 cheaper than the initial allocation using Vogel's approximation. If the reallocation had a negative number in an unallocated square, then another plus and minus type change would be accomplished and the new allocation checked. The procedure is continued until no negative numbers are found.

Constraints. The transportation linear programs can be easily adjusted for constraints imposed by management, labor unions, etc. As-

SECOND OPTIMIZATION CHECK					
1	Minneapolis 40	Chicago 35	Dallas 42	Los Angeles 43	
0 San Diego	40 / 200	48 / +	49 / +	44 /	200
6 Houston	46 / 100	41 / 300	49 / +	50 / +	400
3 Cleveland	43 / 200	47 / +	45 / 400	46 / 300	900
3 Boston	48 / +	42 / +	45 / 200	47 / +	200
57 Dummy	100 / +	100 / +	100 / +	100 / 100	100
	500	300	600	400	1800

Figure 6

sume, for example, that a labor union provision states that the Dallas plant cannot supply the Houston market. This can be accomplished by placing an artificially high cost in the Dallas-Houston square. The problem is then solved using the above procedure and the Dallas-Houston square will not be allocated because of the high cost involved. Alternatively, assume that the Cleveland customer *must* be supplied by the Minneapolis plant. This is achieved by placing an artifically low cost figure in this square.

FIGURE 7   Cost of the Reallocation

$40	×	200 units	=	$ 8,000
46	×	100 units	=	4,600
41	×	300 units	=	12,300
43	×	200 units	=	8,600
45	×	400 units	=	18,000
46	×	300 units	=	13,800
45	×	200 units	=	9,000
(Dummy row is ignored)				$74,300

Computer Application. While the above allocation problem was solved manually, the typical procedure involves programming a computer to follow the same logic and procedures. As a rule-of-thumb, matrices larger than ten rows by ten columns become sufficiently complex to warrant the introduction of a computer to do the time-consuming procedures involved.

ROUTING TECHNIQUES

A typical problem in scheduling vehicles is to determine the route which will minimize the time required to stop at each destination. This type of problem is often known as a "traveling salesperson problem" because it is an important consideration for salespeople in the scheduling of their activities.[2]

The Listing Method. A proven and uncomplicated procedure involves determining the time or cost involved between each point that has to be covered. We will only look at the travel times in the example because it is assumed that the delivery or service times are the same at each stop. Figure 8 illustrates the seven locations and the travel times between all six customers and the warehouse in a given city. The travel times are also listed in a matrix. Remember that *times* are listed and not miles. Thus, for example, the time from Customer A to Customer D is less than the time from Customer A to Customer B because the travel from A to D is on an all interstate route, whereas A to B is travelled on local roads.

The driver must start at A, the company warehouse, and return there after delivering to each of the six customers. To start, add destination

[2] For a complete discussion of this type of problem, see: Robert L. Karg and Gerald L. Thompson, "A Heuristic Approach to Solving Travelling Salesman Problems," *Management Science* (January, 1964), pp. 225–248.

THE TIME (MINUTES) BETWEEN EACH LOCATION

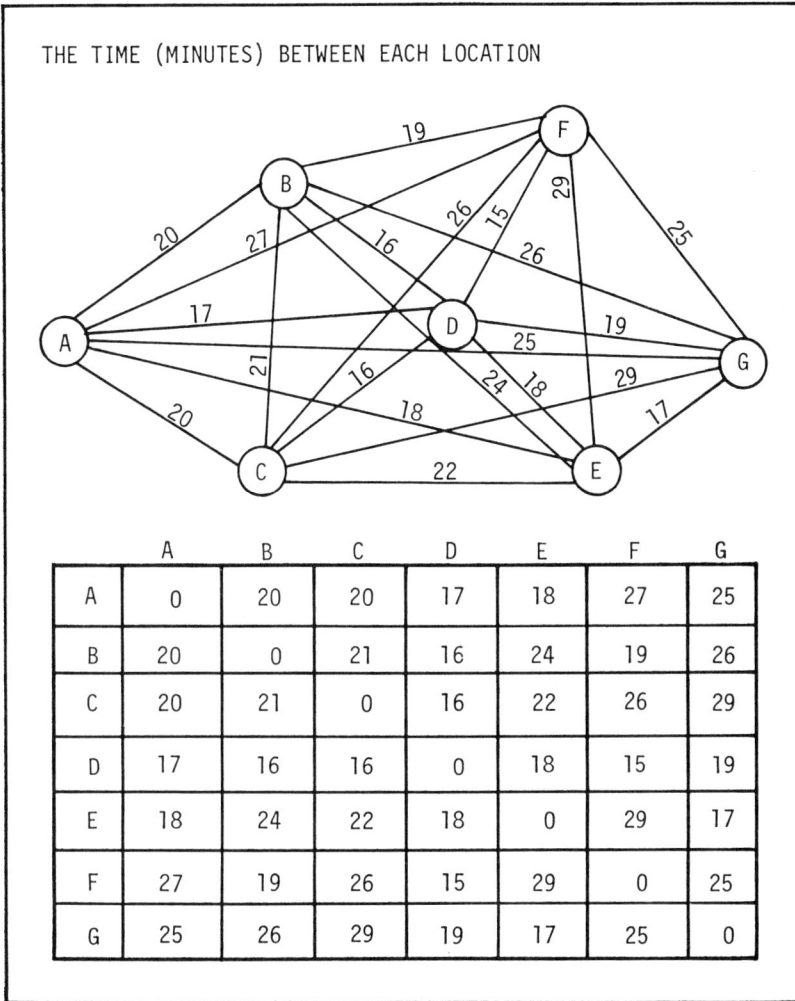

	A	B	C	D	E	F	G
A	0	20	20	17	18	27	25
B	20	0	21	16	24	19	26
C	20	21	0	16	22	26	29
D	17	16	16	0	18	15	19
E	18	24	22	18	0	29	17
F	27	19	26	15	29	0	25
G	25	26	29	19	17	25	0

Figure 8

B to the route which must start and end with A. It is A-B-A and it has a travel time of 40 minutes (A to B is 20 and B to A is 20). Next, add destination C and insert it between each point in the A-B-A route. A-C-B-A has a value of 61, (20 + 21 + 20). The other possible combination is A-B-C-A and it also has a value of 61, (20 + 21 + 20). In the case of a tie, such as this, select either alternative and add destination D and insert it in all possible locations. (When one route yields a lower travel time than the other, of course, continue this method with the swifter route.) Figure 9 illustrates the addition of destination D to route A-C-

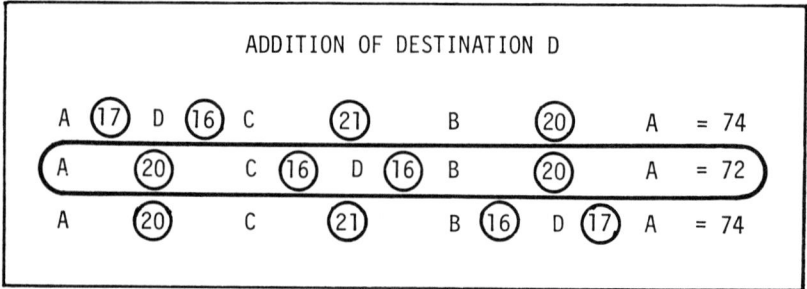

Figure 9

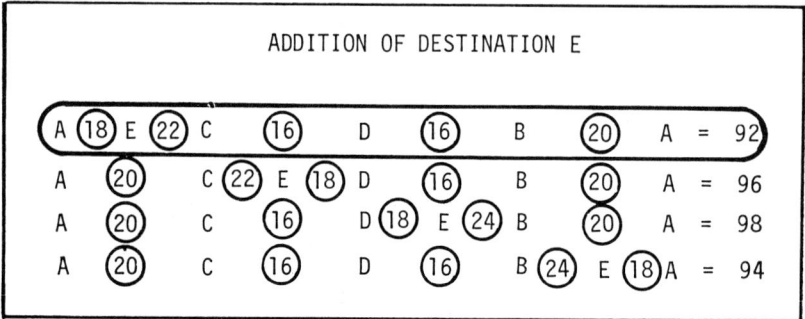

Figure 10

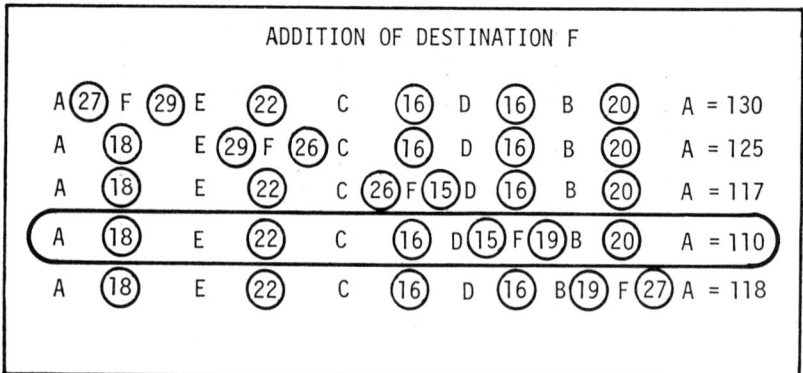

Figure 11

B-A. The circled numbers are the times between locations. The route A-C-D-B-A has the *lowest* travel time and it is used when destination E is added. Figure 10 indicates that route A-E-C-D-B-A has the lowest travel time. Destination F is added to this route in Figure 11. The lowest cost route is A-E-C-D-F-B-A. Finally, destination G is added in Figure 12. Notice that a tie results and that either route A-G-E-C-D-F-B-A or route A-E-G-C-D-F-B-A result in the lowest travel time.

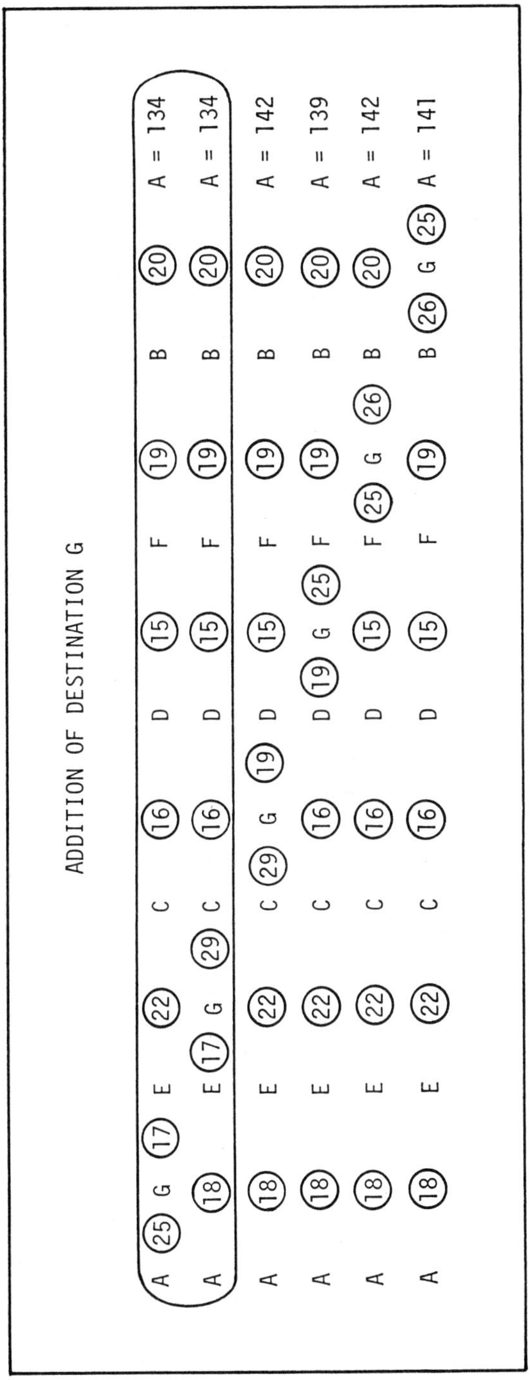

ADDITION OF DESTINATION G

FIG. 12

The above methodology is a *heuristic* procedure. Hinkle and Kuehn have defined a heuristic procedure as ". . . a short cut process of reasoning . . . that searches for a *satisfactory, rather than an optimal solution.*"[3] The above procedure will produce a very good solution to the scheduling problem, although it will not usually produce the optimum solution. In the above example, the optimum solution found by checking every possible alternative route is A-C-E-G-D-F-B-A or A-B-F-D-G-E-C-A. Each of these solutions has a travel time of 132. The simplified heuristic procedure produced a solution (134) almost as accurate as the optimum solution. Remember that the value of a heuristic procedure is when the complexity of the problem is great. If the above problem had 156 destinations that had to be serviced, the problem would obviously be too complex to be performed manually. A computer would be utilized, and the program would be based on the heuristic methodology discussed.

The Pin and String Method. Another heuristic technique helps to solve the problem of how many vehicles are needed to cover the delivery requirements and which route each vehicle should use.[4] Although this technique appears simplistic, the logic of the procedure is sound and it will produce solutions that are reasonably close to the optimum.

Assume a company processes film and every day the company must pick up unprocessed film from each retailer and also drop off processed film. Five hundred locations must be serviced each day. All the locations are within 100 miles of the processing plant. The unprocessed film must be back at the processing plant by 6:00 p.m. each day. The retail locations can be serviced in any order.

The procedure involves using a large scale map which represents the service area involved. Next, convert the mileage scale to *hours* by using a "reasonable" average speed for an eight-hour day. Twenty miles per hour will be assumed to be a reasonable and obtainable average speed. Therefore, any two points on the map can be read as hours and fractions of hours apart.

String is then cut into the equivalent of eight-hours of travelling at an average speed of twenty miles per hour. If the map scale was one inch equals ten miles, each piece of string would be sixteen inches long.

To start scheduling, tack one end of a string at the processing plant and stretch the string to a destination and place a pin through the string at that destination. Take the bight (the remainder of the string) and stretch it to another destination and pin it down. The procedure is

[3] Charles L. Hinkle and Alfred A. Kuehn, "Heuristic Models: Mapping the Maze for Management," *California Management Review* (Fall, 1967), p. 61.

[4] This discussion is based on W. W. Abendroth, "A Dirty Shirt Method for Scheduling Vehicles," *Transportation and Distribution Management* (August, 1972), pp. 24–26.

again followed, being sure that each string eventually returns to the processing plant. Follow this procedure with additional 16-inch lengths of string until all destinations have been pinned. Each string represents a vehicle and its route. When completed, the solution to the entire scheduling problem has been found. However, a better solution can usually be found.

Remember that vehicles can "work" on the way to the furthest point and deadhead back, or they can drive directly to the furthest point and "work" in, or they can make stops during the entire trip. The *best* solution possible by this procedure is obtained when the totalled bight left over from all string is *less* than 16 inches long. For example, if the combined bight was 20 inches, then by rearranging the routes, one vehicle and its route could be eliminated.

CAPITAL BUDGETING TECHNIQUES

The traffic manager, as well as all physical distribution executives, should be familiar with the concept of capital budgeting.[5] It involves selecting from available long-term projects those projects which offer the best advantages to the firm. This discussion will deal with two commonly used capital budgeting techniques—average rate-of-return and payback.

Average Rate-of-Return. This capital budgeting technique is generally considered to be the most commonly used approach for evaluating proposed capital expenditures. Its appeal is based on the fact that the information needed to calculate the average rate-of-return is often available from accounting data.

The formula is:

$$\text{Average Rate-of-Return} = \frac{\text{Average Profits After Taxes}}{\text{Average Investment}}$$

The average profits after taxes are found by adding the after-tax profit for each year of the project's life and dividing by the number of years the project will function. The average investment is determined by dividing the cost of the project by two. The average investment assumes that straight-line depreciation is used over the economic life of the project.

Assume the traffic manager has $60,000 to spend on capital assets in 1978. He or she must decide between two projects, both of which cost

5 For a complete discussion of capital budgeting, see: Lawrence J. Gitman, *Principles of Managerial Finance* (New York: Harper and Row Publishers, Inc., 1976) and J. Fred Weston and Eugene F. Brigham, *Essentials of Managerial Finance* (3rd ed.: Hinsdale, Ill.: The Dryden Press, 1974).

approximately $60,000. The first involves the purchase of *pallet racks* which will enable the present warehouse height to be more effectively utilized. With the racks, pallet loads can be stored three or four high, compared to only two at present. The racks will save $10,000 per year that would have been spent on public warehouse space. Assuming a 50 percent corporate tax rate, the after tax profit is $5,000 per year and the racks should last 20 years. Average profit after taxes for the project is:

$$\frac{\$5,000 \times 20 \text{ years}}{20 \text{ years}} = \$5,000.$$

The average investment is $\dfrac{\$60,000}{2} = \$30,000.$

With this information, the average rate-of-return can be calculated. It is:

$$\frac{\$\ 5,000}{\$30,000} = 16.67 \text{ percent.}$$

The second project is the purchase of a tractor-trailer unit for a private trucking operation. The private truck total cost (vehicle, fuel, labor, taxes, etc.) would be $145,000 per year. However, the firm would terminate the usage of a motor common carrier on the route involved. The annual cost of payments to the motor common carrier would be $150,000. The life of the tractor-trailer is six years. The annual difference between the common carrier rates and the private truck is $5,000 times a 50 percent tax rate equals $2,500. The average profit after tax is:

$$\frac{\$2,500 \times 6 \text{ years}}{6 \text{ years}} = \$2,500.$$

The average investment is: $\dfrac{\$60,000}{2} = \$30,000.$

The average rate of return is: $\dfrac{\$\ 2,500}{\$30,000} = 8.33 \text{ percent.}$

The traffic manager then compares the average rate-of-return on each project and selects the one with the higher return—the pallet racks in this example.

Average Payback Period. This is another commonly used capital budgeting technique. It is the average number of years required to recover the initial investment. The average payback period formula is:

$$\text{Average Payback Period} = \frac{\text{Cost of Investment}}{\substack{\text{Average Annual Cash Inflow or} \\ \text{Average Annual Cash Savings}}}$$

Using the information from the previous example, the average pay-back period for the *pallet racks* would be:

$$\frac{\$60,000}{10,000} = 6 \text{ years}$$

For the *private truck* the average payback period is:

$$\frac{\$60,000}{5,000} = 12 \text{ years}$$

The project or investment with the *shorter* average payback period is preferable. Again, the pallet racks are chosen using the average pay-out period criterion.

QUEUEING THEORY

Queueing theory is an analysis of the probabilities associated with the length of time an individual or object must wait in a line or queue.[6] Because of the nature of this analysis, it is also called *waiting line theory*. There are many applications of queueing theory in physical distribution. Should the firm have one, two or three shrink wrap machines[7] in the warehouse? How many desks should there be in the warehouse which hand out the orders to be filled by the warehouse employees? How many inspectors should check the accuracy of the assembled orders?

A traffic management application will be illustrated. The traffic manager is trying to decide if the receiving area for the plant should have one dock or two. It presently has one and he or she is wondering what the effect of adding a second receiving dock would do to the waiting times of delivery vehicles.

To analyze the above problem, a complementary procedure to queueing theory will also be used. *Monte Carlo* simulation involves recreating real-world elements by using probability. The name Monte Carlo comes from picking events at random, such as would take place if a roulette wheel were used.

To analyze the receiving dock situation, it is necessary to study the actual arrival times of trucks at the receiving dock. An employee with a stop watch notes the time between arrivals for a reasonable length of time. Assuming that the period studied was representative, Figure 13 can be generated. The vertical axis is the *cumulative* probability of the time between arrivals. Thus, 25 percent of all delivery trucks arrive

---

[6] This discussion is based on a discussion in William A. Spurr and Charles P. Bonini, *Statistical Analysis for Business Decisions* (2nd ed.; Homewood, Ill.: Richard D. Irwin, Inc., 1973), Chapter 15.

[7] This machine is discussed in Chapter 10.

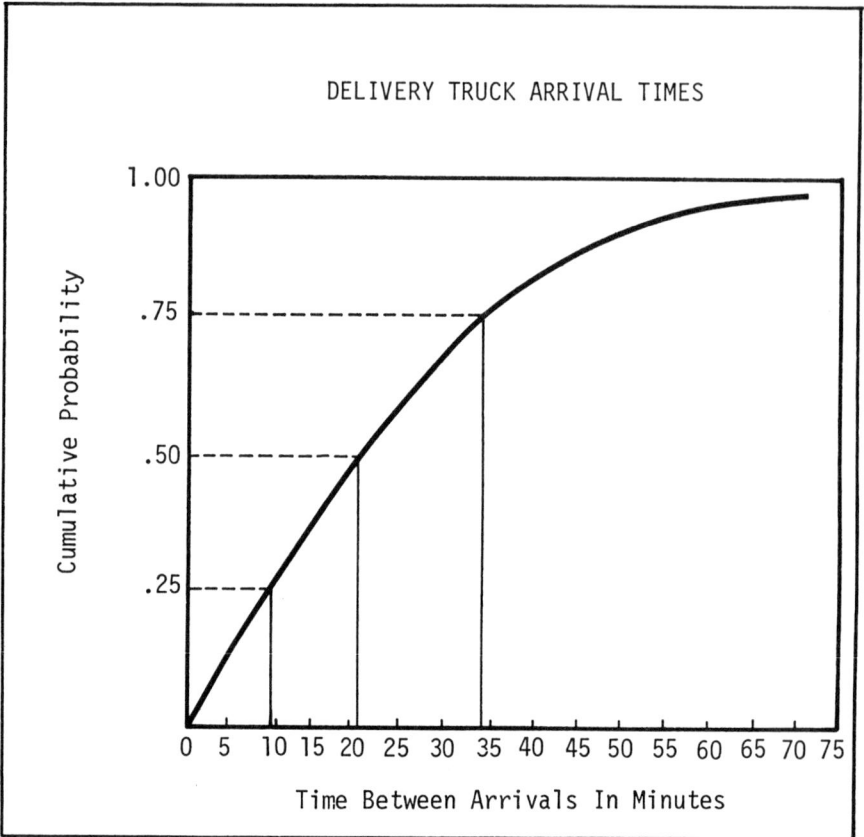

DELIVERY TRUCK ARRIVAL TIMES

Figure 13

slightly less than ten minutes after a previous truck has arrived. Fifty percent arrive within about 20 minutes after the previous truck and 75 percent come within 34 minutes after the previous vehicle.

The traffic manager can simulate, via the Monte Carlo technique, a queueing problem. Since Monte Carlo requires a number of random events, a *table of random numbers* (Table 1) will be utilized. This is a listing of numbers, typically generated by a computer, which are totally random in order. The table of random numbers will be used to generate twenty arrival times. In a real problem, a computer would be used and probably 1,000 arrivals would be tested. Using the first number in the upper left hand corner of the table—05—the time for its arrival is 2 minutes. This figure is determined by treating the 05 as .05 probability (meaning 5% probability) and reading .05 on the vertical axis of Figure 13, then the time between arrivals is approximately two minutes. In this problem, assume that once a truck is cleared to enter a delivery dock, it takes each truck an average of 20 minutes to unload the freight and drive out of the dock area.

TABLE 1   Table of Random Numbers

05	04	31	17	21
43	06	61	47	78
31	85	99	63	92
10	47	39	30	36
39	80	05	45	53
94	20	87	97	04
63	43	14	33	07
99	50	51	80	11
65	29	51	29	85
80	83	09	53	45
87	16	71	77	59
77	58	82	37	85
24	40	43	03	94
99	07	39	40	71
05	17	36	22	20
08	04	63	25	15
63	71	78	62	46
05	67	76	50	85
07	55	97	43	99
49	17	34	63	62
39	56	01	25	83
91	19	08	99	68
22	61	19	61	08
03	67	69	29	02
51	91	76	33	80

The time of the second arrival is determined by the second number in the table of random numbers. It is 43 and we use .43 for Figure 13 to see that the second truck arrives 17 minutes later. With only one dock, the second truck must wait because the first truck is still unloading. The second truck is delayed three minutes and then it starts to unload. Table 2 presents the waiting times for 20 arrivals, for both one dock and two docks. Continuing for the case of a single dock: Truck three arrives 13 minutes later and it must wait ten minutes before the dock is free. Notice that a significant bunch-up takes place with the arrival of the fifteenth truck. Because the trucks are arriving fairly frequently, the waiting time starts to significantly increase.

TABLE 2 Monte Carlo Simulation

		Arrival		1 Dock		2 Docks	
Arrival Number	Random Number	Time Between Arrivals (min.)	Time of Arrival	Time Service Starts	Waiting Time (min.)	Time Service Starts	Waiting Time (min.)
1	05	2	:02	:02	0	:02	0
2	43	17	:19	:22	3	:19	0
3	31	13	:32	:42	10	:32	0
4	10	4	:36	1:02	26	:39	3
5	39	16	:52	1:22	30	:52	0
6	94	60	1:52	1:52	0	1:52	0
7	63	28	2:20	2:20	0	2:20	0
8	99	75	3:35	3:35	0	3:35	0
9	65	30	4:05	4:05	0	4:05	0
10	80	42	4:47	4:47	0	4:47	0
11	87	50	5:37	5:37	0	5:37	0
12	77	35	6:12	6:12	0	6:12	0
13	24	10	6:22	6:32	10	6:22	0
14	99	75	7:37	7:37	0	7:37	0
15	05	2	7:39	7:57	18	7:39	0
16	08	4	7:43	8:17	34	7:57	14
17	63	28	8:11	8:37	25	8:11	0
18	05	2	8:13	8:57	44	8:17	4
19	07	4	8:17	9:17	60	8:31	14
20	49	20	8:37	9:37	60	8:37	0
		Total Wait in Minutes			320		35
		Average Wait in Minutes			16		1.75

The two-dock situation is illustrated by the right-hand two columns. Because two docks are available, the waiting time is significantly lower. The first truck arrives at :02 and is unloaded at that time. The second truck arrives at :19 and it proceeds directly to the second dock for unloading. The third truck arrives at :32 and it proceeds directly to the first dock which was empty 20 minutes after the first truck arrived at :02. The fourth truck arrives at :36 and it must wait. Why? Because the second truck began to unload at :19 and it will not be finished until :39. Therefore the fourth truck must wait three minutes. The fifth truck arrives at :52 and it does not have to wait because the dock used by the third truck just became available. Notice that with two docks and both being used, the time for the next free dock alternates. When the sixteenth truck arrived, it had to wait 14 minutes. The dock was free, *not* after the fifteenth truck had unloaded, but when the fourteenth was finished.

The average waiting period can be calculated for one dock and two docks. They are 16 minutes and 1.75 minutes respectively. The Monte Carlo approach to this queueing problem does not tell us whether the second dock should be added. It does, however, tell us how much truck delays will be reduced.

PROBLEMS USING QUANTITATIVE TECHNIQUES

1. Using the transportation linear program method, solve the following matrix.

PROBLEMS USING QUANTITATIVE TECHNIQUES

Plants

		A	B	C	D	E	
C		40	47	43	44	44	
U	1						1100
S							
T		48	48	41	45	49	
O	2						700
M		43	46	46	45	47	
E	3						400
R							
S		100	100	100	100	100	
Dummy							100
		500	100	600	400	700	2300

2. Solve the following problem using the transportation linear program.

Plants

CUSTOMERS	A	B	C	D	E	F	
1	69	63	62	63	61	64	800
2	65	64	69	63	62	68	1200
3	64	68	65	66	67	68	300
4	67	62	67	61	60	65	800
5	66	66	72	61	71	60	400
Dummy	100	100	100	100	100	100	200
	600	300	400	500	1100	800	

3. Solve the matrix in problem two subject to the following three constraints:
   (a) Plant C must ship to Customer 3.
   (b) Plant A must supply Customer 5.
   (c) Plant E cannot supply Customer 4.

4. Below is a figure showing the travel time in minutes between five locations. The delivery vehicle must start and finish at location A. Using the listing method heuristic technique, what is the optimum route? Is this the optimum solution?

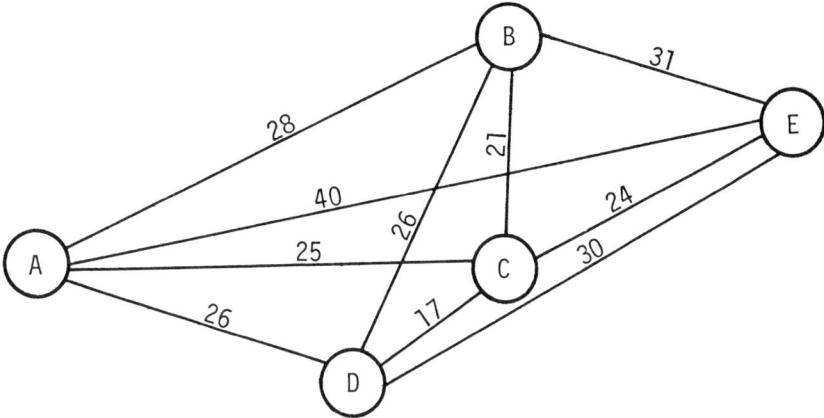

5. Using the listing method routing heuristic, solve the diagram below. Again the vehicle must start and finish at location A.

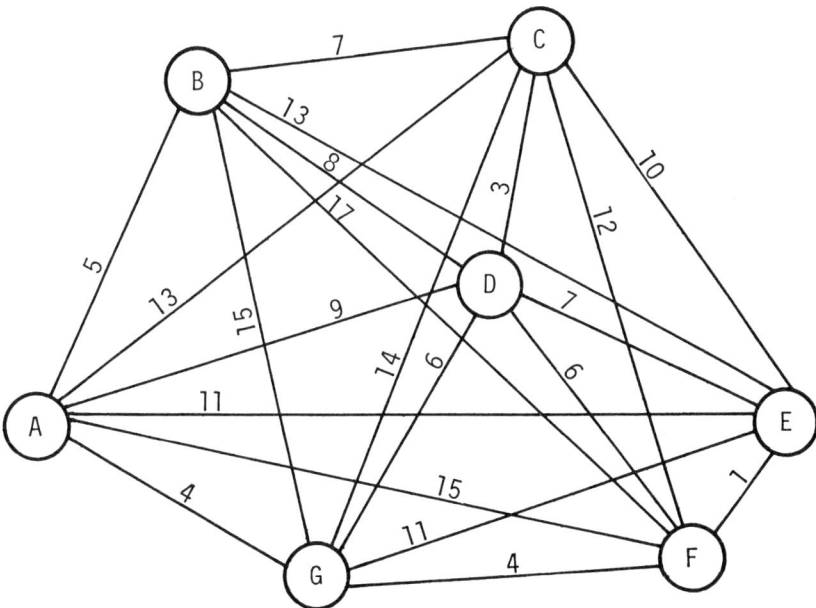

6. Obtain a large, detailed map of your city and randomly locate 100 customers that must be serviced from your warehouse, which is also randomly chosen. Using the "pin and string" method, determine the number of vehicles needed and their respective routes. Assume the average speed of the vehicles is 10 miles per hour.

7. You are the traffic manager for the Walstad Company. You must decide which of three projects to fund in 1978. The first is a purchase of 18 high speed fork-lift trucks. The second is a series of pallet racks. The third alternative is to replace the engines on 15 delivery trucks in order to increase their miles per gallon of fuel.

	18 Fork-Lift Trucks	Pallet Racks	15 New Engines
Annual Profit or Saving Before Taxes	$11,400	$ 9,800	$12,700
Tax Rate	50%	50%	50%
Economic Life	15 years	20 years	6 years
Cost of Project	$63,000	$58,000	$72,000

Based on the information above, which of the three projects should be chosen?

8. A traffic manager must decide among one of the following four projects. Using the average rate-of-return capital budgeting concept, which project should be chosen?

	Computerized Tariff File	100 Reusable Metal Pallets	Pallet Racks	Shrink-Wrap Machine
Annual Profit or Savings Before Tax	$ 27,500	$ 26,700	$ 25,000	$ 24,800
Tax Rate	48%	48%	48%	48%
Economic Life	5 years	10 years	20 years	8 years
Cost of Project	$172,000	$150,000	$120,000	$105,000

9. Utilizing the figure below, use Monte Carlo simulation on this queueing problem. Assume that each vehicle is serviced in 60 minutes and Table 1 can be used for the random numbers. Simulate 25 arrivals for both the one-dock and two-dock situation. What is the average waiting period for each configuration?

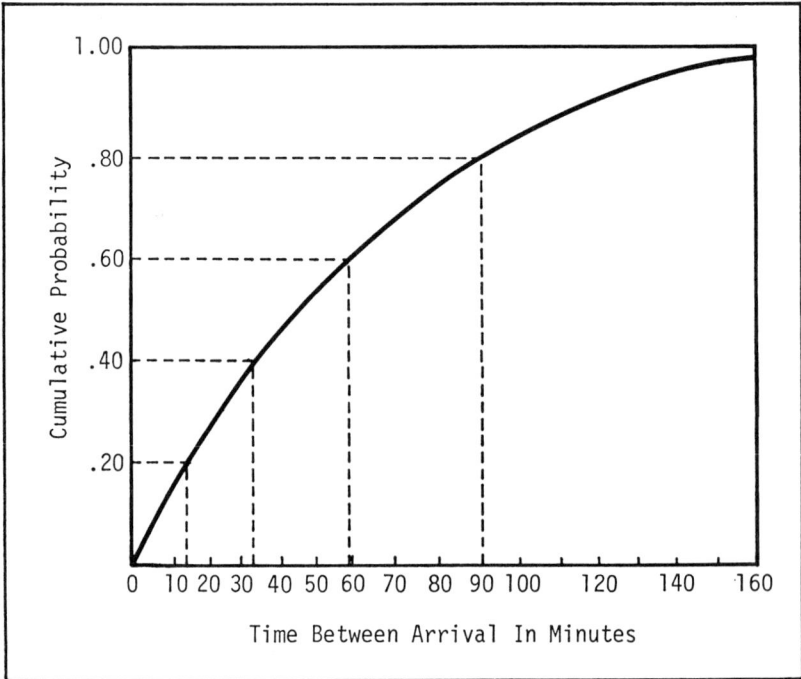

Time Between Arrival In Minutes

Name Index

Subject Index

PETROLEUM PUBLISHING COMPANY
Tulsa, Oklahoma

PPC
BOOKS